IRELAND TODAY

Anatomy of a Changing State

Gemma Hussey

TOWNHOUSE   VIKING

TOWNHOUSE

First published in Ireland by Town House and Country House,
42 Morehampton Road, Donnybrook, Dublin 4
in association with Viking, 1993

1 3 5 7 9 10 8 6 4 2

Typeset by Datix International Limited, Bungay, Suffolk
Printed in Great Britain by Clays Ltd, St Ives plc
Filmset in Monophoto Sabon

A CIP catalogue record for this book is available from the British Library

ISBN 0-948524-66-9

PUBLISHER'S NOTE

Every reasonable effort has been made to keep the facts in this book up to
date, within the constraints of the publishing schedule. We apologize for
any information which is not so at the time of publication.

PHOTO CREDITS

The author and publishers are grateful to the following copyright holders
for permission to reproduce photographs: Government Information Services,
inset pages 3, 5, 6; The Irish Times Ltd, inset pages 4, 5, 7, 9, 11, 12,
13, 14, 16; Pacemaker, Belfast, inset page 2.

In memory of my mother and father

Patricia Rogan and Jim Moran

CONTENTS

INTRODUCTION

While the attention of the world is engaged by the unprecedented political transformation and turbulence in Eastern and Central Europe, a small island behind an island on the western edge of Europe is experiencing its own metamorphosis.

Irish society has changed more in the two decades leading up to the 1990s than in the whole of the previous one hundred years, going back to the Great Famine of the mid nineteenth century. An inward-looking, rural, deeply conservative, nearly 100 per cent Roman Catholic and impoverished country has become urbanized, industrialized, and Europeanized. Its political and social institutions are challenged by the realities of today, and in many cases are proving unequal to the challenge.

And still the hunger for change is there: if politics are any indication, and in highly political Ireland they are, the results of Ireland's January 1993 elections show a marked acceleration of a trend away from the politics of a finally forgotten civil war towards a younger, more European style of social democracy. Politicians of the old school who failed to appreciate what was happening paid the price of their blindness. For the first time in the history of the State, the leaders of the two main parties have no family connections with civil-war leaders. The old guard has passed on. But the electoral system, in a form which imposes an impossible life-style on politicians and actively militates against good planning and good government, persists.

Ireland today is a country where a national leader, elected by popular franchise, having no political power, unattached to any political party, nevertheless enjoys an unprecedented position of great moral authority. The fact that the President of Ireland is a woman in her forties with a strong liberal record on human and civil rights, particularly on matters concerning women and sexuality, underlines that impetus which propels the new Ireland, helter-skelter, towards the twenty-first century. Twenty women in the

Dáil (12 per cent) represent another sign of the fading of old prejudices, while Ireland's first female Supreme Court judge breaks down yet another barrier.

Three and a half million people live in the Republic of Ireland, occupying three-quarters of a green and fertile land. The top right-hand corner of the island belongs to the United Kingdom, though the Constitution of the Republic claims Northern Ireland as its own. The reverberations of the island's division in the early decades of the century, and the historical legacy of oppression, are felt in the Republic in sorrow, unease, and accompanying apathy, born of despair. As the 1990s opened, the Republic's government joined with the United Kingdom and with politicians from Northern Ireland in long and difficult talks in the search for peace, a renewed effort to end the shocking violence in the northern corner of the country. The violence has spilled over to the British mainland, causing a fierce backlash from outlawed loyalist terrorists, whose ferocity matches that of the Irish Republican Army (IRA).

The days of Ireland's ability to cut itself off from the rest of the world and close its eyes to the realities of modern living are over. In 1992, the country was brought face to face with its own hypocrisy: the abortion issue, avoided and condemned for so long, crystallized in the form of a fourteen-year-old pregnant girl forbidden by the State to join the thousands of other Irish women travelling to England for an abortion. The crisis brought out the best in Irish people, revealing compassion and realism in equal quantities. On divorce, the new government in 1993 promised to hold a referendum at an early date, a referendum which has every chance of bringing change about.

The Catholic Church, for so long the dominant force in Irish life, and the main educator and opinion former, faced a crisis of its own when one of its most prominent and popular bishops was discovered to have had a love affair and a child, and to have been sending money to meet maintenance costs for his hidden family. The Church, whose teachings had concentrated so much on the sins of the flesh, and which was already much weakened, found itself confused and damaged. Its younger nuns and priests (though few in number) have long since eschewed authoritarianism, and have worked among the poor and marginalized: they have been prepared, along with the rest of the country, to acknowledge their own uncertainty.

Other complacencies are being shaken too: business and political scandals have taken centre stage since 1991, culminating in a long, public, and shocking judicial tribunal on the affairs inside one of the country's biggest industries. Political connections and apparent irregular practices, official blind eyes and alleged double-dealing with European Community institutions – the rich tapestry of Irish life has been shown to have a dark thread running through it.

While the country comes to terms with these fundamental changes, a great vibrancy in the population stems from the demographic profile. Forty-four per cent of the population are under twenty-five years of age, and nearly one million young people are in the education system with its traditionally high standards. This young population gives Ireland its great modern reputation for rock music, starting with the international success of the U2 rock group. Sport increasingly attracts Ireland's lively young men and women, who follow most contemporary sports while enthusiastically supporting the unique Irish hurling and Gaelic football, which are flourishing today more than ever.

In this generation, a youthful new approach to Irish traditional music, theatre and art has led to an explosion of activity all over the country – and to the popularization of Irish culture across the western world. The repression of artistic freedom in earlier generations has been forgotten, and the interaction with cultural movements in the wider world gathers pace. The ancient Irish language struggles with difficulty to find its place in this cultural revival.

The down side of the high birth rate in Ireland is the tragedy of large-scale unemployment, with its resultant by-products of poverty and crime. The economy has not been able to provide the growing population with work, while world recession has closed off the safety valve of emigration. More than 300,000 were officially on the dole as 1993 began, some 21 per cent of the workforce. All other main economic indicators were healthy: the country asked itself why it had been able to improve competitiveness, increase exports, reduce the massive burden of debt in relation to GNP, keep inflation down to a European low, and not find enough work for its people. Ireland is, sadly, the 'best little jobless economy in Europe'. Did the absence of an entrepreneurial spirit come from the diktat of an education system which told the people what to think and what to believe, and forbade them to entertain alternatives?

The nature of the great transformation in a couple of generations in Ireland is illustrated by the St Patrick's Day parade in New York. The descendants of Irish emigrants who organize the parade refuse to allow Irish homosexual men and women to march in it. By contrast, those groups march on the same day down Dublin's main street, carrying a banner reading, 'Hello, New York!' Irish governments have been trying for years to convince Irish-Americans that the IRA are not heroes or freedom fighters, but are held in contempt at home, where under 2 per cent of the electorate cast their votes for the political allies of the IRA, the Sinn Féin Party.

Society in Ireland is not rigidly stratified into identifiable class structures as in neighbouring Britain. The last vestiges of an Anglo-Irish aristocracy form a very small part of Irish society: the country is generally divided into those who have been lucky or clever enough to get a good education, and those who have fallen through the social-services net, which though extensive in Ireland is not well coordinated. There is little conspicuous wealth in Ireland, but a problem of poverty which is exacerbated by poor urban planning and long-term unemployment.

Ireland is a country which despite its problems loves to laugh. It is even beginning to be able to laugh at itself, when it isn't morosely reflecting on its turbulent past. Irish people enjoy meeting strangers, and take pleasure in drink, good talk, and pubs and theatres. Tourists, who come to Ireland in their hundreds of thousands every year (and disappear easily into the lovely uncongested countryside), consistently rate 'the friendly people' as the main positive element of their visit.

The days of the sexually frustrated bachelors and old maids, the days of de Valera's happy maidens and frugal comforts, are well gone. Sex, which was surrounded by fear and ignorance, is no longer the bogy that it was. Self-esteem has been restored after decades of repression imposed, since 1922, not by a foreign power but from within. Ireland stands on the threshold of a new era when its potential may be fully realized.

This book looks at where the Irish are today, how they got there, and what they might do tomorrow.

ACKNOWLEDGEMENTS

I am in the debt of many people who gave their time and thought to helping me in the writing of this book. First, I should like to thank the Taoiseach and Leader of Fianna Fáil, Albert Reynolds; the Tánaiste, Minister for Foreign Affairs and Leader of the Labour Party, Dick Spring; John Bruton, Leader of Fine Gael; Des O'Malley, Leader of the Progressive Democrats; and Proinnsias de Rossa, Leader of the Democratic Left, for talking to me. Many other politicians helped in one way or another, mostly by finding time to talk to me, and by putting information at my disposal through their very helpful offices. Among them were: Tom Kitt TD, Minister of State at the Department of Foreign Affairs, Mary O'Rourke TD, Minister of State for Labour, Mary Harney TD, Deputy Leader of the Progressive Democrats, Frances FitzGerald TD, Senator Brian Hillery, John Hume MP, MEP, Leader of the SDLP, MEPs Mark Killilea, Pat Cox, Willy deClerq, and especially Mary Banotti MEP for her particular interest and help. The press offices of all the political parties gave most useful information quickly and efficiently.

Ray MacSharry, former EC Commissioner, Terry Stewart and the Dublin EC office, Jim O'Brien and the Dublin European Parliament office, the Institute for European Affairs, John Temple Lang, Una O'Dwyer, Tom Garvey, Tom O'Dwyer, Claus Ehlermann, Liam Hourican, Neville Keery and Ruth Hussey were also most helpful on the European connection.

Many civil servants put themselves out to assist the work: Pádraig Ó hUiginn of the Department of the Taoiseach, Frank Murray, Secretary to the Government, along with Dr Tom Arnold, Larry Bond, David Gordon, Paddy Heffernan, Pat Macken, Patrick Nolan, Seán Ó hÉirgeartaigh, and Michael Scanlon. The press and information offices of all government departments approached were more than obliging, as were the following: Bride Rosney, Special Adviser to the President of Ireland, Tom Savage, Special Adviser in the

Taoiseach's office, the staff of the Leinster House Library, Mary Prendergast of the Institute of Public Administration Library, Seán O'Riordan, Ronald Long, Coillte Teoranta, the Higher Education Authority, the Independent Radio and Television Commission, the Employment Equality Agency, the Council for the Status of Women, the Irish Rugby Football Association, Danny Lynch of the Gaelic Athletic Association (GAA), Pat Hickey of the Olympic Council of Ireland, Bord na gCon, Bord na Gaeilge, Comhaltas Ceoltóirí Éireann, the Central Statistics Office, the Society of St Vincent de Paul, the Combat Poverty Agency, the press offices of the Defence Forces and the Garda Síochána, Dr Bernard Moran and the Chief Librarian of the Michael Smurfit Graduate School of Business, University College, Dublin, and An Taisce.

Further help was generously given by the Catholic Press and Information Office, the Council for Research and Development, St Patrick's College, Maynooth, Fr J. Dargan sj, Fr Dermot Lane, Fr Billy FitzGerald, and Fr John Byrne.

For advice, material, and/or informal talk on some of the many areas I needed to investigate in this book, I would particularly acknowledge the following distinguished Irish people from many fields who were unfailingly responsive: Bruce Arnold, Dr Philip Bourke, John Bowman, Peter Cassells, Professor Frank Convery, Conor Cruise O'Brien, Seán Dooney, Eileen Doyle, Maurice Doyle, Martin Dully, Ronan Fanning, Dr John FitzGerald, Dave Guiney, Kevin Healy, Carmencita Hederman, Dr Gerard Hogan, Séamus Hosey, Dr Áine Hyland, Jack Jones and Áine O'Donoghue, Dr Eileen Kane, Brendan Keenan, James Larkin, Frank McDonald, Jimmy Magee, Kieran Mulvey, Adrian Munnelly, Derry O'Donovan, Lochlann Quinn, Dr Yvonne Scannell, Professor Séamus Sheehy, Paul Tansey, and Brian Walker.

To Peter Sutherland, former EC Commissioner and Chairman of AIB Group, now Director-General of GATT, and Brian Farrell, Associate Professor of Politics, University College, Dublin, a special word of appreciation for their particular interest and guidance.

To Audrey Conlon, who carried the main burden of research over two years, my deepest gratitude. John Fanagan read every section as it was being drafted and gave invaluable advice. Doreen Dalton interpreted the mysteries of word-processing for me and was always on hand, with back-up from Linda Cummins and

ACKNOWLEDGEMENTS

Stuart Hart. Anne Johnson and Dee Johnstone were generous with their time. My agent Jonathan Williams calmed me with confidence. Treasa Coady of Town House and Country House Publishers was responsible for getting me involved at all with this most interesting challenge, and shaped the book with great skill. I acknowledge the assistance of all these persons and bodies, but the views expressed in this book are solely mine and do not purport to represent the views of any of those persons or bodies.

And finally to my husband Derry, who once more had to support his wife through a time- and energy-consuming obsession, thanks.

CHAPTER 1

The Presidency

Presidents of Ireland were all quiet, fairly passive and rather elderly men, until the early 1970s. Their successors were not quite so old, and not quite so passive, but still men, until 1990. Then Mary Robinson,* a woman who was by no means elderly, became President. The significance of the transition is much more than that of changes of sex and age alone: Ireland elected in 1990 not only its first woman Head of State, and the first not approved by Fianna Fáil, Ireland's dominant political party, but also a liberal former Senator and constitutional lawyer, with a history of espousing human rights and women's issues. She has a strongly European outlook, backed by considerable expertise in EC legislation as well as a broad and tolerant approach to the old divisions on the island. In 1985, she felt so deeply about the failure to consult the Unionists of Northern Ireland on the Anglo-Irish Agreement that she resigned from the Labour Party in protest. President Mary Robinson therefore epitomizes a range of attributes and attitudes which aptly illustrate the new Ireland.

She was elected in November 1990 after a national campaign which had elements both of tragedy and farce, idealism and political smear tactics, and was like no other presidential campaign in Ireland. In all, 612,000 people voted for her, 38 per cent of the poll and enough to see her overtake Brian Lenihan† on the second

* Mary Robinson (née Bourke), b. 1944, comes from Ballina, Co. Mayo. Educated by the Sacred Heart nuns in Dublin, and at Trinity College, Dublin (BA, MA, LlB), King's Inns, and Harvard University, she was a law professor (at Trinity College), a barrister, and a senator. An unsuccessful candidate for Dáil Éireann twice (1977, 1981), for the Labour Party, she is known at home and abroad as an expert on Irish and European law. Her list of honours and achievements is lengthy and her record on human and civil rights is outstanding.

† Brian Lenihan, b. 1930. From Athlone and a political family, he became a lawyer (University College, Dublin, and the King's Inns) and had a long and distinguished political career with Fianna Fáil, holding many ministerial portfolios. A very popular man, his serious illness in 1989 contributed to his political disaster in the presidential campaign of 1990.

count with transferred votes from the third candidate, Fine Gael's Austin Currie.* A 'rainbow coalition' of left, centre left, liberals, Greens, and women came together in sufficient numbers to ensure that her first-preference vote was enough to see off a challenge from Lenihan, the hitherto highly favoured candidate of the political establishment, who only a few months earlier had been confidently expected to romp home. For a country which had become used to considering the presidency as peripheral, dull and not relevant to real life, the excitement of the closing stages of the election, as well as the symbolism of a fresh, liberal and female candidate pitted against the older, male, conservative power-bloc of national politics, was intoxicating.

The history of the Irish presidency had not been turbulent earlier. Éamon de Valera designed the post in Ireland's Constitution of 1937, to replace an office called the governor-generalship that had existed since Ireland gained her independence from Britain in 1922.† There have been seven Presidents, including Mary Robinson (see table). It is fair to say that until 1990, Irish Presidents came from the ranks of men who were considered to have their active public life behind them, and who would be 'a safe pair of hands' in what was always a quiet low-profile role. In the twenty or so years up to 1990, there were many discussions in the Irish media about whether or not the office of President was either justified or necessary.

The President is elected directly by the people, although in reality the post has not always been contested. The presidential election of 1990 was the first since 1973, when Erskine Childers‡ was elected on 30 May. His early death a year later saw the unopposed election

* Austin Currie, b. 1939. Born and educated in Northern Ireland, Austin Currie had a distinguished and courageous career in Northern Ireland politics for the constitutional nationalist party, the Social Democratic and Labour Party (SDLP). He became involved in Irish politics in the Republic in 1988 and was elected to the Dáil in 1989.

† The Governor-General, under the 1921 Agreement between Britain and Ireland, was the representative of the Crown in Ireland, on the model of the Governor-General of Canada.

‡ Erskine Childers (1905–74) was the son of a famous father, Erskine Childers, who sailed the yacht *Asgard* into a Co. Dublin harbour with German arms for the Irish volunteers in 1914. Childers was executed in the Irish civil war in 1922. Erskine Childers junior served in several Fianna Fáil governments between 1956 and 1973.

Presidents of Ireland	
President	Term of Office
Dr Douglas Hyde	1938–45
Seán T. O'Kelly	1945–59
Éamon de Valera	1959–73
Erskine Childers	1973–4
Cearbhall Ó Dálaigh	1974–6
Patrick J. Hillery	1976–90
Mary Robinson	1990–

of Cearbhall Ó Dálaigh,* who was followed by Dr Patrick Hillery:†
these three were all the nominees of Fianna Fáil.

The first President of Ireland, Douglas Hyde, combined
Protestantism, academic brilliance, and wide Gaelic scholarship. He
was a prominent and dedicated member of the Gaelic League,
founded in 1893 to revive the Irish language. Born in 1860, he was
unanimously elected President by the Dáil in 1938. He suffered ill-
health for most of his term of office, and spent his last years in
retirement in his native Roscommon until he died in 1949. He
was a much-loved, dignified, and gentle person. He was succeeded
by a staunch Fianna Fáil activist and early fighter for independence, Seán T. O'Kelly, who held office safely and unremarkably
until 1959.

Éamon de Valera (1882–1975) ended his long political career by
serving in the presidency from 1959 until 1973. For many of those

---

* Cearbhall Ó Dálaigh (1911–78). A Fianna Fáil supporter, linguist, and Celtic
scholar, he was Attorney-General before being appointed Chief Justice of Ireland
in 1961, and Irish member of the EC Court of Justice in 1972. His term of office
as President ended abruptly in 1976 after a confrontation with a minister of the
government.

† Patrick J. Hillery, b. 1923. From Co. Clare, he practised as a medical doctor in
his native county until being persuaded to enter national politics for Fianna Fáil
in 1959. He held a range of senior ministries, and as Minister for Foreign Affairs
led the negotiations for Ireland's entry to the EC in 1973, becoming the country's
first EC Commissioner.

years, his advancing age and semi-blindness prevented him from developing the office, although in the early years he still exercised considerable influence over Fianna Fáil. Since he had designed the presidency himself, he was punctilious in observing the constitutional requirements of the office. By the time he left office, at the age of ninety, the presidency seemed a distant and obscure office to most people, suitable as a final resting place for the elder statesmen of Ireland.

In the parliamentary debates on that 1937 Constitution which established the presidency, de Valera had made the limits of the office quite clear: 'He [the President] is there to guard the people's rights, and mainly to guard the Constitution.' In guarding the rights, certain – very few – powers are left to the President's own discretion.

The Irish Constitution of 1937 sets out those powers. The office is largely ceremonial, rather like a constitutional monarchy, with very little leeway for exercising discretionary powers. One of the few powers in that category allows the President to refer a government bill to the Supreme Court to test its constitutionality after 'consultation' with the Council of State:* she is under no obligation to take advice from the Council of State, which is largely a symbolic body. It was one such reference to the Supreme Court which caused the only really severe disagreement between government and President, leading to the resignation of the President in 1976.† This power of referral is the only discretionary power to have been regularly used – in fact, eight times, and otherwise uncontroversially, by Irish Presidents.

---

*The Council of State is a body made up of the Taoiseach (prime minister), Tánaiste (deputy prime minister), Speaker of the Dáil and Chairperson of the Senate, Chief Justice and President of the High Court, Attorney-General, former Presidents, and Chief Justices, and seven other people directly appointed by the President of the day. (The author served on the Council of State from 1989 to 1990.)

†A government minister, Patrick Donegan (Minister for Defence), annoyed at the President's (totally correct) reference to the Supreme Court of an Emergency Powers bill strengthening the power of the security forces to deal with subversives, arising from the Northern Ireland crisis, called him 'A thundering disgrace' in a public speech. After some confusion, and the failure of the Taoiseach to dismiss the minister (who apologized swiftly for his remark), President Cearbhall Ó Dálaigh resigned. President Hillery was his successor.

A second discretionary power is that of calling a referendum: but this can be exercised only if the President is petitioned by a majority of the Senate (an unlikely occurrence because of the inbuilt government majority in the second house) and a third of the Dáil.

Another possibility for freedom of action lies in the provision for the President to convene a meeting of either or both Houses of the Oireachtas (the legislature) – but since the government controls what the President might say to them, it has not been considered as amounting to very much. Mr de Valera, as President, convened both Houses in 1969 to mark the fiftieth anniversary of the first Dáil. In 1992, another President convened a special meeting of both Houses simply as part of the pattern of a new and active presidency. This event will be described later in this chapter.

The most interesting – while hitherto totally unused – power of Irish Presidents is the right to refuse a dissolution of the Dáil to a Taoiseach who has 'ceased to retain the support of a majority in Dáil Éireann'.[1] It was this provision which, indirectly, put paid to the electoral prospects of Brian Lenihan, Fianna Fáil's candidate for the presidential election in 1990, and gave a massive boost to the campaign of Mary Robinson. It is also this provision which has such ambiguity about it that legal and political commentators have called for its clarification. Garret FitzGerald, a former Taoiseach, described the wording of this Article as 'an inappropriate lacuna' in the Constitution. The concern centres around the question of precisely how and when the President is to judge if the Taoiseach has lost the support of a majority in the Dáil, or if another person could attempt to obtain a majority without a dissolution of the Dáil.

For fourteen years before the election of Mary Robinson, the old white house in Phoenix Park was occupied by Dr Patrick Hillery. After the débâcle of the 1976 insult to the President by the Minister for Defence, and the ensuing angry resignation of President Ó Dálaigh, Fianna Fáil called on Dr Patrick Hillery, who was serving as Ireland's EC Commissioner, to come back to Ireland a year early to serve as President. Dr Hillery was a medical doctor in general practice in his native Co. Clare, who held several ministerial offices before taking up Ireland's first Commissionership when the EC was enlarged in 1973. He had strongly opposed the 'republican' wing of Fianna Fáil during the crisis of the Arms Trial in 1970,* which left deep divisions in the party and propelled it into opposition in 1973. So, in 1976, the Fine Gael and Labour parties, which made up the coalition government that had been responsible for the Donegan mess, wisely decided not to cause an election by nominating another candidate. Dr Hillery was sworn in, and served quietly and diligently for two seven-year terms, leaving office in 1990. He has reflected in public only minimally on his fourteen years. They were not easy; he found the office stifling of self-expression. For a lot of his time, relations may have been strained with the government of the day because of earlier political disagree-ment with Charles Haughey (Taoiseach for seven of those fourteen years). His years as President imposed '. . . a much bigger strain on the personality than being a Minister. It's visibility without having policies to enunciate.'[2] Because of his quiet style, and partly no doubt because of a public sensing of his reluctance to accept the second term when he was strongly pressed to do so in 1983, there was criticism of the low profile he adopted in the later years. He feels that politicians have failed to support the presidency, particularly when refusals of invitations are on the instructions of government, and instances an unfortunate episode in November 1980 when he was advised by the Taoiseach's office not to attend a Remembrance Day ceremony in St Patrick's Cathedral organized by the British Legion. Having therefore refused, he had to watch the government later deciding to send a junior minister, who said, 'It was only a religious occasion . . .' Such are the constraints of the office of President that Dr Hillery felt he could not clarify the issue in case it might seem like a disagreement with the government. 'I felt I was dropped through the trapdoor.'[3] It is generally recognized in Ireland that Dr Hillery's presidency had a stabilizing effect on the institution, and he feels proud of that himself. 'After Cearbhall [Ó Dálaigh] resigning, things were very shaky. It's much more stable now.'[4] It was only during the 1990 election campaign that a full picture of the reliability and steadiness under pressure of

* Two government ministers in the 1969–73 Fianna Fáil government were charged in the courts with importing arms for use in Northern Ireland. They were acquitted. The 1970 Arms Trial, as it became known, marked the beginning of a period of eclipse of Mr Charles Haughey, one of the ministers, who later became Taoiseach.

President Hillery emerged. Ironically, that revelation was made because of the maladroit handling by Fianna Fáil of an episode of phone calls to the President in 1982, in an attempt to get him to use Article 2.2: the power to refuse a dissolution of the Dáil. Ronan Fanning, Professor of Modern History at University College, Dublin, said of Dr Hillery: '. . . the remarkable contribution of Patrick Hillery has been lost to view.'[5]

THE 1990 PRESIDENTIAL ELECTION CAMPAIGN

'There will be a woman candidate for the Park for the first time since the institution of the presidency was established. Very much the outsider, Mrs Robinson will be aiming at a good showing, as she has no realistic chance of winning out at the end of the day . . .' In his book, *Mary Robinson – A President with a Purpose*, Fergus Finlay, press officer for the Labour Party, chose to place the above newspaper extract first. That opinion from the *Sunday Press* of 8 April 1990 was a fair reflection of majority thinking in Ireland at the time.

It was an instinct of the leader of the Labour Party which made sure that Ireland would in fact have an election in 1990 for President. Having done well in the general election of 1989, Dick Spring, the Labour leader, felt that his party and the generally liberal views it held on a range of issues could be strengthened by giving people an opportunity to express themselves through a candidate who would embody those views. Mary Robinson was persuaded to accept the Labour Party's nomination, and the official launch of her candidacy took place, appropriately enough, on May Day 1990.

The Workers' Party, the Green Party, and the Women's Political Association quickly declared their support for her. For Fianna Fáil, the candidate's mantle had long passed to Brian Lenihan, who 'fitted comfortably into the models of previous Presidents nominated by Fianna Fáil'.[6] A much-liked and highly experienced elder statesman of his party, and Minister for Defence, his popularity had been enhanced by his courageous demeanour through a serious illness, necessitating a liver transplant: Lenihan had always personified the bluff 'can-do', hard-living but conservative, side of Fianna Fáil. Some alarm bells should have rung in the Lenihan camp, however, when Ireland's most popular TV chat-show* devoted a whole programme to him earlier in the year and invited the country to be amused at tales of pub-crawling while on duty, alleged threats of transfer to police officers for trying to enforce the licensing laws, and other such episodes. That sort of story had usually been the stuff of a certain kind of Irish politics which had begun to lose its appeal to an increasingly educated and sophisticated electorate. Perhaps sensing that times were changing, Mr Lenihan himself looked embarrassed as these revelations unfolded: they were crowned by an amused exhortation on videotape from a former European colleague, remembering Lenihan's sociability and *bonhomie*, to '. . . take better care of this liver than you did of the last one . . .'

Fine Gael, the main Opposition party, already slipping heavily in the opinion polls, belatedly nominated Austin Currie, a former SDLP politician from Northern Ireland, much respected and liked, but not at all well known to the Irish public at large. His candidacy was seriously damaged by the previous frantic efforts of the party leader to persuade several party 'heavyweights' like former Taoiseach Garret FitzGerald and former Foreign Affairs Minister Peter Barry to accept the nomination, before finally settling on Currie, who therefore appeared even to his own party as very much a 'lame duck' third choice. He worked hard in the campaign, gained considerable personal credit, but never looked like overtaking Robinson.

Mary Robinson, starting in the spring in a windswept village in the beautiful south-west of Ireland called Allihies, toured the country quietly, indefatigably, with her totally supportive husband Nicholas at her side, and a talented, diverse and devoted campaign committee behind her. She conducted this tour long before the other candidates were even nominated. Since it was not reported widely in the national media, the population – and the principal political establishment – were not aware of the ground swell of support she was tapping.

In September 1990, the official campaign proper with all three candidates began: it was dull enough, with predictable noises about expanding the presidency, bringing it closer to the people, opening

* RTE Television's *The Late Late Show*.

16

up Áras an Uachtaráin* to the arts, to the travellers (Ireland's modern name for the nomadic people formerly called 'tinkers'), to emigrants. Polls were showing Robinson in second place, Currie a very poor third, with Lenihan well ahead – so far ahead that even with Ireland's proportional representation system, he couldn't be caught by Robinson. To most commentators, it looked like a foregone conclusion, despite the gradual rise in Robinson support. The election date was set for 7 November – in early October, she was narrowing the gap, though still depending on an unlikely nearly 100 per cent transfer from Currie to have a chance. Election day was a month away.†

Then something happened which gave Mary Robinson a massive boost, and meant that her hard work to establish her position as strong second runner was to be rewarded. Brian Lenihan, inexplicably, started to deny an already documented occurrence, which had passed almost without comment since it was first publicly written about in a book in 1985, and a newspaper article in 1982.[7]

He denied that he had been one of those to telephone President Hillery on the night of 27 January 1982, in an attempt to persuade the President to exercise his power under Article 2.2 of the Constitution and refuse a dissolution of the Dáil to the outgoing Taoiseach Garret FitzGerald.

The vehement and repeated denial was arguably unnecessary: in the uncertainty and close-voting situation in the Dáil at that moment in 1982, with a government having fallen by one vote and a possibility of the Opposition leader garnering enough votes for election within the Dáil as Taoiseach without going to the country, telephone calls of an informative kind to the President could have been defended. However, by a combination of poor communications within the Fianna Fáil campaign team, and the confused recollections of Mr Lenihan, the whole incident became a national obsession and a disaster for Mr Lenihan. He compounded his

* The President's official residence in Phoenix Park, Dublin; almost in the city centre, the house sits on seventeen acres. Built originally in 1751, it became the residence of successive representatives of the British Crown in Ireland and was known as the Vice-Regal Lodge until 1922.

† A Market Research Bureau of Ireland poll, taken on 4–5 October, showed Lenihan at 45 per cent, Robinson at 32 per cent, and Currie at 19 per cent.

mistake by denying on nationwide television the evidence of his own voice telling a young research student on tape that he had made the calls. Few will forget Brian Lenihan's haggard face, turned to the camera, asserting that 'on mature recollection' the account he had given to the researcher the previous May was inaccurate.[8] (He was later to assert in his own account of events that he had been on such heavy medication at the time of his interview with the student that his mind was totally confused. 'The interview was given at a time when the state of my health, both physical and, for those few short days around the time of the interview, mental, left a lot to be desired.'[9]

But in October 1990, worse was to befall him: the Progressive Democrats, junior partners in the coalition government, took an extremely serious view of their ministerial colleague contradicting himself in this way, demanded his resignation, and threatened to vote against the government in a vote of confidence on 30 October. The Taoiseach, Charles Haughey, himself looking wretched by now, had to dismiss his old friend Brian Lenihan – who refused to resign – from his Cabinet or face a general election. A week before the national vote, the leading candidate was dismissed in disgrace. In one of the most dramatic political 'finales' in Ireland in modern history, Lenihan's poll ratings plummeted, Robinson's soared. A surge of sympathy for the hapless Lenihan and his family led to a late recovery, only for his campaign to be knocked off balance by an unfortunate sexist attack on Mary Robinson on national radio by another minister, Pádraig Flynn, a few days before the vote: he attacked Mary Robinson by accusing her of only recently discovering an interest in her husband and family.[10] Again, an incredulous country listened to Fianna Fáil throwing away an election, and to the barrister chairman of the Progressive Democrats scathingly cutting the minister down to size. From then on, it was all coasting home for the Robinson camp. On 7 November, the country voted, and Mary Robinson became Ireland's first woman president.

THE ROBINSON PRESIDENCY: SYMBOL OF A COUNTRY'S TRANSITION

Mary Robinson could be the Irish President until the year 2004, if she serves two terms – and she will then be only sixty years of age. In a discussion of power and influence in Ireland, it would not, up to now, have been necessary to dwell at any length on the presidency. This presidency may be quite different. John Bowman, historian, broadcaster and journalist, described her election in these terms: 'A watershed victory with youth on its side . . . the central message of Robinson's success is that the electorate is ready to embrace a more open pluralist society.'[11] Professor Joseph Lee of University College, Cork, a noted historian, said: 'The election has already entered history as a milestone in the slow progress of Irish women to full equality.' He went on: 'Her track record does not suggest Mary Robinson will be satisfied with a do-nothing role. She is more a performer than a possessor.'

On the night of her victory, the President-elect made a memorable speech. She spoke of her six months' odyssey criss-crossing Ireland, 'a journey of joy and discovery of myself, of my country, of the people of Ireland'. Nobody had ever heard of an Irish politician confessing to such a thing. She said: 'I was elected by men and women of all parties and none, by many with great moral courage who stepped out from the faded flags of the Civil War and voted for a new Ireland. And above all by the women of Ireland – *Mná na hÉireann* – who instead of rocking the cradle rocked the system, and who came out massively to make their mark on the ballot paper, and on a new Ireland.' Which victorious politician in Ireland had ever sounded like that?

The inaugural address of the new President in St Patrick's Hall, Dublin Castle, on 3 December 1990, conveyed in five minutes a series of beliefs and hopes which climaxed in W. B. Yeats's translation of an ancient Irish poet: 'I am of Ireland . . . come dance with me in Ireland.' She spoke clearly and firmly of her friendship and love for both communities in Northern Ireland, her wish to be a symbol of a 'Fifth province – a place within each one of us, that place that is open to the other – this reconciling and healing Fifth province'; and, 'As a woman, I want women who have felt themselves outside history to be written back into history – finding a voice where they found a vision.' The speech was full of poetry and idealism, written in consultation with some people close to her and her view of her new role: and it moved the whole distinguished gathering.

By this stage, there were very few critics of the new President. As the months went on, Mary Robinson approached her new office with skill and energy, disarming any critics who remained. It was, however, clear in the first year that relations with the Taoiseach and government were not always smooth: understandable, perhaps, after the bitterness of the campaign and the shock for the main government party of losing the office they had always considered their own. In June 1991, for example, it became known that the government had refused permission for her to deliver the influential Dimbleby lecture on BBC television. Rumours abounded of snubs and sulks, of Mr Haughey preferring not to attend sporting events which the President had decided to attend, and observers wondered if Fianna Fáil would ever come to terms with the new President in the Áras. The President could, of course, afford to be calm about these temporary set-backs, secure as she was in her seven-year term of office, and aware that the Taoiseach's political life-span would certainly be considerably shorter. As it happened, it was short indeed: in January 1992, Mr Haughey was forced out of office, to be succeeded by a new Taoiseach with whom relations were much more cordial. By April 1992, the President was paying a warm tribute to the new government and Taoiseach after earlier 'problems of adjustment to a more active Presidency' ... 'I have had very good support from Mr Reynolds [the new Taoiseach], his ministers, and officials.'[12] The following month, Pádraig Flynn, the politician who had cast the slur which arguably cost Fianna Fáil the presidential election, was saying on national radio, 'She's a good President, does us proud . . .'[13]

This presidency was immediately conducted with maximum visibility: by December 1991, her husband was joking that he had listened to her delivering 750 speeches in a year. The presidential residence has been thronged with visitors from every kind of background, invited for a cup of tea: the disabled, the unemployed, the travellers, groups from both sides of the Northern Ireland divide, women's groups. The President embarked on a tour of the country, revisiting, as she had promised, places and people she had encountered on that first campaign in 1990. In a gesture promised in her election campaign, a light is kept burning in a window of Áras an Uachtaráin, a symbol of her consciousness of Irish emigrants.

This is the first President of Ireland to embark on constant and frequent foreign travel. Apart from State visits to Portugal, the Netherlands, Australia, and France, and less formal visits to the United States, Mrs Robinson is the first President also to visit England and Scotland, the first President to meet British royalty officially (initially Prince Edward at an international rugby match) and most significantly, the first President to make Northern Ireland an important part of her itinerary. Despite the inevitable rebuffs from the extreme end of the Ulster Unionist spectrum in Northern Ireland, because of the claim in Ireland's Constitution over the northern counties, the President has impressed Northerners with her patent sincerity as she seeks reconciliation. In two visits in 1992, to Belfast and Derry, she was warmly welcomed by women's groups and community and peace groups that include both religious and political traditions in their membership.

One of the most dramatic examples of how in tune the presidency has become to Irish people was the national reaction to Mary Robinson's visit to Somalia in October 1992. Her initiative in going, her obvious and unashamed emotion at what she found there, and her impassioned plea to the world's leaders on behalf of the starving people caused a wave of admiration and a fever of fund-raising in her own country. An editorial in a serious Sunday newspaper, the *Sunday Tribune*, on 11 October 1992, caught the general mood: 'She has the great gift of being able to convey respect to people. She has done this to enormous effect both during her Presidential campaign and during her Presidency in Ireland to date. She did so again in Somalia, bringing respect to the destitute of the earth whom she met.' Irish people were irritated that her visit to Somalia was virtually unreported in any country outside Ireland: in truth, by the time the necessary security and other arrangements had been made for the visit, Somalia had already been top news across the world for some weeks. It is perhaps natural that Ireland, so fascinated by this new President, should imagine that the world would be fascinated too.

The President's establishment costs the Irish taxpayer about IR£1 million a year, inclusive of salaries, travel, transport, and security – 'good value' according to the chairman of the Dáil Public Accounts Committee, Gay Mitchell, on receiving the report of the 1991 presidential budget (March 1992). Four army officers take turns as aides-de-camp (including the first woman ever to hold such a position), police drivers and security escort the President, thirteen administrative staff run the official side of things, the household staff amounts to ten people, and the Office of Public Works looks after the handsome gardens and grounds. By Irish standards, this is lavish indeed: it is symptomatic of the impact Mary Robinson makes that nobody criticizes the establishment or its cost. The voices which in the past questioned the validity of having a President at all are silent.

This President is a new phenomenon in Irish public life. She has literally reached out to include every kind of person in her anxiety to show that the presidency has real significance for the country, can be a focal point for diverse strands of society, and has real potential for leadership. The *Irish Times* on 7 November 1991 quoted an admiring woman in the west of Ireland trying to express what she felt about the President: 'For me . . . the State has always been somewhere else . . . but I think she has put a new face on it. In that way, she is subversive and I think it's wonderful . . .'

On 8 July 1992, Mary Robinson addressed, on her own initiative, a joint meeting of the two houses of the Irish Oireachtas. The speech reflected on Ireland as a member of the European Community, from a woman who by her experience and understanding of European issues was peculiarly well fitted to deliver it. It was also a remarkable examination of Irish identity, from the 'great humanizing service rendered to society by the Celtic people of Ireland in the childhood of European civilization' to James Joyce creating 'the uncreated conscience of my race', to the rich experience of diverse traditions in Northern Ireland. It is not often that the Dáil chamber, more used to the point-scoring of political jousting, has heard an Irish person deliver such an eloquent, reflective, and inspired speech, inviting politicians to think about their role in a changing Ireland.

Shortly after that occasion, a normally severe critic of the political establishment,[14] writing about Mary Robinson's ability to appeal to all kinds of people, and her redefinition of the role of President, said: 'She has done much more than simply redefine the presidency ... she has taken steps to move it into the heart of the vacuum of moral leadership resulting from the drift of modern politics.' When the coalition government of Ireland fell apart in November 1992 amid a welter of accusations of dishonesty, that vacuum seemed deeper, and the presidency seemed more central, than was ever envisaged in the 1937 Constitution.

No single event since Mary Robinson's election in 1990 epitomized change in Ireland as much as her meeting with Queen Elizabeth of England in May 1993. The President had just returned from a visit to the United States, where she met President Clinton and was garlanded with awards for her work in Somalia. Before that, she had undertaken a State visit to Spain, which was glowingly reported as having been a particularly successful occasion, with the President briefing herself thoroughly in order to be relaxed and on top of every aspect of a heavy schedule. She still kept up a punishing rota of meetings and visits and speeches at home, ac- companied as often as not by the tall, bearded and dignified figure of her husband. Unusually for Ireland, it was hard to find anyone to criticize her – instead, people just worried that she was getting too thin. Two and a half years after her election, she was still rising in the estimation of the Irish people: no President of Ireland had ever enjoyed anything like it.

When the announcement of the impending meeting with the British monarch was made, no one doubted that the President herself had had something to do with it; such a national asset as this articulate, energetic, and concerned example of the new Ireland could do nothing but good for Anglo-Irish relations. It was the first such meeting ever, heavy therefore with symbolism, unthinkable even in recent history. It was remarkable that criticism hardly surfaced at all. Mary Robinson was overcoming yet another ancient obstacle to progress, and doing so with style and intelligence.

But the President's next mould-breaking initiative, a handshake with Gerry Adams, leader of the nationalist Sinn Féin Party, in Belfast on 18 June 1993, caused the first major controversy since her election. She visited a deprived area in west Belfast and met about one hundred community leaders at a private reception. Among them was Adams, whose hand, like scores of others, she shook before passing on. The British government disapproved strongly, the Irish government seemed confused about their exact stance, and the Fine Gael Party were outraged. This risky action, taken in the context of this presidency being, from the outset, 'inclusive', showed how independent-minded Mary Robinson had become. If it were not for her impeccable credentials as a peace-maker and fair-minded interest in justice for all sectors of society, the reaction might have been much more negative. By June 1993, however, she had achieved such popularity that the banner headlines in the mass-circulation *Star* tabloid newspaper, addressed to her critics on 22 June, came as no surprise: 'Hands off our Mary!'

NOTES

1. Bunreacht na hÉireann (Constitution of Ireland), Article 2.2.
2. Interview with Joe Carroll, *Irish Times*, 3 August 1991.
3. ibid.
4. ibid.
5. *Sunday Independent*, 21 October 1990.
6. Eoin O'Sullivan, 'The 1990 presidential elections in the Republic of Ireland', *Irish Political Studies*, vol. 6, 1991.
7. In a book by Raymond Smith called *Garret the Enigma*, a biography of Garret FitzGerald, Smith stated that three Fianna Fáil front-benchers, including Brian Lenihan, had telephoned Áras an Uachtaráin on 27 January 1982, after the fall of the Fine Gael–Labour coalition on their Budget, in order to explain to the President that an alternative government could be formed without recourse to a general election. None had managed actually to speak to the President. Earlier than that, on 7 February 1982, in the *Sunday Tribune*, political correspondent Geraldine Kennedy had made the same statement about the telephone calls; her report was never denied.
8. *'Six-o-One' News*, RTE Television, 25 October 1990.
9. Brian Lenihan, *For the Record*, Blackwater Press, 1991.
10. *Saturday View*, RTE Radio, 3 November 1990.
11. *Sunday Times* (London), 11 November 1990.
12. *Irish Independent*, 17 April 1992.
13. Pádraig Flynn, on RTE Radio (*The Gay Byrne Show*), 8 May 1992.
14. John Waters, in the *Irish Times*, 28 July 1992.

CHAPTER 2

Government and Cabinet in Ireland

Ireland, for several centuries before the twentieth, was linked with, dominated, and ruled by England and England's system of government. During those long years, Irish political thought and political structures were formed in the shadow of the mother of parliaments at Westminster: Ireland, after all, was insulated from mainland Europe, an island behind an island. The British Lords and the Commons, the prime minister and the party system, and the kings and queens of England all presented a model which was the inevitable standard for imitation. This became all the more inevitable as the foundations and shape of a new Irish independent State were hammered out at the conference table in London between Lloyd George and the Irish representatives in 1921. The result, set out in Article 12 of the Constitution of the Irish Free State, 1922, was a legislature 'hereby created to be known as the Oireachtas. It shall consist of the King and two Houses . . .' The first Constitution went on, in Articles 51 to 55, to describe the basics of the government which Ireland still has today. In 1922 the government was called the Executive Council, with its head described as President. Today it is called the Government, with its head known as the 'Taoiseach'. As the State developed, flexed its independent muscles, and distanced itself more from Britain, Ireland left the Commonwealth, replaced the King with a President, increased the number of government ministers to fifteen, but preserved the essential characteristics of the British structure of government.

The strength of the British system of government was eloquently demonstrated when it was adapted to Irish conditions to fit the new State in 1922, a State which had been born in protracted turbulence and bloodshed, culminating in that London negotiation to establish Irish independence. The Constitution served the country well from 1922, after the years of struggle against Britain, until 1937, when the people adopted a new one, which was to reflect a new government's more nationalistic outlook and bring

Catholic social thinking of the day to bear on the shape of a new Ireland. Éamon de Valera designed the 1937 Constitution of Ireland (in the Irish language, the first official language of the state: Bunreacht na hÉireann).

When he was working on it, he decided that the kind of Cabinet government which had been put in place in 1922 had served its purposes well, seeing the fledgeling new Ireland off to a good solid start. Indeed it had – to the point where it had withstood the strains of de Valera's own 'slightly constitutional' behaviour since 1927,* the year he and his Fianna Fáil party had finally, grudgingly, and suspiciously entered the democratic processes of parliament, not without guns under their coats. However, by 1937, ten years later, democracy had well and truly established itself in Ireland; the same men who had carried guns in the tragic civil war of 1922/3, and later carried them into parliament in secret, were now fully ensconced in government. And that government felt it was time to throw off the constraints which the first administration had had to work under: the 'Free State' Constitution had, after all, been drafted under the eye of the British, following the Anglo-Irish Treaty of 1921.

Nowhere in either of the State's Constitutions does the word 'Cabinet' appear: the earlier document had an 'Executive Council' as the central committee of government, while the present Constitution, that of 1937, uses the term 'the Government'. However, Irish commentators freely use the term 'Cabinet' to describe the fifteen people who are the executive arm of government. The role and function of the government is set out in the twelve sections of Article 28 of the Constitution. The system is a Cabinet one, modelled on British lines, but admirably simple and clear in most respects. It may not be a total description of what actually happens, and in some ways (notably section 10, discussing the procedure governing a dissolution of the Dáil) it is inadequate, but it has worked, and worked well. 'In a community like Ireland, in which the vast majority are constitutionalist and law-abiding, the Constitu-

---

*See pp. 154ff in Chapter 7 below. De Valera refused to accept the treaty which his negotiators in London brought back, and when his group was defeated on this in the first Dáil, led them into civil war. He then refused to take part in parliamentary life until 1927.

tion provides a reference point when questions of competence, demarcation of functions, or abuse of powers arise.'[1]

A government of Ireland may not exceed fifteen in number; they are chosen by a Taoiseach (the word means chief) who is elected by the Dáil after a general election, and will be the nominee of the group (or groups) who have gained a majority in the House. They are the executive arm of the State, in the tradition of separation of powers; the government is required to act as a collective authority, and a Tánaiste (deputy leader) is appointed by the Taoiseach; the government must all be members of either the Dáil or the Senate, but not more than two can come from the Senate, while the Taoiseach, Tánaiste and Minister for Finance must be members of the Dáil; the Taoiseach has sole power to appoint and dismiss ministers, and to decide on a date for an election.

So far so good: Article 28.10 leaves some uncertainty, however, about termination of office of a Taoiseach: 'The Taoiseach shall resign from office upon his ceasing to retain the support of a majority in Dáil Éireann.' And the uncertainty is compounded by Article 13.2 regarding presidential powers: 'The President may in his absolute discretion refuse to dissolve Dáil Éireann on the advice of a Taoiseach who has ceased to retain the support of a majority in Dáil Éireann.' The question arises: what is the definition of 'ceasing to retain the support of a majority in Dáil Éireann'? Is it an ordinary vote, or a special vote of confidence? Nor does the Constitution enlighten us about what further actions the President might take if she or he decided to refuse a dissolution. These questions have never quite come to testing point in modern Ireland. It is worth noting, however, that in 1982 an Opposition Front Bench tried to contact the President after the government had fallen (on a budget resolution) to ask him to refuse a dissolution: the President did not take the telephone calls, and the election was duly called. On another fairly recent occasion – 1989 – an outgoing Taoiseach failed to resign on being defeated on a vote for Taoiseach: he pleaded that the Constitution permitted him time to consider his position, but the combined Opposition were adamant and resign he did.*

---

*Mr Charles J. Haughey, leader of the Opposition in January 1982 when a government fell on a Budget vote, tried to make contact with President Hillery to get him to exercise his prerogative to refuse to dissolve the Dáil. In June 1989, Mr

In today's Ireland, government meetings normally take place twice a week, at Government Buildings in Merrion Street on the south side of Dublin, just beside Leinster House. In addition to the members of the government, those attending include the Attorney-General, the government chief whip (who is usually a Minister of State – a junior minister) and the only civil servant present, the Secretary to the Government.* Occasionally, another Minister of State may attend to explain or elaborate on a matter which has come under the special attention of his or her ministry.

The central power and influence of the Taoiseach is first demonstrated by his control over the agenda for the meeting: it is prepared under his direction, the order in which items are placed is his prerogative, and if he wants a particular item put on to the agenda, it will duly appear: no other minister has that power. In a coalition government, of course, the agenda will be – or should be – worked out between the Taoiseach and the leader of the other party or parties in government. By 1993, with the idea of coalition government well established, a new and powerful Tánaiste's office was established by the leader of the Labour Party, which held six cabinet posts in a Fianna Fáil–Labour coalition government. A painful lesson had been learned during the previous two years, when accusations were made against the Fianna Fáil Taoiseach that there was little or no cooperation in the closing months of that government. In all of this, the Secretary to the Government will play an important advisory role.

In a room connected with the Cabinet room there is a tea/coffee area: ministers may start the meeting with an informal chat over the cups. In another room across the corridor, a civil servant sits, ready to take messages for ministers which, depending on their urgency, may be handed in to the Cabinet room through double doors.

On the formal agenda, there will be proposals for legislation which have been through a process of examination and comment

---

Haughey had failed to get an overall majority in a general election: when all candidates for Taoiseach were defeated, there was some uncertainty about the constitutional position. However, Mr Haughey resigned and was later elected as Taoiseach on going into coalition with another party.

* See Chapter 4, 'Civil Service: Not So Very British'.

by each minister's department before arriving at a Cabinet meeting. There will be many other areas on the list too, such as reports by ministers on developments at EC meetings in different areas; some ministers may ask for approval for new policy initiatives of a sensitive nature; there may be new appointments for the judiciary or for State boards to be considered;* a major report from a government-appointed commission; perhaps the initial discussion of a developing budgetary policy; some delicate point in relation to Northern Ireland . . . the list is endless. All of these must take the form of a memorandum, from the minister concerned, which has been circulated to the whole Cabinet three days before the meeting. (Ministers go around with bulging briefcases, the contents of which they are desperately trying to read before the next Cabinet meeting.)

As well as this kind of agenda, the government has to have enough flexibility to be able to deal with the unexpected: to cater for that, there is a period set aside for 'twelve o'clock items' (the term has its origins in the fact that it was at midday that these matters were usually brought up by ministers). Immediately after the meeting, the Secretary to the Government conveys decisions to the private secretaries of the ministers concerned, so that departments will initiate whatever action is required. The government's press secretary will be briefed, in order to prepare whatever information will be given to the media. With such a massive workload, it is not surprising that sometimes there have to be short cuts: an 'incorporeal' meeting may be held on the telephone, with a short note on the subject-matter sent around before the Secretary to the Government rings the minister at a prearranged time. Minutes of Cabinet meetings only record decisions taken, not the discussions held. If a vote is taken, only the result is minuted. Under the Archives Act of 1985, minutes are available for public inspection after thirty years.

Collective Cabinet responsibility is a fundamental principle of

---

* These appointments are very jealously watched by government ministers, as they are an important part of political patronage. During the interregnum after the election of November 1992, before the coalition arrangement was agreed with Labour, the caretaker Fianna Fáil government filled 200 posts, ranging from Supreme Court appointments and posts on university boards to membership of the Broadcasting Complaints Commission.

Irish government: in theory, a minister who is fundamentally opposed to a Cabinet decision should resign. This does not always
happen, by any means. In 1979, a minister made public his opposition to a government family-planning bill but neither resigned nor
was asked to; a Taoiseach and his minister for education voted
against their own government's 1974 bill (on the same subject) and
remained in Cabinet, and in 1992 it was quite clear that there were
big differences between the two parties in government on a range
of issues – but the government only fell when the Taoiseach
publicly accused his Cabinet colleague from the coalition party of
dishonesty.

Discussions at Cabinet are directed by the Taoiseach, with the
Minister for Finance taking an active part, since so many decisions
have spending implications. The discussion will usually be a three-
way one, between the minister proposing the subject under consideration, and the Taoiseach, who consults the Minister for
Finance if there are financial areas involved, and asks questions
himself. But a great many issues are more complex, and in a
coalition situation, the political/ideological delicacies come into
play. It is clear that the development of new ways of managing
government business in Ireland has not kept up with the increasing
complexity of the work: hence the frequently deplored lack of long-
term planning by Irish politicians. There is simply no thinking time.
In the words of Brian Farrell,* an expert and indefatigable investiga-
tor of Irish government systems: 'The complex, the controversial,
and the insoluble compete with the current, the commonplace, and
the critical for scarce time and attention on the government
agenda.'[2] In the wide-ranging proposals of January 1993 for
restructuring of government, as a new coalition administration of
Fianna Fáil and the Labour Party took office, a proposal was made
to appoint a group of advisers to ministers who could discuss
contentious matters in advance of Cabinet meetings, thereby clearing the ground for a less cluttered and time-consuming Cabinet
agenda. Such ideas have been mooted before, but have disappeared
under the weight of civil-service misgivings or second thoughts by
politicians. However, on this occasion, the partners in government

* Associate Professor, Government and Political Science, University College,
Dublin. Author, and doyen of political broadcasting on Irish television.

proceeded to make those appointments. Each minister appointed a 'partnership programme manager', whose salary was about IR£40,000. Collectively, the work of these officers was described as overseeing the implementation of the joint programme for government agreed before the formation of the government in February 1993. Extra appointments were made by the Tánaiste and leader of the Labour Party to his own office, which for the first time in Ireland became more than just a title. The majority partners in government contented themselves with appointing mostly civil servants to the new programme manager posts, and the new team was to be chaired by the former private secretary to the Taoiseach. All of these innovations could and should have been greeted as overdue modernization of the machinery of government. Instead, they were greeted with hostility and public condemnation for two reasons. The first was a failure to prepare public opinion in any way for the appointments, and the second – much more serious for the Labour Party – was the confusion and disquiet created by other appointments at a much lower level. Several ministers and junior ministers made family appointments to secretarial and driving positions on their staffs. Most of these appointments were quite in order, and most of the people concerned – secretaries – had been working in those capacities before their employers became ministers. However, the Labour Party had made such a big issue of ethics in government and high standards in high places that public opinion was outraged: and there appeared to be a vacuum in the public-relations department of the Labour Party, who attracted most of the odium while the media had a field day.

The lives and day-to-day activities of Cabinet ministers in Ireland are very much related to their roles as Dáil Deputy and constituency worker. They are certainly not full-time managers of their departments. A typical day might follow this kind of pattern: an early awakening, a short time with spouse and children and current affairs on the radio, before the telephone starts ringing with calls from those few people close enough to catch the minister at home (or those who aren't close, but think they are). These calls will usually be on constituency matters. The driver arrives with the car, the minister climbs in with briefcases, messages, and newspapers and tries to catch up on some reading on the way to Leinster House (the parliament building) or to his or her department headquarters.

Depending on their home location, this could be anything from ten minutes to an hour. Ministers from further afield either will have stayed in the city, or will leave home in the small hours.

Since the ministers may have attended a party function the night before (which might go on half the night) or an official dinner of some major interest group, they are already behind with their reading of Cabinet documentation and have no more than a hazy idea of what will come up for discussion. They proceed into the Dáil chamber in single file behind the Taoiseach, and each minister prepares for unexpected or contentious questions lobbed across the chamber by the Opposition on the order of business (the first few minutes of each sitting day). Since standing orders restrict unrehearsed questioning, they will field the questions and make a note for their officials. Into Cabinet they go then (at busy times, or in coalition governments, it is not often possible to limit government meetings to twice a week). The minister will do his or her best to contribute meaningfully to Cabinet discussions, and will wonder how the Taoiseach can possibly find the time to have mastered all the items on the agenda. Then to lunch, perhaps in the rather dingy ministerial dining-room in order to escape the attentions of Dáil Deputies looking for new schools, better water systems, an upgraded hospital . . . and into the Dáil chamber again because it's Question Time, from 2.30 until 3.45 p.m. Here, the minister has two helpful features: the written replies prepared by civil servants which will give as little information as possible in order not to raise any hares; and the standing orders which allow waffling and prevarication. Then, with a bit of luck, there will be an hour or so to look into the business of whatever department of state the minister is supposed to be running, perhaps to sign the many scores of letters which must be scrutinized before the minister's signature goes on them, or to catch up with the secretarial side of constituency work. In Ireland, ministers must attend and vote at all parliamentary sessions. This will be interrupted by deputations: groups of people from Kerry, or Donegal, or Cork, looking for particular things for their area, most of which cost money. They are accompanied by Deputies and Senators from the minister's and Opposition parties, so the minister must sound interested, be well informed, and above all sound sincere. After that, perhaps an important group of constituents have come all the way to Leinster House on a visit, and must be talked to and entertained with food and drink (costly as well as fattening). Finally, some time between eight and nine in the evening, the minister will get back into the car and set off to yet more meetings, social functions, fund-raising events (if possible in the constituency: there are other Deputies and local councillors of his own and other parties, all with high profiles, at home looking for his seat) before falling into bed some time after midnight. The life will vary slightly when the House is not sitting, in that more time will be available for the minister to work in the department, and to sit in upstairs rooms in halls and pubs in his or her constituency dealing with scores of local people and their local concerns. At weekends, the constituency demands high visibility (not to mention the family, who usually come a poor second or third in the priorities). If ministers fail to do this local work, they will suffer the consequences. The leader of the Labour Party, Dick Spring, who had a very traumatic and difficult time for more than four years in government as Tánaiste between 1982 and 1987, and had to try to look after his distant Kerry constituency at the same time, held his Dáil seat by a margin of only four votes in 1987. Two ministers lost their seats after the 1973–7 period of government, despite the fact that they were both considered excellent ministers* in a national sense.

Cabinet meetings are, naturally, confidential gatherings. Irish ministers do not discuss the detail of Cabinet meetings with the public, or with a wide circle. The normal minister/secretary relationship, however, is a different situation: it would be difficult not to discuss meetings with, for example, secretaries of government departments, or the senior civil servants in a particularly specialized area. The author, when a Cabinet minister, frequently found it necessary to tell her senior civil servants and/or special adviser how the Cabinet's mind was working on some areas which were under discussion, in order to get their advice on how to counter the arguments for or against her point of view. She was aware, of course, that this was normal procedure. Historians and writers on politics, as well as former politicians, have illustrated their work with general pictures of the evolution of Cabinet thinking, and

---

*They were Conor Cruise O'Brien, Minister for Posts and Telegraphs, and Patrick Cooney, Minister for Justice.

important Cabinet discussions on particular points of historical interest. At a more immediate level, informal briefing of the political correspondents by the government information and press officer on background Cabinet discussions have been an integral part of democratic interchange in Ireland, as elsewhere.

In 1992, that all changed in Ireland. In July, a former government minister was asked, at a judicial tribunal of inquiry into the beef industry, if certain matters had been discussed at Cabinet meetings of 1988. Counsel for the State, acting on the Attorney-General's instructions, objected, on the grounds that Cabinet discussions were, under the Constitution, completely secret. This presented the tribunal with a dilemma: it had been set up by the Dáil to investigate, among other things, allegations of political favouritism in State support of the beef industry. The case went to the High Court, and Mr Justice O'Hanlon found that the plea of confidentiality could not be used in the tribunal. However, the Supreme Court, on 21 August, overturned that decision, and in a 3–2 decision, declared that Cabinet confidentiality was an absolute, never to be breached, and that no government or member of government could waive this right when it came to discussions of previous or present governments. Apart from the immediate matter of the spancelling of the tribunal, which caused great unease among the media and the Opposition in the Dáil, the blanket protection of ministers, when in Cabinet, against any accountability was another concern. For example, if an Irish Cabinet minister decides to resign from government, is he or she now forbidden to explain publicly what lies behind the resignation? If some ministers in a Cabinet involved themselves in discussions about criminal wrongdoings in which they were involved, would a court of law be unable to hear evidence from their honest colleagues in order to bring them to justice? These and other questions* were raised by many lawyers, commentators, and politicians. The questions remain unanswered. The leader of the Labour Party immediately wrote, without avail, to

---

* The questions included concerns about the only three books of memoirs written by retired Irish politicians, all of which in one way or another apparently breached this blanket prohibition on discussion of Cabinet deliberations: Noel Browne's *Against the Tide*, Garret FitzGerald's *All in a Life*, and the author's *At the Cutting Edge: Cabinet Diaries 1982–87*. However, all three are still on public sale.

the Taoiseach asking for the recall of the Dáil to consider the situation. When a sudden general election took place in November 1992, the Labour Party included in its manifesto an undertaking to have a referendum to reverse this Supreme Court ruling: but when, two months later, they published their joint *Programme for a Partnership Government, 1993–97* on going into government with Fianna Fáil, there was no mention of Cabinet confidentiality or referenda. Back in August 1992, in the Supreme Court judgement printed in full in many newspapers, there was a minority judgement by Mr Justice Niall McCarthy.* He said that the Supreme Court were not offered '. . . a single instance in a modern nation enjoying democratic rule under a rigid constitution where such an absolute rule has been found', and went on to say, 'if absolute confidentiality is not expressed in the words of the people's Constitution, then it does not exist'. However, since 21 August 1992, it has existed in Ireland.

The nine Irish prime ministers since independence have all been male, Catholic, middle class, and married, none separated or divorced, all educated in single-sex religious-run schools, and all with third-level education (except for the present leader, Mr Reynolds, and Seán Lemass).

That list might imply a terrible sameness, yet nothing could be further from the truth. Incumbents of the Taoiseach's office have varied from the austere, autocratic revolutionary with a mathematical bent who inspired devotion and hatred in equal amounts – Éamon de Valera – to the flamboyant and charismatic *bon viveur* who obsessed the Irish people with his controversial personal, business and political life for two decades, Charles J. Haughey. In the late 1950s, when Ireland seemed doomed to eternal stagnation, ruled by tired, post-revolutionary old men, an economic visionary called Seán Lemass took office and kick-started an economic revival; for the first decade of independence, W. T. Cosgrave courageously put in place the foundations of Ireland's modern democracy with quiet strength in the face of threats of assassination and civil mayhem; in 1970 an apparently mild Taoiseach (Jack Lynch) dismissed two senior ministers suddenly, on hearing of their alleged involvement in gun-running to Northern Ireland. Garret FitzGerald

* Mr Justice McCarthy was considered a liberal in the Irish Supreme Court. See p. 111 below.

burst upon the Irish political scene in 1973 with a virtuoso performance as a polyglot Foreign Minister: he went on to revitalize his
party, Fine Gael, attempted (and failed) constitutional change on
the liberal social agenda, but engaged Margaret Thatcher of Britain
in talks leading to the historic Anglo-Irish Agreement of 1985.

Irish politics are often a family affair: even in the short list of
Irish prime ministers there is a father and son (W. T. Cosgrave and
Liam Cosgrave) and a father-in-law and son-in-law (Charles J.
Haughey married the daughter of Seán Lemass). Another Taoiseach,
Garret FitzGerald, was the son of Ireland's first Minister for
Foreign Affairs (then known as External Affairs) Desmond
FitzGerald. In 1993, however, a sign of the changing times in
Ireland was that, for the first time, neither of the leaders of the two
main political parties, one of them holding the office of Taoiseach,
had any family connections with the founding fathers of the State.

Four of those Taoisigh came from Fine Gael (or its earlier
incarnation, Cumann na nGaedheal) and five from Fianna Fáil,
whose first leader de Valera held the office for twenty-one years.
The Fine Gael Party has held power for just one-third of the State's
seventy-year existence, and mostly has had to go into coalition to
achieve that. The first Fianna Fáil Taoiseach to take his party into
coalition with another party was Mr Haughey in 1989, having
failed in five elections to gain an overall majority for Fianna Fáil.

The style of Cabinet chairmanship of each of these men has
naturally varied. Charles Haughey conducted Cabinet meetings in a
brisk, no-nonsense manner, in contrast to Dr Garret FitzGerald in
the 1980s who was so anxious to get consensus among his loqua-
cious coalition colleagues that meetings frequently extended late
into the night. Taoisigh have been described as being chairmen,
chiefs, or bosses in their relationships with their Cabinets: de
Valera was the quintessential chief, who was held in respect border-
ing on awe by his colleagues; Mr Haughey was a boss, conducting
short and efficient Cabinet meetings and brooking little argument;
Dr FitzGerald a slightly too accommodating and discursive chairman, Albert Reynolds falling somewhere in between. Reynolds,
finding himself in January 1993 with six Labour Party ministers at
the oval mahogany Cabinet table, including a formidable Tánaiste,
would have to lean more towards the FitzGerald style if harmony is
to be the order of the day.

Irish Prime Ministers and Their Parties		
Year	Taoiseach	Party
1922–32	W. T. Cosgrave	Cumann na nGaedheal
1932–48; 1951–54; 1957–9	Éamon de Valera	Fianna Fáil
1948–51; 1954–7	John A. Costello*	Fine Gael
1959–66	Seán Lemass	Fianna Fáil
1966–73; 1977–9	Jack Lynch	Fianna Fáil
1973–7	Liam Cosgrave*	Fine Gael
1979–81; 1982; 1987–92	Charles J. Haughey*	Fianna Fáil
1981–2; 1982–7	Garret FitzGerald*	Fine Gael
1992–	Albert Reynolds*	Fianna Fáil

* In coalition.

THE MODERN IRISH PRIME MINISTER

For most of 1992, a coalition government made up of Fianna Fáil and the Progressive Democrats formed the administration of Ireland. It was replaced in January 1993 by a new combination of parties: Fianna Fáil and the Labour Party. In that twelve months, signs of change in Irish political thinking had developed into strong trends. The sudden surge of the popular vote for the Labour Party brought a new strong force to Irish parliamentary life, which was to change the way governments were formed. This watershed for Labour came after the country had been astonished for eight months at upheavals emanating from Government Buildings.

On 11 February 1992, Mr Albert Reynolds* was elected

*Albert Reynolds, b. 1935, Rooskey, Co. Roscommon. Married to Kathleen Coen, with two sons and five daughters. First elected to the Dáil in 1977; Minister for Posts and Telegraphs, and Minister for Transport, 1979–81; Minister for Industry and Energy, 1982; Minister for Industry and Commerce, 1987–8; Minister for Finance, 1988–91. Elected Taoiseach February 1992, and again in January 1993.

Taoiseach in Dáil Éireann, having become the new leader of Fianna Fáil. He immediately demonstrated the strength and power of the Taoiseach over party and government by sacking eight serving Fianna Fáil ministers on that day: an astonished Dáil and country watched while senior Fianna Fáil party figures, with impeccable family dynasties in the party, were summarily consigned to the back benches. He was acting thus after five months of protracted political crisis and public scandals on the business front, during most of which his predecessor was fighting for political survival. The scars were deep and enduring. The new Taoiseach thought that, by having a clean sweep of most of those associated closely with the former leader, he could exorcize the ghosts of times past and bring Fianna Fáil back into government with an overall majority after a decent interval.

Albert Reynolds is the first Irish prime minister from the midlands of Ireland; from a small farming background, he pulled himself up in the world by observing and grasping opportunities in business, first in the rural ballroom scene in the late 1950s and 60s, and then by going into pet-food production. The residual aura of a bland 'country and western' approach was temporarily resuscitated when, on the night of his election, British television played a 1980 film clip of Mr Reynolds in full cowboy gear crooning into a microphone: that image had been put firmly behind him by 1992. His homespun, no-nonsense, almost aggressively unsophisticated style was given respectability by his record of personal business success and by its contrast with his predecessor's worldly, complex and often arrogant air. Reynolds was '... a pragmatist with entrepreneurial flair, no visionary, no idealist, and no claims to be either'.[3]

For some commentators, Reynolds showed that Fianna Fáil was no longer a party of ideologues and idealists, but certainly one of pragmatists. Not for him the cold-as-charity proscriptions of the past. A historian and political commentator observed: 'While Éamon de Valera, Fianna Fáil's founder, idealized an Ireland of comely maidens dancing jigs at the crossroads, its latest leader became a millionaire by enticing the comely maidens in out of the cold to the ballrooms he built at many of those same crossroads.'[4] His 'fix-it' philosophy on matters economic was well known; the only note of concern was his failure to keep exchequer borrowing on a downward path in 1991 as Minister for Finance. Affable at the outset, but reserved, living in discreet comfort, a family man through and through, he could not have been more of a contrast to Mr Haughey. 'He doesn't drink, doesn't smoke, has no expensive hobbies or colourful friends,' wailed a journalist.[5] The country, observing his style, hoped that his dullness would be at least safe, after twelve years of the exciting Mr Haughey, for seven of which he held the prime ministerial portfolio.

The political honeymoon which Albert Reynolds might have expected did not materialize: the day after his accession to power, on 12 February 1992, a story appeared in the Irish media, and then all over Europe, about an injunction in the Irish High Court which had been obtained at the behest of the Attorney-General to prevent a fourteen-year-old girl, pregnant after alleged rape, from travelling to England for an abortion, reopening that long-standing and controversial subject in Ireland. 'A fortnight into the job', said the *Irish Independent*, 'he found himself struggling with the language of the labour ward.'[6] This presented huge political problems which, no matter what course of action would be adopted, would inevitably be protracted and deeply divisive. While that issue was unfolding daily, he became locked in combat with Opposition leaders and trade unions, as well as the unemployed, about a 'national forum' for tackling the unemployment crisis in Ireland, the figures heading towards 300,000 or 21 per cent of the labour force; and a month later – in March – one of Ireland's largest employers in the job-starved west of Ireland, United Meat Packers, ran into financial difficulties with the threatened loss of more than 600 jobs – in Albert Reynolds's own constituency heartland – with accompanying demands for rescue by government. In the first month of his office, a national bank dispute slowly escalated towards threatened full closure of all banks. As the referendum on Maastricht approached in June, he had to deal with the fall-out from an unwise protocol inserted by his predecessor into the Maastricht Treaty on European Union, which had the effect of entangling the abortion issue with Maastricht. In the event, and not without difficulty, the problem was solved by all-party undertakings to put things right in the autumn, and the Maastricht Treaty was approved by a handsome majority.

An early sign of Albert Reynolds's determination to provide a new kind of 'open government' was his announcement that the elegant, refurbished Government Buildings in Merrion Street in Dublin would be opened to the public on Saturdays from June 1992.

This Edwardian edifice in Portland stone, the last of the great buildings left by the British in Ireland, was lavishly and quite tastefully restored at a cost of IR£17·6 million by Mr Charles Haughey;* it includes a helipad, and many Irish works of art, as well as modern examples of Irish craftsmanship in carpeting, wood, marble, and tiling. When Mr Haughey was criticized for spending so much, he defended himself on the grounds that Ireland should have such a seat of government as a sovereign nation with a proud history, and a country which in the modern world has to play host to more and more visiting heads of state and dignitaries. The place was highly praised by most people who visited it.

Mr Reynolds made that promise about open government in his speech to his party's annual conference on 7 March 1992: other statements in that first major public discourse of the new Taoiseach were indicative of what might be expected. A willingness to move forward on Northern Ireland, 'a constant personal grief to me'; a refreshing view of government's role in social issues, 'the government cannot function as a paternal authority seeking to control the decisions of its citizens relative to personal morality'; and a fierce determination (after the convulsions of the previous months) to have clean government, '. . . no inside tracks; no privileged circles; the same rules should apply to everybody . . .' The party slogan for that first Ard-Fheis† of Albert Reynolds's term of office was 'A New Beginning'. He wound up his speech with a flourish, essential for any party leader: 'Confidence is restored, the dark clouds are starting to clear. Ireland is on the move again. The new beginning has already started.'[7] The rafters rang with applause, the standing ovation was duly rendered. Not on the agenda at that point was the ruling on Cabinet confidentiality, which was to make government

---

*Dubliners, on its completion in 1990, called it 'The Chas Mahal' or alternatively, 'Château Charlemagne'. When Mr Reynolds moved in, they renamed it 'The Albert Hall'.

†'Ard-Fheis' is the Irish term for a high-level conference. It is used by Fianna Fáil and Fine Gael for their annual party conferences.

under Albert Reynolds the most secretive ever known. If the media thought it was to be open season on the Taoiseach, they were mistaken. He let it be known, by issuing legal letters, that open government did not mean he would be ignoring anything written or spoken which he considered legally unacceptable.

A Taoiseach is very powerful in Ireland. But if the government is formed by two or more parties in coalition, that power is obviously diluted in direct proportion to the number of Cabinet seats which have to be conceded to the partners in coalition. Four of Mr Reynolds's predecessors have directed coalition governments – but it is a relatively new experience for Fianna Fáil. Two parties formed the government after the election of 1989, for the Progressive Democrats provided enough seats to give Fianna Fáil the support it needed: Fianna Fáil had seventy-seven, the Progressive Democrats just six. However, in the hard bargaining which preceded the eventual formation of the government, the major party had to concede two Cabinet seats out of the fifteen, plus one junior ministry ('Minister of State').*

So Mr Reynolds, as he contemplated his Cabinet appointments in the few days before taking up the new job in 1992, had to appoint a group of twelve, as well as an Attorney-General and a government Chief Whip. The big changes were made, and the new Cabinet assembled for the smiling photograph with President Robinson, probably congratulating themselves on either survival (not many) or restoration and/or elevation. The country presumed that what they were seeing was a government which would last for another two years at least; little did they think that it would be such a temporary arrangement. Little more than eight months later, a general election took place.

There are many criteria which an Irish prime minister must consider when appointing a Cabinet: rewards for the loyal, appeasement of powerful party groups, attractiveness to the electorate, a geographical balance, and fitness for the post. In recent

---

* The leader of the Progressive Democrats, Desmond O'Malley TD (Teachta Dála – a Deputy of the Dáil), became Minister for Industry and Commerce; Mr Bobby Molloy held the other Cabinet Progressive Democrat post, as Minister for Energy. Ms Mary Harney was appointed Minister for Environmental Protection, in the junior ministerial ranks. All three were confirmed in those positions in the reshuffle following Mr Reynolds's accession as Taoiseach in February 1992.

years, there has always been one woman.* Some leaders have placed more emphasis on one or other of these attributes: Mr Haughey was considered to be fiercely loyal to his friends, sometimes to the detriment of the quality of his Cabinets. Such was his own broad knowledge and expertise on the whole gamut of national affairs that some of his ministers were seen as mere ciphers.

Not too many ciphers appeared in the Cabinet appointed by Albert Reynolds on that dramatic February day in 1992. Those new ministers who were noted for their loyalty to the new leader also, happily, were considered to be capable politicians and well able to master their new briefs. The men (and one woman) chosen represented a judicial mix of innovation and caution, with an element of risk befitting Mr Reynolds's entrepreneurial background. One of the features which signalled a lessening of old prejudices was that some of the ministers were publicly known to have had a marriage breakdown. In former days, such personal difficulties would have been carefully hidden or, if publicly spoken about, would have disqualified the husband or wife from ministerial office. The Irish public has become less rigid and more compassionate in its views on the behaviour of individuals encountering problems in their private lives.

The most important post in government after the Taoiseach is that of the Minister for Finance. To that job Mr Reynolds reappointed Mr Bertie Ahern,† one of the youngest members of the Cabinet. Quiet-spoken, pointedly emphasizing his rich, working-class Dublin accent, he represents a predominantly working-class central Dublin constituency and achieves a personal vote which has consistently been among the highest in the country (in 1989, it was 13,589) and which he jealously fosters. In Ireland's multiseat constituency system, a personal vote of half that number is considered high.* Known as 'the great facilitator' he brought considerable personal negotiating skills to industrial-relations

---

*That particular barrier was overcome with the next government in January 1993, when two women joined the Cabinet.
†Bertie Ahern, b. 1951 in Dublin. Obtained diplomas in taxation, business administration, and computer studies at University College, Dublin, and the London School of Economics. Before entering politics, worked as an accountant in hospital management. First elected to the Dáil in 1977.

problems while he was Minister for Labour from 1987 to 1991, and to the first-ever Fianna Fáil coalition negotiations with the Progressive Democrats in 1989. When Albert Reynolds declared himself for the Fianna Fáil leadership race in January 1992, Ahern's uncharacteristic hesitation and apparent indecisiveness damaged his prospects, until then very real, of assuming the leadership himself. His relatively bland first budget in January 1992 (condemned by the business community as damaging to enterprise) gave no clues about his potential of handling Ireland's escalating fiscal problems, the resolution of which must inevitably affect his own constituents. After Reynolds took the country into a general election in November 1992, Ahern was once more called into action as a negotiator of the new coalition between Fianna Fáil and Labour. Reappointed in January 1993, he then had to grapple with the European currency crisis and took a super-cautious line.

An appointment which was considered risky but interesting in the February 1992 Cabinet was that of the Minister for Social Welfare, Mr Charles McCreevy. Born in 1949, and known universally as Charlie, he comes from the same sort of background as his Taoiseach, a small farm. A clever man, he surmounted the family poverty to become a chartered accountant, and went into politics where he had a very public love–hate relationship with his leader, Mr Haughey, for many years. A frank and courageous figure, he opposed the free-spending policies of Mr Haughey between 1979 and 1982, led several revolts against him, was expelled from the parliamentary party, then accepted back and promptly increased his vote by fifty per cent in the February 1982 election. For the following years he continued to criticize openly many of the Haughey government actions. McCreevy, a self-professed betting man and follower of racing, is gregarious and a popular figure. More liberal than his party on social issues, and articulately conservative on economic issues, his appointment to Social Welfare was, at the very least, a gamble. The vagaries of Irish politics saw him survive a fairly tough policy stance on social-welfare spending,

* See Chapter 3, 'Houses of the Oireachtas: the Irish Parliament', for a full description of Ireland's multi-seat proportional-representation system.

to be reappointed to government in 1993 to the more comfortable post of Minister for Tourism and Trade.

A Taoiseach is aware that his team of ministers is going to have to carry out an enormous range of activities. As we have seen earlier in this section, '. . . in Ireland's type of cabinet government, ministers' functions in their range and ubiquity transcend those of almost any rulers in any democratic country'.[8] In the relations between government and Dáil, the ordinary member of the Dáil, particularly if he is a back-bencher, has almost no power or influence over government actions. Ministers act in their corporate capacity as a Cabinet, as the political heads of their departments, as party leaders both inside and outside the parliament, as proposers of legislation and deciders of public spending, unhampered by the parliamentary committees, which have very little power, and none to summon ministers before them. If the distinguishing feature of modern democracy is 'the spectacle of a large number of men obeying, within a defined territory, a small number of other men',[9] then Ireland has brought it to a fine art.

Ministers answer parliamentary questions in the Dáil on three days a week, usually from 2.30 until 3.45. The Taoiseach takes questions on two of those days, at the beginning of the period. As in the British system, questions must be submitted in advance in writing, with some supplementary questions allowed at the discretion of the Ceann Comhairle (Speaker or Chairman) of the Dáil. Government back-benchers rarely ask oral questions, except carefully 'planted' ones. While standing orders allow Deputies, therefore, to put questions to ministers, there is nothing in law or orders obliging ministers to give complete or frank answers or, indeed, any answer.

Cabinet members in Ireland are also the victims of the multi-seat proportional-representation electoral system. Their constituents, far from expecting their local representatives-turned-ministers to devote themselves to their national responsibilities, are more usually determined to make use of the perceived enhanced power and influence of the minister. The burden this places on ministers is a factor which has always diminished their real influence on decisions, and has given considerably more power to the civil service. As early as the 1940s, an accusation of 'excessive bureaucratic control' on decision-making was made by the Commission on Vocational

Organizations ('Ministerial responsibility is a convenient fiction'[10]). The demands of the Irish political system mean that ministers, therefore, are not and cannot be full-time policy-makers in their various departments. But because they must take responsibility in the Dáil and the media for the actions of their departments, such time as they can spend on departmental work is often employed in scrutinizing administrative detail and finding out what is actually happening. This set-up is not conducive to careful planning, thoughtful working out of policy, or long-term perspectives. The permanent element of government, the civil service, plays in Ireland a central role in policy formation and implementation. So the first real attempt to give ministers the kind of personal support they need in policy and planning was the 1993 appointment of the new layer of advisers to the Fianna Fáil–Labour coalition government.

In a country which does not enjoy great wealth at any level, except for a restricted circle, great excitement follows the allocation of the ministerial State car and police driver to the local politician-turned-minister, particularly in small towns and rural areas. The arrival of the sleek expensive vehicle at a local funeral in any part of Ireland outside Dublin is carefully noted, its absence noted too. If the politician has been made a junior minister, there won't be quite the same cachet about it all, but nevertheless it is widely appreciated. Until Garret FitzGerald in the 1980s abolished the practice of allocating the same full facilities to junior ministers as to their senior cabinet colleagues, the junior minister's equally splendid car was referred to colloquially as 'the half-car'. More important, the appointment of a Cabinet minister means that the constituency can expect great benefits in the form of schools, roads, housing, factories. Cork city has never forgotten nor forgiven the loss of their Taoiseach, Jack Lynch, in 1979 to Dublin man Charles Haughey's vaulting ambition for power. As Ireland's second city, Cork people are united in their belief that there should always be at least one full minister from the city. The argument has been made that since Cork city and county provide one-eighth of the seats in Dáil Éireann, they should, pro rata, get two full Cabinet ministers. In 1993, Cork city was still without its minister, though the Minister for Agriculture, Food and Forestry came from rural Cork South-West.

The Taoiseach and Cabinet have only in recent years begun to appreciate the need for extra advisers to provide more than the civil service could or should be doing. The system of outside advisers has by no means reached the European *cabinet du ministre* style, where a minister has a team of his own choosing around him, but the question is no longer a serious source of civil service suspicion or public disapproval. The brief furore about the appointments made by government in early 1993 was caused more by maladroit handling and presentation than by any deep-seated public disapproval.

'A cross between sidekick, guru and scout with invaluable knowledge of the tricky terrain ahead'[11] – the special adviser can be 'special' in the minister's departmental area, or in press and public relations, or in general political know-how. Mr Reynolds has a team of 'specials' – not civil servants – whose contracts expire when he leaves office. They are usually discreet back-room characters, not given to personal publicity. An exception to this rule in the 1987–92 government was Mr Haughey's government press officer, P. J. Mara, who entertained the press with his witty and sometimes faintly scandalous *obiter dicta*. On one occasion he announced that the party wouldn't stand for rebels 'nibbling at my leader's bum'. On another, deploring public dissidence in the party, he said that there should be 'Uno duce, una voce'. With his usual sense of humorous irony, when he was asked about his plans after the ousting of Mr Haughey, he replied that he '. . . would probably be like Cincinnatus, the fourth-century Roman statesman who saved Rome from invasion and the empire from destruction, then selflessly relinquished authority and returned to work on his small farm'.[12] While the image of his boss, Mr Haughey, had sunk very low in the opinion polls by February 1992, very few people in Ireland disliked P. J. Mara: like most people, they admire someone who makes them laugh.

On Mr Reynolds's team there is a mix of special advisers: Dr Martin Mansergh joined the former Taoiseach from the Department of Foreign Affairs as Northern Ireland adviser, but widened his brief to include EC affairs and international relations. The government press officer, replacing P. J. Mara, is Seán Duignan, an experienced broadcaster (and the son of a former Fianna Fáil Deputy) while Tom Savage is communications adviser. Part of a husband-and-wife team who run a firm which trains people in all forms of communications,* Mr Savage works part-time for Mr Reynolds, while his wife has contracts with other members of the Cabinet. Ministers in other government departments are also finding it necessary to appoint specialists, partly because of the increasing work-load involved in European Community membership, and partly to deal with a country whose people are used to a better standard of communications, and in which interest groups are improving their own systems of convincing the public of their right to be heard.

THE PRICE OF GOVERNMENT

Taoisigh and ministers are paid generously by Irish standards. The Taoiseach gets IR£77,845, his Tánaiste IR£66,477, and other ministers IR£61,930. They have State cars at their full-time disposal with two police drivers. Junior ministers receive IR£47,182, and the State pays for two civilian drivers for their own cars.† The most controversial aspect of politicians' remuneration has been the ministerial pension. Up to and including the 1989 election, ministers and Taoisigh became eligible for pensions after four years in office, and the pensions were payable in addition to their Dáil salary if they continued to serve in parliament. Thus a former Taoiseach still serving in the Dáil since 1989, Dr Garret FitzGerald, was receiving in 1991 a pension of IR£20,859 as well as his ordinary Deputy's salary of IR£29,000. His Tánaiste, Dick Spring TD, got IR£10,242; Brian Lenihan, a former minister of many departments, was receiving IR£15,892.[13] This was one of the issues immediately highlighted by the Progressive Democrat Party on their foundation in 1985, and pursued with vigour subsequently. The debate raged furiously up and down the country, with ministers and former ministers being attacked by the public as well as their own supporters. Given the kind of lifestyle imposed on office-holders by the Irish electoral system, as well as the cold wind of

* Carr Communications, one of the first such enterprises in Ireland, founded by Mr Bunny Carr, one of Ireland's early home-grown television personalities. Tom Savage's wife and business partner, Ms Terry Prone, continued to advise her most senior client, Pádraig Flynn, when he became Ireland's EC Commissioner in January 1993.
† These figures refer to January 1993.

insecurity (there were three general elections over the two years 1981 and 1982), many felt sorry they had ever gone into politics. The leader of the Progressive Democrats, and one of his colleagues who was also a former minister, publicly repudiated their ministerial pensions, thus making a strong point by forgoing several thousands of pounds a year each, and by personal example setting a precedent for other politicians.

The consistent pressure of the Progressive Democrats finally bore fruit, their hand having been strengthened by two years in government as coalition junior partner. On 17 December 1991, changes were announced by the Minister for Finance in the Dáil. After the next general election, ministers would not qualify for pensions until they reached the age of 55, or, at a reduced rate, the age of 50. A new scale of service-related pensions would apply, with a minimum rate of 25 per cent of salary for an office holder with three years' service, rising at a rate of 5 per cent of salary for each additional year to a maximum of 60 per cent of salary for an office holder with ten years' service or more. The two former ministers who had repudiated their ministerial salaries announced in March 1993 that they would now accept their ministerial pensions, having achieved the reforms they had sought.

THE FIANNA FÁIL/LABOUR COALITION GOVERNMENT OF JANUARY 1993

The first Reynolds coalition government from February to November 1992 was fractious and dogged by disagreement. It seemed as if Albert Reynolds felt sure he could behave as if there was no coalition sensitivity to be taken into account. Overshadowing the government all the time was a judicial tribunal into the beef industry, which carried within it the potential for destruction of the government, since the Taoiseach and his senior coalition Cabinet colleague were scheduled to give conflicting evidence to it. It was the tribunal which indeed finished off the government, amid a welter of accusations and recrimination. The Taoiseach, on 27 October, under oath, accused Desmond O'Malley, his Minister for Industry and Commerce and the leader of the Progressive Democrats, of being 'reckless, irresponsible, and dishonest'. It was the word dishonest, repeated carefully again by the Taoiseach, which made it impossible for the Progressive Democrats to remain in government. Desmond O'Malley has a reputation in Ireland of being scrupulously honest, and his party has made honesty and integrity in politics a central part of their platform.* O'Malley had played a definitive role in having the tribunal established in 1991 to investigate '. . . vital issues relating to the conduct of big business, its relationship with government, and the effectiveness or otherwise of the regulatory agents of the State . . .'[14]

As the Dáil lurched towards a vote of confidence on 5 November, which the government had to lose, it was clear that the decision to impugn O'Malley's honesty must have been a deliberate provocation by the Taoiseach. Further provocation was offered on 1 November when the Taoiseach described accounts of difficulties in his Cabinet relations with O'Malley as 'crap, total crap' on radio and television. This was yet another grave error of judgement, and was to have catastrophic electoral consequences for Fianna Fáil, who lost nine seats in the ensuing election, while the Progressive Democrats added four to their six.

The vote of confidence was duly lost, and the Taoiseach travelled the ten minutes to Áras an Uachtaráin to hand in his resignation to President Robinson.

During that vote of confidence debate in the Dáil on 5 November 1992, a particularly strong attack was made on Fianna Fáil by the leader of the Labour Party. He could not imagine how anyone could go into coalition with such a party, and accused them of practically every sin in the book, including all kinds of unethical dealings in government. Even allowing for parliamentary hyperbole, it was a bitter attack. It may have swayed the electorate, who on 25 November 1992 took nine seats away from Fianna Fáil and awarded the Labour Party thirty-three as against their fifteen at the dissolution of the Dáil. The campaign was marked by a bitter last few days of attacks on the Labour Party by Fianna Fáil, who warned

* It was all the more painful for him therefore when it was revealed in early 1993 that back in the 1970s his wife had received some minor financial assistance from her brother, who was involved in a mining company for which O'Malley had ministerial responsibility. Nobody seriously believed there had been any impropriety, but it was seized on with glee by some opponents.

that Labour in government would mean an explosion in borrowing, a collapse in economic growth, new and punitive taxes. Those attacks appeared to have been counter-productive. But they certainly led Fine Gael to believe that they would be the natural allies of Labour in a new coalition.

There followed the longest interregnum between governments ever known in Ireland. It was not until 12 January 1993 that the new government was formed. Seven weeks of intense political manoeuvring, a new experience in Irish politics, finally brought together Fianna Fáil and Labour in a 'partnership' government. The astute and triumphant leader of the Labour Party, Dick Spring, the new kingmaker, set his demands high at the outset, insisting that if he went into coalition with anyone, there would have to be a 'rotating Taoiseach'. Fine Gael, who had proposed a three-party coalition of themselves, Labour and the Progressive Democrats, refused to consider this concept, as well as refusing to consider any coalition involving the most left-wing party in the Dáil, the small (four seats) Democratic Left, with whom Labour had already started to talk. Dick Spring, with the memory of the personality clashes with the Fine Gael leader in a previous coalition still fresh in his mind, finally turned to the Fianna Fáil Party, whose leader had wisely kept silent. After some more weeks of comprehensive discussion of policy, and agreement on a wide-ranging programme for government in which Labour policies were clearly to the fore, the Dáil met on 12 January and elected Albert Reynolds once more as Taoiseach.

There was no more talk of a rotating Taoiseach, but Labour had got six Cabinet posts, five junior ministries, a restructuring of government, and a new office of the Tánaiste, as well as the Ministry for Foreign Affairs for the Labour leader. The government included new ministries for Equality and Law Reform, Employment and Enterprise, and Arts, Culture and the Gaeltacht, and a regrouping of some others. It looked like an astonishing victory – it was hard to remember that the Labour Party had achieved not sixty-eight seats like Fianna Fáil, not forty-five like Fine Gael, but had come third with thirty-three. Dick Spring brought into this government some of his colleagues who, because of their radical views and decidedly left-wing stance in the party, had never been considered as ministerial possibilities: the new Minister for Equality and Law Reform, Mervyn Taylor, and the Minister for Arts, Culture and the Gaeltacht, Michael D. Higgins, were particular examples. Each of the government parties appointed a woman to Cabinet, and when the junior ministerial portfolios were handed out, three more women were appointed. It looked as if tokenism in government appointments was coming to an end.

Fianna Fáil, though hating the concessions, would have hated opposition more, and Albert Reynolds, who had almost had to go into opposition and face his party's retribution, got a second chance. Fianna Fáil were prepared to go along with undertakings which the country recognized as Labour's bottom line, in particular a set of new legislative safeguards for ethics in government. In his speech at the Labour Party meeting in January which gave him the assent he needed to go into this new coalition, Dick Spring declared: 'The government will stand or fall on the issue of trust, and no one should be mistaken about that . . . it will be a policy-driven government and not a scandal-driven government. If it does not conform to the highest standards of accountability and openness it will cease to exist . . . ethics in government is a way of life and not just a statement of policy.'[15]

Fine Gael observed this new and unexpected alignment with a mixture of rage and despair, as they contemplated yet more years out of government, and the difficult task of asserting themselves in opposition after such a bruising electoral contest.

If the new Taoiseach had learned something from the débâcle of his last short-lived attempt to work with and lead a government, the partnership with Labour might give Ireland the stability and breathing space she needed. The economy was rocked by the storms of European currency swings, threatening employment even further in a country which approaches the highest unemployment rate in Europe. It would need all the ingenuity, tact, and goodwill of both partners to make this alliance work.

And the honeymoon was short-lived. Many factors combined to dethrone the Labour Party in government from the much-favoured place it had held in public esteem in the dying months of 1992 and the period of negotiation for government. Unemployment figures soared again; the public perception of how the currency crisis of early 1993 was handled was negative; there was a perceived confusion and disappointment over some major environmental issues;

Parties and Ministers in the Fianna Fáil/Labour Party Partnership Government, Appointed 12 January 1993

Fianna Fáil		Labour	
Taoiseach	Albert Reynolds	Tánaiste and Foreign Affairs	Dick Spring
Minister for:			
Finance	Bertie Ahern	Employment and Enterprise	Ruairí Quinn
Agriculture and Food	Joe Walsh	Equality and Law Reform	Mervyn Taylor
Social Welfare	Michael Woods	Arts, Culture and the Gaeltacht	Michael D. Higgins
Justice	Máire Geoghegan-Quinn	Health	Brendan Howlin
Environment	Michael Smith	Education	Niamh Bhreathnach
Defence and Marine	David Andrews		
Tourism and Trade	Charlie McCreevy		
Transport, Energy and Communications	Brian Cowan		
Chief Whip	Noel Dempsey		

Attorney-General: Harry Whelehan

the new government's first budget was considered unhelpful to job creation and negative on taxation, while the public-relations blunder of Labour's family appointments to their staff put the final nail in the coffin. By the beginning of March, Labour contemplated an unaccustomed unpopularity: public alienation from government (but particularly from the Labour element) was at its highest level for six years; 68 per cent expressed dissatisfaction with government in a major poll, while the Labour Party's leader suffered a catastrophic drop in his personal popularity from 71 per cent to 36 per cent. In the Ireland of the 1990s, a new volatility in political allegiances made the business of government even more difficult.

NOTES

1. Basil Chubb, *Cabinet Government in Ireland*, Institute of Public Administration.
2. Brian Farrell, 'The Irish Cabinet system', in Jean Blondel and Ferdinand Müller (eds.), *Cabinets in Western Europe*, Macmillan, 1988.
3. *Sunday Independent*, 21 June 1992.
4. John Bowman, *Sunday Times*, 9 February 1992.
5. Brenda Power, *Sunday Press*, 9 February 1992.
6. *Irish Independent*, 26 April 1992.
7. Quotations from Albert Reynolds's speech to the Fianna Fáil Ard-Fheis, 7 March 1992, reported in the *Irish Times*, 9 March 1992.
8. Chubb, op. cit.
9. ibid.
10. *Understanding Contemporary Ireland*, Breen, Hannon, Rottman, Whelan, Gill & Macmillan, 1990.
11. *Irish Independent*, 7 February 1991.
12. *Irish Times*, 1 February 1992. Mr Mara, in fact, far from taking up farming, joined the much more exciting Guinness Peat Aviation company.
13. Figures printed in the *Irish Times*, from a written answer to a parliamentary question, 18 December 1991.
14. *Dáil Report*, 10 July 1992.
15. *Irish Times*, 11 January 1993.

CHAPTER 3

Houses of the Oireachtas: the Irish Parliament

The 226 members of the Irish houses of parliament meet in the grand eighteenth-century Georgian town house of the FitzGerald family (the Dukes of Leinster) which faces on to Dublin's Kildare Street; its lawns on the other side of the building border the wide sweep of one of the finest Georgian squares in the city, Merrion Square.* Leinster House, as it is called, is guarded by a discreet army and police presence, and manned by a group of officials called ushers.

Inside, in a small, graceful semicircular blue room, complete with musicians' gallery (now allocated to a tiny number of members of the public, strictly enjoined to silence), sit the sixty Senators, engaged in debates which by tradition (and because of the limited influence of the Senate) are conducted in a low-key, quite courteous manner. Away on the other side of the house, down purple-carpeted corridors and up stairs, in a large semicircle, a former lecture theatre added on to the original house, the 166 members of the Dáil meet more often than the Senate, and in a more noisy and confrontational atmosphere.

The constitutional basis for the Irish houses of parliament is the description laid down in Articles 15 to 27 of the Irish Constitution. Article 15.1.2 includes the President: 'The Oireachtas [an Irish word for a general meeting, adapted to mean parliament in modern usage] shall consist of the President and two Houses, viz. a House of Representatives to be called Dáil Éireann, and a Senate to be called Seanad Éireann.' In practice, nobody in Ireland conjures up a picture of President Mary Robinson when the Oireachtas is mentioned, because her impact on the legislative process is almost completely confined to the signing of bills. Presidential power to

---

*Leinster House was built as a town house in 1745 by James Fitzgerald, twentieth Earl of Kildare, later to become the first Duke of Leinster. In 1815, the house was sold to the Royal Dublin Society and, in 1924, made over to the State.

refer bills to the Supreme Court for decisions about their constitutionality is rarely necessary.*

The constitutional Articles give the Oireachtas 'sole and
exclusive' powers to make laws and the right to raise armies, and
to its members the right to be protected from arrest going to or
from Dáil Éireann or Seanad Éireann (except in cases of treason,
felony, or breach of the peace); the Dáil can, in addition, set its
own pay scales and travel allowances, revise constituencies at least
every twelve years, and 'consider' estimates for expenditure. The
Senate cannot stop a bill altogether but can suggest amendments (as
long as it is not a money bill – such bills cannot be tampered with).
These and a host of minor procedural powers and duties form the
bulk of the constitutional Articles. Article 27, however, gives a
majority of the Senate, together with not less than one-third of the
Dáil, the power to petition the President to refer a bill directly to
the people (for a referendum) if 'it contains a proposal of such
national importance that the will of the people thereon ought to be
ascertained'. That Article has never been used, though in a situation
involving abortion in the maelstrom following the Supreme Court
decision of February 1992,† it lurked on the borders of possibility.

HOW IS THE DÁIL ELECTED?

In the years leading up to the establishment of the Irish Free State,
the forerunner to the Republic of Ireland, the Electoral Reform
Society was active in Britain. During discussions with the Irish
delegation in London, in preparation for the Anglo-Irish Treaty of
1921, the British side were most anxious that the Protestant and
Unionist minority would be included in every possible way in the
new State. As a result, the system of proportional representation,
with the single transferable vote in multi-member constituencies,

*See Chapter 1.

†The Supreme Court decided in February 1992 that abortion was permissible in
Ireland if there was a grave risk to the mother's life. This was an interpretation of
Article 40.3.3 which took the nation by surprise. The ensuing public and political
arguments centred on whether there should be another referendum to ensure that
abortion could not be permitted, or whether there should be legislation to define
the circumstances under which abortion should be available. A parallel debate
concerned the implications of the Maastricht EC Treaty for Irish abortion law.
(See Chapter 18, 'Women and Life in Ireland'.)

was agreed as the electoral system for the Free State, and appeared in the Government of Ireland Act 1920. That concern about the minority also influenced the establishment of the second chamber, the Senate.

The number of Dáil constituencies and the number of seats in each one, together with the constituency boundaries, are decided by an independent Dáil Constituency Commission. It has not always been so; Ireland, like many countries growing into political maturity, has seen manipulation of boundaries and seats to suit particular parties. Gerrymandering has been the order of the day, and no political party could claim to be above it. However, the pressures of public opinion have, so the optimists hope, put paid to any such attempts in the future. One of the welcome commitments in the Programme for Government published by the incoming coalition government of January 1993 was to establish an independent Electoral Commission on a statutory basis, which would consist of the Secretary of the Department of the Environment, the President of the High Court, the Clerks of the Dáil and Senate, and the Ombudsman. In 1990, the commission was composed of mostly the same personnel: the President of the High Court, a former Governor of the Central Bank, the Secretary of the Department of the Environment, the Clerk of the Dáil and the Clerk of the Senate.* They confirmed the forty-one constituencies then in existence, with slight boundary changes to account for shifts in population, and decided that the number of Deputies would continue to be 166, giving 21,329 voters per member (this comes close to the maximum number of Deputies allowable under the Constitution). The number of Deputies per constituency was allocated thus: four-seaters, 15; five-seaters, 14; three-seaters, 12.

An Irish voter in a general election (who must have reached her eighteenth birthday) has, therefore, a range of options when standing in the voting booth: the options are all centred around the expression of preferences: she can declare for the person she would most like to see elected, but not only that. She can go on to show who comes second in her preferences, who comes third, and so on. The constituency will return three, four, or five members to the

---

*They were: Mr Justice Liam Hamilton; Dr T. K. Whitaker; Mr Thomas Troy; Mr Éamon Rayel; Mr Kieran Coughlan.

Dáil, and there is usually a minimum of seven candidates, with up to a maximum of ten or eleven, on the voting paper. So the Irish voter does not use 'x' but instead uses numbers; she puts the figure '1' beside her first choice, '2' beside the next, and so on down through all the candidates listed if she so wishes. The larger parties will usually put forward two or three candidates, so their devoted supporters will give their own party candidates their top two or three votes, and only then pass on down to the others.

Fianna Fáil supporters have always been noted for their belief in voting only for their own candidates, and ignoring the rest. Fine Gael, since it has usually been seeking coalition with other parties, normally exhorts its supporters to continue to the next favoured party (never Fianna Fáil). Labour in the past has reciprocated this voting pact with Fine Gael, though as its strength and confidence has increased, it has supported other candidates and parties of the left. The smaller parties' lower preference votes are extremely valuable to marginal candidates and will be carefully canvassed for that reason. It was only in 1989, after Fianna Fáil made the difficult decision to enter coalition for the first time,* that a possibility arose of future voting transfer arrangements involving Fianna Fáil and other parties. In 1992, Fianna Fáil, despite privately admitting during the election campaign that an overall majority was a non-starter, could not yet bring themselves to any kind of transfer arrangement.

This is an extremely democratic electoral system, despite its apparent complexity, but its critics consider that it encourages extravagant clientelism (members' heavy dependence on individual voters' goodwill), imposes a time-consuming and unproductive drudgery on Dáil members, and consequently lowers the calibre of representative. A debate emerges every summer in the pages of the newspapers, during the 'silly season', and seems to die with the summer leaves. In 1987, however, an outgoing Taoiseach, Garret FitzGerald, raised a question about the suitability of the system for a modern democracy in his party's election manifesto: he expressed concern at 'the excessive concentration on this kind of activity [constituency work] which is forced upon the TD not merely by the normal competitive process between parties, but also by

* With the Progressive Democrats.

Cork South-Central

Seats 5	1st Count	2nd Count	3rd Count	4th Count
		Transfer of Abbey of the Holy Cross Fitzsimon's and Coleman's	Transfer of Cogan's	Transfer of Lynch's
Quota 8,937	Votes	Votes	Votes	Votes
ABBEY OF THE HOLY CROSS FITZSIMON, William (Ind)	150	− 150 −		
*BARRY, Peter (FG)	7,791	+ 184 7,975	+ 203 8,178	+ 182 8,360
COGAN, Barry (FF)	3,652	+ 79 3,731	−3,731 −	
COLEMAN, John Kevin (PD)	1,679	−1,679 −		
CORR, Jim (FG)	5,899	+ 210 6,109	+ 124 6,233	+ 188 6,421
*DENNEHY, John (FF)	5,586	+ 52 5,638	+ 1,496 7,134	+ 238 7,372
LYNCH, Kathleen (WP)	4,457	+ 76 4,533	+ 78 4,611	− 4,611 −
MARTIN, Micheál (FF)	6,564	+ 48 6,612	+ 682 7,294	+ 391 7,685
*O'KEEFFE, Batt (FF)	6,012	+ 56 6,068	+ 686 6,754	+ 128 6,882
*O'SULLIVAN, Toddy (Lab)	6,300	+ 93 6,393	+ 141 6,534	+ 2,558 9,092
*WYSE, Pearse (PD)	5,527	+ 963 6,490	+ 194 6,684	+ 487 7,171
NON-TRANSFERABLE		68	127	439

Example of a single-constituency general-election count, Cork South-Central, 1989

Cork South-Central

5th Count	6th Count	7th Count	Elected	
Transfer of **Corr's**	Transfer of **Barry's**	Transfer of **Wyse's**	Toddy O'Sullivan (Lab)*	4th Count
			Peter Barry (FG)*	5th Count
			Pearse Wyse (PD)*	6th Count
			Micheál Martin (FF)	7th Count
			John Dennehy (FF)*	7th Count
Votes	Surplus	Surplus		

Voting by Party

1st Preference	Number	%	% 1987
Fianna Fáil	21,814	40.68	32.81
Fine Gael	13,690	25.53	21.78
Labour	6,300	11.75	8.64
Workers' Party	4,457	8.31	4.18
Prog Democrats	7,206	13.44	24.97
Others	150	0.28	7.62

Statistics

Population	114,253	
Electorate	78,385	
Total Poll	54,172	69.11
Spoiled Votes	555	1.02
Valid Poll	53,617	68.40
Seats	5	
Quota	8,937	
Candidates	11	

Seats

FF	2
FG	1
Lab	1
PD	1
No Change	

Count transfers (left columns)

	5th Count (Votes)	6th Count (Surplus)	7th Count (Surplus)
	+ 4,483 / 12,843	− 3,906 / 8,937	
	− 6,421 / –		
	+ 180 / 7,552	+ 108 / 7,660	+ 357 / 8,017
	+ 232 / 7,917	+ 157 / 8,074	+ 384 / 8,458
	+ 138 / 7,020	+ 110 / 7,130	+ 258 / 7,388
	– / –	– / –	– / –
	+ 1,152 / 8,323	+ 3,502 / 11,825	− 2,888 / 8,937
	236	29	1,889

FF 40.68%
FG 25.53%
OTHERS 0.28%
PD 13.44%
WP 8.31%
LAB 11.75%

Source: Platform Press, Dublin

competition between TDs of the same party.'[1] FitzGerald has continued to criticize the system ever since. That debate did not engage the nation's attention in the 1987 election campaign, which was directed to economic issues, but more and more voices of politicians and former politicians have since echoed these concerns. Another Taoiseach, Charles Haughey (who didn't know at the time that he would be outgoing within two months), raised the question: 'The Government must now give mature consideration to the adoption of single-seat constituencies elected by proportional representation together with a list system.'[2] Just before becoming Taoiseach in 1992, Mr Albert Reynolds urged the need for electoral reform on a nationwide radio programme,[3] and repeated it after becoming Taoiseach.[4] Trenchant words from a former Minister for the Public Service added to the debate: 'The present electoral system has outlived its usefulness. In fact it is now the single greatest factor inhibiting the development of the Dáil as a strong parliamentary chamber . . . clientelism is not just confined to servicing the needs of individual voters. Organized groups from residents' associations to the committee of the Twirling-Majorettes-Marching-Band will use their perceived muscle to "play off" the multi-TDs against each other . . .'[5] A former Labour Party deputy wrote: 'There are politicians in all parties who know in their hearts that a combination of real devolution of power to local authorities, a smaller Dáil, and single-seat constituencies with the transferable vote would make politics in this country less of a life-threatening condition and more of a rewarding profession.'[6] Academic political writers are wary of these complaints, and suspect laziness on the part of Dáil Deputies; their remedy for the problems is the provision of more and better citizens' advice bureaux and better administration of the public service. 'Lack of consumer-friendly public service access points, coupled with an unassertive persona, produce a system where recourse to a go-between is the surest option.'[7] The debate appears to have started, therefore, but since change can only be achieved by constitutional reforms initiated and passed through the Dáil and Senate, inertia seems sure to continue. Most TDs and Senators hold their positions thanks to the present system, and it would need a strong concerted all-party effort to change things.

The opinions of the Fine Gael leader on the subject imply

that no such all-party approach will be forthcoming: he 'cautioned against any rapid movement towards changes in the electoral system ... the priority is for Oireachtas reform and not changes in the electoral system ...'[8] In the meantime, what the *Irish Times* editorial writer described as an example of 'the wilder shores of Irish clientelism'[9] was glimpsed when Dáil Deputies were outraged in 1992 that the officials at the United States embassy in Dublin would no longer accept letters from them guaranteeing that their constituents would return if given a holiday visa to the USA. The practice was, apparently, widely abused (i.e. the young people did not return but joined the multitudes of illegal Irish immigrants). Anyone well acquainted with the pressures on Dáil members would realize that to refuse to give such a letter for a constituent's son or daughter would be dangerous indeed. One of the Dáil members involved is supposed to have said plaintively: 'If elected public representatives can no longer give guarantees on behalf of the people they represent, then what are they there for?'[10] A good question, indeed.

Irish people, despite the lack of any legal compulsion to vote, have traditionally been enthusiastic democrats. In 1989, however, the percentage poll at a general election fell below 70 per cent for the first time in twenty years. It reached 76 per cent in 1969 and 1981, but fell by some five percentage points between 1987 and 1989, to 68·51 per cent. A further fall to 64·14 per cent in 1992 confirmed this slightly worrying trend. Convergence of economic views between the three 'centre' parties and the almost complete disappearance of early civil-war divisions, with consequent voter apathy in a vacuum of ideologies, are put forward as the most reasonable explanation for this fall in enthusiasm. Given the distressingly high unemployment figures of the early 1990s, which touch every family in the country, the further drop in voter interest in 1992 must also signal a lack of faith in the ability of the political process to solve this problem. Add to that the repeated expression of cynicism and distrust of politicians in opinion polls following the outbreak of political and business scandals in 1991, and the country's daily exposure to startling revelations at a public judicial tribunal into the beef industry, all during 1992, and drop in turnout is all too understandable.

Before a candidate's name appears on the ballot paper at all, there is considerable drama. The parties hold selection conventions in each of the forty-one constituencies, chaired by a party elder from outside the area. These can be as hotly contested as the subsequent public election, or even more so. Several hundred party members, delegated by their branches, gather in local parish halls or hotel ballrooms across Ireland to pick their candidates, after the general election has been called. (Sometimes the conventions are held before the election is called, if the party feels it necessary to give its candidates extra time in the public eye.) Canvassing of delegate votes, personal and painstaking, is a matter of great skill and seriousness, with a large question mark over whether or not a delegate can be believed. (The author was advised by experienced party members, when counting assurances of support before the first convention in which she was a candidate, to divide the numbers by two, 'and even then subtract a few more'.)* The criteria for voting for any candidate can vary from personal friendship, old indebtedness, to local loyalty, to judicious decisions on what would be best for the party. Delegates are sometimes mandated by their branches to vote in a particular way, but ballots are secret. So the last-minute orations of the candidates, as well as the exhortations of those proposing and seconding them, can be influencing factors. The number of candidates to be chosen will have been laid down by the national executive of the party, based on a judgement involving numbers of seats and local conditions. The national executive reserves to itself the right to add (but not subtract) candidates after the convention: this can be a source of dissension within parties.

Before the votes are cast, and in an atmosphere of high tension, the aspiring candidates must sign the party pledge – to affirm loyalty to the party, promise only to canvass 'the party ticket' and generally to eschew individuality in favour of party advantage. This is more honoured in the breach than in the observance, because the competition for election between candidates of the same party (particularly if the contest is a tight one) leads inevitably to personal canvassing instead of the dutiful asking 'for the one and two in order of your choice'. Strictly speaking, the party canvassers must

---

* This took place in spring 1981, when the author was a candidate before a Fine Gael selection convention in Rathdrum, Co. Wicklow.

not favour one candidate above another unless that is defined party strategy in certain areas. In practice, rules are thrown aside, arguments erupt, tempers rise, 'illegal' literature (leaflets, letters) in favour of individual candidates gets pushed through letter-boxes, friends become enemies, posters are torn down, money is spent on drinks and meals for loyal workers ... It is not unknown to see canvassers outside polling stations on election day exhorting their own party supporters to give no votes to one of their own candidates – and the other parties begin to seem like colleagues instead of rivals. This is an inevitable result of the multi-seat system. All during election campaigns, each party's headquarters are deluged with complaints and accusations from all over the country as the familiar battles break out within party organizations. After the election is over, an uneasy peace usually breaks out until the next time, although the competition for favour in the constituency goes on. Peace doesn't always return, and there have been occasional court cases arising out of election disputes.

Counting of votes at the conventions is carried out under the same proportional-representation system as the subsequent general election. Complicated it is, exciting too. Counting centres at general elections are places of intense interest, full of people with calculators and, nowadays, computers; and anxious candidates waiting for the experts to tell them their prospects as names are elected or eliminated and votes are distributed.

The counting involves first establishing a quota – the number of votes a candidate must reach in order to be elected. This is done by dividing the total votes cast by one more than the number of seats available, and adding one. (In a three-seat constituency, for example, where the total number of votes cast is 24,733, one-quarter of the total vote is 6,183$\frac{1}{4}$, so the quota is 6,184.) Candidates who have fewest 'number-one' votes are eliminated, and their votes are distributed to those candidates who got their 'number two'. Candidates who have exceeded the quota of 'ones' on the first count watch proudly while their surplus votes are distributed to the 'number twos' on their list. (It may be the job of strong party candidates, like ministers, to achieve a high enough vote to ensure a second seat for their weaker colleague; sometimes the party asks a more difficult task of them – to encourage voters to distribute their number-one votes evenly among party candidates in order to maximize the number elected. Such a high-risk strategy demands skill and selflessness not often on offer.) It was notable in the 1992 election that many Labour Deputies achieved such high numbers of first preferences that the party planners had missed several opportunities to gain second seats, since nearly all of their candidates were standing as the only Labour person on the ticket: a luxury which is comfortable for the candidate, but poor strategy from the party's point of view.

The dual process of elimination and distribution continues until all the seats have been filled. It can take a very long, nail-biting time for this counting process to be completed – some counts continue from early morning late into the night and on to the following day. However, the parties have skilled forecasters called tallymen who at an early stage can predict with great accuracy the end result. They position their workers at the place where the votes are opened out and spread, face up, on the table. Each tallyman watches where the ones and twos are going, and reports back to the party 'guru' at a central table; as the reports come back from all over the counting centre on all the candidates, the pattern emerges and faces brighten or cloud over. Newspaper, radio and television reporters crowd around the tallymen and their teams in order to let the country know what's going to happen: the tallymen are rarely wrong.

The most dramatic illustration of the extreme democracy of the Irish electoral system was seen in 1992 in the constituency of Dublin South-Central, where the final result was only achieved after nine days of counting. A handful of votes separated Ben Briscoe (Fianna Fáil) and Eric Byrne (Democratic Left) for the final seat. Count after count showed tiny discrepancies, the gap narrowed; Ben Briscoe had conceded defeat three times and started to clear out his desk, when yet another count reversed the decision and Briscoe replaced his files. The result was significant for the shape of the next government, because if the Democratic Left had gained that seat, subsequent negotiations for coalition government between Labour, Democratic Left, Fine Gael, and Progressive Democrats might have had quite a different complexion.

Who are these people who put themselves through such ordeals in order to reach Leinster House? Dáil Deputies are mostly men* (146 out of the 166 in the 1992 election) and as in every other area of Irish public life, very largely from Catholic backgrounds. After the 1992 general election, among the handful of Deputies of other religions, a medical doctor of South African Indian origin, a Muslim, was swept into the Dáil in the Labour upswing. In modern Ireland, three Jewish Deputies have outnumbered Protestants in the Dáil.† Many Deputies are related to former members or have family connections, like brothers or sisters, in the Dáil. Nearly 70 per cent have third-level education; the biggest single occupational group (former occupations) is the forty former teachers, who can get secondment and a right to return to their job. Farmers and clerical-type workers make up a large section (twenty farmers). There are significant numbers of former lawyers, and some accountants, but a marked absence of former industrialists, entrepreneurs, or managers. Most Dáil members have pursued a long apprenticeship in local government before getting to national politics and, as shown in the part of this book on local government (Chapter 5), most back-benchers continue to hold the dual mandate and serve on local authorities.

A day in the life of a typical back-bench Dáil Deputy (called TD by most people, signifying 'Teachta Dála' – Dáil Deputy) would find him or her taking early telephone or personal calls from constituents; collecting petitions, letters, messages, and driving to Leinster House; attending the opening few minutes of the session ('the Order of Business') and if possible succeeding in raising some matter of local or national interest before being told by the Ceann Comhairle (Speaker) that it is not admissible; retiring to the bar for a coffee, or going straight to his/her office where a secretary will be waiting. Most of the day will be spent answering correspondence

---

*The twenty-seventh Dáil, elected in November 1992, had an all-time record number of women Deputies. Twenty (12 per cent) of the Deputies were women, an increase from only thirteen. They were a lively and exceptionally able group of politicians, and after the senior and junior ministers were picked, five of them had appointments. Most of the other women hold front-bench positions in Opposition. However, several other prominent women either lost seats or retired from politics in recent times.

†Alan Shatter, lawyer and prominent spokesperson for Fine Gael; Mervyn Taylor, also a lawyer, of the Labour Party, appointed Minister for Equality and Law Reform in January 1993; and Ben Briscoe of Fianna Fáil, formerly an auctioneer, son of a popular former Lord Mayor of Dublin, Robert Briscoe.

from constituents, ringing various government departments, attending a parliamentary party meeting or a Committee of the House,
perhaps grabbing half an hour to prepare something to say on a bill
or a motion in the House, entertaining constituents who have come
to visit, accompanying a deputation or two from the constituency
who have come to petition a minister about something like a school
or hospital, and occasionally being called to the House for a vote*
– the subject-matter of which may not be known in advance –
before getting back into his/her car and driving to the constituency
for a series of meetings, 'clinics' (advice sessions for individual
constituents) or social functions for fund-raising or party morale-
boosting, residents' associations or parents' bodies, at most of
which the Deputy will meet the other TDs, including ministers
and/or junior ministers, who also represent the constituency. Such
is the life of an Irish politician: the variation occurs if the Dáil is
not in session, which is at least half of the year, when constituency
affairs take over almost entirely. The long Dáil recesses are heavily
criticized, which shows the lack of public understanding of the
inevitable character of Irish politics given the fierce competition for
attention back in the constituency.† If the politician is a front-
bench spokesperson for his or her party in Opposition (in Ireland
the expression 'shadow minister' is not used) he or she will have the
added responsibility of Dáil work, with almost no research back-up
facilities,‡ and will also take on the extra duty of representing the
party leadership at functions around the country, unpaid, with no
expenses. If and when there is a by-election in any part of the
country, the call is 'all hands on deck': back-benchers and front-

*In the Dáil, voting is conducted by the time-consuming process of filing
through the 'Yes' and 'No' lobbies; despite talk of installing electronic voting,
deputies, including ministers, still spend up to thirty minutes at each vote.
†By the end of January 1993, TDs had only twenty-eight sitting days in Dáil
Éireann since resuming work after the 1992 long summer recess. It seemed as if
the political year 1992/3, by the time it ended in early July 1993, would be the
shortest ever, with only ninety-two days of sittings. The election of November
1992 was a major contributory factor to this pattern.
‡The library in Leinster House has no trained librarians, despite a helpful staff,
and is very poorly stocked. There is no purchasing policy for new books, except
when specifically requested by a member. It is noticeably quiet and unoccupied,
even when the Houses are sitting. There has been considerable cutting of its
budget in recent years.

benchers are required by their party to descend on the by-election constituency, particularly at weekends, to direct and participate in the party effort on the doorsteps – for this there is no pay or expenses either. There is not much room in that life for family – except that wives (since most husbands of women parliamentarians are already working in jobs) are expected to play a major role in funeral-going, message-taking, and handshaking, as well as washing the socks and raising the children.

The Dáil member is paid IR£30,100, with an allowance for the expenses of secretarial assistance, travel and office equipment. There is a mileage allowance for car use for journeys up to and back from the Dáil, and some recognition of travelling expenses within constituencies. Overnight allowances for nights spent in Dublin while the Dáil is sitting complete a package which the Deputies themselves consider poor, but which is criticized as too much outside the Dáil, particularly in the context of the Dáil's infrequent sittings.

The only member of the Dáil who is released from this life is the Speaker or Chairman, Ceann Comhairle; by virtue of the office, the incumbent is automatically returned to the Dáil at the following election without going through the election process. The Ceann Comhairle is elected by the Dáil at its first meeting after a general election: in a tight situation, it naturally suits an incoming govern-ment to reduce the number of 'wild cards' – independent or Opposition members – by establishing one of their number in the Chair. This can lead to a choice being made on criteria of numbers in the Dáil rather than on the potential for filling what could be an important interpretative and developmental role in the conduct of Dáil business, since the Ceann Comhairle also serves as Chair-man of the Dáil Committee on Procedures and Privileges. After the last three elections, a former Labour Party member who had become an Independent, Mr Sen Treacy,* was nominated as Ceann Comhairle. Fianna Fáil (1987) and then the Fianna Fáil/Progressive Democrat coalition (1989) proposed him to serve as Ceann Comhairle. In 1992, when the Dáil had failed to elect a Taoiseach,

---

*Sean Treacy, b. 1923. A conservative, he was one of the old guard of the Labour Party, and represented Tipperary South in the Dáil for them from 1961 to 1985 when he parted company with them on the contraception issue. He has never held ministerial office.

the only thing that could be agreed upon in early January was to reappoint him. He had served in that post between 1973 and 1977 as a nominee of the Fine Gael/Labour coalition, when he was still a member of the Labour Party. The Ceann Comhairle is paid the same as a government minister – IR£60,000 (in 1992) – and enjoys the 'perk' of a State car and driver. The holder of the post is expected to take no part at all in party political matters either in his constituency or elsewhere. His role has been confined to peacekeeper and preserver of the status quo.

The Dáil, given absolute power in the Constitution to make laws, in reality has very little power, and is entirely subservient to the government. Ireland's most prolific writer on constitutional politics in Ireland, Professor Basil Chubb of Trinity College, Dublin, is in no doubt about the divergence between constitutional aspiration and reality: '. . . the government has a virtual monopoly of new legislation and policy changes; and by its control (by means of its majority) of the timetable and of divisions, it governs the processing of bills into law in large measure unaltered, at least in essentials.'[11] Bills are prepared in government departments, agreed in Cabinet, and presented to the Dáil for approval. Private Members' bills are rarely if ever passed, the government preferring to preserve its own monopoly, usually assuring the House that it will bring forward its own legislation on the area in the near future. A rare exception to this was achieved by one of Fine Gael's formidable lawyer Deputies, Alan Shatter, who prepared and steered through the Dáil two significant family-law bills in the late 1980s which addressed in some measure the morass of matrimonial law in Ireland. Questions of money are firmly controlled by the government, despite many attempts in recent years by Oppositions to involve parliament more in expenditure decisions. 'The poor performance of the Oireachtas arises from first, a general acceptance by members of the dominant role of the government as policy-maker, and second, the pre-occupation of many members with their own local position.'[12]

Again, it can be put succinctly: '. . . there are four interlocking ways in which the government controls the Dáil: 1. Control of a voting majority. 2. Control of parliamentary time. 3. Control of the generation of legislation. 4. Control of information.'[13] There is not much incentive there for the lively, questioning mind or the real democrat who wants to represent his electors. More seriously, this 'democratic deficit' inherent in the Irish governmental system could lead to worse dangers. 'The potential for the executive to pursue its own interest, whether consciously or unconsciously, at the expense of the general interest is possibly the most compelling argument which exists for strengthening the legislature in the modern state.'[14] As a succession of alleged financial scandals erupted in late 1991, involving semi-State bodies and friends and acquaintances of the then Taoiseach, plus interlinking decisions by government ministers, those words seem prophetic. Procedures do not exist for obtaining immediate answers on major areas of public concern, since ministers are protected by standing orders from having to deal with un-rehearsed questions. Question time in the Dáil, for seventy-five minutes three times a week, is unsatisfactory since ministers are under no obligation to give full answers to questions, and their civil servants preparing the answers have preferred to approach their task in the spirit of giving as little rather than as much information as possible. This practice was strongly criticized in 1992 by the chairman of the judicial tribunal of inquiry into the beef industry who observed that the tribunal might never have been necessary if Dáil questions had been comprehensively answered when they were asked.

One of the most consistent advocates of reform of the Dáil is Mr John Bruton,* who was responsible for a flurry of reforming measures in the middle 1980s, and continued his efforts in Opposition afterwards. These included the much earlier debating of government expenditure estimates, some changes to the parliamentary question system, and broadcasting, leading to the televising (in 1990) of debates in both Houses. The most striking, and potentially the most effective, was a great increase in Dáil committees, some of considerable significance.† Not all survived after the change of

---

*Leader of Fine Gael, principal Opposition party, since 1990. Minister for Finance, 1981–2 and 1986–7; Minister for Industry, Trade, Commerce and Tourism, 1983–6; Leader of the House (with special responsibility for Dáil reform), 1982–6. Former occupation: barrister and substantial farmer; b. 1947, was one of the youngest Dáil Deputies when first elected in 1969 for the Co. Meath constituency. Survived as party leader after the 1992 election despite continuing unpopularity with the general public.

†The Joint Committee on Marriage Breakdown involved all parties in the first deep discussion of the chaotic nature of Irish marriage law; its report has had considerable influence.

government in 1987, but there are now many more committees of
the House than there were before 1982 (usually joint committees
with the Senate), but they have not been able to deal with obstacles
which seriously interfere with their effectiveness: one is the issue of
privilege for witnesses, which fundamentally blocks their ability to
arrive at significant facts; another is the lack of personnel resources
for research; but perhaps the most dispiriting is the lack of
parliamentary time. Since Deputies have to devote so much time to
constituency work (or suffer the electoral consequences), the House
has usually sat only for three days a week, though with the advent
of a new government in 1993, Friday sittings for Estimates debates
and committees began to take place.* Rarely have the reports of its
various committees been given full debates. Another feature of the
Irish parliamentary committee system is the difficulty of getting
enough members to attend to form a quorum at all: the author
when chairing from 1987 to 1989 the Joint Oireachtas Committee
on EC Legislation frequently found herself pleading with members
to attend, or dispatching the clerk of the committee around the
House looking for likely attenders. This arises not because Deputies
are sitting with their feet up in the Dáil bar, but because there are
so many conflicting demands on their time. The quiet, in-depth
investigative and reporting work of a committee may not hold
much attraction for members who would like media attention for
their parliamentary time. An outstanding exception to that rule was
Senator, now President, Mary Robinson, who was the most expert
and assiduous member of the Joint Committee on Secondary Legislation of the European Community from its establishment in 1973
until she retired from the Senate in 1989.

In 1993, a new impetus towards improving the operations of the
Dáil and its committees was signalled in the Joint Programme for
Government. Four standing committees of thirty members each
were to be established, 'properly resourced' with paid chairpersons,

* The Dáil adjourns for three months in the summer (July to October), and
usually for at least a month at Christmas and three weeks at Easter. It never sits
on Mondays, rarely on Fridays, with normal agreement that votes will be confined
to Wednesdays; if Monday is a public holiday, the House waits until Wednesdays.
In 1992, when St Patrick's Day fell on a Tuesday, the House did not sit at all that
week. Despite regular public criticism, and the frequent excuse of 'scarce Dáil
time' for delayed legislation, there has been no decision to change the system.

and these committees would take the committee stage of all bills going through the Dáil. In addition, there would be a new Foreign Affairs committee, which would join the Procedures and Privileges, Public Accounts, Selection, Joint Services, and State-Sponsored Bodies committees. There was a promise of new powers and legal strengthening of the committees, and all of this was to be in place by January 1994.

By the summer of 1993, the new committees were indeed in place. The Labour component of the new government, determined to reform rapidly where reform was possible without major political or ideological confrontation, was considered mainly responsible for the new departures, and the unusual speed of the changes. Three select committees of the Dáil, seven joint committees of Dáil and Senate, and four legislative committees were put in place (see table overleaf). Other bodies which involved membership of Deputies and Senators were the Council of Europe, the British/Irish Parliamentary Body, and the Irish Parliamentary Association. All four of the new legislative committees were chaired by government back-benchers.

There are many factors which inhibit reform of the virtually powerless Dáil: the first, and arguably the most intractable, is the proportional representation multi-seat electoral system. Another is the adversarial party-political system which has traditionally obtained in the Irish parliament: this discourages Deputies from working together harmoniously in committees. A third, related element is that the successful 'point-scorer' in heated political debate is more likely to succeed in reaching the top of the political ladder than the quiet parliamentary worker. Some political analysts speculated about the reasons for the introduction of even the limited reforms of the mid-1980s: '. . . it could be argued that the new committees were introduced mainly to provide political insurance to the government of the day by allaying the frustrations of a new generation of young and dynamic TDs and by generating some measure of consensus on controversial issues.'[15] The analyst in question drew back at such an inference about the reforming Mr Bruton, but not about his associates: '. . . such a case does a disservice to the authors of the reforms, if not necessarily to all of those involved in their realization'.[16]

With the arrival of Mr Albert Reynolds as Taoiseach in 1992,

Committees of the Dáil and the Senate, Summer 1993	
Select Committees of the Dáil	**Chairpersons**
Committee of Selection	Noel Dempsey TD, Government Chief Whip
Committee of Procedure and Privileges	Seán Treacy TD, Ceann Comhairle
Committee of Public Accounts	Jim Mitchell TD
Joint committees of Dáil and Senate	
Joint Committee on Irish Language	Mary Coughlan TD
Joint Services Committee	Senator Pat Magner
Joint Committee on Commercial State-Sponsored Bodies	Liam Kavanagh TD
Joint Committee on Consolidation Bills	n/a
Joint Committee on Standing Orders	n/a
Joint Committee on Women's Rights	Theresa Ahearn TD
Joint Foreign Affairs Committee	Brian Lenihan TD
New legislative committees	
Legislation and Security Committee	Dan Wallace TD
Enterprise and Economic Strategy Committee	Toddy O'Sullivan TD
Finance and General Affairs Committee	John Ellis TD
Social Affairs Committee	Séamus Pattison TD

and his declaration of a new style of 'open' government, some hopes rose for more involvement of Dáil Deputies in decision-making. However, one of the first political arguments in his term of office was a protracted disagreement, starting in February 1992, about a proposed new parliamentary committee on employment. Fine Gael, led by the same John Bruton, strenuously objected to the committee format, and demanded that government ministers should be obliged to appear before any such committee in order to prevent it becoming 'just another talking shop'. The inference in that whole debate (unremarked by politicians) was that all other Oireachtas committees were exactly that: powerless groups whose words meant nothing. The government pleaded that ministers were precluded by the Constitution from answering to Oireachtas committees. It was an illuminating debate. The new legislative committee system established in the summer of 1993 could greatly change the way Irish politicians do their public business: if Opposition Deputies were to use the opportunities given to them closely to question ministers in these four committees, the Dáil might begin to seem more relevant to the population at large. Undoubtedly, the extra time demands on Deputies promised to highlight the conflict between constituency work and legislation. The parliamentary observer of the *Irish Times* put it thus: 'Have no doubt, the same electorate which demands a "legislative input" from its TDs is the first to reward the constituency slogger when it comes to voting. Which backbencher will leave his constituency colleague free to roam the constituency while he slogs it out, probably unreported and unnoticed in committee session?'[17]

THE SECOND HOUSE – SEANAD ÉIREANN

Seanad Éireann, often referred to as the 'Upper House', meets less frequently than the Dáil, and is constantly under attack for its very existence. The Senate meets at most on two days a week. Its complicated and indirect system of election, its lack of power, the presence among its numbers of a high proportion of defeated former Dáil members or obvious aspirants to the Dáil, all combine to make it uninteresting to either the public or the political commentators. Except for six members, representing most of the country's university graduates, and occasionally outstanding direct appointments by the Taoiseach, the political composition mirrors that of the Dáil.

The powers of the Senate are rigidly circumscribed, and amount to the ability to discuss and amend legislation: but their amendments can be ignored by the Dáil if not liked. Money bills cannot be interfered with at all. The House sits much less frequently than the Dáil, with little attention paid to it by the media. In 1992, it sat for sixty days of the year. From time to time over the years, some outstanding minds have improved legislation in the Senate, or some important issue has been highlighted in a particularly effective manner:* however, these are the exceptions. 'The prestige of the Senate suffers from the fact that, by and large, it is merely another selection of party politicians chosen in an unnecessarily complicated and not particularly democratic manner.'[18]

The first Irish parliament in 1919, in the throes of the independence movement, had no second chamber. However, when establishing the new Irish State during negotiations with the British, a second chamber was decided upon in order to allow for representation of the Unionist/Protestant minority in the parliament. That first Senate of 1922 was always unsatisfactory, and had a chequered career. 'When it exercised its right to hold up legislation that had been passed in the Dáil, it was immediately open to the accusation of not only thwarting the real representatives of the people, but of being un-Irish as well.'[19] It was finally abolished, and was replaced under de Valera's 1937 Constitution with the Senate which exists today. De Valera took care to ensure that a built-in government majority would almost certainly prevent any such hold-up occurring again. 'He had no intention of permitting his new Upper House an effective mind of its own.'[20]

To understand the basis of the Senate's electoral system one must appreciate that de Valera was trying to respond in 1937 to something called 'vocationalism' that had been propounded in a papal encyclical, Pope Pius XI's *Quadragesimo Anno*. The idea of involving various vocational groups in the running of a country was adapted by de Valera to a format which paid lip-service to the concept. 'He could hardly publicly denounce an ideology commended by the Papacy. He would instead smother it in his embraces by incorporating vocational representation in his new Constitution.'[21] Article 18 of that Constitution created a Senate of sixty members. Eleven were to be nominated directly by the Taoiseach, six elected by the universities. No fewer than forty-three were to represent vocational interests. However, Article 19 said that the

---

*In the mid-1970s, the Senate hotly debated the issue of the destruction of an archaeological site of Viking Dublin by the building of civic offices on the site. Wood Quay, as the site was called, became a national *cause célèbre*, and marked the first massive public interest in environmental issues: the Senate flared briefly into life as it brought this issue to public attention.

forty-three members 'might be elected by any functional or vocational group or association' but only if the Oireachtas so decided. In the absence of such decision, the forty-three members are elected from five panels of broadly based vocational interests, and the electorate are politicians: Dáil Deputies and county councillors. As a result, 'the genuine vocational representatives were swamped beneath the avalanche of party loyalists'.[22]

An Irish Senate election for one of the forty-three 'vocational' seats is something of particular skill and difficulty for candidates. It is also an exquisite form of humiliation for politicians who are already suffering the psychological trauma of general-election defeat, for a great many candidates come from that group. The electorate for each seat is, in practice, a couple of hundred people, since Dáil Deputies are often county councillors too, and they don't get two votes, thereby reducing the number of electors. The candidates are aware that only their own party county councillors will vote for them, so they concentrate on contacting each one personally. In the period following the Dáil elections, aspiring Senators struggle for nominations from party or vocational bodies,* before setting out for an epic journey all around Ireland. Finding the councillor is the first task: the farmer might be out on the far fields, the publican behind the counter, the teacher in the classroom ... spouses and families are courted, hard-luck stories of narrow Dáil defeats are given, financial ruin pleaded, cups of tea or glasses of whiskey tossed back, presents handed out ... and at the end of the day, in some local hotel or friendly guest-house, promises are counted because each one in such a tiny electorate is vital. The folklore includes the story of five aspiring Senators accidentally meeting in a rural pub after a hard winter's day of canvassing. They were all on the same panel, and after a few drinks their mutual confidences revealed that a local TD and councillor had promised each of them his number-one vote. A natural reluctance to disappoint (or moral cowardice, depending on the point of view) means that a flat 'no' is hardly ever given. It is salutary to watch the shock on the faces of some candidates at the count in Leinster House for Senate elections, as they realize that the pleasantries and

---

* For example, a candidate who had been a teacher could seek a nomination on the Cultural and Educational Panel from one of several vocational bodies listed on that panel.

half-promises in country kitchens, front parlours, and back rooms in public houses were not what they seemed. It is during that campaign that local councillors come into their own, as the party powerful beat a path to their doors: the candidates have often included prominent front-benchers or former ministers. Even de Valera's most virulent detractors could hardly credit that he foresaw the travesty which Senate elections would become, when he visualized his new second House. Another element which distances the Senate from real political life is the bias towards rural Senate candidates in an increasingly urbanized country. An analysis of the 1991 local elections shows that 69 per cent of the councillor votes represent areas with fewer than the average number of voters, mostly in rural areas. The extreme comparison is found between Dromahaire in Co. Leitrim, with one councillor for every 914 voters, and Dublin city's Pembroke Ward, with 8,376 voters per councillor. Successive governments have failed to address this problem. 'The effect is the election of a rurally biased Senate with unrepresentative, predominantly rural values and interests.'[23]

Senators therefore arrive in that pleasant blue Georgian room in Leinster House by three different routes: local councillors, the wishes of the Taoiseach, and the voting preferences of some 90,000 university graduates. This last category has provided some of the best parliamentarians in the second House, including not only the present President of Ireland, but also a variety of historians, outstanding lawyers, international statesmen, and the only self-professed homosexual male in Irish politics.* In the Senate elections of early 1993, Trinity College returned another woman in something not unlike the Mary Robinson mould of the previous decades: Dr Mary Henry, whose public stance on the need for clarity and change in the abortion area, as well as her clear liberal views on a range of other social issues had brought her to public attention over the previous few years. Dr Henry had been Mary Robinson's election agent for most of Mrs Robinson's political career. She was upholding the good record enjoyed by Trinity of always electing, since the 1960s, strong liberal women.

The electorate for the three seats from the National University of

---

*Senator David Norris, representing Trinity College in Seanad Éireann since 1987.

Ireland numbers over 70,000; for the three seats from Trinity College, more than 20,000. This imbalance has been considered justified over the years because it favoured the minority religion at a time when Trinity College was almost entirely Protestant in its student body and graduates: it has never been changed, perhaps because of the undoubted quality of the Trinity College Senators. The élitist concept of university graduates having a vote at all has been questioned from time to time, but it has never become a major issue: the comparative obscurity of the Senate itself, and the reluctance of the Irish political establishment to interfere with the status quo, has seen to that. The decision to change the Constitution in 1979 to allow wider third-level representation in the Senate (the seventh Amendment) presaged a possible change, but nothing was done.

The Taoiseach's eleven nominees have usually filled a simple criterion: their appointment was almost entirely to do with political advantage. If the appointment could possibly lead to another Dáil seat next time round, or was needed to reward party 'old faithfuls', then it was made. Traditionally, however, an exception was made for two or three of the nominees, who came from the fields of culture or other unrepresented areas, or had given distinguished service to the community, and were not political.* However, the appointees of the coalition Taoiseach, Mr Haughey, made jointly with his partner in government, Des O'Malley, in 1989 did not include any such non-political personalities. But in January 1993, Taoiseach Albert Reynolds chose Gordon Wilson† from Enniskillen in Northern Ireland as one of his eleven, to general public approval. Such useful gestures notwithstanding, the Senate in the 1990s might be described as an endangered species because of the failure of both its members and Irish governments to address its lack of purpose.

*

* Thus, in 1987, Mr Haughey appointed well-known environmentalist Éamon de Buitléir, archaeologist George Eogan, and playwright Brian Friel. In 1982, Garret FitzGerald appointed three Northern Ireland Senators: Bríd Rogers, John Robb, and Stephen McGonagle.

† Gordon Wilson, a quiet Presbyterian businessman, leapt to international fame and admiration in 1987 when he behaved with great personal dignity amid deep emotion, as he described for the world the death of his daughter Marie, holding his hand as they lay under the rubble of the IRA bomb destruction at Enniskillen in November of that year.

The Dáil, however, born out of armed rebellion and civil war, is a highly democratic body of people, which has given the country political stability since 1922, despite the potentially destabilizing effect of Northern Ireland violence. But the demanding and frustrating life of its members, caused by an electoral system which forces huge concentration on local issues, leads to an increasing reluctance of talented people with good business and professional prospects to involve themselves. The powerlessness of the ordinary member of the Dáil adds to the frustration. These factors, coupled with insecurity of tenure and relatively poor pay, in turn lead to a narrow range of talents available for government, with negative consequences for the standard of legislation and planning, as well as management of the public service. A young Fianna Fáil TD from Cork, Michael Martin, voiced this concern and frustration: 'You will never have Dáil reform without fundamental electoral reform ... the system is woefully wasteful and creates a bureaucratic monstrosity ... the interests of politics, as well as the interests of Fianna Fáil, demand that change comes now and should not be put on the long finger.'[24]

It is fortunate for Ireland that some men and women of undoubted talent and patriotism have taken up the profession of politics; and it is a pity that they have not used their gifts to improve and modernize the system under which they have been forced to work. Lack of political education in schools has contributed to the stagnation of Ireland's political processes.

Dáil reform was in the wind again as a new government took office in January 1993, but neither Dáil nor electoral reform featured in the list of principal objectives at the beginning of the *Programme for a Partnership Government, 1993–97*. However, later on in the document, as has been mentioned, all sorts of reforms were considered, including a register of Dáil and Seanad members' interests. The comprehensive committee system, with particular emphasis on four standing committees for all bills, and detailing numbers and subject-matter, would involve 120 members of the Dáil. The document acknowledged that all these changes would involve changes in procedures, sitting times, 'etc.', to improve efficiency for Dáil sitting time.

The length of Dáil sessions would be fixed, and Friday sittings would be a regular feature. More accountability of ministers, by an increase in the number of items which can be raised at the end of each day's sitting, and time limits on early speeches on new bills were promised.

So far so good. Turning to the section entitled 'Electoral reform', one hoped to find that Dáil Deputies were going to be elected by some new process that would make it possible for them to be born-again, efficient legislators under the new regime. But no: the only electoral reform in the real sense of the word refers to the future electoral procedure for Members of the European Parliament that will be agreed throughout the EC. There was no mention at all of the topic which the Taoiseach himself had brought up before becoming Taoiseach in early 1992, and which many Deputies from different parties, including several ministers in the new government, had identified as being at the heart of the Dáil's inadequacies: the demands of the multi-seat proportional-representation system. In conversations with the author, most political leaders as well as politicians of the back benches expressed concern about the effects of the electoral system, but showed no interest in actually tackling the question.

Until some other system is introduced in Ireland, it is difficult to see the country enjoying a parliamentary process suitable for a modern European democracy. In the words of a practitioner of Irish political life (anonymous): 'Politicians will go around like groundsmen at a football pitch, putting cushions under the people while there's six inches of muck on the field.'

A last word to Garret FitzGerald, deploring the silence of the Programme for Partnership on the issue: 'It is to be hoped that the new Government's leaders will at some stage examine a problem that is fundamental to the effective working of our democratic system at national level.'[25]

NOTES

1. *Breaking Out of the Vicious Circle*, Fine Gael election manifesto, 1987, written by Garret FitzGerald. Ironically, Dr FitzGerald is a former vice-president of the Electoral Reform Society, which advocated multi-seat PR in Britain.

2. Mr Charles Haughey, government statement, reported in the *Irish Times*, 29 November 1991.

3. *Liveline*, RTE Radio; 16 January 1991.

4. *Irish Independent*, 7 February 1992.

5. John Boland (Minister for the Public Service, 1982–6) writing in the *Sunday Business Post*, 11 August 1991.

6. John Horgan, former Labour TD and subsequently lecturer in communications at Dublin City University, writing in the *Sunday Independent*, 6 June 1992.

7. Frances Gardiner, lecturer in political science, Trinity College, Dublin, writing in the *Irish Times*, 30 December 1991.

8. *Irish Times*, 16 August 1991.

9. op. cit., 10 July 1992.

10. ibid.

11. Basil Chubb, *The Government and Politics of Ireland*, 2nd edn, Longman, 1982.

12. ibid.

13. Dunne, 'Politics of institutional reform', *Irish Political Studies*, 1989.

14. ibid.

15. ibid.

16. ibid.

17. 'Drapier' column, *Irish Times*, 1 May 1993.

18. Chubb, op. cit.

19. ibid.

20. Joseph J. Lee, *Ireland, 1912–1985, Politics and Society*, Cambridge University Press, 1989.

21. ibid.

22. ibid.

23. John Colgan, 'Local elections: behind the results', *Administration* (Journal of the IPA), vol. 39, no. 4, 1992.

24. Article by Michael Martin TD in the *Sunday Tribune*, 4 August 1991.

25. *Irish Times*, 16 January 1993.

CHAPTER 4

Civil Service: Not So Very British

The first Irish government took the British model of civil service in
Ireland and improved on it. Despite the bloody and bitter Irish civil
war which had just ended, the incoming 'Free State' government in
1922 was determined to establish a politically impartial civil service,
appointed on independent criteria; in this, they departed from the
British practice of filling all senior posts in Ireland with imported
Scottish and English university graduates 'who could be relied upon
not to undermine Unionist principles in dealing with Irish local
authorities'.[1] A key figure in this Irish achievement was Joseph
Brennan, the Secretary of the Department of Finance, who worked
under the instructions of Irish government ministers to root out
political patronage of any posts above the rank of messenger.
'Considering the ingrained Irish propensity to use political pull at
every opportunity, this was a striking achievement.'[2] And so it
remains today: recruitment is through the independent Civil Service
Commission.* A former senior civil servant remarks: 'Even politicians, who spend a great deal of their time making representations
to other civil service offices, have discovered the waste of time in
approaching the Civil Service Commission.'[3] Such purity is good:
but there are so many question marks over the morale, organization,
and performance of the Irish civil service today that the lack of
modern outside personnel expertise in the recruitment process is
becoming more noticeable.

The Irish civil service is close to government and ministers, and
is at the hub of public affairs, with the dual role of advising and
administering. The whole structure, with Departmental Secretaries
at its head, widening as it goes downwards through Assistant
Secretaries, Principal Officers, Assistant Principal Officers,

---

*The Commissioners are the Ceann Comhairle (Speaker) of the Dáil, the
Secretary to the Government, and an Assistant Secretary in the Department of
Finance.

Administrative Officers, Higher Executive Officers, Executive
Officers – and all below them – numbers some 27,000 (in 1992)
and is very powerful in Irish life; that power, and the influence of the
civil servant, is closely related to, and determined by, the strength
and efficiency of the Taoiseach and individual ministers.

Ireland's multi-seat electoral system places such a heavy burden
of local demands and party responsibilities on ministers that even
the best of them are much more reliant on their permanent officials
than in other countries. They rush from their constituency to the
Dáil, and to Cabinet meetings and back to their constituency, trailed
by anxious officials looking for decisions ... any decisions. Seán
Dooney, former civil servant and co-author of *Irish Government
Today*, says: 'A Civil Servant wants his Minister to be courteous,
appreciative, but above all decisive.' The life of ministers is rarely
understood by those who have never experienced it; one comment
from a distinguished former Finance Secretary is succinct: 'Only
those who work at, or close to, the centre, can have any idea of the
maelstrom in the middle.'[4]

Until 1993, the appointment of outside advisers for ministers was
sporadic and rare enough. On 7 July 1992, a parliamentary question
was put to the Taoiseach and each minister of the government by
an Opposition Deputy asking for the number of 'special policy
advisers' in each department, and their area of expertise. For all of
the fifteen ministers and fifteen ministers of state, including the
Taoiseach, the total number was nineteen: and it was clear that the
vast majority of these were in the category of political helper for
constituency work rather than anything to do with the specific
portfolio of the minister. Neither does the civil-service structure
include any provision to assist ministers to prepare for Cabinet
discussion of matters that do not involve their own departments.
Steps to deal with this were taken in 1993, when the new government appointed a set of 'programme managers' to assist ministers
with their work on the implementation of the elaborate *Programme
for a Partnership Government*. They were recruited at the equivalent
of civil-service principal-officer level (two steps below departmental
secretary) and paid between IR£35,000 and IR£40,000. This was
the first indication ever in Ireland that movement towards the
European *cabinet du ministre* system might become part of the
Irish governmental structure. Some ministers, notably in Fianna

Fáil, appointed civil servants to these posts, while the Labour Party, returning to government after a break of six years and wary of its bigger partner in government, brought in non civil servants. These appointments were in keeping with the new government's announcement shortly after taking office that ministers could appoint a special adviser (maximum salary IR£40,500), a programme manager (maximum IR£40,500) as well as the previously accepted personal assistant and secretary, in addition to the normal ministerial office staff. The logic of making provision for specialist and political advice from outside the civil service might have been quietly accepted were it not for the badly handled appointments by several ministers of family members to lower posts such as secretaries and drivers.

However, government ministers took a deep breath and hoped that the fruits of the labour of the new advisers would eventually silence criticisms. It was yet another sign of changing Ireland that the new government of 1993 had appointed the biggest political staff in the history of the State.

The Secretary and Assistant Secretaries in most government departments are strong and influential figures in forming and implementing national policies: it is worth studying who they are, how they got there, and how they work.

Most recruitment to the administrative civil service is of school-leavers with very high grades in their final examinations, with a small number of university graduates recruited for Third Secretary posts in the Department of Foreign Affairs, or for administrative officers in the Department of Finance. Recruitment has, however, slowed down to very small numbers in the climate of retrenchment since 1980. It is argued (notably by Joseph Lee, a prominent historian who casts a very cold eye on many Irish institutions) that the practice in the early days of bringing in young people – it was mostly young men – from similar backgrounds in rural Ireland, products of the Christian Brothers or other similar religiously run schools, whose families couldn't afford third-level education, led to a deeply conservative, non-innovative service whose officers' only ambition was a secure job with assured promotion if they were there long enough. Recruits for the first forty years of the State were, said Lee, 'the victims of the general intellectual constipation of the wider society during those decades. The educational system reflected this ethos as it generally interpreted its mission as a duty to drill derivativeness into pupils, and to discourage innovative thinking as virtual insubordination.'[5]

This may be overstating the case, but it is clear that there evolved a stultifying working atmosphere, as bosses without management training and with a deeply conservative culture, centred upon risk-avoidance, imposed their ethos on the younger intake: the words of a former civil servant, in conversation with the author in 1992, who joined the service in the early 1970s, confirmed this: 'I was so bored, so frustrated, no one ever asked me if I was enjoying the job, no one cared about any of the young civil servants, that I wrote a memo called "A Monkey Could Do My Job". It was completely ignored, I heard nothing at all about it.' She acquired two university degrees by study at night, and left the service as soon as she could, succeeding brilliantly in her studies and her subsequent distinguished legal career.

Not many take that way out, preferring to conform in the interests of long-term security. However, there have been increasing demands internally for reform and improvement of the working conditions and therefore the performance of the service in general. As well as this, the leap into central economic planning spearheaded by an outstandingly able Secretary of the Department of Finance, Dr T. K. Whitaker,* in the 1960s, raised questions about the ability of civil-service structures to respond to the challenge of modern economic and social conditions. Alas, the history of civil-service reform in Ireland is a sorry one: two major initiatives, the so-called Devlin report of 1969,† and the Government White Paper of

* Regarded as the 'father' of modern Irish economic planning by the State, Dr Whitaker has held not only the highest positions in the public service, in the 1960s, but also has been Governor of the Central Bank, Vice-Chancellor of the National University of Ireland, a Senator (by appointment of the Taoiseach) and is currently a member of the Council of State, appointed by President Robinson in 1991. His pioneering work on Irish economic planning was done under the government of Seán Lemass, successor to Éamon de Valera and father-in-law of Charles Haughey. If asked to name an outstanding Irish civil servant, most people will come up with Dr Whitaker's name.

† The Public Services Organization Review Group under the Chairmanship of Liam St John Devlin tried to improve ministerial functioning by distancing ministers from the responsibility to answer in the Dáil for every tiny detail of their department (the 'Aireacht' concept). It was never really tried. The Devlin proposals for management advisory committees within departments were half-heartedly accepted, and likewise were never properly used.

1985,* have had minimal impact on the structures of the service. Politicians and commissions produced these ambitious reports and plans, and then failed to carry them through. After the White Paper of Minister John Boland, which had far-reaching proposals for reform, needing close monitoring for their implementation, the Ministry of the Public Service was abolished and the department was put back under the aegis of the Minister for Finance.

Even allowing for trade-union hyperbole, the degree of cynicism expressed by the Association of Higher Civil Servants about their political masters and their attempts at reform are striking. In a survey of their members in May 1990, 80 per cent felt that initiative went unrewarded in the civil service, 83 per cent said that management grades were not encouraged to be innovative or to take risks, while 93 per cent said that morale was bad in the civil service.[6] In the author's discussions with civil servants in 1992 – unattributable at their uniform request – I found widespread confirmation of those findings. It was sad to hear senior civil servants firmly determined that their children would not go into the civil service. Two further factors contribute to the general level of unhappiness: the continuing government embargo on recruitment for and filling of vacancies (brought in as a clumsy but effective way of keeping a ceiling on numbers and cost of the service in the economic crises of the early 1980s), and the discontent about levels of pay.

Politicians did achieve some reform; the method of promotion at the top levels of the service has been changed, to get away from the damaging effects of appointment only by seniority, and within rather than between departments. In his autobiography, Garret FitzGerald recounts the struggle to get this decision through Cabinet. Rather than have civil servants convince their ministers that it was a bad idea ('senior civil servants would try to brainwash their ministers against what I saw as a long overdue reform'[7]), he persuaded the Minister for the Public Service to bring the suggestion straight to the Cabinet table. A Top-Level Appointments

---

* The White Paper, *Serving the Country Better*, was published by Mr John Boland, Minister for the Public Service in the FitzGerald government, 1982–7. It laid heavy emphasis on management systems and personal responsibility for results, costs, and services.

Committee* now takes applications from across the service for vacancies at the Secretary and Assistant Secretary level, while many more interdepartmental competitions are held for posts lower down.† Career breaks were introduced – but have trickled almost to a halt because of falling numbers; the establishment of the office of the Ombudsman and many other improvements at the point of public counter-service have ensured more consideration for the public; and certain financial incentives for performance have at least paid lip-service to the concept of encouraging initiative.

The political impartiality of the civil service is not in question. Despite the inevitable suspicions by some incoming governments of the people who were close to outgoing administrations of long standing, it has been generally accepted that the Irish civil servant keeps his politics to himself. Seán Dooney writes: 'There was no political talk, I never knew how my colleagues voted.' Indeed, there have been examples of disdain by civil servants for those few colleagues who transgress this principle: they can find themselves icily isolated by colleagues as well as government when power changes hands.

The independence of the service, and its freedom from corruption from whatever source, is jealously guarded. Some unease has therefore been expressed about the pressures which might possibly come upon Secretaries of departments, who under the new appointments procedures must retire from the post after seven years. The lack of a rule preventing them taking up appointments, immediately upon retirement, with private interests whose activities they were previously regulating is a source of unease; as is the effect on them of the possible influence of their minister on future appointments to boards or commissions to which they might aspire.

Lower down the scale, there has been a wholesale 'head-hunting' of serving Department of Finance officials and tax experts by the private financial sector. The author experienced an example of this

* Established in 1984.

† The new top-level appointments procedure does not always meet with acceptance from within departments, which see 'outsiders' getting big promotions. The Department of Education expressed its senior officers' disappointment to the minister when the TLAC appointed a new secretary from the Revenue Commissioners in January 1993.

shortly after becoming Minister for Social Welfare in 1986. One of the most brilliant of the senior officials who had come to Social Welfare from the Department of Finance was wooed into the private sector by a growing firm of stockbrokers. His move was entirely understandable on many grounds, not least the virtual quadrupling of his salary by his new employers. This episode has been echoed in many ministerial offices; its effect on those left behind, and on the general levels of ability within the service, causes some concern. From the Department of Foreign Affairs a veritable flight of talented senior officials, leaving to join Guinness Peat Aviation, took place in the late 1980s.*

Within the civil service, young recruits have shown their abilities by getting university degrees and a myriad of diplomas and certificates, mostly gained through study outside working hours. In July 1992, about 1,400 were getting financial help with their fees for third-level courses, and 300 were on educational career breaks.[8] It is unusual for a candidate for a post as Principal Officer (the third grade from the top) to present himself or herself without at least one degree to his or her name. The present cohort of Secretaries of departments, and the Secretary to the Government, between them hold a great array of degrees and postgraduate distinctions. It is a moot point whether this academic achievement gained during working years counterbalances the effect, already mentioned, of a uniformity of background, lack of mobility inside and outside the service, and a lack of the socio-economic mix within the service which might broaden minds and enrich attitudes. At this point, the absence of women at senior level in the system should also be mentioned as an impoverishing factor, as well as an indication of attitudes. Women were forced to leave the civil service upon marriage until 1973. In August 1992, women's representation in the general grades of the Irish civil service was as shown in the table overleaf.[9] Despite the existence of an Equal Opportunity Policy and Guidelines for the Public Service, no targets are set for the employment of men and women at any level of employment.

---

*They include former Secretary and Ambassador to the United States, Seán Donlon; former senior officer Richard O'Toole; and former co-principal negotiator of the Anglo-Irish Agreement, Michael Lillis.

Representation of Women in the General Grades of the Irish Civil Service, 1992	
Grade	Percentage of females in the grade
Secretary	Nil
Deputy Secretary	Nil
Assistant Secretary	3
Principal	10
Assistant Principal	23
Administrative Officer	24
Higher Executive Officer	32
Executive Officer	50
Staff Officer	66

'Over-supervised and under-managed' – that judgement of Dr Dónal de Buitléir on his former colleagues in the civil service[10] comes from someone who left the taxation area in the service to join one of Ireland's two dominant bank groups, Allied Irish Banks. He makes the point that investment in the development of potential future senior managers in the civil service is very low by private-sector standards. 'We expect gifted leadership from people who have had little or no preparation and most of whom never worked or studied anywhere outside their own department, let alone outside Ireland or the public sector.'[11] He describes the male, middle-class and middle-aged preponderance in the Irish civil service and says, of the failure to promote women: 'No organization can exclude 50 per cent of its talent and prosper in the modern world.' Efforts to ensure the acquisition of skills and understanding of other sectors in the economy and society by civil servants have not been pursued: only six civil servants in July 1992 were on secondment to private industry or business.[12]

Given the failings of politicians, the embargo and the brain-drain, it is clear that only civil servants themselves will find ways to improve their internal organization and structures. And they have tried. An example of willingness to change was the establishment of a small but lively internal civil-service journal in 1979. Called *Seirbhís Phoiblí*, it provides a forum for debate and vigorous exchange of ideas, and one of its early contributors wrote a strong paper on possibilities of achieving greater productivity in the service.[13] He became Secretary of the Department of the Public Service, and played an important role in the efforts of the reforming minister who pushed through the new senior appointments system in the middle 1980s. Looking at the comparative youth of most of the present group of Secretaries of departments, and the undoubtedly beneficial effect of international interaction with Europe and elsewhere, which increases all the time, there must be hope for their future. But enough people who don't want change, politicians as well as civil servants, may find, as they always have, more convincing reasons why it can't be done. The status quo is hardly satisfactory in terms of unfulfilled potential and consequent poor performance, for the Ireland of the 1990s. The toing and froing on civil-service reform has gone on for a long time. 'It reminds me of the man with a headache who convinces himself that by combing his hair he is getting close to the problem, failing to recognize that he is as far away as ever from a solution.'[14]

The triumvirate at the apex of civil-service power in Ireland are the three key central secretaries: Government, Taoiseach, and Finance. Garret FitzGerald relied very heavily on the quiet skills, patience, and minute attention to detail of Dermot Nally, the Secretary to the Government from 1980, in his negotiations with Margaret Thatcher on the Anglo-Irish Agreement. He was generally spoken of as the quintessential public servant, much admired by colleagues and ministers alike. His quiet, inscrutable presence never betrayed any emotion other than a general benevolence during the four years that this writer observed him at close quarters in government in the mid-eighties. In late 1992, he retired and was succeeded by Frank Murray,* who had served for nearly ten years as Assistant Secretary to the Government, and had therefore often taken Nally's

---

*Frank Murray, b. 1941 in Co. Leitrim. Educated by the Presentation Brothers in Carrick-on-Shannon, and at University College, Dublin (BA, DPA). Entered the civil service in 1960, and progressed steadily upwards, serving a Fine Gael Taoiseach as private secretary from 1974. Served as Assistant Secretary to the Government from 1983.

place at government meetings. He is in the mould of hard-working, utterly reliable and discreet public servants, with a delicate job: that of the only civil servant present in the Cabinet room during the ebb and flow of government drama.

Patrick (Paddy) Teahon was appointed Secretary of the Department of the Taoiseach's in March 1993, to take effect from 1 May. He was succeeding an outstanding civil servant, Pádraig Ó hUiginn, who was considered a classic all-rounder, and served under both Garret FitzGerald and Charles Haughey as secretary of their department. Ó hUiginn, whose retirement had been postponed twice because of his perceived value to two Taoisigh (Haughey and Reynolds), was appointed chairman of Bord Fáilte, the Irish Tourist Board, on his retirement from the civil service. Teahon, at forty-seven, has had a reputation for astuteness throughout his civil-service career and had been in charge of the development of Temple Bar, the major scheme for renewal and revitalization of one of Dublin's oldest quarters.

The powerful position of Secretary of the Department of Finance is filled by Seán Cromien (since 1987). A reclusive bachelor in his social habits, interested in bird-watching, he is not known outside his working life except as a defender of the civil-service status quo in various public-service magazines, and as a slightly acerbic man of dry humour as befits his status as observer and resister of the spending ambitions of politicians. Speaking to a New Zealand conference on 'Public Service Senior Management' in April 1991, on the subject of new challenges for the public service in many countries in the 1990s, he was giving nothing away when he concluded his speech with an account of the first outing of the Irish Department of Finance Hill-Walking club:

A small group of hardened and very competitive young men pushed ahead into the distance, not to be seen again till the evening when the others reached the pub that was the inevitable destination for the day. Behind them were earnest but slower walkers, and behind them again were those who thought it was only going to be a stroll and had not even brought the right footwear. I hesitate to say which group Ireland is in this analogy . . .

The Men at the Top: Senior Irish Civil Servants by Department (Spring 1992)			
Department	Name	Age (1992)	Origin
Taoiseach	Paddy Teahon	47	Kerry
Government	Frank Murray	52	Leitrim
Finance	Seán Cromien	63	Dublin
Agriculture and Food	Michael Dowling	47	Kerry
Defence	Seán Brosnan	60 +	Kerry
Education	Don Thornhill	45	Dublin
Transport, Energy and Communications	John Loughrey	45	Dublin
Environment	Brendan O'Donoghue	49	Cork
Foreign Affairs	Noel Dorr	59	Mayo
Arts, Culture and the Gaeltacht	Tadhg Ó hÉalaithe	44	Cork
Health	John Hurley	47	Cork
Tourism and Trade	Seán Dorgan	41	Kerry
Justice	Tim Dalton	50	Kerry
Employment and Enterprise	Kevin Bonner	45	Donegal
Social Welfare	Edward McComiskey	51	Dublin
Equality and Law Reform	Bernard McDonagh	41	Tipperary
Marine	Fionán Ó Muircheartaigh	41	Kerry

CIVIL SERVICE PAY SCALES

The highest-paid civil servant is the Secretary of the Department of Finance, who gets IR£64,500 per annum. He is followed by the Secretary to the Government on IR £64,000 and the Secretary of the Department of the Taoiseach at about IR£61,000. The normal salary for the head of a department is IR£57,850. Assistant secretaries get from IR£36,880 to IR£45,700. So it goes all the way down, ending up at the cleaner's wage of IR£166.* The public-service pay and pensions bill amounted to IR£3·4 billion in 1991, and absorbed 54 per cent of voted non-capital expenditure, rising to IR£3·7 billion in 1992. Public debate rages about the extent of increases given to senior civil servants, which have been well ahead of inflation over several years: a departmental secretary got IR£37,501 in 1987. The difficulties of attracting and keeping first-class people have to be balanced against the continual knock-on effects of awarding special pay increases to any sector in the public service. The public-service pay arbitrator, a barrister and senior counsel, was appointed to the High Court in late 1992, opening up the possibility of a change in the terms of reference for any new appointee, allowing him or her to take the state of the national finances into account.

Changes are taking place in the public service, though not as speedily or dramatically as in other sectors of Irish society. The Revenue Commissioners, those hitherto feared and secretive people who collect the people's taxes, presented their sixty-ninth annual report in glossy bright colours for the first time and showed that more modern methods of working with increased flexibility had increased the tax take by more than IR£400 million in 1991. This new style of presentation and openness was greeted with surprise and pleasure by the public. In spring 1993 they announced a new office complete with soft furnishings and piped music which would be a 'one-stop shop' for people to call in to discuss any tax queries. Changed times indeed.

In June 1992, reflecting the continuing interest of their leader in public-service reform, the Fine Gael party produced a policy document with new proposals for the civil service, including allowing all

* All figures as of early 1992.

ranks of civil servants to become involved in politics, and increased mobility in and out of the civil service.

A new and unhappy element in the relationship between civil service and government was the conflict of evidence between them during the hearings in the judicial tribunal of inquiry into the beef industry in Ireland in 1992. The Taoiseach challenged the sworn evidence of senior civil servants about decisions and instructions given by ministers in 1987 and 1988. Not since 1970, when civil servants found themselves in a similar situation concerning another judicial process,* also involving the Fianna Fáil party, had there been such a conflict. In 1992, the white heat of a general election resulted from disputes between ministers at that tribunal – with civil servants caught in the middle, and the Taoiseach, almost in an *obiter dictum*, announcing that in future no statement or decision by a minister would be recorded without being endorsed by the minister in question. The implication of mistrust and lack of confidence in civil servants conveyed by that remark was not calculated to improve morale or motivation. Garret FitzGerald, writing about the affair on 7 November 1992, expressed great concern about the effects of these actions on the normal relationship of trust and confidence between government and civil servants, and on the process of decision-making. He concluded: 'One of the first concerns of the next government will have to be how to restore the previous relationship between politicians and civil service.'[15]

---

* The Arms Trial of 1970, when the Secretary of the Department of Justice was embroiled in evidence concerning the actions of government ministers.

NOTES

1. Eunan O'Halpin, 'The civil service and the political system', *Administration*, vol. 38, no. 4, 1991.
2. ibid.
3. Seán Dooney, *Irish Government Today*, Gill & Macmillan, 1992.
4. C. H. Murray, *The Civil Service Observed*, Institute of Public Administration, 1990.
5. Joseph Lee, 'A third division team?', *Seirbhís Phoiblí*, vol. 6, no. 1, January 1985.

6. Association of Higher Civil Servants (AHCS), *Special Bulletin*, May 1990.
7. Garret FitzGerald, *All in a Life*, Gill & Macmillan, 1991.
8. Answer to a parliamentary question to the Minister for Finance, 7 July 1992.
9. Information from the Minister of State for Women's Affairs, August 1992.
10. Dónal de Buitléir, 'Reflections on management in the public service', *Seirbhís Phoiblí*, vol. 12, no. 2, December 1991.
11. ibid.
12. Answer to a parliamentary question to the Minister for Finance, 7 July 1992.
13. Kevin Murphy, *Seirbhís Phoiblí*, 3 January 1982.
14. Murray, op. cit.
15. *Irish Times*, 7 November 1992.

CHAPTER 5

Local Government

'Neither local nor government' – with a sigh, this description of the Irish system of local authorities comes up again and again in conversation with people in Ireland who would like to see 'real' democracy in action. The person who personifies reform in local government is an articulate, energetic septuagenarian, Tom Barrington, who entered the civil service in 1942 and has been working for its reform ever since. He is most identified with the Institute of Public Administration, a staff college for civil servants, whose director he became in 1960 and which he steered for seventeen years. The institute was intended to emulate the École Nationale d'Administration in France, and to have the same invigorating effect on the Irish civil service. Tom Barrington says it didn't succeed to anything like the same degree because 'we suffer from the absence of an intellectual tradition, an intellectual community'.[1] This and many other trenchant comments on the performance of Ireland have given him the reputation of something of a crank. 'No people', he said in 1992, 'have had to endure as much frustration as the Irish for lack of opportunity to govern their collective lives'.[2] His energy was channelled in 1990 (at the age of seventy-five) into chairing an expert advisory committee to the government on the structures and functions (but not the funding) of local government. The resulting report, naturally known as the Barrington Report (published in March 1991), would if implemented have changed the whole character of local government in the country, as well as touching on other areas of public life. However, given the long history of Irish government declarations of intention to reform, and subsequent inaction in this area, not too much was expected as a result and not too much happened. When legislation appeared in 1991, it did not tackle the central question of the lack of financial power of local government. Its main provision was to enable the postponed local elections for county and county borough (city) councils to proceed, and it made certain changes about planning applications which are dealt with later in this chapter.

LOCAL GOVERNMENT STRUCTURES

It was an American idea which gave Ireland the character of its local government structures; the idea of running municipal affairs on a business model had influenced US systems since the early part of the century. It was taken up in Ireland when the process of establishing new public institutions was under way in the 1920s. Thus the city and county manager system was started: experienced whole-time managers run the local authorities in tandem with the elected representatives, who are essentially part-time and almost unpaid.

Travelling expenses and an allowance for actual attendance at meetings, including special provision for longer meetings, and allowances for meetings away from home form the main financial rewards of the elected members of local authorities. These are modest indeed, but can mount up if meetings become frequent, or continue for long periods. In early 1993, local-authority members expressed indignation at a ministerial proposal that there should be a ceiling on the number of meetings for which expenses could be claimed. Equally, some local authorities or subcommittees from outside Dublin have been suspected of involving themselves in a considerable number of all-expenses-paid delegations to see government ministers in the capital. Conferences at home, involving a few days at a good hotel and suitable travelling expenses, are another bonus for the local councillor. A continual source of public scepticism is the regular revelation in the media of delegations travelling abroad to conferences, in what seem large numbers and at considerable expense; since their local councillors have such little power, taxpayers do not always appreciate why they need to go to these conferences on something like urban development. Despite all this negative publicity, however, there is little money to be made by serving as a local councillor. It is difficult to pinpoint motivation for serving on local authorities at all in Ireland: personal satisfaction from service to the community, enjoyment of what little power and prestige there is, and making a start on the road to Dáil Éireann seem to be the driving factors.

*

In trying to explain present-day powerless Irish local government to an international audience in 1991, Tom Barrington starts out by referring to the Irish 'predicament',[3] which has been caused by 'the steady working out of the logic of a set of values, implicit and explicit, in what is largely an intellectual vacuum, in conditions not of dialectic but of drift'. This 'predicament' is only such if you approach it from the Barrington position of zealous reformer; if, on the other hand, you are a senior official in the Department of Finance, the powerlessness of local elected representatives is perfectly acceptable because they do not raise the money locally which they are so anxious to spend. That is the nub of the issue.

Since the 1920s, the number of local authorities in Ireland has been drastically and rapidly pruned – from 460 before Irish independence to 117 today. These are: 27 county councils (Tipperary has two); 5 county borough (city) councils and 6 borough corporations; 49 urban district councils; and 30 town commissions. Elections are held about every five years, and the electorate is composed of people over eighteen years of age who are ordinarily resident in the State (Irish citizenship is not necessary). The number of members of each kind of authority varies, usually according to the numbers of residents; county councils range from twenty to forty-six, county borough councils from fifteen to fifty-two. The least powerful bodies, representing smaller units of population, are urban district councils and the town commissions with a membership of nine. The latter are the subject of impending review and possible changes, so the election for their renewal, due in 1991 at the same time as the county and city elections, has been postponed.

Also in the 1920s, the system of managers was introduced; more and more financial controls by central government were imposed; and the *coup de grâce* was delivered in the late 1970s and early 1980s by the abolition of, first, the domestic rates system, and then the agricultural rates system as a method of local financing. But even as early as 1967, the Maud Committee on the Management of Local Government in Britain, having examined seven countries, could conclude that in Ireland 'central control is the most stringent of all'. That committee was reporting ten years before the two main political parties in Ireland embarked on what Barrington described as 'a disgraceful auction'[4] in 1977 before an election, and abolished domestic rates. This was followed by legal action by farmers which removed the other main source of revenue – farm rates – and left the local government system more emasculated than ever. Very little power lies in the hands of locally elected councillors: more, much more, in the offices of the city or county manager, but most of all in the offices of the Minister for the Environment, surveying the scene from the gracious Gandon-designed Custom House in the centre of Dublin which is the headquarters of the ministry.

Ironically, side by side with the gradual erosion of power of the local authorities, successive governments have made strong statements of intent to reform and strengthen the system. A White Paper in 1971, a government discussion document in 1973, an undertaking in the 1987 government programme to bring in reforms, and the Barrington report of 1991 were all followed by minimal changes.

In Opposition, national politicians are keen to reform: Jim Mitchell, Fine Gael spokesperson on the Environment,* said in 1991: 'Centralization puts a stranglehold on local decision-making; power must be delegated down as low as possible; we must get back to some form of property taxation, but it must mean a simultaneous and equal reduction in central taxation.' He suggested that as well as returning the power of local revenue-raising to the elected representatives, local authorities should be allowed to impose an energy tax for environmental and conservation work. These suggestions went further than any reform proposals in recent years; but in the light of experience, it was hard to see them getting anywhere. And since Fine Gael failed to achieve government in the November 1992 general election, Mitchell's suggestions remain only suggestions.

Ireland's thirty-five city and county managers are appointed by the Local Appointments Commission† which, like the Civil Service

---

*Dáil Deputy (since 1977) for Dublin West, former Minister for Justice, Transport and Communications, Posts and Telegraphs. Has served on Dublin City Council before and after ministerial office, and was Dublin's youngest Lord Mayor (at twenty-nine) when elected by his colleagues in 1976.

†Established in 1926, its members are the Ceann Comhairle (Speaker) of the Dáil, the Secretary of the Department of the Environment, and the Secretary of the Department of Health.

Commission, operates independently of any political pressure. The managers in 1992 were all male, and always have been since the foundation of the State, with a background in the central civil service or various positions in other local authorities. They were seen in the beginning, by governments which were deeply intolerant of the concept of politics being brought into local administration, as 'skilled technicians, applying the antiseptic standards of scientific administration to matters previously dealt with in the unsavoury gutter of local politics'.[5] The managers have had to expand their role greatly with the growth and complexity of government spending channelled through them to local authorities, with new developmental and environmental protection roles, and with regional planning for disbursement of EC structural funding as part of their function. Their pay ranges from IR£60,000 for the city manager of Dublin to IR£40,000 for ordinary county managers.

The local-authority service is similar in structure of employment to the civil service, with a standard pattern of grades for each authority and uniformity in methods of recruitment, pay, and conditions of service. The hierarchy has the manager at its head, followed by the county secretary, finance officer, administrative officer, senior staff officer, and so on down to the clerical assistants and clerk-typists. There are technical officers too: engineers, architects, librarians, fire officers.

Local authorities employ nearly 30,000 people, and spend over IR£1 billion a year. The central exchequer input is by far the largest amount of this money,* followed by revenue raised from house-loan repayments, water and service charges, refuse-collection charges, planning applications, and employees' pension contributions; the third category of revenue is in rates on commercial property, which is the only rating system in existence, and annoys the business community intensely. They often consider themselves to be the 'soft targets' of local councillors seeking to avoid difficult decisions that involve sensitive spending cuts.

The money is spent on eight broad programme areas (see pie chart overleaf), well over half going on programmes 1 and 2 –

---

* Specific grants from central government amount to approximately 80 per cent of capital expenditure.

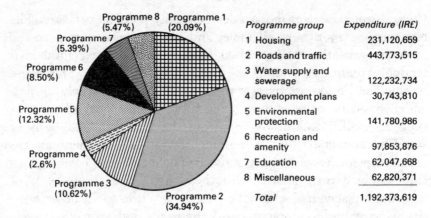

Programme group	Expenditure (IR£)
1 Housing	231,120,659
2 Roads and traffic	443,773,515
3 Water supply and sewerage	122,232,734
4 Development plans	30,743,810
5 Environmental protection	141,780,986
6 Recreation and amenity	97,853,876
7 Education	62,047,668
8 Miscellaneous	62,820,371
Total	1,192,373,619

Local-government expenditure by sector (programme group), 1992
(*source:* Press Office, Department of the Environment)

housing, buildings, and roads – and nearly all controlled by central-government decisions. In recent years, a growing expenditure area is environmental protection, a new departure for Ireland, which gained momentum with the appointment of a special junior Minister for Protection of the Environment in the government of 1989. That appointment was renewed in January 1993, but with a new minister.*

The specific functions allocated to Irish local authorities by central government are considerably less than in most western democracies; in a list of fourteen Council of Europe members in 1991, Ireland was bottom of the list for local responsibility. The sectors for which no real local autonomy exists include: urban road transport, ports, airports, agriculture, forestry, fishing, hunting, electricity, commerce, tourism, security, police, justice, education, hospitals, personal health, and family welfare services.[6] Any functions carried out by local authorities in these areas are strictly controlled by central government.

It was expected in the early days of the system that tensions might arise between the managers and the elected representatives. In fact, a very smooth *modus vivendi* has been worked out. Managers are very careful to retain the goodwill of their councillors, and recognize the political exigencies governing their elected colleagues'

* Details of the amounts spent on each programme can be seen in the diagram.

lives. Even though they are not required legally to tell councillors everything, they are circumspect with communications about constituents' affairs. There is seldom a real clash between the sides, though 'there may frequently be a semblance of conflict when councillors at meetings may wish to be seen as championing the interests of those who elected them as against the tyranny of the bureaucracy'.[7] Thus, an outcry against the siting of a rubbish dump may involve agonized table-thumping by councillors, with murmurs of agreement from the public benches, while privately the councillors know that no alternative is open to the county manager. At openings of sewerage schemes or new tourist amenities, the manager in his speech will be careful to praise the hard work and input of the councillors.

This friendly arrangement avoids any tensions arising from a system which reduces the councillors to 'almost the role of supplicants, seeking dispensation for individual constituents in matters like the allocation of public authority housing'.[8] Such resentment as there is is directed at national government which has rendered the councillors powerless.

WHAT POWERS DO THE ELECTED REPRESENTATIVES HAVE?

Speaking in Seanad Éireann, Senator Carmencita Hederman described a meeting of Dublin Corporation at which councillors demanded that a colleague should stop smoking; they cited a decision which the members had made a month previously to ban all smoking at their meetings. 'We were told rather sheepishly by one of the unfortunate officials that the no smoking rule could not be implemented because the Minister had not yet sanctioned it.'[9] Local authorities receive their powers through legislation, and in the Irish context those powers are very narrow, and, as we have seen, do not touch on areas such as health, training and manpower, transport, policing, and education. Most important, their powers to raise revenue are extremely limited. Neither do they control when their own elections will be held; central government decides that, and has often postponed elections, usually for reasons which have more to do with national political trends and fear of a trouncing than with any other reason. Thus, they were postponed in 1965, 1972, 1984, and 1990. There was virtually no public protest.

The power and functions reserved to the elected members cover the adoption of the annual expenditure estimates, the fixing of the annual rate (in practice on commercial properties only), the amount to be borrowed (again, strictly controlled), the making of development plans, local by-laws, housebuilding programmes, and assisting other local authorities in providing services and amenities. Any resolution which does not conform to the legal powers is considered *ultra vires* and would incur heavy penalties. This was somewhat modified under the 1992 Act, when members were empowered to 'take action in the interests of the local community'. If an authority fails to agree its expenditure estimates, it can be abolished by the minister, who will then appoint a commissioner to carry on with the work.

PLANNING: ABUSE – REAL AND IMAGINED

One of the most controversial powers of the councillors is that generally referred to as 'Section 4'. This is when the decisions of the manager can be overturned by use of Section 4 of the City and County Management (Amendment) Act 1955, to require the manager to carry out some action desired by the councillors for example one that concerns planning, particularly in expanding urban districts like greater Dublin involving millions of pounds in added value for land which is rezoned from 'agricultural' or 'amenity' to 'residential' or 'industrial'. The continuing rash of ribbon development outside cities and towns, the construction of Spanish-style houses in scenic areas which were supposed to be amenity areas – a great deal of this failure can be laid at the door of Section 4 motions.

The Local Government Bill 1991 amended the powers of the councillors to employ Section 4: in future, three-quarters of the members generally (plus three-quarters of the members in the particular ward or district concerned) will have to sign and support such a motion, and also any motions calling for 'material contravention' of the development plans for the area. Tom Barrington's report had, however, firmly recommended that Section 4 motions in the area of planning should be abolished. This is one of the areas in which public disquiet is being continually expressed, with suspicion that financial incentives for councillors and officials alike are available from property owners, that political favours are done by getting the permissions, and that planning decisions are made for entirely the wrong reasons. 'Out there, local government is merely a device for distributing money, advantage, and patronage along strict party lines. A lot of very stupid men implement the wishes of a handful of corrupt ones.'[10] A widely read and respected columnist in an Irish daily newspaper wrote those words just after the local elections of June 1991: she gave examples of (anonymous) cases of planning corruption, abuse of travel grants of councillors – a talking point in Ireland for years – and a conviction that 'Ireland, except for parts of Dublin, is run by two Mafias, Mafia Fáil and Mafia Gael'. The Irish public hold that unshakeable view. Asked in December 1991 about the extent of corruption in Irish public life, 65 per cent said it was 'widespread and serious'.[11] No legal case has been brought against any local councillor, despite persistent rumours, and the only case brought against a paid official did not stand up in court.

Just before the new regulation curbing the worst aspects of Section 4 decisions came into force, a rash of last-minute planning applications were passed across the country. When the new Dublin City Council took office (a disparate 'rainbow' coalition, displacing the Fianna Fáil majority), moves were immediately made to rescind many of these decisions. In discussion of this issue, an elected representative in Dublin (against whom no accusation of any kind of corruption was ever made) defended others in local government by saying: 'They're treated so badly in every other respect by national government, can you blame them for going over the top on one of the few powers they have, the Section 4 thing . . .?' The councillor didn't want to be named.

The controversial nature of planning applications was well demonstrated by the heated debate in the Dublin County Council chambers in the spring of 1993, when intense lobbying and public wrangling took place on the subject of north County Dublin. Large areas of this part of Dublin are the subject of applications by developers for rezoning of green areas to residential and industrial use. The developers present their case to councillors and residents' associations, frequently putting forward attractive carrots like new sports facilities and parks to sweeten the pill. But an exasperated Minister for the Environment, having accused local councillors in

Dublin of making bad and irresponsible plannng decisions over the years, pointed out finally that 5,000 acres of land in the county was available, already zoned for private development, but was not being taken up by developers. Why? Because a series of bad decisions had resulted in massive single-class housing developments, ensuring that too many social problems were concentrated in certain areas, making adjacent land unattractive for private development. Meanwhile, in the Swords area of north County Dublin, in the week leading up to 23 May, the councillors made decisions which would mean 17,000 new houses in the area, against the advice of the planning officials of the county council. The minister castigated councillors of all parties, including his own, and accused them of allowing zoning to be 'developer-driven'.[12]

LOCAL LINKS WITH NATIONAL POLITICS

A power invested in county and borough councillors which might seem innocuous, but which has huge implications for national politics, is that of voting for members of Seanad Éireann. Councillors, in fact, constitute the majority of the electorate. Membership of the second House of Ireland's bicameral legislature is either the consolation prize for defeated Dáil Deputies, where they rest and enjoy prestige while mustering resources for the next electoral battle, or the stepping-stone for a bright political future. Councillors are courted and respected by Senators and Dáil Deputies, as well as ministers . . . on the principle that you never know when you might need them; they are also needed to ensure a government majority in the second House. This may well be a major part of the explanation for the delicacy with which local-government reform is treated, and why governments constantly swear confidence in the local representatives (while drawing the line at giving them real power, which since it involves raising local taxes is not all that welcome to many local party stalwarts anyway). A description of the exquisite torture endured by those in search of the county councillors' votes in the Senate elections will be found in Chapter 3 above.

THE DUAL MANDATE

In recent general elections in Ireland, about two-thirds of the 166 successful candidates for Dáil Éireann were, or had been, members of their local authority. This dual mandate has been criticized and deplored for decades; there was a succinct recommendation in the 1991 Barrington report that no Dáil Deputies, Senators, or Members of the European Parliament should be simultaneously members of local authorities. The reasoning behind this was that no clear-cut and separate role for local government could be achieved while the dual mandate persisted. This recommendation was ignored in the Local Government Bill of June 1991. Therefore 'local issues are largely decided, in so far as they are decided at all, nationally ... local issues are hawked prominently around the national political arena ... it is less the intensity of localism that is peculiar to Ireland than the mechanisms devised to elevate the local to the national'.[13] The cause of this national intrusion into local affairs is, of course, the Irish multi-seat electoral system, which makes it imperative for each national legislator to relate minutely and on a daily basis to his local area, and not to allow any other aspirant to, or member of, Dáil Éireann any advantage whatsoever. The Dáil, therefore, never meets on Mondays, when local-authority meetings all over Ireland are held, and if a Deputy wears a local mayor's or chairman's chain, he will have special 'pairing'* arrangements in the Dáil. An Irish Senator vehemently condemned the dual mandate just before the June 1991 local elections: 'We all share a portion of the guilt ... we get plenty of pretty parochial TDs ... we are promoting clientelism and clinics† ... has anyone got the guts to sacrifice a few council seats in the national interest?'[14] (The same man bowed to the realities of Irish political life, decided to try for a Dáil seat at the next election, and stood for election himself to a county council the following month; he was successful.)

At local elections, the turnout of voters is always lower than in

---

* 'Pairing': the system whereby members of opposing parties in parliament can be absent from a vote, provided the Whips know in advance that the numbers of absentees will be equal.

† The political clinic: an elected representative advertises her presence in a pub/ parish hall/hotel at certain hours so that local people can come with problems to be solved.

general elections,* while the electoral performance of independents and smaller parties is usually much better than in national contests. The big political parties get heavily involved in local elections, for a variety of reasons: they serve as a barometer of public opinion between general elections; they serve to activate the local party workers, to keep them 'in trim' for the big national joust; they recruit new members and bring forward new talent for future Dáil elections; and, crucially, they provide the Senate votes. Local elections 'might reasonably be regarded as merely ersatz versions of general elections . . . they are a minor battleground where the same parties which dominate national politics engage in the same type of contest as at national elections'.[15]

Prime ministers and ministers trail around the country encouraging the voters, while spending promises are made to coincide with voting day in marginal areas. Thus, in June 1991, Co. Cork was promised a tunnel under the River Lee, and the Central Statistics Office was to be moved to Cork city: however 'the wrath of the cynics did not gain momentum . . . until Tullamore, Portlaoise, Wexford, Longford, Kilkenny, Waterford and Dundalk were also promised hordes of de-centralized Civil Servants at a press conference on June 12th'[16] (two weeks before polling day 1991). The civil-service unions were not impressed, and accused the government of attempting 'to give out their members like Smarties in lieu of factory openings'.[17]

WINNERS AND LOSERS: 1991 LOCAL ELECTIONS

In 1991 the vote for Fianna Fáil, the main government party, slumped dramatically compared with the total cast for it in both the 1989 general election and the 1985 local elections. The electorate were rapping the knuckles of the ruling party. Fianna Fáil's share of the vote went down to 37·8 per cent from a 1985 high of 45·5 per cent. It gained 358 of the 883 seats contested.

Fine Gael, undergoing a long-drawn-out decline in recent years, did not benefit from Fianna Fáil's misfortune: its 26·6 per cent compared badly with the already low 1985 figure of 29·8 per cent. Its seat total was 270.

* It was 55·1 per cent in 1991.

The Labour Party continued its gradual improvement: from 7·6 per cent in 1985, it improved to 10·6 per cent and ninety seats. This foreshadowed its huge increase in seats at the next general election, in 1992, when many of its new councillors were elected to the Dáil.

The Progressive Democrats achieved 4·9 per cent, the Workers' Party 3·7 per cent, the Greens 2·4 per cent, Sinn Féin 2·1 per cent, and others 11·9 per cent. All these small parties got 166 seats between them, out of the grand total of 883.

Thus, Fianna Fáil's control of the local authorities was swept away in 1991, leaving them in absolute control of only four: Clare, North Tipperary, Westmeath, and Laois. Such power as there is went to a mixture of small parties and Independents in most of the others, which did not augur well for any imminent legislative moves to give local politicians more power.

The anxieties of the reformers remain: the suspicion that Ireland's very low degree of real local involvement has been a major factor in the economic and social problems facing the country today. It is worth quoting the Barrington report on this issue: 'In terms of economic growth, providing for our population, and social equity, Ireland has performed relatively badly in comparison with most other Western countries ... the other more successful small countries have governmental institutions far less centralized than Ireland's ...'; our excessive centralization has a bearing on our poor performance 'by not stimulating and harnessing local initiative and energy ... this also tends to foster a dependency culture ... a further problem is the degree of rigid uniformity, which tends to limit the options for choice'.[18]

Professor Frank Convery, Director of the Environmental Institute of University College, Dublin, summed it up thus: 'What you want is a system which allows people to make a contribution; government from the top down hasn't worked. The whole thing requires drastic re-organization.'[19]

The issue never goes away; in January 1993, yet another set of promises was made, another list of reforms set out in a programme for government. The incoming government of Labour and Fianna Fáil undertook 'to accelerate the devolution of funding from Central Government to Local Authorities so as to give greater scope for local initiative in decision-making'.[20] Three new county councils for the huge greater Dublin area were to be established in 1993, statutory controls 'on various functions' were to be removed so as to give greater freedom to act, and new legislation was to give greater autonomy to local authorities in such areas as traffic control, land acquisition and disposal, and by-laws. The Barrington Report got its mandatory mention in promises of additional devolution, the reform of local government at sub-county level was back on the list, and new regional authorities were promised for 1993. If that package is put into place, and if the new government can overcome the pitfalls, resistance and inertia inherent in any attempts to carry out institutional reform, Ireland may yet achieve government at local level for the people and by the people.

NOTES

1. *Irish Times*, 20 April 1991.
2. *Irish Times*, 27 October 1992.
3. T. J. Barrington, 'Local government in Ireland', in: Batley and Stoker (eds.), *Local Government in Europe*, Macmillan, 1991.
4. ibid.
5. Eunan O'Halpin, 'The origins of city and county management', *City and County Management. A Retrospective 1929–1990*, Institute of Public Administration.
6. Institute of Public Administration, *Administration Yearbook and Diary*, 1992.
7. Seán Dooney and John O'Toole, *Irish Government Today*, Gill & Macmillan, 1992.
8. Micheál Gallagher, 'Local elections and electoral behaviour', *Irish Political Studies*, 1989.
9. *Seanad Report*, 11 December 1991, Col. 1575 (debate on ratification of the UN Charter on Local Self-Government).
10. Nuala Ó Faoláin, *Irish Times*, 1 July 1991.
11. 'IMS opinion poll', *Irish Independent*, 28 December 1991.
12. *This Week*, RTE Radio, 23 May 1993.
13. J. J. Lee, *Ireland, 1912–1985, Politics and Society*, Cambridge University Press, 1989.
14. Senator Shane Ross, *Dublin Tribune*, 16 May 1991.
15. Gallagher, op. cit.
16. Maol Muire Tynan, *Irish Times*, 22 June 1991.
17. ibid.

18. *Local Government Re-Organisation and Reform*, Report of the Advisory Expert Committee, December 1990.
19. *Irish Independent*, 14 May 1991.
20. *Programme for a Partnership Government, 1993–97.*

CHAPTER 6

Law and Order: Justice, the Police, and Defence

IRISH JUDGES AND JUSTICE; THE LEGAL PROFESSION

Under the Irish Constitution, the three powers of government are set out, and each one – legislative, executive, and judicial – is subsequently defined in different Articles. The courts system, with the Supreme Court at its head, is laid down in Article 34, including the appointments of judges and the independence of the judiciary. There has been a constant stream of judgements over the years from the Supreme Court, interpreting the Constitution and dealing with matters of great importance to the people. These judgements can be of extraordinary significance to the whole direction of society, and nowhere was this more obvious than in the early spring of 1992. The nature and composition of the Supreme Court, and its distinguished if slightly less exalted partner, the High Court, are therefore central to the process of transition of Ireland towards the next century.

The year 1992 was expected to see a fairly low-key public debate about the Maastricht Treaty for closer European union, and its ratification by Ireland with a constitutional referendum. It was far from that. It turned out to be the year when the Supreme Court threw a bombshell at the government – and many citizens – in the form of a judgement in February 1992 on the question of abortion. It concerned a case which will go down as a watershed in the legal and social history books of twentieth-century Ireland, known as X v. *the Attorney-General*, concerning the right of a fourteen-year-old girl, a victim of alleged rape, to travel to England in order to have an abortion. The question was whether an article in the Constitution, the Eighth Amendment,* could be relied upon to prevent Miss

---

* The Eighth Amendment, Article 40.3.3, reads: 'The State acknowledges the right to life of the unborn, and with due regard to the right to life of the mother, guarantees in its laws to respect, and as far as it is practicable, by its laws to defend and vindicate that right.'

X from travelling to the UK for the termination. The Supreme Court ruled that not only could she have travelled, she could have had an abortion in Ireland. This reversed a High Court decision only days before, that Miss X should be prevented from travelling. The Supreme Court judgement centred on the question of a 'real and substantial risk to the life of the mother' if the pregnancy continued. Since the unfortunate girl at the centre of the case had threatened to take her own life, and this threat was taken seriously by the Supreme Court judges when they heard the evidence, Ireland suddenly found itself needing urgently to face difficult choices. What kind of evidence of 'real and substantial risk' to the life of a pregnant woman would be needed to permit an abortion to be carried out in Ireland? Or should there be another constitutional amendment to undo the Supreme Court's judgement? The unravelling of that dilemma is described in Chapter 18 below ('Women and Life in Ireland').

One of the judges* also found it necessary to castigate the executive and the legislature – parliament and government – for not addressing this question over the years since the insertion of the 'pro-life' Eighth Amendment into the Constitution in 1983. Mr Justice McCarthy said, with some acerbity, in his judgement published on 6 March, '. . . the failure of the legislature to enact the appropriate legislation is no longer just unfortunate, it is inexcusable . . . the amendment remains bare of legislative direction'.[1]†

The general Irish public, not normally *au fait* with senior judicial personnel, quickly wanted to know who these judges were who interpreted their Constitution in this way. They had had a sudden sharp reminder of reality, in an Ireland which had preferred to close its eyes to the question of abortion. It had been possible to adopt this ostrich-like stance because the safety valve of travel to England – near, and relatively cheap to reach – had conveniently removed nearly all the pressure for legalizing abortion.

---

* Mr Justice Niall McCarthy (1925–92). He served on the Supreme Court from 1982, after a distinguished and outstandingly successful career as a barrister. His liberal judgements were often minority ones. He was killed, with his wife, in a car accident in Spain in September 1992.

† For notes on this section (Irish Judges and Justice . . .'), see page 130.

Supreme Court judges do not normally seek the light of publicity, but Ireland in 1992 brought them firmly into the public eye.

The Supreme Court

The Supreme Court is the final court of appeal under the Constitution for all civil and criminal matters, including constitutional validity of law. It is composed of six judges (until December 1992, they had been all male – no woman had ever served on Ireland's Supreme Court), mostly elderly, with long legal experience as barristers in Irish courts before becoming judges, usually Catholics, and nearly all from solid middle-class families. The sixth, *ex officio*, member of the Court is the President of the High Court. Five judges out of the six sit on each case. They share many characteristics with most of those who wield power and influence in Ireland: maleness, Catholicism, of middle age or older, of middle-class and/or moneyed background, Catholic single-sex education (and, frequently, membership of all-male sporting/social clubs).* As such, they can often be relied upon to reflect a set of conservative values which has been bred into their very bones. This was one of the reasons why the interpretation of Article 40.3.3, as giving rights to the mother of the unborn as well as to the child, caused such astonishment among people who had cocooned themselves into thinking that such a question would never have to be addressed at all.

The X case was an example of how, despite its members' homogeneous background, the Supreme Court has nevertheless proved to be a strong force in law reform. Perhaps this is because it has had to resolve issues which successive governments have failed to address, and a vacuum has had to be filled. This has been the case particularly in areas where liberal views on social issues conflict with those of Catholic conservatives. It was the Supreme Court, for example, which declared that contraception was a matter for private decision and not public laws, that women should serve on juries, that married women were discriminated against under taxation laws. The legislature has been slow to follow the example of the

---

*In the 1991 edition of *Who's Who in Ireland*,[2] most of the judges listed are members of clubs which in 1992 still refused full membership to women.

Court, so that the Irish Supreme Court's many constitutional interpretations are very slowly, if ever, put into legislation. Interest groups seeking law reform find the delay and inaction of the legislature extremely frustrating.

Meanwhile, as we saw in Chapter 3, the legislature has operated at a snail's pace (for various reasons, including the infrequency of sittings). There is also a reluctance among politicians to come to terms with decisions requiring legislation in so-called moral areas (mostly to do in some way or other with sex). Thus, it took until 1979 before the first (and very restrictive) legislation allowing for the importation and sale of contraceptives passed through the Dáil, despite a Supreme Court decision six years earlier. It is a mark of the rapid change in Irish attitudes that the Dáil and Senate passed legislation in 1993 providing for almost total availability of condoms in retail outlets, including vending machines. The public debate about the AIDS virus played some part in this change of attitude, but AIDS notwithstanding, the legislation would have been unthinkable ten years previously.

Sometimes, where the Court's decision does not require full legislation for its implementation, things happen more quickly. For example, in 1982 a married couple challenged the constitutionality of the tax regulations, which had the effect of taking more tax from a married couple than an unmarried pair. Since the Constitution pledges to guard the institution of marriage (Article 41.3), it found that the regulations contravened the Constitution, and they were changed very quickly.

An important decision in 1991 established that, despite some legal protection for a spouse's interest in the family home, it is not automatic that each partner is entitled to half of the home. This was deemed to be depriving people of their constitutional right to private property (Article 43.1). Shocked by this bald statement, which dismayed most women in the country, promises were made that legislation would be immediately forthcoming. By late 1992, no such legislation had appeared. When a general election was called in November 1992, and seven weeks elapsed before a new government was formed, hopes for such legislation in the short term were dashed. A new promise was made in the programme of the new government for 'legislation to give each spouse an equal share in the family home and household belongings'.[3]

The High Court and Lower Courts

The High Court is the next rung down the legal ladder, and like the Supreme Court has the power to test the constitutional validity of laws, while not having the final say. It has full original jurisdiction and power to determine all matters of law or fact, civil or criminal. Of its seventeen members, the overwhelming majority are, of course, male and Catholic. However, there is usually a leavening of other traditions, that has included a Protestant and a Jew, and in recent times, a woman. In Ireland, such labels are important.

The Circuit Court, with seventeen men on its bench, has limited civil and criminal jurisdiction. Some more serious criminal cases are brought before the Central Criminal Court (this in fact is the High Court, exercising criminal jurisdiction).

Given the particular circumstances of Ireland, with its extra criminal element of the terrorist IRA and allied paramilitaries, with all the intimidation of witnesses and juries which that implies, there is a Special Criminal Court (established in 1972), which sits without juries. This handles cases involving those who are ready to subvert normal legal procedures: it is a dangerous assignment, and the judges working in this court are given police protection. A panel of judges supplies the three sitting on each case, one each from the District, Circuit, and High Courts.

District Courts hear cases of a relatively minor nature, and are placed around the country. There are more than forty of them, and in 1992 a handful of women were listed among their judges.

The Judiciary

The Constitution confers independence on the judiciary, in that it gives the higher courts the absolute right to decide on the validity of any laws passed by the legislature, and states clearly that 'all judges shall be independent in the exercise of their judicial functions and subject only to this Constitution and the law' (Article 35.2). Technically, the President appoints all the judges, but she does so on the advice of the government. In practice, the government usually seeks the advice, if it needs it, of the Attorney-General, who is its own legal officer, and knows who is who in the legal world. The judges are chosen from barristers of high standing. Most of the Supreme Court and High Court judges can be identified as former strong supporters of one party or another, and given the dominance in government over the years of the two main parties, Fianna Fáil and Fine Gael, most judges have come from those political stables. An anecdote illustrates the acceptance of this: a young law lecturer told the author that he innocently enquired from a barrister colleague about the likely successor to a retiring High Court judge. 'I've no idea,' he was told; 'it depends who comes out of the hat in Mount Street.'* However, the consensus among the legal profession, the politicians, and the media is that the judges, once appointed, do not exhibit any hint of political bias or favouritism in their judgements. That is not to say that their attitudes (where they are ascertainable) to important issues of the day are not major considerations to those appointing them.

The incoming government of January 1993 promised the establishment of a Judicial Commission, comprising the presidents of the various courts and the Attorney-General, whose functions would be the general overseeing of the running of the courts, the fixing of the financial needs, streamlining of court services, review and reform of court practices – a package of potential which would go a long way towards sorting out many of the complaints which are made about the legal system in Ireland today.

There are reservations too about the appointment of judges. A serious Sunday newspaper editorial gave a sample of the occasional reservations which come to the surface – 'it is not right that five people should have such crucial influence over our private and public lives without ever having to go through any process of accountability or scrutiny . . .'[4] There are calls from time to time for a system of public hearings, or an independent committee or commission of some kind to oversee judicial appointments. However, notwithstanding the private opinions of some barristers and the public opinion of some commentators, no serious public debate in Ireland has ever taken place on the issue. Apart from (carefully) anonymous comments from young lawyers such as, 'it's wrong to be able to stack up the Supreme Court', no debate seems likely.

*In conversation with the author; Mount Street contains the headquarters of both of the dominant political parties, Fianna Fáil and Fine Gael. In the instance referred to, the party in question was Fianna Fáil.

The events surrounding judgements on abortion in 1992 may change public opinion on that.

The Legal Profession

The legal profession in Ireland is exercised by two branches of practice: barristers who plead in the courts; and solicitors who brief them. Later in this section, the procedures for qualification in each area will be looked at. There is a movement in Ireland, as in Britain, for fusion of the two branches.

Solicitors do not understand why they are not eligible for appointment to the higher courts, whose judges are all picked from the ranks of senior barristers. 'We would like to see a situation develop where all lawyers would be eligible for a judicial appointment based on their suitability for the position,' said the 1991–2 President of the Incorporated Law Society,* Adrian Bourke.[5] Solicitors at present are only appointed to the District Court, something which they feel is not only a slight on their profession, but limits the choice of the government to a small group of senior barristers who are specialists in restricted areas, for appointment to the higher courts. They point out that this restriction excludes 80 per cent of practising lawyers from consideration for higher judicial appointments. In July 1992, the junior minister at the Department of Justice pleased the solicitors' governing body, the Law Society, by saying that he himself would be supportive of a change. It was expected that this would be incorporated in a bill to come before parliament in the autumn of 1992. Unfortunately for the solicitors, the Dáil was dissolved suddenly in November, thus putting all such new legislation back for an unknown length of time. In the new programme for government announced in January 1993, there was no mention of such a bill.

Irish solicitors rarely exercise their right (which they have enjoyed since 1971) to plead in the higher courts, leaving that field to the

---

*The Incorporated Law Society is the representative body of the solicitors' profession. Currently, 3,700 solicitors practise in Ireland. It is responsible for the education, admission, enrolment, discipline and regulation of the profession. It administers a statutory compensation fund, which in 1992/3 came under extreme pressure owing to some very heavy claims from people and institutions suffering from legal malpractice.

barristers. In delving for the reason for this, it is whispered that a solicitor who has the temerity to appear in the higher courts may risk incurring the displeasure of the presiding judge, himself a former barrister . . . but no one says it out loud.

Irish Supreme Court Judges (in March 1993)

Chief Justice: Thomas Finlay (sixty-nine). From a legal and political family (Fine Gael), he was a Dáil Deputy for Fine Gael himself from 1954 to 1957. Educated at the Jesuit boarding-school Clongowes Wood College, and University College, Dublin (UCD), his first nomination to the High Court came from a Fianna Fáil government in 1972. (Governments sometimes appoint from the 'other side' in order to 'project an image of objectivity'.)[6] Considered to be a very clever lawyer, a conservative, and a good judge, he has the respect of the legal profession in general. He agreed with a 1985 Supreme Court judgement against homosexual-law reform, and delivered during the 1980s the judgements against the Well Woman Centre and Open Line Centre,* forbidding them to give Irish women information about abortion facilities in Britain. In 1992, of course, the latter cases seemed to require reopening following the abortion case in February, and the carrying of a referendum allowing information in late 1992.

Mr Justice Anthony Hederman (seventy). A strong Fianna Fáil supporter, and a former Attorney-General to a Fianna Fáil government, Mr Justice Hederman is a bachelor, educated at Castleknock College (an up-market Vincentian boarding-school for boys) and UCD. A member of the Supreme Court since 1981, he is known as a conservative and quiet judge. His was the dissenting voice in the February 1992 judgement allowing 'Miss X' to travel on the grounds of threatened suicide. In late 1992 he was appointed President of the Law Reform Commission, which means he will sit less on the Supreme Court but will still be available to them, making a seventh

---

* As part of their work in helping women in Ireland with crisis pregnancies, both of these agencies gave counselling on all the options facing the woman, and if she decided that abortion was her definite choice, she was supplied with addresses of clinics in Britain, and helped both with travel arrangements and contacts with the clinics, as well as post-abortion counselling if necessary.

judge available for the time being. The announcement of his replacement on the Court was delayed when the general election of November 1992 was called.

Mr Justice Séamus Egan (sixty-seven) was appointed to the Supreme Court in 1991. A well-liked, quietly liberal and distinguished lawyer, he is a product of Blackrock College (Holy Ghost Fathers this time) and UCD. He is one of the judges without strong previous affiliation to any political party.

Mr Justice Hugh O'Flaherty. At fifty-three, O'Flaherty is relatively young; he comes from a Kerry Fianna Fáil background, and was an adviser to a Fianna Fáil leader, Mr Charles Haughey, in the 1970s and early 1980s. The only one of the main Supreme Court judges not to attend a major establishment boys' school (he attended St Brendan's College in his home town of Killarney), he is generally spoken of as one of a 'new breed' of senior judges, and said to be extremely clever.

Mr Justice John Blayney. Born in 1926, and educated by the Jesuits and the Benedictine monks (Belvedere College and Glenstal Abbey), University College, Dublin, and the King's Inns. A former rugby player (he once played for Ireland) and, in 1981–3, legal adviser on a professional basis to the 'pro-life' campaign. Upon his appointment in late 1992, to replace Niall McCarthy, who was killed in a road accident, there was concern about his supposed conservatism, and praise for his excellent legal brain.

Mrs Justice Susan Denham (b. 1945). Educated in Alexandra College (Ireland's best-known Protestant secondary school for girls), Trinity College and Columbia University, New York. Mrs Justice Denham had only spent one year as a highly regarded High Court judge when she was appointed, on 9 December 1992, to the Supreme Court. In making this important appointment when they were only in a caretaker capacity as a government, Fianna Fáil might have expected heavy criticism: but such was the regard for Mrs Justice Denham's excellence, added to the fact that she was a woman, that there was an enthusiastic welcome.

The *ex officio* sixth member of the Supreme Court is the President of the High Court, *Mr Justice Liam Hamilton* (b. 1928). Educated by the Christian Brothers in Mitchelstown, Co. Cork, and University College, Dublin, here is someone whose political roots are, unusually, in the Labour Party, but whose legal career has progressed steadily upwards through the years, whether or not the Labour Party were in government. In 1991, he was given the full-time task of presiding over a tribunal of inquiry into the beef industry, which grew and grew in length and complexity and kept him away from the courts. 'A gregarious, witty man, popular with colleagues.'[7] A female solicitor wryly remarked to the author, 'Yes, he's one of the lads . . .'

The sharp line between legislature and judiciary has seldom been breached or even become a matter for discussion in modern Ireland. It took the abortion issue to bring it up in 1992, and it became part of the agonized public discussion around the subject. A High Court judge,* who had just been appointed President of the Law Reform Commission,† and who was considered by barristers and the legal profession generally to be astute, careful, and often brilliant in his judgements, gave a trenchant opinion about abortion, and suggestions for a new 'pro-life' constitutional amendment in an article in the April 1992 edition of the *Irish Law Times*.‡ He went on to emphasize and expand on his views in a newspaper interview despite having raised eyebrows with the first intervention, and gave it as his opinion that membership of the EC was 'not worth it if it means having to vote for lawful abortion in this country'.[8] The government of the day was, to put it mildly, unhappy about this intervention coming as it did in the middle of a most difficult and delicate political and legal process which looked like endangering the referendum on the Maastricht Treaty due to be held in Ireland.

* Mr Justice Rory O'Hanlon (b. 1923), a much-respected member of the Bar, was appointed to the High Court in 1981. His membership of the Catholic organization Opus Dei was apparently common knowledge among colleagues, but not publicly known until the April 1992 incident. He is the father of twelve children.
† The Commission continually examines areas needing new laws and recommends action to the government. It is also invited by governments to propose legal action on matters referred to it.
‡ Mr Justice O'Hanlon's suggested wording was: 'The unborn child from the moment of conception shall have the same right to life as a child born alive.'

The judge went to see the Taoiseach (having made it clear that he could not be 'summoned' to do so) and was dismissed from his position as President of the Law Reform Commission on 9 April 1992, but not dismissed as a High Court judge. A judge of the Supreme or High Court can only be removed 'upon resolutions passed by Dáil Éireann and by Seanad Éireann calling for his removal'.[9] In the letter dismissing the judge from the Commission, the government said they no longer had confidence in him. The question was then raised, '. . . can a government decide it cannot depend on someone's judgement in one respect, but can have confidence in him in another respect? You either have plenary powers as a High Court Judge or you don't . . .' said a 'senior member of the judiciary'[10] in one of the plethora of newspaper articles following these unprecedented events. A feature of these comments was their anonymity, reflecting both professional caution and the small size of the tightly knit legal community in Ireland. An editorial in one of the country's leading newspapers was in no doubt about the issues: '. . . he is laying down value judgements on social, political and economic questions which are emphatically not the business of the judiciary. It would be no less indefensible if his convictions lay the other way and he were urging the opposite.'[11] At the end of 1992, the judge defiantly stated his views very strongly again during the course of the referendum which was held on the question, and urged the population to vote against the government's proposals. But the idea of proceeding to ask the Dáil and Senate to remove Mr Justice O'Hanlon from office would present an appalling vista indeed.

The only woman judge of the High Court was mentioned during this controversy too:* she was appointed chairperson of the second Commission on the Status of Women by the government in 1990, with a brief to report on all matters concerning the rights of women, and to make recommendations to government. Her commission entered the abortion controversy earlier than her male colleague did, with a recommendation that women's right to travel and

---

*Miss Justice Mella Carroll (b. 1934), the first female High Court judge, appointed in 1980. She serves on the administrative tribunal of the International Labour Organization, and is one of the judges spoken of approvingly by nearly every legal practitioner.

information had to be safeguarded. Most commentators felt that this intervention was perfectly in keeping with the brief she and her Commission had been specifically given by government, and that no conflict of roles was in question.

How Judges are Paid

In 1993, the Chief Justice had the same salary as the Taoiseach (IR£77,845); the other Supreme Court judges receive about IR£65,026. High Court judges are paid a little over IR£60,000. It is certain that all of these people were earning considerably more in their private legal practices. Circuit Court judges earn IR£47,919, and the judges of the District Court IR£40,194. (All of these rates are as of 1 January 1992.) An official car and driver are available to only a very few judges, usually those working in areas like the Special Criminal Court whose lives are possibly in danger. In April 1992, an independent public-service review body (known as the Gleeson Committee, because of its chairperson, a senior barrister called Dermot Gleeson) recommended increases for all ranks of judge: for example, the Chief Justice was recommended a further IR£13,000, a High Court judge a further IR£11,000 and so on down. Gleeson stated that judges' salaries should not be allowed to fall too far behind earnings in the legal profession, otherwise the State would be hindered in its efforts to recruit high-quality individuals to the bench. But given the huge bills and impending trouble the government had to face in 1993 over public-service pay, it was hard to see the Gleeson package being implemented. And so governments will go on having some difficulty in filling some of the vacancies with the very best legal brains.

The Attorney-General

The legal adviser to the government* is not a member of the

* The Attorney-General since September 1991 is Harry Whelehan SC (b. 1944). A genial and well-liked barrister, with identifiable political leanings towards Fianna Fáil (otherwise he would not have been nominated), he was appointed by Charles Haughey in the last few months of his term of office, and reappointed by Albert Reynolds in February 1992, and again in January 1993 on the formation of the Fianna Fáil/Labour coalition.

government, but, like the judges, is appointed by the President on the advice of the government. He is usually a senior counsel, whose exact functions, and the degree of discretion he enjoys in carrying them out, became a source of great public interest in 1992. He it was who instigated the attempt to stop 'Miss X' travelling to England, and who started the process in July which culminated in a decision by the Supreme Court that Cabinet discussions enjoyed total confidentiality in perpetuity. Attorneys-General are chosen almost invariably from barristers who have been supporters of the political party in power.

There has never been a woman in the office, although in 1984 there was speculation that a Labour Party member and distinguished constitutional lawyer called Mary Robinson might be appointed. In the event, the Labour Party chose someone else.

The Constitution states: 'All crimes and offences . . . shall be prosecuted in the name of the People and at the suit of the Attorney-General or some other person authorized in accordance with law to act for that purpose' (Article 30.3). The Attorney-General attends government meetings, giving his opinion when asked for it. He oversees the drafting of new legislation. His two roles, as legal adviser to government on the one hand, and guardian of the public interest on the other, have seldom aroused much controversy. That is, until 1992, the year when so much of public importance happened in Ireland.

It was the Attorney-General, Harry Whelehan, who applied in February 1992 for the injunction to prevent the pregnant fourteen-year-old from travelling for her abortion, thus unleashing a series of events which were to convulse the country in 1992 and beyond. The Supreme Court judges emphasized, in their judgement, that though they did not grant the injunction, he had acted in full accordance with his duties, and had correctly exercised his discretion. And later in 1992, on a different matter, he again exercised his discretion by applying for, and getting, a total ban on the disclosure of any discussions held at any Cabinet meeting in the past. This was in the context of evidence being given by former government ministers to the tribunal of inquiry into the beef industry. Despite the government's insistence in both instances that the Attorney General had acted entirely on his own initiative, the Taoiseach contradicted this in the Dáil on 24 June, by assuring the House on the X case issue (and particularly women, who were very anxious at this stage) that 'there would be no further injunctions sought by the State in relation to the right to travel'. Understandably, public questions were raised: if the Attorney-General had acted on his own initiative, and was told by the Supreme Court that he had no choice but to do so, how could a Taoiseach instruct him about hypothetical future events? The Taoiseach appeared to have put the Attorney-General in a wasteland where the law is what the government says it is.

The complex question of exactly how the Irish Attorney-General can be expected to fulfil two apparently conflicting roles was thrown into sharp focus by these events. Those two roles are: legal adviser to the government, and guardian of the public interest in the legal field. After 1992, the general public in Ireland was very confused about what their principal legal officer was supposed to do. And the Attorney-General has no platform upon which to enlighten the public. Suggestions are put forward that the two functions should be separated into two different persons and offices,* and that the Attorney-General should be automatically given a seat as one of the Taoiseach's nominations to the Senate to provide him or her with a public platform for explanation.

The Accessibility of Irish Justice

'What matters to the citizen facing the government is, first, the accessibility of the courts ...'[12] Not until 1962 was a general provision made for free legal aid in Irish criminal cases, and that system works reasonably well. However, Ireland had to be forced by the European Court of Human Rights to provide a system of free legal aid in civil cases: the government was found in breach of the European Convention on Human Rights when a brave Mrs Josie Airey fought her case all the way to Strasbourg, with the help of a young woman barrister called Mary Robinson (later to be elected President of Ireland in 1990). Finally, in December 1979, a

* Most notably by Professor David Gwynn Morgan of the Law School of University College, Cork.

Legal Aid Board* was set up to provide such legal aid on a means test. It has been bedevilled by lack of resources ever since.

In 1969, students and young lawyers had set up and run an organization called Free Legal Advice Centres (FLAC) to provide for the deficiency in free civil legal aid. Their agitation for a State system did not succeed in the face of the financial fears of successive governments, and it needed the European legal case to achieve their objective.

FLAC still exists and works, because of what its supporters consider to be the inadequacy of the State system. That system provides legal services in cases of civil debt, matrimonial cases, and negligence; it does not cover areas such as unfair dismissals and all of social welfare. FLAC costs about IR£90,000 annually to run, more than half of which is supplied by the legal profession itself through voluntary levies, and from a range of fund-raising activities; the rest is given by the State. As with so many small agencies supplying public services, continual financial crisis dogs the group: in 1992 it was run from a small office above a snooker hall in central Dublin, with eight staff, a mixture of part-time, trainee, and young lawyers, and once again, a threat of closure because of uncertainty about the State grant.

With a budget of nearly IR£2·5 million in 1992, employing thirty solicitors, the State's Legal Aid Board has very long waiting-lists. A former Board member, solicitor Ernest Margetson, resigned from the Legal Aid Board when he was President of the Incorporated Law Society in 1990, saying it was ineffective. His resignation was an echo of the resignation of yet another member, this time its chairperson, in protest at inadequate funding.† When the Minister for Justice‡ announced an expansion of the State system in May 1991, he was not given the plaudits he might have hoped for. 'It is a small step, and there is an awful long way to go ...', said Margetson.[14] When FLAC undertook a survey of the situation

---

*The Legal Aid Board, whose chairperson is Vincent Landy (a former senior counsel), was established 'to administer the scheme for Civil Legal aid and advice, and to make the services of solicitors and barristers available to persons of modest means'.[13]

†Niall Fennelly, Senior Counsel, chaired the Legal Aid Board from 1983 until his very public resignation in 1990.

‡Then Mr Ray Burke, of Fianna Fáil.

nationally in March 1992, they found that the fifteen State law centres could only take on new cases if they were considered emergencies. 'The situation in Dublin is that an applicant requiring legal aid for a [domestic] barring order, maintenance, custody or judicial separation will not be able to see a solicitor through the legal aid service this year.'[15]

The Law Society and worried individuals in the legal profession want the Board to be able to use the services of private solicitors rather than their own full-time employees, thus giving the system greater flexibility; they argue that rather than paying a Board solicitor to travel fifty miles to move a case adjournment, for example, a local lawyer could be hired at a fraction of the price. It seems, in the absence of major changes, that Irish justice is not yet accessible to the poor.

Wigs, Gowns and Divisions – Irish Barristers and Solicitors

A government minister in 1992 described the wigs and gowns of the Irish barristers as 'that rather quaint 250-year-old attire'.[16] It was one of the verbal exchanges in a battle between a minister full of zeal to reform and modernize the legal profession, the Bar in particular, and a profession which traditionally seems to take a very dim view of being criticized. But he was not the first: as far back as 1987, a Supreme Court judge revealed his dislike of the 'post-colonial servility' enshrined in elements of the courts system, including the dress: he said he had heard it suggested that the wigs afforded barristers 'a sense of protection against their clients as if they were a sort of forensic condom'.[17] When the Fair Trade Commission* reported on the legal profession in 1991,[18] the *Irish Law Times* thundered: 'This journal questions whether Mr O'Malley [the minister in question], who has shown a distrust towards the Irish Bar since his first ministry in 1970, is the right person to decide on the future of the legal profession in Ireland vis-à-vis the Fair Trade Commission Report.'

Barristers control entry to their profession: young people

---

*The forerunner of the present Competition Authority (established by the Minister for Industry and Commerce in October 1991), whose chairman is Patrick Lyons.

usually acquire a primary degree in law, then attend lectures in the late afternoon at the King's Inns, the barristers' college, before taking their examinations. Fees are expensive, and there are uncomplimentary comments – again, anonymous – about the academic standard of the lectures. A newspaper reporter, trying to gather material on legal education, commented: 'Students spoken to for this feature – none of whom felt they could risk being named for fear of victimization – were critical of the repetitive nature of the training, the indifferent quality of the lecturing and inadequacy of the course generally.'[19] The author's experience in speaking to students or young barristers mirrors the findings of that journalist, including the unwillingness to be quoted. Students are also expected to 'eat dinners' – that is, to dine regularly at the college as part of an old tradition – and this is also seen by the younger members as archaic. Once through that process, the student barrister becomes a 'devil' – an apprentice with a senior barrister for a year, with no pay. Then a young barrister embarks on what may be many years of penury, before beginning to reap the rewards of long years of preparation. Small wonder that Irish barristers come from families who can afford to support the many years of study and apprenticeship: that class structure as seen in the composition of the Supreme Court is reflected at all levels of the Bar and the higher judiciary.

But rewards there eventually are; even though a survey in 1990, commissioned by the Bar Council itself, found Ireland's 800 barristers earning only an average of IR£14,200, figures from the Department of Industry and Commerce show that for 1990, barristers earned IR£30 million from personal-injury cases alone.[20] The department's figures would imply earnings of IR£37,000 each for that year. But of course it is not evenly divided. It is obvious that the more successful older practitioner can earn a great deal, while the younger barrister must depend on family or other subsidy to survive.

For State briefs (which are frequently less well paid than others), a senior barrister can expect to earn about IR£1,200 for the first day, and about IR£600 for each subsequent day of the case. In the case of a tribunal, or a specially big court hearing, it is the length which will determine the fee – and the more days there are, the better the fee. In March 1992, after fifty-six days of one of the Irish

State's biggest public tribunals of inquiry* (presided over by Mr Justice Liam Hamilton), it was reckoned that IR£5 million had already been reached in legal costs. Most of this would go to the senior and junior barristers involved, with a considerable amount also for the backing solicitors, estimated at IR£5,000 per week.[21]

Solicitors generally progress through a university degree, although other preliminary courses are being developed, then continue to the Law Society's own legal courses at Blackhall Place in central Dublin. These courses are combined with periods of practical apprenticeship in a law firm – which are paid. Courses are taught by practitioners. Some years ago, the Law Society itself was successfully sued by students alleging irregularities in the way examination scripts were graded. The Law Society was suspected of limiting access to the profession of solicitor by regulating the number of students who would pass examinations. The entry examination was then dropped, and relative harmony and satisfaction reigned in the academic side of the profession.

To approach the courts, the public must first deal with a solicitor, who will then brief barristers. The Fair Trade Commission Report recommended a very broad range of actions to bring fusion – or, at least, rationalization and streamlining – between the professions of solicitor and barrister, to simplify and allow access to barristers by persons involved in legal proceedings, and generally to modernize the whole legal process. Both the Law Society (solicitors) and the Bar Council are busily working on any areas where they feel they can meet some of the criticisms. After many years of quiet immobility and undisturbed autonomy, the Irish legal profession – like the British – is being forced to respond to long-voiced criticisms of its monopolies and privileges and other restrictive practices. The minister who so much annoyed the barristers spoke of his determination when he addressed the third joint Conference of Young Solicitors and Young Barristers just after the Fair Trade Commission Report had appeared: 'My one clear objective is to create conditions in the legal profession that enable its users to obtain the necessary services at a cost which is not inflated by restrictive practices or inefficiencies.'[22]

In 1975, the Law Reform Commission was established, as an

* Tribunal of Inquiry into the Beef Industry. For details see Chapter 12.

independent statutory body corporate. Its job is to keep the law under review, to carry out research and examination, and to issue proposals for law reform. A president, who must be a senior judge, and four commissioners, all appointed by the government, are prolific in telling the government what should be done. In late 1992, the newly appointed president was the seventy-year-old Supreme Court Judge Anthony Hederman, who succeeded the High Court judge who fell foul of the government (as we saw above) with his pronouncements on abortion prior to the Maastricht ratification. One solicitor, a senior psychologist, a professor of law, and a barrister made up the Commissioners.* They have a staff of nine, and in 1992 the State grant was IR£416,000.

The Commission is regarded as efficient and very useful in the work it does; but its members criticize successive governments for their failure to act on their reports, of which less than a quarter have been put into law. It has published eleven working papers, forty-one final reports, five consultation papers, and thirteen reports up to 1992.

Happily, Irish judges enjoy a reputation for incorruptibility, but there is much criticism of the legal system. It is expensive and mostly unavailable to those without means to pay for it. It is dominated by the male middle class, many of whom are considered to be in a close-knit clique, and gains no credit for being seen to cling tenaciously to old habits. A country like Ireland, in transition in so many areas, has a lot to do in reforming one of its most important institutions. In early 1993, the legal profession from top to bottom was facing a new low level of public esteem. Repeated revelations about very high fees for work on State inquiries continued to surface, culminating in a court battle because of strong language used in the media; a solicitor was facing ten charges under the Forgery Act involving over IR£100,000, while the irregular affairs of another who had committed suicide in 1992 were reckoned to total some millions of pounds; barristers had come under public scrutiny because of a public controversy over alleged remarks made by a barrister concerning beef-tribunal evidence in a hotel bar. A High Court judge was taken to a Garda

* They are: John Buckley, solicitor; Simon O'Leary, barrister; Maureen Gaffney, psychologist, and Professor William Duncan of Trinity College, Dublin.

station in the small hours from outside the same hotel in the week after he had given a controversial sentence in a particularly distressing sex case ... and in the general climate of distaste for such goings-on, it was forgotten that many legal people give their services free to impecunious clients on important cases of public interest, and many private ones too.

As well as the appointment of the first woman to the Supreme Court, and a known liberal at that, the Taoiseach Albert Reynolds followed it up – in January 1993 – with the appointment of the first woman to the Ministry for Justice. Máire Geoghegan-Quinn,* a hardy and experienced politician from Galway, is identified as on the liberal wing of her historically conservative Fianna Fáil party. Because of her considerable ministerial experience in various areas, and her closeness to the Taoiseach, Geoghegan-Quinn is expected to be a formidable holder of this difficult portfolio. The ongoing violence generated by the Northern Ireland situation is a central and difficult area, as is the continual public disquiet about violent crime in Dublin city.

One of her first challenges was how to deal with Ireland's unsatisfactory machinery for review of miscarriages of justice. The Irish, in celebrating in recent years the eventual vindication of several Irish people who had been wrongly convicted by English courts, have now to deal with some worrying cases which went through Irish courts. The most pressing case of alleged miscarriage of justice has been simmering since the 1970s, after a train robbery at Sallins, Co. Kildare. The new government set about processing legislation which would 'provide for review of alleged cases of miscarriage of justice, and to give a statutory right to compensation for such miscarriages'.

One of the most lengthy, detailed, and ambitious sections of the *Programme for a Partnership Government*, published at the beginning of the 1993 coalition government of Fianna Fáil and Labour, dealt with the general area of crime and law reform. If even half of the programme were implemented in a four-year term of office, it would be an immense achievement.

Another avenue through which the Irish public may pursue justice is via the office of the Ombudsman. Established by legisla-

* For biographical details, see page 439n.

tion in 1980, the office was not filled until 1984. The Ombudsman deals with complaints about administrative actions, delays or inaction which affect people who have to deal with government departments and offices, local authorities, health boards, and the post and telephone companies. Ireland's first Ombudsman has been an unqualified success: Michael Mills,* a newspaperman and a highly respected public figure, was unpopular with the leader of the Opposition at the time of his appointment – Charles Haughey. This was because of Mills's political writings and comments during the period of Mr Haughey's often-disputed leadership of his party and his country in the early 1980s. It looked for a while in 1987 as if his office would have to stop taking new complaints as it was starved of resources after Mr Haughey had returned to government: however, a political row ensued and the Ombudsman was given staffing. He professed himself satisfied with his budget of IR£1 million and his thirty-three staff in 1992; the number of complaints had levelled off at some 3,000, with 49 per cent coming from civil-service clients – mostly in Social Welfare. The news that he intended to retire at the end of his term in October 1994 was greeted with regret. His office, so reluctantly established by the politicians, has been one of the legal success stories in Ireland.

* Michael Mills (b. 1927 in Co. Laois) came from the media world: he was chief political correspondent of the *Irish Press* newspaper.

NOTES ('IRISH JUDGES AND JUSTICE ...')

1. Mr Justice Niall McCarthy, *Irish Times*, 6 March 1992.
2. Maureen Cairnduff (ed.), *Who's Who in Ireland – The Influential 1,000*, 2nd edn, Hibernian Publishing Co., 1991.
3. Fianna Fáil and Labour, *Programme for a Partnership Government*.
4. *Sunday Tribune*, 20 October 1991.
5. *Irish Independent*, 28 December 1991. Ireland is a small society: Adrian Bourke, who held the office of President of the Incorporated Law Society for the year ending in October 1992, is the brother of the President of Ireland, Mary Robinson née Bourke.
6. P. Bartholemew, *The Irish Judiciary*, Dublin and Notre Dame, 1971, quoted by Basil Chubb, *The Government and Politics of Ireland*, 2nd edn, Longman, 1982.

7. Cairnduff, op. cit.

8. *Sunday Tribune*, 5 April 1992.

9. Constitution of Ireland, Article 35.4.

10. *Irish Times*, 13 April 1992.

11. ibid., 6 April 1992.

12. Chubb, op. cit.

13. Institute of Public Administration, *Administration Yearbook and Diary*, 1992.

14. *Irish Times*, 16 May 1991.

15. ibid., 27 March 1992.

16. Desmond O'Malley TD, Minister for Industry and Commerce, *Irish Times*, 10 April 1992.

17. The late Mr Justice Niall McCarthy, *Sunday Tribune*, 3 May 1992.

18. Fair Trade Commission, *Study into Restrictive Practices in the Legal Profession*, July 1990.

19. *Irish Times*, 10 April 1992.

20. ibid., 27 March 1992.

21. *Sunday Independent*, 22 March 1992.

22. Desmond O'Malley TD, Minister for Industry and Commerce, reported in the *Irish Times*, 19 November 1990.

*

GUARDIANS OF THE PEACE – THE IRISH POLICE (GARDA SÍOCHÁNA)

In 1922, 'the young Irish leaders kept their heads and formed a protecting arm to shield her [Ireland] from rapine and ruin' – one of the early heads of the Irish police force described thus the setting up of the force after the foundation of the modern Irish State. It was indeed one of the many achievements of the early politicians of that new State after 1922 to establish and gain acceptance for an unarmed police force, despite a recent and murderous civil war. Today, that force is a national, unified one: all uniformed sections of the force are unarmed, and only detectives, in plain clothes, carry arms. The decision not to arm the police force proved to be a wise one. In the twenty years from 1970 to 1990, just twelve police officers were murdered, leading the Gardaí themselves to conclude, in their own publication of 1990, that 'violent crime has not been a major feature of Irish life'.[1]* It is worth noting that most of those murders were connected in some way with the IRA and associated paramilitary groups, often referred to by the Gardaí as 'subversives'.

According to historians, it was virtually unprecedented in a post-civil-war situation for the police to be disarmed as part of the search for a stable society. Those first leaders, however, felt that there had to be a clear separation between the civil police and the military in order to restore peace. So, in February 1922, the first meeting of the new government to set up the police was held, decisions were taken quickly, and by the end of that month the force was established, and their members were called Civic Guards. They had a most difficult first decade – 'they were shot at, ambushed on patrol, and stripped of their uniforms. Their barracks were attacked, and ten policemen were killed in the first ten years.'[2] Part of the difficulty was the need to come to terms with the existence of the previous police force. This had operated under British rule, but its officers were, none the less, Irishmen. The force was called the Royal Irish Constabulary (RIC) – and it was their translation into the new Civic Guards which caused a mutiny in Kildare shortly after the foundation of the Gardaí. However, over the decades, as the Irish institutions of democracy gradually

---

* For notes on this section ('Guardians of the Peace . . .'), see page 142.

strengthened and settled down, the Garda Síochána developed into a solid, well-respected, modern police force.

The strength of the force today usually stands at or a little above 10,500, made up of over 8,500 uniformed personnel and 1,700 detectives. The Garda Síochána – usually shortened to 'the Guards' – employ about 500 civilians, mostly doing clerical work.

The headquarters of the Garda Síochána is in a handsome old stone building in Phoenix Park, one of the largest municipal parks in Europe, just on the western side of the city of Dublin. This is where the head of the force, known as the Garda Commissioner,* has his office. Further into the city, the Dublin headquarters is housed in a large modern red-brick complex at Harcourt Street, near St Stephen's Green and the Department of Justice. The Commissioner, though technically appointable from outside the force, is normally someone who has risen right through the ranks of the Guards before his appointment by the government. His boss is the Minister for Justice, who is in turn accountable to the Dáil for the activities of the Gardaí.

The police force of Ireland is generally highly regarded by the population, behaving with responsibility and observing suitably rigid high standards. Good relations exist between the Gardaí and the population in most areas. In a special 1992 newspaper supplement to mark the seventieth anniversary of the foundation of the Guards, a public-opinion poll was proudly quoted showing that 85 per cent of the population had a high opinion of the Gardaí; this is part of a pattern of polls whenever the public is asked that question.[3] A European Values Poll, in September 1991, gave the same figure, comparing it to a European average of 63 per cent.[4]

There are, as in most countries, pockets of distrust, and there are also accusations of unnecessary violence being used. In a force numbering nearly eleven thousand, it would be surprising if there were not some problems of this kind. There is both an independent Complaints Board and a Complaints Appeal Board, created by

---

*The Garda Commissioner, appointed in January 1991, is Patrick Joseph Culligan (b. 1936). A much younger man than the normal holder of the office, with very broad and successful experience, the Commissioner also holds an MSc in organizational behaviour from Trinity College, Dublin.

legislation initiated in 1984, but only reaching finality in 1987, to deal with complaints from the public about improper conduct of police officers. The Boards include barristers, solicitors, and lay people as well as senior Gardaí.

The complaints initiatives were not popular inside the force: when the legislation was first published in 1984, there was resistance in the Garda Síochána to the establishment of an independent tribunal. Public opinion was, however, uneasy, following widespread earlier accounts of the existence of a group of Gardaí, known as 'the heavy gang', who were allegedly prepared to use unacceptable methods of questioning suspects. Garda objections were overruled. The Boards have been continually hampered by lack of staff, but the new system is considered on the whole to have worked well and to have contributed towards the much higher reputation enjoyed by the Gardaí today. 'There was undoubtedly an element in the Gardaí who were allowed go their own way and developed undesirable and undisciplined habits in dealing with suspected offenders ... that is much more under control today.'*

The Garda Commissioner is assisted by two deputy commissioners, six assistant commissioners, and so on down through chief superintendents (thirty-eight), superintendents, inspectors, sergeants, and Gardaí. The first policewoman was taken into the force in 1959; only in 1990 was it decided to stop calling women officers 'Banghardaí' (women police officer) and to use the ordinary title of Garda. Women make up about 400 members of the Gardaí.

The country is divided into twenty-three divisions, for policing purposes, five of them in Dublin united under the heading Dublin Metropolitan Area. The smallest administrative unit is called a substation; usually run by a single officer, it is attached to a parent station. There are continual calls for more policing in every area, particularly towards local election time, as election candidates seek to persuade the Minister for Justice to put a full-time presence in every town and village.

As crime of all kinds increases in complexity,* accompanied in

* The words are those of a criminal lawyer who did not want to be named, in conversation with the author.

Ireland by the crimes of violence associated with the Provisional IRA and its splinter groups, the State has tried to equip its police with both the skilled personnel and the equipment considered normal in modern western democracies – not easy in a country with huge borrowings and massive unemployment.† However, the specialist services include the latest technology and training: in serious crime detection; the drug scene; fraud; and security for local and visiting VIPs. The image of the slow-witted, bulky neighbourhood policeman on his sturdy upright bicycle and with thick rural accent is rapidly fading.

Ireland has its own share of drug-related problems and criminal activities, which has led to the establishment of the special Drug Squad within the Garda Síochána. It is based at Garda Headquarters, and has an international as well as domestic area of operations. Up to 1992, more than 400 Gardaí have had special training in drugs detection. The Drug Squad is one of several special units; another is the Fraud Squad. This has had a difficult development period: shortcomings of personnel and legislative back-up were dramatically exposed as a result of a bank collapse in 1982 that left 600 depositors carrying a loss of IR£1·3 million.‡ After investigations that lasted six years the Director of Public Prosecutions eventually announced that he was not taking action. The official court-appointed liquidator to the failed bank, chartered accountant Paddy Shortall, publicly deplored the situation and commented on the inadequacies of the Fraud Squad, brought about by personnel shortages and lack of specialized skills. The failure to pursue a prosecution was unfavourably contrasted with the situation in Northern Ireland, where the same company was successfully prosecuted. The deficiencies in the Fraud Squad were further

---

*In 1990, there were 87,658 indictable offences recorded (an increase of 1 per cent on 1989); 28,985 were detected, or 33·1 per cent. Fifty-six per cent of total crimes occurred in the Dublin Metropolitan Area (where 29·5 per cent of the population live). There is a very high detection rate in murders; of seventeen murder cases in 1990, only two remained unsolved. The lowest rates of detection are in the categories of armed and unarmed robbery.

†The 1992 estimated expenditure on the Garda Síochána was IR£339,570,000. This was an increase of 4 per cent over 1991, very slightly more than the rate of inflation.

‡Merchant Banking, controlled by Patrick Gallagher.

exposed in the hearings of the Beef Tribunal (see Chapter 12) in early 1992, when 'a picture emerged ... of a Garda Fraud Squad which was at the time [the mid-1980s] woefully understaffed'.[5] This exposure led to a considerable improvement: personnel have been upgraded, numbers increased, and a budget provided for access to specialized financial professionals outside the force. It also led to new legislative back-up to deal with the kind of evidence admissible in court.

The Garda Síochána are deeply involved with the national effort to deal with the subversive elements in the country, the IRA and their offshoots. Duty on the border between North and South is an essential part of this, and there is full and friendly cooperation with the Northern Ireland police force, the RUC (Royal Ulster Constabulary), on the other side of the border. The Garda Commissioner attends meetings of the Anglo-Irish conference, along with the Chief Constable of the RUC, under the terms of the Anglo-Irish Agreement of 1985. It is fair to say that the Gardaí are particularly anxious to act against the paramilitaries, who have shown themselves in the past to be ready to use arms against the police.

Recruitment to the force is of young people between the ages of eighteen and twenty-six who reach a certain minimum height and level of medical fitness, and whose educational attainment is at least that of the Irish school-leaving certificate. Unlike the Irish Army, there is only one tier and one kind of recruitment, which, because it is not considered suitable for a modern police force struggling to fight crime in an ever more sophisticated world, has been frequently commented upon – no specialist intake, no graduate intake, and no sign of it. The Garda training college in Templemore, Co. Tipperary, where the training courses were revamped and considerably modernized following a review in the early 1980s, is run by a chief superintendent. The courses involve a mixture of in-house theory and training, with periods of practical work in Garda stations, and last a total of three years.* The college is also

---

* The Minister for Justice said in October 1991 that he was asking the Garda Commissioner to examine the idea of giving university-degree status to Garda training, treating the sixty-two-week basic training as a foundation year for further academic training in criminology and law-enforcement studies.[6]

used for in-service training activities for all ranks. One of the first statements of the new Commissioner in January 1991 was that comprehensive management courses would start in Templemore for Garda Superintendents and Chief Superintendents.

Ireland has also joined the international trend of community interaction with the police force: systems of 'neighbourhood watch' and 'community alert' (for urban and rural areas respectively) have been flourishing since the mid-1980s, in an attempt to control housebreaking and other domestic-related crime. At the end of 1990, there were 995 Neighbourhood Watch schemes, involving nearly 200,000 households. There were 221 Community Alert Schemes.[7] One of the most admired activities of the Gardaí is the work of making contact with and gaining the confidence of disadvantaged young people – the 'Juvenile Liaison Scheme', under which designated police officers, men and women, take charge of young first offenders, and involve themselves in youth clubs, meetings of schools and parents, and all sorts of sporting and social initiatives. In the difficult sprawling housing estates of certain parts of Dublin, where unemployment reaches 70 per cent and more, their work is essential and sometimes nearly impossible.* In 1992, there were about forty men and women involved in this scheme, and it is growing and expanding to more areas. Despite the lack of specialized intake, the police have understood and interacted with social agencies well: the director of Dublin's Rape Crisis Centre reports an increasingly close and satisfactory relationship with the Garda Síochána. 'Of course, the women police officers are the most suitable, but the men have made great strides. In my nine years as Director, working with the Gardaí in hundreds and hundreds of cases, I have had to make a complaint only twice to the Commissioner about individuals . . .'[9]

---

*In November 1991, considerable trouble erupted in the west Dublin suburb of Ronanstown, a public-housing area not dissimilar from others spreading around the city. Youngsters rioted and attacked firemen, residents were intimidated, and violence spread rapidly. With an unemployment rate of nearly 70 per cent, local clergy, social workers, and politicians deplore the lack of schools, Garda presence, training schemes, but most of all jobs. An advisory group of civil servants from six government departments was established to examine and report on this and other similar areas. The *Irish Times* advised the group to look at the kind of schemes undertaken for Liverpool in the aftermath of the Toxteth riots in 1981.[8]

Irish police are prohibited by law from taking strike action, but all ranks are represented by associations when it comes to making claims for better pay and conditions. The biggest of these is the Garda Representative Association, with a membership of some 9,000. The Association of Garda Sergeants and Inspectors, with 2,000 members, comes next, and the Superintendents and Chief Superintendents are each represented by their own associations. The basic pay – excluding allowances, perks and overtime – of the Garda Síochána ranges downwards from the Commissioner's IR£55,092 (the same as the Army Chief of Staff) to the new recruit's IR£10,101 on leaving Templemore.* The pay and conditions are obviously attractive to Ireland's young people, who apply in their many thousands every time there is new recruitment to enter the Garda Síochána; the competition in Ireland's high-unemployment climate has become so intense that applicants today are of an increasingly high calibre, and many already have other jobs or hold university degrees. In 1991, 13,000 young people applied for 1,000 places.

There is in Ireland continuous debate about the extent of political interference in the recruitment and promotion of the Garda Síochána, as well as in the operations of the force. Families approach politicians on a regular basis to look for admission to the Gardaí for their son or daughter; serving officers approach, directly or indirectly, politicians looking for promotion. Government strenuously denies any favouritism; but who is to check a quiet call on a senior officer who is known to be politically sympathetic to the government? It is not too long since Irish television audiences, in an RTE mass-audience late-night show devoted to the career of a government minister who had recovered from a liver transplant, were invited to be amused at the account of a Garda being threatened with transfer to a remote area because of his wish to take names of politicians caught 'drinking after hours'.[10] In December 1982, the national broadcasting station's main current-affairs programme presented a lengthy report on allegations that a Minister for Justice, Mr Seán Doherty, had used his position 'to interfere directly in Garda matters in his Roscommon constituency . . . the programme included the attempt to transfer Sergeant Tom

* At 1 January 1992.

Tully to Ballyconnell after the raid on Keaney's pub . . .'[11] This is the kind of incident which has left the legacy of a suspicious public and an aggrieved body of Gardaí.

Since 1987, as a result of new regulations, the government's role in senior promotions has been limited to assenting to the appointment of all ranks from superintendent upwards, after an interview process involving not only senior Garda officers but including a civil servant. The government directly appoints the Commissioner.

Perhaps the most dramatic example of suspected political involvement with the police was in 1982, when two journalists' telephones were irregularly tapped, and when a very senior Garda supplied a tape recorder to a minister for the purpose of secretly recording a conversation with another minister.*

Another bizarre incident involved the detention by the Royal Ulster Constabulary in Northern Ireland of a man who was thereby prevented from giving evidence against a Garda, the brother-in-law of the Irish Minister for Justice, on a charge of assault.† These incidents took place over the period of office of a short-lived government in 1982, under the leadership of Charles Haughey of Fianna Fáil. A new word entered the Irish political vocabulary: 'GUBU', derived from the words grotesque, unprecedented, bizarre and unbelievable. These were epithets used by Mr Haughey when, as a sort of culmination of strange events in that year, a wanted murderer was found hiding in the apartment of the Attorney-General. (The acronym was coined by writer Dr Conor Cruise O'Brien.)

Ten years later, at the 1992 annual conference of the Association of Garda Sergeants and Inspectors, the president of the body seemed to imply that, despite the 1987 changes in promotions

* Commissioner Patrick McLaughlin and Deputy Commissioner Joseph Ainsworth resigned from the Gardaí on 29 January 1983, following the discovery of the tapping of two journalists' telephones during the term of office of the previous government under Charles Haughey, and the revelation that the Garda Deputy Commissioner had also been involved in the secret recording by one government minister of a conversation with another.

† In September 1982, Garda Tom Nangle, brother-in-law of Minister for Justice Seán Doherty, was due to appear in Dowra in Co. Cavan on a charge of assaulting a man in Blacklion, Co. Cavan, the previous December. The complainant, Jimmy McGovern, never appeared. He had been detained by the Royal Ulster Constabulary, questioned, but charged with nothing.[12]

procedures, there was still political interference and spoke about 'the re-emergence of the GUBU period'.[13] This was strongly denied by both the Minister for Justice and the Garda Commissioner. 'Political influence plays no part whatsoever in the Garda selection process, and the decisions made by the interview board are final . . .'[14]

The Irish police establishment are a faithful reflection of the country they serve: the great bulk are solid, conservative people, with personal high standards of integrity. They are moving into the modern era of sophisticated crime fighting, and are having to deal with the unhappy results for Irish society of modern urban living and massive unemployment black spots, as well as with terrorism, drug pushers, and financial fraud. The Commissioner no doubt echoed the thoughts of police chiefs in every western democracy when he said: '. . . the duty of maintaining law and order should be seen as placed fairly and squarely on the community – aided by the Gardaí – rather than on the Gardaí, occasionally aided by a small number of public spirited citizens.'[15]

Ireland has one police person per 323 of the population. This compares favourably with most of western Europe, according to the Minister for Justice, speaking in the Dáil on 26 June 1992. His office gave the following figures: Germany has 300 people per law officer, Denmark 350, and Sweden 500.

Women, having been admitted to the police force in 1959, have made very slow progress indeed in becoming a sizeable part of the force. In 1992, according to figures from the Taoiseach's office, there were 501 women, amounting to 4.8 per cent of the total. The highest rank held at that point was superintendent. It was only in September 1992 that women police officers were finally allowed to wear trousers: and then, the regulations stipulated that it would only be from October to May, 'or at the discretion of the divisional officer'. There seems to be some kind of misunderstanding of the principal reason for women to wear trousers – the active pursuit of criminals. Questions about the restrictions on the wearing of trousers to the Garda press office from the author met with a continual reiteration of such phrases as 'there are always regulations about the wearing of uniforms, it is never at the discretion of the Gardaí themselves . . .' Nevertheless, any trousers at all for women must rank as a breakthrough.

In May 1992, the Deputy Commissioner of the Garda Síochána told a meeting of a European Forum for Victim Services that European statistics show that Ireland still has a low crime rate compared with her EC neighbours, including the lowest homicide rate in the EC. She also has fewer assaults per head of the population. Serious violent crime has been falling steadily over the 1981–91 decade: from 2,478 in 1981, to 1,435 in 1991, a drop of 42 per cent. Within those figures, however, there are some disturbing trends: reported violence against women had more than trebled in the period (110 rapes in 1991, and 245 indecent assaults). Common assaults of a minor nature amounted to 5,950 in 1991 – up from 4,291 in 1976. Assaults on police officers, and arrests for 'aggravated drunkenness', showed similar increases. Ireland, therefore, while not a scene of violent gangs and casual murder, has the same trend of urbanized crime, mostly committed by young men from difficult backgrounds, as in other western democracies. Its police force faces the same kind of challenge. Its prisons hold an average of 2,100 people daily, in conditions which have been gradually improving but are continually criticized for over-crowding.

In general, therefore, Ireland relies on a steady and sure police force which has lived up to the hopes placed in it at its foundation. If there is serious current criticism, it is directed more at the politicians and top managers than at the Gardaí themselves. A psychology lecturer at Dublin's Trinity College deplores the lack of ongoing ordered research in Ireland into crime, criminal justice, the lack of any department of criminology in the Irish university system, and the fact that, by February 1993, the last annual report on prisons was that for 1988. In his broadside at the Department of Justice, he concludes: 'This scandalous failure to publish a statutorily required report, which has been largely ignored by the media, is symptomatic of a political and bureaucratic disdain for the public. It also suggests a preference for secrecy and for avoiding being hamstrung by facts and well-argued analysis.'[16]

A five-year plan for development of the Garda Síochána was published by the Garda Commissioner in April 1993, and welcomed by the new Minister for Justice, Máire Geoghegan-Quinn. It covered the whole range of issues affecting a modern police force, from the need to develop a 'service ethic' among members, to increased recruitment, new management structures, greater recruitment and use of women members, and a general strategy to make the Irish police force 'the best police service in Europe'.

NOTES ('GUARDIANS OF THE PEACE . . .')

1. Community Relations Section, Garda Síochána, *An Garda Síochána – Ireland's Police Force*, 1990.
2. *Irish Times*, 18 August 1992.
3. ibid.
4. Gallup Poll conducted for the European Values Group, reported in the *Irish Independent*, 24 September 1991.
5. *Irish Independent*, 23 January 1992.
6. *Garda News*, vol. 10, November 1991.
7. Commissioner, Garda Síochána, *Report on Crime 1990, to the Minister for Justice.*
8. *Irish Times*, 27 November 1991 (editorial).
9. Ms Olive Braiden, in conversation with the author, April 1992.
10. *The Late Late Show*, in spring 1990, devoted a whole programme to the career of Mr Brian Lenihan, a formerly very popular minister. Mr Lenihan subsequently was his party's candidate for the 1990 presidential election, and was narrowly defeated by Mary Robinson.
11. For a description of these events and what happened to the Fianna Fáil government in March–December 1982, see Joe Joyce and Peter Murtagh, *The Boss: Charles J. Haughey in Government*, Poolbeg Press, 1983.
12. A full account of the incident and others involving the Gardaí in 1982 can be found in Joyce and Murtagh, op. cit.
13. *Irish Independent*, 14 April 1992.
14. *Irish Independent*, 15 April 1992.
15. *Irish Times*, 1 February 1992.
16. Dr Paul O'Mahoney, *Irish Times*, 4 February 1993.

*

THE DEFENCE FORCES

On 11 November 1960, eleven Irish soldiers were ambushed by spear-carrying Baluba tribesmen in the jungle of Niemba, in the former Belgian colony of the Congo. The Irish unit was among the early battalions of Irish soldiers serving on United Nations peace-keeping missions. Eight of the group were killed, one died later, and two survived. When the patrol was suddenly surrounded, the commanding officer, Lieutenant Gleeson, in the best traditions of the United Nations, called out a peaceful greeting, 'Jambo', and help up his left hand in a peaceful gesture. The historian of the Irish Army describes what happened next: 'He got an arrow right through it. Encircled and menaced, the patrol had no option but to open fire.'[1]* But they had no hope.

The shock and mourning which followed when the bodies of the killed were brought back to Ireland could be said to mark the newest phase in the life of the Irish Army, a phase given pride and legitimacy by its status as part of the United Nations worldwide army. Since those first Congo days, the Army has served with distinction in troubled areas all over the world. United Nations peace-keeping duty has become a central element in its activities – no officer could seriously expect to be promoted today unless he had a record of UN service.

The strength of the Army in August 1992 stood at 13,005 (all ranks),† including some 1,500 officers. That is a far cry from the hordes of exhausted, strife-ridden irregular forces which had come through a rebellion against Britain in 1916, a type of guerrilla war-fare between Britain and Ireland in 1916–21, and then a civil war. They were indeed a motley and disorganized Army, and had never known what it was like to be a peacetime Army, subject to a demo-cratically elected government and accepting the principle of the primacy of politics. Ireland's first independent government set about the difficult job of putting their military house in order, not an easy undertaking in a post-civil-war atmosphere. One of the early moves was to enact the Defence Forces (Temporary Provisions) Act 1923, which put the Army on a statutory footing under the law.

*For notes on this section ('The Defence Forces'), see page 151.
†Figure supplied by the Department of the Taoiseach.

In its early years, given the turbulent state of the country, the role of the Irish Army was clear: it had to deal with perceived threats from within rather than outside its borders. Civil security was the primary concern, and set the tone of 'assistance to the civil power'.[2] There was even an early threat to the State by a mutinous group of military men in 1924, in an Army which had been swollen in size to 55,000 men and 3,300 officers. It seemed as if this mass of men might cause a threat to the new State, because of their grievances over large-scale demobilization and reorganization, and also because they differed politically from their civil rulers. However, the mutiny was dealt with by careful negotiation not confrontation, and died away. But over the years, as the country settled down to peace, and because the early Irish Army wanted to keep a low profile in order to minimize any possible comparisons with the British garrisons, a number of which they had taken over, its role became blurred and uncertain for the Irish people. Numbers and expenditure were severely reduced, morale plummeted, leading to a situation in 1939, on the outbreak of the second world war (a period sometimes referred to as 'the Emergency' in Ireland, because of the declaration of a state of national emergency in 1939), in which the country had a weak, poorly equipped Army, and virtually no Air Force or Navy. Confusion and public apathy about the necessity for any Army at all, and consequent governmental neglect and penny-pinching, had left Ireland vulnerable to attack. 'In the event of invasion, the Irish forces would have paid the price for a policy of long-term neglect of national security.'[3] It was just as well that the country had decided to be neutral in the circumstances, but the Irish neutrality policy could not be compared with that of the Swiss or the Swedes: '. . . they both pursued a policy of armed neutrality, Ireland pursued, at most, a policy of half-armed neutrality.'[4]

Declaring neutrality was one thing; preserving it was another, and the government continued to neglect the Army during the war, relying on de Valera's ingenuity and international statesmanlike skills to make sure that no country, least of all Britain, felt it was worth launching an invasion of Ireland. The British had acquired a certain respect for the capabilities of the fighting Irish after the years of guerrilla fighting in the early decades of the century. Despite this, they nevertheless must have felt that the Germans would find virtually defenceless Ireland no trouble at all. Those

Germans after all 'had ways of dealing with recalcitrant populations that made the Black and Tans* seem a boy scout brigade'.[5] The end of the war came without an invasion of Ireland, and with an Army which had done its best to present a determined and well-organized front, under the command of General Dan McKenna. They had made up for their poor numbers and equipment by excellent discipline and the nuts and bolts of hard-graft soldiering.

After the war, and all the excitement which had given the Army at least a *raison d'être*, the years between the mid-1940s and the beginning of active service with the United Nations in the 1960s were quiet and dispiriting. 'The exciting times of the Emergency were forgotten, and slipping back into the old pre-war rut seemed inevitable.'[6] Demobilization and poor pay compared with other sectors were not good for morale, and successive governments paid little heed to the pleas and warnings of Army chiefs. And then the United Nations requested Ireland's help with peace-keeping initiatives, while the IRA intensified attacks around the border between the north and the south of the country. Gradually the Army, Naval and Air Corps began to come into the twentieth century. The UN Congo mission gave the Army a new image, better morale, new uniforms and equipment, and a pride in their new sense of purpose. The ferocity of the IRA and its potential threat to internal security gave governments the jolt they needed to examine their conscience about the treatment of the Army over too many years.

The Irish Army of the 1990s is a sharper, better-equipped, better-dressed, better-trained fighting force than ever before in its history. Its ordinary soldiers are more carefully recruited (gone are the days when judges might recommend a trouble-maker to join the Army and 'be made a man of') and they have at last the beginnings of caring social services for dealing with problems among the soldiers and their families.

But because of financial constraints, recruitment came to a virtual full stop in 1990. By August 1992, there was a backlog of 11,500 applicants waiting to get into the Army. The average age of a

---

* The 'Black and Tans' were an auxiliary force sent to Ireland by the British during the War of Independence between 1920 and 1921, made up of undisciplined, often drunken members who terrorized the population. They were so called because of the colour of their uniforms.

soldier was twenty-eight years – compared to the eighteen- and twenty-year-olds who fought for Britain and the United States in the Gulf War. Ireland's massive unemployment problem mean that few men leave the Army, making little room for new recruits.

Army officers are impressive, trained at the Military College and university, the Army's equipment is modern (though according to one international defence specialist, the new purchases amount to 'little more than a few examples of the best equipment')[7] and its domestic and international standing is high. As well as acting in support of the civil power to assist during floods or other natural disasters, accompanying large cash movements, assisting with the air ambulance service, and supplying essential personnel in certain kinds of strikes, it also plays a most important role in border duty, supporting the Garda Síochána in the perennial struggle with the IRA. Permanent military guards stand on duty at Portlaoise and Limerick prisons, and because of the terrorist threat, they provide guards at special courts and at the British Ambassador's residence. Also, of course, they supply officers for aide-de-camp duty, as well as staffing, for the President of Ireland, who is their commander-in-chief. Immediately after her inauguration in 1990, President Robinson appointed the first woman from the ranks of military officers to serve as her junior aide-de-camp.*

International service has become a feature of life in the Irish Army. In October 1992, a total of 846 Irish soldiers were serving in thirteen countries. Many thousands over the years have therefore seen service abroad. Thirteen have been killed in that kind of active service. Lebanon has consistently taken up most of these troops, but as the world erupts in more and more trouble spots, Ireland responds to more UN calls for personnel. The European Commission has entered this arena too, calling for Irish help in places like the desperately troubled former Yugoslavia. This has meant a great revitalization of morale in the Irish Army, as it is seen that Irish soldiers are sufficiently highly regarded to be in demand for trouble spots as far away as El Salvador, Iraq–Kuwait, Cambodia, and Afghanistan.

There are still areas of discontent in the force – of which

* Captain Colette Harrison.

stagnation of promotion prospects for young officers is one.* Pay was becoming an extremely serious bone of contention until 1989, when the government was forced by the public agitation of a new and unexpectedly effective fighting force – the National Army Spouses' Association – to set up an independent commission under the chairmanship of Dermot Gleeson SC.† That commission was wide-ranging in its recommendations for modernization, some of which got an official frosty reception at first, but were eventually carried out. Others have not yet succeeded. Army pay was increased by between 16 and 30 per cent, but most important, the soldiers were allowed, like the Gardaí, to set up their own representative bodies to fight for better pay and conditions. The Permanent Defence Forces Other Ranks' Representative Association (PDFORRA) and the Representative Association for Commissioned Officers (RACO) have swung into action on behalf of their members: one suspects that senior Army personnel are having some difficulties in coming to terms with this new democracy.‡ Small eruptions occur, like a difficulty about members of PDFORRA having to wear their uniforms when meeting the Chief of Staff in his office, leading the Irish Conference of Professional and Services Associations to accuse the Army management of 'living in the past and behaving like Colonel Blimps'.[8]

Basic pay now ranges from the Chief of Staff's IR£55,000 (the same as the Garda Commissioner) down to the (roughly) IR£150 per week for the new recruit coming in as a private, rising to about IR£200 per week after training. A second lieutenant starts at IR£12,579 a year, while a commandant earns a maximum of IR£25,000 after training. The generals in charge of the four geographical commands in the country each earn IR£40,000 a year.§ Apart from pay, there is some concern among armed forces about the

---

* As a result of the sudden quadrupling of Army cadet recruitment as a response to the UN and border requirements of the early 1970s, there has been a build-up of 400 officers (240 at captain rank), who cannot be promoted to the very few vacancies at the next rank of commandant.

† Senior Counsel.

‡ PDFORRA has 12,000 NCOs and privates in its membership, while RACO takes in about 1,200 people between the ranks of second lieutenant and colonel.

§ At 1992 rates.

compensation for personnel killed or injured on service abroad, which is not as generous as that available to the police.

Among the other Gleeson recommendations were that management consultants should be brought in to examine the way the Army was run (Gleeson discovered that, at any one time, only 15 per cent of personnel on duty were engaged in operational duties) and that the Army should manage its own budget (instead of civil servants doing it). Gleeson wanted an end to stop–go recruitment policies, more input on decision-making by NCOs, and easier progression to officer rank for enlisted men. All these recommendations are being considered, and progress is being made on the way senior officers are appointed, with the establishment of interview boards and a move towards promotions based on merit instead of seniority.

In April 1992, a new Chief of Staff of the Defence Forces was appointed. Major-General Noel Bergin, aged sixty, was an obvious choice for his solid achievements and wide experience in all the right areas: the United Nations, border duty, and with additional training in the USA and the UK on top of his university degree. His term of office will conclude in late 1994. It is generally considered that, following the Gleeson report, Major-General Bergin will be the last Chief of Staff to be appointed so late in his career.

Why does a small, neutral country need an Army? Why does the taxpayer have to finance it to the tune of IR£326 million (the figure in the 1992 government estimates)? After many years of confusion about that question, the IRA and the United Nations have supplied the answer. Government is making a response to the self-evident need for an Army, albeit one which does not please the military top brass (one can only infer that they are far too circumspect in every way to articulate any discontent). The excellence of Army training, with the allied benefit of interesting international and domestic experience, together with the increasing awareness among the public of the potential threat of the IRA and corresponding Loyalist paramilitary forces, has resulted in an Army in which most Irish people now take pride. They were proud to watch an Irish officer working as chief EC negotiator in Sarajevo,* and found it an extra

* Commandant Colm Doyle (b. 1947). Served in Lebanon and Cyprus with the Irish Army/UN. Asked by Lord Carrington to undertake the work of chief negotiator for the EC in Bosnia-Herzegovina, he was the first non-diplomat to hold such a position.

bonus that he should be working in particularly close cooperation with a representative of 'the old enemy' – Britain's Lord Carrington. It is a source of some puzzlement to Irish people that its Army should be so much in demand for peace-keeping abroad when the country seems unable to achieve peace on its own small island. Commandant Doyle apparently did not see any irony in the situation when he told the *Irish Times*: 'The popularity of the Irish with their hosts in peace-keeping missions around the world is also partly to do with our neutrality and because the Irishman is a natural peace-keeper.'[9]

The Air Corps of the Defence Forces flew well over 25,000 missions in 1991: the number of aircraft rose to forty-four that year. In 1970, it flew 8,600 missions. The increase in activities, involving many helicopters, has two main sources: the Northern Ireland security problems, and the considerable intensification of EC business for the ministerial air services. The Air Corps dates back to the days of the negotiation of the original treaty setting up the Irish Free State in 1921, when an aircraft was based in London in case the formidable Michael Collins, Army Chief of Staff, needed urgent passage to Dublin. The role of the Air Corps is varied: it works in support of the Army, the Naval Service, and the civil power. It carries organ transplants for the Department of Health, and helps to survey forest and wildlife; it operates helicopter ambulance services; it helps to protect Ireland's fishing rights; and it participates in search and rescue operations. The complement of pilots in 1991, according to Brigadier-General Cranfield,* GOC of the Air Corps, was eighty-nine. The Air Corps flying school turns out its own pilots, at the rate of about five a year. The total personnel of the Air Corps in 1991 was under 1,000: 800 of these work at the main base, Baldonnell Airport near Dublin. Smaller bases are found at Gormanston, Co. Meath, Shannon, Co. Clare, Finner Camp in Donegal, and Monaghan, the last two conveniently near the border with Northern Ireland.

The Naval Service, also under the control of the Army, has to patrol 136,000 square miles (nearly 25 per cent of the European

---

*Brigadier-General Patrick Cranfield (b. 1940), with training in Ireland and with the Royal Air Force, appointed as GOC in 1989.

Community's waters) in the interests of the fishing industry. It does so with a small fleet of seven ships, manned by some 900 officers and ratings 'of fine quality, as anyone here or abroad with any knowledge of the sea who has had contact with them will testify'.[10] The *Le Eithne* is the star of the fleet, equipped with a serious-looking Bofors gun and an up-to-date operations room, and carries an SA 365 Dauphin helicopter. This fleet of ships was quickly acquired and manned after Ireland's entry to the EC, and the establishment of a 200-mile economic zone off its coasts made Irish governments aware of the poor state of the Naval Service. 'We need a minimum of twelve ships . . . we need at least 400 more men . . . need to allow the flag officer commanding the service to put its requirements directly to government without filtration through the Army hierarchy which inevitably regards naval needs through land-oriented eyes' – thus spake Ireland's most prominent old salt of the sea in 1991.[11]

The flag officer of the Naval Service is Joseph Deasy, born in 1932, noted as the first trained diver in the service, and the last seagoing officer to span the old and the new, having commanded corvettes, minesweepers, and patrol vessels.

Unlike countries whose armies might be key players in world conflicts, Irish Ministers for Defence are not usually considered heavyweights in Irish governments. The appointment is regarded both within and without the Cabinet as something of a sinecure for a senior politician nearing retirement, but who will have a 'safe pair of hands'. In the Reynolds government of Ireland, appointed in February 1992, the department was combined with that of the Gaeltacht (responsibility for the Irish-speaking districts) and given to a senior Fianna Fáil party figure, Mr John Wilson, who also held the position of Tánaiste (deputy government leader). The only severe political test for any Minister for Defence in recent years was when the agitation for better pay and conditions broke out in 1989, and rapidly escalated under the leadership of the extremely determined spouses of Army personnel, working on behalf of their husbands who could not by law agitate for themselves. The issue was well handled by the minister of the day, Brian Lenihan, despite his frail state of health at the time. His long experience in politics and many ministries showed, and his efforts resulted in the Gleeson report with its seminal recommendations for reform and modernization of the Defence Forces' structures and conditions.

In 1993, the minister appointed to the Defence brief was David Andrews.* A Defence portfolio was held for the first time in many years by someone considered to be a political heavyweight: he described himself as the 'Minister for Fish and Ships' since he was also given the portfolio of the Department of the Marine.

In October 1992, only 115 women served in the permanent defence forces, with another 192 in the part-time auxiliary force. The highest rank was commandant. In early 1992, a decision was announced to open all areas of the Defence Forces to women, instead of confining them to 'suitable' non-combatant roles. The minister undertook that the basis of selection in all areas like operational and ceremonial duties, assignment to military courses, and promotion would be suitability rather than sex. This is another move towards modernizing the Defence Forces of which their Commander-in-Chief, Ireland's first woman President, no doubt thoroughly approves. She would no doubt thoroughly approve too of the new minister's decision not to exempt Army personnel from the lifting of the ban on homosexual acts in legislation which went through the Dáil and Senate in summer 1993, an eloquent testimony to the profound changes under way in Ireland today.

*David Andrews (b. 1935), barrister by profession. Long-time opponent of former Taoiseach Charles Haughey, which kept him out of government until appointed to the Cabinet by Albert Reynolds. When the Fianna Fáil–Labour coalition took the place of the FF–PD government, he lost his Foreign Affairs portfolio, in which he had been considered excellent, to the leader of the Labour Party, Dick Spring.

NOTES ('THE DEFENCE FORCES')

1. John P. Duggan, *A History of the Irish Army*, Gill & Macmillan.
2. Professor John Jackson, *Irish Times*, 23 July 1991.
3. ibid.
4. ibid.
5. Joseph Lee.
6. ibid.
7. Adrian J. English (Irish correspondent for *Jane's Defence Weekly*), *Irish Times*, 23 July 1991.

8. *Irish Times*, 27 November 1992.
9. *Irish Times*, 9 May 1992.
10. John de Courcy Ireland, *Irish Times*, 23 July 1991.
11. ibid.

A child wonders where his father is: a scene typical of the
Northern Ireland tragedy

Ian Paisley MP, leader of the Democratic Unionist Party (*left*), and
John Hume MP, leader of the Social Democratic and Labour Party

The leaders of the coalition government of Ireland which took office in January 1993. (*Left*) Taoiseach and leader of Fianna Fáil, Albert Reynolds TD, and Tánaiste and leader of the Labour Party, Dick Spring TD

Mrs Justice Susan Denham, first woman member of the Irish
Supreme Court, appointed in 1992

Four former Taoisigh of Ireland: (*left to right*) Jack Lynch, Garret FitzGerald,
Liam Cosgrave and Charles J. Haughey

John Bruton TD, leader of
the Fine Gael Party

Proinnsias de Rossa TD,
leader of the Democratic
Left Party

Desmond O'Malley TD,
leader of the Progressive
Democrats

Wearing the trousers at last: (*left to right*) Gardaí Joy Treacy and Alice Kennedy
modelling the new Garda uniforms in September 1992

Taoiseach on the campaign trail: Albert Reynolds joins the 48A bus in Dublin during the 1992 general election campaign

Sheep crammed into the foyer of the Department of Agriculture offices in Dublin during a farmers' protest in June 1992

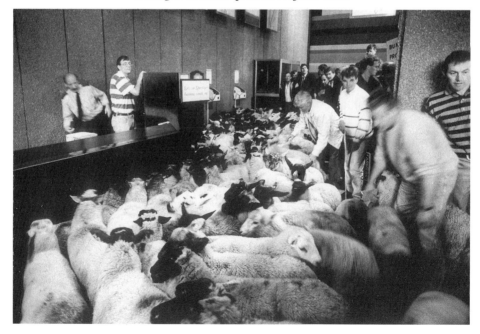

CHAPTER 7

Tools of Democracy: Political Parties in Ireland

Born out of armed rebellion against Britain and ensuing civil war during the first two decades of this century, the party political system in Ireland took a very long time to arrive at what might be called normal political exchange. When party loyalty depends on who thinks they love their country more, or who did what terrible deed in a bloody civil war, the ideology of class struggle or higher political philosophy takes a back seat. Sloganizing and sacred cows take the place of serious debate. Given the inauspicious start to modern democracy in Ireland, it was to the country's credit, however, that once the State was established on a sound footing, the handing over of power to an opposition whose members had been deadly, armed enemies only a few short years before was accomplished calmly and correctly.

By the 1990s, few vestiges remain of the armed struggle and civil-war legacy. At the first general election of the new decade, in November 1992, the change to modern politics seemed to be complete. The parties whose origins lay on opposite sides in the civil war had catastrophic election results, while the main party of the left surged to become for the first time major political power brokers. In many ways, this was a continuation of the political ground swell for change which had been demonstrated so convincingly in the election of Ireland's first woman President in 1990.

Two parties have dominated Irish politics and government since the foundation of the State: Fianna Fáil (FF) and Fine Gael (FG). The oldest party in the country, the Labour Party, remained small, only sometimes finding a place either in government in coalition with Fine Gael, or supporting a Fianna Fáil minority administration. These parties have been joined in the last decade by some smaller groups, a sign of the shifting nature of Irish political thinking, and the dispersal of votes: the Progressive Democrats (PD), right of centre economically but liberal socially; the Democratic Left (DL), which has been through a metamorphosis from revolutionary Marxism to 'soft left' social democracy (changing its name several times on the way – in the 1989 and 1987 elections it was known as the Workers' Party, or WP); and the Green Party, a close relation of the international environmentally concerned movement. The last time any party had an overall majority of seats in Dáil Éireann was in 1977, when Fianna Fáil went into government with an unprecedented majority of 20. Ireland has been governed by minority governments or coalitions since then.

After the general election of 1989, change had really taken hold: Fianna Fáil for the first time went into coalition (with the Progressive Democrats), thereby abandoning what was always considered a 'core value' of the party, i.e. that Fianna Fáil would never join another party in order to govern. This 'core value' arose from the well-known conviction of Fianna Fáil over the years that they were somehow the natural party of government, a 'great national movement' which could not and would not envisage any other party having any legitimacy in government: until recent times, defeats for Fianna Fáil were considered an unfortunate accident, a quirk of the electoral system. The party tried twice to change the electoral system to the British 'first past the post' but the Irish people drew the line at that.

By the end of the 1980s, the trends of modern Irish politics were clearly established: Fianna Fáil slowly declining from its dominant position, Fine Gael languishing a poor second, and the Labour Party beginning to recover from its difficulties (see charts opposite). The strength of the parties in Dáil Éireann after the 1987 and 1989 general elections is shown in the table on page 156.

FIANNA FÁIL

'In our house, every great Irishman, including St Patrick, was automatically assumed to be an early Fianna Fáiler.'[1]

That fervent spirit of Fianna Fáil* members, their conviction that they were the natural party of government for Ireland, has always astonished and annoyed their political rivals. Fianna Fáil is in fact the youngest of the three main parties, and yet has dominated Irish politics, in or out of government, since the foundation of the State.

---

* Fianna Fáil means 'warriors of Ireland'.

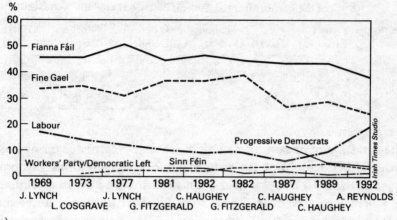

(a)

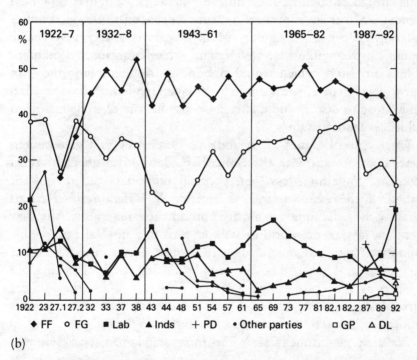

(b)

[a] Electoral support (%) for the Irish political parties, 1969–92 (*source: Irish Times*, 28 November 1992)

[b] Parties' share of the vote (%), 1922–92 (*source:* Richard Sinnott, *Irish Voters Decide: Voting Behaviour in Elections and Referendums, 1918–92,* Manchester University Press, forthcoming)

State of the Parties after the General Elections, 1987 and 1989					
Election	Fianna Fáil	Fine Gael	Labour	Progressive Democrats	Workers' Party	Others
1989	77	55	15	6	7	6
1987	81	51	12	14	4	4

The giant figure of Éamon de Valera (1882–1975)* was synonymous with Fianna Fáil from its foundation in 1926 until his death in 1975. Born in New York of a Spanish father and an Irish mother, de Valera was a born leader of men, filled with intense conviction about his country's destiny, brooding, dogmatizing, often rationalizing, tough enough to take up the gun when he felt it right and turning on former comrades-in-arms when constitutional politics beckoned. He had a singular vision of a thirty-two-county Gaelic republic – the whole island of Ireland – free from foreign domination of any kind, which would embody in itself simple virtues and sturdy self-reliance, speaking its own language (which by 1921 had come close to death) and eschewing what he saw as malign foreign influences from Britain.

When his colleagues in Ireland's revolutionary first government concluded a treaty with the United Kingdom government in 1921, accepting something less than political unity and full republican status for the whole island of Ireland, de Valera refused to go along with it. Despite a majority vote in the country's first parliament in favour of working with the treaty, de Valera and his supporters marched out, leading the country into civil war. That war, short and sharp, laid the foundation for the long-lasting old enmities between two camps: anti- and pro-treaty – and the political parties of Fianna Fáil and Fine Gael respectively. De Valera and his followers refused to become involved in the new parliament.

The first government after the treaty held firm, the civil war

*De Valera (1882–1975) was brought to Ireland in his very early years, educated in Limerick, Dublin (Blackrock College) and University College, Dublin. First elected head of the government in 1932, he held that post with some interruptions until 1959. Author of the Constitution of Ireland, in 1937, and President of Ireland 1959–73.

ended, and a few years later, de Valera realized that parliamentary politics and a party structure were the only ways to put him in a position to achieve power. He had spent a year in prison, thinking about his future, and, rather in the spirit of de Gaulle in later years, he pondered on the state of Ireland without him: 'Never again would he serve in another man's army; never again would he, the most subtle Irish intelligence of his generation, be kept waiting outside while those he deemed political illiterates pondered whether even to admit him to their primitive counsels.'[2] He formed his anti-treaty supporters into a new party, Fianna Fáil. Unfortunately, he was faced with a dilemma: in order to enter parliament, participants had to take an oath which included a reference to the British Crown. His resolution of that dilemma marked the first great somersault of Fianna Fáil on what was apparently a 'core issue', which was echoed down through the decades of the century on many other occasions, culminating in the landmark decision of 1989 to enter government as part of a coalition. To get around the difficulty of the oath, de Valera and his followers signed the book containing the oath, while placing the Bible face downwards in the furthest corner of the room, and covering the words of the oath while actually signing their names. Thus, in August 1927, the Fianna Fáil members felt able to circumvent their consciences and take their place in Dáil Éireann.

The party and the leader assumed power in 1932, and were to hold it, with occasional interruptions, for most of the next four decades. That first period of government lasted until 1948. So it is worth looking at what kind of party it was, and how it evolved.

'Fianna Fáil's Ireland was a nation set apart by Catholicism and nationality: the interlocking relationships of Church and politics helping to define a unique, God-given way of life.'[3] 'The long fellow', 'the chief' (de Valera), in a St Patrick's Day broadcast in 1935 was eloquent about his country and where he wanted it to go: 'Ireland remains a Catholic nation, and as such sets the eternal destiny of man high above the isms and idols of the day . . . the State will be confined to its proper functions as guardians of the rights of the individual and the family, coordinator of the activities of its citizens.' In that set of priorities, de Valera was not at odds with prevailing opinion in the country at large at that time. His *magnum opus* was the Constitution which he masterminded in 1937, and which remains in place today, without any fundamental changes. It embodied Catholic social thinking of the day, but also 'proved to be a formidable bulwark against any tendency towards a tyranny of the majority'.[4] Among its articles was one which recognized the 'special position' of the Roman Catholic Church (Article 44.2) and another two which claimed jurisdiction over Northern Ireland (Articles 2 and 3). Article 44 was abolished without fuss by a referendum in 1972, but Articles 2 and 3 remain at the centre of heated debate in both parts of the island. They represent another 'core value' of Fianna Fáil, and were still constituting a central difficulty for the party in talks on the future of Northern Ireland in the 1990s.

Through the 1930s and 1940s, and right up to the early 1960s, Ireland seemed asleep: a low level of economic activity, a gradually increasing unemployment and emigration rate, a stultifying censorship of literature and the arts, and a seemingly immortal old man in a long black coat, peering short-sightedly through schoolmasterish round glasses, were the dominant features. De Valera, dominating his party, had kept Ireland out of the second world war, announcing a policy of neutrality which became yet another 'core value' which modern international realities are gradually wearing away. The party, better organized and better managed than any other, never slipped below 40 per cent in its share of the national vote, and was usually well above it.

And then a second leader came to Fianna Fáil in 1959. Seán Lemass,* with an impeccable background in old republican battles, married to a determination to pull Ireland out of the trough of despondency of the 1950s, was a pragmatist par excellence. In order not to alarm the old faithful Fianna Fáil following, who had believed in protectionism and isolationism, Lemass presented his new, outward-looking economic and industrial policy not as what it was, a determined effort to undo the economic mistakes of the past, but as a continuation of the long struggle of Irish people to obtain independence. Lemass has entered the pantheon of Fianna

---

* Seán Francis Lemass, 1899–1971, a Dublin man and activist in the struggle against Britain and in the civil war. A founder of Fianna Fáil, he was a long-serving minister in several de Valera governments, mainly in industry and commerce. Taoiseach 1959–66. One of his last initiatives was the foundation of a parliamentary committee on the Constitution which sought to make the Republic's claim on Northern Ireland aspirational.

Fáil leaders as a sort of Kemal Atatürk of Ireland, the man who led his country out of the desert of economic depression and social isolation. He also blazed a trail to Northern Ireland when he sat down in 1965 with a Northern Ireland prime minister, Terence O'Neill, breaking that mould with quiet, no-nonsense realism. The party acquired new young men, and new methods: young turks of business in mohair suits set up high-powered fund-raising systems. Lemass's genius was in bringing the party along with him, perhaps because they knew that he was motivated primarily by fervent nationalism. As Fianna Fáil won election after election in the 1960s, pushing up its share of the vote to 47 per cent in 1965, it seemed as immovable as the rock of time.

Lemass moved on; and the party acquired a deceptively mild, pipe-smoking former Gaelic Athletic Association hurling and football hero as leader: Jack Lynch.* A barrister from Cork city, he moved into place in 1966 as president of a party which had chosen him instead of two thrusting younger men, one of them Seán Lemass's son-in-law. Generally regarded as one of the most agreeable and pleasant leaders ever to be Taoiseach, Jack Lynch is unfortunately also remembered as an instigator of Ireland's first major shift into 'auction politics' in 1977. Fianna Fáil abolished rates on domestic dwellings and taxes on private cars after an election campaign which ignored the signs of incipient serious financial difficulties for the country, and marked the beginning of really massive borrowing to finance current budget deficits.† Lynch won a massive victory for Fianna Fáil in that election, achieving 50.6 per cent of the vote and a majority of 20 seats. It was to mark the last hurrah for his party's pre-eminence in Irish politics.

Jack Lynch is also remembered as the Taoiseach who was faced with the eruption of the modern phase of the Northern Ireland problem: this spilled over into his own party and government in 1970, forcing him to dismiss several ministers. Two of them were

* Jack Lynch (b. 1917, Cork) entered the Dáil in 1948, and held a plethora of ministries before being elected Fianna Fáil leader and Taoiseach in 1966. He held the unique distinction of winning six All-Ireland medals in a row, in two Gaelic Athletic Association games: hurling and football.

† The outgoing government, a coalition between Fine Gael and Labour, were not blameless in this auction either, but did not carry promises to the excesses of Fianna Fáil.

prosecuted for alleged arms smuggling to Northern Ireland. They were cleared of the charges, and one of them took the leadership of the Fianna Fáil party from Jack Lynch nearly ten years later.

The traumas of that period marked the beginning of deep differences within Fianna Fáil between hawks and doves on the Northern Ireland question. Lynch retired in 1979, leaving a party facing a challenge from an opposition party – Fine Gael – which was, for the first time, highly organized, well-financed, and using modern electoral techniques at the same level as – or better than – Fianna Fáil traditionally employed.

Fianna Fáil entered, under its new leader in 1979, further turbulent and difficult years. Charles J. Haughey* presided over a party which had been returned in 1977 with 20 seats more than the combined Opposition, but the rumbling storms in Northern Ireland had deeply affected the party, and the residual bitterness of the Arms Trial and its aftermath in the early 1970s had not been eliminated. The country began to question the conservative values of the old-style Fianna Fáil, as the women's movement and a new liberalism brought voters towards other, more appealing parties. Distrust of Haughey and Fianna Fáil on Northern Ireland, and a growing concern about spiralling borrowing and inflation, all led to a drop in the party's support to 45.26 per cent in the June 1981 election from 50.6 per cent in 1977. Fianna Fáil found itself out of power, but not for long. As Ireland went through one of the most politically unstable periods in its history, two more elections followed quickly: in February 1982, Fianna Fáil with 47 per cent of the vote and 81 seats formed a precarious minority government, dogged by scandal and continuing internal upheaval; in November 1982, yet another election saw the party back in opposition. Charles Haughey, who was at the centre of continual suspicion about his political and personal probity, survived leadership challenges, and led vociferous opposition to a coalition government which was itself facing internal strains.

---

*Charles Haughey (b. 1925 in Co. Mayo, reared in Dublin), from a chartered-accountancy background, was first elected to the Dáil in 1957, and held many ministries with distinction. He married the daughter of Seán Lemass, and was admired, loved, feared and hated: people were never indifferent. *Bon viveur*, with unexplained sources of wealth, he survived many challenges to his leadership of Fianna Fáil between 1979 and 1992.

In 1985, Fianna Fáil had to watch the old enemy, Fine Gael, conclude a historic Anglo-Irish Agreement with Great Britain on Northern Ireland. The first instinct of the Fianna Fáil Party was to oppose it: however, on regaining office in 1987, pragmatism triumphed easily, and the party enthusiastically espoused and operated the Agreement, as well as turning a new leaf in fiscal responsibility. But the days of overall majorities for Fianna Fáil were apparently over, and the minority 1987 government (with 44.15 per cent) faced the electorate again in 1989, through a decision of the leader himself which was considered to be a mistake. With the same percentage vote as in 1987 (44.2 per cent) but four fewer seats (77), the party over several traumatic weeks came to terms with the necessity to take another party into government if power was to be regained. Worse was to follow: the presidential election of 1990 brought defeat for the Fianna Fáil candidate, and for the first time ever, the President of Ireland did not come from its ranks. Fianna Fáil was seriously weakened once more by a series of alleged financial scandals in 1991 which involved associates of the party or government appointees. A Tribunal of Inquiry had been set up to investigate apparent grave irregularities in the multi-million-pound beef industry, which was damaging Fianna Fáil every day it sat. Mr Haughey finally lost out when a former ministerial colleague alleged that he had been personally aware of illegal telephone-tapping of journalists in 1982. Faced with the wrath of his party, he resigned.

Fianna Fáil, rocked from all these momentous happenings, elected a new leader, Albert Reynolds, a self-made successful businessman from rural Ireland. He apparently carried no ideological baggage and, compared with his immediate predecessor, appeared approachable and low-key in style. Almost on his first public appearance as Taoiseach, he set out all his personal financial circumstances in order to emphasize his integrity, and he declared that he wanted to 'let in the light' and have open government. He was, however, immediately plunged into controversy over abortion, the Maastricht Treaty, some major industrial disputes, and rapidly climbing unemployment figures. Neither was he as skilful or pragmatic as Haughey in handling his coalition partners, with whom relations became increasingly tense. It was quickly recalled that he had referred to the government partnership, when he was Minister for

Finance the previous year, as 'a temporary little arrangement'. As the clouds gathered, the country braced itself for an election.

FINE GAEL

The difficult birth of modern Ireland as an independent nation had for its midwives a group of men who felt that the attainment of the possible was better than the bloody pursuit of the impossible: thus, the small majority of parliamentarians who supported the 1921 treaty with Britain were themselves pragmatists. At the very beginning of their work, two leaders died: Arthur Griffith* from natural causes, and the formidable Michael Collins† from an assassin's bullet in an ambush on a country road in Co. Cork. Collins was such a strong figure that he would probably have challenged Éamon de Valera in national prominence had he lived. His death left a sorry vacuum.

The party of those treaty supporters was Cumann na nGaedheal (from 1933 Fine Gael). As well as being the upholders of the treaty, theirs was also the party of law and order, and Commonwealth status. 'As such, it was more attractive than Fianna Fáil to the business world, to many shopkeepers and professional people, and to the more prosperous farmers who relied on British markets.'⁵ As well as the gulf of policy between them on the national question, Fine Gael and Fianna Fáil were therefore initially separated by intellectual/social barriers, urban and rural. Those characteristics persisted for decades, but have almost disappeared today.

The first leader of the party, founded in Dublin's Mansion

---

* Arthur Griffith (1871–1922), a thinker and activist politically and militarily since his youth, led the delegation from the Dáil to London for the treaty negotiations. Like many of his colleagues, he had suffered imprisonment and internment under the British. After the treaty was accepted by the Dáil he was elected President of the Dáil in 1922, but died of a cerebral haemorrhage later that year.

† Michael Collins (1890–1922) came from Cork. Worked as a clerk in London, returned to Ireland in 1915 and fought in 1916. Organized the Irish intelligence system against Britain in the Anglo-Irish war. Minister for Home Affairs, then Finance, in the Provisional Government to 1922. He was one of the delegation to negotiate the treaty with Britain in 1921. Commander-in-chief of government forces in the civil war. Known as 'the big fellow', he was strikingly good-looking, inspired great devotion, and was shot and killed in August 1922.

House (Lord Mayor's house) on 27 April 1923, was W. T. Cosgrave,* a quiet man, little known in many parts of the country. A participant in the Easter Rising, he was unanimously elected as President of the Executive Council (i.e. prime minister). There was nothing dominant or masterful about him. He was a clear but not an exciting speaker. There was no trace of the orator in his make-up. There was nothing in him to suggest the 'daring pilot of extremity'.[6] Neither was there much in him to ensure an efficient and widespread national organization for his party, a failing which was to have predictable consequences for Fine Gael in the long and weary decades of opposition which followed their first ten years.

Since de Valera had stormed out of the Dáil, and plunged the country into civil war, the remaining politicians had the mammoth job of putting a whole new administrative and legal machine into place while fighting a mercifully short-lived civil war at the same time. They had ten years in power to do it, which was the length of time it took Fianna Fáil to get really started and to enter constitutional politics. The civil war brought ferocity out on both sides; in ending it, the Free State government used the utmost severity, a factor which added to later bitterness in politics.

Naturally enough, the dominant preoccupation of those first years in the Free State was the establishment of a country without British control, without British cultural power as well as political power. 'The rigorous conservatism of the Irish Free State has become a cliché.'[7] There was a heavy emphasis on the Gaelic nature of the State – perhaps because at the same time the politicians had to insist on loyalty to the treaty, with the republican forces of Fianna Fáil breathing down their necks. Compulsory regulations for learning Irish in schools were put in place, and educationists were urged to inculcate national pride and respect in the teaching of history in particular.

The first Constitution designed by Cumann na nGaedheal in 1922 was ostensibly a liberal one, but the government itself was

* William Thomas Cosgrave (1880–1965), born in Dublin. President of the Executive Council 1922–32, after fighting in 1916 and a spell of imprisonment under the British, he was Minister for Local Government in the first Dáil, leading Cumann na nGaedheal until it became Fine Gael in 1933; he led Fine Gael in 1935–44, retiring in 1944.

authoritarian and conservative. A most dramatic illustration was the cutting of the old-age pension by a shilling a week. The most notorious statement of a Free State minister remained that of Patrick McGilligan (Finance Minister): 'People may have to die in the country, and die through starvation.'[8] The political fallout from actions and statements like these was only weathered because in the absence of Fianna Fáil there was virtually no official political Opposition.

Under Cosgrave, the work of establishing the Army, the Gardaí, the justice system, the civil service, and an energy supply all reached successful conclusions, despite the immense instability preceding the State's establishment and continual threats of assassination. 'Under the cautious rule of William Cosgrave, the discourse of Free State politics remained dogmatically buried in the issues over which the civil war had been fought, and practically obsessed between steering a conservative, rural, strongly petit-bourgeois State through the rocks and shoals raised by fiscal autonomy and international economic instability.'[9]

While the business of government went on, not enough attention – if any – was given to the work of party organization. The lack of nationally organized structures for Cumann na nGaedheal, in contrast to Fianna Fáil, contributed to its continual defeats at the polls in and after 1932. That 1932 election saw the genesis of an organization which subsequently became known as 'the Blueshirts' – a name which is bandied about nowadays as a jocose description of Fine Gael people. The political meetings of the 1930s were rumbustious affairs, and some Cumann na nGaedheal people felt they needed protection in order to ensure freedom of speech. A sudden election in 1933 saw a particularly bitter campaign, and an organization was formed whose adherents wore blue shirts and marched in military style. To this day people argue about whether or not it was a fascist body in the European mode of the 1930s. Historian J. J. Lee has no doubts: 'Blueshirts were simply traditional conservatives, decked out in fashionable but ideologically ill-fitting continental garb. Fascism was far too intellectually demanding for the bulk of the Blueshirts.'[10] Whatever the truth of that, 1933 saw the fusion of Cumann na nGaedheal, the Blueshirts, and the Centre Party (a small group which had tried to steer clear of both sides in the civil war) into a new organization, Fine Gael. The new leader was Eoin

O'Duffy,* whose period in charge was short-lived as the Blueshirts behaved more and more badly and without regard for the law. Cosgrave re-emerged as leader, the Blueshirts were shrugged off, and the party settled into protracted opposition ... the decade 1938–48 was to be the most dismal in Fine Gael history, until the period from 1987 to the early 1990s threatened to be even more inglorious. In the ten years after 1938, the party's share of the vote never exceeded 33 per cent but usually hovered around the low 20s. During the elections up to and including 1948, the party lost more and more seats (hitting an all-time low of 30 in 1944). However, Cosgrave retired and Richard Mulcahy† took over, and coalition government suddenly emerged, almost by accident, in 1948. Between that year and 1957, there were to be two 'interparty' governments, each led by a Fine Gael Taoiseach, John A. Costello.‡

After 1959, with a new leader, James Dillon,§ the party once again faced a long period out of government, which by now had begun to seem its natural state. There was still no hunger for power, no national electoral machine, both of which were permanent features of Fianna Fáil. Fine Gael did not have the tight network of *cumainn* (branches) in every corner of the country and the strict hierarchical structures combined with great national gatherings, which were part and parcel of the Fianna Fáil persona. To complicate life further for Fine Gael, the differences between Fine Gael and Fianna Fáil began to diminish as the civil war

*Eoin O'Duffy (1892–1944), from Co. Monaghan, was an engineer. First Commander of the Garda Síochána, 1922–33. Dismissed by de Valera. Became leader of the Army Comrades' Association (the Blueshirts) in 1933. First President of Fine Gael 1933–4. Led pro-Franco Irish brigade to Spain in 1936–7.

†Mulcahy (1886–1971) was never Taoiseach, because his conservatism was unacceptable to the coalition partners in two governments; however, he served as Minister for Education in both of them (1948–51 and 1954–7). Like his colleagues in Fine Gael of that time, he had an honourable record of bravery against the British in pre-independence days.

‡Costello, a barrister before and after his political career, was Attorney-General 1926–32. He was the man who suddenly declared an Irish Republic at a dinner in Canada in 1948, prompting the British government to pass the 1949 Ireland Act, copper-fastening the separate status of Northern Ireland as part of Britain.

§Dillon (1902–86), a sonorous orator and a bridge between the old British-oriented National Centre Party and modern Fine Gael, was expelled for a period for opposing Irish neutrality in the second world war. Never Taoiseach, but twice Minister for Agriculture.

bitterness receded and the Blueshirt pedigree was forgotten. With the advent of new blood on both sides of the Dáil, the seeds were sown for the later blurring of the distinctions between the two main parties. 'Despite Fianna Fáil affectations about their radical roots vis-à-vis the bourgeois antedecedents of Fine Gael, there was next to no difference in the social background of Dáil TDs on each side.'[11]

At the end of James Dillon's period, a Fine Gael policy document appeared called *The Just Society* which, though eminently middle-of-the-road by today's standards, nevertheless seemed then a major step forward in radical social thinking. Its author was Declan Costello, son of the former Fine Gael Taoiseach, who eventually became a High Court Judge after a fairly short political career. The party was not yet ripe for conversion to radicalism however, and the next leader was in the old conservative mould. Liam Cosgrave,* the son of the party's first leader, became leader in 1965 on Dillon's retirement. In spite of Cosgrave's conservatism, the party revival took on a little more pace, as a younger generation of talented men began to take their Fine Gael politics more seriously than their elders. Their opportunity came when Fianna Fáil was rocked in 1970 by the Arms Trial scandal. The year 1973 saw Cosgrave leading Fine Gael into coalition government – with 35 per cent of the popular vote – with the Labour Party, and marked the beginning of the end of Fianna Fáil's long stranglehold on power. That government's term was marked by Fine Gael's stern treatment of the IRA, the early years of EC membership (and the surge in prosperity for Fine Gael's friends, the bigger farmers), and the whirlwind international *tour de force* of Garret FitzGerald,† the kind of Foreign Minister Ireland had never before experienced. It also saw the first major initiative in new Northern Ireland structures – a short-lived power-sharing experiment launched at Sunningdale in England, but scuttled by a combination of British lack of

---

*Born in 1920, he was a Dáil Deputy from 1943 until retirement in 1981. Leader of Fine Gael 1965–77, and Taoiseach 1973–7. The son and father of politicians, his father was Ireland's first prime minister; his son (Liam too) has had an uneven career, but was safely elected to the Senate in 1989.

†Born 1926, the son of Desmond, a minister in the first Irish government up to 1932. Economist, polyglot, he was Minister for Foreign Affairs under Liam Cosgrave 1973–7, leader of Fine Gael in opposition 1977–81, and Taoiseach in 1981–2, and again in 1982–7. Held his seat in 1987 and 1989, accepted several directorships, and published his autobiography in 1991.[12]

commitment and Unionist intransigence. It was marked too by the growth of public disquiet about some sections of the Garda Síochána and 'strong arm' tactics, a gross insult to the President by Cosgrave's Minister for Defence,* and a beginning of government borrowing to counter the effects of the first international oil crisis. Cosgrave voted against his own government's bill of 1974, which was designed to legislate following a Supreme Court decision that the importation and sale of contraceptives must be allowed, alarming many of the new recruits to the party. Cosgrave finally became somewhat overconfident, even arrogant, as by-elections and early opinion polls seemed to indicate another victory for the coalition.† No such victory happened; Fine Gael was soundly trounced at the election of 1977, and the party strength dropped by 11 seats to 43, its share of the national vote going down to 30.5 per cent.

Cosgrave promptly resigned, ushering in the era of Garret FitzGerald, who was to lead the party until 1987.

A transformation of Fine Gael took place in a few short years, as FitzGerald and his party's general secretary, Peter Prendergast, toured the country, inspiring the faithful and attracting new members in large numbers, including women and young people. They were drawn in by a combination of FitzGerald's new emphasis on liberalism and pluralism, and a fear of increasing national debt and financial instability as Fianna Fáil tried to spend its way out of trouble, first under Jack Lynch but with a sudden acceleration under Charles Haughey from late 1979. Prendergast was ruthless in weeding out the inactive occupants of safe seats, forcing them to accept new running mates with real chances of gaining seats. For the first time, Fine Gael had branches and structures as efficient as Fianna Fáil's, with election machines using all the latest technology and gimmicks. Catchy election songs,‡ visually clever party-political broadcasts – the public were treated to an overdose of persuasion.

---

* See page 12n.

† An unfortunate unscripted turn of phrase in his 1977 Ard-Fheis speech, televised nationally, to the effect that 'blow-ins . . . could either blow up or blow out' was taken as a reference to a prominent journalist, Bruce Arnold, originally from England, who was critical of his government.

‡ Fine Gael's 'Fine Gael, Fine Gael/ a bright new future we hail/ go with Garret the man you know . . . ' was matched by Fianna Fáil's 'Arise and follow Charlie'.

The political contest was highly personalized between leaders FitzGerald and Haughey, a feature of Irish politics which remains firmly in place today, albeit with different personnel.

All of this effort, combined with that of new party strategists (who became known as 'national handlers'), catapulted Fine Gael into contention for power (with the Labour Party) during the three elections of 1981 and 1982. Its national share of the vote went to an all-time high of 39·22 per cent in November 1982, and saw Fine Gael back in government. Four years of mixed success followed, while the government tried to come to grips with the financial results of ten years of budget-deficit borrowing, the increasing ferocity of the Northern Ireland crisis, and the desire of FitzGerald to push out the frontiers of social progress. Uncertain leadership, strains internally, public wrangling between the coalition partners, and implacable opposition from Fianna Fáil to all initiatives saw two referendum defeats for the government on social issues (abortion and divorce), unrest and hostility from unions, particularly teacher unions, to cost-containment measures, and plummeting popularity. FitzGerald and Fine Gael, however, could claim one significant achievement: the signing of the Anglo-Irish Agreement in 1985.* This was Fine Gael's second major initiative on Northern Ireland, in a political culture which had always associated Fianna Fáil with nationalist concern. It was not enough, however, to counteract all the negatives, and to shore up anything like sufficient support when facing an election.

Fine Gael, having been built up to fighting strength before 1982, was once more defeated in 1987, declining to a 27 per cent share of the vote, losing a calamitous 19 seats and its leader to boot – FitzGerald quickly resigned. The new leader, after a three-way contest between three attractive candidates, was Alan Dukes,† a former Eurocrat and youthful Minister for Agriculture, Finance, and Justice under FitzGerald. The party was now composed of a

* See Chapter 8 ('Northern Ireland').

†Dukes, born in 1945, represents Kildare in Dáil Éireann. An economist, he was appointed a minister on his first day in Dáil Éireann in 1981. His background includes periods as chief economist for the Irish Farmers' Association, and Brussels Cabinet member of Irish EC Commissioner Richard Burke 1977–80. Since losing the leadership, he has been an active back-bencher with every appearance of ambition.

growing number of 'liberals', added on to the more traditional wing, of whom Dukes was one.

In 1987, Alan Dukes declared that Fine Gael would not bring down the minority Fianna Fáil government as long as it followed the responsible fiscal path espoused for so long by Fine Gael: this strategy* was admired by the business community and many commentators as a breakthrough in political responsibility, but put an increasing strain on the parliamentary party. It did not gain much for the party electorally either: despite massive cuts in public expenditure, and the resulting growing unpopularity of Fianna Fáil, only four more seats were gained by Fine Gael in 1989, bringing Fine Gael to 55. Alan Dukes became the shortest-lived leader of his party since Eoin O'Duffy in the 1930s, when the party's candidate in the 1990 presidential election came a poor third and the demoralized and disappointed TDs turned on him. He was unceremoniously ousted, leaving many of his supporters, and the liberal wing of the party, very uneasy.

One of those who had contested the 1987 leadership battle, John Bruton,† won the ensuing contest easily. A well-to-do landowner from Co. Meath, with a legal qualification and considerable experience in politics dating from his first election to the Dáil at the age of twenty-two, Bruton is energetic and forceful, and, naturally, desperately anxious to strengthen his party again. He represents a bridge between the old Cosgrave days and the modern party, and is considered conservative. Both he and his party are caught, however, in the swirling tides of political change in Ireland, where votes are dispersing away from the large centrist groupings, and where the distinction – economically or socially – between the three parties in the centre (Fianna Fáil, Fine Gael, and the Progressive Democrats) is becoming less and less clear. Since the advent of the essentially pragmatic Albert Reynolds to the leadership of Fianna Fáil, that distinction is even more blurred. Fine Gael showed

---

*Known as the Tallaght Strategy, after the west Dublin suburb where it was announced in late 1987.

†Bruton, born in 1947, represents Meath in the Dáil. He lists his former occupation as 'farmer' but holds a barrister's qualification. An indefatigable worker, with a loud braying infectious laugh (not heard so much since assuming leadership), he is considered a clever and original thinker, with great zeal for reforming institutions. Despite his comparative youth, he has held office in various governments since his first junior ministry in 1973.

no signs of recovery from its low position after the shocks of 1990, while Bruton himself seemed launched on an irreversible slide in public popularity, failing to capture the interest of the Irish public in any of his considerable plans and projects for their future.

The oldest party in Ireland, the Labour Party pre-dated Irish independence, and emerged as the political wing of the Irish labour movement in 1912. The motion for its establishment, at a meeting in Clonmel, Co. Tipperary, came from James Connolly on behalf of the Belfast branch of the Irish Transport Workers' Union. This was the first union to combine political as well as industrial aims: and when a great lockout took place in 1913–14, the fallout saw the establishment of the Irish Citizen Army, whose first leader was James Larkin – known as 'Big Jim'. The result of the lockout was 'a short material victory for the forces of capitalism, but a moral victory for the forces of Labour'.[13]

James Connolly was badly injured in the Easter Rising of 1916, and had to be propped in a chair for his execution by the British government. This and other executions carried out by the British turned the tide of Irish public opinion in favour of nationalism, but it deprived the Labour Party of its founder and foremost activist.

Since 'Big Jim' Larkin was away in the United States, and Connolly was dead, no national elections were fought by Labour until 1922. After that, a group of twenty-two TDs, led by Tom Johnson, were the de facto opposition because of the refusal of Fianna Fáil to enter the Dáil. But it was a desperately difficult time for a Labour Party caught in a new State which was conservative and rural and intensely nationalistic in its obsessions.

In 1923, Jim Larkin came back from America, and there ensued one of the classic Irish splits, which saw another party being formed and the Irish Transport and General Workers' Union disaffiliated from the party. Despite instructions to the contrary, from the union, this new party – the National Labour Party – entered the first inter-party government in 1948.

From then on, the Labour Party had the problem of finding its niche, and a narrow one it was, in the broad sweep of Irish political life. Its candidates often resembled either Fianna Fáil or Fine Gael in profile, and the phenomenon arose of Labour Party seats held not on Labour philosophy or loyalty, but rather like independent fiefdoms. There was no constituency in the country as a whole for doctrinaire, or even watered-down, socialism. However, in the 1960s, along with the fresh winds blowing through the other parties, new faces appeared, with an intellectual stature not previously experienced in Labour. That decade 'brought the Labour Party an access of intellectual window-dressing, in the shape of some prominent academic candidates and supporters'.[14] A painfully slow process of building up support was hampered by the undeniable fact that Fianna Fáil had traditionally attracted most of the working-class votes in Ireland. The year 1969 saw the first general election in which Labour contested every constituency; they fielded ninety-nine candidates, but lost seats, dropping from 22 to 18. However, their share of the vote reached 17 per cent, which was not to be seen again until 1992.

Despite its leader's* brave assertion that the 'seventies would be socialist', the 1969 result was a crushing blow, and caused a rethink about coalition possibilities. And the desired result came about: the party went into government three times in coalition with Fine Gael, despite apparent enormous divisions between the two parties. In 1973, 1981, and 1982, Labour sat at the Cabinet table with Fine Gael. The first time was under the leadership of Brendan Corish, the second time with Micheal O'Leary,† and the third time under its present leader, Dick Spring.‡

---

*Brendan Corish (1918–91), leader of the Labour Party 1960–77. Minister for Health and Social Welfare 1973–7. Member of a well-known Wexford family, Brendan Corish was a local-government official before entering politics in 1945, following his father's death.

†After four years as Minister for Labour in the 1973–7 coalition government, O'Leary became deputy leader then leader of the Labour Party. However, in a showdown with his own party at a party conference in 1982, he was defeated on the question whether the parliamentary party or a national party conference should decide electoral strategy (he favoured the former). He immediately left, and joined Fine Gael.

‡Dick Spring (b. 1950) became leader of the Labour Party in 1982, and Tánaiste (deputy prime minister) a few weeks later in Garret FitzGerald's coalition government. A barrister and former international rugby player, Dick Spring, when a junior minister in 1981, suffered severe back injuries in a car accident on his way to Dublin from his Kerry constituency. In 1993 he again became Tánaiste, as well as Minister for Foreign Affairs.

One of the best parliamentary performers in the Dáil, as well as being the youngest of the party leaders, Spring's self-confessed aim is to bring all the left-wing Deputies in Dáil Éireann together under the Labour banner, and to build up enough strength to challenge Fine Gael for its place as second biggest party in the Irish parliament. The Labour Party was bruised after its four years in government in the 1980s, and lost 4 seats – descending to 12 in 1987 but climbing back up to 15 in 1989, helped greatly by the astute performance of its leader in the Dáil, where he was generally considered to be 'the real leader of the Opposition', much to the chagrin of Fine Gael. The question of coalition has always caused dissension within the Labour ranks; in 1992 the party leader refused to speculate on what might happen in the future. 'If the whole movement took off like Mitterrand did, you'd never know, I might be Taoiseach . . .'[15] Today its links with trade unions are less close, though some funding is made available to the party – IR£25,000 in 1992.

THE DEMOCRATIC LEFT

Like the two big Irish parties, Fianna Fáil and Fine Gael, the Democratic Left's origins are bound up with 'the national question' – the division of Ireland. At the outbreak of severe trouble in the North in 1969, the Irish Republican Army – which had been simmering for years, and occasionally erupting into violent campaigns – broke into two, the Official IRA and the Provisional IRA. The former was socialist/revolutionary, the latter would have none of that communist stuff. A year later, the political wing of the IRA – Sinn Féin – followed suit, and a party known as Official Sinn Féin emerged.

By 1977, the name had been changed to Sinn Féin the Workers' Party, with more and more branches springing up in working-class areas, and more and more strength apparent in the Republic of Ireland. By this time, the depth of hostility between the old Sinn Féin Party and this more communist-oriented group was obvious; it was dramatically in evidence outside polling booths, where party workers from the other groups watched while ugly scenes took place between the rival groups.

It was during the politically turbulent opening years of the 1980s that Sinn Féin the Workers' Party (SFWP) won its first seat in Dáil

Éireann, increasing the number to three in February 1982. A feature of the modern party, which became firmly established by the 1990s, is the constant condemnation of violence, particularly violence emanating from their old enemy, the Provisional IRA. In the second 1982 election, the Dáil representation was reduced to two, rising to four in 1987, then seven in 1989. In 1992, after a bitter but democratically fought battle for control of the party and yet another split, six of the seven Dáil members formed themselves and their supporters into the new Democratic Left. Since a party needs seven members in the Dáil to be recognized as a fully fledged political unit, this reduction weakened them in terms of parliamentary time and the State money that goes with each grouping (in the case of the former Workers' Party, it was IR£96,000 – a considerable amount for a small party).

The upheavals of 1992 were part of a pattern which marked the distancing of the group from unsavoury elements in Northern Ireland. Connections between the Workers' Party and criminal Official IRA groups in Northern Ireland were constantly rumoured. Tensions arising from these accusations, made by many respected people in Northern Ireland, dogged the party over several years. Politicians in Dublin often referred to the Workers' Party as 'the Stickies' – to signify a group of Official IRA members who sold Easter Rising commemoration badges with sticky labels, as opposed to the Provisional IRA who used pins ...

In June 1991, a BBC *Spotlight* television programme alleged, with case histories, that people in the criminal section of the Official IRA were also members of the Workers' Party. All of this led to the final split in 1992, and the birth of the Democratic Left on 28 March 1992.

The party is now firmly in the mould of mild left-wing politics. It has also disowned its previous attachment to the Soviet Communist Party, which many believed financed the early days of the Workers' Party. It is led by Proinnsias de Rossa,* a serious hard-working man. The party is ultra-liberal on all social issues, and uses terms like liberty, equality, and fraternity with insouciance. Relations

---

*De Rossa, born 1940, represents Dublin North-West in the Dáil. He added an MEP's job to his workload in 1989, but relinquished it, as promised, to a party colleague in 1992.

were extremely strained with the Labour Party until recently. The older party resented the claims of the new group to be the real representatives of the working classes. Despite the Labour leader's relaxed optimism about a possible future merger, statements of de Rossa are not positive: '. . . the Labour Party has no real core values in terms of the kind of Ireland it wants to see evolve or develop . . . it hasn't produced any new documents or policies . . . to my mind it lacks the intellectual energy to do so in any event.'[16]

However, as usually happens in Irish politics, pragmatism will no doubt prevail when the time comes. It triumphed in late 1992 when a prospect of government was in sight. In the meantime, de Rossa leads a small group of impressive, industrious and articulate parliamentarians whose presence in the Irish political system provides an interesting and provocative stimulus to older, larger parties which in their efforts to 'catch all' can fudge issues or simply ignore them.

THE PROGRESSIVE DEMOCRATS

The same might be said for the Progressive Democrats. This small, right-of-centre party, with only six Dáil members, negotiated itself into government with Fianna Fáil in 1989 with great skill. It demanded and got two Cabinet seats out of fifteen, one junior ministry, and three Senators (out of the Taoiseach's eleven nominees).

The party sprang straight out of Fianna Fáil, having its origins in a long-running feud between Desmond O'Malley* and Charles Haughey, which began at the time of the Arms Trial in 1970, continued through the undermining by Charles Haughey of Jack Lynch later in the 1970s, and culminated in the expulsion of O'Malley from the party after a magnificent speech in Dáil Éireann in February 1985. The issue which finally caused the crisis was a government bill liberalizing the laws on the sale of contraceptives:

---

*Desmond O'Malley (b. 1939) comes from a well-known Limerick family with long Fianna Fáil connections. A lawyer by profession, O'Malley entered the Dáil in 1968 and immediately became close to the leader, Jack Lynch. He held several senior ministries (where he was known as an acerbic hard worker). In 1989 he was appointed Minister for Industry and Commerce by Charles Haughey in Fianna Fáil's first coalition.

O'Malley used it to deplore the kind of extra-parliamentary lobbying of TDs that was going on at the time, and excoriated the undemocratic nature of the extremist Catholic pressure groups in Ireland, refusing to vote against the measure despite the party whip. 'There is a choice of a kind that can only be answered by saying that I stand by the Republic and accordingly I will not oppose this Bill.'[17] It was always sensational, because of being almost unheard of, when a Fianna Fáil member, most of all such a senior person as O'Malley, bucked the party whip.

By the end of 1985, O'Malley was in a position to announce the formation of a new party, with himself and a lively young woman, Mary Harney,* as the two Dáil members. They were followed later by two more former Fianna Fáil members, and a Fine Gael TD. From the outset it claimed to transcend civil-war politics, and laid great stress on the increasingly difficult and worrying financial situation of the country. It particularly stressed the need for high standards in high places and from the outset, too, tax reform was a central platform of the party. It has always held that high personal taxes had a lot to do with unemployment, and it supported the government in matters like a pay dispute with the powerful teachers' unions in 1986. Because of the refreshing nature of its broadly liberal stance on social issues, combined with conservative economic theories, the party attracted huge middle-class crowds to public meetings in the early days. Its crisp enunciation of social and economic policy was in stark contrast to the stumbling and seemingly uncertain approach of Fine Gael, whose new liberal supporters were rapidly becoming disillusioned.

Opinion polls showed the party's ratings jumping to 21 per cent of the 'voting intentions' polls in February 1986. To the dismay of the two big parties, the Progressive Democrat support was mostly coming from them, though more from embattled Fine Gael voters – punch-drunk from the unpopular decisions of their party in government – than Fianna Fáil's. In 1987, when Fine Gael lost 19 seats, the PDs achieved 14 Dáil seats, a staggering success for its first

---

*Mary Harney (b. 1953), when Jack Lynch appointed her to the Senate in 1977, became the youngest ever member of the second House. A forthright and fluent speaker, she became Minister of State (junior minister) with special responsibility for the protection of the environment in 1989. One of her first initiatives was to clean up Dublin's air by banning smoky coal.

outing. Despite a fine parliamentary performance during the 1987–9 period, the PDs fell back to 6 seats in 1989 – a casualty of the new fiscally correct policy of Fianna Fáil. (From a high of 11·9 per cent of the popular vote in 1987, it sank to 4·7 per cent in 1992, but won 10 seats.)

However, in 1989, since Fianna Fáil found itself short of a majority, Desmond O'Malley's team of negotiators agreed to go into coalition in July 1989: once more, O'Malley found himself 'knees under the table' with his old arch-enemy, Charles Haughey. And until Haughey's final ousting in 1992, the two men worked together in Cabinet efficiently if not amicably. The PDs faced down their larger government partner on several issues, most notably the crisis surrounding the Fianna Fáil presidential candidate in 1990. The Progressive Democrats, in particular their leader, gained a reputation as the party which kept Mr Haughey in check, as it were: a sort of watchdog on the man who couldn't quite be trusted. This understandably irritated the whole Fianna Fáil Party intensely. And so, as the political climate grew stormier in spring 1992 around the abortion debate and its confusion with the Maastricht referendum, while an impending legal clash loomed between the Taoiseach and his PD Minister for Industry and Commerce at the tribunal of inquiry into the beef industry, another election threatened.

THE IRISH GREENS

An undoubted success of the Green Party in Ireland was the 1989 establishment of the special environmental junior ministry in government. This response to the surge of interest in Ireland in the whole 'green' area may, of course, be the Green Party's un-doing, as the minister set about addressing a wide range of issues in her area of responsibility, and in particular established an independent Environmental Protection Agency which is intended to be a strong watchdog on all matters environmental.

The Green Party has existed in Ireland in a variety of forms since 1981. Founded as the Ecology Party of Ireland, it has progressed through various name changes to its present 'Green Party/Comhaontas Glas'.

In 1989, the party scored its first victory in a national election, when Roger Garland* was elected for the constituency of Dublin South, slipping into a seat formerly held by a prominent Fine Gael member who had retired from politics. The middle-class suburban constituency was typical of the areas where the Greens have drawn their support, and their first and only Dáil member was nearly to be accompanied by a colleague in the neighbouring constituency: however, clever use of the electoral system by Fine Gael ensured two Fine Gael seats and held off the challenge of the Greens.

THE PARTIES IN THE 1990S

Fianna Fáil still dominates Irish politics in the 1990s just as it has since first coming into government in 1932. It had wild swings in opinion polls over the Haughey years, but until 1992 never looked like losing its position of strength. It is a 'catch all' party, drawing support from all social groups, including the lowest socio-economic groups, a party which is intensely pragmatic in its modern phase, and will change its policies if that seems to be the right thing, politically, to do. It inspires in the 1990s, as it always has, a loyalty verging on the fanatical in many of its supporters, though that number is falling. Financially, after two elections in the late 1980s, and a massively expensive presidential election campaign in 1990, the party owes money, and has to engage in non-stop fund-raising, since the State does not support the party in government (and only minimally supports parties in Opposition). Its debt at almost IR£3 million is bigger, as is only fitting, than any other party's. Because of a desperate last-minute attempt to stem the rising tide of support for the Labour Party in the closing days of the November 1992 general election, when financial controls were abandoned as expensive advertisements were placed, the last IR£700,000 of that debt was incurred. Fianna Fáil's membership total of 75,000, with 3,000 branches,[18] is more than three times larger than that of its nearest rival.

Fine Gael, on the other hand, has limped along in a very poor second place since leaving government in 1987. By 1992, its standing

---

*Born in 1933. A former chartered accountant, Garland has been a member of the Green Party since 1982, and unsuccessfully contested the general elections of November 1982 and 1987. Lost his seat in 1992.

in the polls was plummeting (see table opposite) so that many of its fifty-five TDs were feeling distinctly nervous about the next election. Despite John Bruton's conviction that Fine Gael should be seen as the party of reform, of high standards, of new and radical policies for dealing with the country's problems, and despite the constant flow of policy documents from the party, the Irish public seems uncertain and uninterested in Fine Gael. In a period when the dominant political philosophy of Ireland was pragmatic and centrist, away from extremes, Fine Gael was getting squeezed in the battle for the middle ground. It claimed 25,000 members and 1,250 branches, and was grappling with a IR£1 million debt, made all the more difficult to deal with because the money was spent with such a poor return (Fine Gael's candidate came a very poor third in the presidential election in 1990). Its performance in the 1992 election was so bad that its leader was considered to be under severe threat; the situation was exacerbated by a maladroit performance in the post-election jockeying for position to negotiate with the Labour Party. John Bruton, a man of undoubted high principle and intellect, nevertheless seemed unable to overcome the public perception of him as humourless, tired, and right-wing. As the new Fianna Fáil and Labour government suffered a reversal of popularity after a short political honeymoon in early 1992, the Fine Gael Party and its leader did not attract any further support in the polls. A new and younger front bench, with an able and popular woman* as deputy leader, were appointed by Bruton in March 1993. It was generally considered that these moves were his last chance to restore the party's fortunes.

The Labour Party, with its attractive and quick-witted young leader, and a clearer line of opposition to government decisions on spending cuts and expenditure priorities, was establishing a steady if slow improvement in its standing, given impetus by the adroit handling of the presidential election in 1990. Since the Democratic Left purged itself of doubtful associates and Marxist philosophies

---

*Nora Owen (b. 1945). First elected to the Dáil for Dublin North in 1981, she has been a prominent figure in the party since her election, and has made a speciality of foreign affairs and overseas development cooperation, chairing the Oireachtas Committee on the latter subject in 1982–7. She is the grand-niece of one of Ireland's giants of history, Micheal Collins, and the sister of Mary Banotti MEP.

Popular Support for the Irish Political Parties, 1989–92				
Party	June 1989	March 1991	September 1991	April 1992
Fianna Fáil	44	54	43	52
Progressive Democrats	6	4	6	4
Fine Gael	29	25	26	21
Labour	10	10	13	15
Democratic Left	5	3	6	3*
Green Party	2	2	3	2
Others	5	3	3	2

* I have, for simplicity's sake, called the former Workers' Party by the new name of the group to which six of the seven former WP members now belong: the Democratic Left (DL). In this April 1992 poll, the DL actually achieved 1 per cent, but this can be disregarded because the party had only just been through its metamorphosis.

in 1991–2, the possible merging of the two parties on Ireland's moderate left means that a coherent and growing Irish left could become a reality. In the 1992 election, Labour's amazing surge in popular support saw them achieving 33 seats, twice as high as any previous Dáil representation.

Whither the Progressive Democrats? Their main platform for support appeared to be the influence they exercised over Fianna Fáil in government from 1989 to 1992, but the high standing of the leader in terms of personal integrity was not reflected in any great surge of popular support. As a general election inexorably approached in 1992, commentators felt that Fianna Fáil – if coalition was forced on them again – might well prefer the Labour Party to the detested former members, who are still seen as betrayers of the great Fianna Fáil cause. As it turned out, a quite different coalition emerged, leaving the Progressive Democrats in opposition, contemplating the prospect of cooperation with Fine Gael.

An opinion poll[19] published in May 1992, carried out between 21 and 27 April 1992, gave figures for 1992 (and comparisons with previous polls carried out by the same agency) (see table).

Irish political parties have annual meetings, which provide a meeting-place and discussion forum for members from all of their units. The biggest, naturally, are those of Fianna Fáil and Fine Gael. The Irish word Ard-Fheis is used to describe the big rallies which these gatherings have become. Unlike their counterparts in Britain, the party rallies in Ireland are movable, and are held whenever the party management thinks the time is right. Dublin is the most-favoured venue. The traditional format for the Ard-Fheiseanna of Fine Gael and Fianna Fáil has been a three-day event, held in a conference centre capable of holding several thousand people. Units of the organization send motions for discussion and debate to a committee which attempts to reflect the wishes of the members in the final Clár (programme) of the conference. This procedure presents ample opportunity for manipulation of the programme, particularly if it is a time of internal dissension in the party. Some members think that the Ard-Fheis is the policy-making body of the party: but in reality policy is formed by the leadership, who will use every means to make sure the Ard-Fheis endorses it. The climax of the party conference, big or small, is the address of the leader, televised to the nation, and attended by the expected masses, with the regulation standing ovation. Drink and dancing are an important part of the entertainment on the sidelines. There are signs that the parties, not to mention the public, are becoming tired of the traditional format. Experiments are tried, to escape the formula, and sometimes fail. Fine Gael, already struggling, had a public-relations disaster in 1991 when they employed a well-known comedienne as part of a new kind of televised political programme; she made what were considered tasteless and hurtful comments about an alleged sexual-harassment incident involving a government back-bencher, which caused uproar and red faces all round.

Ireland, a country whose young population has been forcing change at a remarkable pace in recent years, underwent a political metamorphosis in November 1992. The pragmatic Albert Reynolds turned out to be less than skilful in handling difficult issues, and less than careful in his public pronouncements. This culminated in a crisis at the end of October, when he used the word 'dishonest' at a sworn public tribunal to describe the actions of his government colleague and leader of his coalition partners, Des O'Malley of the Progressive Democrats. Understandably, a deeply offended O'Malley asked for an apology and retraction, which was not forthcoming. During a few tense days, the Taoiseach used the word 'crap' on television to describe allegations that he had been continually difficult with O'Malley in Cabinet. Fianna Fáil, having exorcised the ghost of Charles Haughey, and the 'Haughey factor' which had dogged them for so long, now faced an 'Albert factor'. Mr Reynolds stumbled over words in an important radio interview, assuring the country – twice – that his Minister for Social Welfare was attempting to 'dehumanize' the social welfare system.[20] The effect of these mistakes was further slippage in the polls. People were embarrassed: '. . . they may like his bonhomie, but they don't want the Taoiseach swaggering around with his hands in his pockets and misusing fairly simple words.'[21] The Progressive Democrats withdrew from government, a vote of confidence took place, and the expected general election was called for 25 November 1992: a short, sharp campaign.

Polls immediately began to show a fascinating change in traditional voting. The most interesting feature was a move towards Labour, which became more marked with each sounding. Fianna Fáil, clearly blamed for causing the election in the first place, started to lose heavily, as did the personal rating for Mr Reynolds. Voters were not, however, turning to Fine Gael, which struggled with poll ratings in the low 20s. Fianna Fáil support was collapsing in the capital city. The Labour Party overtook Fine Gael in Dublin, while Dick Spring's personal-satisfaction rating, well over 60 per cent in most polls, was double that of Reynolds and Bruton. Two issues which concerned the electorate most were unemployment and the general credibility of ministers. On both of these, Labour scored: in particular they were not blamed for the dole queues approaching 300,000. A head-to-head television debate between the outgoing Taoiseach and the Leader of the Opposition had a slight air of unreality about it, since Dick Spring was not included. It became clear that Fianna Fáil were not only failing in their bid to get an overall majority, but that they were going to be further weakened. And the same looked certain for Fine Gael. Fianna Fáil in desperation launched a bitter attack on Labour in large newspaper advertisements in the closing days of the campaign. 'In the end, it has been the despair of the country's largest and most successful

Parties' Share of Seats Obtained in the Irish General Elections, 1989 and 1992			
Party	1989	1992	Percentage vote
Fianna Fáil	77	68	39·1
Fine Gael	55	45	24·5
Labour	16	33	19·3
Progressive Democrats	6	10	4·7
Democratic Left/ Workers' Party	7	4	2.8
Others	5	6*	9·6

* Includes one Green and the Ceann Comhairle (Seán Treacey), who was automatically returned without election.

party which has been the most astonishing aspect of this election campaign,' said a senior political commentator.[22]

The policy platforms of the main parties played a curiously small part in the election campaign, which was more about perceptions of parties and their leaders than about serious policy discussions. Because unemployment was such a central concern, the parties all put forward ideas on the subject. Fianna Fáil promised to devote the proceeds of rapid privatization and new EC funds (IR£750 million) to embark on large employment-creating initiatives. Tax rates would come down, borrowing would be stabilized at present levels. Fine Gael proposed to guarantee that anyone who took a job would get at least IR£25 per week more than social welfare; they would halve PRSI (Pay-Related Social Insurance) for employers in certain areas; borrowing would be strictly controlled at rates suitable for EC requirements. The Labour Party proposed IR£350 million more borrowing for jobs; no more privatization; better personal allowances in the tax system for the low-paid; and child benefit to be increased to IR£40 per month per child. All these policies were put forward with due solemnity and fanfare by the parties, but since it became clear at an early stage that there would be some kind of coalition, not too much serious attention was paid to them.

When the counting was over (and it took nine days, because several recounts were held in one constituency) Fianna Fáil and Fine Gael were left contemplating electoral disaster. Fianna Fáil had lost heavily, Fine Gael even more heavily, while the Labour Party had surged to become a major force in Irish politics.

It will take another election to establish whether or not there is a genuine realignment in Irish politics. The nature of the Labour vote – strong among the young, urban population, and not confined at all to the working class – shows it may be a volatile vote which has swung wildly in several elections. An interesting feature of the result was the failure of the Labour Party to anticipate the huge swing to them. They ran single candidates in several areas where, with Ireland's multi-seat proportional representation system, they could have obtained two seats. For example, in Dublin South, Eithne FitzGerald* of Labour polled 17,000 first-preference votes (the highest in the country), that could and should have meant two seats if it had been divided between two candidates. Labour, if it is to build on the 1992 success, will have to persuade its Deputies, so accustomed to being sovereign and single in their constituencies, to accept running-mates and the kind of vote-sharing exercise which the larger parties know all about.

The 1992 Labour vote may be a continuation of the Robinson phenomenon of 1990. If so, why did Labour remain so low in the 1991 local elections, and fare badly in opinion polls of early 1992? That will all be clearer next time round. As the Labour Party went in to government with Fianna Fáil in January 1993, having conducted the long (seven weeks) interregnum negotiations with toughness and confidence, they looked like a group that planned to stay, with a leader firmly in control, bringing some previously troublesome Deputies from the slightly militant left into both Cabinet and junior ministerial positions.

Fianna Fáil ceded six Cabinet posts to Labour, as well as five

---

*Eithne FitzGerald (forty-one) was a candidate five times before winning her seat. An economist, she was well known for her strong feminist and left-wing views. The daughter-in-law of former Taoiseach Garret FitzGerald, she was elected Chairwoman of Dublin County Council in 1992. After her impressive election victory, she might have legitimately expected a Cabinet position, but instead was given a key junior ministerial role in the Tánaiste's office and the Department of Finance.

junior ministerial positions, and Albert Reynolds, like Houdini, escaped the wrath of his party – for the moment – and remained as Taoiseach. The Fine Gael Party, the all-round biggest loser, licked its wounds and re-elected its leader in late January, appointing a 'commission' to help to sort out its problems, in opposition once again.

NOTES

1. Charlie McCreevy, quoted in the *Irish Independent*, 14 October 1990. McCreevy was made Minister for Social Welfare in February 1992 by Taoiseach Albert Reynolds. He had spent many years on the back benches because of outspoken differences with the former Fianna Fáil leader, Charles Haughey, principally on economic matters. In January 1993, he became Minister for Transport and Tourism.
2. J. J. Lee, *Ireland 1912–1985, Politics and Society*, Cambridge University Press.
3. R. F. Foster, *Modern Ireland: 1600–1972*, Allen Lane, 1988/Penguin, 1989.
4. Gerald Hogan, 'Church–State relations in Ireland', *The American Journal of Comparative Law*, vol. XXXV, No. 1, winter 1987.
5. Basil Chubb, *The Government and Politics of Ireland*, 2nd edn, Longman, 1982.
6. Stephen Gwynn, writing in the *New York Times*, July 1923, quoted in Maurice Manning, *The Courage to Succeed*, Fine Gael, 1986.
7. Foster, op. cit.
8. ibid.
9. ibid.
10. Lee, op. cit.
11. Foster, op. cit.
12. Garret FitzGerald, *All in a Life*, Gill & Macmillan, 1991.
13. Ray Kavanagh, *Labour from the Beginning*, The Labour Party.
14. Foster, op. cit.
15. In conversation with the author.
16. In conversation with the author, 4 March 1993.
17. *Parliamentary Debates, Dáil Éireann*, 20 February 1985, Col. 285.
18. All figures on membership, branches, etc. supplied by the parties, May 1992. In Fianna Fáil branches are called *cumainn*, the other parties

refer to them as branches. Structures are similar in all the main parties: branches, districts, and constituency executives; an elected national executive works closely with the parliamentary party. The Labour Party has continual upheaval about which is the final deciding body, the parliamentary party or the administrative council, representative of the party as a whole.

19. Lansdowne Market Research, commissioned by the *Sunday Press*, and published on 3 May 1992.
20. On RTE Radio's *This Week* programme.
21. *Sunday Tribune*, 1 January 1993.
22. *Sunday Tribune*, 22 November 1992.

CHAPTER 8

Northern Ireland

Ever-present, even if sometimes only hovering at the back of the mind, but at other times dominating thought and word, the continuing Northern Ireland crisis is a constant reality to every Irish person in the Republic. It is not easily explained: it is a common experience for Irish people, invited to analyse the 'Northern Ireland problem' for bewildered foreigners, to find the discussion descending into a disagreement between the Irish themselves. Perhaps the attempt to explain it here will suffer the same fate. The result of this uneasiness with the subject is, frequently, to try to forget it. In very few opinion polls in the last decade has the Northern Ireland question been high on the people of the Republic's list of concerns. In March 1993, a reporter* returning from three years' work in Northern Ireland for the *Irish Times* wrote about his frustration at the lack of interest he found in the Republic on the whole question: he frequently found that most people just had not bothered to read his piece.

Only when some particularly appalling outrage occurs, or when there is a rare breakthrough in political terms, does the North emerge into everyday conversation. Thus, in 1985, when the Anglo-Irish Agreement† was signed, an otherwise deeply unpopular government of the Republic found itself – very briefly – basking in 59 per cent public approval (29 per cent broadly disapproved, 12 had no opinion).[1] An interesting feature was that 43 per cent of supporters

---

* Mark Brennock.

† Signed at Hillsborough, Co. Down, by Margaret Thatcher and Garret FitzGerald, on 15 November 1985, the Agreement gave the Irish government a small but mould-breaking role in the internal governing of Northern Ireland through an intergovernmental conference co-chaired by Irish and British ministers, served by a permanent secretariat based in Maryfield outside Belfast; it also recognized the principle of consent of the people of Northern Ireland before any constitutional change could come about. It carried the first-ever statement that Britain would legislate accordingly if a majority of the people of Northern Ireland wanted constitutional change.

of the Opposition Fianna Fáil registered their approval. It was not to last for long, however. Pádraig O'Malley[2] had accurately remarked in 1983, 'the most remarkable feature of the last fifteen years has been the lack of popular support in the South for the nationalist cause in the North'. He talked of the people's 'sullen passiveness' in the face of Northern violence, and points out: 'Each time a Government party has tried to make Northern Ireland an election issue the electorate has rejected the attempt, making it clear that the state of the economy in the South concerns it far more than the state of the state in the North.' That remains true today. People are jolted into an anguished reaction to something like the IRA massacre of eleven civilians in Enniskillen in 1987;* hopes rose publicly in 1975–6 with the People's Peace Movement, the Anglo-Irish Agreement, and again in 1991 and 1992, when it looked as if the patience of British Secretaries of State for Northern Ireland might be rewarded in meaningful talks leading to some kind of settlement. There is concern for Irish relations and friends in Britain when the IRA destroys and kills over there; there is shame and anger at the IRA when particularly grotesque events shatter the lives of English people, as in the murder by bombing of two children at Warrington on 20 March 1993, pity and outrage when seven workmen die horribly in a bomb-blast in Co. Tyrone in January 1992, unease and anger at gross miscarriages of British justice – but the long failure of politicians, British, Northern Irish and Southern Irish, and the relentless slaughter by the IRA, compounded by the violence of Loyalist paramilitaries, has caused general weariness, apathy and lack of interest.

In April 1991, only 41 per cent of Irish people considered the question of Northern Ireland to be 'very important', while 78 per cent felt that emigration was very important.[3] Apathy rises and falls with the roller-coaster of events across a border just eighty miles from Dublin. Writing in the *Irish Times* on 15 August 1990, Andy Pollak criticized one form of that apathy: the failure of Irish political leaders to attend the funerals of murdered Protestants, civilian and official, while noting that an Irish Minister (Dr Rory

---

*This resulted in, among others, the death of a young nurse, whose father Gordon Wilson moved the world when he described her dying moments, holding his hand, under the rubble of walls blown down by an IRA bomb-blast.

O'Hanlon) and the Lord Mayor of Dublin attended the funeral of a Catholic nun, one of four people murdered by the IRA outside Armagh the previous month. Remarking that no government representative attended the Enniskillen funeral services in 1987, 'because of fears of a hostile reception', Pollak concludes: 'The dictionary definition of that response is cowardice.' Obviously, advice is given to Irish politicians by the RUC about visits to Northern Ireland at tense times like funerals, but Pollak feels that the potential value of such a gesture to Unionists should outweigh such consistent caution. The absence of such visits is a feature of a general exasperation and weariness among the people about Northern Ireland, the most extreme example of which is the comment, 'it [the North] should be cut off the island and sent out to sea' – echoes of a British attitude almost two hundred years ago when British prime minister Pitt said that Ireland in turmoil was 'like a ship of the line that was on fire: it had to be extinguished or cut adrift'.[4]

A more interesting attitude of an ordinary Republic of Ireland citizen is that overheard in the crowd on its way to an international rugby match at Lansdowne Road in Dublin on 18 January 1992, the day after seven workmen were killed in their minibus at Teebane Cross in Co. Tyrone by the IRA: 'And they want us to be united with that crowd of murderers . . .! They must be joking . . .' However, a sizeable majority of Southern Irish people questioned in surveys over recent years would like to see a united Ireland, but only achieved by peaceful means, with the consent of the Northern people. Most of them expect that to happen only in the very long term. In 1987, 60 per cent saw Irish unity as unlikely ever to happen, or not for at least 100 years, a reflection of depression and disappointment after the violence following the Anglo-Irish Agreement.[5] There was more optimism about in April 1991, when that figure was reduced to 39 per cent. In that same 1991 poll[6] 82 per cent were prepared 'to postpone unity if postponing it helped to bring about an internal settlement in the North'.

The new President of Ireland, following her declaration at her inauguration of interest in reconciliation on the island, set about trying to bridge the gulf in interest and understanding between North and South as she began a series of visits to community groups in Northern Ireland, both in Belfast and Derry. Her reception by those courageous organizations, a great many of them women's groups, who work for quiet reconciliation and peace was one of delight. Extreme Unionists distrust any visit by an Irish head of State, naturally enough, despite her record of conciliatory gestures. The President's handshake with the President of Sinn Féin in Belfast on 18 June 1993 was a milestone in her contacts with all Northern Ireland's communities.

BRIEF HISTORY OF THE MODERN NORTHERN IRELAND CRISIS

In 1968, the tide of social revolt against authoritarianism which was sweeping around the world reached the North of Ireland. Civil rights, a new catchphrase in Ireland, was the demand of an angry movement of educated and embittered Northern Irish Catholics. They were finally – and they intended, peacefully – demanding an end to a political and social system which since the British Government of Ireland Act of 1920 (effectively setting up the Northern Ireland State), the Anglo-Irish Treaty in 1921* and the partition of Ireland had been grossly unjust.

With comprehensive job discrimination against Catholics, gerrymandering of constituencies, gross corruption in the allocation of public housing, continual harassment – and worse – by police and auxiliaries (the infamous 'B-Specials', a force of Protestant civilians set up in support of the police, whose attitude and methods were anything but impartial or peaceful) – the system was described in somewhat restrained terms in the New Ireland Forum report of 1984:† 'The fundamental defects in the resulting [after 1921] political structures and the impact of ensuing policy led to a system in the North of supremacy of the Unionist tradition over the nationalist

---

*The Anglo-Irish Treaty, negotiated between a team of Irish provisional government ministers and Lloyd George's British government, ended the bloody guerrilla-type warfare between the countries which had been waged since 1916. It allowed for the subsequent partitioning of Ireland, and stipulated an Oath of Allegiance to the British King for Irish parliamentarians, establishing an Irish 'Free State' within the British Commonwealth. The President of Ireland's fledgeling Dáil and government, Éamon de Valera, repudiated the treaty and started Ireland's bitter civil war when a majority of the Dáil accepted the treaty.

†The Forum was an initiative by Garret FitzGerald, with the intense encouragement of John Hume of the SDLP, to bring the political parties on the island together for formal discussions on the realities of the Northern Ireland issue, as a prelude to pressing for discussions with the British government. It met first in 1983, and reported in May 1984. It was ignored by Unionists in Northern Ireland.

tradition. From the beginning, both sections of the community were locked into a system based on sectarian loyalties.'[7] Conor Cruise O'Brien,* emphatically not a 'republican' writer, is in no doubt: 'The great losers by the settlement of 1921 were undoubtedly the Catholics of Northern Ireland'[8] and 'what developed in Northern Ireland from 1921 to 1969 was an institutionalized caste system'. Nearly fifty years later, as the 1970s approached, a combination of furious overreaction by the Northern authorities and the mostly Protestant police and special constabulary to the civil-rights demonstrations and the ensuing state of siege of sections of the Catholic community led to the emergence of the new, well-armed and funded IRA and the arrival of the British Army. The British people watched in disbelief, as they saw Belfast burning under their eyes on their television screens, while the British political establishment was stunned at the mess at their own back door. So began the modern chapter of ruthless terrorism, sectarian tit-for-tat violence, crass wrongdoing and often disastrous mistakes by the British, and fierce resistance by the Ulster Unionists to almost all pleas for discussions or agreement on a possible new way of governing the province. Roy Foster describes the events after 1968 and the catastrophic slide into disaster: '. . . by 1972, then, half a century of the Protestant supremacist state had come to a bloody and chaotic end.'[9] It was in January 1972 that the British Army shot and killed thirteen civilians in Derry, writing another disaster into Anglo-Irish history. 'Bloody Sunday', as it is called, was commemorated twenty years later in 1992 with bitterness and anger: Bishop Edward Daly, a priest at the time, and present at the massacre, who is still furious at the Widgery Tribunal report which exonerated the Army, reflects also that one of the effects of this catastrophe was immediate and widespread recruitment into the IRA.[10]

And today, in the last decade of the century, fear and hate which have their origins in the historical mist of battles for land and souls between the native Irish in Northern Ireland, the British Crown, and the imported Scottish Presbyterian and English Protestant

* Conor Cruise O'Brien (b. 1917) is a former senior civil servant in the Department of Foreign Affairs; United Nations Representative in Katanga, 1962–5; Minister for Posts and Telegraphs, 1973–7; Pro-Chancellor, Dublin University (Trinity College); and a noted international historian, scholar, writer and newspaper columnist both in Ireland and abroad.

landlords and smallholders of several centuries ago, still dominate in Northern Ireland. The New Ireland Forum report in 1984 pointed out the staggering costs to the Irish economy of this new phase of Northern trouble since 1969, taking into account tourism losses, industrial investment forgone, extra security costs, costs of duplication of infrastructure (in energy, transport, agriculture) – and arrived at a figure of IR£6·6 billion (in 1982 money values). In January 1992, the Irish Minister for Justice said 'the additional security costs for the Republic in 1991 arising from the Northern troubles would be in the order of £180 million'.[11] Given the stranglehold which the crisis has exercised on an already weak economy, coupled with the tide of human suffering in Northern Ireland witnessed since 1969,* it is a measure of the depth and intractability of the problem that the people of the Republic of Ireland metaphorically turn their back on it most of the time. A notable exception is the President of Ireland, who has set about making reconciliation and cross-border contacts one of the central themes of her term of office.

IRISH POLITICS AND THE NORTHERN QUESTION TODAY

In his New Year's statement of 2 January 1992, the Leader of the main Opposition party in Dáil Éireann, John Bruton of Fine Gael, called for 'changes in Articles 2 and 3 of the Irish Constitution,† in order to get talks really moving with Unionists and all the constitutional non-Unionist parties on the island of Ireland'. He affirmed that this would be 'his personal priority' for 1992.[12] This symbolizes the principal difference between the two main parties in

---

*On 3 February 1992, in a written answer in the House of Commons, London, the following figures were given by British Minister Brian Mawhinney: 3,200 lives lost in Ireland, Britain and Europe as a result of Northern Ireland troubles since 1968, 2,969 of them in Northern Ireland. That figure passed the 3,000 mark later in 1992.

†Article 2: 'The national territory consists of the whole island of Ireland, its islands, and the territorial seas.'

Article 3: 'Pending the re-integration of the national territory, and without prejudice to the right of the Parliament and Government established by this Constitution to exercise jurisdiction over the whole of that territory, the laws enacted by that Parliament shall have the like area and application as the laws of Saorstát Éireann and the like extra-territorial effect.'

Irish politics on the Northern question. Fianna Fáil have traditionally been more 'republican' than any other party, but have shown
themselves to be pragmatic and realistic when in power: after an
initial condemning of the Anglo-Irish Agreement when he was
leader of the Opposition in 1985, Mr Charles Haughey found it
possible to take the Agreement on board on achieving government
in 1987; he then assiduously preserved it as the main tool of
government policy on Northern Ireland. A lessening of the
constitutional claim to the whole territory of Ireland would only be
contemplated by Fianna Fáil if there were very major concessions
on offer by the British and the Unionists. The position of the
successor to Mr Haughey as Taoiseach and leader of Fianna Fáil,
Albert Reynolds, is pragmatic and reiterates the position as being
open and constructive; he threw another element into the bargaining
when he said that Articles 2 and 3 couldn't be discussed unless the
Government of Ireland Act 1920 was up for discussion too. In April
1993, Bruton accused the Taoiseach of 'putting internal Fianna Fáil
considerations ahead of the national interest'. He gave the view
that 'the people of the South would agree to any settlement reached
between the two communities in Northern Ireland. In the light of
this, we should not be in the business of putting down claims over
and above the heads of the people who live in Northern Ireland.'[13]

There is generally a careful consensus among the political parties
of the Republic on the main features of Northern Ireland policy.
Distrust, disagreement, or difference in emphasis have occurred
over the years, but the extent and ferocity of the violence has
welded a solid central repugnance for this kind of coercion. Fianna
Fáil's policy is not quite as limited or pragmatic as described by
Garret FitzGerald in his autobiography: 'Fianna Fáil had always
conceived itself as having the particular role in Irish politics of
voicing the aspirations of traditional Irish nationalism in such a
way as to attract away from the IRA and to constitutional politics
as large a proportion of "republican" opinion as possible.'[14] While
Fianna Fáil certainly attracts the support of more nationalistic-
minded people than Fine Gael, the core republicanism of the party,
and its origins in the civil war in Ireland in the 1920s when it took
the anti-treaty side, are values in themselves and not a façade to
attract a particular kind of voter. Mr Haughey, so long a dominant
figure in Fianna Fáil, could always be described as a conviction

politician when it came to the North; it led to his temporary political eclipse between 1970 and 1977 after his alleged involvement in a controversy about sending arms to the IRA in the midst of the mayhem of the outbreak of violence in 1969–70.

⌊Fine Gael, on the other side in the treaty war, has evolved a policy more concerned to understand Unionist fears, more condemnatory of violence. This came to its apogee in the Anglo-Irish Agreement, which reflected the deep concern of Garret FitzGerald to enshrine in an international agreement an undertaking that no constitutional change would come about without majority consent in Northern Ireland. This did not impress the Ulster Unionists, who mounted a fierce and unrelenting campaign against the Agreement. An example of the range of Irish opinion on all things pertaining to Northern Ireland is the resignation of the then Trinity* Senator Mary Robinson from the Labour Party (one of the partners in the FitzGerald coalition) because she felt that the Unionist position had not been sufficiently considered.

After going into Opposition in 1987, Fine Gael saw Fianna Fáil not only accept the Anglo-Irish Agreement but frequently extol its virtues as being an extremely useful tool in that it undertakes, with the British government, talks with all constitutional parties on the island. Fine Gael watches carefully the attitude of Fianna Fáil on matters such as extradition of wanted IRA people to Britain, which has been complicated by the revelations of gross miscarriages of justice in Britain. The Birmingham Six, the Guildford Four † – these and other cases seriously damage the efforts of British and Irish governments to work together against the IRA (whose culpability in allowing innocent people to suffer so long for the crimes they committed themselves has got lost in the welter of outrage against the perversion of British justice). In 1993, John Bruton urged the government to adopt a more conciliatory approach towards Unionism in Northern Ireland, and to move away from any rigid position

---

*She represented the graduates of Dublin University (Trinity College) in the Irish Senate.

†Both cases of convictions of Irish people for bombing offences in Britain committed in the 1970s. Having served long sentences in British gaols, the ten people were exonerated and set free when the British courts finally accepted evidence that the convictions were unsafe, with implications for corruption among the police. These were only two instances of miscarriages of justice.

which might give Unionists good reason to refuse to engage in any real dialogue on the future of the province.

The Labour Party, with an old and honoured tradition of national-ism from James Connolly, one of the executed leaders of the 1916 Rising, follows a centrist Northern Ireland policy. Its leader, Dick Spring, was part of the government which signed, in 1985, the Anglo-Irish Agreement with Margaret Thatcher's British govern-ment. In the new government of 1993, Spring took the post of Minister for Foreign Affairs as well as being Tánaiste, and was given responsibility for Northern Ireland, an interesting new develop-ment, since that area was usually reserved for the Taoiseach of the day. In his new role, he became the person to deal with the British Secretary for the North. He made an important speech on 5 March in Dublin, signalling a softer, more conciliatory line towards Northern Ireland, and said he had never considered that Articles 2 and 3 were 'cast in bronze'. Neither did he consider that the Constitution of the Republic of Ireland should be '. . . an obstacle to mutual understanding on this island'.[15] A few days later, Sir Patrick Mayhew pronounced himself 'heartened' by his contacts with Mr Spring.

The Workers' Party (with 4.9 per cent of the 1989 vote) was very vociferous in its condemnation of the IRA: since its origins stem from the splinter group (the 'Officials') which broke away from the IRA in the early 1970s, it has felt the need to protest greatly at the actions of the old republican enemy. It began life in constitutional politics as 'Sinn Féin the Workers' Party'. In 1982 the Sinn Féin prefix was dropped. In 1992, the party was still struggling with the differing ideologies of its North and South branches and faced a breakup.* Most of its members left and formed a new party, the Democratic Left, which continued to condemn IRA atrocities and urge reconciliation and dialogue.

The Northern Irish politician with whom people of the Republic most easily identify is John Hume.† One of the instigators of the ill-

---

* See pages 172–4.

† John Hume MP (for Derry), MEP (b. 1937). Leader of his party, of which he was a founder member, since 1979. Has made attempts to persuade the IRA to stop their campaign, sometimes incurring the suspicion of both Irish and British governments. He has travelled widely in the USA both to attract investment to Northern Ireland and to keep Irish-American opinion on his side. Recognized as a

fated but significant civil rights movement in 1968, this dogged and articulate former teacher from Derry* has dominated Nationalist politics in Northern Ireland since those stormy years. With a degree of personal courage, and a huge amount of perseverance, he explores, with his party (the Social Democratic and Labour Party), every possible avenue of hope for a peaceful solution, all the time being threatened by the political support in Northern Ireland for Sinn Féin. He seeks 'agreement on how we share the island, an agreement between the Unionists and the rest of the people of Ireland, with whatever ensuing constitutional changes North and South that would entail.'[16] A referendum, North and South, on the agreed proposals is an essential part of his programme. In spring 1993, he alarmed many of his admirers by embarking on a series of meetings with the president of Sinn Féin, Gerry Adams, arranged initially by some priests. It was only two years before that he had dismissed the idea of involving Sinn Féin in talks: 'You can't expect anyone to sit around a table with somebody who reserves the right to pull a gun if he doesn't get his own way.'[17]

The Irish government, and many other commentators, hoped that John Hume, an experienced man in the ways of Northern Ireland, knew what he was doing as he involved himself in these talks, during the run-up to the May 1993 local elections. An Irish government spokesperson was cautious: 'The Government as a general principle approves of approaches by clergymen and other morally concerned individuals to paramilitaries or people who might have influence with them to try and persuade them of the futility of violence.'[18] Hume works closely with whatever Irish government is in power: and treads the difficult path between the fiercer nationalism of his deputy leader, Séamus Mallon, and his own more pragmatic approach. During the negotiations towards the Anglo-Irish Agreement in the 1980s, ministers of the Irish government were acutely aware of the importance of their relationship with John Hume, and his party: an importance reflected in the account by

---

brilliant, articulate and courageous leader of constitutional nationalism in Northern Ireland.

*Derry is known as Londonderry to Unionists and the British, and is referred to as such in, for example, BBC news programmes. To citizens of the Republic of Ireland, as well as Northern Nationalists, it is always known as Derry.

Garret FitzGerald of an emotional dinner-party with the SDLP leadership just before the signing of the Anglo-Irish Agreement in November 1985, where the relief of the then Taoiseach at the acceptance by the SDLP of the full Agreement was palpable.[19]

Sinn Féin, the political party which supports the concept of 'armed struggle' against the British 'occupying forces' is personified for people in the Republic of Ireland by its intensely articulate Belfast President, Gerry Adams. His defeat – after a bitter struggle – in the general election in Northern Ireland of April 1992 by Dr Joe Hendron of the SDLP was generally hailed as a victory for constitutional nationalism over the supporters of violence. He is a native of Belfast, and was a barman there when he became involved in violence during the outbreak of trouble in 1969. Interned and gaoled several times, Adams cannot be seen or heard on Irish television and radio because of legislation in the Republic banning Sinn Féin from the air waves (legislation confirmed by the Irish Supreme Court in 1982 as not only being constitutional, but imperative as part of the duty of government to defend the state).* Dublin Corporation voted in December 1991 to refuse Sinn Féin the use of the Lord Mayor's Mansion House for their annual conference – an event and venue which had been an irritant for many Dubliners for a long time.

Gerry Adams said in 1990, when asked about the killing policy of the IRA, 'I believe that the IRA is morally justified in doing this, and I believe I am morally justified in supporting their right to do it.'[20] He told his party's Ard-Fheis in January 1989 that accidental killings of civilians by the IRA must stop because they 'retarded' the Republican struggle. He then went on to support the IRA campaign generally. The electorate in the Republic of Ireland rejects that thinking (making no distinction, unlike Sinn Féin, between 'legitimate targets' – police and soldiers – and 'innocent civilians') and regularly rejects Sinn Féin at the polling booth, where its vote consistently hovers below 2 per cent. In tables of election results in the Republic of Ireland, Sinn Féin is usually found buried among 'others' – a disparate group of independent, sometimes single-issue candidates whose total vote in Irish general elections has not reached 7 per cent since 1973.[21] This has been the case

---

* But see Chapter 14 ('The Media in Ireland') for 1992 developments.

Results since 1983 of General Elections in Northern Ireland (%)					
Year	OUP	DUP	SDLP	SF	Alliance
1983	34·0	20·0	17·9	13·4	8·0
1987	37·8	11·7	21·1	11·4	10·0
1992	34·5	13·1	23·5	10·0	8·7

OUP = 'Official' Unionist Party (slightly moderate Unionists).
DUP = Democratic Unionist Party (extreme Unionist/Loyalist).
SDLP = Social Democratic and Labour Party (moderate Nationalist).
SF = Sinn Féin (extreme Nationalist, with IRA links).
Alliance = moderate Unionist/centrist party.

despite the party's efforts to establish itself as more than a single-issue group, involving itself in working for its poorer constituents in local-authority fields such as housing and social welfare. In the Republic's local elections in June 1991, Sinn Féin saw its vote sink to 1·7 per cent; it gained only 7 seats compared, for example, with the Workers' Party's 24 and the Green Party's 13.

On the other side of the border with Northern Ireland, Sinn Féin's vote is, by contrast, a major factor, though it suffered a severe blow in the April 1992 general election, losing its only Member of Parliament, and seeing its vote descend to barely 10 per cent.

The debate within the Republic on Northern Ireland takes many forms. Sinn Féin argues within itself about how much the IRA connection is damaging it, and as new waves of violence gathered ferocity from 1991, there was more and more speculation on a possible split in the ranks of the 'Movement', as increasing mention was made of the prospect of joining in official talks if the campaign of violence stopped. Far from stopping, however, a series of bombs and murders in Northern Ireland, and a wave of smaller blasts in the London area in late 1992 and early 1993, claimed as their handiwork by the IRA, hardened political attitudes towards Sinn Féin. Churchmen embarked on a series of semi-secret talks with Sinn Féin, apparently to no avail. The breakthrough of the Hume/Adams talks came, therefore, as a sign that perhaps all was not lost.

Gerry Adams made a statement of Sinn Féin policy in May 1993, following his talks with John Hume. In an article in the *Irish Times* on 3 May, he studiously avoided any reference to the IRA, the bombs, and the murders. In curiously soft language, he spoke of forgiveness, of 'embracing each other as neighbours'. A significant statement of policy aims is worth quoting: 'What is needed is a strategy for change and peace. This means London adopting a policy aimed at ending partition and which seeks, with Dublin, to achieve this in the shortest possible time consistent with obtaining maximum consent to the process, minimizing costs of every kind, and recognizing the centrality of inclusive dialogue in this process.' This insistence on a unified Ireland as the only possible solution did not bring matters much further, in most people's eyes. But John Hume in discussions with Adams had restated his own and his party's position that the Irish people had a right to national self-determination: as the only politicians with links simultaneously to the Unionists (through the ongoing, if tortuous talks process), the Irish government, the British government, and – through Adams – to the Provisional IRA, he was in a unique position to tease out how far everyone could go in the search for, and indeed the definition of, 'self-determination'.

The intense discomfort of the people of the Republic of Ireland with the IRA and with violence manifested itself in a minimalist commemoration of the seventy-fifth anniversary of the 1916 Rising against the British rule of Ireland on Easter Sunday 1991: the brief ceremony with Taoiseach and President at the General Post Office (where the patriot rebels centred their efforts) was an expression of the fear that more elaborate celebrations might give an impression of support for armed violence and the IRA. Such thinking was heavily criticized by a group of radical academic and literary figures as showing both cowardice and confusion about Ireland's modern identity. Referring to the ceremony, historian Máirín Ní Dhonnchadha and poet Theo Dorgan remark: 'There are those of us who feel that, as a reaction, amnesia – private or communal – is both unhealthy and dangerous.'[22]

But all Southern Irish politicians must tread carefully in dealing with Northern Ireland. The massive efforts of British Secretary for Northern Ireland Peter Brooke in 1990 to bring all the Northern political parties together were watched anxiously, the Dublin government playing a constructive sidelines role. After the British general election in the spring of 1992, a new team was appointed to the Northern Ireland office by Prime Minister John Major. Headed, as Secretary, by a former Attorney-General, Sir Patrick Mayhew,* it included Michael Mates MP† – both appointments considered slightly provocative in that both men had been considered hard-liners on Northern Ireland.

In 1984, Garret FitzGerald as Taoiseach suffered a humiliating public rebuff from Margaret Thatcher in a summary 'out, out, out!' dismissal of the conclusions of the New Ireland Forum (one of the many British mistakes in this modern chapter of Irish history), but he showed remarkable calm and astuteness in resisting the pressure put on him to engage in a war of words with the British prime minister, and a year later signed the historic Anglo-Irish agreement with her. Peter Brooke (quintessentially a polite English gentleman of the old school, though with Irish ancestry) showed the same kind of patient forbearance, often sorely tested by Unionist vilifica-tion, dramatically seen when he reluctantly but foolishly agreed to sing two verses of an old song on Ireland's most popular television chat show a couple of hours after the Teebane Cross massacre by the IRA in January 1992. A measure of how much Mr Brooke had gained the sympathy and trust of most Irish people was the immedi-ate public reaction in the South, which contained more anger against the host of the show, Mr Gay Byrne,‡ than against Mr Brooke: there was relief when the British prime minister rejected Mr Brooke's resignation offer, and satisfaction when Gay Byrne apologized for having pressed Mr Brooke so hard to sing. But a weakened Brooke had to preside over the obsequies of his talks initiative on 27 January 1992 in London: the impending general

---

*Sir Patrick Mayhew (b. 1930). British Attorney-General since 1987, during a period when many tensions arose between the British and Irish governments on extradition of IRA suspects. He is considered, however, as a skilled, urbane, and clever man, and has Irish connections on his mother's side. *The Economist* magazine described him in July 1992 as '. . . a toff with Anglo-Irish connec-tions'.

†Michael Mates MP (b. 1935), who served for twenty years in the British Army (including a period served in Northern Ireland), was described as a sort of 'Colonel Blimp' by many when he was appointed. He is MP for East Hampshire, was chairman of the Select Committee on Defence, and co-chairman of the Anglo--Irish All-Party Parliamentary Committee at Westminster. He resigned in 1993.

‡See pages 349–52.

election in Britain and the consequent heightening of tension and distrust finally put paid to that stage of his effort. The meeting and the agreed statement afterwards were, however, encouragingly low-key and positive. But suspicions were surfacing that the Conservative Party in Britain was contemplating a possible 'arrangement' of some kind with the Northern Ireland Unionist MPs in the event of a hung parliament after the 1992 election; in the absence of convincing denials by Brooke or John Major, it was not surprising that the talks were getting nowhere. In the event, John Major needed no help from the Unionists at Westminster after the election of April 1992.

The dogged perseverance of the British government, taking Northern Ireland and its problems with great seriousness, was seen again in the resumption of talks in April 1992. All of the parties in Northern Ireland (with the exception of Sinn Féin, with whom no one at present wants to sit down), plus the Irish and British governments, took up the process again. A senior Irish government minister, deputy prime minister (Tánaiste) John Wilson, was sober about the challenges in the months ahead, when he spoke in July 1992 of the dangers of failure: 'Because [the meetings] are an almost unprecedented opportunity, failure would give rise to a correspondingly deep sense of despondency ... no one needs any reminder of the evils that flow from political despair in relation to Northern Ireland.'[23]

An outside chairman, Sir Ninian Stephen,* who is a former Governor-General of Australia, was eventually accepted by all sides. Delicate and tortuous steps, involving various parallel strands, saw history being made as Northern Unionists were seen officially in Dublin in September 1992 talking about Ireland with Irish government ministers for the first time. In the search for some kind of agreed formula for the future government of Northern Ireland, meetings took place in Dublin, London and Northern Ireland, with occasional outbursts of suspicion, accusation of leaks, and threats of withdrawal – mainly emanating from the Democratic Unionist

* Sir Ninian Stephen (b. 1923 in England) went to Australia at seventeen. A barrister and solicitor, he became a judge in 1970. He accepted the governor-generalship in 1982, in which post he distinguished himself as skilful and caring. He was approached by the Irish Ambassador to Australia and the British Deputy High Commissioner in 1991 and immediately accepted the chairmanship.

representative and leader, the Reverend Ian Paisley.* For the Democratic Unionists, however, it was simply too much to talk in Dublin, so they stayed away from the Dublin meeting of 21 September 1992, refusing to accompany their mainstream Unionist colleagues on that visit.

Hopes of any dramatic breakthrough in 1992 were gradually dampened, as thoughts centred on the possibility of 'heads of agreement' – no matter how vague – being drawn up before Christmas 1992. It was hoped that all parties could be persuaded to put their names to some sort of document, entitled 'elements of agreement', so that the next phase, whenever it took place, would at least have an agreed starting-point. The talks were tedious, occasionally tendentious, but astonishing in that they were taking place at all. As winter approached, however, it was clear that little if any progress had been made, despite trojan work by Sir Ninian and a very large investment of time and energy by the Dublin government, as well as the other participants. Ministers travelled to Belfast and to London constantly. The 16th of November loomed close – the date upon which a much-postponed meeting under the Anglo-Irish Agreement format was due to be held. And then the Irish government fell, at the wrong moment, and the Dáil was dissolved on 5 November. Ministers and politicians continued for the next few days to try to tidy up the talks and at least put a respectable gloss on the outcome, but the last talks session was held on 10 November 1992 in Belfast with only the publication of a joint statement showing interest in further talking to show for eight months' work. The depth of the problems facing the parties was demonstrated by recriminations about whose fault the impasse was, and even by different interpretations among Nationalists of what the talks were about. The Irish Minister for Foreign Affairs

---

*Ian Paisley MP MEP (b. 1926). Son of a Baptist Minister. Founder of a Free Presbyterian Church. Since 1963, he has been protesting vigorously against any kind of gesture to Catholics or Nationalists by Britain or Northern Ireland officialdom. In 1971 he set up the Democratic Unionist Party to replace, he hoped, the already existing Unionist Party. His larger-than-life personality, loud hectoring manner and occasional association with semi-military Loyalist groups have made him a feared figure. He has been a huge vote-getter both in Westminster elections and elections to the European Parliament, where he has worked with the nationalist MEP John Hume in the interests of Northern Ireland.

Percentage of First Preference Votes Obtained by Each Party in Northern Ireland in Local Elections, 1989 and 1993

Year	UUP	DUP	SDLP	SF	Alliance
1989	30·4	17·7	21·2	11·3	6·8
1993	29·0	17·2	21·9	12·5	7·7

UUP = Ulster Unionist Party   SDLP = Social Democratic and Labour Party
DUP = Democratic Unionist Party SF = Sinn Féin

declared in the Dáil that they had been about 'peace and reconciliation, about sidelining the gangster and the gunman'.[24] Séamus Mallon, at the SDLP's annual conference on 7–8 November, said they were about 'confronting the failure of partition'[25] and John Hume said at the same conference that they were about 'agreed realities' and 'a better understanding of our differences'.[26] The Joint Statement of 10 November, signed by all the participants, at least accepted that the dialogue had been valuable, and that further dialogue was both necessary and desirable. Sir Patrick Mayhew said that talking must resume as soon as possible. It was generally felt that the stumbling-block to any kind of agreed statement was the position taken by the Irish government and the Unionists on Articles 2 and 3 of the Republic's Constitution, claiming jurisdiction over Northern Ireland. As the Republic's new government took office in early 1993, it was felt that yet again an election would hold up progress towards dialogue: local elections in Northern Ireland, held in May 1993, are not the gentle exercises in democracy enjoyed by most peaceful democracies. Politicians in Northern Ireland, Britain and the Republic of Ireland are acutely aware that statements by any leaders can and will influence the degree of support within and between the tense factions in Northern Ireland as they try to exercise their votes against a background of armed threats and intimidation by paramilitaries on both sides. Twenty million pounds' worth of damage was done by four massive IRA bombs in Northern Ireland in the week leading up to the local elections. And the result was largely a restatement of the status quo, with a slight shift to the Nationalists (perhaps reflecting population changes since 1989) and a slight increase for Sinn Féin (for the first time in ten years), counterbalanced somewhat by a small increase for the moderate Alliance party.

Church leaders of the main religions are unequivocal in their joint condemnations of violence, and their unanimous urging of politicians to persevere with real talks. Again, a difference of emphasis emerges. Cardinal Daly suggested in his first words of 1992 (a measure of his hands-on experience of the situation on the ground in Northern Ireland): 'If the campaign of violence is called off, I believe that there is a clear responsibility on the Irish and British governments to find some means whereby the Sinn Féin tradition of republicanism can be fully represented at the conference table.'[27] The Protestant Archbishop, Dr Robin Eames, hurried to explain that there would need to be a considerable time-lapse after a cease-fire before any such trust could be established.[28] Ian Paisley, the personification of Ulster loyalism, in reply to the Cardinal's statement, retorted: 'Such a suggestion only fuels unionist belief that the Cardinal is the IRA's chaplain.'[29] The Archbishop of Tuam, Dr Cassidy, suggested that the time was approaching when excommunication of the IRA might have to be considered: though he soberly remarked that it probably wouldn't make any difference.[30] Churchmen like Bishop Edward Daly, of Derry, and Fr Denis Faul have played an essential role of keeping in touch with all sections of their Catholic flock, while speaking out against both paramilitary violence, and the security forces, if they deem the police or Army to have acted badly. It is a delicate balance: the late Cardinal Tomás Ó Fiach was believed by Garret FitzGerald's government to have erred on the side of republicanism. (In her Cabinet diaries for 1984, the author noted his 'extolling Sinn Féin's work for housing and refusing to denounce them or membership of the party. His silence speaks volumes.')[31] The leaders of four churches in Northern Ireland – Church of Ireland, Catholic, Presbyterian and Methodist – have made a point of travelling together to the United States to speak jointly to Irish Americans on the need for reconciliation and peace.

WHO ARE THE UNIONISTS?

In short, the Unionist tradition springs from the descendants of Scottish, English and Welsh settlers in Northern Ireland, 'planted' by the British since the sixteenth century in their troublesome neighbouring island. Huge estates of the continually defiant native

Irish nobility were dismembered and distributed, with more intensity after the 'Flight of the Earls' in 1607, when the owners had to flee to Catholic Europe. Religion, not race, separated the Scots and Welsh from the native Irish. Natural and inevitable barriers arose between colonizer and colonized, with enforced dispossession and social and economic apartheid adding to the religious divide. Wave upon wave of immigration from Scotland, England and Wales followed, particularly after the Protestant Williamite victory at the Battle of the Boyne in 1690. And gradually all these groups became Irish, with a mixture of religions and even some strong believers in a united Ireland, although a noted anti-Catholic bias was evident among a great many of them. A majority of the descendants of Scottish settlers in Ulster see no contradiction in being both Irish and British. 'They would consider themselves to have created a good, fertile, and prosperous land out of what was barren and primitive' – writer Finlay Holmes considers this a myth, but with elements of truth, just like 'the alternative Irish myth, which portrays the Scots as greedy robbers of Irish land'.[32]

Unionism can be divided into two strands today: Ulster Loyalism, and Ulster British. The definition of Ulster Loyalism? 'It approximates a closed system, resisting refutation by experience or argument. In its deep structure it derives its intelligibility and power from the evangelical fundamentalist religious tradition. Its core assumption is that the only alternative to Ulster Loyalist dominance is Ulster Loyalist defeat and humiliation.'[33] Its most well-known, vocal and extreme exponent is the Reverend Ian Paisley. In its violent manifestation it encompasses the Ulster Defence Association, the Ulster Freedom Fighters and, from time to time, other groups. The Orange Order (the Loyal Orange Institution) includes members from both of the Unionist strands, and celebrates on 12 July every year, with frequently good-humoured pageant with fife and drum, but occasionally triumphalist marches in sensitive areas, the victory of King William over Catholic King James at the Battle of the Boyne in 1690. To observe some of the celebrations on that day, an outsider would be forgiven for imagining that the famous battle had happened last year rather than 300 years ago.

On the other hand, Ulster British ideology, with its political expression in the mainstream 'Official' Ulster Unionist Party, is not so easily defined, but can be described as strongly British in orientation, not primarily bound up with religion. The traditional nationalist opposition to British rule is thus seen by Unionists as incompatible with the survival of their own sense of identity. But, as the Forum report pointed out in 1984, they generally also regard themselves as being Irish, even if this does not include a willingness to live under all-Ireland political institutions. Moreover, said the report, the Unionists 'have a widespread perception that the Roman Catholic Church exerts or seeks to exert undue influence in the civil and legal organization of society [in the Republic] which Protestants consider to be a matter of private conscience'. They would see themselves as liberal and progressive, open-minded and essentially fair. An articulate spokesman in recent years has been barrister Robert McCartney: he believes that 'the true and essential Union is not an exclusive Union of loyalists or Protestants, but a Union between people who believe in liberal democracy and civil and religious liberty for all in the fullest sense of a pluralist society'.[34] If these admirable sentiments, as well as the doughty hardiness and undoubted work ethic of the Ulster Protestant, had been available to the whole island of Ireland, instead of being isolated in Ulster after the Treaty of 1921, there might have been a better and more balanced society on both sides of the border: but the gradual division and build-up of distrust deprived both societies of a healthy leavening of differing views and attitudes. In other sections of this book, the effects of that division on the society of the Republic of Ireland will be clear.

One of the deepest fears of Ulster Unionism centres on the growing size of the Catholic population: in the 1991 census, 38.4 per cent of the population of Northern Ireland was Catholic (605,639). Membership of the three largest Protestant churches together (Presbyterian, Church of Ireland, and Methodist) is 42.8 per cent. Other denominations, including Ian Paisley's Free Presbyterian Church (with 12,363 members), amount to a further 7.8 per cent.

THE VIEW FROM THE REPUBLIC

Media coverage in the Republic is almost totally condemnatory of violence and supportive of peace initiatives. Dr Conor Cruise O'Brien writes passionately, frequently, and consistently of his hatred of the IRA, his distrust and dislike of Fianna Fáil (and its former leader Mr Charles J. Haughey in particular) and his belief that the British government for several years has been hatching a plot to get out of Ireland with the minimum of international opprobrium. 'The waters surrounding the Brooke talks may be deeper and murkier than Gerry Collins* may suspect. I suspect that Mr Brooke, in concert with certain senior officials in London, mostly in the Foreign Office, is patiently preparing the way for an eventual British declaration that unless the Unionists, by a given date, accept policies laid down by Her Majesty's Government with the approval of her Parliament, Northern Ireland will cease, by a named date, to be part of the United Kingdom.'[35] O'Brien's is the doomsday scenario of British withdrawal and ensuing full-scale civil war in Ireland.

When further violence erupted in England and Northern Ireland in March 1993, O'Brien once again urged internment without trial as an essential safeguard of peace. A widely reported remark of Mr Brooke's in the House of Commons, not long after Mr John Major's accession to power, certainly gave rise to a deal of speculation in Ireland, North and South: 'The British Government has no selfish strategic or economic interest in Northern Ireland' (9 November 1990).

Historian and writer Ronan Fanning seems to share some of that suspicion: 'The relentless pursuit of Britain's national interest – not any intrinsic concern for Irish or for the harmony of Anglo-Irish relations – has always characterized the Irish policy of the British Government.'[36] He goes on to illustrate the concern of the British continually to impress the Americans, above all, with the correctness of their approach on Northern Ireland. '... and it was to the United States that Peter Brooke hastened with the news that his initiative had culminated in the talks which have now begun'[37] – those talks which looked promising in May 1991, which were aborted after a long summer of fruitless hair-splitting, and further destabilized in the pre-election atmosphere in Britain and Northern Ireland of the winter of 1991/2, revived and revitalized from March 1992, and halted again after November 1992.

*Minister for Foreign Affairs, 1987–92, co-chairman with Peter Brooke of the intergovernmental conference under the Anglo-Irish Agreement. He was succeeded by David Andrews, appointed by Taoiseach Albert Reynolds in February 1992.

An example of the kind of anger expressed in the mass media on the subject of the violence done in the name of ordinary Irish people is given by Frank Byrne, writing in the *Sunday Independent*. Describing the murder of Constable Louis Robinson, who was abducted while on holiday in Dingle, Co. Kerry, in the Republic, in August 1990, Byrne invites his readers: 'Follow me now to the execution. I want you to be there to see the spurting of blood, the splintering of bone. Steel yourself for the last plaintive cries. I want you to be there because it was done in your name. You have a moral right to witness.'

Mary Holland, writing in both the London *Observer* and the *Irish Times*, has been one of the most perceptive analysts of the Northern tragedy. She wrote with intense feeling about the murder of two British soldiers by an uncontrolled mob in Belfast in 1988; and, later, about the attributes of Peter Brooke. She found him to be different from the usual British minister in Ireland, as he was characterized by an encyclopedic knowledge of, and sympathy for, Irish people of both traditions who were trapped in the coils of history. As the 1992 marathon of talks on Northern Ireland closed in November 1992, and the Irish Republic became enmeshed in an unwanted general-election campaign, she deplored the low priority given to Northern Ireland matters during that campaign. She reminded readers of the *Irish Times* of the unfashionable truth that a large part of the roots of violence in Northern Ireland 'lie in the way that this State abandoned the nationalist minority in the North . . . it was the sense of isolation experienced by Northern Catholics, the discrimination that was practised against them, which led first to the civil rights movement and later to the violence of the IRA'.[38]

With the even-handed view that she has become respected for, she deplored the failure of the Taoiseach to respond to the 'historic resonances' of a big ecumenical occasion in May 1993: the unveiling of a memorial to Erskine Childers, the second Church of Ireland President of Ireland. Noting that the Protestant community of Northern Ireland has been suffering 'a corrosive feeling of near-despair' she criticized the lack of generosity of the Irish Taoiseach, speaking in the magnificent St Patrick's Cathedral, a powerful symbol of the divided history of Ireland, in confining himself to the consideration only of the Childers contribution: 'What was missing was any sense that this was an occasion of contemporary significance, and one which Mr Reynolds could have used to reach out to the broader Protestant community at a time when many of its members feel a profound sense of uncertainty and fear about their future.'[39]

Northern Ireland sickens, wearies, worries and alienates the population of the Republic of Ireland. Their exasperation and bafflement at the obduracy of the Unionists is matched by their anger and shame at the deeds of the IRA, carried out in the name of 'a united Ireland'. That anger and shame was seen again in March 1993 when spontaneous demonstrations for peace took place all over the country in the wake of the killing of two children in Warrington in England. Yet another peace movement was started, with the rhetoric echoing that of the Peace Movement of the mid-seventies, and the outpouring of sorrow after Enniskillen in 1987. They fear any spilling-over of the conflict to the South, and in 1993 these fears were fuelled by the new ferocity of the UFF, who killed five Catholic workmen as a riposte to the Warrington killings.

British tourists are welcomed as old friends and polite visitors, and Irish people wish that someone, somewhere, would solve the problem for once and for all. They would like – in theory – the island to be united politically, but not at the cost of higher taxes or a dramatic change in laws or practices in, say, the question of abortion. They most emphatically do not want to be involved militarily in any way with Northern Ireland, and distrust any politician who sounds too 're-publican'. All of this adds up to a grave temptation for Irish political leaders to put the whole question to one side: and indeed politicians are unhappily aware that Northern Ireland and its problems are not vote-getting issues in the Republic. It is fortunate that the two dominant figures of the 1980s in Irish politics both felt strongly enough about the question to make it a central policy issue for them-selves, despite the aversion of the population. Garret FitzGerald, the son of a Northern Protestant mother and Irish Catholic father, and Charles Haughey may not have made huge progress, they may have come to the problem from different viewpoints, but they cannot be accused of that greatest of political sins: despair. Despite the failure of the Anglo-Irish Agreement to lessen the violence in Northern Ireland, it nevertheless sowed the seeds of the great efforts made since 1990 to break through centuries of distrust by political dialogue.

It has been clear, unfortunately, over the last few years that past centuries of warfare, and this century's history of injustice and bloodshed, have left a gulf between the communities in Northern Ireland which the best diplomatic efforts of British and Irish governments, and the encouragement of the United States, have failed to bridge. In the year 1992, up to the end of December, over 100 people died violently in Northern Ireland or Britain at the hands of the IRA or one of the Loyalist paramilitary groups, or in incidents involving the security forces. As 1993 arrived, no pause in the bloodshed was evident.

What is to fill the dangerous vacuum left by politicians' failure to reach any kind of agreement? As 1992 closed, a former senior civil servant, highly respected and skilled, and one of the leading negotiators of the Anglo-Irish agreement, broke silence* to urge a new government and the Irish people to put Northern Ireland back at the centre of their thoughts, words and deeds. Michael Lillis's thesis was that the Anglo-Irish Agreement's machinery has not been used to anything like its full potential to achieve harmony and understanding between Nationalist and Unionist in Northern Ireland. Pointing out that nothing happens unless Dublin proposes, he urged vigorous and creative action on at least 100 proposals from the new government, so that the men of violence – whose motives are often selfless, despite the gangsterism in their midst – could begin to see advantages from putting down the gun. Deploring the low priority given to Northern Ireland in Dáil debates, he asked for unrelenting pursuance of government by Opposition on the issue. And he pointed out that the public dealings and debates and government policies in the Republic of Ireland are followed intensely by people in Northern Ireland, much more so than the other way round: therefore great care is needed in considering the effects that actions and words in the Republic have on the North. He concludes: 'Of course, there are no votes in it, but there are, most definitely, lives.'

*Michael Lillis, writing in the *Irish Times* on 30 December 1992. A former diplomat in the Irish Department of Foreign Affairs, Lillis joined Guinness Peat Aviation in 1991 after serving some years as Irish Permanent Representative to the UN, in Geneva. He was the first head of the Anglo-Irish Conference secretariat at Maryfield, outside Belfast, from 1986, and was head of the Anglo-Irish Division of Foreign Affairs.

For the first time since 1987, a Cabinet committee on Northern Ireland was established by an Irish government in January 1993. Composed of the Taoiseach, the Tánaiste, and the Minister for Justice it was interpreted as an effort to avoid any rift between the parties in government on the approach to the whole question.

Any leader of a Fianna Fáil party has to be wary of any steps towards compromise with Unionism – and it was no surprise that there should have been some rumblings from Fianna Fáil back-benchers in March 1993 as Dick Spring stamped his new conciliatory stance on this area. In the continuing work of trying to open doors which have been closed for seventy years, Fianna Fáil sensitivity is only one of the minefields to be crossed by politicians from all sides.

Those political sensitivities were once more demonstrated when a new and major examination of the Northern Ireland problem was published on 9 June 1993. A group of distinguished people, chaired by an international civil rights lawyer, Professor Torkel Opsahl of Norway, spent thirteen months receiving and pondering submissions made by organizations and individuals from every spectrum of Northern Irish life. The Opsahl Report argues for an official recognition by the British government of nationalist aspirations in Northern Ireland, a 'parity of esteem'. It urges that a government of Northern Ireland with real power-sharing should be put in place, before discussions with the Irish government could be pursued; it concludes that the British government should open discussions, directly or indirectly, with Sinn Féin with a view to ending violence. The Opsahl Report was yet another sign along the appallingly difficult road to some agreement, some overall design, which might persuade extremists on both sides to escape from the past in order to build the future. By that time the Minister for Foreign Affairs had begun to show signs of impatience with what he saw as Unionist intransigence and refusal to resume talks.

NOTES

1. *Public Reaction to the Anglo-Irish Agreement*, Market Research Bureau of Ireland/*Irish Times* survey report, November 1985.
2. Pádraig O'Malley, *The Uncivil Wars*, Blackstaff Press, 1983, pp. 75–6.

3. MRBI/*Irish Times* poll, April 1991.
4. Quote from *The Economist*, 25 January 1992.
5. MRBI, 25th Anniversary survey, 1987.
6. MRBI/*Irish Times* poll, April 1991.
7. *New Ireland Forum Report*, 1984, chap. 3, para. 3.3 (Stationery Office, Dublin).
8. Conor Cruise O'Brien, *States of Ireland*, Panther, 1974, p. 128.
9. R. F. Foster, *Modern Ireland: 1600–1972*, Allen Lane, 1988/Penguin, 1989. (See Chap. 23, p. 592 in the Penguin edition.)
10. *Irish Press*, 23 January 1992.
11. *Irish Times*, 24 January 1992.
12. Statement by John Bruton TD, Fine Gael Press Office, 2 January 1992.
13. *Irish Times*, 20 April 1993.
14. Garret FitzGerald, *All in a Life*, Gill & Macmillan, 1991, p. 492.
15. Speech by Minister for Foreign Affairs and Tánaiste, Dick Spring, to the Irish Association in the Mansion House, Dublin, 5 March 1993.
16. Interview with Frank Millar, *Irish Times*, 27 March 1991.
17. ibid.
18. *Irish Times*, 12 April 1993.
19. FitzGerald, op. cit., p. 566.
20. *Sunday Tribune*, 24 June 1990.
21. Ted Nealon, *Nealon's Guide to 26th Dáil and Seanad, Election '89*, Platform Press.
22. *Revising the Rising*, Field Day, 1991.
23. *Irish Times*, 29 July 1992.
24. Dáil Éireann, 4 November 1992.
25. *Irish Times*, 9 November 1992.
26. ibid.
27. New Year Statement, 1 January 1991.
28. *Irish Times*, 6 January 1992.
29. *Irish Times*, 2 January 1991.
30. *Irish Times*, 18 January 1992.
31. Gemma Hussey, *At the Cutting Edge, Cabinet Diaries, 1982–87*, Gill & Macmillan, 1990.
32. Patrick Loughrey (ed.), *The People of Ireland*, Appletree Press/BBC, p. 110.
33. Jennifer Todd, 'Two traditions in Unionist political culture', *Irish Political Studies*, vol. 2, 1987.

34. R. McCartney, *Liberty and Authority in Ireland*, Field Day, Derry (Field Day Pamphlet no. 9, 1985).
35. Conor Cruise O'Brien, *Irish Independent*, 21 December 1991.
36. *Sunday Independent*, 12 May 1991.
37. ibid.
38. *Irish Times*, 19 November 1992.
39. *Irish Times*, 13 May 1993.

CHAPTER 9

Ireland and Europe

In February 1992, in a small Dutch town called Maastricht, twelve European heads of government signed a treaty signalling their intention to take new and major steps towards the political, economic and social union of their countries in the European Community. It was an important moment for Europe and the world. Its importance was such that it needed the consent of the parliaments and/or the peoples of each signing country. Three of those countries held a referendum of their people, and Ireland was one of them.* Ireland's referendum was set for 18 June 1992.

On the face of it, why should there be any difficulty whatsoever with the Irish vote? Since joining the European Common Market (as it was then known) in 1973, Ireland has been 'a good European', subscribing wholeheartedly towards the ideals of the founding fathers of the Community, endorsing entry to the Community in 1973 by 83 per cent of the votes cast in a 71 per cent electoral turnout, joining the European Monetary System as soon as possible (thereby breaking the historical link of the Irish pound and sterling) and voting for the Single European Act in 1987 – the last great leap forward – decisively, if not as enthusiastically as in 1973.

To understand the impact on Irish life of its membership of the European Community, and contemporary Irish attitudes to Europe, an examination of the Irish debate in 1992 about Maastricht will be illuminating.

One of the country's fifteen Members of the European Parliament summed up in his customarily pithy way a dominant feature of the Irish/Europe debate: 'Ireland, after two decades of EC membership, must develop a vision for Europe that is more sophisticated than milking a cow.'[1] The European cow has indeed been a source of rich bounty for the country; the Maastricht debate featured a heavy

* The other two were Denmark, which finally ratified Maastricht in May 1993, having narrowly rejected it in June 1992, and France, which gave it a 'petit oui' – accepting Maastricht narrowly, in 1992.

emphasis on the financial transfers the country has enjoyed since 1973. On the principle that 'eaten bread is soon forgotten', there was an even heavier emphasis on the munificence to come in the next few years, the figure of IR£6 billion so often repeated that it became part of the country's everyday vocabulary. By 1993, that figure had grown to IR£8 billion.

The total amount of financial support which Ireland received from the European Community between 1973 and 1991 amounted to IR£14 billion.[2] In 1991, Ireland paid IR£348·3 million towards the Community, and received IR£2·2 billion in return. In the context of estimated total Irish government spending on running the country in 1992 of IR£7·6 billion,[3] this size of transfer has major significance for Ireland's economic viability. For every pound that Ireland sends to help run the Community, it gets over six pounds back. Irish farmers and their organizations, and the whole agriculture sector, despite ongoing public quarrels with aspects of European administration and reforms in their area, were in no doubt about where their interests lay in the referendum of 18 June, and urged their members to vote 'yes', well aware that the lion's share of that IR£14 billion had come to the agriculture sector: IR£10·3 billion of it. Infrastructural support on a massive scale, as well as for training and education, and a range of social and cultural supports accounted for the not inconsiderable remainder.

Irish political leaders and pro-Europe spokespersons in 1992 were adamant that not only was the country benefiting from Europe's generosity in straight transfer terms, but that the opportunities for trading into this tariff-free market of 320 million people were something which had already had a huge impact on Irish exporting achievements and employment patterns. A former Irish Commissioner in Europe deplored the undue emphasis on incoming monetary flow and highlighted other aspects: 'We are winning the trade battle ... take our relations with Germany: in 1991 our exports were close to double our imports, and represented 13 per cent of our total as against 5 in 1973. In addition we have 155 German production firms here employing 11,500 people: they are here because they see Ireland as part of, and permanently part of, the EC.'[4] He might have reminded his listeners that Ireland's huge dependence on trade with one country – the United Kingdom – has been transformed since 1973, as shown in the table.

Changes in Irish/UK Trade since 1973 (%)		
	1973	1991
EC minus UK	17·6	42
UK only	56	32

The Minister for Industry and Commerce gave figures for employment which he attributed directly to Ireland's membership of the EC: 'Overseas-owned, internationally mobile businesses employ over 90,000 people directly in Ireland, and indirectly support a similar level of employment in the services sector ... if Ireland stepped aside from the development of Europe many of them might find it in their better interest to re-locate.'[5]

The Taoiseach gave an exhaustive list of advantages to Ireland of EC membership when he opened the Maastricht referendum debate in the Dáil on 5 May 1992. Despite Ireland's alarming unemployment rate, touching 21 per cent, which he ascribed mainly to demographic factors, he reminded the House that over the twenty years since joining the Community, Ireland had experienced one of the highest growth rates: per capita income 'which has grown by nearly a half in real terms, is now 69 per cent of the EC average instead of 59 per cent in 1973 ...' Implying that even fewer people would have work without EC membership, he gave the figure of 70,000 more people at work than there were in 1973. With a healthy trade surplus of IR£500 million with the country's EC partners even in the first two months of 1992, 75 per cent of Ireland's exports going to Europe, and the promise of greater things to come, as well as the IR£6 billion in the European pipeline, the country's prime minister was in no doubt as to Ireland's need for continued European loyalty. This Dáil debate was one of the few major Irish discussions of the implications of closer union in Europe – the European dimension has never been a central subject for the Irish media and public. As late as April 1991, the governor of Ireland's central bank described this ostrich-like attitude of the Irish thus: 'A process akin to sleep-walking.'[6]

However, the numerical strength and political clout of the supporters of Maastricht in the spring of 1992 drowned out other voices questioning the wisdom of closer union: 'We are asked to believe that Irish entrepreneurs, who have never in this century produced an economy that can gainfully employ and satisfactorily maintain three and a half million people, will now in the face of a single European currency, foreign competition selling freely into Ireland, and the anti-periphery pressures of the Birmingham–Milan–Hamburg triangle, suddenly manage it.'[7] The answer normally given to these soothsayers of doom is that however bad things were in Ireland in 1992, they would be infinitely worse were it not for membership of the Community.

The strict economic arguments were not the only ones in favour of maintaining and strengthening Ireland's ties with its European colleagues: Irish women workers, and workers generally, were reminded that European legislation on pay and conditions, access to employment, social security, and protective labour legislation had been the main inspiration for progress in these areas in Ireland. The five directives concerning various aspects of equality policy represented progress for Irish women which might not have been made otherwise. (They were not reminded that on some of these issues, like equal pay for equal work in the mid-1970s, Irish governments had fought against their imposition, causing Irish women to take to the streets to demonstrate and collect signatures in order to get at home what other European women were enjoying.)

In February 1992, a few days after the Maastricht Treaty had been signed, there was an abrupt awakening from the sleep surrounding European debate in Ireland when the treaty was found to contain a 'protocol' (an explanatory clause) inserted at the request of the Irish government at the time of its negotiation in late 1991, which emphasized that European law would not interfere with the application of the anti-abortion constitutional provision in Ireland.* When the protocol† had been inserted during the negotiations leading up to the signing of the treaty, it went unremarked in Ireland because it changed nothing and apparently was just a

---

* The Eighth Amendment to the Constitution (Article 40.3.3), passed in a referendum in 1983, reads: 'The State acknowledges the right to life of the unborn, and with due regard to the equal right to life of the mother, guarantees in its laws to respect and, as far as is practicable, by its laws to defend and vindicate that right.'

† The protocol: 'Nothing in the Treaty on European Union or in the Treaties establishing the European Communities, or the Treaties or Acts modifying or supplementing those Treaties shall affect the application in Ireland of Article 40.3.3 of the Constitution of Ireland.'

safeguard against any assertion by the pro-life movement that Europe would somehow foist abortion on Ireland. However, just a few months later, things did change: after a dramatic and unexpected Supreme Court interpretation of the Eighth Amendment in February 1992, stating that abortion should be available in Ireland in cases of grave risk to the mother's life, and casting doubt on whether Irish women had the right to travel outside Ireland for abortions unless their life could be proved to be at risk, a huge and far-from-sleepy campaign began. Anti-abortion groups saw the Maastricht protocol as introducing abortion to Ireland *à la* Supreme Court, while pro-choice groups and women's organizations saw it as threatening the freedom of movement of Irish women (who have been leaving Ireland to obtain abortions in England at the rate of at least 4,000 a year, according to clinics in England, figures not seriously disputed in Ireland). Women also resented the ban on information about abortion clinics in England which previous Supreme Court judgements, based on Article 40.3.3, had imposed.

There was a hurried but unsuccessful attempt by the Irish government to get the other eleven governments of the EC member states to agree to amend the protocol to clarify that freedom of travel and information would be assured, but the European partners, appalled by the prospect of reopening a treaty discussion which had been so painstakingly constructed and successfully concluded in February 1992 (and understandably dumbfounded at the mess which Ireland had managed to get itself into), refused. So instead, the government had to settle for a 'Solemn Declaration'* from its partners affirming

---

*The Solemn Declaration: 'The High Contracting Parties to the Treaty on European Union signed at Maastricht on the 7th day of February 1992. Having considered the terms of Protocol No. 17 to the said Treaty on European Union which is annexed to that Treaty and to the Treaties establishing the European Communities hereby give the following legal interpretation:

'That it was and is their intention that the Protocol shall not limit freedom either to travel between Member States, or in accordance with conditions which may be laid down, in conformity with Community law, by Irish legislation, to obtain or make available in Ireland information relating to services lawfully available in Member States.

'At the same time, the High Contracting Parties solemnly declare that in the event of a future constitutional amendment in Ireland which concerns the subject-matter of Article 40.3.3 of the Constitution of Ireland and which does not conflict with the intention of the High Contracting Parties hereinbefore expressed, they will, following the entry into force of the Treaty on European Union, be favourably disposed to amending the said Protocol so as to extend its application to such constitutional amendment if Ireland so requests.'

that no one had ever any intention of stopping Irish women from travelling or getting information. It was, then, an ironic twist that the protocol, originally inserted into the Maastricht Treaty to prevent any coupling of the abortion issue with the treaty referendum, seemed to have achieved exactly the opposite result. Naturally therefore, during the approach to the Irish referendum on 18 June, anti-abortion groups called for a 'no' vote, while worried women, in particular the influential Council for the Status of Women, and other groups like the trade-union movement called for an additional referendum before Maastricht to ensure travel and information rights. An exasperated Taoiseach announced somewhat desperately that abortion had nothing to do with Maastricht and that the two issues were entirely unrelated. Acres of newsprint, hours and hours of broadcasting time, and a succession of street demonstrations and public meetings disagreed with him. In his speech of 5 May in Dáil Éireann there was not one word about abortion, protocols, solemn declarations, rights to travel and information, showing that an Irish Taoiseach can be a proficient sleep-walker when he wants to be. To frustrate him and the political pro-Maastricht side further, a post-office industrial dispute blocked plans to circulate one million pro-Maastricht explanatory leaflets to Irish homes. The leader of the Democratic Left, explaining why his party (with only six Dáil Deputies) was going to vote against Maastricht, gave as one of his reasons 'the spectacularly inept handling' of the whole abortion affair by the Taoiseach.[8] As if to tighten the vice, just before the Dáil debate on Maastricht, newspapers reported that a man had walked into a Garda station in Dublin asking that his former girlfriend be stopped from travelling to England for an abortion: a collective frisson ran through the country, which held its breath waiting to see if the case would be pursued. The Council for the Status of Women immediately renewed its call to the Taoiseach to publish, before the referendum day of 18 June, the wording and date of a referendum guaranteeing travel and information rights. A cabinet subcommittee laboured over the whole abortion issue, and the Taoiseach declared that he didn't know if the women's demands could be met. He could take some comfort from an opinion poll published a few days after his Maastricht Dáil speech showing 61 per cent in favour of the treaty, only 11 per cent against, with 28 per cent 'don't know'.[9]

The pro-Maastricht groups were once again shaken when on 21 May 2,000 copies of one of the most respected of the British newspapers coming into Ireland, the *Guardian*, were not distributed because the agent had been told that it carried an advertisement for an abortion clinic in Britain; a police presence watched the arrival of the newspapers at Dublin airport, 'to ensure there would be no breach of the peace'.[10] As the public contemplated this development, Irish customs officials temporarily confiscated twenty-five copies of the newspaper which an activist in the 'pro-choice' movement had ordered for herself, and she was detained for a short time in a Garda station. The reason given for the confiscation of her property was that the officials had thought they were a commercial assignment. The leader of the Democratic Left gave it as his opinion that Ireland was descending into 'an infantile theocracy'. The reason for the alarm of the pro-Maastricht majority was that the protocol in the treaty had the effect of preventing any European court from intervening in the application of these laws in Ireland, something which deeply concerned more and more women as each incident took place.

Confusion reigned. Radio Telefís Éireann, the national broadcasting station, in its current affairs *Questions and Answers* programme on 25 May featured a government spokesperson fervently advocating a 'yes' vote for Maastricht (and asserting that the abortion issue was entirely unconnected with it), the leader of the Democratic Left advocating a 'no' vote for a variety of reasons, a well-known artist and self-confessed revolutionary socialist* opposing Maastricht for roughly the same reasons as the Democratic Left, while a former government minister (the author) supported Maastricht but reserved a decision on voting 'yes' until the situation was clarified on abortion information and travel rights.

As the twelve EC member states in 1992 prepared to strengthen their union, aware that aspiring new members were getting ready to opt in to this increasingly important club, another issue

---

*Robert Ballagh (b. 1943). Musician, artist, stage designer. Best known for his hyperrealistic portraits, murals, posters, stamp designs and book covers, he has exhibited extensively in Ireland and abroad – mainly in Lund, Warsaw, Moscow, Sofia and Varna.

resurfaced to disturb further the smooth countdown to ratification. Ireland since before the 1939-45 world war has been a neutral country. That concept is not terribly clear to most Irish people, except that it meant in 1939 that an Irish Army did not fight alongside the English, thus incurring the wrath of Britain's leader Winston Churchill. Ireland has not been a member of Nato, though firmly, if somewhat tacitly, on the western side in the long grey days of the cold war against the godless Soviet Union. The neutrality issue never moved to centre stage, principally because there was never any need for it to do so; most Irish politicians and political parties had not addressed the issue in serious terms. Fianna Fáil had a certain sensitivity about neutrality, since it was first promulgated and established by their founder Éamon de Valera, much revered and long-serving Taoiseach and third President of Ireland. At the outbreak of the second world war, the scars of the old Irish battles with Britain over Ireland's independence as well as over the continuing division of the island were still fresh; de Valera saw neutrality as representing 'the final proof of the south's sovereignty'.[11] Declarations by successive Fianna Fáil Taoisigh from Seán Lemass to Charles Haughey sealed the link between neutrality and the partition of Ireland. For many years the subject lay dormant, and achieved a sort of 'sacred cow' status. There were some trenchant opinions expressed from time to time about Irish neutrality by courageous Irish politicians, most notably John Kelly TD* (speaking in Galway in 1985): 'It scarcely makes sense to talk about a traditional policy of neutrality, when in fact in sixty-two years of independence, there has only been one juncture at which anyone needed our help and at which we thought it right to refuse it. This was during the Second World War; and while in hindsight, it is no credit to us to have stood aside from civilizations's efforts to put down the

---

* John Kelly (1931-91) was an outstanding academic lawyer who lectured at both Trinity College and University College, Dublin, becoming Professor of Jurisprudence and Roman Law in the latter. A Senator, Dáil Deputy, junior minister and minister, as well as Attorney-General in various Fine Gael-led governments, he was extremely witty, an entertaining and sometimes acerbic debater, and considered the best speaker in the Dáil of his generation. A man of strong convictions and integrity, his early death in 1991 shocked political friends and foes alike.

Nazi regime, we can admit that the Government of the time –
supported by the Opposition – had what seemed adequate reasons
for neutrality.'[12] A few years later, in 1988, John Kelly referred
in less than enthusiastic tones to a message congratulating Ireland
on its neutrality sent from Mikhail Gorbachev as he flew over
Ireland, 'small wonder, since, nice man though he appears to be,
it is the Soviet system which is the gainer from our leaving this
gap in the defences of the west'.[13]

Ireland's Army has been helped by its government's neutrality,
or perhaps more accurately its non-aligned status, to achieve
considerable standing and desirability as an acceptable United
Nations peace-keeping force in troubled areas around the world.
As part of a European defence alliance, that status might
change – on the other hand, the Irish Army would very much
welcome the certain improvement in its salaries, equipment
and European standing which a new strong European military
association would give it.

Defenders of Irish neutrality asserted in 1992 that if Ireland
voted 'yes', the spectre of conscription would come to haunt the
homes of Ireland – this was rejected as nonsense by the Taoiseach
among others. 'Neutrality is not an issue. The Treaty does not
require us to change our policy of non-participation in military
alliance.'[14] But in a clear indication that such a position might
not always hold, and that Ireland could – and surely would –
change its position with changing circumstances, the Taoiseach
said: '. . . in the context of a developing foreign and security
policy, the eventual formation of a defence arm cannot be ruled
out.'[15] The gradual change in the stance of all political parties
towards Ireland's traditional 'purist' position on neutrality has
been well noted. In the days leading up to the signing of the
Maastricht Treaty in 1991, a leading political commentator
observed: 'By the end of the Maastricht summit, Ireland will
have started on a road which will almost certainly end the neutrality which has long been waved as evidence of our independence
. . . it will almost certainly be an irreversible process.'[16] Such is
the new pragmatism of most parties on this issue that even the
Labour Party has expressed a preference to deal with international
military problems from inside a European union rather than
powerlessly, from outside. Fine Gael, the main Opposition party,

has no problems with a future military involvement. 'Ireland must be prepared to join with the other EC member states in a mutual pact to defend Europe if we want to claim the full benefits of Community membership,' said its foreign-affairs spokesperson in April 1991.[17]

The prospect of full European integration, therefore, brought about a major change in this hitherto untouchable area, as voters in Ireland contemplated the logic or otherwise of voting against a union that other neutral countries in Europe (which had stayed out of the Community in 1972/3 because of their neutrality) such as Austria, Finland and Sweden were now clamouring to join. As referendum day approached, the Taoiseach was seen as finally burying the traditional reluctance to identify with Europe in all its aspects; neutrality was dead. The *Irish Times* was clear about the new position: 'It [neutrality] was laid to rest by our Taoiseach with no more than a passing nod as to how well it had served us in times past, and without even a mention of Dev himself; times change, said Albert, and we must change with them. And what's more, he said, if this means even closer defence involvement after the 1996 inter-governmental conference, then that too is on the table.'[18] Many people are wary about, or hostile to, the abandoning of a position which gave Ireland a certain stance in the modern world, even after passions had subsided on the partition issue, finding expression in a foreign policy which opposed nuclear weapons, played an honourable and valuable – if limited – role in world peace-keeping, gave a special understanding between Ireland and former colonies in the Third World, and as John A. Murphy, a distinguished historian and independent Senator, put it, 'generally seeing international issues quite distinctly, if not differently from most of our Community partners'.[19] Senator Murphy concluded that for that reason he had no choice but to vote 'no' to Maastricht.

The referendum date was set for 18 June. The Danes voted 'no' in their first referendum on 2 June, and the shock waves swept across Europe. The Irish state of preparedness for this set-back was extremely bad, just as it was in the rest of Europe, despite the clear indications for some weeks in the polls that the Danish result was in the balance. As the news from Denmark was covered in depth by Irish television and radio, rumours spread that the Irish vote would be postponed because of the uncertain status of Maastricht in this situation. A hapless government minister, in charge of the 'yes' campaign, spoke on national radio on the morning of 3 June and could only make general supportive remarks about Europe while waiting for meetings at various levels in Europe to find out what exactly Ireland might be voting for. In the vacuum which had been allowed to exist, all groups opposed to Maastricht declared the whole thing a charade, calling for the abandonment of the referendum. Danish opponents of Maastricht arrived in Dublin to urge a 'no' vote. However, on 9 June, the Council for the Status of Women reluctantly urged Irish women to vote 'yes'. This was, they said, 'on balance and in the long term, in the best interests of Irish women'. Their statement was made possible by a joint public undertaking by the leaders of four of the five political parties that the right to travel and information would be restored by a referendum in the autumn of 1992, and that the main issue of abortion would be dealt with by legislation and/or a referendum at the same time. The trade unions similarly came out in support of the treaty.

A nervous Europe watched the closing stages of the Irish debate, fearing that a negative vote from another country, however small, might throw the whole Maastricht process into a tailspin. In the event, Ireland endorsed Maastricht by a substantial majority. In a turnout of 57.25 per cent, 69.05 per cent voted 'yes', with 30.95 per cent voting 'no', so that the Taoiseach could go to the Lisbon EC summit a week later and bask in the glow of approval from his colleagues. Ireland took its lap of honour at the summit, enjoying the attention until the prime ministers were distracted by the sight of the Danes, having vanquished Maastricht at home, beating one of Europe's giants in a 2–1 victory over Germany to take the European Cup football title.

THE IRISH BRIGADE IN BRUSSELS

The highest level of functionary in Europe is the office of European Commissioner, one of that eminent group whose responsibility is the formulation and carrying through of policy throughout the Community. Seventeen Commissioners are appointed from the twelve members. Since 1973, Ireland has had six European Commissioners in Brussels (one of them served twice). This is a list of them, with their areas of responsibility:

1973–6   Patrick J. Hillery: Social Affairs, and was one of the Vice-Presidents of the Commission.

1977–80   Richard Burke: Transport, Taxation, Consumer Protection, Relations with the European Parliament, Research, Education and Science.

1981–2   Michael O'Kennedy: President's delegate, Personnel and Administration, Statistical Office, Publications Office.

1982–4   Richard Burke: Roughly the same package as O'Kennedy's.

1985–9   Peter Sutherland: Social Affairs (for the first eighteen months until Spain acceded), Competition, Relations with Parliament.

1989–92   Ray MacSharry: Agriculture, Rural Development.

1993–   Pádraig Flynn: Social Affairs and Employment, Relations with the Economic and Social Committee, questions linked to immigration, internal and judicial affairs.

It is generally conceded that the country has not always used its best talent in this crucial and powerful position, where immense skill, hard work, and strength of personality are needed, first to obtain important portfolios, and then to operate them successfully. It is interesting that one of the most successful Irish Commissioners – both in terms of achievement in his own field of responsibility and in gaining a worldwide reputation for his skilful performance – was the only one not to come from the ranks of senior Irish politicians. This was Peter Sutherland,* who had served as a young Attorney-General in 1981 and again from 1982 to 1985, and had been defeated in his only electoral outing for Dáil Éireann in the 1970s. He was, as Commissioner, Ireland's most prominent voice in Europe from 1985 to 1989. 'A European of stature, an unpretentious man of great ability and charm.'[20]

Sutherland's portfolio was initially Competition and Social Af-

---

*Peter Sutherland (b. 1946). A barrister and unsuccessful Fine Gael Dáil candidate in 1973. Attorney-General, 1981, 1982–5; Commissioner of the European Communities 1985–9; chairman of the AIB group from 1989; holds several directorships, honours, and decorations. Became Director-General of GATT in June 1993.

fairs. His legacy in the latter field, which he was in charge of for only eighteen months until an incoming Spanish Commissioner took over, is the Erasmus programme (which in 1992 saw 60,000 young Europeans taking a year of their university studies in another Community country) and the COMETT programme – the university/industry initiative. It was in the exercising of the supranational powers of the Competition portfolio, however, that Sutherland really made his mark, assaulting uncompetitive behaviour and imposing huge fines, breaking up cartels and monopolies (most notably tackling airlines' practices) and confronting the Community's wealthy nations about their practice of huge subsidies to new industries at the expense of poorer countries. In the course of his work, he became close to M. Jacques Delors, President of the Commission (who referred to Sutherland as his 'sheriff'), and played a major role with Delors in shaping the Single European Act of 1987. For his work on relations between the Commission and the European Parliament, he was the first and, so far, the only Commissioner to receive that parliament's gold medal. Like most countries, but especially a small island country, Ireland savoured the unusual experience of hearing a compatriot praised in the international meetings of the powerful. Not since Garret FitzGerald careered around the world as foreign affairs minister in the 1970s had Ireland felt it had a statesman well fitted to deal on a level with the world's best.

The contribution of the first Commissioner, Dr Patrick Hillery, who had negotiated Ireland's entry to the Community, and who had developed the social-affairs portfolio in a way which was ahead of its time, has been undervalued in Ireland. It is sometimes forgotten that in the course of this work, Dr Hillery had to face down the Irish government of the time, which was strenuously opposing his work, particularly for women. Dr Hillery became President of Ireland in 1976, just as his time in Europe was drawing to an end, which is one of the reasons why his role was never properly discussed in public.

A second distinguished Commissioner was Ray MacSharry,* who

* Ray MacSharry (b. 1938) was educated at Summerhill College, Sligo. First elected to Dáil Éireann in 1969. Held ministerial portfolios in Agriculture and Finance, with a spell as a member of the European Parliament from 1984 to 1987. Was Tánaiste (deputy prime minister) as well as Minister for Finance from 1987 to 1989.

was Irish Minister for Finance from 1987 to 1989. His portfolio of Agriculture meant immediate confrontation with farmers all over Europe as he brought forward reforms of the Common Agricultural Policy – a policy which had resulted in massive surpluses and stockpiles of European (including Irish) beef, milk and cereal production as farmers enjoyed the security of the Community's intervention-price policies. He pursued that reform with single-mindedness, despite being described as various kinds of a traitor by Irish, French, and many other farmers. On the world stage however, it is his achievements in the massive effort to conclude the much-delayed Uruguay round of the GATT agreement which might ensure his place in history. The closing stages of those negotiations provided an interesting battle between MacSharry and Commission President Delors. The Irishman resigned on 5 November 1992 as the EC's GATT negotiator because, apparently, of Delors's interference in attempting to reduce the impact of the agreement on French farmers. He told the *Irish Times*: 'Nobody undermines me; I do what I have to do.' Against the background of mounting world concern about US threats of economic sanctions, the rest of the Commission backed MacSharry, who withdrew his resignation, flew to Washington, and went on with the deal. There followed instant deification of MacSharry by much of the British media, whose dislike of Delors was legendary. Describing him as 'Europe's Hero of Gatt', the London *Independent* quoted, with approval, an unnamed Irish official in Brussels: 'The thing about MacSharry is that he doesn't give a shit for anyone. You see Ministers from some of the most powerful governments in the world cowering before this guy from the arse-end of nowhere.'[21] Ray MacSharry had already announced that he would not be accepting the Irish Taoiseach's offer of a renewal of his appointment from January 1993, but intended to return to Ireland to the private sector, which he did. By one of those twists in public fortunes, his predecessor Peter Sutherland was appointed Director-General of GATT in June 1993, and set out to try to finalize the Uruguay Round of the GATT agreement in the face of French and Irish governmental hostility. Sutherland's GATT appointment was warmly welcomed in Ireland, which was pleased to see one of its own again taking centre stage internationally.

The political attitude in Ireland towards the appointment of Commissioners has been coloured by two things: first, the huge prestige and considerable financial rewards – by Irish public service standards – of the job* mean that the appointment is seen as a particular plum, to be offered only to very loyal and devoted members of the Taoiseach's team and party. The second criterion is usually the conflict between wanting to have an able person in Europe and the desire to keep exceptional talent at home. Other factors have entered into the equation: in 1982, the Taoiseach of the day made the appointment of Richard Burke – who came from the Opposition – on purely political grounds, hoping that the resulting by-election for Burke's seat in Dublin would give the government the majority it desperately needed in the Dáil. The ploy failed, the Opposition won the by-election, and the government had given away this coveted job for nothing.

Peter Sutherland's appointment by Garret FitzGerald in 1985 was also unusual; in fact the idea came from FitzGerald's influential wife, Joan: 'It was Joan who came up with the answer ... she suggested Peter Sutherland.'[22] The government had a dilemma, in that Dr FitzGerald, a committed European and most anxious to send a really high-powered person to Europe who would be taken seriously and would be influential in the Commission, admitted: 'I could not spare one of my Ministerial heavyweights, nor did I wish to face a by-election which we might easily lose.'[23] Sutherland was not a minister and did not hold a seat in the Dáil. Even though he held the central job of Attorney-General, he was not seen by the Fine Gael rank and file as really 'one of them'. However, such was his subsequent performance in Europe that when it came to replacing him in 1989, there was an unprecedented public demand that he be given a second term. The man expected to replace him, Ray MacSharry, had been doing a very good job as Minister for Finance since 1987, hauling the country back to economic realism with toughness. However, perhaps because MacSharry had been promised the job by his Taoiseach in 1987, there was a change of Commissioner, to the surprise and regret of the Europeans and the resigned

---

*Estimated at IR£120,000 in 1992, with generous pension entitlements and other perquisites such as assistance with house expenses, education expenses, the provision of a car and driver, etc.

puzzlement of many in Ireland. A cartoon of him at the time was captioned: 'Only one man knows where the Irish economy is going, and he's leaving.'[24] The Taoiseach, Mr Haughey, may have baulked also at the prospect of awarding the post for the second time to a member of the Opposition, despite public pressures on him to do so. As it turned out, the appointment was extremely successful. Two very different Commissioners, from very different backgrounds, have performed well in Brussels and on the world stage, and brought pride to their country.

The surprising appointment of Pádraig Flynn to the Irish Commissionship to succeed MacSharry came about, it was generally held in political circles, because of two factors: the front-runner for the post, Justice Minister Máire Geoghegan-Quinn (who had performed very well as Minister of State for EC Affairs for some years) had an unsafe seat in her constituency of Galway West which might be lost in a by-election. The more widely held theory was that the Labour Party, going into coalition with Fianna Fáil in January 1993, would have found it difficult to deal with Pádraig Flynn at the Cabinet table, because of his deeply held conservative views on the many social issues facing the new government. Whatever the reason, Commissioner Flynn's appointment to the Social Affairs brief was greeted with some concern by Irish groups hoping for innovation and liberalism from Europe on social issues. There was, however, no doubting Flynn's abilities as an experienced and politically astute politician.

THE EUROPEAN PARLIAMENT

Ireland elects, by multi-seat proportional representation, fifteen members of the European Parliament. The elections are held every five years, and so give a welcome security of tenure to the Parliament members, by contrast with the unsettling volatility and more frequent electoral outings of Dáil Éireann. The country is divided into four constituencies: the city and county of Dublin (four members); the provinces of Leinster, outside Dublin (three members), and Munster (five members); and the amalgam of Connaught and that part of Ulster not governed by Britain (three members). Because of shifting population, it was expected that Dublin might gain another seat for the 1994 European elections,

The 1989 European Elections: Ireland				
Constituency	Fianna Fáil	Fine Gael	Labour	Progressive Democrats	Other
Dublin	1	1	1		1
Leinster	2	1			
Munster	2	1		1	1
Connaught–Ulster	1	1			1

involving perhaps a loss of one seat for Munster. In Northern Ireland, there are three seats.

In the 1989 European elections, ten of the fifteen seats went to the two big parties, but the rest were widely scattered (see table). The voting turnout at 68·3 per cent was the highest ever for a European election: but this is explained by the fact that, on the same day, the people were voting in a general election too. In 1984, the turnout was 47 per cent.

Irish representatives sit with various groups in the European Parliament, which sometimes leads to strange anomalies, such as the curious alliance in the Parliament between the small conservative group, the European Democratic Alliance, and Ireland's biggest political party, Fianna Fáil. This came about because Fine Gael's very Europe-minded Garret FitzGerald identified quickly his party's most natural allies – the Christian Democrats – and joined them in the European People's Party in 1976. Fianna Fáil could hardly join the Socialists along with the Irish Labour Party, and having missed the centre-right boat, so to speak, ended up with the French Gaullists. Labour's only representative sits with the largest parliamentary group, the Socialists. The Progressive Democrat sits with the Liberal, Democratic and Reformist Group (as does one of the Irish independents); the Democratic Left sit a little uncomfortably with the United Left group, the Labour Party having made it quite clear to their European friends that they would not have the rival left-wing party in the same group; while the remaining Irish independent, a fiery former republican Fianna Fáil member, sits with the Rainbow group.

European elections have not been considered very important or interesting by the ordinary Irish voter. It was thus in 1989: because of speculation about the possible calling of a general election to coincide with the already fixed date of the European elections, such interest as there was in the European one took a back seat. The European campaign, issues and all, was increasingly marginalized. In various polls to establish what issues were regarded as important by the electorate, European issues hardly appeared at all. The electorate was much more concerned with unemployment, emigration and similar domestic issues which they did not connect with Europe.

The election results showed a decline in support for candidates from the two main parties* and an increase for small parties (except Sinn Féin) and independents. Thus, Ireland is represented in the European Parliament by five parties and two independents sharing the fifteen seats – depending on one's point of view, that might mean a richness in the range of Irish views being expressed, or a waste of the already small opportunity to make an impact in the bigger, more powerful European parliamentary groups.

Two Irish MEPs since 1989 have made a bigger impact on the national stage in Ireland than the thirteen others. The only woman, Mary Banotti,† whose first elected office was that of MEP, and the Munster MEP Pat Cox,‡ the sole representative of the Progressive Democrats – and whose first election was also that for Europe, in 1989 – have both managed to combine effective European activity and a high profile nationally. Banotti has made a speciality of environmental issues, for which she is best known in Ireland (in June 1989 she was named by the European Environmental Bureau as one of the ten most influential legislators on environmental

*Fianna Fáil dropped 7·7 per cent and Fine Gael 10·6 per cent from the previous European elections, and 12·7 per cent and 7·7 per cent respectively from the coinciding general election.

† Mary Banotti MEP (Fine Gael, a Dublin constituency) (b. 1939). Formerly a nurse and industrial social worker, an MEP since 1984.

‡ Pat Cox MEP (Progressive Democrats, Munster constituency) (b. 1952). Formerly a lecturer in economics, and current-affairs broadcaster, general secretary of Progressive Democrats 1986–9. Astute negotiator between Progressive Democrats and Fianna Fáil on programmes for government in the coalition government from 1989. Elected to Dáil Éireann in November 1992. Seen as a possible future leader of his party.

protection). Cox concentrates on economic and Irish political issues, and is ubiquitous in the Irish media, putting forward his views with force and clarity.

Apart from these two, Ireland's MEPs do not enjoy high national profiles, though many have high profiles in their constituencies upon which they prefer to concentrate. Neither is the European message brought to Irish people by its MEPs. Most of them did not come from the ranks of currently prominent or influential politicians. The European Parliament is seen – accurately – as a relatively powerless body, albeit with a faint air of foreign glamour about it, and not for people who really want to make it in politics at home. Pay and conditions are very good by Irish political standards. A certain coyness is encountered in trying to ascertain exactly how much Irish MEPs can earn. The elaborate European system of allowances and expenses intervenes – MEPs are paid the same as Irish Dáil Deputies (IR£29,000 in 1992) and also have secretarial, information and travel allowances both within their constituencies and between Brussels, Strasbourg and their home base. It has been estimated that a thrifty and wise MEP can bring home at least IR£70,000 a year after tax by judicious juggling of international air fares and accommodation allowances.

Part of the reason for Irish indifference to their MEPs lies in the national parliament. Small wonder that apathy and ignorance surround a great deal of the European debate in Ireland: the MEPs have no formal links with the Irish parliament, no forum in which to communicate nationally the matters which occupy them in their work. They had the right to attend as non-voting observers the Irish parliamentary committee on EC legislation, but rarely managed to do so because its sittings coincided with their absences. Because of the multi-seat nature of their elections to date, they must translate as much as possible of their work into local issues, and therefore play down broad European and international issues. It would be a bad month for any Irish MEP when his or her name did not appear several times in the local newspaper linked with some local initiative which is hoping for European cash.

All of this may change if the European Parliament begins to acquire real power in the new Europe after Maastricht, and if the voting systems are standardized to a list system. This would relieve some of the obligation presently on Irish MEPs to court their local areas in order to survive.

THE IRISH PARLIAMENTARY COMMITTEE ON EC LEGISLATION

In 1973, a Joint Committee of Dáil and Senate was established on a statutory basis 'to strengthen the degree of control of the Oireachtas over EC secondary legislation'.[25] It was subsumed in 1993 into a new Joint Foreign Affairs Committee, with a much wider brief. The original committee, which survived for twenty years, with eighteen Dáil members and seven Senators, was originally intended to have ten MEPs among its membership, but the above-mentioned difficulties in attendance soon meant that the MEPs' entitlements were diluted to attendance, participation in debates, but not full membership. The chairperson of the committee was drawn from the Opposition.* The committee invited interest groups that would be affected by proposed EC directives to attend subcommittee meetings, and then prepared reports for the main committee. The committee's final reports were then 'laid before both houses of the Oireachtas' and could be debated in the Dáil.

The reality, however, was that the committee's reports were largely ignored by the Dáil, the meetings were poorly attended because the subject-matter was seen as dull and not newsworthy (the hapless clerk to the committee could be found searching for prospective attenders in order to get a quorum to start the meeting at least) and the staff supplied by government was inadequate in numbers for the complex work of examining and dissecting the proposals coming from Brussels. Very few members had the specialist knowledge to enable them to operate without much more help; a distinguished exception to this rule was the present President of Ireland, Mary Robinson, who, as a Senator and lawyer with specialist skills, served on the legal affairs subcommittee of the Joint Committee for almost all of her years in the Oireachtas until 1987.†

The idea of the committee was undoubtedly a good one, but it totally failed in its aim of alerting the Oireachtas, or the public, to what was coming out of Brussels. Ireland's electoral system discour-

---

*In 1989, Peter Barry TD of Fine Gael, a former Minister for Foreign Affairs, was appointed to the chair. The author held the chair from 1987 to 1989.

†She also founded Ireland's first Centre for European Law in Trinity College, Dublin.

ages parliamentarians from devoting time and energy to this kind of work when local issues demand – and get – their attention. The committee was notably silent during the Maastricht campaign. Denmark is the only other country to have such a committee, where it is much more powerful and effective.

In the aftermath of Maastricht a specialist in modern European history deplored the lack of monitoring structures within Ireland about what is happening in Europe. Speaking to a summer school on 'Employment and Unemployment in the Europe of Maastricht' Professor Dermot Keogh of University College, Cork, proposed the setting up of a series of Oireachtas committees in fields such as social welfare, agriculture, competition policy. Harking back to the Maastricht debate in Ireland, he felt that the quality of the debate was depressingly low, and he particularly criticized the level of secrecy surrounding Irish dealings at Council of Ministers meetings, and the consequent lack of knowledge and understanding of Europe either by politicians or people: 'Such secrecy ... is a danger to the operation of a healthy democracy and it would not be tolerated for a second in an open democracy like that of the United States.'[26] As the new Joint Committee on Foreign Affairs was beginning its work in the summer of 1993, it hardly seemed likely that legislative proposals coming from Europe, or control over them, would get any more attention from Irish parliamentarians than they had in the past.

MOMENTS OF EUROPEAN GLORY

Ireland has held the Presidency of the Community on four occasions since 1973.* It is a challenge for a very small country, involving extraordinary extra demands on a civil service as special meetings have to be arranged between different groups of ministers, formal and informal, from all twelve countries, not to mention the responsibility of arranging, chairing and directing the procedures at all of these meetings as well as those of heads of governments. On the shoulders of the presiding country falls the administration of all this, not to mention the expense (which, in 1990, was estimated to

* January–June 1975; July–December 1979; June–December 1984; and January–June 1990.

have exceeded IR£2 million). The Taoiseach and his Minister for Foreign Affairs carry the main burden of work.

The 1990 presidency was a flamboyant affair, conducted by the then Taoiseach Charles Haughey with flair and intense personal direction. It was lifted out of the ordinary by the convulsions of the breakup of Eastern Europe as an Iron Curtain monolith, the immediacy of German reunification, and the acceleration of progress towards community union. An Irish professor of politics saw an EC presidency as a kind of opera: 'It provides opportunities for making a lot of grand noise up front, with all sorts of people strutting centre stage, but is also susceptible to squabbling prima donnas, indifferent librettos, and collapsing scenery.'[27] He went on to say of the 1990 Irish presidency: 'If this is opera, the score is richer, the libretto more inventively incredible, and the stage more crowded than on any of the three previous performances.' Haughey's presidency of Europe (for it was presented as such in Ireland, with much satirical reaction describing him as Emperor of Europe ...) was efficiently run, gaining the admiration of his European colleagues. In answering criticisms about the expense of the huge PR arrangements and press and television facilities, the Junior Minister for European Affairs said 'we have not only to do a good job, we have to be seen to do a good job'.[28] The TV cameras of Europe saw ministers meeting in Ireland's most scenic locations and staying in Ireland's most luxurious hotels.

The first Irish presidency, in 1975, in contrast was approached with some trepidation because of the newness of the undertaking. It was, unexpectedly, a triumph for both the then Minister for Foreign Affairs, Dr Garret FitzGerald, and his recently expanded Department of Foreign Affairs. 'The personal impact of Dr FitzGerald both on his own team and on his sometimes patronizing foreign counterparts was a notable feature.'[29] Euro-Arab dialogue was greatly helped by FitzGerald's initiatives, and progress towards the first Lomé convention was made.

The 1979 presidency was hampered by the convulsions inside the government party (Fianna Fáil) with the sudden departure of Taoiseach Jack Lynch before the presidency was complete and a subsequent bitterly fought leadership battle distracting everyone. Margaret Thatcher had arrived on the scene too, casting something of a cloud over progress towards European unity.

The third Irish presidency occurred in 1984, when the architect of the first success was now in place as Taoiseach. His problems were many, including plummeting popularity for his government, a sharp and painful rebuff from Margaret Thatcher on his initiatives for Northern Ireland* and a slowing-down in the progress towards European unity. However, the enactment of the Dooge† report – an important blueprint for progress which subsequently influenced the shape of the Single European Act in 1987 – helped to give Ireland's 1984 presidency some solid achievement.

CONCLUSIONS

There is no argument about the benefits Ireland has gained economically from membership of the European Community. Neither is there an argument about the progress made socially through enlightened legislation for workers and women. A beneficial side-result has been the increase in international skill and competence of a range of civil servants who had led a very sheltered life up to the 1970s. There is some argument that Ireland was discouraged from establishing new and competitive industries in the food sector by the cotton-wool effect of subsidies and guaranteed prices: but there is no way of knowing if the country would have developed those industries outside of Europe.

Ireland's failure to develop its own manufacturing industry in or out of the community suggests structural weaknesses which must be addressed. 'The very similarity between the failure of Irish policy under protection (1932 to 1965) and under free trade (1965 to the present) suggests that the key question is not free trade (EC membership) versus protectionism (leaving the EC).'[30] In 1992, those major questions about Ireland's domestic industrial and economic policies were addressed by the Culliton report (details of which can be found in Chapter 11).

---

* The famous 'out, out, out' rejection of the conclusions of the New Ireland Forum report setting out options for the future governance of Northern Ireland, delivered by Mrs Thatcher at a press conference in London in November 1984.

†Prepared by a European committee headed by Professor Jim Dooge, a long-standing Senator and adviser to Dr Garret FitzGerald, and a hydrologist of world standing. He served briefly as Minister for Foreign Affairs in 1981, one of the few Senators to serve in an Irish Cabinet.

Convergence Criteria Set by the Maastricht Treaty, 1992 (%)		
Item	Maastricht Guide	Ireland 1992
Total debt as percentage of GNP	60	99·8
Current borrowing as percentage of GDP	− 3	− 2·3
Member State's inflation rate	4·3	3

The future closer relationship of Ireland with its European neighbours in a monetary union, should it come about, will bring some disciplines to Irish domestic financial management which can only be welcomed by the majority of politicians: the policy of building up the national debt as an alternative to self-discipline was as destructive for the long-term prosperity of the country as it would be, if continued, for the financial cohesion of Europe.

The convergence criteria established by the Maastricht Treaty in 1992 will present Irish leaders with a challenge that will test politicians' capacity for good government (see table).

As barriers across Europe fall, and borders become blurred, the central national question of the Republic of Ireland's relationship with Northern Ireland may be eased. On 13 May 1992, a leaked document from ongoing talks in Northern Ireland set out a suggested method of governing Northern Ireland: there would be a commission of six people, three elected in Northern Ireland, one each nominated by the Dublin and London governments, and one nominated by the European Commission. The leader of the political party behind these suggestions – John Hume, leader of the North's Social Democratic and Labour Party (SDLP) – is also a member of the European Parliament. So is the leader of the Democratic Unionist Party (DUP), Hume's most outspoken opponent, Ian Paisley. Hume's suggestion was, of course, instantly turned down by the Unionist parties, who have never been enthusiastic workers for a united Europe, for obvious reasons. But it has been a notable feature in Europe that the two men have worked well together for Northern Ireland's economic interests in the European Parliament, while implacably opposing each other on political issues at home. It is interesting to speculate where a newly united Europe might lead them in their search for acceptable ways to govern Northern Ireland, so as to squeeze out the violent groups, who thrive in a power vacuum.

As 1993 began, a new government in Ireland looked towards Europe for help in dealing with the growing crisis caused by the European currency maelstrom, which was causing considerable upheaval in businesses trying to export to Britain in particular. As sterling weakened against the Irish pound, and interest rates rocketed, support in hard cash rather than fine words was needed. The much-needed lowering of German interest rates was not about to happen, so the government looked for soft loans from its European allies in order to help businesses and building societies to survive the shocks. All of this European currency instability, which had started in September 1992, took some of the gilt off the gingerbread of a greatly increased structural fund bonus for Ireland. After the Edinburgh European summit in December 1992, a beleaguered Taoiseach Albert Reynolds, in the throes of a difficult election campaign and considerable personal unpopularity at home, was able to announce Ireland's achievement of IR£1·14 million a year from Brussels until the end of the decade.

Despite criticism of the highly centralized manner in which Ireland draws down structural funds from Brussels – tightly controlled by the Department of Finance – most people in Ireland have not taken too great an interest in the exact mechanisms of how the money is spent. Like a great many things in modern Ireland, that *laissez-faire* attitude is gradually giving way to more knowledgeable concern about the actions of central government, and about what Ireland could and should expect from Europe. Resentment has been expressed at what was considered lack of local consultation on the spending of the earlier funds from Europe to Ireland. The new government appointed a powerful junior minister to the Department of Finance with specific responsibility for overseeing the national plan to be submitted to Brussels for drawing down the IR£8 billion in structural and cohesion funds. A strong-minded Labour Party economist, Minister Eithne FitzGerald, set about consultation with regional committees and declared that this fund would have to 'make a difference to the lives of families and of communities which have been hit by chronic unemployment ... these projects will have to be looked at in the context of a net increase in economic activity on this island ... when the last ecu has been spent, we want to ensure that something permanent will have been left behind to assist our ability to grow and to produce jobs'.[31] The minister was not about to listen too carefully to advice from some quarters that Ireland would do better to use the money towards paying off the national debt. The main defender of this argument is Dr Seán Barrett of Trinity College, Dublin, whose pronouncements often attack government spending policies. Using the Brussels money to pay off the debt 'would be superior to the present EC policy of co-funding expenditure which is exacerbating Ireland's economic problems rather than solving them' he told a seminar in Dublin in March 1993.[32] Another economist from another university feared that proposals for spending the EC money 'would relate to the perceived needs of spending agencies themselves and not to any major analysis at the centre of government'.[33]

NOTES

1. Pat Cox MEP, *Irish Times*, 28 April 1992. He was elected to the Dáil for the Progressive Democrats, in the general election of November 1992.
2. Figures from the European Commission Office in Dublin, May 1992.
3. *Revised Estimates for the Public Services, 1992*, Government Publications (Stationery Office).
4. Peter Sutherland, Irish Commissioner in the EC 1985–9, *Irish Times*, 28 April 1992.
5. Desmond O'Malley TD, Minister for Industry and Commerce, *Irish Times*, 28 April 1992.
6. Maurice Doyle, *Irish Times*, 20 April 1991.
7. Desmond Fennell, *Irish Times*, 4 February 1992.
8. Dáil Debate on Maastricht, 5 May 1992.
9. *Irish Independent* poll, 9 May 1992.
10. *Irish Times*, 22 May 1992.
11. John Bowman, *De Valera and the Ulster Question*, Oxford University Press, 1982.

12. John Fanagan (ed.), *Belling the Cats. Selected Speeches and Articles of John Kelly*, Moytura Press, 1992.
13. ibid.
14. Dáil speech by Albert Reynolds TD, Taoiseach, on 5 May 1992.
15. ibid.
16. Gerald Barry, *Sunday Tribune*, 3 November 1991.
17. Jim O'Keeffe TD, *Irish Times*, 3 April 1992.
18. *Irish Times*, 23 May 1992.
19. *Irish Times*, 5 June 1992.
20. Maureen Cairnduff (ed.), *Who's Who in Ireland – The Influential 1,000*, 2nd edn, Hibernian Publishing Co., 1991.
21. *Independent* (London), 21 November 1992.
22. Garret FitzGerald, *All in a Life*, Gill & Macmillan, 1991.
23. ibid.
24. *Irish Independent*, 23 January 1992.
25. Seán Dooney and John O'Toole, *Irish Government Today*, Gill & Macmillan, 1992.
26. Report from Patrick MacGill Summer School, *Irish Times*, 11 August 1992.
27. Professor Patrick Keatinge, Trinity College, *Irish Times*, 19 June 1990.
28. Máire Geoghegan-Quinn, Minister of State for European Affairs, 1987–91, *Irish Times*, 19 June 1990.
29. *Irish Times*, 19 June 1990.
30. Patrick Keatinge (ed.), *Ireland and EC Membership Evaluated*, London, Pinter Press, 1991.
31. *Irish Times*, 18 March 1993.
32. *Irish Times*, 5 March 1993, reporting on a seminar of the Statistical and Social Enquiry Society in Dublin.
33. Joe Durkan, University College, Dublin, economist, reported in the *Irish Times* on 5 March 1993.

CHAPTER 10

The Irish Economy: National Finances

'Take a tiny, open, ex-peasant economy. Place it next door to a much larger one, from which it broke away with great bitterness barely a lifetime ago. Infuse it with a passionate desire to enjoy the same lifestyle as its former masters, but without the same industrial heritage or natural resources. Inevitable result: extravagance, frustration, debt.' This was *The Economist*'s analysis of Ireland in a broad survey in January 1988.

Irish people, like most others, do not enjoy negative assessments from outside on how they should conduct their affairs, particularly when the lecturer is one of the old enemy – in Ireland's case, the British. That *Economist* survey caused some offence and anger in Ireland, since it used headlines like 'Nouveau Riche, Nouveau Pauvre' and was less than respectful about the then Taoiseach, making quite personal and insulting attacks on Mr Haughey's reputation. It mattered little that such comments were part of the everyday political gossip inside Ireland, or that many would concur with the descriptions in the same magazine of the two main political protagonists in the Ireland of the 1980s: Charles Haughey as a 'Peronist romantic', Garret FitzGerald as 'humane, honest and uncharismatic'. FitzGerald, quintessentially the intellectual, was said to have remarked of some new idea: 'That's all very well in practice, but how does it work in theory?'

However, on the economic side of things, the hurt was perhaps more acute because of the accuracy of the criticism in 1988, referring as it did to the previous fifteen or so years of inglorious Irish economic history.

The first decades of Irish independence after 1922 saw painfully slow progress towards any kind of economic prosperity. Post-colonial Ireland was indeed a small peasant economy, virtually without industrial infrastructure or development, heavily focused on agriculture, and locked by British subsidy policy into a total dependence on Britain for trade. Early Irish governments were

understandably obsessed with civil reconstruction and the establishment of durable political, judicial and administrative structures in
difficult circumstances. Then there was a world depression in the
early 1930s, coupled with an 'economic war' with Britain. The so-
called economic war stemmed from the uneasy relationship and
distrust between the British government and de Valera's Irish
government (which had been elected in 1932) and had as its catalyst
the decision by de Valera to withhold payment of moneys to the
British Treasury which were due under agreements made after
landlordism had been abolished in Ireland in the early years of the
century. In short, the British retaliated by imposing tariffs on
incoming Irish goods, causing even more unemployment and
poverty, and confirming the 'ourselves alone' policies of de Valera,
increasing isolationism and protectionism.

During the second world war, in which the country followed a
policy of neutrality, deeply unpopular with Britain, Ireland was
able to endure the economic privations because of the home
industries (these subsequently proved to be fragile) which had been
built up behind tariff walls. These tariffs were, to quote one of the
most innovative of civil servants ever to hold high office in Ireland,
Dr T. K. Whitaker,* 'both generous and indiscriminate'.[1]

In very many ways, Ireland followed a recognizable post-colonial
pattern: initial commitment to and obsession about getting
structures of self-government into place, a desire for economic self-
sufficiency (accompanied by isolationism in many other facets of
national life like censorship), no export-led economic policies, all
exacerbated by Ireland's geographical location as an island off an
island off a continent.

In the 1950s, as the generation of revolutionary politicians of the
1920s inevitably gave the lethargic and unimaginative leadership of
old men, the country had settled into economic doldrums and
despondency: dependence for agricultural sales on a single market

---

*Thomas Kenneth ('Ken') Whitaker (b. 1916), Secretary of the Department of
Finance 1956–69; Governor of the Central Bank, 1969–76; President, Economic
and Social Research Institute, 1970–85; Chancellor, National University of Ireland,
since 1976; recognized and admired as a major contributor to the economic and
cultural life of the State; this was acknowledged in his appointment to the Senate
by a Fianna Fáil Taoiseach (1977) and, subsequently, a Fine Gael Taoiseach
(1981).

– Britain – which had a low-food-price policy and simultaneously protected her own farmers and forced Irish people off the land; indigenous industry, artificially protected for too long, had failed to grow and prosper, underlining the gap between Ireland and other European countries which had had an industrial revolution in the last century; and serious balance-of-payments deficits that ate into the sterling reserves Ireland had been forced to accumulate in two world wars. Massive emigration took place, that sad outflow of young people to the United States, Australia, Canada, but most of all to Britain; the population declined miserably. Thirty years on, in 1986, Dr Whitaker described the mood of Ireland in the 1950s: 'The community was experiencing a dark night of the soul in which doubts were prevalent as to whether the achievement of political independence had not been futile.'[2]

The descent into economic and social depression presaged a sort of rebirth. Two men are today credited with having had the energy and vision to pull Ireland out of the depths of the 1950s: the new and dynamic Secretary of the Department of Finance, Ken Whitaker, and his Taoiseach, Seán Lemass. Between them they recognized certain realities, and persuaded their colleagues and the wider population to do likewise. Whitaker designed Ireland's first Programme for Economic Expansion in the years 1957–8. The Programme was solid, simple and achievable. Nearly twenty-five years later, in Dáil Éireann, it was still praised for its 'calm, jargon-free assessments, devoid of political trumpeting, its statement of priorities, not all of them popular; its setting of simple, modest, credible targets'.[3] The Programme recognized the hard realities: protected manufacture for a tiny (and then dwindling) home market gave no hope for increased employment; such employment as there was would be at unacceptably low wages in an increasingly competitive world; the only hope for new jobs was to start exporting on an increasing scale, and to do that meant internal aids and incentives, as well as dismantling tariffs and finding new markets. The simple concept of attracting multinational firms to Ireland rather than see young Irish people travelling abroad to work for them was accepted. Grassland and its products were to be vigorously developed in agriculture rather than protected home production of wheat – 'grass before grain'. A general policy of development through a coherent expansion of manufacturing, foreign as well as Irish, was an integral part of the strategy of those early Irish development plans. De Valera, old and blind and now President of Ireland, presided benignly as his young successors changed utterly the economic direction he had imposed for so long.

Whitaker had the great satisfaction of seeing his grand economic strategy yielding abundant results for his country, but Lemass retired in the mid-1960s and died a few years later, too soon to see its full realization. As a result of the new thinking during the 1960s, economic growth per annum doubled to 4 per cent; tourism prospered; emigration abated; and by 1966 the population had risen to 66,000 above its lowest-ever level of 2·8 million in 1961, and went on growing. This was all achieved without any major financial deficits in any area, and with moderate inflation, as befitted the careful stewardship of Ken Whitaker. In 1971, Ireland's total national debt was just IR£1 billion (59 per cent of GNP). More recently, the debt stood at IR£25 billion (104·7 per cent of GNP) by 1992.

Those optimistic days when Ireland began to seem at last like a place where its young could find work for life, when foreign investors crowded in to take advantage of both generous tax incentives and a lively young and literate workforce, when politicians presided over a well-ordered and growing economy were halted by a combination of external economic upheavals at the end of the decade, and internal weaknesses of resolve to deal with those problems independently. Inflation rose internationally and Ireland's rate with it (to 8 per cent for the years 1968–72). Irish ministers and trade unions, having become accustomed to the prosperity of the 1960s, wanted to have it all – and more – in the 1970s, despite clear evidence that it could not go on. As Whitaker approached retirement, and the political competition in Ireland heated up, he had to watch while 'ambitious ministers jibbed at being kept prisoners of a plan and cut free with novel and expensive initiatives. Trade unions favoured planning of everything except wages.'[4]

This new spirit of profligacy, the opposite to Whitaker's carefully managed expansion, gave rise to the breaking in 1972 of the tradition of never running a current budget deficit. The euphoria attending Irish entry to the European Economic Community in 1973 deflected attention from growing financial mismanagement.

Then, at the end of 1973, the world was plunged into uncertainty and economic disorder by the quadrupling of the price of oil. The Irish finance minister, like so many around the world, feared the possibly catastrophic deflationary effects of the oil crisis on the Irish economy if it was not cushioned by borrowing. This was the main reason for the start of really serious deficit budgeting to meet current expenses: expenses which had a lot to do with ambitions to set and keep Irish social welfare and health standards on a par with her large and formerly dominant neighbour Great Britain, despite the lack of domestic revenue to pay for them. This has been a consistent problem in Ireland: a demand for equality in all social services with much wealthier nations despite a much smaller GDP per capita. An example of the kind of political thinking of the time was the sudden announcement of free secondary education in 1966, without warning or advance planning. Growth did not keep up with these demands, and so between 1973 and 1977 the aggregate budget deficit was IR£750 million, mostly borrowed abroad. The coalition government in 1977 – soon to be outgoing – made a last-minute return to more conservative budgeting by trading tax concessions and investment in job creation for moderate pay increases, but it went out of office in what was subsequently considered one of the most economically damaging election contests the country ever knew.

The 1977 general election was one of bread and circuses: promises were made – and duly fulfilled – of the abolition of domestic rates on dwellings and of no more car tax; and a government swept into power committed to higher spending and more borrowing. It was a campaign which did no credit to any participant.

Opinion differs as to whether the new Taoiseach, Jack Lynch of Fianna Fáil, and his economic guru Martin O'Donoghue, a former economics lecturer at Trinity College, Dublin, were genuinely convinced that high spending (borrowed) would 'kick-start' the economy into growth and therefore enough buoyancy to deal with repayments of the additional borrowing, or whether the whole programme was pure political auctioneering. The truth probably lies somewhere in the middle, as it usually does. Whatever the motivation, the results were negative for the economy, and the position deteriorated further when two years later, at the end of 1979, a new Taoiseach, Charles Haughey, took over from Lynch.

By that stage, a national malaise had well and truly set in, as high spending on social services – health, education and social welfare, as well as on public-service pay – had become an accepted part of the way governments did their business.

The early 1980s saw an extraordinary period of political and economic upheaval in Ireland. The political parties battled it out in three general elections over eighteen months in 1981 and 1982.

Charles Haughey, in a famous and solemn television address to the nation in January 1980, had warned that hard decisions would have to be made, that the country was living beyond its means, that difficult times lay ahead: it was tightening-the-belt time. Economic analysts and worried financial institutions were relieved; they felt that this man with a tough reputation would pull the country back from the slide into unmanageable debt.

But, in a volte-face as astonishing as it was damaging, Haughey added enormously to the debt as he used current deficits to finance massive public-service pay increases in the face of strike threats and added thousands to civil-service numbers in a bid to bring down unemployment figures. By June 1981 when he finally faced the electorate, there was a major economic debate raging. *The Economist* accurately described Haughey's legacy: 'When Mr Haughey took over from Mr Lynch in 1979, the public sector was already in rapidly growing deficit. In the following eighteen months, public spending and borrowing shot up, helped by Mr Haughey's habit of promising new hospitals or protected jobs wherever he travelled ... the public sector borrowing requirement and the exchequer borrowing requirement reached their peaks, at 20.3 per cent and 15.9 per cent of GNP respectively, in 1981.'[5]

A feature of that 1981 general election was the new awareness of ordinary householders of the seriousness of the country's financial problems. Party canvassers found worried women and men everywhere who bandied phrases like budget deficits, national debt, interest payments, the International Monetary Fund: and Mr Haughey failed to achieve a majority, having inherited a 20-seat majority a mere eighteen months before. The public debate on the economy in Ireland, the first such phenomenon ever seen, was caused by a combination of a revitalized Fine Gael under Garret FitzGerald, whose dual platform of economic realism and social liberalism appealed to the urban middle classes, and the alarm signals sent out by the Central Bank, whose bulletins gave the more serious economic commentators ample material for their articles.

Two more elections in 1982, with the consequent stop–go pattern of economic policy formation, did nothing to improve matters. When a coalition government with a working majority finally took office in December 1982, the debt had reached IR£12 billion, unemployment was rising steeply, and inflation was climbing higher and higher. The annual exchequer borrowing requirement had rocketed from under 10 per cent of GNP in 1977 to 15 per cent in 1981.

In this crisis situation, Garret FitzGerald and his Labour Party deputy prime minister faced decisions which would prove nearly impossible to implement. The flair which FitzGerald had shown in resuscitating his Fine Gael party in Opposition was not carried through into determined leadership of his country when in office. There was an early indication of strains between the parties in government: in January 1983, the Minister for Finance had warned that cuts of IR£500 million would be the minimum needed in that year to start on the road to restoring financial stability. From his hospital bed, where he was having treatment for a troublesome back injury, the young Labour leader quickly issued a contradictory statement denying that any such agreement for this scale of cuts had been made by the government. It boded ill for the future; such public disagreements became a feature of that government, leading to ill feeling and distrust inside the Cabinet room and uneasiness between the parties in the Dáil. Naturally, this was exploited by an Opposition that vigorously condemned any suggested cut in public spending.

By 1986, the ageing but still highly respected Dr Whitaker was deploring, yet again, the failure of government to deal with the continuing crisis. Noting that the original government target of eliminating the current budget deficit by 1987 had been abandoned in favour of reducing the deficit to 5 per cent of GNP by that date, he said sadly: 'Procrastination merely piles up the agony for the future, increasing the risk that solutions will be imposed from outside rather than chosen by ourselves.'[6] In 1986, unemployment had risen to 230,000, while emigration on a large scale was once again denuding the countryside. Sad stories abounded of towns unable to field a hurling team because the young men had gone, of airports and ports witnessing scenes of family partings reminiscent of the depressed 1950s. Trade unions were militant, and among the most difficult were the powerful 40,000-strong members of the teachers' unions, who had been awarded a substantial special pay increase in 1985 by the independent arbitrator on public-service pay. The government, having initially stood out against this addition of more than IR£100 million to the already disastrous level of borrowing, failed to sustain a strong line, and fudged the issue sufficiently to confirm the view of it as a weak and divided force. Concessions were made, a calamitously handled Cabinet reshuffle reinforced the general perception of confusion in government, and the gains made on the economy, such as much-reduced inflation, were not sufficient to amount to real progress. It was not a period calculated to encourage investment and growth.

A government plan, produced in late 1984, was called 'Building on Reality': apart from easing some of the targets like the ratio of GNP to deficits, its major aspirations were unrealized. It has been a feature of modern Irish economic planning, or lack of it, that plans are produced with great solemnity ('Building on Reality' was launched in considerable style in the magnificent Iveagh House, headquarters of the Department of Foreign Affairs) and then fail through lack of any serious implementation plan, or because governments lack the political will to put in place the hard decisions in order to be able to make the easy ones.

By 1987, great progress had been made on inflation, which stood at 2·6 per cent (compared with 15 per cent in 1982). But unemployment had doubled, from 9 per cent to 18 per cent of the labour force in those same years. And the national debt had reached IR£24 billion, doubling in those years.

The best way to describe the years of coalition government between the end of 1982 and the beginning of 1987 is to use the analogy of yet another economic war. The major party in government, Fine Gael, faced several opponents: first, the parliamentary opposition, Fianna Fáil, who refused to recognize any need for either containment or curtailment of public spending and opposed every government move. This was normal Opposition behaviour in Ireland. Second, the more powerful interest groups, led by the public-service trade unions, had not accepted the message of three elections and resolutely refused to tailor their demands to what the government felt was appropriate. Marches, demonstrations, pickets outside the Dáil and constant tight votes and bitter recriminations inside, angry scenes at the clinics of government Deputies – the pressure was relentless.

Third, and most seriously, the minor party in government had considerable difficulties in bringing its parliamentary Deputies through the 'yes' lobbies in those frequent Dáil votes forced by the Opposition. This led to vacillation, last-minute changes of policy, and lack of firmness, so that Garret FitzGerald was unable to achieve the kind of financial discipline he had promised, though making progress on some elements, like inflation. However, he could certainly claim to have made the financial running of the country a central issue once again. Looking back on that period, some economists consider that the government of FitzGerald was unduly harshly criticized: 'Seven irresponsible years – 1975–82 – had to be followed by seven desperate years of trying to turn the ship around,' said one of them.[7] The ship had indeed proved very cumbersome and unresponsive.

Finally, the gravity of the deteriorating situation caused the two parties in government to part company: the Fine Gael Minister for Finance prepared a 1987 budget which the Labour Party found unacceptable. It left the government, and Fine Gael went to the country in late January of that year. After an election campaign which centred around Fianna Fáil's condemnation of all spending cuts (the slogans read, 'Health cuts hit the old, the poor, and the sick . . .' and 'There is a better way'), the result was, not surprisingly, a considerable loss of seats for Fine Gael, gains for Fianna Fáil and a surge in seats for a new party, the Progressive Democrats, which promised financial rectitude and social liberalism. Significantly, however, Fianna Fáil could only achieve government in a minority situation. There was a historic moment for Ireland in the television coverage of the election count, when the outgoing Taoiseach offered the Opposition's support to the incoming minority Fianna Fáil government; the condition was that they should make the right decisions to bring the economy back to order. This marked a turning-point in economic as well as political history.

FitzGerald then retired as leader of Fine Gael. His undertaking was reinforced later in 1987 when the new leader of Fine Gael, Alan Dukes, expounded the 'Tallaght strategy' (named after the

THE IRISH ECONOMY: NATIONAL FINANCES

town in west County Dublin where the strategy was explained).
For the first time ever, the country observed an Opposition refusing
to use its voting strength to topple a government which was making
unpopular decisions.

Fianna Fáil, a party which had always been able to make
pragmatic decisions on the day, not only executed a 180-degree
turn on economic policy, but adopted the budget of the outgoing
government and even added more cuts to it. A new and determined
Minister for Finance, Ray MacSharry,* pursued the kind of policy
which hadn't been seen in Ireland in modern history. Discipline
was rigidly enforced, backed by the Taoiseach, who had put on the
mantle of fiscal rectitude. *The Economist*, marvelling at this
Damascus-like conversion, described the new atmosphere of
expenditure-cutting in the Irish corridors of power: 'Mr Haughey's
backing is essential; civil servants who complain that it cannot be
done are told: "The Taoiseach will be sorry to hear that" – they
turn white and do their sums again.'

Pressure groups and trade unions were dumbfounded as their old
allies in Fianna Fáil deserted them. Fine Gael, because of the new
strategy of supporting the government, couldn't agitate on their
behalf as Opposition politicians had always done, and frequently
came in for as much obloquy as government Deputies. This was a
new and strange role for Opposition politicians, which was resented
by many inside Fine Gael. The new leader, Alan Dukes, found
himself slipping in popularity among his own party parliamentarians and rank and file, as well as in the public-opinion polls.

By 1989, the current budget deficit was down to IR£263 million
(1·3 per cent of GNP) compared with IR£1,180 million (6·5 per cent
of GNP) in 1987.[8] Fine Gael's gesture in supporting the government
was, however, doing them no good at all with public opinion; the
party sank lower and lower in the polls, despite the unpopularity of
the government's spending cuts. In the next general election of
1989, the government party lost 4 seats, but Fine Gael gained only
4, and was in no position to form a government. This was a grave

---

*Ray MacSharry (b. 1938), Dáil Deputy for Sligo–Leitrim 1969–84, Member of
the European Parliament, 1984–7, Minister for Agriculture 1979–81, and Finance,
1982, again from 1987 to 1989; Irish Commissioner at the EC 1989–92. Retired
from the Commission and from public life in December 1992. For more on Mr
MacSharry, see pages 225–8.

set-back for the party, which had had high hopes of regaining many more of the 19 seats lost in 1987. It was a further indication of the blurring of identity between the parties of the centre–right, presaging yet worse results for the future. Perhaps the most serious implication of the result was, however, that there was no electoral reward in Ireland for an Opposition which had put the national interest first and helped to set the economy on the right road.

Despite approving comments from business leaders and even occasionally from Fianna Fáil, Alan Dukes did not survive his next test, the 1990 presidential election, and was unceremoniously dumped in favour of John Bruton, a man with a reputation for conservatism on both financial and economic issues. It was in 1990 that the change occurring in the political outlook of the Irish was further marked by the election of Mary Robinson to the presidency; she was backed by the parties of the left, and had been an outspoken member of the Labour Party herself.

As the 1990s dawned, Ireland was managing its economy much better than in the previous decade and a half. In terms of economic growth, borrowing, inflation, balance-of-trade figures, budget deficits, interest repayments of national debt, interest rates, numbers at work . . . all these indicators were positive, all signs of a healthy economy. International economic upheavals apart, it seemed as if Irish maturity and good sense had at last put the country on a straight road.

The dark side – and some would say the central failure – is unemployment, and its accompanying spectre of poverty, street crime and violence. Large pockets of Dublin and other bigger cities suffer unemployment rates of up to 70 per cent and more, leading to ghetto-ized black spots and self-perpetuating generations of unemployment and deprivation. In this situation, the social-welfare cushion assumes a great importance. Expenditure on social-welfare support at over IR£3 billion and 12·8 per cent of GNP (and 28 per cent of total expenditure in 1992) is a major drain on resources. Ireland has more than kept pace with inflation in social-welfare support systems, which are well up to international levels. This has led to a situation where there is concern that the lowest-paid workers would be better off financially if they remained idle, particularly married men with several children. The central problem

Selected Irish Economic Statistics (30 September 1992)			
Subject	1971	1981	1991
Labour-force unemployment*	61,000	126,000	215,000
As percentage of labour force	5·5	9·9	16·1
Live register unemployment	60,875	149,063	253,950
As percentage of labour force	5·5	11·7	19·0
Inflation (%)	9·0	20·4	3·2
Exchequer borrowing requirement (IR£ million)	128†	1,721	501
As percentage of GNP	6·8	15·9	2·1
As percentage of GDP	6·9	15·2	1·9
National debt (IR£ million)	1,114	10,195	25,387‡
As percentage of GNP	59·2	93·9	104·7
As percentage of GDP	60·0	89·8	94·1
Interest repayments on debt (IR£ million)§	112†	885	2,353
As percentage of GNP	6·0	8·2	9·7
As percentage of GDP	6·0	7·8	8·7
Social welfare expenditure (IR£ million)¶	113·7†	1,182·7	3,092·5
As percentage of GNP	6·0	10·9	12·8
As percentage of GDP	6·1	10·4	11·5
Public-service pay (IR£ million)	155·5†	1,664	3,406
As percentage of GNP	8·3	15·3	14·0
As percentage of GDP	8·4	14·6	12·6
Emigration‖	5,000	− 2,000	1,000

* Mid-April estimates (based on Labour Force Survey).
† Converted from financial-year basis to calendar-year basis.
‡ Provisional.

§ Service of public debt.
¶ Gross expenditure on social welfare.
‖ Estimated net migration (negative figure equals inflow).

Sources: Central Statistics Office; Central Bank of Ireland; Department of Finance; Department of Social Welfare.

is, of course, that even if the State is relatively generous with rates of support, it does not amount to anything like prosperity for a huge section of the population, and engenders poverty, depression and crime.

Governments hesitate about the best way to deal with what is variously described as a poverty trap or a disincentive to work. Between the years 1972 and 1987, when governments spent enormously of money which was not theirs to spend, unemployment rose from 70,000 to 247,000. It has continued to rise inexorably, and by early 1993 reached 300,000 – 21 per cent of the labour force, or 17 per cent after changes were made in 1992 in the method of calculation. The new Minister for Finance, Bertie Ahern,* reluctantly agreed with forecasts of further rises in a newspaper interview in March 1992.[9]

In early June 1992, the Central Statistics Office announced a change in methodology. In future, those working on a week/on, week/off basis would no longer be included; self-employed people claiming assistance would likewise disappear from the figures; and an extension of a government pre-retirement scheme accounted for the disappearance of yet another group. Overnight, 7,500 people disappeared from the unemployment figures. In future, the unemployment figures would be calculated using the annual labour-force survey instead of the numbers of those signing on the live register. The economics editor† of the *Irish Times* mused with some amazement on 6 June: 'Last month the Irish unemployment rate was 21 per cent. It is now below 16·5 per cent. And that is official.' The editorial writer of the same newspaper on the same day reminded his readers that the Economic and Social Research Institute was forecasting that 'numbers on the live register this year will average 284,000, up 30,000 on last year and nearly 60,000 on the preceding year'. Ireland's historically high birth rate combined

---

* Bertie Ahern (b. 1951), Minister for Labour, 1987–91, and Minister for Finance from 1991. A skilful, low-key, modest-sounding politician from the heart of old Dublin. His rich Dublin accent and empathy with 'the working man' seemed to fit him peculiarly for the job of Minister for Labour. Deceptively quiet, he tops the poll at most elections which means endless seven-days-a-week cultivation of his constituency. He almost challenged Albert Reynolds for Fianna Fáil leadership in 1992, but backed off at the last minute, damaging his reputation somewhat.

† Cliff Taylor.

with the return of emigrants from the recession-hit economies of the UK, the USA, and other English-speaking countries, as well as the continued migration from agriculture to the cities, caused this acceleration in these gloomy figures. A debate rages in Ireland about contributory causes and possible remedies.* With the massive help of the European Community, Ireland provides a network of training centres for the unemployed, without which the figures would be even more disastrous.

The government which took office in 1989 was a coalition between Fianna Fáil and the Progressive Democrats, both committed to keeping the economy in order. The successful Minister for Finance, Ray MacSharry, was by now established in the Irish Commissioner's office in Brussels, and was succeeded by the equally pragmatic Albert Reynolds, from whom fiscal rectitude was confidently expected. But trouble was looming ahead, and the stern resolve of the 1987–9 period seemed to be less stern. One of the major features of the new policy was the negotiation of the 'Programme for Economic and Social Progress' (PESP). This was a national agreement between government and the 'social partners'† on pay and a wide range of policy issues, and followed on an agreement concluded in 1987 called the 'Programme for National Recovery' (PNR). Opinion in Ireland differs about the value of these agreements, some economic commentators feeling that they amount to little more than public-service pay agreements accompanied unnecessarily and expensively by expenditure undertakings, others conceding that order was re-established in the 1987–9 period with the valuable help of the PNR. Those opposed to them feel that governments only need to keep inflation low, and pay demands should be reasonable as a result.

The indubitable fact is that public-service pay has become a huge factor in escalating government expenditure in recent years. One of the foremost economic journalists in the country wrote in September 1991: 'The special pay awards for public servants due under pay deals past and present are causing the Minister for Finance major headaches.'[10] Ray MacSharry had left a legacy of deferred public-service increases, and the 1989 government added more

* See Chapter 11.
† Farmers, trade unions, employers and government.

Trends in Public Service Pay, 1987–92			
Year	Public-service pay bill (IR£ million)	Percentage increase on previous year	Consumer price inflation (%)
1987	2,759	5·1	3·1
1988	2,845	3·1	2·1
1989	2,914	2·4	4·1
1990	3,160	8·4	3·3
1991	3,406	7·8	3·2
1992	3,722	9·3	3·0

Source: Sunday Tribune, 6 December 1992.

commitments in two budgets. By mid-1991, a serious budget overrun was causing concern. And one of the principal bugbears in the system was the method of determining public-service pay. While few would use the colourful expression of Trinity College economist Seán Barrett to describe it – 'public service payola'[11] – the freedom of the independent arbitrator to give special awards without reference to the state of the public finances sat uncomfortably with the need to contain expenditure. The arbitrator, a barrister, was appointed as a judge of the High Court in December 1992, giving the government an opportunity to alter the terms of reference with a new appointee, if the public-service unions could be persuaded to agree.

Another economist worried about the size of the pay bill: 'Public service pay passed 50 per cent of public spending some years ago, and is moving towards 60 per cent. There'll be only pay and no services if this goes on. The arbitration system has to change.'[12] In the budget of 1992, the Minister for Finance announced that current public spending was to rise by 7·7 per cent – more than twice the estimated inflation rate for the year. He also announced that public-service pay would amount to IR£3,726 million in 1992, an increase of 9 per cent on 1991, well over double the rate of inflation.[13] Government signalled that an attempt might be made to change the method of determining public-service pay changes.

As this former peasant economy looks into the next century, it can claim – despite structural problems proving difficult to put right – to have achieved certain goals and to be well placed to make rapid improvements, if international factors were at least benign. A positive growth rate of at least 2·5 per cent in 1991 in the context of a grave international recession, and indications of a 1992 growth of 3·5 per cent, represent a considerable economic feat. The chronic structural problem of the Irish economy – its inability to create jobs at a sufficient rate to absorb the high natural increase in the labour force – would be eased if, as the Economic and Social Research Institute forecast in 1992, a 6 per cent per annum rate of growth could be achieved and sustained for some years. The ESRI calculates that 30,000 new jobs a year should be possible with this rate of growth. This bullish forecast, made in early summer 1992,[14] was based on a very healthy current-account surplus, and the spillover effect into increased confidence and investment in the Irish economy. In the opinion of the ESRI economists, the growing surplus is 'a measure of the under-utilization of Irish labour'. The simple fact of the matter is that Irish exports have performed extraordinarily well even when their main markets have been in recession; there is no telling how much better things could and would be when the world comes out of recession. The ESRI reckoned that total exports rose by 6 per cent in volume in 1991 (a nearly 5 per cent increase in value) and in 1992 they were expecting the volume increase to be over 9 per cent. With price increases, the value of the increase in exports should be 12·5 per cent in 1992. (Total money value of 1992 exports is expected to be IR£18,797 billion.) In a note of realism, the economists of the ESRI remind their readers that unemployment figures are such 'that a merely good economic performance is inadequate to deal with the employment crisis. What is needed is an outstanding performance, sustained for several years.' Not too many economists were prepared to share the optimism of the ESRI, and as a currency crisis erupted in late 1992, accompanied by an unsettling and unnecessary general election, a growth rate of even 3 per cent in 1993 began to look unlikely.

With the exception of the 'unavoidable corrective period of the mid-80s'[15] Ireland's economic growth did indeed average about 4 per cent over every five-year period since 1960. If Ireland could take advantage of increased trade prospects opened by the Single European Act, and the possibilities of closer and stronger links with a new Europe despite the hesitations over Maastricht, it should achieve good growth. That confidence factor, given such a boost by the return to fiscal sanity in the late 1980s, and dependent on its continuance, could well be the key to meeting the needs of the young arrivals on the Irish labour market. The national debt, which loomed so large and threateningly in the 1980s, was at last proving to be a manageable entity, as interest payments decreased as a percentage of GNP – down to £2,200 million in 1992, or 8.5 per cent of GNP, a considerable and progressive improvement on recent years. The target set by Maastricht for countries hoping to be part of Europe's monetary union at the end of the century – national debt approaching 60 per cent of GDP – seemed to be attainable without desperately severe measures if trends since 1987 could be sustained.

Those years in the 1970s and 1980s when Ireland might have made much more progress instead of wasting years of potential growth by overspending and borrowing, and the subsequent years of damaging wrangles and delays in remedying the crisis – need they have happened? A generation of young people emigrated or languished in the dole queues while politicians desperately tried to cut back on expenditure and poured scarce money into international-debt repayment. One school of thought asserts that the Fianna Fáil government from 1977 cost the country some ten years of economic growth. However the blame should be apportioned, the fact remains that between 1975 and 1982 Ireland's international reputation and creditworthiness, as well as international investment confidence, plummeted. It took nearly seven more years of slippage before stability, confidence and fiscal reason were fully restored. What caused that apparently blind and uncontrolled political irresponsibility?

A feature of Ireland's political/administrative system is the absence of interchange with business and academic life. There is an almost complete lack of interaction between groups which should be working together – business, industry, universities, civil service, politicians. No politician in Ireland moves alternately as a matter of course between any of these different areas, and very few civil servants spend any time at all experiencing life in the machine-rooms of the economy. An almost inflexible structure of public administration, political and civil service, is ill-fitted to meet the complex challenges of a sophisticated and developing Europe. Even the simple procedure of bringing special advisers into ministerial offices has been virtually non-existent and very different from the practice in most modern western democracies. There is not much evidence in Ireland of the 1990s that any serious concern exists about the resultant vacuum in real understanding, dynamism and development of the broad picture of the economy. A breakthrough in the area of special advisers was made in early 1993, when a new government appointed a range of advisers, particularly on the Labour side of government.

The Irish Central Bank enjoys nearly total autonomy, and has usually confined itself to a narrow brief, maintaining the external integrity of the Irish currency, juggling around interest rates with inflation. There is an unwritten but firmly institutionalized practice of appointing the retiring Secretary of the Department of Finance as Governor of the Central Bank: with the resulting scenario of trenchant criticisms of state financial policy emanating from the Central Bank headquarters, made, of course, by people who have been relieved of the obligation to carry out that policy under a succession of governments. Both the Central Bank and the Department of Finance suffer a continual 'brain drain' to the private sector because of lack of reward, in either monetary or promotional terms, in their work. As the Central Bank celebrated its fiftieth birthday in 1993, its reputation for independence was praised by financial commentators, but not so its penchant for secrecy. Despite occasional forthright speeches by its governor, the bank is not accountable to any Dáil committee, and is not open to questioning in any public forum. 'It is probably the only central bank in Europe that has no press office, and in the last five years its only press conferences have been to launch new notes or coins,' said a disgruntled economic commentator.[16]

Faced with difficult decisions, Irish governments in the late 1970s and right up to the mid-1980s proved inadequate: the Department of Finance lost control, while powerful interest groups, mainly trade unions and farmers, quickly wore down the resolve of politicians battling for power. The apparent recovery of the early 1990s followed so many years of failure that it might have been expected that lessons would have been learned and institutional arrangements examined. It remains to be seen if the discipline required from closer links with Europe and European systems will bring about the modernization which Irish politicians domestically seem unable and/or unwilling to contemplate themselves.

When, in November 1992, a sudden general election was called, clouds had already started to gather on the financial horizon. The most serious one was the currency crisis affecting the Irish pound. Irish people found themselves with a pound that was, for the first time, worth more than the English one. This followed the turbulent events in Europe over the previous months, and led to speculative pressure on the Irish pound. As exports rocketed in price, the government announced a IR£50 million fund to help Irish exporters survive this shock. Calls for devaluation of the Irish pound were made by the Confederation of Irish Industry, but the Minister for Finance gritted his teeth and said no.

The election showed a surge towards the left in Ireland, but more significantly, there was no decisive result; and the careful progress towards economic strength seemed stopped in its tracks. What is more, the form of the campaign – promises of high spending to give employment a boost – alarmed some economists. Was this a sensible idea, given the relatively low exchequer borrowing requirement, or was it a return to the disasters of the late 1970s? The problems caused by the currency crisis implied the need for severe adjustments – including lower pay rises across the board – to preserve jobs in the aftermath of the crisis. None of the parties seemed to want to address the question of how Ireland was to deal with the crunch issues of high interest rates and sterling weakness. It was clear that the economic climate had changed utterly. The incoming administration faced low growth, rising unemployment, punishing interest rates, and a tight budget position: no easy options. The optimistic forecasts of the summer of 1992 no longer seemed sustainable. When the currency crisis started to develop, Ireland got sympathy instead of criticism from its neighbours: the *Sunday Times* of London, in what Irish people would call a backhanded compliment, commented: 'Poor old Ireland: for once, the authorities are struggling with a financial crisis not of their making.'[17] Observers at home hoped that domestic decisions would not exacerbate it.

What kind of people make the essential financial decisions for Ireland? The inner circle around the 1992 Minister for Finance was extraordinarily small. Their identity became a matter of public curiosity in the autumn of the year, when European currencies went into the maelstrom, and the Irish pound came under severe pressure.

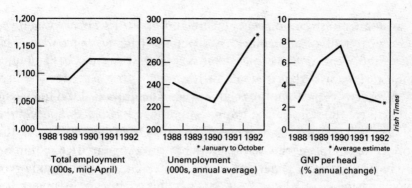

Total employment
(000s, mid-April)

Unemployment
(000s, annual average)
* January to October

GNP per head
(% annual change)
* Average estimate

Key economic indicators, 1988/92 (*source: Irish Times*,
18 November 1992)

Five men – for no woman has reached the heights in the financial management of Ireland – who had all spent most of their working lives inside the Irish Department of Finance met almost daily with the minister. They had all studied economics at University College, Dublin, between the 1940s and the 1960s, and none of them had ever worked in the private sector. They faithfully mirror the dominant characteristics of all power blocks in Ireland: middle-aged, middle-class, Catholic, and male. The minister himself, from a more sturdily working-class background, nevertheless followed the inclination of his predecessors, signalling a reluctance to widen the net of advice and consultation available to him.

The five were:

Maurice Doyle, Governor of the Central Bank. Born in Dublin in 1932, he graduated in economics from UCD, then qualified as a barrister, and joined the Department of Finance. Part of his early work in the department was on the first Programme for Economic Expansion, under the redoubtable Dr Whitaker. He became a tough Secretary of the Department of Finance in 1981, though even he was defeated by the refusal of politicians to make the really hard decisions. In 1987 he followed the pattern of assuming the governorship of the Central Bank, where his intellectual sharpness, dry wit, and energy, as well as his penchant for straight talking, have annoyed politicians. He was part of the Delors Committee at the EC which drew up the blueprint for economic and monetary union – a fact which did not stop him warning against complacency in Ireland about its effect. When the currency crisis of September 1992 put the Irish pound under pressure, the Central Bank raised interest rates by 3 per cent despite ministerial noises that it would be less.

Another former top official of the Department of Finance is crucial to the ministerial think-tank: the chief executive of the National Treasury Management Agency, *Dr Michael Somers*. His job is to manage the national debt, standing at IR£25 billion in 1992, and he is generally considered to be an acute analyst of world currency markets. Born in 1942, his doctorate in economics from University College, Dublin, led him to the Department of Finance, through which he progressed to seniority with a short spell in the Central Bank. The Agency was established in 1990 by Taoiseach Charles Haughey, and was welcomed as at least one step in improving the flexibility of the state's financial management.

In 1992, the country's most powerful civil servant, the Secretary of the Department of Finance, was *Seán Cromien*.* His financial astuteness is admired, as is his single-mindedness. He follows the conservative pattern of his predecessors, 'which has often frustrated the big spenders in other Departments, but which has meant that priority is always given to the defence of the punt [pound] in foreign exchanges'.[18]

The other two senior men advising the minister during that crucial currency crisis in 1992, which saw the country slipping into a general election in the middle of it, were *Maurice O'Connell*, Second Secretary of the Department, and *Tom Considine*, a principal officer in the monetary area. O'Connell, a Kerryman and member of the EC's powerful monetary committee, had a reputation of staunchly defending the Irish pound and holding a very hard line on government spending. Considine, his assistant, who is from Co. Clare, opted to stay in the Department of Finance when the National Treasury Management Agency was established in 1990.

A formidable and talented group then, and one which carries enormous clout with Irish Ministers for Finance, who are not

* See page 90 above for a profile of Seán Cromien.

usually people with financial expertise or experience themselves. The problem is the narrow range from which these officials come, unleavened by entrepreneurial business skills, or any wide experience of the world of private investment and industrial decision-making. The ministers can – and do – accept almost unquestioningly the diktat of the finance mandarins, but then go on to confer in the Taoiseach's office or Cabinet meeting where they frequently lose the argument, to the unspoken – in public at least – disquiet of those who advise them.

In a country with Ireland's unemployment problem, and its resulting poverty and social alienation, the later 1990s will require something extra, something more than what has gone before.

The general election was held on 25 November 1992. Seven weeks – the longest interregnum ever in Irish government – elapsed before a new administration was in place. In that period, the pound was under severe pressure, with Central Bank and acting government battling to stave off speculators and preserve the value of the currency.

A curious episode took place on Tuesday, 5 January, when the Minister for Finance, Bertie Ahern, unexpectedly implied that the government were about to consider the devaluation option; despite later vigorous denials by himself and his officials, the London *Financial Times* reported his words and caused big selling of the Irish pound. Analysts concluded that Ahern's poor timing was caused by his anger at news of a French and German bilateral currency arrangement which would appear to have left the Irish pound 'to hang out to dry'. Whatever the cause, it would have been much better to have kept silent.

Political, if not financial, stability returned with the appointment of a government, on 12 January 1993, composed of a newly invigorated Labour Party (which more than doubled its Dáil representation, getting 33 seats) and a chastened Fianna Fáil Party, who were down to 68 seats from 77. Irish business and employers were aghast as sterling weakened and Irish exports lost their competitiveness in the huge British market. The Minister for Finance was reappointed, and launched a diplomatic offensive in Europe, seeking support for the government's position. Soft loans were obtained from the European Investment Bank to provide interest subsidies for industry and householders. It became crystal clear that the big Europeans were not disposed to do anything to help support the Irish pound, illustrating Ireland's vulnerability yet again. Against a chorus of conflicting advice from unions and business, the threat to Irish employment was uppermost in the minds of politicians and major interest groups. Ireland's small open economy struggled to protect employers from the massive and continuous threat to jobs as sterling's weakness persisted.

The *Programme for a Partnership Government, 1993–97*, which was agreed between the two parties as their working document for their term of office, contained no reference at all to the currency crisis, which had been well established before and during the period of its negotiations. The programme seemed to consider that the twin burdens of high interest rates and the appreciation of the Irish pound were temporary problems – 'heroic assumptions on which to construct a programme for government' said the *Sunday Tribune* economist.[19] The gathering clouds of increasing unemployment, erosion of competitiveness, and failing demand in the European Community in 1993 pointed to grave difficulties ahead. In the first week in January, the Industrial Development Authority announced that job losses had outnumbered gains in the companies it supported. It would need considerable ingenuity and resolve on the part of the new government if its members were going to be able to work together to bring Ireland through 1993 and beyond.

After five months and four runs on the Irish pound, and repeated assurances that there would be no surrender, devaluation of 10 per cent was announced on 30 January 1993. Among the recriminations which followed, the failure to involve the Department of Foreign Affairs in the diplomatic offensive for support in Europe was identified as one blunder. A sober assessment was made of the real help Ireland could expect from Europe in a crisis. Exporters, however, were relieved that their markets could return to normality, and interest rates began a slow descent.

Budget day in Ireland, as in Britain, is something of a media event. The Department of Finance had, as usual, issued dire warnings of hair shirts and hard realities: in the event, after Bertie Ahern had posed in his office with his briefcase, and outside his office with his children and with his mother, the package was very much 'no change'. Since the catch-phrase from the Labour Party during the November election, and all during the negotiations for government had been, 'The people voted for change', it was something of a disappointment, and added to the shortening of the political honeymoon of the new administration.

Their first budget was unveiled at the end of February, and was generally regarded as no more than a holding operation. With record unemployment apparently spiralling out of control, there was little sign of real imagination. However, a borrowing requirement of 2·9 per cent of GNP (IR£760 million) was a reassuring sign of stability to the investing community. The wisdom of some of the means used to achieve this were questioned: a 1 per cent levy on all incomes over IR£9,000 while increasing the public-service pay bill by more than 7 per cent was seen as foolish if not unfair to the taxpayer in the private sector, as well as flatly contradicting the advice of a major review committee on industrial policy which had recommended reduction of personal tax on the low-paid. The inclusion of IR£150 million in government income from the proposed sale of government shares in some privatized companies was considered uncertain. Current government spending was increased by 6 per cent, a figure nearly three times that of projected inflation, accounted for by the pay increases across the public service, and the continuing escalation in social-welfare spending. The minister forecast growth in Ireland's GDP of about 2·5 per cent in 1993, and was happy that this would be well above the OECD and EC average.

In its summer bulletin of June 1993, the Central Bank forecast GNP growth of 2 per cent in 1993 (an increase on the actual growth of a disappointing 1·75 per cent in 1992). Employment would be almost static at 1,126,000, while unemployment would increase to an average 310,000 from the 1992 average of 283,000 (the new figure was described as just under 18 per cent of the labour force, according to the new way of calculating the live register). It declared that the aim of monetary policy was to ensure a stable, low-inflation environment in order to encourage the development of the real economy. And as interest rates established a healthy downward trend, with the currency crisis well behind it, the Irish economy looked ready to benefit from the much-anticipated alleviation of the international recession. As ministers battled with each other and with the Department of Finance to decide where the money would be spent in the National Development Plan 1993–9 (a total of IR£12 billion between EC and Irish exchequer funding), Ireland's real economy could be facing a new and expansionary period.

NOTES

1. Kieran A. Kennedy (ed.), *Ireland in Transition*, RTE/Mercier Press, 1986 (the Thomas Davis lectures).
2. ibid.
3. John Fanagan (ed.), *Belling the Cats. Selected Speeches and Articles of John Kelly*, Moytura Press, 1992.
4. ibid.
5. '*The Economist*' *Survey on Ireland*, January 1988.
6. ibid.
7. Brendan Keenan, Financial Editor of the *Irish Independent*, in conversation with the author.
8. Figures from the Institute of Public Administration, *Administration Yearbook and Diary*, 1992.
9. *Irish Times*, 10 March 1992.
10. Paul Tansey, *Sunday Tribune*, 22 September 1991.
11. *Sunday Independent*, 7 July 1991.
12. Brendan Keenan, Financial Editor of the *Irish Independent*, in conversation with the author.
13. Financial Statement of the Minister for Finance, Dáil Éireann, 29 January 1992.
14. Economic and Social Research Institute, *Quarterly Economic Commentary*, spring 1992.
15. ibid.
16. *Irish Times*, 29 January 1993.
17. *Sunday Times*, 20 September 1992.
18. *Irish Times*, 19 September 1992.
19. Paul Tansey, *Sunday Tribune*, 10 January 1993.

CHAPTER 11

Unemployment, Industrial Policy, Performance, and the Poverty Trap

INDUSTRY

'One of the most successful unemployed economies in the world.'[1] That was one respected economic commentator's view of Ireland as she faced the early 1990s: rapid growth every year (averaging 5 per cent between 1987 and 1992); low inflation, never more than a 5 per cent rise since 1985 and down to 3 per cent by 1992; huge surpluses in the balance of payments; government borrowing under control and 'slimmed to a shadow of its former scale'.

But 'we did everything like the rest of western Europe except control the size of our families,' a successful Irish businessman muses to the author about one of the contributing factors to Ireland's chronic unemployment problem, for that is the fly in the economic ointment. By mid-1993, unemployment had passed 300,000 (21 per cent) on the lists used for calculation, the Live Register. A further 55,000 people over fifty-five years of age who had no work were not included on the register because they do not have to sign on for their support. Thirty thousand more people who were taken off the register because they were on training schemes or social employment schemes brought the real total of the unemployed to some 380,000. Even at 300,000, Ireland's unemployment is among the two highest in the EC; the depressing and continual rise in this statistic is in contrast to the recent buoyant growth rates in exports and healthy balance-of-trade figures, the sharp rise in manufacturing industry to the point where it easily outstrips agriculture as the dominant source of exports, and the continual improvement in tourism earnings – all of which would present a picture of a country prospering and confident, were it not for the lengthening dole queues. Ireland today presents a picture of a small, open, vulnerable economy struggling to find its niche in European and world markets, with an unusually young population

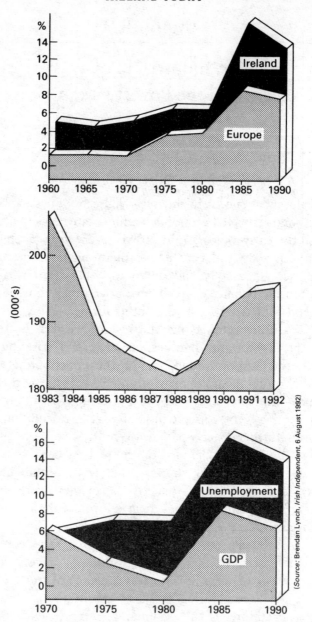

(a) Unemployment rates, Ireland and Europe, 1960–90
(b) Manufacturing employment (numbers employed in manufacturing industry) in Ireland, 1983–92
(c) Unemployment and GDP in Ireland, 1970–90

Sector	Employment in 1991		Total employment 1991	Percentage change	Number of firms
	Indigenous companies*	Overseas companies*			
Electronics and engineering	23,893	37,676	61,569	0.8	1,867
Food	26,918	7,379	34,297	0.3	867
Chemicals	3,307	11,443	14,750	3.8	277
Paper and printing	11,258	1,898	13,156	−0.5	382
Miscellaneous industries	7,153	5,546	12,699	−0.2	674
Clothing, footwear	8,158	3,966	12,124	11.0	451
Non-metallic minerals	7,152	2,357	9,509	−4.8	391
Textile industry	2,986	6,478	9,464	−4.0	276
Timber and furniture	7,917	425	8,342	−2.4	708
Drink and tobacco	2,068	4,579	6,647	−3.5	92
Grant-aided services	5,355	6,225	11,580	10.7	599
Total	106,165	87,972	194,137	−0.2	6,584

* Companies in the Industrial Development Authority (IDA) regions do not include those under Shannon Development and Udras na Gaeltacta programmes.

Source: 'IDA Employment Survey', IDA Annual Report 1991.

posing a challenge to government and business as it crowds on to the job market year after year.

It was not always an open economy; the 1930s and 1940s saw the long-failed experiment of protectionism and isolation. But the 1950s marked the transition period in Irish industrial development; decisions made at the end of that decade and policies put in place at that point were to shape events for the next twenty-five years. At the outset, it should be remembered that Ireland had missed out on the industrial revolution of the mid nineteenth century. It had remained a poor agricultural country.

In the 1950s, Irish manufacturing industry consisted of firms producing for a home market protected by extensive tariffs and quotas; exports were mainly of live animals, unprocessed meat, dairy products. The economy was stagnant, and the level of emigration was massive. The sad reality was that the majority of those emigrating were aged between fifteen and thirty: up to one-third of those in this age bracket in 1951 had left the country ten years later. This haemorrhage of the young and able seemed unstoppable: the population of Ireland plummeted during the fifties to its lowest ever at 2.8 million. There was even talk of the disappearance of the Irish as a race – a series of essays appeared published in America called *The Vanishing Irish*.[2] But even though so many left, there was still significant unemployment at home: the figure reached 95,000 in 1957.[3]

Ireland and its leaders finally awoke to the implications of the long crisis and started remedial action: the first economic programme at the end of that disastrous decade bore fruit in time. Incentives in the form of grants were put in place, new agencies mushroomed to handle and guide the transition to international trading, and the Irish found themselves in the heady and challenging era of free trade at last. Between 1960 and 1973 the volume of manufacturing industry doubled, though employment grew more slowly, by about one-third over this period. Chemicals, mineral products, metals and electrical equipment were leading the expansion of industry, while the older, formerly protected industries grew more slowly and sometimes went to the wall, unable to adapt to the new conditions.

A free-trade agreement with Britain in 1965 put an end to the long and damaging tit-for-tat economic/political trade disputes with Ireland's neighbouring and biggest market, and 'in the flowering climate of optimism and self-confidence'[4] Ireland looked forward to joining the European Community in 1973 (an earlier attempt foundered on the rocks of Britain's rejection by de Gaulle). Ireland, therefore, witnessed an almost phoenix-like resurrection, which involved not only these major economic changes, but also a profound political transformation of the dominant political force in the country, Fianna Fáil, which had led Ireland into protectionism and isolation in the first place. '. . . it involved Fianna Fáil in reversing the policy of economic nationalism which had first brought it to power in 1932 and which sustained it in government for much of the next generation.'[5]

This reversal of the apparently immutable political philosophy of Fianna Fáil is generally attributed to the skill and pragmatic outlook of Seán Lemass, as well as his most able civil servant lieutenant, T. K. Whitaker; the other political parties gave enlightened support, while the business community – those who saw where the future lay – enthusiastically backed it up.

These years of optimism also brought the Industrial Development Authority (IDA) into prominence.* This body had been established during one of the rare non-Fianna Fáil administrations, in 1949, amid some recriminations because it was suspected that it was a plot to take power away from the government Department of Industry and Commerce. Its brief was 'to investigate the effects of protective measures', 'to initiate proposals and schemes for the development of Irish industry', and to 'advise on steps necessary for the expansion and modernization of existing industries'. By 1970, with new powers of funding, a new IDA was deeply involved in the industrial blossoming of Ireland, and was considered to be a dynamic and positive force for progress.

The first international oil crisis, in 1973, coincided with Ireland's entry to the EEC. By then, Ireland and the IDA had established a track record of attracting foreign industry by strong incentives that included generous tax concessions and capital grants. These industries had fared well in Ireland and were profitable; labour was plentiful, educated and adaptable; and the prospect of having free

---

*IDA became an autonomous State-sponsored agency in 1970, under the Department of Industry and Commerce.

access to Europe's 250 million consumers seemed supremely fortuitous. The IDA was bullish about its chances of creating 10,000 jobs a year in manufacturing alone, which together with other new jobs across the economy might make the holy grail of full employment a real prospect.

However, disturbing trends had appeared: older, home industry had responded badly to free trade and was shedding jobs rapidly. With heavy reliance on mobile foreign investment for job creation, Ireland suffered from the international recession as investment faltered, and manufacturing output fell by one-tenth in what was, fortunately, a short-lived depression. But by 1976, progress had once again started up, a good stream of new international projects flowed into the country, and despite a sluggish growth in employment because of the job losses in older industries, Ireland looked set to reap the advantages of EEC membership.

The world went into shock in 1979 as another, more serious depression resulted from the second oil crisis. Ireland's continual vulnerability to world trends was shown dramatically as stagnation set in in the hitherto booming field of manufacturing production: 1980, 1981, and 1982 were static years. Investment slackened badly, and – most ominously – foreign firms in Ireland were also losing jobs just like the older native Irish industries.

Since those years, the debate on industrial policy in Ireland has been continual and heated. Long before the trough of the second oil crisis, as far back as 1973, the National Science Council published an analysis of industrial policy by economists Charles Cooper and Noel Whelan. Its main thesis was that the heavy concentration on attracting foreign industry had meant that no Irish scientific and technological base was being developed, the foreign plants were simply using the country as platforms, taking advantage of generous grants and other favourable Irish factors. Little or no relationship was being established with the rest of the economy, and Irish research and development (R&D) was not being promoted at all.

Other critics surfaced, but little attention was paid by governments as long as things were going along nicely on a day-to-day basis. However, by the end of the 1970s, it was conceded that a major review was necessary: this led to the Telesis Report (named after the American consultancy firm who produced it), commissioned by the National Economic and Social Council and incorporated into their *Review of Industrial Policy* (1984). This report is considered one of the milestones along the path of modern Irish industrial development. It praised many aspects of the IDA's work, but centred its recommendations on the need to foster strong indigenous industry, with high-quality marketing, innovation, and the development of native skills. Its authors pointed out that no country had succeeded in developing high levels of industrial income without developing a strong indigenous sector. That argument, and the argument about the degree to which Ireland has succeeded or failed, still rage in the 1990s. Various reorganizations and amalgamations of agencies, the creation of new junior ministries, and the publication of reports and reviews had occurred in the intervening years, and still the unemployment grew.

The numbers out of work had fallen to relatively low levels during the period of growth in the 1960s, helped not only by progress on the job front, but also by the introduction of free secondary education in the mid-1960s and the resulting removal of pressure on the labour market. The population continued to expand, and former emigrants began to return. Ireland was, remarkably, in a situation of net immigration. A minor population explosion saw the numbers of Irish people in Ireland rising to 3·4 million by 1981 – a level last reached in 1890. The healthy rise continues: most recent census returns (1991) show a population of 3·5 million.

However, this increase in population could not be absorbed into employment and the numbers on the dole queues grew; at the height of the first oil recession the figures had reached an unprecedented 110,000 in 1974. Then came the economic madness of the 1977–82 period, when government policies were designed in desperation to inflate artificially the numbers at work: 60,000 additional workers between 1977 and 1979. These jobs were bought at a very high price: public expenditure and new tax concessions, all achieved by foreign borrowing. Even with this increased employment, the population and labour-force growth were such that no real dent was made in the spiralling unemployment figures. And when the 1979 recessionary shock hit the country, Ireland had no scope left for getting out of it: 'We had, as it were, used up too many of our economic chips, and the impact on our economy was all the more severe.'[6]

The Live Register – those receiving unemployment assistance

Live Register 1980–91		
Year	Thousands	As percentage of labour force
1980	101·5	8·1
1983	192·7	14·7
1987	247·3	18·4
1990	224·7	17·2
1991	253.9	19·0

Source: Institute of Public Administration, *Administration Yearbook and Diary*; Central Statistics Office.

from the State – tells its own story since 1980. It has seen a steady and inexorable climb in numbers, the chronicle of an economy unable to give work to all its children, despite all the grants, all the growth, and all the industry bodies and training agencies.

As well as unemployment, that other yardstick of a sick economy – emigration – started in earnest again in the mid-1980s, reaching a peak of 46,000 (net migration figure) in 1989, before sharply descending to almost nil from 1991 as international labour markets felt the cold wind of yet another recession. In the years 1983 to 1990, the total number of people at work changed too little to make any impact on the growing unemployment figures, and the number at work in 1990 was 1·126 million, in 1991 it was 1·125 million,[7] while the Central Bank estimated the figure for 1993 at a return to 1·126 million. Labour force numbers varied too over that decade, as emigration peaked and fell, and more and more people entered the various training courses and social employment schemes provided with considerable help from the European Social Fund.*

The factor which goes some distance towards explaining the gap between industrial expansion and unemployment is the Irish birth

---

*The State training agency, FÁS, provides a huge range of courses for unemployed people. A staff of about 2,000 runs a network of sixty offices and training centres. A budget of more than IR£218 million provides training for more than 56,000 people, largely funded by the EC.

Birth Rate: Live Births per 1,000 Average Population in Six Countries				
Country	1970	1980	1987	1990
Austria	15·0	12·0	11·4	11·7
France	16·7	14·9	13·8	13·5
Ireland	21·8	21·8	16·5	15·1
Netherlands	18·3	12·8	12·7	13·2
Spain	19·6	15·3	11·0	n/a
United Kingdom	16·2	13·4	13·6	13·9

Source: Central Statistics Office figures, 1992.

rate, consistently higher than that in most of western Europe, or indeed most of the western world. Ireland shares this characteristic with other traditionally agriculture-based conservative societies like Spain and Portugal, though its birth rate has dropped more slowly than theirs. In this strongly Catholic, conservative, farming nation, mothers stayed at home and contraception was taboo. In an unusual outburst on the subject, the Church of Ireland (non-Catholic) Dean of Christ Church cathedral in Dublin observed in August 1992: 'The population increase over the last thirty years has been almost identical to that of the unemployment figure ... if there had not been the increase in population, we might not have had the problems with the economy we are having.'[8] Only after 1981 did the downturn begin, so that by the end of that decade primary-school numbers were beginning to fall. It will take until just after the turn of the century for that fall in the birth rate to show in the young adult population, when unemployment may ease. Some commentators in 1992 dared to predict that full employment in Ireland might at last be in sight in 2010. Politicians were more circumspect, fearing the understandable wrath of parents who could not wait for twenty years.

Ireland may have been late in following birth-rate trends of the rest of the western world, but because of proximity and close ties to the United Kingdom, she gave herself standards of social and public services which many economists and commentators feel were extravagant and unjustified since they had to be paid for by borrowing. Supporters of the services argue that, without them, not only would emigration have been much worse, but poverty would have been unacceptable.

Ireland has indeed developed social services which either match or come very close to those of her nearest neighbour Britain, and are well up to European standards in social welfare, health care and education. But poverty exists, and it can be seen most vividly in the large housing estates outside some of the bigger cities of Dublin, Cork and Limerick, where unemployment is almost endemic, and is well above the national average. Social structures are so damaged by this that communities become grossly disordered. The country has not developed sufficiently expert or well-funded support and intervention systems to deal with this serious blot on its progress. It has not been enough to give relatively generous financial support to the individuals affected by unemployment and family breakdown. Millions of cinema-goers throughout the world will have seen typical scenes of this deprivation and neglect in the film *The Commitments** – which was greeted with a mixture of pride and shock by most Irish people.

Within Ireland, there are some very severe critics of the performance of the economy and those who have directed it since the foundation of the state. None is more severe than historian Joseph Lee from Cork, who considers Ireland's long-term performance since independence as 'sub-European'. In 1986, he was fulminating in what was a preview of his major work *Ireland 1912–1985: Politics and Society* (Cambridge): 'Even in terms of per capita income we have fallen much further behind every other state, except Britain, that was ahead of us sixty years ago . . . every state then below us from the Atlantic to the Urals, and from the Baltic to the Mediterranean has either narrowed the gap significantly with us or overtaken us . . .'[9] He joined in the criticism, still being made in 1986, of Ireland's industrial policy with its heavy emphasis on

* *The Commitments*, directed by Alan Parker, dealt with a group of unemployed youngsters in one of Dublin's poorer suburbs, who come together to form a rock band, achieve the beginnings of success, and then fall apart unable to develop any further. It was adapted from a book of the same name by Roddy Doyle, a schoolteacher.

the attraction of foreign-owned business, and which was demonstrating large levels of profit-repatriation along with uncomfortable dependence on decisions being made in boardrooms far away in the United States or Japan.

By 1987, foreign companies in the Irish economy were playing a central role. Forty-two per cent (78,000) of Irish people who worked in manufacturing companies were working for foreign firms; 65 per cent of net manufacturing output was from those same foreign companies (the vast bulk of them from outside Europe). And the domination of certain industries by foreign firms was almost total: 99·6 per cent of office and data processing, 97 per cent of pharmaceuticals, 90 per cent of electrical engineering were all undertaken by non-Irish companies.[10] In the 1991 IDA annual report, the employment figure for those in foreign manufacturing companies had jumped to almost 50 per cent. When asked in a 1992 survey, 'Overseas Investment in Ireland', by the Allied Irish Banks group why they had come, two-thirds of the ninety-two foreign chief executives surveyed gave the not unexpected answer that the finance package/incentives offered by Ireland had attracted them. The English language and the educated/skilled workforce figured next on the list.[11] Thus it was clear that the IDA's policy of persuading government to give incentives on a par with or better than other competing countries was certainly attracting the business; the core of the debate is whether the country is getting sufficient return from what is by any standards massive investment in terms of grants and tax forgone. That investment is itself the subject of varying standards of measurement: taking into account grants and special tax concessions, one could estimate the Irish exchequer's input to job creation at IR£4·48 billion between 1981 and 1990. In that time, the total number employed in industry increased by only 7,000, after balancing job losses and gains. In 1991, depending on how tax reliefs to industry are calculated, industrial promotion cost the State a minimum of IR£750 million or a maximum of IR£1,650 million (including contributions from Europe).[12] The IDA claimed in 1992 that each job created cost the exchequer IR£14,300; this is disputed by various commentators, who apply different measurements and arrive at the figure of IR£500,000 per 'sustainable' job – net jobs which survive after closures and redundancies.

As unemployment soared to unprecedented heights in the new decade of the 1990s, critical eyes therefore were turning towards the IDA, the State's main tool for job creation. A new (1989) Minister for Industry and Commerce, Desmond O'Malley, with a reputation for toughness and acerbity, who had left memories of sharp words and short fuses behind him when he previously held that portfolio, set about scrutinizing the State's investment in job creation. To help him, he appointed a small group of efficient, plain-speaking, mostly business people with records of achievement. The chairman was a man who as well as being one of Ireland's more successful business chiefs had already shown his breadth of ability as chairman of the national broadcasting authority in the late 1980s. The group was called the Industrial Policy Review Group, and the chair was held by Jim Culliton:* the report is referred to in Ireland as the Culliton report.

The Culliton team appointed consultants at home and abroad to report to them rapidly on various aspects of Irish industrial investment, performance, and potential. And so, in January 1992, this latest group to ponder Ireland's industrial potential and the employment shortfall produced their conclusions, which, in summary, are the following:

1. The tax system in Ireland needed reform – it was full of unproductive tax reliefs while bearing too heavily on personal income tax particularly for single persons with modest earnings. It stifles enterprise. (This has been said *ad nauseam* for several years, and is a central feature of the policy of the Progressive Democrats.)
2. Infrastructure, transport and energy costs need decisive government action to improve Irish competitiveness. Too much State interference and inbuilt costs exist for good operation.
3. The Irish education and training system has serious gaps in filling the technical, vocational, and production skills needs. Curriculum changes, and more emphasis on vocational qualifications in education, together with a major institutional reform

* Jim Culliton (b. 1934); Chairman, Unidare PLC, Chairman, RTE Authority 1986–9. In summer 1993, he was named as next chairman of Allied Irish Banks in succession to Peter Sutherland.

of the main training agency FÁS would have to be undertaken.

4. The EC structural funding for science and technology should be steered, using greater involvement of industrialists, towards more R&D spending to ensure employment and growth in this area.

5. A new look was needed at the grant structures for attracting foreign industry, and greater emphasis should be laid on taking equity rather than giving grants. The food industry should be singled out for priority, and clusters of industry should be fostered, building on leverage points of national advantage. The degree of international mobility and the extent to which firms have significant management roots in Ireland should be points taken into consideration when considering foreign grant applications.

6. Structures within the Department of Industry and Commerce itself were inadequate and too concerned with operational matters rather than policy formulation and evaluation. The supports for the development of indigenous industry were too diverse and need to be harnessed and integrated into a new agency, while a distinct agency should promote all types of internationally mobile investment in Ireland.

7. A Task Force should be set up, reporting to the Taoiseach, to ensure quick action.

The last, being easy, was done first. The Task Force was immediately set up, with a surprising choice as chairman: Paddy Moriarty,* a man who had run the monopoly Irish State electrical company for many years, strongly connected with the public rather than the private sector, and of post-retirement age. Private fears were expressed that this was the Taoiseach's riposte to the high-profile, highly praised work of the Culliton group, who were chosen by his government colleague but political rival O'Malley. However, the new chairman's experience and popularity, his undoubted toughness, and his wide range of interests and background of service supported the view of those who held that

---

*Patrick Moriarty (b. 1926). With the ESB (Electricity Supply Board) since 1945. Rose to chief executive in 1981, and Chairman thereafter. Chaired the RTE Authority (as did Jim Culliton – Ireland is a small place); an Irish-speaker and supporter of the Gaelic Athletic Association, as well as a golfer.

such attributes would be needed if the fundamental and difficult decisions required by Culliton had any hope of being achieved.

The Culliton report met with approval from most quarters, accompanied by many exhortations to action, and fears of delay or timidity. 'Much of what the report requires to be done will necessitate a political commitment beyond the norm for Irish governments – simply because the change will cause pain ...'[13] The financial editor of one of the country's main daily newspapers, welcoming Culliton's principal recommendations, expressed a general worry in succinct terms: 'The policies will succeed only if the inertia of the Irish political and administrative system is tackled.'[14] Former prime minister Garret FitzGerald had a warm welcome for it: 'The report deserves the ultimate accolade so rarely given to the report of a commission or committee in the Republic – actual implementation ... I would endorse almost all the proposals made by Jim Culliton and his colleagues.'[15] Referring to the area of expertise, or lack of it, within key government departments – in this case the Department of Industry and Commerce – FitzGerald noted that attempts to attract people on secondment to the Irish civil service from Irish industry have notably failed in the past. Neither, of course, does the civil service ensure that its own people spend time in industry; a mere handful of civil servants were on secondment to industry in July 1992 (see Chapter 4).

Culliton himself, on launching the report, put the size of the problem in context: 'We were disheartened to find that after an expenditure of many millions of pounds of State grants over the last twenty years, there are still only 20 Irish companies employing 500 people or more, and only 150 companies with sales of £5 million or more. That is tiny by international standards ... our problems won't go away by themselves, they have to be tackled with vigour and imagination ... between now and the year 2000, there will be an extra 20,000–25,000 entrants to the jobs market each year, but our average manufacturing job creation rate over the past three years was only 3,800 jobs per annum.'[16] In a *cri de cœur* appealing for action on the report, one of Ireland's most thoughtful columnists in the *Irish Times* developed that theme: 'We have a shortfall in the immediate future of about 168,000 jobs; on top of the present 260,000. How in the name of God would we even begin to tackle a problem so big? Yet, how can we live with it either?'[17]

While Culliton was being absorbed by government and institutions, politicians, under attack about the unemployment figures, were wrangling. Fine Gael suggested a 'jobs forum' which would involve politicians and major interest groups and be a national catalyst for ideas on how to deal with what was being widely referred to as the unemployment crisis; the government resisted that format, and in the end established in May 1992 a parliamentary committee on unemployment, chaired by a professor of industrial relations who was also a Fianna Fáil member of parliament.* This committee was boycotted by Fine Gael, who felt that ministers should have to involve themselves in this national effort but were not required to appear before a parliamentary committee. The country was not amused by the spectacle of politicians disagreeing about how they should discuss things, while the dole queues grew and grew.

On 4 May 1992, Fine Gael published *Towards the Jobs Economy*, a considerable document which bore the hallmarks of many strands of thinking the party had been developing since John Bruton became its leader in 1990. It was the result of six months' work by a task force of academics, business people, and politicians, and contained proposals for every branch of public administration, budgetary practices, new social-welfare work incentives, regulating monopoly powers of State services, new tax structures – a host of original ideas, and others echoing some of Culliton. At the launch of the document, Bruton declared: 'We want strong enterprises, not strong agencies . . . Ireland has failed to perform to its potential over the past twenty years of EC membership . . . our new venture capital ideas will put an end to the dependency culture . . . if Ireland can gain just an extra half of one per cent of the European market, we can overcome unemployment . . . all it needs is the introduction of a sustained, strong competitive drive to every aspect of our society.'

In 1992, therefore, there was no shortage of proposed solutions on the table for Ireland's unemployment problems. Because Culliton

---

*Dr Brian Hillery TD (b. 1937), Professor of Industrial Relations, University College, Dublin, and Fianna Fáil Deputy for Dún Laoghaire-Rathdown, Co. Dublin, from 1989 to 1992. He was appointed to the Senate in 1993 by Taoiseach Albert Reynolds.

in many respects echoed the main recommendations in the Telesis report, which in turn had repeated the main concerns of Whelan and Cooper in the early 1970s, it would be understandable if a certain weariness was felt about prospects for concerted government action. Fine Gael, slipping in the opinion polls over several years and looking unlikely to be in a position strong enough to implement its radical proposals, could only be one part of the public debate.

Like many another democracy, Ireland's capacity for grasping the nettle of major and controversial reform is limited by political realities, rendered in Ireland's case even more intractable because of the inbuilt inertia of the electoral system itself. The facts and figures, the ideas and proposals, the fine blueprints for a great future may all remain merely markers on the way to the solution which will inevitably arrive in its own good time as the young population drops to the European norm.

By the end of 1992, a general election had halted the progress towards grappling with the recommendations of the Culliton report. The country had been regaled with leaked accounts of differences between the sponsoring Minister for Industry and the Taoiseach and leader of the main party in government, Fianna Fáil, over some of Culliton's ideas. The breakup of the government in some mutual hostility and disarray at the beginning of November 1992 seemed to confirm those rumours. However, by that time the chairman of the Industrial Policy Review Group, Jim Culliton himself, had welcomed the intention of the government to set up a 'super-agency', with two distinct divisions for home and foreign industry, despite the difference between that and his original recommendation. There had also been a welcome for the establishment of new County Enterprise Boards with IR£100 million seed funding for the encouragement of local enterprise. The Taoiseach and several government ministers had affirmed commitment to the 'thrust and the policy' of Culliton, and the Task Force on Culliton was busy producing work plans for its implementation. In an upbeat declaration in late October, the Minister for Industry and Commerce promised that legislation to implement the main recommendations of Culliton would be through the Dáil by the end of the year.[18] He was not to know that the whole process would be thrown into the melting-pot within days of that declaration, as the Dáil dissolved.

The currency crisis which engulfed several members of the EC from September 1992 deepened during the political interregnum. It was yet another damaging factor for Irish jobs, as sterling weakened against the Irish pound and exporters demanded help from government. A special fund was set up to provide cheap loans to industry suffering from the twin effects of high interest rates and damaged competitiveness; when devaluation finally took place in January 1993, the relief on the jobs front was shattered by the announcement from one of the largest and most prestigious of the multinational computer companies in Ireland, Digital, that it was shedding 780 jobs in its Galway plant.

The new government held its first meetings in January 1993 with the jobs and industry dilemma at the top of its agenda: how to give its people jobs that will last, that are rooted in the Irish economy, in commercial, successful and competitive industry. The actual number of firms has to be increased, and those already in existence have to be expanded. Culliton, at the end of a long line of advisers, told the politicians what instruments could achieve those aims.

Ireland is a small place, with a small community. The new minister for the employment area was Ruairí Quinn, Minister for Enterprise and Employment.* As a Labour minister, it was feared that he might not have the ideological commitment to the implementation of the market-oriented Culliton report: but since he is the brother of one of the members of the small Culliton team, and has been known as a centrist in his party, those fears were not great. The economics editor of the *Irish Times* wondered in March, 'Is there a stake in the heart of Culliton?'[19] and concluded that Culliton was not quite dead and buried, but needed emergency treatment from the new minister.

And that is what Ruairí Quinn set about trying to do. He issued the government's responses to the Culliton report and to the Task Force's recommendations in a wide-ranging and firmly worded document, conveying a long-overdue sense of urgency. The document, called *Employment Through Enterprise*, was launched at

---

*Ruairí Quinn (b. 1946). Deputy leader of the Labour Party, an architect by profession. Held posts of Minister for Labour and Minister for the Public Service in the Fine Gael/Labour coalition government, 1982–7, and Junior Minister for the Environment, 1982–3. An articulate, popular and energetic politician.

Dublin Castle on 3 May 1993. The range of decisions he managed to get his government colleagues to agree to, many of them controversial, amounted to a massive programme of action to be taken as well as legislative intentions, covering every part of Culliton. Despite the initial set-back for Culliton in the increased taxation provisions of the February budget, and the separation of marketing from his own department into a new Department of Trade and Tourism, no one could doubt Quinn's sincerity and determination to grasp the myriad nettles so clearly set out in the Culliton report. As the spring of 1993 dawned, there was some hope that the Irish people might, for the first time since the economic renaissance of the 1960s, see a real and coordinated effort being made by their leaders to transform the economic scenario of their country. Whether that effort would surmount the political sensitivities of dealing with Culliton's strong and unequivocal recommendations on the tax area, or would deal with such thorny but significant questions as releasing the electricity company (ESB) from its obligation to purchase energy from Bord na Móna (thereby threatening jobs in the midlands), remained to be seen. The economics editor of the influential *Irish Times* was sceptical: 'The Government has decided to dine à la carte on the Culliton Report, despite the recommendation of Mr Culliton who said, when he presented his report, that it was a set menu, to be implemented as a package.'[20] Eighteen months after Culliton, with unemployment still rising, the hard decisions really had yet to be taken.

TOURISM: A HUNDRED THOUSAND WELCOMES

The economic and social importance of tourism to Ireland can be measured by three facts: (1) it provides employment for 87,000 people; (2) it contributes about 7 per cent of GNP; and (3) in 1991, it contributed a net surplus of over IR£500 million to Ireland's balance-of-payments position.

Ireland's unexpected pleasures – space, timelessness, small courtesies, small pubs and wide smiles, slumbering old country mansions, clean and green hills and valleys, clear and open waterways – some or all of these features of an island far out on the western edge of Europe prompted a writer in Britain's *Observer* newspaper to exclaim after three weeks in the country: 'Ireland –

the last paradise of Europe. It is true.' Romany Bain, writing on 26 January 1992, after three weeks touring the south and west of the country, by car and boat, was evidently bowled over. As was Christopher Somerville, recounting his adventures walking in the far west of Ireland enjoying the pubs, the wild scenery, 'The music, the chat, the stories, the hospitality . . . all this open exchange goes under the generic name of "crack": if the crack has a spiritual home anywhere in Ireland, it's in the pubs.' Even more convinced was a cycling holidaymaker, describing his journey along country lanes beside the sea in Co. Cork: 'The sun was sometimes out . . . the Atlantic rose and fell and sighed. Seals snoozed. The tree roots were swathed in moss. There were hedgerows (whatever happened to hedgerows?) Our way was lined with flowers . . .'

What music in the ears of Ireland's State Tourist Board, appropriately named Bord Fáilte (the welcome board) which claims credit for attracting three million visitors to Ireland in 1991, and tourist revenue of £856 million . . . but could anywhere so near western Europe possibly be so idyllic? And if it were, why were there not treble the number of visitors clamouring to spend time on this paradise island?

The answer to the first of those questions is yes and no; the answer to the second is slightly more complex – a combination of horrendously negative publicity arising from violence in the northern part of the small island of Ireland, difficult and relatively expensive access, high internal costs, uncertain climate, ignorance of Ireland's very existence, and certain self-imposed impediments. The chairman and chief executive of the tourist board might well describe Ireland as 'a hard sell' as he contemplated the difficult tourist season of 1992.

The most noteworthy of the self-imposed impediments is the 'Shannon stopover' – the Irish government's requirement that any transatlantic air traffic may not land directly in the capital city in the east of the country, but must first land at Shannon airport, in the west of Ireland. Imposed first to protect the industrial and tourism facilities which had grown up around the airport at a time when it was the necessary first European landfall, the stopover was considered by Bord Fáilte and the national airline, Aer Lingus, to be a serious impediment to growth in the American tourist inflow. Political debate raged around the subject, with Dáil Deputies from the counties which surround Shannon joining with the local bodies in fiercely opposing any change. In 1989, the most prominent of the politicians from the area joined a new government as head of the minor coalition partner, becoming Minister for Industry and Commerce, and in 1992 a western Dáil deputy became Minister for Tourism, Transport and Communications. One of that minister's early actions was to instruct, by letter, the chairmen of the boards of tourism and transport bodies to refrain from any more public statements on the subject, and to instruct their staff to do the same. When challenged in the Dáil on 1 July 1992 about the heavy-handedness of such an edict, the minister gave a reply which cast a sharp light on a certain kind of political thinking at the time: 'It would have been much easier for me not to send a letter, and instead to call in the chairmen of each semi-State company and give the directive orally. There would not have been any record of it, and I could have denied it at any time.' Despite the fact that this reply was reported on radio and television in the normal coverage of Dáil questions, hardly any political or public comment was made. However, the instruction had the desired effect and the semi-State critics fell sullenly silent.

In October 1992, the minister announced that the government had decided not to change the status quo. She did not announce, but everyone understood, that she had been reminded forcibly by posters on the roads to Galway every time she travelled home that her electorate were very interested in the subject. A few days later, just as the sudden general election of November got under way, a poll showed that her decision was not popular nationally: 43 per cent of all those questioned would have preferred the stopover to go, 33 per cent preferred it to stay, and 24 per cent said they didn't know. However, she had made the decision just in time: she held on to her Dáil seat by a very narrow margin indeed. When, in early 1993, Aer Lingus was forced to produce a survival package because of mounting debt and continuing losses, the plan included a change in the compulsory stopover: jumbo jets would be parked and serviced at Shannon, and would fly to the USA via Dublin, stopping at Dublin on the way back. Uproar ensued, and the country once more speculated whether a government would have the courage to proceed with this modification. But proceed it did.

Ireland is a sparsely populated island (only 50 inhabitants per square mile in 1989, compared with 233 in Britain) where the majority of the population cluster in Dublin and some other urban areas, leaving vast tracts of open, wild, and peaceful country dotted by farmhouses: the whole western rim of the island from Donegal in the north-west to Kerry and Cork in the south-west offers a range of natural phenomena from spectacular seascapes, cliffs, limestone hills and plateaux, small stone walls and glorious lakes, to rolling fields and challenging mountains. The midlands, flatter but undulating, present rich agricultural land, historic old houses and estates, thriving and interesting towns and villages, and world-famous horse-breeding stud farms – and more lakes, as well as the largest inland waterway in the British Isles; the eastern rim is the more populated and developed, particularly around Dublin, which has a population of about one million, nearly a third of the whole.

Dublin itself is not today a beautiful city, though beautifully situated between the hills and the sea, with easy access to the wild scenery and rural quiet of County Wicklow which borders it on the south and west. A city which boasted magnificent Georgian streets, squares and terraces, with some fine and noble buildings, it did not sufficiently protect itself from destruction by demolition and developer, private and public. There are still many remnants of the old graciousness, and some noble public buildings and street scenes – but Dublin's charm mainly lies in its old and friendly pubs, its theatres, its art, its literary traditions and landmarks, and the vitality of its people. The vitality comes from the unusually large young population thronging the streets, something particularly noticeable for example in the newly restored heart of old Dublin, Temple Bar, where restaurants of all kinds, art galleries, film centres, pubs and small shops as well as living accommodation have given a fillip to the city.

The capital city is not the flagship of national tourism, as it is in so many European countries. Only recently has the city woken up to the need to call a halt to the destruction of its architectural heritage, and to preserve the ancient medieval traces of its past. A chaotic traffic problem and an inadequate public transport system add to the difficulties for the tourist. The failure to capitalize on the worldwide appreciation of James Joyce, George Bernard Shaw, and other Dublin writers is exemplified in the disappearance of

7 Eccles Street, the home of Joyce's Bloom. However, an increasingly important celebration on the 16th of June – 'Bloomsday' from Joyce's *Ulysses* – is celebrating Ireland's best-known writer. Shaw's decrepit home in Synge Street was only just rescued in time ... such neglect led the *Irish Times*'s environment correspondent to despair: 'A city which treats its architectural heritage with such contempt can hardly hope to attract the new breed of "cultural tourists".' A report commissioned by the City Centre Business Association of Dublin in 1992 found that Dublin was attracting only half the number of visitors who went to Edinburgh every year, and only one-fifth of those going to Amsterdam. A combination of many factors, not least the increased environmental awareness of the citizenry, has led to improvements in this situation. With European funding assistance and powerful advocates in the Dublin City Council elected in 1991 (and the support of the popular husband of the President of Ireland, Nicholas Robinson), new projects and preservation of Dublin's architectural heritage have started all across the city, and there are plans for great improvements in the traffic situation ... if sufficient European funding can be obtained. In that context, the announcement after the EC Edinburgh summit in December 1992 that Ireland would get IR£8 billion in European Structural Funds was good news.

Leaving Dublin, every kind of tourist accommodation is available around the country. There are not too many hotels (but some) on the grand scale of major international cities or resorts, but there is an abundance of good hotels, gracious country mansions and houses, more modest inns, and everywhere farms and homes which take guests in for bed and generous Irish breakfast. Food in Ireland has been revolutionized by the example and teaching of people like Myrtle Allen of the famous old country mansion, Ballymaloe in Cork, as well as by the Irish State's training schools for the tourist industry. Irish restaurants feature in small but growing numbers in international good food guides, its hotels and country homes in most good visitors' handbooks. Ireland is not a cheap holiday destination, but it features in or around the middle of any list of European countries for cost of food, accommodation, alcohol, and petrol ...

Despite the three million visitors claimed by Bord Fáilte, tourists have not yet impinged too much on either the landscape or the facilities of the country. The kinds of foreign tourist whom the country attracts tend to be quiet, individualistic, and increasingly European. There is nothing at all to resemble mass tourism, since Ireland's gentle but damp climate means it was never part of the 'north to south' traffic in search of sun. The only group movements one could detect at the height of the season might be occasional busloads of elderly Americans in search of their ancestral roots, some buses with culturally oriented Europeans, or the chattering of foreign students on the streets of Dublin's suburbs. Other tourists are mainly fishing, shooting, walking, motoring, or golfing.

Everywhere the visitor will find Irish people who are mostly pleasant, humorous, interested, polite. That is a recurring feature of any survey of tourists carried out in recent years: Ireland's attractions are described as, first, the scenery, and high on the list after that comes 'friendliness of the people'. The man who will 'go the road' with you instead of merely giving directions, the woman who will sit and chat with you in her farmhouse kitchen while she fills you full of Irish bacon, sausages and eggs, the ready conversation in the pub or the willingness to sing an old song, the genuine enquiries about your welfare and curiosity about your origins – surely that is what was meant by a foreign journalist's remark: 'Such are the courtesies in one of Europe's last redoubts of civilized behaviour.'

Is Ireland the paradise which Bord Fáilte would like to project? There are negatives just as there are in every developing country. Not all towns and facilities are as clean and tidy as they should be. The charm of a place which in many ways 'is like the beginning of the century' can wear thin when there is a shortage of clean public lavatories; planning laws have been slow to control indiscriminate building in scenic areas, resulting in 'bungalow blight' on the outskirts of some towns – the road to Spiddal outside the city of Galway is an unfortunate example; some extraordinary decisions were made which defy explanation – a massive, reddish, concrete 'viewing tower' was erected on the site of an old mansion in the middle of a beautiful forest park in Leitrim; a whole long terrace of Georgian houses was torn down in the centre of Dublin to make way for new head offices for the State electricity board; two enormous modern buildings were erected on top of the remains of the Viking city of old Dublin . . . Ireland has been slow to wake up to its responsibilities towards its environment, and to realize the damage such neglect does to the tourism industry as well as to the birthright of its own citizens. Happily, with the emergence of a strong environmental movement, accompanied by improved planning laws and European involvement and financing of better projects, such unfortunate lapses are becoming rarer. However, in 1992 arguments raged between environmentalists and the Office of Public Works about proposed interpretative centres in the centre of wild and beautiful areas. The importance of Europe in Irish affairs was seen when the finance for the centres from Brussels was threatened after Irish appeals to the relevant Commissioner. And finally, the charm of the people may not be entirely universal, since Dublin includes a criminal element like any city of its size in western Europe, causing the police to design and issue leaflets to incoming tourists counselling care and attention of belongings and cars in city areas.

Bord Fáilte, with a budget of IR£22 million in 1992 and a staff of 231 (both falling steadily in the cost-conscious Ireland of the 1990s), markets Ireland in any way it can. Such is human nature, it also markets itself, not without some justification. It was set stringent targets by the government in 1987, to be achieved by the end of 1992: to double the number of visitors (from 2·1 to 4·2 million), increase revenue by IR£500 million and create 25,000 new jobs. This required growth of 15 per cent per annum.

The visitor number target was missed, and in 1992 was projected to reach just over 3 million. The revenue target was missed too, and instead of the desired IR£1 billion it was expected to be some IR£855 million. But the jobs target – the most important of the three – was met, and reliable independent estimates agree that 25,000 new jobs directly arising from tourism were created between 1987 and the end of 1992, bringing to some 87,000 the number of people working in the industry. (The importance of the industry can be judged by comparison of this figure with the estimated total of 90,000 people working in foreign-owned industry in Ireland.) Tourism represents some 7 per cent of Ireland's GNP.

There is great room for expansion and development of tourism in Ireland, without killing the goose that lays the golden egg. The debate in Ireland centres around the kind of tourist Ireland should be aiming for: the 'quality' market or a more basic low-spending visitor. The trend is towards quality: rapid growth in the number of golfers coming to play on Ireland's quiet and often beautiful courses, walkers who want comfort as well as challenge, and cyclists likewise; fishing enthusiasts who stay in good country inns, environmentalists and literature students of all ages interested in the folklore, heritage, and historical and archaeological remains all around the country: the thinking holidaymaker. Interestingly, one of the trends running through the public debate in early summer 1992 on the Maastricht Treaty was the fear that Ireland, if she doesn't learn to stand on her own two feet industrially without eternal cash transfers from Europe's centre, might become the clean, green, relaxing 'theme park' and golfing, shooting, and fishing playground for Europe's tired businessmen, where the natives would become a race of waiters, golf caddies and hotel-keepers, telling amusing stories to entertain the visitors while Irish youngsters left the country to run the industries in the lands from where the tourists came.

In October 1992, a 'Tourism Task Force' reported to the Minister for Tourism, Transport and Communications. This Task Force, headed by the ubiquitous and able Pádraig Ó hUiginn, the Taoiseach's top civil servant, had been established because of perceived untapped potential in the tourism area. Their report started out with the view that 'the sector has potential to provide an additional 35,000 jobs with a 50 per cent increase in foreign earnings from tourism over the next five years, if the commercial core of the industry can be significantly strengthened and new institutional arrangements put in place'. As is so often the case in Ireland, one of the central recommendations was for the establishment of yet another body, the Tourism Council of Ireland, 'to unify and co-ordinate the activities of the industry from planning and policy formation through product development to marketing the product . . .' and so on. If Bord Fáilte felt that the wheel was being re-invented, they wisely kept their counsel, in public anyway. Amid a range of recommendations, many of which had already been advocated by Bord Fáilte (like measures to lower the cost of car hire, developing 'new product lines'), the report also recommended that transatlantic flights should be allowed to land in Dublin as well as Shannon, and it counselled against the abolition of Regional Tourism Boards, which had been due to be absorbed into new County Enterprise Boards.

Bord Fáilte set about drawing up its own Tourism Development Plan 1993–7. And in the welter of statistics and documents emanating from different areas of the public sector, one had the uneasy feeling that all this energy could be more wisely used in getting on with the job on the ground rather than in engaging in battles to impress government and the public. This range of official claim and counter-claim left people actually working in the field, trying to earn their living, somewhat sceptical. An Irish manufacturer of quality craft products, who runs a very large shop and busy restaurant in a lovely old white house on the quiet edge of an inlet of the sea in western Ireland, and deals with thousands of tourists every year, said to the author: 'In more than ten years since we took over and expanded this business, nobody from Bord Fáilte has ever called in to talk to us about the business, the numbers, the kind of facility we offer, the feedback from tourists . . .'

In 1993, Pádraig Ó hUiginn, who had articulated his healthy scepticism about tourism statistics in the past, was made chairman of Bord Fáilte. It was expected that he would be a vigorous new broom.*

THE COMMERCIAL SEMI-STATE SECTOR

Shortly after the new Irish State began to function, it became clear that there were desirable activities which should be got under way, activities unsuited for direct day-to-day control by ministers and civil servants, but that looked unlikely to be started without State involvement. Among the first needs to be identified were the proper supply of electricity and the financing of agricultural expansion: in 1927 the Electricity Supply Board (ESB) and the Agricultural Credit Corporation (ACC) were set up. Many others were established, and are still being set up; one of the latest is the forestry development body, Coillte, established in 1989 because it was considered that the work of establishing a dynamic, commercial, and growing forestry industry had been proved to be unsuitable for civil-service structures inside the Department of Energy, while the private forestry industry was still in its infancy and unable to undertake the huge planting programme required. Thus an Irish government

---

* See Chapter 4, 'Civil Service: Not So Very British'.

belatedly set about using a resource which had been grossly neglected since the foundation of the State. (See Chapter 12, 'Agriculture'.)

By 1992, there were twenty-five of these bodies (the number fluctuates slightly all the time as amalgamations or changes happen), employing 72,000 people. Each of them is set up under legislation, the regulations differing according to the job to be done by the new body. They include companies which provide an essential infrastructural service which was either commercially impossible or unattractive for the private sector at the time of its setting up, like the national air company, Aer Lingus, and the electricity board. The wish to develop natural resources like Ireland's extensive fuel-producing boglands, or to exploit and use natural gas, lay behind the establishment of Bord na Móna and An Bord Gáis, respectively.

Most of these companies have part-time boards of directors, all of whom are appointed directly by the relevant minister, and this is a constant source of controversy in Ireland. Appointments to most of the boards are coveted as status symbols (symbols only: there is rarely any remuneration for service except expenses for attending meetings). It is common practice, though diminishing, for ministers to appoint party supporters to the boards, with or without the best kind of qualification for the work. Perhaps it would be better to put it this way: it is rare to find a minister appointing a supporter of any party other than his own to a board. When it comes to a board such as the authority which controls the national broadcasting company (RTE), governments consider it such a highly sensitive area that the political sympathies of the chairperson and board must be broadly in line with those of the government party or parties.

However, there is a trend away from appointment of blatantly unsuitable people, partly because many of the newer bodies have seats reserved for the nominees of various interest groups which are active within the company's area of responsibility, and partly because government has been advised strongly by the trade unions to desist from such practices. The social partners insisted on the insertion of the following in the State Programme for Economic and Social Progress, 1991: 'The primary considerations which should apply in the appointment of directors to State companies are the experience and expertise of the individuals concerned' and went on to lay down that the chairman of the board should be consulted before directors were appointed. These provisos, together with a more exigent public opinion, have combined to improve greatly the standard of appointments to such boards and bodies.

Other controversies arise in the running of the semi-State companies which cause public agitation and government embarrassment. For example, An Post, which runs the postal system and is instructed by the government to be self-financing, wanted in 1991 to close tiny rural post offices around Ireland, and in 1992 to take part-time workers in just for peak periods while cutting down on their overtime bill. The first plan was shelved when local government elections were pending, and the second led to a protracted and bitter dispute which stopped postal services for over a month. The degree to which the government is prepared to finance what the company says is a purely social, uneconomic activity is as yet unknown, and is rarely permanently defined. Similar difficulties arise in the public transport companies, which struggle to make profits while under government stricture not to close all the rural railway stations or bus routes. It is not surprising that chairmen and chief executives complain about the impossibility of efficiency in the face of political pressures.

There is a constant debate about accountability and control of semi-State bodies: a parliamentary committee (Joint Oireachtas Committee on Commercial Semi-State Bodies) selects bodies for examination, calls in chief executives and chairmen for public questioning, demands reports and documents, and generates considerable publicity when controversies arise. Its influence and power is minimal, however – the committee has no power to call ministers, and its reports are never debated in parliament. There is an Ombudsman whose remit extends only to An Post, and Telecom Éireann (the telecommunications board). All in all, therefore, 'the accountability and control of the State-sponsored body is as yet an unresolved problem, and the failure to devise a precise and comprehensive system has meant that the level of control tends to depend on such factors as the political visibility of an organization, its geographical spread, its financial performance, and the attitudes of individual ministers and boards.'[21]

UNEMPLOYMENT, INDUSTRY AND POVERTY

Privatization, that word which first became current in the late 1980s in Ireland, has not as yet been really tried. As international comparisons and information become more readily available, and consumerism becomes a more powerful force, questions arise about the cost of energy in Ireland, the price of getting from Dublin to London by air, the creaking and ageing school buses trundling around the country, energy costs affecting industry ... as in other countries looking at their public companies, more and more questions are asked about the imposition of political and public-service trade-union attitudes and practices on what should be money-making modern services. Governments begin to ask why the companies cannot go to the private sector for funds for improvement and expansion. The beneficial or malign effects of competition on performance are hotly disputed. As in most things, Irish governments have taken a pragmatic rather than an ideological point of view on this issue. The experiment of introducing competition into the broadcasting area (see Chapter 14) proved controversial, unpopular, and unsuccessful in its main aim: State fingers were burnt. As yet, the Irish Sugar Company and Irish Life Assurance Company remain the only two full-scale privatizations undertaken. With the arrival of a new and stronger Labour Party into government in January 1993, with its declared ideological antipathy to any further privatization, it looked as if the State would continue its close involvement with most of the State and semi-State companies. When rumours emerged that there was a possibility of the giant Cable & Wireless buying part of the semi-State telecommunications company (Telecom Éireann) in May 1993, the deputy prime minister and leader of the Labour Party took a strong public stance and announced that there would be no sale of any part of Telecom Éireann and no further privatization of any other such body.

The State-sponsored bodies played a most valuable role when they were introduced and for a good while afterwards. 'In an unstructured, unplanned sort of way ... they contributed very effectively to the development of the country.'[22] As Ireland has emerged into the new world of international competition, with new generations of educated and able managers, and business demanding economical and efficient infrastructure and services, the challenge of modernization and adaptation of those companies will require at

Some of Ireland's Commercial Semi-State Bodies	
Name and function of body	Year of foundation
Electricity Supply Board: monopoly on generation and provision of electricity	1927
Voluntary Health Insurance Board: a system of provision of all kinds of health insurance	1957
Aer Lingus: air services to and from Ireland	1936
Córas Iompair Éireann (and Iarnród Éireann and Bus Éireann): public road and rail services	1950
Radio Telefís Éireann: radio and television services (succeeded the national radio station)	1960
Irish Steel Ltd: steelmakers and corrugated coated-sheet manufacturers	1947
Agricultural Credit Corporation: to provide finance for the agricultural sector	1927
Custom House Docks Development Authority: to secure the re-development of this large old site on the estuary of the river Liffey	1986
National Stud: farm for breeding thoroughbred horses and providing first-class stallions	1946
Bord na Móna: developing the country's peat resources	1946

least as much energy and imagination as it took to set them up in the first place. The resolution of some of the worst difficulties in the sector, like those of the heavily debt-ridden national airline, Aer Lingus,* which became an election issue in November 1992, will test the ingenuity of government in the late 1990s.

* Aer Lingus with debts of IR£550 million and operating losses of IR£100 million forecast for the year to March 1993 is in deep trouble. On 9 March 1993, the chief executive was allegedly forced to resign, and the government appointed the chairman to take over the executive role. On 29 March, the board appointed Peter Owen, formerly of British Airways, to take the job of reorganization of the airline. Political storms surrounding job losses and the compulsory Shannon stopover for transatlantic flights to Ireland epitomize the kind of dilemma in aviation facing Irish governments.

POLITICS AND BUSINESS: THE INTERACTION

Ireland was, until recently, relatively scandal-free: its people have watched the revelations of the Mafia corruption in Italy, the intrigues of Greece, the big-money machinations in Japan, and while not feeling complacent, at least felt that in the corruption league Irish politicians and business people were small fry. Despite rumours and speculation surrounding Charles Haughey during his political life, nothing untoward was ever proved about him. The top Irish businessmen kept a relatively low profile and a good working relationship with the two big political parties. It was known that some financial support was given to the parties by business, but nobody, except the Labour Party and the smaller and newer Democratic Left (with its roots in the Marxist-oriented Workers' Party), got really worked up about it. There was not much ostentatious luxury expenditure within Ireland by the small group of really rich people.

Then in the autumn of 1991 a series of revelations about practices and personalities in the realm of business and politically linked companies descended upon the Irish public. The trails uncovered led mostly to the door of Mr Haughey and/or his colleagues, cast possible doubts on the probity of government appointees to State boards, or indicated failure of control and accountability by those entrusted with running State companies. The total amount of money which the Irish taxpayer appeared to have given away in deals which, at the very least, were questionable amounted to many millions. Coming as they did just four months after a judicial tribunal had begun to investigate shocking allegations of malpractice, fraud, and political favouritism in the beef-exporting industry,* these new developments marked the decisive beginning of the end of Mr Haughey, and seriously damaged public confidence in politics. Haughey finally fell four months later, while the reverberations for the general body politic were to go on and on . . . snaking slowly through the courts amid appeals to both the High and Supreme Courts. The businessmen involved in these matters were foremost among the Irish success stories, and were household names by the time the revelations broke.

* See section on the Beef Tribunal on pages 313–16.

The first story concerned the privatization of the Irish Sugar Company, which had been turned around to profit by its tough and efficient chief executive.* The chief executive was allegedly involved in a company which had been lent money by Irish Sugar to buy 49 per cent of another company of which Irish Sugar already owned 51 per cent. A year later, Irish Sugar bought back the company for IR£8·68 million, giving its owners a IR£7 million profit extremely quickly. The allegations of scandal centred around a potential conflict of interest between the public and private roles of the chief executive, and the apparent failure of his board, or the Department of Agriculture, or the Department of Finance to spot what was going on.

The Cabinet decided to call in High Court inspectors to enquire into all this, since there was increasing public disquiet on the subject.

The next revelation concerned the purchase by Telecom Éireann – the semi-State telecommunications board – of a property for its new headquarters. The price paid was some IR£9·4 million, despite the State Valuation Office's view that it was worth about IR£6 million. The scandal arose because of allegations that the government-appointed chairman of the Telecom Board† had a possible connection with the company selling the property to Telecom Éireann, of which he was the chairman. Some of the same business names that had featured in the Sugar Company affair also appeared in this. Another inquiry was set up.

Hard on the heels of these two events came another shadow on government and business relations. An educational complex of buildings, formerly a teacher-training college, was bought for University College, Dublin, by the government. Its price was IR£8 million, despite the fact that it was on the market only months earlier for IR£6·5 million.

While the public considered all these issues, controversy simmered over the revelation that agricultural land owned by the Taoiseach Mr Haughey in the suburbs of Dublin was provided with sewerage facilities after two interventions in 1987 by his Minister for the Environment to alter the opposition of the senior planning officials.

* Chris Comerford.
† Michael Smurfit.

The provision of these expensive pipes greatly enhanced the value of Mr Haughey's land.

A stockbroker who had allegedly been involved in two of the stories outlined above was implicated in yet another extraordinary event. He sent information about the helicopter activities of Aer Lingus, by whom his firm, NCB, had been retained as an adviser, to one of their principal commercial rivals, Celtic Helicopters. This helicopter company is owned by the son of Mr Charles Haughey. The disclosure of the documents was made public when it became known that through a 'postal error', the stockbroker had sent the information he was giving to Celtic Helicopters to Aer Lingus. That story died relatively quickly when the Board of Aer Lingus decided that it did not need any further investigation.

Mr Dermot Desmond,* the stockbroker in question, found himself on the public rack again when a letter from his company to a French company was made public. In it he justified a IR£2 million fee for his services to the French company who were involved in buying the big Irish Distillers whiskey and drinks group, by citing his ready access to the highest political level and consequent influence over official attitudes to the deal.

All these sensations, coming hard and fast over a period of a few months, led to suspicions that a 'golden circle' of businessmen was in control of too much public money, and that standards – to put it mildly – appeared to have slipped to an unacceptable level. By Christmas 1991, 65 per cent of those asked in a public opinion poll if 'corruption was a widespread and serious problem amongst our elected politicians' answered 'yes'. Sixty-eight per cent said they had little respect for politicians. Those with strongest suspicions about honesty, and with least respect for politicians, were the young.[23] Not surprisingly, when a general election was called eleven months later, the issues of standards and credibility in politics were central.

---

*Dermot Desmond (b. 1950). A talented and slightly flamboyant businessman who took the Irish world of stockbroking and finance by storm when he founded National City Brokers (NCB) in the early 1980s, and brought it rapidly to the forefront of Irish financial dealings. He was generally considered one of Ireland's modern success stories, often seen in company with Charles Haughey and other powerful figures. He resigned as executive chairman of NCB in October 1991 in the face of all these events.

THOSE WHO CAN'T MAKE A LIVING: POVERTY IN IRELAND

Like many western European countries before the modern age of relative enlightenment in social thinking, Ireland experienced abject poverty among its lowest social groupings. The famine of the mid nineteenth century in Ireland, caused by repeated failure of the potato crop, is perhaps the strongest folk-memory of real poverty, when literally millions died. Things could hardly get worse, and so they gradually improved; there were still harrowing scenes of deprivation to be seen in old drawings and even ancient photographs of evictions of peasants from their meagre holdings in which they had scraped a subsistence living from someone else's soil. But as kinder times came to Britain, the nearest neighbour, they came to Ireland too. Until relatively recently, it was rural poverty which sprang to mind as an Irish problem: the poetry of Patrick Kavanagh (quoted below on page 303), about the hard life of the small farmer in Co. Monaghan, was eloquent witness to it.

Nowadays, with the flight from the land continuing apace, and the search for work in the bigger cities just as much an Irish phenomenon as elsewhere, a generation of urban poverty has been witnessed by a country increasingly disturbed by the social problems it brings with it. This is not to say that there are not pockets of poor farm families still, but they have been joined by their urban cousins in Cork, Limerick, Galway, and most of all in the relatively recent large public-housing developments on the outskirts of Dublin.

Most discussions of the extent of poverty in Ireland today are based on an extensive research project carried out by Ireland's Economic and Social Research Institute (ESRI) in 1987. According to those working in the field, there has not been much change in the essentials, the quantity and type of poverty, since then. What is new is the dramatic increase in unemployment, from 250,000 at the time of the project to the figure of 300,000 and rising since early 1993. Mitigating factors are the gradual improvement in social-welfare rates,* which, however, while alleviating distress in some

* These rates were identified as far too low by a Commission on Social Welfare which reported in 1986 – the first study of the complex and often baffling system of welfare in Ireland. In 1993, the rates of unemployment assistance were still below what the Commission recommended as the minimum acceptable.

areas of particularly acute poverty, do not amount to much more than a maintenance of the status quo, and the improvement in farm incomes (which had been particularly bad in 1986, the reference year). There always seems to be a negative when a positive appears: and so a phenomenon of new rural poverty and deprivation is the isolation and parlous position of the older population in sparsely inhabited areas like some parts of Connemara, where the young and active, along with their children, have left.

Some of the principal social-welfare payments, after the budget of 1993, were:

Unemployment assistance (personal rate) (long-term)		IR£59·20
Unemployment assistance (with adult dependant)		IR£94·70
Old age and blind pension (personal rate)		IR£59·20
Old age (with adult dependant)		IR£94·70
Child benefit (monthly rate): For one child		IR£20·00
	two children	IR£40·00
	three children	IR£60·00
	four children	IR£83·00
(and so on up to:)	eight children	IR£175·00

Full eligibility for free health services is established by income levels, and those fully eligible are known as 'medical card holders'. Some examples of income limits for full eligibility (at January 1993) are:

Single person living alone (per week)	IR£81·50
Married couple (under sixty-six)	IR£118·00
Allowance per child under sixteen	IR£14·00
Married couple aged sixty-six to seventy-nine	IR£131·50

In 1987, then, it was found that 23 per cent of the population (or 810,000 people) were living at or below 50 per cent of average disposable income, adjusted for family size: this is the commonly used EC standard of measurement of poverty. Over a million people were found to be living at or below 60 per cent – some 30 per cent of the population. One of the most dramatic findings of the research team was that over the fourteen years since 1973, the numbers living in poverty had increased by 53 per cent: and since the Irish population had grown considerably, the actual numbers living in poverty had dramatically increased.

Putting this in a European context, the severity of the Irish poverty problem can be understood more clearly when it is realized that average Irish living standards (GDP per capita in 1990) are only 69 per cent of the EC average: above Portugal and Greece and behind everyone else. Spain was immediately above Ireland at 77 per cent, and every other EC country exceeded the European average.[24]

A feature and a result of poverty is homelessness; Ireland has its growing problem in that area too. In 1991, 23,242 households were assessed as being in need of housing, and 2,751 adults were assessed as being homeless. Focus Point, one of Ireland's major voluntary organizations dealing with this problem, found that more than 6,000 adults use the adult hostels in Dublin annually, with 550–600 persons per day. In the first nine months of 1992, Focus Point dealt with 368 young people under seventeen years of age, an increase of 38 per cent on the same period in 1991.[25]

The new 1993 government included a specific action programme on homelessness in its *Programme for a Partnership Government* and appointed a junior minister at the Department of the Environment to have special regard for housing and homelessness.

Focus Point is one of a large and growing list of voluntary organizations working in the area of poverty and health. It is unusual for a weekend to pass without an army of volunteers taking to the streets with collection boxes and a range of ingenious ways of extracting money; and Irish people are generous, both for domestic charities and Third World appeals. In 1985, Bob Geldof of Ireland organized the international 'Live Aid' television event for Ethiopia. Irish people contributed more than IR£9 million, far outstripping any other country in the scale of their response. The official policy of government is to work with voluntary organizations, contributing to their funds and often to their staff, but allowing the organizations to set the pace. The Department of Social Welfare works with the Combat Poverty Agency, which advises the minister, initiates and evaluates projects, and works on research and public information about poverty: it also works with the EC Commission on the EC Poverty Programme.

There has been a failure in coordination of public services for the disadvantaged in Ireland: despite the considerable expenditure on social welfare, health and education, the services have not been able to translate all their efforts into a comprehensive unified support system for the poor. It is the author's contention that this failure is another aspect of the paucity of planning and lack of dynamism at the core of our political system. The saddest results of this are seen as they affect those who cannot help themselves.

NOTES

1. Paul Tansey, *Sunday Tribune*, 16 August 1992.
2. John A. O'Brien (ed.), *The Vanishing Irish*, McGraw-Hill, 1953.
3. Figures from J. J. Sexton, 'Employment, unemployment, and emigration', in Kieran A. Kennedy (ed.), *Ireland in Transition: Economic and Social Change since 1960*, RTE/Mercier Press, 1986 (the Thomas Davis lectures).
4. ibid.
5. ibid.
6. ibid.
7. Institute of Public Administration, *Administration Yearbook and Diary*, 1993.
8. *Irish Times*, 29 August 1992.
9. J. J. Lee, 'Whither Ireland: the next twenty-five years', in Kennedy, op. cit.
10. Institute of Public Administration, *Administration Yearbook and Diary*, 1992.
11. *Sunday Tribune*, 28 June 1992.
12. *Sunday Tribune*, 10 May 1992.
13. *Sunday Tribune*, 12 January 1992.
14. Brendan Keenan, *Irish Independent*, 11 January 1992.
15. *Irish Times*, 18 January 1992.
16. *Irish Independent*, 11 January 1992.
17. Nuala Ó Faoláin, *Irish Times*, 16 March 1992.
18. *Irish Times*, 23 October 1992.
19. *Irish Times*, 5 March 1993.
20. *Irish Times*, 4 May 1993.
21. Seán Dooney and John O'Toole, *Irish Government Today*, Gill & Macmillan, 1992.

22. T. J. Barrington, *The Irish Administrative System*, Institute of Public Administration, 1980.
23. *Irish Independent*/IMS Poll, 28 December 1991.
24. Larry Bond, *Ireland in the EC*, Social Europe, Institute of European Affairs, 1993.
25. Focus Point pre-Budget submission 1993.

CHAPTER 12

Agriculture

Clay is the word and clay is the flesh
Where the potato-gatherers like mechanical scarecrows move
Along the side-fall of the hill – Maguire and his men.

The opening lines of Irish poet Patrick Kavanagh's epic *The Great Hunger*[1] set the tone for one of the most searing descriptions of the life – or perhaps long slow death – of the small farmer in the Ireland of the 1930s and 1940s. A hard life with little money earned from the sparse produce, no chance of marriage while mother and sister lived in the smallholding and had to be supported, the rites of life and death marked by the seasons on his farm: he muses on what it might be like in his coffin –

. . . he remembers names like Easter and Christmas
   by the colour his fields were.

and

He'll know the names of the roots that climb down to tickle his
   feet

Patrick Kavanagh was describing the period of Irish agriculture between the wresting of independence from Britain in the early 1920s almost up to entry into the European Economic Community in 1973.

Ireland's independence was preceded by a succession of acts of the British parliament which, after centuries of landlordism, restored ownership of the land of Ireland to Irish people. For nearly three hundred years the pattern of farming had been determined by the iniquitous system of absentee landlordism, which had pernicious results for Irish agriculture: neglect of the land, with consequent financial loss; no leadership or guidance of the farming community; unscrupulous agents and rack-rents stultifying all will to produce; and the growth of rage and anger at the grotesque differences between the privileged landlord class and the wretched tenants on their tiny units.

By 1800, 95 per cent of the land was owned by settlers. These were mainly Scots and English landowners introduced in periodic large-scale transfers of land to non-Irish and therefore reliable loyal ex-soldiers and other settlers: among them were many absentee landlords. By 1870 there were 527,000 'yearly tenancies' – terminable at six months' notice without compensation for improvements. About 90 per cent of all holdings were under twelve hectares. Then, the cruel and cruelly pursued evictions, growing political unrest, agrarian crime and governmental coercion brought Parnell* and Davitt,† two of Ireland's giants of history, into the fight for reform of the whole sorry system of Irish landownership. It is no wonder that Irish farmers still have a fierce possessiveness about landownership. It was well illustrated by the Kerry dramatist, John B. Keane, in his play, *The Field* (later made into a film of the same name), about land obsession, leading to murder.

After several Land Acts over many years, substantial land reform had taken place by the time of Irish independence. The new native Irish government set about accelerating the process, using compulsory measures to give full ownership to tenants. It took powers to acquire land compulsorily, and distributed land to create economic holdings. The agency which was used to carry out this work was the Land Commission, first established in 1881. Its work was adapted by the independent Irish government after 1922 to concentrate on creating viable farms, out of the patchwork of tiny holdings, particularly in the west of the country. The former

---

*Charles Stewart Parnell (1846–91), b. Avondale, Rathdrum, Co. Wicklow. A Protestant landlord himself, he was first President of the reforming Land League, 1879. He led the Irish Party in Westminster from 1880; became revered throughout Ireland; secured Gladstone's conversion to Home Rule for Ireland; and died in the arms of his new bride, divorcée Katharine O'Shea, fourteen weeks after their marriage. His celebrated romance with her, and his citation in her husband's divorce proceedings, contributed greatly to his rejection by most former admirers and supporters.

†Michael Davitt (1846–1906), b. Co. Mayo. A lifelong worker for land reform, he lived in England and America, and spent years in prison for his Irish agitation. He founded and organized several national movements for land reform and wrote *The Fall of Feudalism in Ireland*, 1904. He, too, turned against Parnell and ran as an anti-Parnellite in 1892.

304

owners of land compulsorily acquired were given bonds instead of money. The new owners paid annuities to the Commission. A decision of the first Fianna Fáil government in the early 1930s to stop paying annuities to the British for land acquired before 1922 led to the foolish so-called 'economic war' with Britain. The Land Commission was abolished finally in 1992, when concentration on more progessive farms, rising land prices, and the growing resentment of owners at the issuing of land bonds all combined to make it an anomaly.

Back in the 1920s it seemed that with political freedom Ireland might at last be able to realize the potential riches from her superb natural resources of soil and climate, so suited to grassland and livestock production. Livestock and livestock products were by then the focus of agriculture, with a growing export market to Britain.

However, political forces were to intervene. Éamon de Valera came to power in Ireland for the first time in 1932, and immediately set about settling old scores with the British. Two stubborn governments locked horns over the old land annuities, leading to the economic war (see Chapter 10). For farming, the result was a change in policy to tillage, using a system of guaranteed prices and import restrictions: self-sufficiency was the aim, using the production of wheat and beet for the home market, and depression of farming the result. In the 1930s, much of rural Ireland would have been recognizable to the Victorian traveller. 'Housing remained dominated by the single-storey cottage, living conditions were basic, families large, emigration and tuberculosis a way of life.'[2] De Valera's particular view of an idealized, noble peasant way of life involved small agricultural units, each self-sufficiently supporting a frugal family. By 1938, there was a huge fall in output of cattle and cattle products, while the value of tillage had not risen proportionately; imports from Britain had declined substantially, but no other markets had been developed.*

---

* Cattle and cattle products declined from IR£54·6 million in 1929–30, to IR£31·1 million in 1935–6. Crop production (excluding potatoes) had risen from only IR£4·1 to IR£5·1 million; imports from Britain fell from 81 to 50 per cent of the total, while exports to Britain were almost static (going from 96 per cent of the total to 91 per cent).[3]

Even as realization dawned that this policy was doomed, the second world war intervened, precluding change.

With the rebuilding of Europe after the war, Ireland joined in international discussions on what was needed in food as part of European recovery. Along with easier relations with Britain after an agreement in 1948, policy was turned once again towards the export market of those products – meat, dairy and eggs – which Ireland was peculiarly well-suited to produce. A succession of policy reviews, particularly in those exciting years of Ireland's new economic planning from 1958 onwards, concentrated on increasing efficiency in production, processing and marketing, improving structures and gaining better access to external markets. But the starting-point was one of such deep depression, with the United Kingdom still dominating the export target area with its low prices, that agriculture remained a poverty-stricken sector needing massive State assistance. By 1972, State expenditure in relation to agriculture and financial aid to poor farmers accounted for one-third of farmers' incomes and was taking up one-sixth of total tax revenue.[4]

Agriculture ministers were therefore centrally important at the Cabinet table. They were continually at the centre of controversy, and the subject of intense and often hostile lobbying and demonstrations by the increasingly powerful farmers' organizations. (The Irish Farmers' Association, the biggest of the farming lobby groups, claimed 85,000 members in 1992, but sees its influence slowly waning as the numbers involved in full-time farming gradually diminish.)

Why is agriculture such a major part of Ireland's economy? A mild climate, averaging about 6 °C in winter and 15 °C in summer, combined with a well-distributed rainfall averaging about 1,000 mm per annum, provides ideal growing conditions, particularly for grass. About 5·7 million hectares (out of the Republic of Ireland's total land area of 6·9 million hectares) is used for agricultural purposes. The remaining area includes woods, forests, bogs, marshes, towns and roads.

It is hardly surprising that the agricultural sector welcomed entry to the European Economic Community (as it then was). The country was entering a high-priced market with guaranteed prices for most farm products. A massive four-to-one majority in the whole country voted for entry in the 1972 referendum, showing, incidentally, the strength numerically of the agriculture and agriculture-related industry. Quite simply, there appeared to be no alternative to membership, a view which is held as firmly today by farmers as it was then. All the farming organizations, except for some small farmers with reservations, were active in urging a 'yes' vote in the 1992 referendum in Ireland which ratified the Maastricht Treaty on European Union. As far as the rural life of Ireland was concerned, EEC accession in 1973 might well be viewed as the most important event in Irish history since independence.

Membership of the European Community has totally dominated and determined Irish agricultural development since 1973. Through its price-support mechanisms* and market-management functions, the Common Agricultural Policy (CAP) of the EC largely determines the market conditions under which Irish farm output is produced and sold. In the 1992 referendum campaign there were a great many reminders by government and farmers alike of the IR£10 billion in various kinds of agricultural support which the country had received since 1973. Not too many wanted to hark back to the other reality – the roller-coaster record of agricultural fortunes since joining the EC, with its price rises and falls, and its reactions to world depressions. Neither was there too much discussion in that campaign about the wider question of whether the direction taken by Ireland in producing huge quantities of unprocessed, and eventually surplus, output because of guaranteed prices was the right one. In 1986, an agricultural economist said: 'Efficiency in agriculture has improved, but some people are asking what kind of efficiency is it that sheds labour to add to the dole queues while unprocessed food piles up in intervention stores.'[5] That neat statement of Ireland's agricultural dilemma became even more relevant in 1992, with the announcement from Brussels of more and more major reforms of the CAP. This reform process, meaning lower prices, lower production, less intervention buying, and lower milk quotas, had implications for Irish farmers and the Irish economy of massive proportions. Irish politicians, as well as

---

*A linchpin of the CAP is intervention: if supply exceeds demand for a particular product, prices fall. If the fall goes below a certain predetermined figure, the Community steps in and purchases the commodity at what are known as intervention prices. It represents a sort of guaranteed minimum price for community producers.

Irish farmers' organizations, had missed a major opportunity to design a long-term strategy for Irish farming during those twenty, mostly halcyon, years of agricultural support by Brussels. No policy was articulated, and there was no development of a real marketing strategy, negligible product research and development, and no optimizing of added value.

In the early 1990s, Ireland's economy still depends to an almost unnerving degree upon agriculture, a sector which faces a most difficult transition to the next century. At the beginning of the decade, 24 per cent of the State's export earnings came from the sector, and an estimated 300,000 of the 1,120,000 people at work rely on the agricultural sector directly or indirectly for their employment. In 1992, the value of agricultural exports, including such things as cream liqueurs and other drinks, was IR£3.395 billion or 24 per cent of total exports.

Beef and dairy produce dominate activity on Irish farms. Both of these are heavily dependent on CAP intervention buying. This led to a situation where, for example, in 1991, 40 per cent of Irish butter went into intervention (adding further to the infamous 'butter mountain') along with more than half – 52 per cent – of beef and 49 per cent of skimmed milk powder.

The shape and pattern of Irish farming follows the geography of the country: the large limestone plain which occupies the centre of the island is ringed almost completely by coastal highlands and mountains. It is here on these central lowlands that the rich rolling cattle farms abound with luxurious grass, while the famous Irish thoroughbred horses thrive. The farms of the east and south-east, with least rainfall and free-draining soil, produce wheat, barley, potatoes, and sugar beet with yields among the highest in Europe. The south and south-west are the principal milk-producing areas. Over on the shallow limestone soils west of the Shannon river, and on the hill and mountain regions of the east and south, sheep farming is the most important enterprise. It is on the small hilly stony farms of the west and north-west coasts – Galway, Mayo, Clare, Sligo, Donegal – that farmers have the most intense struggle to survive, needing continual State supplements to their income; it is from these areas too that the migration is most marked, with all its implications for rural life in Ireland, and social change in the whole society. The farmers in the smaller units are older and less

Total Population and Numbers Engaged in Agriculture in Ireland,
1971, 1981, 1990

Numbers	1971	1981	1990
	millions	*millions*	*millions*
Total population	2·9782	3·4434	3·5027
Total labour force	1·1195	1·2636	1·3050
	thousands	*thousands*	*thousands*
Farmers	181·6	138·8	122·2
Relatives assisting	52·9	24·2	17·3
Employees	46·9	28·8	23·3
Total	281·4	191·8	162·8
Percentage of labour force	25·1	15·2	12·5

Sources: Central Statistics Office, Labour Force Surveys.

willing or able to change. The typical profile of Irish farm size is one of about 23 hectares of owner-occupied land, with most of the farm in grassland. It has two or more farm enterprises and in nine out of ten cases it is operated by the farmer and his family.[6]

Despite the importance of agriculture to the economic life of the country, the pattern of flight from the land which is common to all developing countries has been no less marked in Ireland. The small, difficult, uneconomic farm units of the western and northern part of the island provided very little incentive for young people to stay, while improved production methods elsewhere meant there was no need for the farm labourer or the extra son around the place. It is also true that 20 per cent of farmers, mostly larger producers, were the beneficiaries of 80 per cent of the Brussels supports over the years, a point frequently made by the reforming EC Commissioner for Agriculture Ray MacSharry. The face of rural Ireland is changing rapidly, while the news of the withdrawal of EC support strikes even more fear into the hearts of those still hoping that their sons and daughters might stay on the land. Young people leave the land and flock to the cities for employment, or leave the country altogether. The 162,000 farmers in Ireland today represent a huge drop in numbers since a generation ago. Commentators accept that the figure of real farmers engaged exclusively in serious agriculture is more probably below 100,000. The table on page 309, drawing on official figures, illustrates the trend.

Towns and villages falter and stagnate, reduced to a population of older people living on smallholdings who get State assistance. This is the description of a small town in inland Co. Galway in 1991:[7]

The town dies with a whimper, not a bang, almost unnoticed as the years trickle by. The local creamery closes, so what milk there is must be brought from elsewhere. The local Garda station closes and the mobile library service stops visiting. A centrepiece of activity, the primary school, loses more children and so faces amalgamation with another small school miles away. Hardly anyone drinks in the pub any more, which will have to close, and the post office is threatened, because the old postmistress died and the postal company says it's uneconomic to provide the service any more. Sunday afternoons settle into silence, since the GAA can't field a team because the lads have left.

What lies ahead? Can Ireland develop new forms of agricultural production which will substitute for the concentration on the easy option of intervention supplies over twenty years? Will the elaborate compensation packages and programme for rural development promised by Brussels succeed in preserving the family farm structures which have been the formative backbone of modern Ireland?

The potent European and GATT cocktail of price cuts and production quotas, with some compensatory sweeteners to curtail surpluses and reduce agricultural subsidies, heralds a new era of Irish rural life. The emphasis and the financial supports are increasingly focused upon alternatives to traditional farming: forestry, cheese-making, agri-tourism, free-range poultry and egg production, organic vegetable growing, deer and horse farming, horticulture (especially mushrooms) and fruit. These are among the new lines in which young farmers are interesting themselves. Agricultural colleges redesign their curriculum to teach entrepreneurial techniques and specialist areas of production. Of these alternative land uses, forestry has a great capacity to make an impact in rural areas.

Four hundred years ago, Ireland had wonderful carpets of forest, amounting to 12 per cent of total land use. By the turn of this century, the total was down to just 1·2 per cent and, without planning or development, it stayed at a very low level until new thinking – or any thinking at all – permeated the planning. With EC encouragement and generous grants, 7 per cent of Irish land was under forest by 1992, compared to an EC average of 24 per cent (which does not include the forests of Scandinavia). The Irish Forestry Board (Coillte) was set up in 1988 to take over the former functions of the civil service in this field of activity, and is charged with managing forestry – and its related activities – on a commercial basis. Coillte owns 400,000 hectares of land, and the realistic annual target for new planting is approximately 23,000 hectares, with some 65 per cent being controlled by the growing private sector. Irish politicians are uncomfortably aware that forestry has been grossly neglected, along with so much else in agricultural enterprise: Coillte says that a further one million hectares are suitable for forestry, and that a realistic target for total forestry in the longer term would be 14 per cent of land use. An Irish farmer can get an EC grant of 85 per cent of planting costs (about IR£800–£900 per hectare) with further grants for maintenance, and very generous tax arrangements for future income. The relationship between the private sector and the public one has been uneasy, characterized by mutual distrust. There has also been resistance in pockets of the countryside to the idea of planting where farming, however uneconomic or neglected, had been carried out before. However, progress continues: the amazing growth rates of trees on much of Ireland's wet mineral sites, notably Leitrim, Cavan, and Clare – a yield class of 26 compared, for example, with Finland's 3 – encourages farmers and the State to forge ahead with this potential major contributor to Ireland's exports and employment.

Some case histories illustrate the new trends in farming: two brothers from Waterford in the south-east of Ireland, farming adjoining areas, concentrated until 1983 on dairy and beef cattle. Jim and Tommy Harty then began to think about diversifying: Jim went into mariculture – oysters – along with his traditional activities, while his brother and sister-in-law took up cheese-making. The oysters are booming, mostly exported to France, and the cheese appears on tables in Germany, Britain and at home in Ireland.

John and Mary Barber's farm of just over 100 acres in Co. Laois in the midlands has been turned into a mixed-enterprise operation too: a small milk quota, 22 acres of sugar beet, 30 acres of spring barley, a calf-to-stores enterprise, and now strawberries, which they started in 1988.[8]

Food-processing is the most important sector of Ireland's indigenous industry. Largely Irish-owned, with high profit retention in Ireland, it accounts for about 20 per cent of Irish exports. There is a group of agricultural cooperative companies, with large farmer shareholding, which has led the way in developing and marketing processed foods, with a strong emphasis on dairy produce. But the five biggest cooperatives in Ireland* are each dwarfed by the ten biggest such organizations in Europe. The aim of the Industrial Development Authority and the Irish Cooperative Organization Society is to get this group to rationalize by merger so that economies of scale will enable them to compete with those massive food conglomerates of Europe; they would like the sector to reduce down to four or five companies, and to develop the fish, beef and pig-meat processing activity alongside the well-developed dairy sector, which employs over 9,000 people and provides exports of IR£1 billion.

After two decades of sheltered, and relatively easy, primary production, the cold winds of real competition are blowing through Irish agriculture. The dangerous – if understandable – decision to take the easy way of selling traditional products at low guaranteed prices rather than developing new products for higher-priced markets has left the country with a huge challenge to meet. It is by no means sure that the agricultural sector will be able to rise to it.

In its forecast of trends for Irish agriculture in the 1990s, the Irish government's Department of Agriculture sounds a sombre note.[9] CAP reforms will continue with further downward pressures on prices and supports, increased EC emphasis on environmentally friendly farming methods, a shift in emphasis to direct payments to smaller and less intensive farmers, and increased support for rural development schemes. The Uruguay round of the GATT (General Agreement on Tariffs and Trade) negotiations will, when completed, have profound effects on the economic environment for farmers. Possible enlargement of the EC to include Eastern and Central European countries will put pressure on the funds available to

* Kerry, Avonmore, Waterford, Dairygold, and Golden Vale.

Ireland, though a positive result might be increased markets for Irish produce.

Dr Séamus Sheehy, professor of applied agricultural economics at Ireland's largest university, foreseeing the gathering pace of change, exhorted the agricultural sector to face up to the challenge and not to waste time mourning the losses: 'It would be tragic if obsession with the losses were to deflect farmers, other agribusiness interests, and the government, from maximizing the prospective gains . . . this will entail the mobilization of all available energies to enhance Ireland's competitiveness . . . a good foundation is being laid which warrants cautious optimism about the future . . . one can only hope that the result will be the successful transformation of the agricultural industry such as that achieved by countries like Denmark and the Netherlands a century ago when they were faced with a similar challenge.'[10]

Farmers had to face even more difficulties in early 1993, as the Irish pound gained sharply on the international exchange and weakened the competitiveness of their exports. The government set about arranging alleviating finance for exporters, amid a cacophony of calls for devaluation.

THE BEEF TRIBUNAL

Irish agriculture in these testing times, relying on its reputation for high-quality produce from a clean, green setting, could do without international scandals about the quality and probity of its beef-exporting practices. The worst possible scandal broke out in May 1991. On 13 May 1991, a British television channel showed a programme on the Irish beef industry, full of astonishing allegations concerning the practices in handling beef, and alleging fraud in obtaining EC subsidies, and favouritism towards some companies by government. One 'beef baron' in particular was picked out, Larry Goodman,* who had enjoyed a reputation as something of a

---

*Larry Goodman (b. 1939), from Dundalk, Co. Louth, where he was educated by the Marist brothers. His rise from a small-town dealer in offal and animal hides was meteoric. He became the country's most important man in agriculture, with an astonishing IR£1 billion turnover by 1989 in the beef-exporting business. His hard work, entrepreneurial expertise and ability to win new markets for Irish beef were legendary. His low profile was carefully guarded too.

wizard as he built up a multimillion-pound beef-exporting business, using the tools of EC subsidies as part of the machinery. He had come close to government in 1987, playing the central role in C. J. Haughey's plans to launch a massive drive for employment in the agriculture and food sector. By 1991, several major business setbacks had plunged the Goodman empire into deep financial trouble; adding to his troubles was the failure of Iraq to pay its bills for beef he had sold to them.

The *World in Action* programme by ITV did not come out of the blue, as there had been rumours and political allegations inside the Dáil for some time. At the centre of these allegations were Charles Haughey and his government of 1987/8, and accusations that political favouritism had been the motivating factor in providing huge export-credit insurance for Goodman's company when exporting meat to Iraq, an extremely risky market. After the television programme, the political storm really broke, and the Taoiseach – still Mr Haughey, but now in coalition with partners, the Progressive Democrats, who made a particular point of absolute integrity in public affairs – was forced to set up a tribunal of inquiry into the beef industry.* The tribunal began its work later that month.

Many feared that a lengthy public tribunal would further damage the beef industry. Ireland's *Sunday Business Post* called on Goodman either to sue the TV programme-makers or resign. 'The programme has probably done immense damage to the reputation of the Irish beef industry,' it said, and in a prophetic statement went on, '. . . this inquiry could result in a massive fudging of the issue, could take several years to complete, and could produce inconclusive findings'. This comment was typical of general reaction.

By the end of 1992, the prophecies seemed accurate. A succession of witnesses and allegations about fraud in the industry had rocked the country every day; former employees of Goodman alleged that the TV programme was correct in its descriptions of falsifying records. Evidence was given alleging that employees were paid

---

* The tribunal, established by the Dáil on 24 May 1991 under Mr Justice Liam Hamilton, President of the High Court, had terms of reference requiring it to investigate allegations in the Dáil and on ITV of illegal activities, fraud, malpractice in or connected to the beef-processing industry, and any matters connected to or relevant to these matters, and to make recommendations.

'under the counter' in order to evade tax. It was also alleged that 38 per cent of the beef going to Iraq was not sourced in the Republic of Ireland, and that 84 per cent of the remainder came out of intervention and had already been processed. Civil servants and politicians trooped in and out of the witness-box; the Taoiseach appeared at odds with senior civil servants on recollections of instructions and conversations; former ministers and colleagues of the Taoiseach when he had been Minister for Industry and Commerce and Finance clashed with him on recollections of what might have been discussed at Cabinet meetings. At that juncture, the State's counsel objected to anyone talking about any previous Cabinet discussions. The High Court overruled the objection, but the Supreme Court ruled in August 1992 that Cabinet discussions about extending export insurance could not be revealed.* Undeterred, the tribunal chairman persevered with the inquiry. Substantial financial contributions to political parties were laid bare, and the Taoiseach, at the end of October 1992, accused his Cabinet colleague, leader of the junior coalition partner, and one of the principal instigators of the inquiry, of dishonesty,† refusing to withdraw it when invited several times. Naturally, this precipitated a general election, held on 25 November – yet another major national change brought about by the tribunal.

The tribunal adjourned for the election campaign, and resumed in December to be informed by some Dáil members‡ who had made allegations about Goodman and about political favouritism that they were claiming parliamentary privilege and refused to reveal their sources. Their right to do this was upheld by the tribunal chairman. Dáil privilege was opposed by counsel for the State, who not only represented the Taoiseach and former government members, but civil servants as well. The legal team representing Goodman objected also, on the grounds that their client had to

---

*The Supreme Court ruling on the absolute secrecy of Cabinet discussions was one of the major national changes caused by the Beef Tribunal.

†This charge related to differences of interpretation about exactly how much money Goodman was claiming in a separate action against the State to recover his losses in Iraq, and strictly speaking was not part of the terms of reference of the tribunal at all.

‡Including the Labour leader, Mr Spring, who was to become Tánaiste and Minister for Foreign Affairs in the coalition government led by Mr Reynolds in January 1993.

know who was making the accusations against him. Yet more cases, on this point, were brought to the High Court; these parties also wished to have the ITV programme-maker, Susan O'Keefe, forced to reveal her sources. In late January, the High Court reserved judgement; it looked as if it was possible that at the end of this latest legal process most of the allegations made in the Dáil and by the television programme could not be pursued if sources were not revealed. Only the allegations made outside the Dáil and to the tribunal by Desmond O'Malley and the Industrial Development Authority (which had been named by Fine Gael's leader as his source) would remain.

The effect of the daily media reports of these revelations, quarrels, legal manoeuvrings, and clashes between senior members of government was, to put it mildly, damaging to the public estimation of both politicians and business, at home and abroad. It was like having a Greek chorus in the background over two turbulent years in the Irish economy and body politic. It touched on many areas of Irish life, and could possibly end without being able properly to investigate all the charges. Taken together with all the other revelations in the autumn of 1991 about big business and political connections,* it marked another stage in the shaping of modern Ireland.

By the summer of 1993, the tribunal still dragged on, punctuated by more clashes between the Taoiseach and his former government colleague Desmond O'Malley about alleged leaks by the Taoiseach of documents calculated to damage O'Malley's credibility. As if to underline the sorry state of things, O'Malley allegedly was physically assaulted at Brussels airport by a relation of Larry Goodman in June. The most pessimistic forecasts of those who had predicted that the tribunal would run into the ground amid a sea of accusations and bitterness seemed to be coming true.

The tribunal's hearings finally concluded on 15 July 1993, after 200 days, the appearances of 600 witnesses, and estimated costs of IR£20 million.

The 1990s would present Irish agriculture with challenges and difficulties, which many hoped would lead to a new and dynamic generation of young farmers bringing change and real progress.

* See Chapter 11.

NOTES

1. Patrick Kavanagh, *Collected Poems*, MacGibbon & Kee, 1964.
2. R. F. Foster, *Modern Ireland, 1600–1972*, Allen Lane, 1988/Penguin, 1989.
3. ibid.
4. Robert O'Connor, 'Agriculture and other natural resources', in Kieran A. Kennedy (ed.), *Ireland in Transition: Economic and Social Change since 1960*, RTE/Mercier Press, 1986.
5. ibid.
6. *Ireland: Agriculture and Food*, Department of Agriculture, 1991.
7. *Irish Times*, 3 January 1991.
8. *Irish Independent* (Farming Supplement), 7 July 1992.
9. *Annual Review and Outlook for the Agriculture and Food Industry 1991.*
10. Dr Séamus Sheehy, *Towards Free Trade in Agriculture*, ICOS (Dr Henry Kennedy Memorial Lecture 1989).

CHAPTER 13

The Irish Entrepreneur

'A high proportion of school-leavers describe their schooling in dismissive terms: they can see clearly its lack of relevance for them . . . the education system has become progressively more academic in nature.'[1] In searching for reasons for the relatively small number of indigenous Irish success stories in the business and industry area, the Irish education system is often targeted, as it was by the report of a government-appointed industrial policy review group in 1992, quoted above. For several years, politicians and business people have urged reform in education.

The Irish Minister for Education in a major Green Paper in June 1992 recognized this widespread demand and included as one of the principal aims of education 'fostering a spirit of innovation and enterprise'. He went on to list areas in which he believed young Irish people were lacking, including 'the critical thinking, problem-solving ability, and individual initiative that an enterprise culture requires'.[2]

Following this train of thought, speaking to Irish people about their own experiences, there is undoubtedly a feeling that individuality, leadership, and innovation were not highly valued traditionally in the Irish school system. It was, of course, until very recently, a system controlled largely by the conservative Irish Catholic Church and a deeply conservative government Department of Education. It is not unconnected with the dearth of innovators and entrepreneurs that Ireland's Catholic Church, despite the high number of religious, was and continues to be one of the most conservative and unquestioning in the world. (See Chapter 17, 'Education in Ireland'.)

A successful businesswoman recounts her experience serving on a government-appointed curriculum-review body in the mid-1980s. She was asked by the group to list three things which should be on the school curriculum, and gave – as her first preference – entrepreneurship. Of forty or so people – mostly experienced and distinguished educationists – at this meeting, she was the only one to mention it, and the only one to vote for it when it came to listing all the suggestions in order of importance. Her experience of educationists, in that situation and on other boards on which she served, was that they were apathetic at best, but usually negative about anything to do with making money and getting into business.

The National College of Art and Design, teaching art, crafts, industrial and other design, film-making, and a range of other skills to hundreds of Ireland's best and brightest every year, has no structured courses for all students on how to plan and develop a small business, using the skills nurtured at great expense to the state. A former student who attended the college during the 1980s remarked to the author that not only was such a thing never mentioned, but there was a positively hostile attitude to anything smacking of commercialism. The Green Paper ran into similar hostility – but then, it omitted any mention at all of arts and creativity as an important part of education. In the public debate on the Green Paper, this lack of emphasis on general creativity and independence of thought was held to be responsible for Irish people's lack of initiative in business. The minister was accused of trying to invent some magic way of turning young people into economic units rather than whole human beings.*

Stories abound of the failure of the school system to recognize and foster initiative and leadership. A male national champion in several sports and, later, business entrepreneur par excellence, was neither given the school captaincy in any of those sports nor made a school prefect. In his fifties today, he runs the kind of medium-size Irish business which the country badly needs. An Irishwoman who started a highly successful business at twenty-two and went on to leadership at national political level was continually denied any position of authority in her convent school.

While all these attitudes prevailed, Ireland was turning out first-class doctors, lawyers, priests and nuns, accountants, and civil servants; the number of accountants trebled between 1971 and 1986, the number of lawyers and auctioneers doubled, but the number of engineers increased by under 50 per cent.

One of Ireland's most astute and acerbic commentators in politics

*See Chapter 17.

spoke in 1989 of the shortage of Irish initiative. Describing the burgeoning of craft-work in the 1980s, such as making harpsichords, or unusual sheep's-milk cheese, he feared that 'more than likely they are being made by foreigners: an Englishwoman running a hotel, a German raising a herd of deer, a Canadian running a shell-fish farm: very rarely will it be a person of native Irish blood who sees an opportunity such as that, and makes the most of it'. He went on to wonder whether it was something psychological in the Irish people and whether 'our education system, including linguistic education and industrial education, needs to be rapidly overhauled before we can have the social and psychological infrastructure on which a healthy economy can be built'.[3]

Small wonder that by 1992, the chairman of the Industrial Policy Review Group gave these disappointing figures about indigenous industry: fewer than twenty Irish firms employing more than 500, fewer than 150 companies with sales of over IR£5 million. Historian J. J. Lee put it like this, describing the position in 1980: 'Sixty years after independence, fifty years after blanket protection, fifteen years after the Anglo-Irish Free Trade Agreement, eight years after entering the EEC, a native entrepreneurial cadre of the requisite quality had failed to emerge.'[4]

Ireland had no industrial revolution; a whole European experience passed by the country which was discouraged, to put it mildly, by its British rulers from starting or developing anything which might compete with nascent British enterprise. Apart from some minor specialities like linen-producing in the north of Ireland, nothing emerged in eighteenth- and nineteenth-century Ireland which could lay the foundations for a business-oriented community, for producing clusters of skills and strengths, for bringing out new abilities, as happened across western Europe.

When the Minister for Education in the 1992 Green Paper announced his intention to bring a new 'enterprise dimension' to second-level schools through a new module in business studies courses, and a completely new subject – Enterprise and Technology Studies – to be made obligatory eventually for all students, he did not spell out how teachers with hitherto academic qualifications only were going to be transformed into inculcators of a whole new outlook. However, the Green Paper's proposals were at least a response to the many years of urging for something to happen.

Given the snail's pace at which reform and renewal of the Irish education system takes place, and the vacillation of policy as different ministers take office, the Green Paper's outline proposals were expected to have a long slow path before making an appearance in the classroom. Its progress would not be helped by the marked strong antipathy to its ideas expressed by many educationists, who feared that the ideas put forward in the Culliton report on new emphasis on vocational training and technology in schools and their echoing in the Green Paper would turn education on its head. The Provost of Trinity College, Dublin, an eminent classics scholar, had this to say: 'The Culliton report was completely wrong in its over-emphasis on vocational studies at second level, and the Green Paper did not correct that . . .'[5]

For years, therefore, many Irish people – but not enough – have noted and worried about values and attitudes which are inimical to entrepreneurship. They identify a colonial and dependent past, a high need for security, the attitudes in schools, an authoritarian Church dominating not only education, a peasant culture which puts more value on professions than on business . . . The author of a book on Irish entrepreneurs remembers thinking in 1984: 'We are not Yeats' swift, indifferent men; the struggle to get cultural legitimacy for enterprise in Ireland is therefore a struggle against odds; we Irish find it hard to stomach the rich; we even find it hard to stomach success; we rejoice in the failure of others.'[6] When a computer company announced the shedding of 780 jobs in Galway in early 1993, an international expert on technology and competitiveness* came to address the despondent workforce, and added his voice to criticism of the Irish education system; young people leaving the system, he said, 'can work in a structured multinational but they are ill-equipped to face the uncertainties of life . . . the system does not imbue them with the sense that with the new knowledge they have acquired they can go back to their communities and revitalize them . . .'

Fortunately, things are changing: many of the factors which were

---

*Dr Mike Cooley, consultant to several governments and large companies, as well as a director of the EC-sponsored Technology Exchange organization, chairman of Technology Innovation Associates, and visiting professor at Tokyo University and Bremen University in Germany.

present in the Irish nation's development period have either disappeared in the 1990s or have been radically altered. No longer isolated on their island, Ireland's young people are mobile throughout Europe and the world; a colonial past means nothing to them. The influence of the Church is lessening rapidly (see Chapter 16, 'Religion in Ireland') and the old, totally academic, tightly controlled static system of education is changing, albeit slowly and somewhat painfully. Most significantly, the number of young people trying to get into third-level business courses exceeds the number of available places, and now is well ahead of the numbers seeking entry into the older professions such as law and medicine, so much so that private business schools are thriving across the country.

One of the most helpful changes has been the arrival in recent years of the hitherto rare Irish species: the successful, visible entrepreneur as role model. A growing number of Irish companies and Irish executives have achieved international success too, which for a small country looking outwards has considerable impact. In recent years, the successes of the Irish indigenous private sector have begun to make an impression on the jobs figures. Former Taoiseach and economist Garret FitzGerald drew on the Central Statistics Office figures for public-sector employment to extrapolate figures for the private sector: he reckoned that some 70,000 new jobs in the Irish private sector had been created between 1985 and 1992, a better performance proportionately than that of the same sector in western Europe and the United States over that period. He firmly rejected the blame placed on the private sector for the present very high unemployment rates: these are caused, he said,

... by the fact that a country whose birth rate fifteen to twenty years ago was nearly double that of the rest of the industrialized world cannot hope to provide jobs at home for the children born then unless it is prepared to significantly reduce its income levels relative to those of competing countries in world markets.[7]

Be that as it may, there are not many household names in the business world of Ireland of the 1990s – and obviously not enough. There are few discernible common features in their background, except the obvious one of their sex. Seventeen of the nineteen entrepreneurs who agreed to be interviewed for a 1991 book about entrepreneurs in Ireland were men; and interestingly the two women (one of whom was not native Irish) did not have children.[8] The other factor common to a majority of the successful people in that book was the completion of at least full-time second-level schooling, and a look at most Irish substantial entrepreneurs of today establishes that all came from what might be called comfortable homes, rarely luxurious, but rarely substandard either.

As an aside, one of the difficulties about the successful business person as a highly visible role model is that he (it is mostly male) may not always represent the most desirable model – in an Irish context – in every aspect of his life. Three of Ireland's very few multimillionaire international entrepreneurs have had highly public marriage difficulties, breakups and/or new partners.* The scion of another Irish business family was convicted in 1992 of drug possession, in Florida, with great publicity, that included the presence of an escort-agency employee in his hotel room.† Gossip columns abound in repeated stories of the reputedly high life and risqué doings of a small number of wealthy business people. All of this is deplored by the quieter, more discreet and private Irish business people – the majority – who are concerned about the effect on public – and political – opinion of this kind of flaunting of questionable standards. Ireland's need for political action to encourage new business and investment, well documented so many times, is so acute that anything which gives the political establishment further reason for inaction is alarming.

This concern of the generally low-profile, hard-working, business community was considerably heightened in the autumn of 1991, when a succession of revelations in the media about various deals to do with property acquisition, allegations of political favouritism to particular business people, and of irregularities inside semi-State company boards, mostly involving prominent men who were close to, or appointed by, the most powerful politicians of the day, caused shock waves throughout the country. These revelations added to the already simmering unease about possible major scandals in the Irish beef industry.‡ Political uproar ensued, official

* Tony O'Reilly, Tony Ryan, and Michael Smurfit.
† Ben Dunne, of the Dunne's Stores international chain of department stores.
‡ For a discussion of these events of autumn 1991, see Chapter 11, 'Unemployment, Industrial Policy, Performance, and the Poverty Trap'.

inquiries were set up (and in early 1993 they were mostly still in train), and the whole sorry saga added to the increasing momentum towards removing the Taoiseach of the day – which eventually happened in January 1992. The damage done to reputations and to the business and investment climate led to great bitterness among the business community, whose general view was expressed by the editor of the *Sunday Business Post* newspaper in September 1992: '. . . daily outpourings of bile . . . infantile columnizing . . . has been used to discredit all business people . . . Irish people will have to decide whether they want a functioning economy or an impoverished debating society.'[9]

IRISH BUSINESS: SUCCESS STORIES

One of the quieter, low-profile, and most unassuming but most successful Irish business people is the head of Glen Dimplex, a group involved in the manufacturing of electric domestic goods. The company, employing 5,000 (more than a thousand of them in Ireland), had a turnover in 1992 of IR£300 million. Martin Naughton started it in 1973. He had left Ireland, one of the huge numbers of 1950s emigrants, with his school certificate and was an engineering apprentice for five years in England. He came back to Ireland, worked his way up until, still only thirty-three, he was able to start his own company. It now owns world-famous brand names in electrical appliances: Dimplex, Morphy Richards, Burco Maxol, Glen and Cromalox, Hamilton Beach in the United States and in 1992 acquired the Belling company. He put his finger on the essential prerequisite for really big business success in a small country like Ireland: 'Less than 2 per cent of our sales are in Ireland, both north and south, but 30 per cent of our employment is in Ireland.'[10] Speaking at a summer school in Donegal on one of his rare public appearances, Naughton identified the violence in Northern Ireland as one of the obstacles to investment in Ireland; he urged lower personal taxation, but enthused about what he described as Ireland's best asset – intelligent, well-educated, English-speaking people who are willing to work hard. Rather than blame anyone else for Ireland's ills, he suggested 'we should look in the mirror and blame ourselves, and get off our backsides and do something about it'.[11] In a country with no State honours system, the accolade of an honorary degree is the nearest Irish equivalent: an honorary doctorate of laws was conferred on Martin Naughton by University College, Dublin in 1991.

On a much smaller scale, but none the less striking, is the story of Geoff Read, who as a young middle-class emigrant in London in the late 1970s was suffering one morning from a hangover after a late night. A customer in the shoe-shop where he was working that day – he had already some success in the shoe business in England – suggested he should drink some mineral water: and from there, the idea of an Irish spring water took root. Geoff Read came home, worked hard and long and doggedly, and introduced Ballygowan Spring Water to Ireland.* It now claims over 70 per cent of the Irish market, and is the fastest-growing brand in the UK market. Its 1992 turnover was IR£16 million, and it employs more than seventy people. In 1993, Geoff Read sold 51 per cent of Ballygowan to Cantrell & Cochrane, a British-owned company. He had, in just over a decade, introduced a mass Irish market to the mineral-water drinking habit.

The highest-paid business executive in the United States – he earned $75 million in 1991 – is an Irishman called Anthony J. O'Reilly. He burst upon the Irish public in the 1950s as a big, redhaired, fast rugby player who thrilled the crowds by playing for his country while still in his teens. A man of considerable charm, erudition, wit and versatility, he emerged from a middle-class Dublin family and law studies into stardom through sport initially (capped for Ireland twenty-eight times) and then as a very young general manager of Bord Bainne (the Irish Dairy Board) and on to the Irish Sugar Company, through which he came in contact with Heinz. His rise therein was meteoric: British managing director, president (US) and chief executive before he was forty, and chairman of Heinz since 1987. In addition, he holds a substantial interest in Ireland's biggest newspaper chain, Independent Newspapers (to which he has added since his initial investment in 1973); he holds 8 per cent in one of Ireland's big investment

*The author experienced Geoff Read's dogged persistence in the 1980s when he haunted her political 'clinics' – he was a constituent – in order to lobby the government for abolition of 'table water' tax and value-added tax on what he claimed was ordinary water out of the ground. He won his arguments.

companies (FitzWilton); and he is part of a consortium which owns the Waterford/Wedgwood group. As well as all this, he and his family control (with 85 per cent) an Australian newspaper group, APN. Past business ventures include an oil-exploration company, Atlantic Resources, once enormously valuable, but which O'Reilly got out of amid controversy in 1991.

His personal fortune, estimated in 1992 at $350 million, is, however, dwarfed by his second wife's: she is Chryss Goulandris, of the Greek shipping and finance family. They were married in September 1991; he is divorced from his Australian first wife and mother of his six children.

O'Reilly, like most of the business community, involves himself in philanthropy; in his case, it is highly visible, very substantial, and heavily weighted towards funding projects to help the disadvantaged and troubled border region between Northern Ireland and the Republic. He has also endowed Dublin's Trinity College very generously. Apart from his imposing Pittsburgh home, O'Reilly lives and entertains when he is in Ireland in some splendour in a large old Irish mansion, Castlemartin, in Co. Kildare (former home of Lord Gowrie), and owns a splendid art collection and a stud farm. It would be extraordinary if he did not come in for some criticism, including a critical (unauthorized) biography called *Oh Really O'Reilly?* by Harry Walsh (published by the author). When asked why the book cost so much (IR£25) Walsh riposted: 'You wouldn't believe the legal fees.'

A story of solid work, opportunities grasped, and quiet success is that of Christopher Jones, who left the country town of Bandon in Co. Cork in the 1940s to be apprenticed as a plumber in Dublin. At twenty-one he took over the management of the small firm in Dublin in which he worked. On the death of the owner, Jones acquired a majority share, and never looked back. As well as building up the original firm, H. A. O'Neill, to become one of the country's biggest mechanical-services operations, Jones and his brothers went into shipping (small oil tankers), manufacturing (radiators and steel tubes), oil distribution, and other allied activities. The company went public in 1973, becoming the Jones Group, and twenty years later employed some 700 people in Ireland, with a turnover of IR£100 million, and owned companies in Britain and the United States. The founding brother, who retired from the chair of the board in 1991, lives quietly in Co. Meath, enjoys racing and farming, and carries out his considerable support of various charities extremely discreetly. Following European trends, the Jones Group in 1993 was owned to the tune of 21 per cent by a Swiss company, and had sold the H. A. O'Neill part of its operations to management.

One of the successes in the attractive world of Irish craft industry is the firm of Avoca Handweavers. Avoca is a village in the south of Co. Wicklow, where Thomas Moore's song 'The Meeting of the Waters' brings tourists to admire the two rivers meeting in the town. It had a tradition of weaving since the eighteenth century, when local farmers brought their fleeces to the mill, which were dyed and spun for weaving yarn. By 1974, however, after many vicissitudes, the company consisted of a couple of leaking buildings, which the owner hoped to sell off for a caravan park. It was bought by a Dublin solicitor and his wife, Donald and Hilary Pratt, for IR£17,000. Skilled weavers were persuaded to come back to the mill; the initial produce was car rugs and bedspreads but the company added clothes to their range quite quickly. Donald and Hilary Pratt devoted themselves to development, carrying suitcases of samples to quality stores in London, Frankfurt, and Paris, opening retail outlets in five prime tourist locations in Ireland, and one each in the United States and Canada. They provided home-cooked snacks and freshly brewed coffee (this activity developed into a popular and profitable restaurant in their largest shop) and employed designers and expert tailors, constantly updating styles and introducing new colours and designs in their tweeds. By 1992, Avoca Handweavers employed 112 people, had a turnover of IR£6 million and exported 50 per cent of their produce, selling most of the rest in their shops around Ireland to tourists. In each retail outlet, they also sell a wide range of other Irish quality crafts.

The world's biggest airline leasing company, Guinness Peat Aviation (GPA), was started by Dr Tony Ryan (the 'Dr' is from an honorary degree in recognition of his contribution to the arts), who began his business career as a clerk with Ireland's national airline, Aer Lingus. Dr Ryan took his company to the market in June 1992, but aborted the flotation at the last moment when the expected international interest did not materialize. It had been valued in advance at about IR£2 billion. The last-minute change was the first real hiccup in the upward momentum of this Irish achiever.

The son of a train driver, Ryan was born in Co. Tipperary in 1936; there were no funds for university, so the young Ryan went to work in Aer Lingus, got himself a business degree in the United States, and gradually conceived the idea of international aircraft leasing. With just IR£50,000 in equity at the beginning in 1975, it was four years before he began purchasing aircraft. In 1991, his GPA portfolio was reckoned to own 349 modern jet and turboprop aircraft, leasing to more than ninety-eight airlines in forty-six countries. It was generally agreed that the extraordinary personal commitment of Ryan himself, plus the unusual demands – accompanied by generous remuneration – made on everybody who works in the company, were essential elements in this success story. The management team was considered to be of an exceptionally high standard. The difficulties experienced by the company as 1993 opened were watched with anxiety by many in Ireland who had admired the worldwide achievements of this Tipperary man. If it were to get into serious difficulties, the sheer size of the financial disaster would be hard to imagine. A massive rescue deal with General Electric announced on 12 May 1993 seemed likely to save the company but transfer ownership and control to GE. It seemed that management failure to anticipate international difficulties in air transport had very nearly brought GPA, one of Ireland's more dramatic success stories, to a sticky end.

The board of directors of GPA in 1993 read like a 'who's who' of international politics: Nigel Lawson, former UK Chancellor of the Exchequer; Peter Sutherland, former EC Competition Commissioner; and Dr Garret FitzGerald, former Taoiseach (who worked in Aer Lingus himself in his early days).

Living on an extensive and beautiful estate in his native Tipperary, Tony Ryan enjoys serious farming and is a significant patron of many different art-forms in Ireland, as well as supporting architectural and historical renovation in his own county, third-level education, and employment-giving local schemes. He has invested in other Irish ventures, not always successfully: Ryanair, the first private airline to take on Aer Lingus, which his sons work in, has had continual financial troubles* but forced the semi-State monopoly to lower prices.

A success story on a smaller scale is that of Dan Tierney, from Limerick. On leaving secondary school in 1956, he joined Esso Petroleum and worked with them for ten years, learning the business and ending up as area manager for Co. Limerick. Tierney always wanted to be self-employed, joined a small company called Golden Eagle, which was the Irish arm of Jet Petroleum, bought it out, and sold it to Continental Oil in 1966. Seeing the inevitability of Ireland joining the EC, and realizing that animal health was going to be an important concern, he bought a small veterinary pharmaceutical company, and then two more. He then moved into human pharmaceuticals, because of his instinct that the genetic industry was about to take off. Looking at modern trends, he has also set up Greenscience Ltd, a company specializing in naturally occurring bacteria for the biodegradation of waste, slurries, and petroleum wax. His companies, known as the Cross Group, employ 350 people with a turnover of IR£25 million of which 50 per cent is from exports. Asked what can be done to nurture more Irish entrepreneurs, he points the finger at the education system: the points system which forces all young people into an academic race, and brands those who do not get high points as failures. He would like more venture capital to be available to young business people.

That cross-section of Irish success stories illustrates the variety of interests in which some Irish people have excelled. There are, of course, a myriad of other initiatives, large and small.

Ireland can and does produce some people with ideas, and with the imagination and energy to carry them through to realization. Ireland produces some people who see the opportunities and do something about them. One of the achievers mentioned in this book, Martin Naughton of Glen Dimplex, reminded his Donegal audience in 1989 that the most successful ethnic group in business in the United States were those claiming Irish descent. The creativity, however, that the Irish at home have shown in literature, theatre, film, and painting has not extended widely enough into

---

* The appointment of former EC Commissioner Ray MacSharry as non-executive chairman of the Ryanair board in January 1993 created some optimism about its future.

business. When Irish people think about creativity, they usually think about people who paint pictures, write poems, or compose music. Why this is so, and what modern Ireland can do about it, is one of the major public debates in the country in the 1990s.

NOTES

1. *Report of the Industrial Policy Review Group* (*the Culliton Report*), Stationery Office, 1992.
2. Green Paper on Education, Irish Department of Education, June 1992.
3. John Fanagan (ed.), *Belling the Cats. Selected Speeches and Articles of John Kelly*, Moytura Press, 1992.
4. J. J. Lee, *Ireland 1912–1985, Politics and Society*, Cambridge University Press, 1989.
5. Dr Tom Mitchell, in conversation with the author, 8 March 1993.
6. Ivor Kenny, *Out on Their Own*, Gill & Macmillan, 1991.
7. *Irish Times*, 5 June 1993.
8. ibid. Gillian Bowler, a travel agent, is English; the other woman was Carol Moffett, a Co. Monaghan head of an engineering company.
9. *Sunday Business Post*, 27 September 1992.
10. Keogh and Mulholland (eds.), *Emigration, Employment and Enterprise*, Hibernian University Press, 1989.
11. ibid.

CHAPTER 14

The Media in Ireland

There has been a continuing battle in the Republic of Ireland which has nothing to do with the IRA, the Unionists in Northern Ireland, or the British. This struggle began in earnest in 1988, though it had its genesis much earlier. It is a war between the Irish national broadcasting network and the print media, with a second battle front involving politicians and broadcasters. One would be forgiven for thinking that politicians, since they hold the trump card of legislation, might have a huge advantage which would see them win decisively. However, decisions by Irish governments in recent years in this area have been hesitant, and mostly ill-judged – no sooner made, they were shown not to work and had to be changed. The issues have been money (revenue from advertising) and power (broadcasters' power to influence voters). By late 1991, a commentator of the print media, in some exasperation, described the position as 'the morass of dithering and muddled thinking that passes for broadcasting policy in Ireland'.[1] A major inhibiting factor on political action has been the power, skilfully used, of RTE (Radio Telefís Éireann) – the national broadcasting body – to influence public opinion against any encroachment on its central position.

During the early 1980s, it became clear that no longer could the traditional Irish blind eye (or deaf ear) be turned towards the growth of pirate radio stations all over the country (reaching about seventy at its peak), but particularly in the Dublin area and other larger urban areas. This anarchy of the air waves drew a bigger and bigger – and mostly younger – audience away from the official state broadcaster, RTE, which was then the only legal broadcasting organization in Ireland. The print media and RTE anxiously watched the inevitable consequence: advertising revenue following the listeners. Governments got worried, not only about the law-breaking aspect of it all, but also about the need to regularize the air waves on an agreed international basis, and about matters like interference with safety and security systems such as those used at airports and by police, ambulance services and fire-fighters. RTE, seeing the trend, established its own popular youth-oriented second national-radio network.

Worried though it might be, the Fine Gael/Labour coalition government of 1982–7 was virtually paralysed by disagreement between the partners, a disagreement which was loosely ideological: the Labour Party wanted extinction of the pirates, the adherence to public-service broadcasting, and the shoring-up of RTE's Irish monopoly. The Fine Gael Party wanted to introduce independent commercial broadcasting on a legal basis, as competition for RTE, who they felt had undue – and not always properly used – influence on the news and current-affairs reporting. Deadlock ensued, and the nettle was ungrasped.

Underlying the political attitude to broadcasting, both in the Fine Gael Party and among the more centrist members of the Labour Party, was a strong suspicion about the extent of the influence exercised by extreme left-wing employees of the station, either members of or closely connected with the Workers' Party. It was felt, and articulated mostly in private, that the Workers' Party had a very definite policy of infiltration of RTE. This view was shared by Fianna Fáil. It was also felt by Fine Gael and Fianna Fáil that the trade unions within RTE had been allowed to get out of hand, ensuring overmanning and restrictive practices at a level much higher than in the BBC, for example.

The current-affairs sector attracted the most suspicion, in which a particularly acute example was a long-standing television programme called *Today Tonight*. When that programme was abolished in the summer of 1992, commentators recalled the general view which had been held: 'Whatever the subject', said a prominent Sunday newspaper columnist, 'this viewer always felt that something less than the full story was being told . . . businessmen seemed to be given a rougher ride than trade unionists, the concerns of strikers seemed to matter more than the suffering of those affected . . .'[2] The programme gained a reputation of being some kind of blood sport, in which politicians of the centre/right, business people, or serious commentators were usually the quarry. In 1992 also, revelations about the contacts between the Workers' Party and the Communist Party of the then Soviet Union seemed to bear out at least some of the suspicions: letters from the Workers' Party

National Adult Daily Radio Reach and Stations Share (%)*

National data†	All adults		Age 15–34		Age 35†	
	Reach	Share‡	Reach	Share‡	Reach	Share‡
Any radio	88	97§	90	94	87	99
Any RTE radio	67	58	66	53	68	62
Radio 1	44	39	21	15	60	53
2FM	28	19	45	37	15	8
Any local station	48	39	53	41	44	37
Home locals	43	34	47	36	10	33
Other locals	9	4	10	5	7	4

* Listened yesterday; Monday–Friday average. All normal scheduled programmes on both Radio 1 and 2FM were off air for the duration of a strike at RTE from 21 January to 16 February 1992 inclusive.
† National adult population estimate: 2,580,000 aged 15 +.
‡ Share = Minutes listened 7 a.m. to 7 p.m.
§ Data for Century Radio, which ceased broadcasting on 19 November 1991, are not included. (Century had a 3 per cent national adult share of listening in the twelve-month period.)

Source: MRBI Ltd (for RTE Audience Research, June 1992), *JNLR Weekday Survey, July 1991 to June 1992*, Table 1A.

to the Soviet Union, dated 1986, discovered in the official archives of the Soviet Communist Party (CPSU), apparently named former senior RTE personnel, including a producer of *Today Tonight*, as being involved with a Workers' Party film company which was seeking financial assistance from the Soviet Union.

In the 1987 general election battle, politicians were warned by RTE trade unions – on pain of 'blacking' their parties – not to use the pirates during the campaign; this led to all sorts of subterfuges as some politicians tried to steal a march on others by 'accidentally' giving interviews to the nearest microphone as they were doorstepped by reporters and subsequently pleading innocence, or the parties sent 'unofficial' spokespeople on the pirates' panel discussions, swearing later not to have known about it. Privately, politicians fumed in resentment at the threats of RTE people to 'black' any who broke the embargo.

Finally, the 1987–9 Fianna Fáil government, who in their own words were 'unfettered by the ideological preoccupations of the previous administration',[3] passed legislation in 1988 which put the pirates off the air, and established a commission to license and regulate the introduction of independent radio and television broadcasting. The commission (the Independent Radio and Television Commission) had a difficult birth. The Fianna Fáil government at first intended the regulation of the air waves and granting of licences to be a government activity, but being in a minority situation in the Dáil, it had to bow to political pressure. A former Supreme Court Judge* was appointed to the chair of the commission, along with nine others from diverse areas. Several of them were simultaneously prominent personalities and distinguished in their own fields. They lost no time in getting down to their work.

The controversies and debate which have raged in Ireland ever since were fuelled by the granting by the IRTC in 1989 of a licence to a new national radio network (Century), which collapsed two years later, losing several million pounds in the process. As it became clear that this new national station was in severe trouble, RTE was deprived in 1990 of some of its advertising revenue, having been threatened with far worse by the Minister for

---

* Mr Justice Séamus Henchy.

THE MEDIA IN IRELAND

Communications,* who drew back from some of his most draconian threats under pressure from the government's coalition partners, the Progressive Democrats.† As a sort of backdrop, it was believed that the Fianna Fáil government wanted to rescue Century Radio not only because of the principle of competition for RTE, but also because of an allegedly sympathetic relationship with the promoters of the station. It was also alleged that Fianna Fáil had been furious with RTE because of what the party considered biased reporting of public reaction to health-service cuts during the 1989 election campaign.

Further controversy ensued when it transpired that the only bidder for a third television channel could not raise the money when the time came for it to take up its franchise. The IRTC found itself therefore in the unenviable position of having granted franchises, after lengthy public examination, to two failed entities. The government had to survey its new broadcasting policy in ruins. It was rumoured, though not yet officially conceded, that government had tacitly accepted the non-viability of a third television channel, despite all the rhetoric at the establishment of the IRTC. The dilemma at the core of the controversy is: how can a small country of 3.5 million people support a plethora of native radio stations and three television channels, given the fact that British television and satellite channels are now available across most of the island? Will RTE lose its second television channel, Network 2, and its popular commercial radio channel, 2FM, to the private sector?

By 1992, therefore, a stand-off situation had developed: RTE's advertising revenue was capped‡ since 1990, but it had earned more than it should, therefore more than IR£18 million was frozen as a

---

*Raphael (Ray) Burke (b. 1943) served in several ministries under Charles Haughey; appointed Minister for Justice and Communications in 1989. Nicknamed 'Rambo' because of his strong approach in dealing with RTE, he was accused in the Dáil of threatening drastic action against RTE in the studios on the night of the election results in June 1989. In February 1992, he was returned to the back benches when Albert Reynolds became Taoiseach.

†Among the original proposals made and then dropped were the diversion of some of RTE's licence revenue to the ailing Century Radio, and the conversion of RTE's second radio channel (2FM) into a serious, totally public-service station.

‡The ceiling for advertising revenue was set under the legislation at IR£103.6 million.

result, while a relatively new minister* pondered the absence of alternative national radio or television which had been the principal *raison d'être* of the legislative upheavals of 1988 and 1990. She also had to ponder the proven might of RTE when it came to defending itself, skilfully using its own nationally popular radio and television personalities to make its case. The associated unanswered question is: who will pay, and how much, for Irish public-service broadcasting? During 1992, the minister indicated that new thinking would see the removal of the cap on RTE and a whole new package of broadcasting legislation. But, eight months after she took office, the government faced a general election that resulted in a new coalition, this time between the Labour Party and Fianna Fáil, not the most comfortable of bedfellows on broadcasting matters.

For the twelve-month period from January to December 1992, the Joint National Listener Research/Market Bureau of Ireland survey on radio listenership reported that independent radio was continuing a trend of taking audiences away from RTE. Fifty-one per cent of the 5,695 people surveyed said that they had listened to independent radio at some stage on the previous day, compared with 41 per cent who had listened to RTE's Radio 1, and 27 per cent to RTE's 2FM. The biggest winners in this changing trend were Classics Hits 98FM, a lively Dublin station, and FM 104, also in Dublin, who jumped to 25 per cent.

A new broom took charge of broadcasting in January 1993, in the person of Michael D. Higgins, a man who was always a strong supporter of public-service broadcasting. His portfolio of Arts, Culture and the Gaeltacht included responsibility for the air waves. And he moved quickly to announce his intention to abolish the 'cap' on RTE's advertising revenue, to sighs of relief from the station, who could abandon a large economy package they had been planning. He enraged the newspapers, who were also faced with an increase in value-added taxation (from 10 per cent to 12·5 per cent) in the 1993 budget, and upset the independent local radio stations. It was generally considered that the minister's principal concern in abolishing the cap was a cultural one, to allow RTE to

---

* Máire Geoghegan-Quinn TD. Appointed Minister for Transport, Tourism, and Communications in February 1992. She was appointed Minister for Justice in January 1993.

use more of the output of Irish film-makers, who have been clamouring for home support more and more vociferously. And so it proved: the broadcasting bill began its passage through the Oireachtas on 4 May, abolishing the cap on RTE advertising revenue, and enjoining RTE to spend a fixed sum of money for the next five years on commissioning work from independent producers. The minister had some strong words of warning to say to RTE: 'Let me be quite clear about this: I will not stand for any abuses by RTE of its position in Irish broadcasting ... RTE was not established to set up markets, to target audience segments or to crush other broadcasters.'⁴ He also indicated that he was preparing proposals for the radical restructuring of broadcasting as a whole, in which he would address the question of developing a strong independent radio sector.

THE BEGINNINGS OF BROADCASTING

'And now, we pause for the Angelus' – at noon and 6 p.m. each day, on the two main broadcasting outlets, RTE 1 television, and RTE Radio One, the bells ring for the traditional Catholic prayer about the annunciation to the Virgin Mary by the angel that she had been chosen as the mother of God. It is a custom sometimes criticized as giving an inappropriate position to one church, but on the whole the attitude is benevolent: it is seen more as a charming traditional Irish custom than as a religious affirmation. It is one of the last remnants of the old style of Irish broadcasting which began in 1926.

In that year, Irish radio came into being, as part of a government department – Posts and Telegraphs. Radio Éireann was tightly controlled, its staff were civil servants, and all its activities were open to parliamentary scrutiny. For its first thirty-five years, a gentle cultural, drama, literary, religious, and sporting service wafted across the Irish air waves from musty corridors and creaking turntables in Dublin's Henry Street, often enlivened by the genuine and sparkling talent of Irish musicians, talkers and writers. News was neutral and brief. The occasional political foray was confined to formal statements of authority figures, like a rare ministerial address from Éamon de Valera.

The main effect of its civil-service status was to insulate the station from any political commentary, controversy, or analysis whatsoever: 'It was a political eunuch.'[5] When the old machinery had been replaced by the 1960 Broadcasting Act, setting up a much more autonomous Radio Telefís Éireann and taking it outside the civil service, the first chairman of the new governing body fondly described the former radio service as: 'One of the worst but best-meaning radio services in the world.'[*]

The 1960 Broadcasting Act charged the new Broadcasting Authority with providing radio and television services, gave it the right to collect licence fees and sell advertising, and to operate all the while under the governing principle of social responsibility, which it is the duty of the State to ensure. It has been the interpretation of that 'social responsibility' by the State and by the broadcasters which has given rise to difficulties and controversies over the years; these tensions are not much different from those arising in Britain and other democratic countries, and follow from the natural suspicion by politicians and other groups of the power of those using the air waves to influence the mass of the people. Thus, both sides watch each other carefully: occasional lapses of objectivity or impartiality on the part of broadcasters have led to recriminations, while occasional apparently overbearing actions on the part of politicians are resented.[†]

All in all, the history of RTE has been one of slow but steady maturing into sophisticated understanding and interpretation of its rights and duties, while powerful pressure groups like the Church, Irish-language enthusiasts, and politicians have made progress towards equipping themselves with the skills they need to communicate effectively, using broadcasting and other communications media. Despite this, wariness and suspicion still exist on both sides, and no doubt always will.

---

[*]Éamonn Andrews, reported in the *Irish Times*, 1 November 1967. Andrews (1922–87) had become one of Ireland's first broadcasting exports to Britain, and was internationally known for his radio and television work in sports and light entertainment.

[†]In the period immediately before the vote on the Maastricht Treaty on European Union, June 1992, the Taoiseach Albert Reynolds exercised his legal right to make a ministerial broadcast in favour of the treaty. The tradition of these broadcasts was, until then, to use them for announcements of a non-party-political kind and not in the context of a voting situation. RTE had no choice but to comply, but gave extra time to opponents of the treaty on its current-affairs programmes that evening.

IRELAND IN PRINT

Ireland enjoys, and always has enjoyed, a free press, and Irish national newspapers sell more than 350,000 copies every day. Newspapers complain about severe libel and defamation laws and what they see as unfair competition from the national broadcasting network, but they operate nevertheless in a relatively healthy environment, without a press council, or any real regulating body. Reflecting the ethos and character of the country, Irish newspapers are not guilty of the worst sexual and sleazy excesses of the British tabloids. There is indeed an interesting unwritten tradition that Irish journalists do not hound politicians about their private lives or sexual transgressions. As the scandal surrounding British minister David Mellor's private life broke in the British press in summer 1992, this principle was restated by one of its strongest proponents, the editor of the Irish *Sunday Tribune* newspaper, in July 1992: 'It [revelations about private lives of politicians] would represent a denial of a fundamental liberty to the individuals concerned that would be intolerable . . . the effect of it would be to preclude all but the least sensitive from public life . . . the media has no function in relation to private lives of public figures . . .' However, the Irish buy more than 100,000 British newspapers every day, the vast majority of them of the 'popular' variety, so perhaps they feel deprived of the more purple strand of journalism.

Four Irish-owned national daily newspapers are read by Irish people (see table of circulation data on page 354). One of them, the *Cork Examiner*, is almost entirely confined to the southern province of Munster but would always be found, for example, in the marked bundle of papers which a government minister might be handed for perusal by the private secretary. As well as the Irish papers, several daily British newspapers circulate widely in Ireland. On Sunday, five Irish national newspapers are sold, and a plethora of British (by far the biggest of these is the *News of the World*, which sold 175,000 copies each Sunday in December 1991).

The history of the Irish newspaper industry mirrors the political history of the country. The oldest newspaper, the *Irish Times*, has its roots in Protestantism and Unionism in the nineteenth century, but long ago became a politically independent, liberal, middle-class 'quality' newspaper 'with a reputation in Europe as one of the great newspapers'.⁶ It was formerly owned and run by Protestant business and professional men, but in 1974 was transformed into a trust, under the unlikely but astute chairmanship of an elderly retired military man, Major Tom McDowell.* As Ireland rapidly emerges in the 1990s from its former conservatism, the *Irish Times* readership steadily increases; it is considered the most influential newspaper in the country because of the pattern of its readership, highest among the higher social groupings. Its circulation approaches two-thirds of the biggest daily seller, the *Irish Independent*. By the 1990s, it had evolved into a well-produced, thoughtful newspaper with a mix of high-quality business pages, liberal and independent-minded columnists, and in-depth reporting and analysis of current affairs, Irish and foreign. It has attracted some of the finest journalists working in Ireland: one of them, Fintan O'Toole, won the country's major award for outstanding work in Irish journalism in 1992 for his work in covering, and analysing in great depth, the Tribunal of Inquiry into the Beef Industry.

The Independent group of newspapers came into being in 1905, founded by businessman William Martin Murphy (who gained an unenviable reputation as the employers' leader in Ireland's first trade-union battle in 1913). Its first daily morning paper, the *Irish Independent*, was the first halfpenny popular newspaper in the country. A staunchly Catholic, socially conservative organization, the Independent group supported the political moderates in the treaty debates – that turbulent period which ended in the 1922 civil war – and thereafter was firmly identified as being in the camp of Fine Gael. The *Irish Independent*, its flagship, was always known for its heavy emphasis on Catholic church news and views, old-fashioned rural values, and the prevailing ethos of the first half-century of politically independent Ireland. It, too, changed as the country changed; by the mid-1970s it had taken the direction of market-orientation, political neutrality, and became 'the most brash, carried the biggest headlines, and gave the most "popular" treatment of all the dailies'.⁷ A sign of the changing times (and of the new thrusting ownership under the chairmanship of Dr A. J. F. O'Reilly of Heinz fame) was its Sunday tabloid, the *Sunday World*

---

* McDowell (b. 1922) may, under the trust, appoint five of the twelve governors, and may remain chief executive until he decides otherwise.

(founded in 1973), complete with page three titillation, which soon outsold all rivals. The *Irish Independent* and the *Sunday Independent* in the early 1990s are a mixture of slightly sensationalized – but efficient and up-to-date – news reporting, some solid financial reporting, a lot of social and business gossip, populist features, heavy sports coverage, juxtaposed with some more thoughtful feature and analysis work. It illustrates the priorities of the newspaper group that the Saturday page of literary reviews was frequently dropped in favour of the latest feature on some topical eye-catcher like a spate of sex crimes, a new 'kiss and tell' book, or film-star scandals, until the establishment of a separate 'Weekender' section restored it to permanence.

On 25 April 1993, readers of the *Sunday Independent* were amazed to find in their newspaper a prominent editorial in the form of an apology to its readers headed 'error of judgement'. It came after two weeks of uproar in all the other media outlets, newspaper and broadcasting, on the subject of a purported interview with the Catholic bishop* who had fled Ireland a year previously after revelations that he had fathered a child in the early 1970s. The bishop had been traced to Mexico, and a writer – Gordon Thomas – had claimed to have interviewed him, at the behest of the *Sunday Independent*. The bishop, it turned out, had been pursued but not interviewed, a private telephone call was intruded upon, and angry denials followed. The whole episode offended a great many people, and outraged journalists who felt that a slur had been cast on their profession. It was generally felt that the abject apology had been extracted from the newspaper by its own journalists, whose views were discernible in sentences like this: 'Were we to undermine the ethics by which good journalism is governed, we would be contributing to the decline in public standards which causes each citizen of this country such concern.'

The Independent group at the end of 1992 was recording a profit of over IR£16 million – a huge increase on the previous year – and had acquired a 2 per cent interest in the late Robert Maxwell's Mirror Group. It had been prevented by government from taking over the *Sunday Tribune* newspaper, and had given that troubled broadsheet a IR£2·4 million loan.

---

*Bishop Éamonn Casey. See Chapter 16.

Back in the early days of the Irish State, it was quite understandable that Éamon de Valera should feel the need of a newspaper to promulgate his and his party's views in the decade of the 1920s when Fianna Fáil was growing into power. Neither of the existing two national dailies was sympathetic to him or interested in his kind of radical politics: quite the opposite. Since 1922, de Valera had wanted a 'national' (in every sense) newspaper, and he eventually raised a considerable part of the money for it in the United States. By astute managing of the American money, including manipulation of American holders of earlier 'Republican bonds' and a speedy combination of their shares with his own, he and his family and their descendants gained total control of the new newspaper, the *Irish Press*. How he did this remains controversial to this day. Be that as it may, on 5 December 1931, the mother of Patrick Pearse,* no less, pressed the button that started de Valera's presses rolling.

And so the powerful Fianna Fáil organ came into being; strictly controlled by the de Valeras and loyally bought by every member and sympathizer of the party, it attained power and prestige and added an evening and a Sunday paper to its stable. It prospered for five decades, and then began a long downturn. Whether the Fianna Fáil Party's faltering fortunes, the wisdom or otherwise of some management decisions, or the fierce modern competitive world of the print media were to blame, by 1992 it looked as if the power of the de Valera dynasty in the Irish press was coming to an end.

In 1982, Dr Éamon de Valera† became managing director of the *Irish Press*, succeeding his father Vivion and his grandfather, Éamon, the founder. Whether it was wise, in the age of fierce newspaper competitiveness and professionalism, for an industrial chemist with no professional newspaper background to undertake the role, can certainly be questioned. His arrival followed several years of his father's illness, during which time the *Irish Press*

*Irish scholar and fervent and ascetic dreamer, author of the proclamation of the Irish Republic, who led the 1916 Rising against the British, occupied the General Post Office in O'Connell Street, and was executed by the British in May 1916, at Kilmainham Gaol in Dublin.

†Éamon de Valera (b. 1950). Graduated in chemistry from UCD in 1972, later taking a PhD. Worked as a researcher then an industrial engineer, and served as a part-time director of the *Irish Press* from 1978.

appeared to fail to meet the challenges of modern newspaper management. A series of disputes with the print unions and the NUJ exacerbated the problems of the Press group.

Despite a more liberal and politically independent editorial policy, circulation figures plummeted severely – by 1992 it was now well behind the *Irish Times* – and the Press group were in trouble. A decision to change to a tabloid format for its daily *Irish Press* failed to slow the downward slide. Americans – in the shape of US publisher Ralph Ingersoll – were once more on the scene, but this time their money was in search of power, and they held 50 per cent of the company in summer 1992. A public feud between Ingersoll and de Valera about control did little to stabilize the paper's fortunes, shared power had not worked, and the losses mounted. The High Court became the stage on which the fate of the Irish Press group was fought over, as bitter battles between the different factions of the deadlocked board of directors erupted, and all the time the sales of all three of the Press newspapers declined. Irish people contemplated yet another sign of a changing country – the possible end of the de Valera connection and control of the *Irish Press*.

In every county in Ireland, a range of provincial newspapers inform their readers about local happenings and comment on the national issues from their local perspective. Great and venerable names like the *Clare Champion*, the *Connaught Tribune*, the *Donegal Democrat*, the *Kerryman*, and the *Munster Express* carry enormous influence among their loyal readers. Most of them appear once a week, and are more anxiously scanned and assiduously courted by politicians than the national dailies, because the Irish parliamentarian is first and foremost a local representative.

The *Irish Farmers' Journal*, a weekly newspaper selling over 70,000 copies, is a lively independent paper.

THE MEDIA BATTLE

Given the circulation battles that rage between the Irish newspapers, as well as the competition from British newspapers, and the gradual downturn in newspaper sales generally, it is small wonder that they look fearfully at the pull of the broadcast media on their advertising revenue. It is this which lies at the root of the hostility of the Irish newspapers towards the national broadcasting station, RTE. The Independent group is particularly hard-hitting, criticizing what they see as the monopoly position of the station, and the 'dual funding' arrangement, by which RTE gets IR£49 million in licence-fee income and about the same in advertising revenue.* In a typically impassioned editorial, the paper declared: 'It is not an exaggeration to say that freedom of the press is undermined when conditions are created by the State which give all the advantages to one side [RTE] and makes life difficult to the point of extinction for the other side.'[8] The nub of their case is that they would like RTE to be given the licence fee only, while their second RTE radio channel, at present operating as a revenue-earning popular music outlet, should be given to the independent commercial sector. They also pointed out that RTE got as much as half of all advertising revenue. They also note that the biggest-selling magazine in Ireland – at around 150,000 copies every week – is the *RTE Guide*, carrying features about RTE's national 'stars' as well as the timetables for all TV and radio stations and substantial advertising.

The riposte of RTE is that dual funding is the norm in most European countries, and while the BBC exists on licence fee only, it operates on a huge scale and with a very much higher licence fee (£87 sterling). Despite an independent report in 1985 which recommended index-linking of the RTE licence fee, by 1992 it remained the same (IR£62) as in 1986. RTE insists that it cannot support activities like two orchestras, Irish-language radio, classical music programmes, and a high percentage of current affairs and political reporting without advertising revenue as well as the licence fee. The broadcasters consider that the newspapers have dual funding too: their purchase price (which annualized works out at much more than the licence fee) and their advertising revenue. Another similarity with the newspaper industry claimed by the broadcasters is the international competition; far from being a monopoly, they say, Irish listeners and viewers have access not only to British stations but up to twenty others. Where television is concerned, RTE's share of peak-time viewers falls to 36 per cent since satellite stations as well as all British channels are available; in the 70 per cent of Ireland which in 1991 received all British channels and not satellites,

* Figures for 1991.

RTE's share was 50 per cent. Radio too is a different animal today: the independent legal local stations licensed since 1989 have claimed 31 per cent of all listeners, and this is growing. Advertising industry figures for 1991 show that RTE could only achieve 36 per cent of all advertising spending. As a new director-general of RTE* took office in July 1992, his colleagues looked to him to defend them against further attacks from government.

The station runs three national radio networks: Radio 1, which is the news/current affairs/discussion/chat-show outlet; 2FM, which is mostly popular music, but features a lighter chat-show format for part of the time; and Raidió na Gaeltachta, which is all Irish-language broadcasting, but shares the frequency with classical music. The National Symphony Orchestra and the RTE Concert Orchestra, as well as choral ensembles, are supported by the station. Regionalization is growing, as competition from the newly licensed local stations eats into the advertising revenue, and criticism of a certain Dublin bias begins to surface in the newspapers around the country. The station is regulated by government legislation, and operates under a nine-person authority appointed for five-year terms of office.

The battle about the air waves is ongoing; politicians hover at the edges. It is a source of great temptation for them to wield their power against the broadcasters, to 'put manners on them' in revenge for uncomfortable questioning, too incisive investigations, or perceived political bias. Ireland is no different in this from many western democracies: the history of political broadcasting, particularly on television, in the view of political scientist Basil Chubb shows 'that governments and politicians generally are inclined to view it with suspicion'.[9] Not long after RTE television was established in 1961, and after the station at last began to move into the world of political analysis and commentary, a Fianna Fáil Taoiseach, the redoubtable Seán Lemass, declared: 'Radio Telefís Éireann was set up by legislation as an instrument of public policy,

---

* Joe Barry joined RTE in 1956. Always in the operational/technical area of the station, his appointment followed three years as director of production facilities. There was comment on his appointment that (a) no non-RTE people were on the interviewing panel, and (b) programme-makers were once more passed over. The *Irish Times* mentioned the 'old feud' between programme-makers and technocrats on 22 July 1992.

and as such is responsible to the Government ... the Government reject the view that Radio Telefís Éireann should be, either generally or in regard to its current affairs and news programmes, completely independent of Government supervision.'[10] It is the extent to which RTE is or is not treated as 'an instrument of public policy' which is at the heart of the continuing debate, and which has caused tensions down the years. In the 1990s, however, lively radio and television discussions, controversy, confrontations between ministers and interviewers are all part of Ireland's daily life. It is RTE's delicate task to walk the path between, on the one hand, independence and responsibility to its public, and, on the other, the big stick in the background which is in the hand of government. The station has become increasingly adept at this job, as both it and the political establishment become more sophisticated in their dealings with one another.*

One area which remains most definitely unresolved is the ban on members of illegal paramilitary organizations, north and south of the border with Northern Ireland, and the political party Sinn Féin, from appearing on any broadcast medium in the Republic of Ireland. First issued in 1971, and further clarified in 1976, the order banning these groups is made under Section 31 of the 1960 Broadcasting Act. It is opposed by the National Union of Journalists, and disliked by senior broadcasting journalists and managers. The point at issue is that Sinn Féin is a legally recognized political party, north and south of Ireland's border, so the ban, as interpreted by RTE, on its members can have strange effects; a local councillor of the party, whose work may be totally concerned with housing, for example, cannot be interviewed on that subject or any subject. There was the added anomaly that in Northern Ireland, Sinn Féin was not banned from the air waves, giving rise to a situation where Southern Irish viewers of the two Northern Ireland channels, UTV and BBC, available over most of Ireland, could see and hear interviews with the Sinn Féin MP Gerry Adams (who lost his seat in 1992), but were denied this access on their own national channels.

---

*Taoiseach Albert Reynolds appointed no less than three people to deal with the media when he took office in February 1992: Seán Duignan, an experienced political broadcaster straight from RTE; Bart Cronin, a civil servant with considerable experience in media matters; and Tom Savage, a director of Carr Communications Ltd, the leading media consultancy firm in Ireland.

The British government introduced a pale imitation of the Irish ban, but it was never as total or as effective.

The argument of the Irish broadcasters against this ban, quite apart from its implied distrust of their work, is that such represssion glamorizes the party, and gives it a propaganda weapon. They feel that the decision should be an editorial one. A legal challenge was mounted against the ban, but the Irish Supreme Court decided that not only was it in keeping with the Constitution, but the legislators had a duty to enforce it. Mr Justice Henchy (later to become first chairman of the Independent Radio and Television Commission) in delivering that judgement in 1982, said that Sinn Féin was 'an integral and dependent part of the apparatus of the Provisional IRA ... therefore the Minister was fully justified in his opinion that a broadcast by Sinn Féin would "be likely to promote, or incite to, crime, or would tend to undermine the authority of the State"'.[11] The Chief Justice of the time was no less definite: 'In my view, it is abundantly clear that the Minister was not only justified in forming the opinion that he did, but that he could not have formed any other.'[12] A further appeal to Europe was similarly rejected.

Dr Conor Cruise O'Brien, who restated and clarified the ban in 1976 as minister in charge of broadcasting, is dismissive of the claims of broadcasters that they would be able to deal effectively with Sinn Féin members: 'The idea of the clever broadcaster who exposes the stupid Sinn Féiner on the box is a myth inculcated by the higher levels of broadcasting in order to keep the government at arm's length ... at lower levels, working broadcasters don't even pretend to believe it.'[13] He firmly believes that the ban has contributed significantly to the very low level of support (less than 2 per cent) for Sinn Féin in elections in the Republic of Ireland, and cites the much higher support in Northern Ireland as partly due to the 'legitimacy' conferred on them by access to the broadcast media. Dr Cruise O'Brien tells the story of an interview with a prominent republican, Martin McGuinness,* by the BBC shortly

*Prominently associated with Sinn Féin in the Derry area of Northern Ireland for the last decade and a half. Has held top positions in the party and in the Provisional IRA, is highly visible at functions like funerals, and has been imprisoned several times; he unsuccessfully contested the Westminster parliamentary seat of John Hume, leader of the SDLP.

after the killing in Gibraltar in 1988 by the British Army of three IRA terrorists: 'The interviewer expected him to be indignant about the shootings; instead, he was quite calm, and said: "We've always said this was war; in this case, the British showed that in their view too, it's war ..." – and there was a long pause ...' Former Taoiseach Dr Garret FitzGerald reminds readers of his auto-biography that: 'The case for the ban has convinced successive Irish governments under four Taoisig during two decades to maintain the order, despite its unpopularity with liberal opinion and media, and notwithstanding the many anomalies to which it has given rise.'[14] In spring 1992, the British and Irish governments and the four 'constitutional' parties in Northern Ireland started to talk to each other in earnest. At the same time it became known that Sinn Féin was talking to churchmen, and – most comforting of all – there was a pause in attacks by the IRA on the security forces and Unionists and Protestants. In such optimistic conditions, refer-ences to inclusion of Sinn Féin in political discussions and the possibility of a change in the operation of Section 31 began to be heard. As hopes rose and the weeks and months went by, a new picture began to emerge. But it did not last long, and by the late autumn of 1992, ferocious violence had broken out yet again.

In a changing scenario, the ban may well disappear quietly. RTE's decision to interpret Section 31 as forbidding any appearance at all by a Sinn Féin member, even to discuss a local issue like a factory closure, was once more questioned in 1992. A trade-union activist who was also a Sinn Féin Councillor went to the High Court to assert his right to appear on RTE concerning an industrial dispute. Mr Justice O'Hanlon on 31 July found that RTE's blanket prohibition on Sinn Féin was in contravention of Article 40 of the Constitution. Support for this decision came from Dr Conor Cruise O'Brien, who suspected RTE of somewhat machiavellian motives: 'It seems possible that the RTE objective was to discredit the Act itself by piling on the restrictions ... if so, a stop should now have been put to that little game by the High Court decision.'[15] By December 1992, RTE had not relented, and had appealed against the decision. The unanimous ruling of the Supreme Court, given on 30 March 1993, was highly significant for Irish broadcasting; the judges found that RTE had gone too far in their interpretation of Section 31, and that they could not keep members of Sinn Féin off the air except if they were to speak about matters like advocating violence or subversion of the State. 'RTE', said the Chief Justice, 'would be entitled, if it apprehended a Sinn Féin member was likely to spontaneously include a prohibited matter in a broadcast, to insist that he not broadcast live.'[16] As the management of RTE digested this decision, it was clear that the complexities of trying to administer it would need further ministerial orders to interpret this new judgement for the guidance of broadcasters. In June 1993, the Opsahl Commission in its report on Northern Ireland (see Chapter 8) recommended the Irish government to look again at Section 31, on the grounds that a policy of exclusion of Sinn Féin from public debate only played into the hands of those who prefer violence. The new minister, a long-time opponent of any kind of censorship, was expected to take a new look at the issue.

Of the influences which have been central in shaping modern Ireland, radio and television are among the most important. And within the broadcast media, one person has dominated sound and vision over twenty years: Gabriel (Gay) Byrne.* Acknowledged to be the foremost broadcaster in Ireland, a position he held – unchallenged – up to and including 1993, Gay Byrne hosted the two most popular talk shows, on radio and television, for decades. A consummate master of the broadcasting medium, similar to but more serious than the legendary Johnny Carson of the United States, he has produced as well as presented the major television programme of each week, *The Late Late Show*, since 1962 – almost since the beginning of Irish television. The radio show, broadcast every morning from Monday to Friday, was also the most popular (only the news programme early in the morning was more widely heard). Remembering that the total Irish population is only 3·5 million people, Gay Byrne's achievement in TAM ratings of 1·342 million viewers for a pre-Christmas show (and figures not much lower than that every Friday night of the year) and consistent morning-radio audiences of 718,000† are remarkable.

---

*Gay Byrne, born 1934 of Dublin working-class parents. Educated by the Christian Brothers in one of their most famous old Dublin schools, Synge Street. Held a few minor jobs before joining RTE in 1958, just before television and the modern broadcasting station took shape.

† These figures are supplied by TAM and the Market Research Bureau of Ireland (MRBI) for 1991.

The formula for his radio work has included many long interviews with people who have brought problems and subjects to public attention for the first time: battered wives, homosexuality, divorce, sexual problems of all kinds, and a wide range of social issues and political debates. Gay Byrne's broadcasting skills, his (mostly) non-judgemental attitudes, and above all his presentation of himself as the ordinary, informed, understanding man gave him a place in Irish society unrivalled by any other: his is undoubtedly the best-known voice and face in the country. It has consistently baffled commentators and critics that listeners (mostly women) through the years have felt able to tell him – and the country – their most intimate fears, worries, and experiences. The television programme too has often reached great heights of drama, pathos, and emotion and caused national debates on subjects hitherto taboo. They have ranged from the deadly serious to the sometimes hilariously trivial. During the 1970s and 1980s, *The Late Late Show* set the headlines for most people's conversations in pubs, workplaces, and shops during the following few days.

A 1966 episode has become part of Irish media folklore, referred to as 'The Bishop and the Nightie' – it seems unbelievable in the Ireland of today that a senior Irish bishop should vehemently denounce the show because a woman confessed in a husband/wife quiz format that she might have worn no nightie on her wedding-night. Huge public controversy ensued. A measure of the times was that RTE and Gay Byrne apologized publicly for the offence they had given. The whole sorry saga was pleasantly resolved when good humour returned eventually, and there was even a private apology made to Gay Byrne by the bishop. It did, however, illustrate both the power of television and the obsessions of Church and people of the time.

In 1985, a fifteen-year-old girl died while giving birth alone and out of doors at a Marian grotto – a shrine to the Blessed Virgin, in rural Ireland. The country was shocked, and in the reaction many conservative elements condemned the huge media debate as exaggerating the problem. A flood of letters poured in to Gay Byrne from women who had had babies outside marriage, often in tragic circumstances; an entire radio programme was devoted to the letters being read out, in calm tones, by two actresses. Assessing the effect that this kind of programme, and many others, had on Irish society, Gay Byrne said in his 1989 autobiography: 'I believe that if the Gay Byrne Show has had influence, this is how it has been done: by doing programmes like this, allowing reality to show through the veils of cant and hypocrisy, because by hearing everyday layers of opinions different to their own, people realize that there are other legitimate points of view, other tolerances, other ways of approach.'

Politicians have been enraged and enthralled by Gay Byrne down the years – enraged at the particular view he often expressed about them and their work, including his continual insistence during the mid-1980s that the country was 'banjaxed' (an Irish expression meaning totally destroyed). A high degree of cynicism about politics and politicians in Ireland has often been attributed to his influence. It is easier to blame someone else, of course, than set about examining whether or not there is any foundation for the cynicism.

In the early 1990s, a mellow Gay Byrne approaches his sixtieth year, sits on the RTE Authority (appointed by Fianna Fáil – his wife is an adherent of the party), and is very proud indeed of an honorary degree from Trinity College. He is said to have refused an offer of the top administrative job at RTE – the director-generalship – in the 1980s, preferring to stick to what he knew he was good at. When the independent commercial radio station, Century, was being set up, it is rumoured that Gay Byrne was offered IR£1 million to join it. He refused, but subsequently asked for, and got, a huge rise in pay from RTE: in summer 1992, the revelation that his earnings could be as much as IR£250,000 a year from RTE caused some ripples among other broadcasting stars.

The man behind the public face appears to be exactly the same as the broadcasting professional: caring, open-minded, not an intellectual heavyweight, enjoying the simpler pleasures of life, without any show of ostentation, interested in a lot of things but expert only in his craft, and still acting as a conduit for the country's opinions. If, after thirty years of continual exposure, his TAM ratings are slipping, particularly among the under-thirty-fives, and his opinions begin to seem old-fashioned and just a little right-wing, it is not surprising. His retirement will mark yet another milestone in the changing patterns of Irish life. Gay Byrne is not used to public disapproval, but had to face a great deal of it in April 1993 when he handled an interview on television with Annie

Murphy* with an apparent lack of impartiality, and with what many angry women and men regarded as a judgemental harshness. Acres of newsprint and hours of radio were devoted to dissection of the interview and criticism of Gay Byrne, who coincidentally was away from the air waves on holiday for the subsequent two weeks, and never mounted a defence. It was a moment in Irish broadcasting which symbolized the new society in which people like Gay Byrne find themselves not always at ease.

There are now many other Irish radio programmes, and some television, which followed the Byrne lead and developed it; there are personalities and programmes which analyse and discuss issues every day which would have been utterly unthinkable thirty years ago; but it is hard to imagine any other broadcaster exercising the kind of influence that Gay Byrne did. He straddled and dominated the coming of age of the Irish broadcast media. His radio work was described by the media correspondent of the *Irish Times*, a writer not normally enamoured of what he saw as Dublin domination of RTE, as 'a mirror which a large part of Irish society held up to itself each morning'.[17] One of the most influential of newer programmes in that genre today is hosted by a woman, Marian Finucane. It is called *Liveline* and is the successor of earlier programmes started in the 1970s when women protested at the lack of attention to areas which concerned them; today, that phone-in programme, going out for an hour from 1.45 p.m. daily, is a barometer of current thinking in a range of areas. An example of its ground-breaking approach was its treatment of abortion in the middle 1980s, when the presenter accompanied one of the thousands of Irish women who go every year to clinics in England. The country was reminded of simple reality in a non-judgemental way, treating an almost taboo subject with great skill. Ms Finucane is gentle, humorous, and compassionate; she was another RTE person who resisted the lure of commercial radio and opted to stay with RTE. In 1993, she was presented with the Publicity Club of Ireland's communications award.

---

*Annie Murphy is the American mother of Bishop Éamonn Casey's child, fathered in the early 1970s. She was paying a much publicized visit to Ireland to promote her book on her romance with the bishop. This subject and its impact are dealt with in Chapter 16, 'Religion in Ireland'.

The island of Ireland, accidental recipient of much broadcasting output and open to all English-language media, is truly caught up in the communications revolution of the last decade of the twentieth century. Its home-grown media have changed as the country has changed; the argument about what causes social change and how much the media contribute to it is still inconclusive but will go on engrossing politicians, sociologists, and the media themselves for a long time to come. The Irish government of 1993, composed of two parties with radically different views on public and commercial broadcasting, has some nettles to grasp if the confusion and uncertainty surrounding broadcasting and its future is to be ended. A last word to the gadfly: 'The media in Ireland is being led through a treacherous bog, and every so often its guide – the Minister for Communications – pitches into a dark squelchy hole and disappears. Soon, another Minister emerges from the mire and sets off in a totally different direction.'[18] It has indeed been a long and inconclusive war.

In the annual readership survey of Irish newspapers, published on 15 August 1992 by the Joint National Readership Research (JNRR),* only two national daily newspapers increased their readership over the year: the *Irish Times* and the *Star*. Eighty-seven per cent of Irish adults read Irish national newspapers on a regular basis, with 88 per cent of those aged fifteen to thirty-four doing likewise.

The *Irish Times* has a readership of 290,000, of which 51 per cent are women, and 57 per cent Dubliners. Seventy-nine per cent of the readers are from social group ABC1 (the most affluent group). The *Star*'s readership is the reverse: 80 per cent of their 292,000 readers come from social group C2DE group, which is almost the same as the *Sunday World*.

The continuing wide appeal of the daily *Irish Independent* is demonstrated by its 578,000 readership, which is more evenly spread across the social groups: 45 per cent ABD1, 37 per cent C2DE. It

*Figures based on twelve months' data collected between June 1991 and June 1992, carried out for the National Newspapers of Ireland by Lansdowne Market Research, the Institute of Advertising Practitioners, and the Association of Advertisers in Ireland. Readership figures are a multiple of circulation figures, based on research into how many people see each copy of the newspaper, as opposed to how many actually buy it.

National Newspapers in the Republic of Ireland: Circulation Figures, January–June 1992*		
Title	Year of foundation	Circulation figure
Irish Independent	1905	150,121
Irish Press	1931	52,167
Irish Times	1859	94,021
Cork Examiner and Evening Echo	1841	55,615
Evening Herald	1891	100,209
Evening Press	1954	74,391
Sunday Business Post	1989	30,119
Sunday Independent	1966	247,360
Sunday Press	1949	185,209
Sunday World	1973	229,919
Sunday Tribune	1983	90,841
Star† (daily)	1989	82,119

* Figures supplied by National Newspapers of Ireland, 10 August 1992.
† English-owned, but an Irish edition printed and published in Dublin by Independent Newspapers.

also reaches rural Ireland much more than the others, with 47 per cent of its readers in that group.

Of the Sunday newspapers, both the *Sunday Independent* and *Sunday World* score over 900,000 in readership. The *Sunday Press* follows with 732,000, the *Sunday Tribune* and *Sunday Business Post* between them managing less than 500,000, and both of them reaching more ABC1s and urban readers.

Middle-class and mostly middle-aged people from Dublin and its surrounding areas continue to dominate the media, which since more than one-third of the population lives there, is hardly surprising. However, they are regarded with a highly critical eye by some commentators. The *Sunday Business Post* was expressing the views of many when one of its senior contributors described the 1990s Irish media in general, and broadcasting in particular, as 'controlled by people who are relatively affluent, forty-something and liberal, who would like to promote secular values, who distrust successful business people, who feel they have a role to play in weakening traditional value systems'.[19] The writer ascribed a lot of these attitudes to the fact that the controllers were graduates of the late 1960s and early 1970s, a time when rejection of the old Ireland was taking hold; and the view was put somewhat differently but not less strongly by a prominent and respected Catholic priest who directs a Church communications centre. Noting that the media in general in Ireland today do not reflect the high level of religious belief and practice in the country, Fr Tom Stack gave some reasons for this: the former inordinate power wielded by the Church, largely buttressed by the State, its obscurantist and oppressive image, and its perceived autocratic attitudes, secretiveness and culture of infallibility. He went on: 'This is bitter folklore for present-day journalists. It makes for an understandable if mildly vengeful subconscious.'[20] In looking at the social and economic history of Ireland over the last fifty years, the overreaction of many writers and opinion formers to the dark days of the 1940s and 1950s is understandable. However, with a new generation taking more and more power, better educated in every way, and with the kind of training in communications which its bosses never knew, a new balance is gradually coming about.

Media policy in Ireland in recent years has been a stop–go affair. There is not much evidence that a cool clear long look has been taken at the big picture, which must include the invasion of Ireland by British and American print and broadcasting media. Since no action can reasonably be taken to control this phenomenon, it behoves government to study how the Irish media can be protected and encouraged to provide the kind of service for Irish people which social, cultural, and democratic considerations require.

NOTES

1. Liam Collins, *Sunday Independent*, 24 November 1991.
2. Éamonn Dunphy, *Sunday Independent*, 30 August 1992.

3. Broadcasting Bill, 1990: Seanad Éireann Official Report, speech by Ray Burke, Minister for Communications.
4. *Dáil Report*, 4 May 1993.
5. Basil Chubb, *The Government and Politics of Ireland*, 2nd edn, Longman, 1982.
6. ibid.
7. ibid.
8. *Irish Independent*, 26 November 1991.
9. Chubb, op. cit.
10. *Dáil Debates*, 12 October 1966.
11. *Irish Law Reports*, 1982.
12. ibid.; Chief Justice Thomas O'Higgins.
13. In conversation with the author, August 1991.
14. Garret FitzGerald, *All in a Life*, Gill & Macmillan, 1991.
15. *Sunday Independent*, 2 August 1992.
16. Judgement of the Supreme Court, 30 March 1993, reported in the *Irish Times*, 31 March 1993.
17. John Waters, *Jiving at the Crossroads*, Blackstaff Press, 1991.
18. Liam Collins, *Sunday Independent*, 6 September 1992.
19. Damien Kiberd, *Sunday Business Post*, 14 June 1992.
20. *Irish Times*, 4 August 1992.

CHAPTER 15

Trade Unions and Pressure Groups

The history of Irish trade unionism in modern times, like many things Irish, has featured a big effort at shaking off British links: Irish trade-union leaders today are unanimous in their conviction that progress towards modern labour relations machinery for Ireland was held up for decades because of the British connection. It was natural, of course, before Irish independence in the 1920s, that as trade unions developed in Britain and Ireland, they should have headquarters and management in the bigger island; and since Ireland had such a tiny industrial workforce in those years, the strength of the British unions was attractive to the comparatively weak and poorly organized Irish. Today, looking back on it, trade unionists in Ireland deplore this influence because, as they see it, Irish social structures were and are so different from the British that the accompanying management/labour relations should have been different too. In short, rigid class structures and insurmountable social barriers between worker and manager formed part of the British style and tradition of confrontation between the two, while Ireland – without that historic class structure – could and should have developed more along continental European lines. Today, that British influence is very much diminished, and only a small number of trade unions in Ireland have their headquarters in Britain, while many cooperate on an all-Ireland basis, north and south.

Irish labour-relations machinery and attitudes are rapidly making up for lost time, eyes are turned towards Europe, and a sense of economic nationalism in the face of the uncertainties of the 1990s is developing, as well as a new realism about inevitable changes in work practices and demands by both labour and management. However, the process of change is not easy against a background of a traditional adversarial culture in industrial relations, and at a time when Irish industry questions the cost of monopoly services like energy and communications whose wage costs and work practices need change. The chief executive of the Labour Relations Commission,* established in 1990 as a new element in peace-making and early warning in Irish industrial relations, is under no illusions:

To attempt to suggest a 'we're all in it together' attitude and thereby elicit a mutual sacrifice within the nation and then translate that to the area of industrial relations is ambitious indeed. And yet we know, at least at leadership level, among the social partners and Government, that this is necessary if not indeed a necessity to ensure our social and economic viability as a nation.[1]

Again and again, the concern is expressed by leaders of both trade unions and employers that, while great progress has been made quite quickly at national leadership level towards understanding the urgent need for modern attitudes, there is still a gulf of understanding on the factory floor.

A characteristic of Irish industrial relations is the strong element of voluntarism surrounding the machinery: Irish governments have been reluctant to use the stick and prefer the carrot in this field. This approach is mostly understood and welcomed by workers and management, although the occasional flaring up of sudden disputes in essential services like an electricity workers' dispute in 1991 leads to calls for anti-strike legislation.

Three principal pieces of state apparatus exist to deal with labour relations: the Labour Relations Commission, the Labour Court, and the Employment Appeals Tribunal. The commission, the newest arrival, is seen as the necessary third arm to work with unions and management before strikes begin, to help establish codes of practice for disputes, and to improve the climate for, and understanding of, modern industrial relations procedures. The Labour Court, established in 1946, has no binding authority except the moral one of examining grievances and handing down decisions, which may or may not be accepted: 'In line with the voluntarism which characterizes the Irish industrial system, the parties are free to accept or reject the Court's recommendations.'[2] Employers have complained incessantly that their willingness to accept Labour

*Kieran Mulvey (b. 1951), former general secretary of the Association of Secondary Teachers in Ireland; generally considered as one of the most militant and formidable trade-union leaders in the country before he turned gamekeeper as head of the Labour Relations Commission.

Court decisions has not been matched by the unions, and have consistently asked for more powers for the court. The quasi-judicial Employment Appeals Tribunal adjudicates on a range of matters arising from labour legislation such as redundancy, minimum notice, maternity leave, and unfair dismissals, and its decisions may be appealed against in the ordinary courts. In 1990, a new Industrial Relations Act repealed and replaced the 1906 Act which had regulated the system; the 1990 Act, in effect, simply clarified modern practices, and ensured that secret ballots would become the norm (Ireland, in fact, was not given to the sort of 'hands up, all out' meetings in the company car-park which became a symbol of what was wrong in British industrial relations). Employers and unions welcomed the Act, while both expressed mild disappointment with it. It did not cause any real problem; whether it solved any real problems is debatable.

Today, some 459,000 Irish workers are members of trade unions: this is nearly 60 per cent of the workforce,* and is among the highest in western economies. The membership has decreased steadily in recent years, mostly as a result of Ireland's soaring unemployment. A new element which is creeping into the labour-force profile is worrying the unions: more and more of the new multinational plants (particularly from the United States) in, for example, the health-care and computer-related industries are resolutely non-unionized and staying that way. 'They offer an extremely attractive staff package, so who'd blame the workers?' is the resigned comment of a union official. Since the workers in these areas are highly educated and skilled, as well as being well paid, the loss is even more keenly felt by the unions.

The vast majority of Irish trade unions are members of the Irish Congress of Trade Unions (ICTU), which has been at the centre of bargaining with government in the two important national pay agreements since 1987.† Both of these agreements involved more

---

* The total 1992 membership of the Irish Congress of Trade Unions was 672,600 in seventy trade unions (a reduction of some 10,000 over the previous year). Some two-thirds are in fifty-three unions in the Republic of Ireland, and one-third in thirty-five unions in Northern Ireland. Eighteen unions have members both in the Republic of Ireland and in Northern Ireland. Fifteen of the affiliated unions with a membership of 59,700 have their head offices outside Ireland.

† The Irish Congress of Trade Unions has as its general secretary one of the quietest but most highly respected figures in Irish industrial relations: Peter

than just pay bargaining, particularly the second one, and had
suitably grandiose names, so that everyone involved would understand the significance of what they had agreed – the first, in 1987,
was called the Programme for National Recovery (PNR),* and the
second was the Programme for Economic and Social Progress
(PESP).

Some disquiet was expressed, and still is, by Opposition parties
to the concept of a relatively small group of people sitting down
behind closed doors to agree not only pay guidelines, but also
measures concerning farming policy, forestry, education, labour
legislation, social welfare, and health expenditure – a range of
activities more properly decided upon, they believe, in the open
democratic forum of the elected parliament. The leader of the
Opposition, in his comments in the Dáil when it came to debate the
ninety-six closely written pages of the PESP, summed it up: 'It is at
this late stage, after all the discussion is over outside this House,
that the elected assembly of the Irish people is finally being asked
to discuss, and approve without amendment, a Programme that
was negotiated elsewhere.'³ Disquiet was not confined to the Opposition; as the PESP was in negotiation in 1991, a back-bencher of the
government party (who was to find himself Minister for Social
Welfare within twelve months) expressed his concern: 'It will be
more important to be elected a trade union leader than a TD, and
people would be better off attending their union meeting or joining
an employers' organization than voting in an election.'⁴ As 1992
went on, and the public-service pay elements of the PESP proved to
be too expensive, and looked likely to be postponed, while
unemployment and its associated social welfare costs soared,
rumours abounded that the new Taoiseach, Albert Reynolds, was

---

Cassells (b. 1949). He is a dogged but reasonable defender of workers' rights: he
worked his way up through many levels of Congress before being elected general
secretary in 1989.

* This name implied, to the annoyance of the parties constituting the outgoing
government in 1987, that the country needed emergency measures to recover from
four years of inept leadership. There is no doubt, however, that by 1987 the Irish
people had finally grasped that an economic abyss was ahead if suitably stern
measures were not adopted. The outgoing Fine Gael FitzGerald government
prided itself on having forced the incoming Fianna Fáil government under Charles
Haughey to accept this reality and act accordingly.

developing misgivings about the whole process of tying in pay negotiations to other spending and policy areas.

Who negotiated the Programmes? Who are the social partners, these people who have put together plans for the broad development of Irish pay and social policies? In summary, they are: government and employers, trade unions, and farmers. The last three are the big groups who carry most clout and to whom government in Ireland must listen, and with whom government confers. Ireland also has its many other articulate and organized lobbies on a range of interests, from large professional bodies and associations to voluntary groups, all clamouring for attention. From church bodies to women's groups, from doctors' organizations and national parent councils to agencies for combating poverty, they range in power and influence.

At the table in Government Buildings when national programmes are being negotiated, the government deploys its key ministers and their civil servants, with the Taoiseach of the day taking a leading role, working with the Ministers for Finance (who is also the Minister for the Public Service), Labour and Agriculture, as well as Industry and Commerce, and others when necessary. It is generally agreed, however, that one powerful civil servant at the head of the Department of the Taoiseach between 1987 and 1992 was the *éminence grise* of both the 1987 and 1989 Programmes – Pádraig Ó hUiginn.* Mr Ó hUiginn had his retirement date twice postponed during those years to allow him to continue his work on the all-important programmes; he had chaired the National Economic and Social Council, which laid the foundation for these programmes. The political correspondent of the *Irish Times* characterized his position: 'He can justly be described as the architect of the two programmes for economic and social development negotiated since 1987.'[5]

For employers, there were three organizations: the Confederation of Irish Industry (CII), the Federated Union of Employers (FUE),

---

*Pádraig Ó hUiginn (b. 1924). Ireland's *Who's Who?* in 1990 described him as possibly the most influential man in the country; known as a superb negotiator, he was close to Charles Haughey (who resigned as Taoiseach in January 1992) and had a range of Irish and international skills and expertise widely admired. He did not enjoy the same influence under Garret FitzGerald between 1982 and 1987.

and the Construction Industry Federation. Of these, the employers are the most central. Employers have only recently in Ireland transformed themselves into a powerful, well-financed and knowledgeable linchpin in the negotiating process through their representative body, the FUE.* In 1992, the FUE boasted 3,250 member companies, as compared with 1,257 in 1960, and by its decision to merge with the Confederation of Irish Industry in late 1992, increased that to 3,700 firms, employing 300,000 people. Almost until the 1980s, the FUE was a body known more for its instant and predictably hostile reactions to all union and labour demands than for its quality of thoughtfulness; as late as the 1960s, it was described as a 'democratic, non-enforcement organization', and could deliver in negotiations only as much as individual interest groups within it would wear.

Its conservative image was further reinforced by its opposition to the European Community Directive on equal pay for women, many of its members genuinely believing that it would be disastrous for the economy. Not until 1979 did the FUE appoint its first 'communications officer', whose functions included relations with the media. Up to then, its idea of public relations seemed confined to ritual lunches for newspaper editors in some private dining-room in Dublin, most probably in a gentlemen's club.

Two things helped the Federated Union of Employers to maturity: one was its participation in the Employer–Labour Conference, established in modern form in 1970. That body, constituted along the lines of the 'social partners', brought about national wage agreements between 1970 and 1976, and then broader national agreements between 1977 and 1980. These were agreements which were unlike anything seen in Irish industrial relations up to that point, and answered the challenge of keeping pay flexible enough to correct anomalies and reward performance, while controlling

* Director-General of the FUE, and of the new IBEC from November 1992, is John Dunne, who joined the organization in 1966. A low-profile personality, he is considered a middle-of-the-road traditionalist in terms of attitudes to industrial relations, a hard worker, and to be cautious by nature. Under his leadership, the FUE has become much more efficient and effective in its operations. On 11 November 1992, the FUE and CII voted to combine into a new organization to be known as IBEC – Irish Business and Employers' Confederation. The CII had been a pressure group for industry.

pay increases to avoid inflation; a prominent academic economist of the time commented that 'the Irish answer in the national agreements was imaginative and for several years was at least moderately successful'.⁶ However, despite some success, strikes and man-days lost soared in 1978 and 1979,* and only started a steady decrease after 1982. Between 1982 and 1987, no national agreements were embarked upon; it is a moot point, much argued, whether the dramatic lowering of inflation achieved during that period was because of the refusal of government to enter expensive deals on pay and social expenditure.

The second element bringing the FUE and other employer organizations into the modern world was Ireland's entry to the European Community. It was quickly realized that a spate of labour legislation would emanate from Brussels, needing both anticipation and expertise, and that no EC country could afford to be without full knowledge of what was going on in the Berlaymont, or without an opportunity to influence developments. A representative and an office were established in Brussels, European employers' organizations were joined, and Irish employers became part of the machinery of the Community. The Irish Business Bureau in Brussels is highly regarded internationally.

The third group among the social partners are the farmers, a powerful bloc in Ireland, represented by four bodies: the Irish Farmers' Association (IFA), the Irish Creamery Milk Suppliers' Association (ICMSA),† the Irish Co-Operative Organization Society (ICOS), and Macra na Feirme, the national organization of young farmers.

The Irish Farmers' Association is the strongest voice for farmers in Ireland, a voice which sometimes is heard in strange and controversial ways. An example of IFA tactics was seen in the summer of 1992, when a large number of sheep were driven into the Dublin city-centre offices of the Department of Agriculture, causing the kind of disruption and disgust which guarantee headlines in all the media; the protest was about reductions in subsidy payments for sheep. Amid fury on the part of civil servants, and condemnation by animal lovers and the urban public generally,

---

* In 1978, 624,000 days were lost; in 1979, 1,464,000 days.
† The ICMSA refused to sign the Programme for National Recovery in 1987.

the IFA refused to condemn the action, although apologies were quietly made to the outraged office workers. There has been much high drama of that kind throughout the years, with demonstrations and sit-ins often ending in legal confrontation and imprisonment – for short periods – of farmers' leaders. The IFA president elected in January 1990 for a two-year (minimum) term* had himself served a prison sentence of twenty-seven days in 1967 for blocking a bridge in Co. Kildare as part of a farmers' rights campaign of that year. Irish farmers joined enthusiastically in the Brussels demonstrations of November 1992 against the GATT agreement, but their tactics have never been as violent as those of some of their continental farming colleagues.

The Irish Farmers' Association is organized efficiently all around the country, and is a political force of considerable standing: it would be a foolhardy Dáil Deputy, Senator or councillor who failed to respond to an IFA summons to attend a meeting on whatever the latest agricultural problem was. In 1985, a government proposal to introduce new forms of farmer taxation led to mass meetings all over the country, and swingeing losses of seats for the main government party, Fine Gael, in that year's local elections. Eighty-five thousand farmers subscribe to the IFA, out of a total of approximately 100,000 who live on the land.† The organization carries out a range of invaluable functions and services for farmers from its well-staffed and equipped headquarters in Dublin.

It is interesting to note that neither in the biographical notes and statement of achievements of its president, supplied to this author by the IFA, nor in the potted history and present structures of the organization, also supplied by the IFA, was any mention made of the organization's role in the negotiation of the two major economic and social programmes which have dominated public policy since 1987, the PNR and the PESP. The private opinion of one trade unionist, a participant in both sets of negotiations, that 'the farmers' only weapon is their vote, their numbers are falling, and their money comes from Europe anyway' and that these factors marginal-

---

* Alan Gillis (b. 1936), from a Protestant middle-class background, who left an engineering career to establish a small farm, which he built up to a 375-acre, 170-cow dairy and beef-fattening farm in west Co. Wicklow.
† Figures supplied by IFA.

ize them at the negotiating table was confirmed, more crudely, by another: 'It's really ourselves, the FUE, and the government doing the negotiating: we decide on the Programme, and then see what grants we'll give the farmers, and then we try as hard as we can to get them to pay a bit more tax.' It is undoubtedly true that because of the Common Agricultural Policy of the EC and the dependence of Irish farmers on it, Irish Ministers for Agriculture have become less important at the Cabinet table, but feature more frequently as whipping-boys for the farmers when negotiations in Brussels get tough, as they have in recent years.

The Irish Creamery Milk Suppliers' Association, with head-quarters in Limerick at the heart of Munster's rich dairy lands, is a smaller independent grouping, describing itself as the family-farm organization; attempts in the past to effect a merger between it and the IFA have failed, and relations are often strained. The Irish Co-Operative Organization Society is the coordinating society of the IR£4 billion cooperative movement which encompasses the fast-growing and increasingly important food industry. Macra na Feirme (literally, farm youth), with 10,000 members and 350 clubs around the country, concentrates on the development of young farmers in both agriculture and on the wider social and political scene, and lobbies on matters like inheritance taxes, agricultural education, and establishment aid for young farmers.

TOO MANY UNIONS?

Despite the trend today towards rationalization and amalgamation, there were still too many trade unions operating in the Republic of Ireland in 1992. This is the consensus of government and trade-union leadership. Just over fifty unions operate today, with power struggles, membership poaching, and sudden strikes as a result of their proliferation. Seventy per cent of all trade-union members in the Republic of Ireland in 1992 were in only eleven unions, each of which had over 10,000 members. At the other end of the scale, twenty-seven unions with fewer than 2,000 members account for a membership of 18,600 or 4 per cent of the total.[7] The Irish Congress of Trade Unions is consistently anxious to see amalgamations and rationalization, and urges members to use the services of ICTU to bring this about. One of the most significant amalgamations of the

1980s was that of two strong old unions, the Irish Transport and General Workers' Union and the Federated Workers' Union of Ireland, to form SIPTU: the Services, Industrial, Professional, and Technical Union, which is now a giant on the industrial scene with 197,000 members.*

Other smaller amalgamations have seen tax officials and customs people joining up with other public servants, postal workers combined with telecommunications engineers, computer operators amalgamated with boilermakers. In another big move, in 1991, the Local Government and Public Services Union joined up with the Union of Professional and Technical Civil Servants to form the Irish Municipal, Professional, and Civil Trade Union (IMPACT), making it one of the big four Irish unions with nearly 25,000 members.†

An amalgamation which has been talked about for many years, but has not materialized, is that of the Irish teachers' unions. There are four, each representing teachers in one of four different kinds of educational establishment. Given the high proportion of young people in Ireland, teachers' unions are numerically strong. Because of permanence of employment, a high standard of education (with resulting articulateness among members) and relatively good wage levels, the unions are well financed and well run, and powerful. They are also very militant. If they were all in one union, they would number more than 40,000. But even as it is, Irish Ministers for Education must deal warily with the teachers, more particularly with the INTO (Irish National Teachers' Organization – 19,000 members) and the ASTI (Association of Secondary Teachers of Ireland – 12,300). The TUI (Teachers' Union of Ireland) represents 8,000 members working in publicly controlled second-level schools and third-level technical colleges, while the small Irish Federation

* SIPTU's joint General Presidents are William (Bill) Attley (b. 1938) and Edmund Browne (b. 1937). Attley is a well-respected, serious, low-profile, experienced trade unionist, who handled the delicate negotiations establishing SIPTU with great skill. He is also devoted to soccer. Browne is a gifted future leader of the trade-union movement.
† IMPACT's joint General Secretaries are Phil Flynn (b. 1940) and Greg Maxwell (b. 1948). Flynn, whose background includes the vice-presidency of Sinn Féin, is from Dundalk, and is a formidable negotiator. Maxwell, from Belfast, came to IMPACT after thirteen years in charge of UPTCS (Union of Professional and Technical Civil Servants). An articulate and professional pair.

of University Teachers has 1,200 members. A feature of Irish life every Easter, covered in great detail by all the media, is the spectacle of the Minister for Education of the day visiting the annual meetings of the teachers' unions in different parts of Ireland, to be publicly harangued by union leaders anxious to impress their members. It is a sort of blood sport, or perhaps, as the *Irish Times* editorial writer described it, initiation rite: 'No Minister for Education is fully initiated until she or he has undergone a ritual baptism of fire at the teachers' conferences.'[8]

IRISH INDUSTRIAL RELATIONS IN THE EARLY 1990S

Ireland enjoys relatively peaceful industrial relations. The number of strikes called, but particularly numbers of days lost, has been declining steadily since the early 1980s. (This gives a boost to the arguments of those who dislike the PNR and the PESP; they point to the steady decline in disputes and days lost even between 1982 and 1987 when there were no national agreements.) In 1992, however, a series of disputes revealed the tensions arising in modernization and adaptation in large organizations; they are described in more detail below.

The exigencies of international recession and all-out free competition in Europe have kept the private sector and Irish industry relatively trouble-free, though one very large private company – Waterford Glass – looked in danger of disintegrating in 1992. (Its 2,000 workers, historically highly militant, and highly paid, with uncertain and weak management over many years, faced possible closure of their workplace: sanity prevailed, and skilful modern management and unions negotiated a radical rescue deal together.) It is, however, in the semi-State public sector – transport, communications, energy – where strikes are a threat in the early 1990s as secure workers resist attempts to modernize and control labour costs and practices. The privatization battle, with the coming to power of the Labour Party in the coalition government from January 1993, seemed to have been postponed. It would be very difficult for Dick Spring, deputy prime minister, to take his party down the privatization road.

There is an unresolved problem in Irish industrial relations, which is not peculiar, of course, to Ireland. It is: what to do about

Table of Strikes and Days Lost, 1982–92		
Year	Number of strikes	Days lost
1982	131	434,253
1984	192	386,421
1986	102	309,178
1988	72	130,000
1990	52	222,916
1992	41	189,623

Source: Labour Relations Commission figures.

essential public services? Police and Army do not have the right to strike, but no such prohibition attaches, for example, to the national electricity supply company, the ESB. In 1991, this problem again arose. The Electrical Trade Union plunged the country into chaos with power cuts, despite assurances to the nation from ESB management, just a few days before, that power supplies would not be affected. The degree of disaffection and ignorance between management and unions displayed by subsequent events was alarming, all the more so since the ESB had supposedly sophisticated industrial relations procedures in place. So also was the failure of the Department of Labour or the Labour Relations Commission to realize that the 'cooling off' period had cooled nothing off. After a week of power cuts and appeals by all parties in the Dáil to the strikers (totally ignored), the dispute was settled not by the machinery of the company or the State for resolving such issues, but by the personal intervention of the Minister for Labour. Amid a media chorus of condemnation of all sides to the dispute, and the urging of government to 'do something' to stop this kind of thing happening again, the general secretary of the ICTU went as far as saying that 'some way would have to be found of ensuring that disputes in essential services do not have such an effect again'.[9] In January 1992, a new code of practice for disputes, including particular measures for essential services, was introduced to the Dáil by order of the Minister for Labour, as part of the new industrial-relations legislation. The provisions, if acted upon in any future disputes, should go a long way towards avoiding disruptions like the 1991 ESB strike. The fact that the code of practice is still essentially voluntary is a measure of Irish government reluctance to 'taking on' the unions with whom they have worked so closely in recent years. In a country which has no access to alternative sources of electricity unlike mainland Europe, and no corps of personnel in the Army capable of running the electricity service, this may be a luxury any Irish government can ill afford.

The year 1992 opened with a succession of strikes that included the national broadcasting network (RTE) and went on to take in the postal service (An Post), and then the commercial banks of the Republic of Ireland. The RTE strike, in January–February 1992, showed up weakness and confusion within the Irish branch of the National Union of Journalists about its role as a trade union and/ or a professional body; some programme editors who were also members of the NUJ considered that they had a duty as managers to pass the pickets and run a skeleton service. The initial strike issue (about technical manning levels) was forgotten as the country had effectively a news blackout while the historic final political ousting of a Taoiseach at the end of January – a huge news story – was in progress. Several weeks later, everyone went back to work but post-mortems got under way as the NUJ and SIPTU tried to enforce sanctions against those who had worked, and bitterness continued. Months after the strike, the recriminations still simmered in the newsroom. A side-effect of the strike was the reinforcement of the view, already widespread among legislators, that a virtual monopoly by RTE of Irish current affairs and news-broadcasting arrangements was not a good idea.

The dispute at An Post, the semi-State body with a monopoly on running Ireland's postal services which is emerging painfully from decades of life within the civil service, was about overtime and temporary staff for peak periods. The chief executive of the company,*

---

* John Hynes (b. 1945). With a reputation for a 'go-for-it' style of management, Hynes tackled outdated work practices at Dublin's Gas Company, then the city's bus system, before taking on the massive challenge of An Post. A new style of manager in the public sector, he told the *Irish Independent* newspaper in the middle of the Post strike of 1992: 'I'm not into crab-like sideways movements where people don't know what you're about.'

who had inherited grievous organizational and financial difficulties, and who was under orders from government to break even financially in 1992, had been trying to introduce a package of measures as a viability plan. Since the closing of small rural post offices was part of it, the government put the whole thing on hold until after local elections in 1991. By early 1992, certain steps had to be taken, including the cutting down of the huge overtime bill and the creation of temporary posts when needed. Backed by the Minister for Communications, the company went ahead with its plans and the Communications Workers' Union* struck. After more than a month of empty letter-boxes and frustrated businesses, a compromise was reached with which both sides were – at least in public – satisfied, although it was privately conceded that the union had not won the battle, and Ireland's postal services are on their way to something near commercial viability.

The IBOA (Irish Bank Officials' Association) affiliated to the Congress of Trade Unions only in 1992. It is a large (13,000 members), powerful and traditionally militant body. Its strike in April 1992 took place in a very different climate from that of previous disputes, which had caused considerable disruption to the economy. In the 1990s technology has so changed the banking world that the strike did not deprive the public of ready cash. The 'hole in the wall' – the automated teller machine doling out money – was easy to deal with, and the other computerized functions of banking meant that business proceeded nearly as usual. The IBOA did not have the total support of all its members; the public observed a group of relatively well-paid employees refusing to accept a Labour Court recommendation, and refusing to open at lunchtime or slightly later in the afternoon, despite not having to work individually for any extra hours and despite an offer of money and extra time off. The ICTU supported the IBOA in its interpretation of what could be given under the PESP (a sign of the new closeness of the ICTU and the IBOA, which was on the brink of finally joining the Congress) and the strike proceeded for three weeks. At the

* The CWU, with 20,000 members, is a strong organization with a strong leader, its general secretary David Begg (b. 1950). A graduate of the tough school of the ESB unions, he impresses as an articulate and determined man. As the Irish postal service enters the 1990s he will need all of those attributes.

end of that time, after the usual lengthy and dramatic day and night meetings, the bank officials voted to go back to work in what amounted to a capitulation, though it was naturally not publicly described as such.

These strikes took place in the public sector, or in the case of the banks, the white-collar sector of relatively secure employment. In none of the three was there a threat to the jobs of the strikers, and all of them were connected in some way to the transition from old to new, from old work-practices to new economic imperatives, from insulated inward-looking company structures to bracing themselves for competition and survival in Europe. They encapsulate the challenges facing trade unionists in Ireland today, not least of which is the emergence of something which is variously described as the new realism or the New Right. Thatcherism in Britain is the most immediate parallel, though Irish people do not like that label, no matter how accurate. In Ireland, the political group most identified with 'the new realism' is the Progressive Democrats, founded in the mid-1980s, who became the small coalition partner of Fianna Fáil after the June 1989 election, but with numerous adherents in Fianna Fáil and Fine Gael too.

As unemployment increased inexorably towards 300,000 and government financial targets for 1993 looked difficult indeed, Irish employers, trade unions, farmers, and pressure groups contemplated European economic integration and international recession with varying degrees of realism. It became clearer and clearer that the lead in realism and skill would have to come in the first place from Irish government.

NOTES

1. In conversation with the author, July 1992.
2. *Industrial Relations in Ireland*, Department of Industrial Relations, University College, Dublin, 1989.
3. John Bruton, Dáil debate on the PESP, 19 February 1991.
4. Charles McCreevy, quoted in the *Irish Times*, 5 January 1991.
5. *Irish Times*, 5 January 1991.
6. Article by Professor Michael Fogarty, 'The two faces of Irish industrial relations' in: Kieran A. Kennedy (ed.), *Ireland in Transition*, RTE/Mercier Press, 1986 (the Thomas Davis lectures).

7. Figures from ICTU *Information Bulletin*, 1992.
8. *Irish Times*, 23 April 1992.
9. *Irish Independent*, 26 April 1991.

CHAPTER 16

Religion

Ninety-three out of every hundred people in the Republic of Ireland are Roman Catholic; and 82 per cent of them go to their church once a week for Mass – they are the most orthodox Catholic community in the western world. The vast majority of the schools – both primary and second-level – in the country are controlled by Catholic management. Many of Ireland's major teaching hospitals, though almost 100 per cent funded by the State, are controlled by Catholic boards and religious orders. The Catholic Church's teaching on divorce and abortion has been enshrined in the Irish Constitution. In 1979, Pope John Paul II visited Ireland and was welcomed in an unprecedented nationwide outpouring of loyalty. Not surprisingly, he exclaimed, 'Young People of Ireland, I love you,' with deep emotion in a vast gathering at Galway in the west of Ireland; his emotion was reciprocated as hundreds of thousands of young people repeatedly interrupted him with songs, cheers and applause. A wave of religious fervour enveloped the whole of Ireland during those three days. At the start of the visit, 1,250,000 people had greeted the Pope in Dublin's Phoenix Park on 29 September 1979 – more than a third of the whole population. They gathered from dawn in the most peaceful and orderly manner, and afterwards the police remarked on the exceptional good humour and trouble-free atmosphere of Dublin on that day.

However, such demonstrations masked the reality of significant signs of change in the Irish attitude to their Catholicism: most dramatically in the falling number of 'vocations' – the numbers of young people entering the religious life, whether as members of religious orders or diocesan clergy. Between 1970 and 1986, there was a 29 per cent drop in the numbers of religious personnel, from 25,172 to 19,113. That decline was to continue, so that in 1989 the number was down to 15,634. Of these, only 557 (3.6 per cent) were under thirty years old. More than half the diocesan priests working in parishes across Ireland are over fifty, and the average age is rising.

This age profile contrasts with the population as a whole, which has nearly 50 per cent under thirty.[1] The table on vocations to the religious life in Ireland between 1970 and 1989 (on page 376) records the decline.

No official data have been released since 1989, but enquiries yield the information that just a trickle of young people are entering the religious life today: the smallest numbers ever. The Jesuit Order in 1991/2 had two novices; the Dublin Diocesan Seminary of Clonliffe, which trains priests for service in the country's largest population centre, had seven young men entering in September 1991, which came down to six by Christmas 1991 as one of them left. (This compares with, for example, a class of forty joining a large bustling Clonliffe college of several hundred students in 1960.) The crisis in vocations is matched by the internal crisis: in 1989, 102 diocesan clergy left the priesthood, while the clergy lost only about half that number through death.

The Catholic Church in Ireland today is facing remarkable change: the 80 per cent church-attendance rates mask a catastrophic fall to somewhere between 5 and 10 per cent in Dublin's huge working-class housing estates; two referendums in the 1980s on issues of deep concern to the Church, despite a result for the status quo, revealed both an abstention rate and a defiance of Church teaching which together made up a majority of the electorate.* Increasingly, there is a rift between the activities and public statements of the thirty-five-strong College of Bishops and the Conference of Major Religious Superiors: the CMRS is the group which represents the thinking of the religious orders in Ireland, who are not subject to the authority of the bishops. The CMRS has taken on a role which approaches the liberation theology of social concern, not previously seen in Ireland. They have eschewed involvement in what seems to have obsessed the bishops, the topic of personal sexual morality. The CMRS represents 207 religious communities of priests, brothers and nuns which have, as we have seen, been decimated in numbers since the 1960s and are, in the

---

* The 1983 abortion referendum and the 1986 divorce referendum resulted in a two-to-one victory for the stated position of the Church, but the low poll in each case plus those voting negatively meant that a minority overall of the electorate actually came out to affirm the Church position. By far the biggest proportion of the 'anti' vote was in the Dublin area.

Catholic Church Personnel, 1989

Category	Total	Diocesan clergy	Priests and brothers	Religious orders	
				Sisters	Brothers
Applicants	634	263	197	152	22
Entrants	322	139	99	75	9
Percentage of applicants accepted	51	53	50	49	41
Balance in number of entrants since 1988	−50 (−13%)	−16 (−10%)	−24 (−20%)	−12 (−14%)	+2 (+29%)
Departures	269	102*	70†	77‡	20§
Deaths	401	58	91	218	34
Balance of total personnel since 1988	−348	−21	−62	−220	−45
Balance as percentage of total personnel in 1988	−1	−1	−1	−2	−3
Total	24,546	3,800	6,325	12,981	1,440

* Nine priests; ninety-three seminarians.
† Four priests; fifty-four unordained; twelve brothers.
‡ Twenty-four professed; fifty-three others.
§ Six professed; fourteen others.

Source: Irish Times: Working and Living, 5 June 1992.

375

Vocations in Ireland, 1970–89

Year	Diocesan clergy	Clerical religious orders	Sisters' orders	Brothers' orders	Total	Percentage change
1970	164	261	227	98	750	−11
1971	179	236	239	81	735	−2
1972	184	246	176	59	665	−9
1973	157	220	153	40	570	−14
1974	144	167	188	48	547	−4
1975	154	191	175	55	575	+5
1976	181	189	188	64	622	+8
1977	206	161	194	40	601	−3
1978	175	179	175	31	560	−7
1979	175	143	161	27	506	−10
1980	195	199	181	33	608	+20
1981	176	212	163	51	602	−1
1982	187	192	173	37	589	−2
1983	154	172	149	49	524	−11
1984	154	187	145	27	513	−2
1985	169	151	123	28	471	−8
1986	170	129	115	18	432	−8
1987	168	127	115	14	424	−2
1988	155	123	87	7	372	−12
1989	139	99	75	9	322	−13

Source: Irish Times: Working and Living, 5 June 1992.

The author with two churchmen: (*left to right*) Most Reverend Donald Caird and Most Reverend Desmond Connell

Church and State: President Mary Robinson with His Eminence Cahal Daly, Catholic Primate of Ireland and Most Reverend Donald Caird, Archbishop of Dublin (Church of Ireland)

Women in government: (*left to right*) Ministers Niamh Bhreathnach TD, Minister for Education, and Máire Geoghegan-Quinn TD, Minister for Justice

A new consciousness of social issues concerning women has brought protesters
on to the streets in both urban and rural Ireland

Changing roles everywhere: Irish women enjoy an increasing
involvement in football

The game of hurling: uniquely Irish

Environmentalists Éamon de Buitléir and Mary Banotti MEP at the Burren, County Clare, in 1992, during a protest against the siting of an interpretative centre in a sensitive area

Celebration of Irishness:
dancers at the 1992 Fleá Cheoil at Clonmel, Co. Tipperary

Three junior ministers: (*left*) Mary O'Rourke TD (Enterprise and Employment), Joan Burton TD (Social Welfare) and Eithne FitzGerald TD (Finance and Tánaiste's Department)(*Below, left to right*)

Pilgrims' progress: the faithful make their way, often barefoot, up Croagh
Patrick in County Mayo during the annual pilgrimage

A pilgrim kisses the cross at the summit

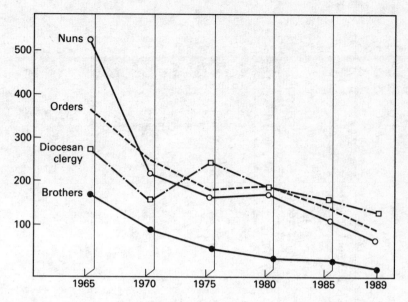

Those entering the religious life (*source: Sunday Independent,*
17 March 1992)

view of many, therefore facing extinction, with profound implications for the future of the Church in Ireland.

Presiding over both the bishops and the diocesan priests and
people of the Irish Catholic Church is the slight but charismatic
figure of Cardinal Cahal Daly, Archbishop of Armagh and Primate
of All Ireland, born in Northern Ireland in 1917, and created
Cardinal in 1991. Next in line is Dr Desmond Connell, Archbishop
of Dublin, tall, stooped and gentle-looking, with the slightly
abstracted air of the professor of metaphysics which was his previous occupation. Archbishop Joseph Cassidy of Tuam, and
Archbishop Dermot Clifford of Cashel and Emly complete the
senior hierarchy. Acting as a representative of the Vatican is the
Papal Nuncio, Archbishop Emanuel Gerada, who conveys to Rome
the state of the Church in Ireland, and has a central role in the
appointment of bishops.

There are not many members of other Churches in this
overwhelmingly Catholic country; the most numerous is the
(Protestant) Church of Ireland, with fewer than 100,000 members.
Presbyterians (12,000), Methodists (about 5,000), and Jews (1,400)

Deaths and Departures, 1980–89: Seminarians, Religious, Priests

Year	Diocesan clergy		Clerical religious orders		Sisters' orders		Brothers' orders		Total	
	D1*	D2†	D1	D2	D1	D2	D1	D2	D1	D2
1980	66	65	89	140	239	125	31	34	425	364
1981	64	40	93	55	295	120	27	36	479	251
1982	93	26	86	76	274	119	21	37	474	258
1983	87	98	83	116	284	101	33	24	487	339
1984	60	46	96	122	242	97	30	44	428	309
1985	80	59	95	142	266	96	28	27	469	324
1986	71	70	81	103	287	93	36	19	475	285
1987	68	84	72	96	251	98	29	27	420	294
1988	74	83	93	81	296	91	32	27	495	282
1989	58	102	91	70	218	77	34	20	401	269

* D1 = deaths   † D2 = departures
Source: Irish Times: Working and Living, 5 June 1992.

make up almost all of the rest.* There is a tiny Quaker group –
about 700 in the Republic of Ireland. Muslims in Ireland are an
eclectic, multiracial group, numbering about 3,000 in the Republic;
there is a small following of the Baha'i faith, and a number of
Buddhist traditions are represented in the country.

Twelve bishops represent the Church of Ireland, headed by Dr
Robin Eames, Lord Archbishop of Armagh and Primate of All
Ireland; his next in line is Dr Donald Caird, Lord Archbishop of
Dublin. The Church of Ireland has seen a slow and inexorable
decline in its number since the establishment of the Irish Republic.
It is estimated to have fallen by 68 per cent in the Republic of
Ireland since a census in 1911. There are various reasons for this
catastrophic decline: in the early years, many were killed in the
Great War of 1914–18; many civil servants left Ireland after political
independence; many left because of fear and intimidation (192
Protestant country homes were burned down in the political upheavals of the second and third decades of the century); many left no
doubt because of the very Catholic laws for a very Catholic people.
And all the while, those who stayed saw their number decline
further because of the Catholic Church's 'Ne Temere' decree which
forced the Catholic partner to an inter-church marriage to promise
in writing that all children of the marriage would be baptized and
brought up in the Catholic faith. In 1970, Pope Paul VI revised the
'Ne Temere' decree; today in Ireland that requirement has been
relaxed by the Irish (Catholic) Bishops' Conference. Today, a
Catholic partner 'is required to make a sincere promise to do all in
his or her power to ensure that all the children of the marriage are
baptized and brought up in the Catholic faith'.[2] Despite its small
numbers, the Church of Ireland is greatly respected throughout the
country. Its bishops and clergy, and their spouses, have been of a
high calibre, giving devoted service to their diminishing flock. The
higher socio-economic group of most of the members also
contributes to the influence of their Church on the life of the
country, although participation rates in public life have been

---

* Figures in the 1981 population census, compared with the figures given by the
individual churches in 1992, show a fall in numbers for all these religions in the
intervening eleven years. The question was not asked in the restricted 1986
census.

minuscule. In the public debates on issues of sexual morality which have so obsessed the Irish in recent decades, the Church of Ireland has taken a more liberal stand, and in the changing Ireland of today that has gained it many friends. The Church of Ireland has doggedly fought for its fine old schools and institutions, many of which now survive (and thrive) by virtue of the influx of children of Catholic parents who appreciate the more liberal education which they perceive to be on offer there.

A long-running and divisive debate on the sensitive issue of the Protestant ethic in medicine came to a resolution in May 1993. A brand-new IR£112 million hospital development in Tallaght to the west of Dublin had been held up because one of the amalgamating hospitals moving to the greenfield site had been the focus for Protestant participation in the health services. The Adelaide Hospital (which, for example, had a fully liberal attitude on the question of female sterilization) fought long and hard for its dominant position on the board of the new hospital, and won that battle under the new young Labour Minister for Health.* The Protestant Archbishop would become president of the new hospital, and would have enough nominees on the board in conjunction with the Adelaide Society to ensure a majority.

The two great ancient and beautiful ecclesiastical buildings in the capital city, St Patrick's and Christ Church Cathedrals, belong to the Church of Ireland; the Catholics, for all their strength, wealth and power, have no cathedral. A 1950s plan to build a new one on the grassy interior of one of Dublin's handsome Georgian squares happily came to nothing. (Some Catholics in private will admit that they consider St Patrick's and Christ Church to belong to them, morally if not in fact, since they are both pre-Reformation.) As if to emphasize the Irishness of his Church, since there is sometimes historical confusion about their real loyalties, the Church of Ireland Archbishop of Dublin Dr Caird is an Irish-language scholar of some distinction and speaks the language with a fluency and flair seldom heard in public figures.

---

*Brendan Howlin (b. Wexford, 1956). Formerly national schoolteacher. First elected to the Dáil in 1987, after four years in the Senate. An articulate and hard-working man, a bachelor, he tackled his new portfolio from January 1993 with considerable energy.

To explain the modern strength of the Catholic Church in Ireland – a strength, conservatism, and orthodoxy so different from the situation in countries like France, Italy, and Spain, where 'believing' and 'practising' are not synonymous – one must look to Irish history. The Catholic Church, during the bitter years of the nineteenth-century struggle for religious freedom, worked closely with the movements for political freedom. Together they won successive battles with the United Kingdom to gain control over schools for Catholics; the Church also evolved a substantial role in the provision of hospital facilities and care for the poor. When the new southern State gained its independence, the Catholic Church could therefore claim to be the true Church of the people. The shared experience of a long and weary fight against Britain gave it a central and pivotal role in the life of the people, who fully identified with it and accepted almost without question its dominance over every aspect of their lives. By then it had become a deeply conservative church, by contrast with the early years of the nineteenth century when a distinguished Irish Catholic barrister, Daniel O'Connell, fought for Catholic emancipation from oppressive laws, becoming known throughout Europe as a great liberal.

The foundation of St Patrick's College in Maynooth, Co. Kildare, in the late eighteenth century, which provided the academic training for the Irish priesthood, contributed however to an inward-looking attitude of Irish clerics at all levels.* In Ireland by the first decades of independence there were hardly any diverse strands and debates or internal questioning and wrangling. The normal tension between a Church and its flock 'often provokes large percentages of atheism, agnosticism, dissent and anti-clericalism'[3] – but Ireland never produced any real debate about the Church or its role in the country's life until very recent times. There was, and is, an almost complete absence of a Catholic intelligentsia.

Despite some tensions between the Church and militant republicans, the new Irish State after 1922 was closely and continually influenced by Catholic thinking. In 1925, Seán Lemass,

---

* The college has developed into a constituent college of the National University of Ireland, with male and female lay and clerical students fully integrated. There is still some unease about the degree of control over the college exercised by the Catholic hierarchy – an area gingerly avoided by successive governments.

later to become one of Fianna Fáil's most dynamic and respected Taoisigh, expressed a little hostility to the political influence of the Church* – but by 1937 Fianna Fáil had changed its view, and: 'Cleverer counsels were to prevail; Fianna Fáil would not destroy the political power of the Church. Fianna Fáil would capture the political power of the Church.'[4] This was the thinking which informed those working on the 1937 Constitution of the fairly new State, now under the firm control of the party which had opposed the treaty with Britain establishing the fledgeling State in 1922, and which would dominate Irish politics and government for many decades to come.

Éamon de Valera's 1937 Constitution, which survives almost intact today, was explicitly religious in its overtones and some of its provisions. It formally affirmed the 'special position' of the Catholic Church (Article 44) – removed quietly, almost without debate, in 1972 – as 'the guardian of the faith of the great majority of the citizens'. Backing up this article was a series of provisions on the family, placing it squarely at the centre of life, and giving it rights 'antecedent to and superior to all law' (Article 41.1). De Valera worked closely with the Catholic Archbishop of Dublin, John Charles McQuaid, on this blueprint for his country.

Women were placed in the home: 'In particular, the State recognizes that by her life within the home, woman gives to the State a support without which the common good cannot be achieved' (Article 41.2.1). Marriage was to be especially protected 'against attack' (Article 41.3.1) and therefore, 'No law shall be enacted providing for the grant of a dissolution of marriage.' It further strengthened the role of the family by designating it as the 'primary and natural educator', emphasizing the parents' freedom to choose their children's schools, and, where the State would assist educators to provide schools, it would do so 'with particular regard to the right of parents, especially in the matter of their children's religious and moral formation' (Article 42.4). Thus was the framework created for the institutionalized denominational education system which survives today.

* In the *Irish Independent* newspaper of 14 March 1925, he was quoted thus: 'We are opening now the campaign against the political influence of the Church. If we succeed in destroying that influence, we will have done good work for Ireland and, I believe, for the Catholic religion in Ireland.'

Until the 1960s, the Church's unrivalled position as the arbiter of social legislation and controller of all matters to do with the family and society remained almost unquestioned. As well as that, Catholic social thinking of the day ensured that private property was enshrined as sacrosanct in Article 43: 'The State acknowledges that man, in virtue of his rational being, has the natural right, antecedent to positive law, to the private ownership of external goods.'

Ireland's political and social history since independence in 1922 and up to the 1970s was therefore a faithful mirror of that conservative Catholic social thinking, with censorship laws which saw writers like James Joyce hunted off the shelves; religious discrimination which occasionally manifested itself openly in cases of refusal of public positions to non-Catholics; obstruction of attempts by legislators to provide free ante- and post-natal care for mothers; refusal of contraception and abortion to Irishwomen; the absence of divorce for couples whose marriages had failed; the refusal to provide legal tubal ligation for women or male vasectomy in hospitals paid for by the State but controlled by the Church; the 'hiring and firing' of teachers on grounds of personal beliefs or lifestyle which had nothing to do with standards of teaching; the prohibition on Catholics' attendance at Trinity College, Dublin. Bishops and priests were accorded an awed respect, and dominated community life, particularly outside Dublin. Any sporting or social activity on a local level needed for its success at least the approval, if not the active patronage, of the parish priest. One of Ireland's most successful modern novelists, John McGahern, who was himself dismissed from his teaching post because the local school authorities – the Church – disapproved of one of his early books, summed it up: 'It was a very simple world of the GAA and the drama society with a very distorted view of life.'[5] At Sunday worship, as if to emphasize the views of the clergy on the proper scheme of things, men and women knelt at different sides of the church. Catholics could not enter a Protestant church even to attend a wedding or bury a friend,* while young people who managed finally to get permission to marry out of the Catholic Church had to make do

* A dramatic illustration of the lengths to which this practice was carried: at the funeral in 1949 of Ireland's first President – Douglas Hyde – a Protestant and much revered Gaelic scholar, the government of the day sat outside the Protestant church in their State cars.

with a furtive, truncated ceremony early in the morning away from the main part of the church building. The two dominant newspapers, the *Irish Press* and the *Irish Independent*, were fearfully respectful of the Church. 'To this day, a life-size statue of the Virgin Mary stands in a corner of the library at Independent House, put there by the staff in 1954 to commemorate the Marian Year.' Those were the days of 'a rubric-ordered world where the Catholic Directory in the newsroom was dog-eared from use and death-notice proofs had to be scanned meticulously for departed CC's or PP's* for obituary material'.[6]

The dominance of the Church, and its deep conservatism in Ireland, may be explained also by Irish colonial history, resulting in a situation where loyalty to the Church was synonymous with loyalty to the country, and where anything 'foreign' was threatening. There was no need for the Church to question or develop its own philosophical base when 'the neo-colonial legacy of unfinished business with Protestant England has given a defensive siege mentality to the Irish level of religious practice, and this to an extent surpassing even the position in Poland'.[7]

The Church strongly denies that there is, or ever has been, any question of enforcing Catholic moral teaching on the State: their position is, quite simply, that it is the Church's role and duty to point out what, in their view, the impact on society would be of any particular proposal by the legislature. Cardinal Daly, when he was Bishop of Down and Connor, developed that thesis in his opening statement to the New Ireland Forum† in 1984:

What we have claimed and what we must claim, is the right to fulfil our pastoral duty, and our pastoral duty is to alert the consciences of Catholics to the moral consequences of any proposed piece of legislation and to the impact of that legislation on the moral quality of life in society while leaving to the legislators and to the electorate their freedom to act in accordance with their consciences.

That frequently used warning mechanism has had – quite naturally – a powerful effect on public opinion and a correspondingly inhibiting effect on legislators. It comes from one of the most conservative

* Abbreviations for Catholic Curate or Parish Priest.
† See page 139.

Catholic Church establishments in the western world, and gives a major boost to the activities of groups of lay people who form themselves into organizations to apply pressure to legislators in support of the Church's arguments. Many of the issues are sexual, and therefore very sensitive in an Irish context, resulting in public debates which have from time to time become extremely heated.

The Catholic Church's control of the education of most of the country's children and young people is mirrored by the same degree of control exercised by the minority Churches in Ireland over their own flocks; Ireland's is an 'aided' education system, and the bodies aided by the State are the Churches. Unlike other countries, where the Churches lost ground to public initiative, the Irish system for historical reasons evolved to the point, at the beginning of the century, 'which was acceptable to, and controlled by the Churches, but was funded mainly by the State'.[8] By the time the country achieved independence in 1922 there was no doubt as to how the Catholic Church viewed its future in education: 'The only satisfactory system of education for Catholics is one wherein Catholic children are taught in Catholic schools by Catholic teachers under Catholic control.'[9] The work done by the teaching religious orders among poor Catholics in the previous century was continued, strengthened, and added to by more orders starting schools, all over the country, until children at all social levels were being educated by the Church. The State provided most of the finance, but at that time the orders still had sufficient personnel and money to give extra facilities and supervision which the State did not have to pay for. Today, there are over 450 'voluntary secondary schools' – that is, schools under the management of the Catholic Church, educating 212,446 students, compared to 129,473 being educated by other types of second-level school, in which the Church has control over about one-third of the students (e.g. Community Schools, a new type of school often resulting from amalgamations of other types of school).[10] The nuns, brothers and priests in the classrooms of those secondary schools now form a small minority of teaching staff. The table overleaf shows the gradual decline in numbers of religious teachers since the early 1970s.

At university level, the Catholic Church until 1970 forbade its members to attend Trinity College, Dublin, and urged instead attendance at the National University of Ireland, founded in 1908.

Numbers of Religious and Lay Teachers, 1970–71, 1980–81, 1990–91			
	Year		
Type of teacher	1970–71	1980–81	1990–91
Religious	2,349	2,106	1,175
Lay	4,923	9,634	10,375

The repeal of that 'ban' was considered to be a pragmatic response to the impossibility any longer of enforcing it, as more and more Catholic families sent their children to the fine old college, redolent of tradition, and no longer – to the new generations – a threat to the faith.

Today, with the virtual collapse of recruitment to the teaching orders, the Church must rely for its power in education on managerial structures which give the bishop or the order the majority on the board of schools, and on its influence on the teachers and parents of Ireland. When the history and influence of the Catholic Church on education is debated in Ireland today, there are two sides to that discussion. There is widespread gratitude and appreciation of the orders that gave such service to the Irish in darker times, but there is also criticism for what is seen as the heavy hand of authoritarianism, allied to excessive physical discipline, which together stifled both freedom of thinking and, in the view of many, a questioning or entrepreneurial spirit.

An emerging debate about Church and State, and their respective roles in education, was stimulated in 1992 by the publication of a Green Paper (a government discussion document) on education. The reaction of the Catholic Church authorities was one of hostility to the tentative suggestions in the Green Paper that control of schools might in future be more in the hands of the community than directly under Church control. A small group called the 'Campaign to Separate Church and State' agitates for clearer demarcation in society generally, but in education in particular. The Constitution is generally considered to be, as yet, not fully interpreted on this issue, and it is not one that governments have felt necessary to tackle. Fr Dermot Lane – until 1992, director of a third-level Catholic College of Education – points out: 'When it comes to third-level education we are faced with the extraordinary anomaly in Ireland that the Christian Churches have no theological place or educational presence in our Universities.'[11] It is indeed a strange lacuna: in the absence of publicly funded theology and/or religious studies at third level, there is very little interdisciplinary contact with serious religious questions in a country where religion has been so central and so influential. This contributes to the lack of intellectual debate on religion which has been so marked. 'How can Universities claim to be Universities and yet exclude the study of the religious dimension of human experience and its revelation in Judaism, Christianity and other faiths? These are questions that the Minister for Education . . . must begin to address.'[12] During the 1980s, when the author held the Education portfolio, it proved impossible to get clear answers from the State's legal advisers about the constitutional implications of assisting theology courses in universities or introducing Religious Studies as a mainstream subject for public examinations at second level.

Almost simultaneously with the publication of the Mac Gréil survey, showing high overall levels of church attendance in 1989, came the announcement of results of a 'qualitative' survey conducted by the Augustinian Order in twelve areas all over Ireland, involving more than 1,000 people. This was conducted a year after the Mac Gréil survey, and was published with admirable candour in 1991. Great care and preparation went into the devising of the questionnaire, which involved interviewing groups of five people at some length in centres where the Augustinians carry out pastoral work. The results, collated by Fr John Byrne, Augustinian Provincial in Ireland, were disturbing for the Church. In his commentary on the section dealing with 'Attitudes to the Church', Fr Byrne says: 'The widespread disillusionment expressed in our survey points to nothing short of a crisis in the Irish Catholic Church today.'[13] The results were not published in the form of percentages, but rather in descriptions of main trends in the results. The principal findings in attitudes to the Church were:

Many responses were dominated by anger, frustration and disillusionment with the institutional Church. Most of the respondents regarded the Church as simply buildings, hierarchy, or just another institution. The Church is perceived as having an autocratic and authoritarian style, distant, and out of touch with the experience of the people. It is narrow-minded, old-fashioned and male-dominated. It is preoccupied with rules, regulations, and rituals. Its position on divorce, contraception and sexual morality generally is out of touch with today's reality and is a source of annoyance to many people. The laity and women in particular are excluded from the life and ministry of the Church. Priests work out of a controlling model rather than a trusting model. Collections and money matters predominate. The middle class security of the clergy puts them out of touch with real life, like finance and family.[14]

When it came to personal beliefs, however, it was different: there was a strong faith in a personal God, and a personal life of prayer. The respondents were asked to put forward their proposals for the future; they asked for better education and information, voluntary (as opposed to compulsory) celibacy for religious, small basic communities, a re-examination by priests of their lifestyles, and the admission of the laity, particularly women, into collaborative ministry. The Augustinians, at their Emmaus retreat house in north Dublin, brought together representatives from all the centres covered in the survey, in February 1991, to work out their plan of action as a response to the findings. In a realistic summary of the choices facing the order (and, undoubtedly, the Irish Catholic Church as presently structured) Fr Byrne said: 'We can either adapt and flourish, or stagnate and perish.'

In February 1992, an *Irish Independent*/IMS survey showed yet again the complex process of separation of religious belief from religious behaviour: 93 per cent expressed a belief in God, while 75 per cent believed that regular Church attendance was important (that figure plummeted to 56 per cent among the under-twenty-fives).[15]

Fr Dermot Lane, former director of the Mater Dei Institute of Education in Dublin, which awards degrees to young people who study theology and other subjects in order to become teachers of religion in Irish schools, explains that there are more lay students of theology than ever before in Ireland. He speaks of the unstoppable movement of religious into small units among the poor of Ireland, and the need to involve the laity in the future ministry of the Church 'not because there will be a crisis of personnel, but because it is the right thing to do'.

The former religious principal of one of the country's biggest and most prestigious convent schools for girls confirmed to the author the wish of the nuns to live among the poor 'and help with the material needs and emotional deprivation of the people'. Looking back on the years of teaching, she regretted having spent so many years 'educating the children of the rich'. She believes that the religious orders had stunted the growth and maturity of the people inside the orders, and therefore they couldn't pass on maturity and growth to their students; she spoke of the anger of many of the older sisters at what they felt was their own oppression as young nuns when they should have been developing and maturing intellectually. She felt – and this was a frequent comment of the religious, both clerical and in orders, that I spoke to – that there would be fewer and fewer people going to Mass but that they would be the really committed, as opposed to the automatic churchgoers who never thought about religion. Her own order was expecting to have no entrant to their novitiate in 1992. Like Dermot Lane, she was optimistic about the involvement of the laity and the new social consciousness of the Church. She preferred to remain anonymous.

Nuns are among the most vocal and progressive agents for social change in Ireland today. Some activists illustrate the new trend: Sister Stanislaus Kennedy has campaigned publicly and vociferously for the poor for twenty years, and now runs Focus Point, which helps young homeless people; Sister Consilio in Co. Kildare works with alcoholics and drug-abusers; Sister Colette Dwyer has achieved major advances in education and training for the travelling population, frequently against fierce opposition from the settled community; and historian and feminist Dominican Sister Dr Margaret McCurtain has been a leader of the new Irishwomen's movement since the 1970s. Fr Joseph Dargan, Secretary-General of the Conference of Major Religious Superiors, says: 'Modern Irish nuns are trying to live out the original spirit of their founders in a much more radical way. They are much more in tune with that spirit than in years gone by. Many of them have put the institutionalized way of life behind them.'

Today, the modern Church is adapting to a new Ireland; sometimes painfully, sometimes reluctantly, the diocesan bishops and priests are finally seeing the needs which the orders identified before them. There is still a reluctance to accept the new trends towards multidenominational education, led by the Cardinal himself, a stand which seems to many to be at odds with his often-expressed and undoubtedly sincere wish for reconciliation and peace in Northern Ireland. Those courageous groups in Northern Ireland struggling to have children from the two traditions educated together have not been helped at all by intransigence from their religious leaders.

Occasional outbursts from the more conservative bishops can cause unease: Dr Jeremiah Newman, Catholic Bishop of Limerick and a volatile and frequent conservative commentator, is regularly found in their ranks. At a ceremony of confirmation in his diocese at the end of February 1992 he gave offence to a number of parents by remarks about Protestants and their apparent belief that nothing was absolutely right or wrong. His Protestant counterpart, Reverend Edward Darling, was forced to issue a statement expressing 'deep sadness'.[16]

The Catholic Archbishop of Dublin, Dr Connell, in a rare interview given two years after his appointment, surprised and offended many Irish people by his affirmation that homosexuality was a 'disorder which afflicts many people as a result of being portrayed as an acceptable lifestyle'.[17] As the Irish parliament prepared to pass legislation in June 1993 decriminalizing sexual activity between consenting adults over the age of seventeen, with little public debate or controversy, the archbishop's attitudes seemed sadly out of date.

Ecumenism has faltered; whereas in England by 1991 there were 600 local ecumenical projects, many of them involving sharing of buildings for services and other activities, there were only twenty schemes in Ireland and none of them included any property-sharing by the Catholic Church.[18] After an initial flurry of activities following the second Vatican Council, bishops, theologians and priests met and talked at Ballymascanlon near the north/south border over several years, but no major structures were put in place to involve ordinary priests, ministers, lay people or students on an ongoing and permanent basis. It is left to individual initiatives by committed people to try to break the log-jam of apathy coming from Rome.

However, signs abound of the new widening of horizons by the Catholic Church. Cardinal Daly is an indefatigable worker for peace, and no one questions his passionate sincerity when he condemns violence in Northern Ireland and urges the politicians and people towards dialogue. Indeed, in a talk given by the Cardinal (then Bishop) to the Knock Methodist congregation in Belfast on 25 March 1990, he showed an openness towards his fellow Christians which was obviously heartfelt, and seems to indicate a new frame of mind:

Whether Protestant or Catholic we profess in our Creed our belief in the 'holy Catholic Church'. The word 'Catholic' connotes a fullness, a wholeness, a comprehensiveness of vision. We Catholics are surely being summoned now to include Protestant spiritual insights in our own way of being Catholic. Protestants are being summoned to include Catholic spiritual insights in their way of being Protestant. The respective communities are being called to respect unionist feelings, interests and rights in a nationalist perspective, and nationalist feelings, interests and rights in a unionist perspective. We are being invited to rejoice as Catholics in Protestant faith and Christian witness and holiness of life, and praise God for them, and be humbly eager to learn from them. We are being invited as Protestants to rejoice in Catholic faith and Christian witness and holiness of life and praise God for them and be humbly eager to learn from them.

A few months later he was appealing at his installation as Archbishop of Armagh and Primate of All Ireland for the end of violence, specifically to Irish republicans: 'You have no sane justification, moral, rational, or political for continuing with your campaign of violence. May Christ . . . enlighten your consciences so that in his light you may, as Saint Patrick puts it, "recover your senses for God".' Cahal Daly, created Cardinal in 1991, has continued at every opportunity to repeat that message. To most observers, he seems much clearer than his predecessor, Cardinal Tomás Ó Fiach, about his total opposition to the IRA and their political wing, Sinn Féin. He is widely respected and admired by the British government, the Irish government, and constitutional Nationalists in Northern Ireland. He is disliked by the IRA, Sinn Féin, and all shades of more extreme Unionist opinion. At his installation, the country noted his great warmth and special smiles as he greeted the newly elected President of Ireland, Mary Robinson, clasping her hands in his – this feminist, liberal woman who had campaigned for years to overturn laws in Ireland which enforced Catholic moral teaching, and who had left the Irish Labour Party in 1985 because Unionists had not, in her view, been consulted about the Anglo-Irish Agreement. Another sign of increasing tolerance and understanding was the attendance of the Cardinal in St Patrick's Cathedral in Dublin in March 1992 to mark its 800th anniversary, where he made ecumenical history by preaching from its ancient pulpit. In September 1992, the Cardinal and the Church of Ireland Archbishop gave a joint interview to RTE Radio to call for further top-level talks on the Northern Ireland situation.

Catholic bishops in the Republic today have begun to speak on issues other than the narrow sexual morality which for so long seemed to obsess them. In the west of Ireland, where unemployment and emigration have their worst effects on the population, the bishops started in early 1992 to agitate publicly for government action, and successfully persuaded the EC Commission to undertake a special examination of the problems of the area. Bishops have also begun to speak out on the question of morality in business dealings, and standards of behaviour in public life, following a spate of business and political scandals which were uncovered in late 1991.

As the unemployment figures approached 300,000 – an all-time high – in late 1992, the Conference of Major Religious Superiors produced a powerful socio-economic review concentrating on unemployment, while on 8 December the Catholic Bishops' Conference issued a 100-page pastoral letter entitled *Work is the Key*. Both documents showed a deep concern about the effect on society of the poverty and despair induced by long-term joblessness.

A sign of how much the times have changed was an article which Conor Cruise O'Brien wrote in February 1992 in the *Irish Independent*, which was for so long a fervent defender and respecter of all things Catholic. Written in the February 1992 period of upheaval and deep public concern at the time of the High Court injunction preventing a pregnant fourteen-year-old girl who wished to have an abortion in England from travelling, Dr Cruise O'Brien addressed an open letter to the bishops, beginning: 'Your Lordships . . .' The bishops, in a terse statement, had welcomed the lifting of the injunction by the Supreme Court, expressing satisfaction 'that the legal issues in this case have been resolved without delay'. Cruise

O'Brien thunders: 'I have never read a statement which so happily combines absurdity, complacency, impudence, incoherence, and incongruity.' Blaming the bishops for causing the incident in the first place, he went on: 'I suggest you refrain for the future from efforts to shape the laws of this State which are for all the citizens and not just for what you call your flock. Your flock is increasingly less flock-like.' And – with a customary O'Brien flourish – he ends, 'I am, Your Lordships, with all the respect that is due from one citizen to any group of fellow-citizens, yours sincerely . . .'

Not too many people in Ireland today would approve of the tone of that article: not because it is irreverent, but because it is accepted that the Church is grappling with immense change, that its religious members are engaged in an agonizing reappraisal of its role in Irish life, that more and more religious are involved in work of great social benefit. Some religious are better than others in communicating their genuine concern, sometimes the bishops exasperate by apparent intolerance, and some groups of the devout laity involve themselves in hyperbole which must embarrass the Church. The next ten years will see a new Church emerging from the crucible of the last two decades.

Nothing that has happened to the Church in Ireland could compare with the trauma of the Bishop Casey* affair in May 1992. It will be seen as a major catalyst in changing attitudes in Ireland. As has been described earlier in this chapter, the people of Ireland have a deep, and mostly simple, attachment to Catholicism. It goes to the heart of the nation. Bishops have been revered as the Pope's lieutenants. None was more prominent, more friendly, more socially concerned, or more conservative on the main teachings of the Church than the attractive and ebullient Éamonn Casey, Bishop of Galway. He had even publicly asked for – and got – forgiveness for that traditionally acceptable Irish failing, 'taking a drop too much' (he had been arrested for it in England, while driving a car). A regular television star, where he might sing a song or tell a story or speak passionately on social injustice, he was chairman of the

*Éamonn Casey (b. 1927, Co. Limerick). Came to prominence with his work for poor Irish emigrants to Britain, in particular in setting up housing agencies. Member of many welfare agencies in Ireland, and prominent in social and academic organizations. Interested in theatre, music, film.

Church's Third World charity, Trócaire. When the Pope came to Ireland, Bishop Casey was prominently and proudly at his side.

In May 1992, Bishop Casey suddenly resigned, and left Ireland hurriedly and secretly. The *Irish Times* simultaneously announced to a stunned Ireland that he had had an affair with an American woman in 1973, and had fathered a child by her. Not only that: it emerged that he had spurned the woman as soon as the pregnancy was revealed, and had refused to acknowledge his child, treating both with apparent coldness, only sending money to the USA for their upkeep with reluctance. As Irish people reeled at these revelations, there was a further controversy about the circumstances in which substantial payments were made by the bishop to his former lover; but at the end of the day steps were taken to ensure that the diocese was at no loss.

The Irish people were shocked to the core. The Church was taken utterly by surprise, for its leaders had only had very short notice of the announcements. Reactions among senior churchmen varied from disbelief to speechlessness; real pain was evident among many, most notably the Cardinal. The reaction of the people was mixed: initially a wave of sympathy for the bishop and his colleagues, changing to anger as the distasteful details emerged. It was clear that this would have a profound effect on the whole body of the Church, and its authority. It had come just a few months after the full panoply of the State had been used against a young pregnant girl, causing an upsurge of emotion which had hardly subsided. The Church had played a central part in urging the constitutional change in 1983 which had caused this event.

May and June 1992 saw a national debate on the Church and its attitudes which showed a rapidly changing spirit among Catholics. A public-opinion poll* taken in the weeks following the Casey affair showed that 69 per cent of Catholics felt that priestly celibacy should be abandoned; 48 per cent said they would have less confidence in the Church's leadership on moral and social issues; only 25 per cent of Catholics between eighteen and twenty-four years of age would have full confidence in the Church, and 19 per cent of that age group, born into the Church, said they no longer

* Taken on 19 May 1992, by Lansdowne Market Research, and published in the *Sunday Press* on 24 May 1992.

believed in or followed Church teaching anyway. On the question of the treatment of women by the Church, 53 per cent of all Catholics felt that women were treated 'like second-class citizens', and 60 per cent felt that women should be ordained, a subject on which the Irish Catholic Church is quite obdurately negative (in contrast to the other Christian Churches in Ireland). It was clear that things would never be the same again.

It was not surprising, therefore, that the bishops refrained from their previous practice of directing people how to vote when the Maastricht referendum was held in June 1992, and later when a further referendum concerning abortion was held in November. Their statements were in considerable contrast to the kind of paternalistic directions the people had come to expect; while still making clear their outright opposition to abortion, they accepted that people had to make up their own minds, and that the questions were not as simple as they might seem. Media interviews with the hierarchy's spokespeople showed a degree of uncertainty never before witnessed, most notably during an interview between a bishop and a newspaper editor on 5 November. The bishop was unable to give a definite answer to the repeated question: should a fourteen-year-old girl who has become pregnant through rape, and who is suicidal as a result, be required by the Constitution of Ireland to have that baby?[19] During the summer of 1992, when a bill relaxing the availability of contraceptives was going through the Dáil, it was interesting that the bishops spoke only after the votes had been cast in the Dáil and Senate, and not before.

The Irish people are emerging from centuries of unquestioning loyalty to the Catholic Church to face a world full of uncertainties. Their dominant Church struggles to come to terms itself with a changing country and its changing people. One of Ireland's best-known public figures, psychiatrist and writer Anthony Clare, identifies one kind of Irish solution to the dilemma: 'Irish Catholics seem to have made their own very personal, idiosyncratic arrangements with their own, very personal, idiosyncratic God . . . it is difficult not to feel that Ireland is closer to being a Protestant nation than anyone appears to appreciate.'[20]

NOTES

1. *Profile of Religious in Ireland. Conference of Major Religious Superiors, Milltown Park, Dublin 6, 27 September 1990.*

2. Wording from Catholic Press and Information Office, 24 September 1992.

3. Máire Nic Giolla Phádraig, 'Trends in religious practice in Ireland', *Doctrine and Life*, vol. 42, January 1992.

4. J. J. Lee, *Ireland 1912–1985, Politics and Society*, Cambridge University Press, 1989.

5. John McGahern (Irish author and playwright), *Sunday Independent*, 23 December 1990.

6. Frank Byrne, *Sunday Independent*, 7 February 1991.

7. Nic Giolla Phádraig, op. cit.

8. Séamus Ó Buachalla, *Education Policy in Twentieth Century Ireland*, Wolfhound Press, 1988.

9. Statement issued by the Catholic Primary Managers' Association, reported in *The Times Educational Supplement*, 29 October 1921 (and quoted in Ó Buachalla, op. cit.).

10. Figures supplied by the Department of Education, for the year 1990–91.

11. Dermot Lane (ed.), *Religion, Education and the Constitution*, Columba Press, Dublin, 1992.

12. ibid.

13. *Irish Augustinians Today*, Easter 1991.

14. ibid.

15. *Irish Independent*, 17 February 1992.

16. *Sunday Press, Sunday Independent*, 2 March 1992.

17. *Sunday Tribune*, 14 January 1989.

18. *Irish Times*, 31 January 1991.

19. Interview between the editor of the *Sunday Tribune* and Bishop Joseph Duffy, printed in the *Sunday Tribune*, 8 November 1992.

20. Extracts from 'Some Psychological Reflections on Irish Catholicism', lecture delivered to the National Library Association on 10 December 1992.

CHAPTER 17

Education

Education 'represents a repository of the aspirations of a people with regard to their future, their view of their heritage, their definition of worthwhile and useful knowledge, and the standards which they consider appropriate in human relations.'[1] Looking at the development of the modern Irish education system, one is forced to the conclusion that in the formative years of the present-day system, during several crucial decades after the foundation of the independent Irish State, the only group in Ireland who had a clear vision of the importance of schools, colleges, and what went on in them, were the churches, in particular the Catholic Church. That vision, and its vigorous pursuance, has shaped the Irish system and gives it the character it has today.

The State did not see itself as a policy-maker in education for a long time after the foundation of the independent Ireland: the constitutional references to education make it very clear that, by 1937, the government under de Valera saw its role as only assisting parents, who were the prime educators. Article 42 summed up the thinking of the day, considered by many to have been heavily influenced by John Charles McQuaid, a Catholic cleric at Blackrock College, a friend of Éamon de Valera, who subsequently became Archbishop of Dublin. The primary educator of the child is 'the Family', with inalienable rights and duties to provide, 'according to their means, for the religious and moral, intellectual, physical and social education of their children'.* Later in the Article we find: the State 'shall endeavour to supplement, and give reasonable aid to private and corporate educational initiative . . . with due regard for the rights of parents, especially in the matter of religious and moral formation'.†

In keeping with this arm's-length philosophy, early Ministers for Education interfered minimally with the system, which was being

* Article 42.1.   † Article 42.4.

run by the religious orders financed largely from the State (but with a considerable input in management and administration from the orders which cost the State nothing); there was 'unrelenting opposition to positive State action in education'[2] and as late as 1949, the then Minister for Education, General Richard Mulcahy, declared: 'It is the function of the Minister to watch out for causes of irritation, and having found them, to go around with the oil can.' Mulcahy perceived his own role as 'a kind of dungarees man, who will take the knock out of pipes, and will link up everything'.[3] There was a determination to keep away from areas which were considered to be part of either the rights of parents or the legitimate authority of the Church. Only in the 1960s, with increasing prosperity, a new openness, and an interest in economic planning, did education become more than an administrative sinecure for ministers. Until then,

The system was one in which the State provided the bulk of the finance while owning and exercising a managerial function . . . over but a small proportion of educational institutions. With the exception of the (small) vocational sector and third level, the Exchequer funded individuals and orders to provide the educational service on its behalf.[4]

The immediate impetus for change was an OECD/Irish government-funded report in 1965, *Investment in Education*, which arose from concern about the relationship between education and a newly industrializing society. That report highlighted the social class and regional differences in educational participation rates, as well as fears that there would be a shortage of trained manpower for the expected needs of the Irish economy in the 1970s. During the years immediately following, great changes were made: new subjects were introduced (Business Organization, Accountancy, Economics, Building Construction, Engineering . . .); new types of schools (the Comprehensive and later Community models) with very broad curricula were started; third-level Regional Technical Colleges were embarked on with the help of the World Bank, and – most dramatic of all – a Minister for Education, Donough O'Malley, immortalized himself in 1967 by suddenly announcing that all children could proceed to second-level education free of charge. Numbers mushroomed overnight, putting an immense strain on school buildings and on the exchequer; education

spending rose rapidly, teacher numbers swelled, building programmes started everywhere, and Ireland arrived at a situation of
near-parity with other western European democracies in terms of
participation rates.

Education today is a central concern of Irish people and politicians: nearly a million children and young people, out of a total
population of only three and a half million, are participants in
education. And the numbers are to continue rising into the next
century, except at primary level (see table overleaf). Given that high
proportion of people in education, which is a result of Ireland's
unusual demographic composition, Ministers for Education have
had for several years the unenviable task of fighting for resources at
a Cabinet table which increasingly wants to reduce spending. The
gross education expenditure for 1992, at IR£1·598 billion, represents
6·4 per cent of GNP, but looks – and is – rather less generous in
terms of spending per capita. An OECD report in 1992[5] placed
Ireland well below the average spending per capita in a list of
countries with centralized education systems like Ireland. It showed
that Ireland spent $1,769 per student compared with Canada's
$5,337, Denmark's $4,656, and the Netherlands' $3,513.

The proportion of the Irish population that falls within the age
range of education – from three to twenty-four – is higher than in
any other similar country. Former Taoiseach Garret FitzGerald
said in November 1991: 'In the latest year for which figures are
available, 41 per cent of our population was in the three to twenty-
four age group, a full 10 percentage points higher than the average
for the rest of Europe.'[6]

Irish politicians, teacher unions, and the Industrial Development
Authority are very keen to praise the Irish education system; as a
result of this continuing paean, there is a firm national perception
that Ireland's young people are not only a match for, but better
than, their young counterparts elsewhere – 'in Ireland, it is quite
easy to be bowled over by our own rhetoric,' said an acknowledged
expert on education. The description of Ireland as the 'island of
saints and scholars' has always been very pleasing to Irish priests
and people. It is true that the Irish have adhered to a firm and solid
traditional method of education, with a history of good discipline,
which can be attributed to the domination of religious orders in the
schools. The collaboration of Church and State produced over the

Numbers of Students in Ireland, 1965, 1991, 2001			
Category	1965	1991	2001
	thousands	thousands	thousands
Primary level	505	553	421
Second level	143	332	334
Vocational training	—	15	30
Third level	21	70	100
Total	669	970	885

Source: Figures from Green Paper, Department of Education, 1992.

years a high-achievement ethos in the academic subjects like English, History, and Latin, and a middle and upper-middle class of well-motivated, highly literate, well-disciplined, conservative young people, destined largely for the professions and the civil service, and, most recently, for management and financial services employment in Ireland and abroad, after some years at a third-level college. The education debate in the Ireland of the early 1990s, sparked off by a major discussion document on education, has as one of its main topics the apparent conflict between a very academically oriented education system and the technological/entrepreneurial requirements of economic Ireland.

The evolution of education in Ireland has also seen teachers' salaries rise to a comfortable level by international criteria, meaning that the profession has generally high standards and enjoys good status in society, with an undoubtedly positive effect on the quality of Irish education. Whether this happy situation has come about from governments actually planning to give teachers more, or simply collapsing under pressure, is a moot point: the view of Dr Garret FitzGerald (who came under fierce pressure from teachers when he was Taoiseach in 1985 and 1986) may be post hoc rationalization: 'We could skimp on teachers' salaries, but we don't . . . we have been wise enough to pay our teachers relatively well, thus avoiding the danger of the lowering of morale and commitment which has affected adversely education in some other countries.'[7] The level of salaries is clear evidence of the success of the three main teachers' unions* in pursuing their central aims of improving pay and conditions of their members. A young teacher starting in the classroom in 1992, with the kind of qualifications normally presented, could expect to earn more than IR£13,000; at mid-career, taking various additional allowances into account, she could expect about IR£18,500; at top level, about IR£22,000; principals of schools could earn up to IR£30,000.[8] There will be about four months' holidays a year, with opportunities to supplement this income, as well as additional payment for supervising and correcting public examinations.

In a country with Ireland's economic problems, such financial achievements by teachers distort the figures for expenditure on education generally; only 22·2 per cent of current exchequer spending is available for all other education requirements, such as equipment, books, grants, running costs, and welfare services. New Zealand, a country comparable to Ireland in population size, spends 46·6 per cent on non-teaching costs.[9] The physical facilities in our schools and colleges are therefore much less lavish than in neighbouring countries, there is very little back-up for teachers in administrative and secretarial help, and student–teacher ratios at all levels (including – in particular – third level) are worse than in most other western European countries. Parents make a considerable contribution, particularly at third level, to the cost of education, and even in primary and 'free' second-level schools, there is constant fund-raising going on to help meet a range of expenses or provide extra facilities.

Only in the last decade have educationists really begun to question the fundamental criteria of excellence in education: has the system failed the bottom 15 per cent of young people? (The National Adult Literacy Agency asserts that between 10 and 20 per cent of young people leave school with inadequate reading and writing skills.)[10] Why is Ireland so poor in modern European languages (fewer than 4 per cent of school students can study German)?

---

*The Irish National Teachers' Organization is the largest of the three major teachers' unions, representing primary teachers; the Association of Secondary Teachers comes second, representing those in the Voluntary Secondary and Community School sector; and the Teachers' Union of Ireland represents the Vocational Community College, and RTC sector. Together they have nearly 40,000 members, an articulate and well-financed executive, and a national network which is used effectively to lobby Dáil Deputies on all contentious issues.

Time Spent at School (Second Level) in Ireland and Twelve Other Countries*		
Category	Ireland	Average time in twelve other countries
School cycle	Five years	Six years
Total time in school	864 days, 5,212 hours	1,217 days, 7,066 hours
Average time in school per year	173 days, 1,042 hours	200 days, 1,166 hours

* Denmark, England and Wales, France, the former East and West Germany, Greece, Italy, Japan, Netherlands, Poland, the former Soviet Union, and Spain.
Source: German Institute for International Educational Research, Frankfurt; printed in the *Irish Times*, 24 October 1991.

Disquieting information emerges from international comparisons: in February and March 1992, an international survey showed Ireland trailing at the middle or lower end of a table of achievements of nine- and thirteen-year-olds in mathematics and science.[11] Citizenship education as a concept is virtually ignored in Irish schools; in 1987 a government-appointed body, the Curriculum and Examinations Board,* presented a Minister for Education with a detailed syllabus for a Politics and Social Studies curriculum for senior-cycle schools. It found no favour and was not heard of again.

Uncomfortable facts are not well received in the world of education. Government and teachers' unions together try to ignore the increasing criticism of the shorter time Irish young people spend in school; a shorter secondary-school cycle and a shorter school year than the international norm have encouraged parents (finally becoming organized in Ireland) to raise this question. The emergence of the kind of figures shown in the table above, published in 1991, fuels the debate.

* The board was established on a non-statutory basis in 1984, as a preliminary to full legislative status. It included representatives from education interests, the arts, business, trade unions, and women, and was charged with renewing and reforming the curriculum and examinations system in schools. It was the first time that outside interests had been asked to contribute to education policy on an official basis. Shortly after a change of government in 1987, the board was abolished; it was replaced by a purely advisory body, the National Council for Curriculum and Assessment.

Teachers' unions have an obvious reason for preserving the status quo of unusually long holidays, and always criticize such international studies. In April 1992, the secondary teachers' union, annoyed by these data about their working conditions, published a survey compiled from the diaries of 419 of their members showing that they worked slightly more than 40 hours every week.[12] Irish governments have become wary over the years of the political dangers of grappling with the powerful teachers' bodies and have allowed the situation to become a possibly immutable norm. The early closing of schools in summer in Ireland (just at the end of May) is also bound up with the almost 100 per cent monopoly by teachers of the invigilation process of public examinations, which begin at that time, and for which they are paid on top of their salaries. Irish teachers on the whole do not enjoy good working conditions inside the classrooms, which entail higher than normal pupil–teacher ratios, poor equipment, sometimes dilapidated school buildings, and lack of secretarial and other support services.

More than 3,000 primary schools, educating children up to twelve years of age, 788 second-level schools taking them on to seventeen or eighteen years of age, and 41 third-level colleges make up the fabric of Irish education.

The primary and second-level systems are almost entirely denominational, controlled mostly by the Catholic Church in their management, with curriculum requirements laid down by the State, which also pays teachers' salaries and most of the running costs. The system is being scrutinized critically as more and more politicians and parents wonder about their lack of control. It was given a cold assessment in 1992 by a former member of the Dáil who also had been editor of an education newspaper: tracing the history of primary education in Ireland back to pre-independence days, he said: 'Its central, colonial characteristic involves the transfer of large amounts of public money into the hands of local tribal leaders who are expected, in return, to administer it in such a way that the natives do not become restless.'[13] In the primary and secondary sector, buildings are owned by the churches, despite being maintained by the State. A small and determined sector of Irish parents has established the nucleus of a multi-denominational sector within the primary-school system: there are ten such schools in existence, with a further three in the offing. Eighty-eight per cent of secondary schools are owned and controlled by the Catholic orders, a further 6 per cent by other denominations. There is a growing sector, in the second-level system, of establishments that are often on green-field sites but sometimes result from amalgamations, called Community Schools or Community Colleges. About sixty of them already exist, and more are added all the time. A wide and comprehensive curriculum is offered, under a management with, however, continuing strong Church input. The vast majority are 'schools' as opposed to 'colleges' – the latter come under the authority of the Vocational Education Committee* of the relevant area. These are unusually large schools by Irish standards, and have achieved a high reputation; their birth in the 1970s was troublesome and controversial, as the Church fought to retain control and the Vocational sector tried to assert a right to manage them. There is an uneasy peace now, while educationists speculate about whether ministers will take any more steps to try to rationalize the dichotomies of State funding without control.

The Irish child will start school at four years of age – early by international standards. Since there exists virtually no pre-school education in the country, parents feel that their children will 'miss out' unless they are involved when very young. Despite efforts over the years by government to persuade parents not to send children to school so young, or legally to dissuade them, the outright opposition of the Irish National Teachers' Organization to a later start has succeeded. In 1981, the efforts of Mr John Boland,† Minister for Education in a short-lived coalition government, were defeated by a national campaign of such virulence and efficiency that the idea was dropped. No government since has taken on the union, despite sound educational arguments that six years of primary education would be quite sufficient.

* Vocational Education Committees are subcommittees of local authorities; they were originally established to provide technical education for children unable to afford secondary schooling. Since the advent of free education, their role has become blurred, particularly since they lost control over the third-level Regional Technical Colleges.

† John Boland, Minister for Education, 1981–2; Minister for the Public Service, 1982–6; Minister for the Environment, 1986–7. Opposition front-bench spokesperson on the environment, 1987–8; lost his seat in Dáil Éireann in 1989; subsequently qualified as a barrister and became a political columnist in national newspapers.

Primary schools vary from the little stone building on the edge of the sea at Connemara in the west of Ireland with one or two teachers to the 800-pupil school in one of Dublin's or Cork's big suburban areas. Managed by the local parish priest or clergyman with the help of a board of management, or by a board of the new multi-denominational kind, the school will teach the three Rs, religion – integrated into the curriculum – the Irish language, elementary music and singing. None of the modern European languages is on the primary curriculum, though the new government of January 1993 promised to consider their introduction.

At twelve, the child proceeds to the second level – and there the choice of school will depend on class, location, expectation . . . The diversity of types of school at second level is Ireland's unsatisfactory historical legacy. From the fee-paying schools in the better-class suburbs of rolling country hills, to the struggling Vocational School in the concrete jungle of badly planned housing estates in Dublin's inner city, the variety is anomalous and a constant source of concern. Irish parents have consistently shown their preference for religious involvement in schools, while some politicians feel that there should be public control. The problems are being solved by sheer facts of demography and social change. As fewer and fewer religious personnel are available and old buildings fall out of use, while the numbers of students from twelve to eighteen begin to fall inexorably, the bright new schools with broader curricula come into their own. The boarding-schools close their doors one after the other, and the schools run by the religious reach out to a wider population than before, in the new Church climate of social concern. The young person will have a good choice of subjects, and will take six or more in the final school examination at the age of seventeen or eighteen. The most popular subjects in 1991 for the student taking the Higher papers were: Irish, English, History, French, Business Organization, Home Economics, Biology, Physics, Accounting, Mathematics, and Art.[14]

Those who drop out after reaching the compulsory school minimum attendance age of fifteen are fewer and fewer, though they still amount to 18 per cent. They may be picked up by FÁS, the State training agency, but they are the largest single group in the unemployment statistics year after year. The Minister for Finance, grappling with the rapidly escalating unemployment figures of 1992, suggested that the State should give consideration to extending the school-leaving age to eighteen or nineteen rather than sixteen which is the present policy; he pointed out that 45 per cent of those who are long-term unemployed left school at or below fifteen years of age.[15]

After many years of gestation, starting with the work of the Curriculum, and Examinations Board in 1984, a new Junior Cycle curriculum which is flexible and modular in character, offering a mix of academic and technical subjects, is in place in schools for the youngster aged between twelve and fifteen. It was introduced nationally in 1992. It is hoped that it will have relevance and attraction for all young people, and will serve as part of a drive to keep students in the schools after the legal school-leaving age.

Despite some grave inequities in access to education, Ireland does not have the kind of rigid, class-based public-school system which is still found in Britain. A table of the kind of second-level school attended by some powerful Irish political, professional, legal, media and business leaders shows a strong bias in favour of the single-sex Catholic religious-run school, but not overwhelmingly by those in the upper socio-economic group. All of the people on the list were educated before free second-level education was available, and therefore before the coeducational, broadly based Community Schools and colleges had become available across the country. The Christian Brothers and the Jesuits played a dominant role in educating future leaders.

THE THIRD-LEVEL EDUCATION ESTABLISHMENT

The third-level system includes seven universities, fourteen technologically oriented institutes, and seven colleges for the training of teachers. The universities are almost entirely autonomous in their management, excluding the considerable financial influence wielded by the State, which pays the piper more and more reluctantly. The Technological Institutes (the Regional Technical Colleges and the colleges of the Dublin Institute of Technology) were until 1992 subject to the politically controlled Vocational Education Committees of the relevant local authorities, though funded by the State. The Colleges of Education are increasingly under threat of amalgamation or closure as the demographic

Schools Attended by Some Top Irish Personalities	
Name and position	School
Mary Robinson, President of Ireland	Sacred Heart Convent, Mount Anville
Albert Reynolds, Taoiseach	Summerhill College, Sligo
Maurice Doyle, Governor, the Central Bank	O'Connell Schools, Dublin
Michael Smurfit, Chairman, Smurfit Group	Clongowes Wood College
A. J. F. O'Reilly, Chairman and Chief Executive, Heinz	Belvedere College
Tony Ryan, Chairman, Guinness Peat Aviation	Christian Brothers' School, Thurles, Co. Tipperary
Thomas Finlay, the Chief Justice	Clongowes Wood College
Martin Naughton, Chairman, Glen Dimplex	De La Salle College, Dundalk
Liam Hamilton, President, the High Court	Christian Brothers' School Mitchelstown, Co. Cork
Gay Byrne, host, the *Gay Byrne Show* and *The Late Late Show*	Christian Brothers' School, Synge Street, Dublin
John Bruton, Leader of the Opposition, Dáil Éireann	Clongowes Wood College
Dick Spring, Tánaiste and Leader of the Labour Party	Mount St Joseph's, Roscrea
Peter Sutherland, Director-General, GATT	Gonzaga College, Dublin
Alan Gillis, President, Irish Farmers' Association	High School, Dublin
Larry Goodman, Chairman, the Goodman Group	Marist College, Dundalk

changes of recent years work their way through the system; since they are denominationally controlled, and have produced generations of articulate and powerful members of teachers' unions, any government moves to rationalize them quickly become *causes célèbres*. The backlash against closure of one of the colleges (half-empty like some others) in 1986 was enough to be a major factor in a government reshuffle, removing the Minister for Education who had had to take on the job.*

The doyen of Irish universities is Dublin University, with its sole constituent college, Trinity. Established 400 years ago by Queen Elizabeth I of England, it occupies a large site in the middle of Dublin city, its walls and halls mellowed by the years. Not the biggest of Ireland's colleges, with 9,400 students (including postgraduates), it is finding it hard to cope with the demand for student places. Trinity College is the most popular first choice for students who file their applications with the university admissions Central Applications Office: 8,280 in 1991. Trinity College is also the best-known internationally of Ireland's universities, because of its age, its connections with the British establishment for so many centuries, and because of its consistently high academic standards. In celebrating its 400th birthday in March 1992, Trinity College conferred an honorary degree on the President of Ireland, Mary Robinson, who is not only a distinguished graduate and former professor at the college, but represented Trinity graduates in Ireland's Senate for many years. She could be said to embody all that Trinity holds dear: a liberal, independent thinker who also involved herself in the public life of the country. Her Catholic religion is a mark of the new Trinity College too, while the election of the first Catholic Provost of the University in 1991, Dr Thomas Mitchell,† emphasizes the new character of the place. Trinity College has attracted funds from other sources in recent times, most notably from the establishment of the O'Reilly Institute, heavily endowed by Tony O'Reilly, in memory of his parents.

* The coalition government announced in 1986 that Carysfort College of Education in Dublin would have to close. The Mercy Order of nuns, who ran the college with State funds, mounted a national campaign against the closure; this, combined with an already tense situation between the minister of the day (the author) and the teachers' unions over a pay dispute, was a precipitating factor in the removal of the minister to a different portfolio. Despite promises, the following government did not reopen the college, which was sold eventually to University College, Dublin.

† Dr Thomas Mitchell (b. 1939). Educated at University College, Galway, and at Cornell University, New York. His speciality is Latin of which he was the professor in Trinity College from 1979 to 1991.

The National University of Ireland encompasses several colleges; despite their linkage under the 'national' title, they are in reality separate institutions, and may well establish this *de jure* as well as *de facto* in the near future. Founded in 1908, when Trinity College was considered by the Catholic hierarchy to be only suitable for Protestants, the National University today is indistinguishable in the type of student intake from the other big university in the capital city. University College, Dublin, on a large and spreading campus, south of Dublin city, called Belfield, is the largest of the constituent colleges, with 13,000 students. Its president is Dr Patrick Masterson,* a former lecturer and professor of ethics and philosophy; elected in 1986, he has undertaken an American-style fund-raising task at home and abroad, establishing alumni associations, and has taken to the work of university administration with an ease and flair not foreseen when he took office.

Cork city and Galway city, as well as Maynooth, Co. Kildare, are the sites of the other National University constituent colleges. In Co. Kildare, St Patrick's College, Maynooth, has grown out of the original Catholic seminary, which still operates on the same campus. Yet another symbol of the complex intertwining of Church and State in Ireland, the college at Maynooth, while enjoying the status of a university, has unclear lines of responsibility and authority when it comes to staff appointments. Progress towards giving each of the constituent colleges of the National University autonomy, with new governing structures, has been held up at least partly because of the delicacy of working out where Church authority begins and ends at St Patrick's College.

The newest of the universities, at Limerick (Limerick University) and Dublin (Dublin City University, to the north of the city), were given their university status in 1989. Having started out as 'National Institutes of Higher Education' they tired of trying to explain their precise standing to their international contacts. With an emphasis on technology, in particular new information technologies, as well as skills like marketing and languages, with strong European links,

---

*Dr Patrick Masterson (b. 1936). Has a background of studies at Louvain, Belgium, and University College, Dublin, in the field of ethics and philosophy. Elected registrar of UCD in 1983, and president in 1986. In 1993, he announced that he had accepted the post of head of the European University at Florence in Italy and would take up the new post in 1994.

they are quickly becoming sought-after centres of study. The agitation for the coveted university name was led by the president of the University of Limerick, Dr Edward Walsh,* who is considered to be an exceptionally achievement-oriented figure, of unlimited energy and great talent, with views on performance in education which are the bane of trade unions, and with a record of setting high standards for students and lecturers in his own university. He is a new kind of university president for Ireland.

Twelve Regional Technical Colleges (RTCs), the Dublin Institute of Technology, colleges of art, colleges of catering, two law schools, a privately funded medical school (the Royal College of Surgeons) and a plethora of private business schools as well as private 'cramming' institutions endeavour to meet the demands of a young population facing Ireland's difficult job market or preparing for emigration: 70,000 students attend third-level colleges in Ireland, a number that will grow for several years more.

Third-level education in Ireland is an expensive business, both for the taxpayer and for the students. Fees vary enormously: from IR£1,307 per year for Arts or Commerce at University College, Dublin, to IR£2,256 for a student of medicine at University College, Cork.† Fees will continue to rise as the State takes steps to generate more income from fees from the universities, and proceeds towards a new system of unit-cost funding. Outside the university sector, most Irish students attending the Regional Technical Colleges pay no fees, and will get a maintenance grant, courtesy of the European Community Social Fund, which makes a distinction between education and training for grant purposes, a distinction that has increasingly baffled educators. There is a grants system in operation by the State to assist students at universities; the means test is severe, and is a contributing factor to the persistent problem of very low take-up by lower socio-economic groups of university places. The table opposite shows the discrepancies (the latest figures available from the Higher Education Authority are for the entry year 1989).

---

* Dr Edward Walsh (b. 1939) has a background of Irish, US and UK engineering studies, academic life, and work in the engineering and energy fields. A member of innumerable international and Irish organizations and a proficient violin and piano player who paints, sails, rides horses, and skis.

† 1991/2 figures.[16]

Socio-Economic Background of Students Entering University				
Year	Semi-skilled	Unskilled	Higher professions	Employers/ Managers
1989/90	119	41	1,492	1,631

Source: The Higher Education Authority.

Sociologist Dr Eileen Kane, commenting on the self-perpetuating cycle of privilege by the higher socio-economic groups who 'know their way around the system,' says of the Irish university education system and its class bias:

... getting through by using a combination of brains, luck, money, strategies and networks, is a preparation for life later on in the upper reaches of society. Those who fail this test fail the 'life test' as well. Maybe this is what we learn in school. The saddest thing of all is that the poor think it's just brains.[17]

In the Trinity College, Dublin, first-year intake in 1990, three students out of the 1,600 admitted were from the lowest socio-economic group. The new Provost of the college, Dr Mitchell, describes this as 'horrific and unacceptable':[18] the college has set up a special outreach programme to identify and nurture young people in disadvantaged areas, starting with six schools initially. The programme is planned to involve other universities and a much wider catchment area.

THE POINTS RACE

Because of the increasing pressure on places at third level in Ireland as the numbers leaving school grew dramatically in the 1980s and early 1990s, there is a fierce competition to do well in the qualifying examinations at the end of school years, in the Leaving Certificate.

The system, devised to make sure that entry to the various faculties is open and on a strictly fair and unbiased basis, is known in Ireland as 'the points system'. Students try to obtain as high a grade as possible, because an 'A + ' will be worth more than a 'B' and so on. A Central Applications Office takes lists of choices from students early each year, based on first preferences of the students, and their own assessment of how they might perform. Such are the complications of the system, and the possible combinations of choices and new levels of points for entry, that a whole information industry in Irish newspapers has grown up around it. Led by Christina Murphy of the *Irish Times*, an acknowledged expert on all things educational, but in particular the Irish media 'guru' on the points race, she interprets and advises parents and students with indefatigable energy, both in writing and on a free phone service. Just after the announcement of the Leaving Certificate results in August, the Central Applications Office publishes its first list of 'offers' in the main newspapers: in 1991, it had 48,000 numbers on its list.

The number of points needed is very high for entry to, for example, the medical schools, the school of veterinary medicine, architecture, all areas where the cost to the State is very high, and the number of places has been strictly controlled. In 1991, Christina Murphy hoped that a trend of levelling-out of points requirements which she noticed among the colleges was an indication that 'the worst excesses of the points system are over'.[19] The colleges have been making great efforts to increase the number of places in recent years for faculties like Arts, Commerce, and Business Studies, with a resulting brake on the escalation of points requirements.

For years, the influence of this heavy pressure to get the right points in the right subjects has been felt right down throughout the years spent at second-level schools. Irrespective of whether or not a young person wanted to go to third level, the whole thrust of studies and subjects in schools was determined by the Leaving Certificate imperative. Despite continual criticism of those harmful distorting effects of the points system,* nothing better has been found to measure the performance of students. As the pressure of numbers eases in the coming years, curriculum and assessment reform may re-emerge as possibilities. Many educationists worry that the strong tendency to 'cram' for maximum points has caused damage to the process of education itself, and stunts the develop-

---

* In a survey of Irish parents carried out by Irish Marketing Surveys for the *Irish Independent* in August 1991, 54 per cent disapproved of the points system.

ment of intellectual maturity and wider mental skills: university entrants may find themselves unable to cope with a new learning environment because of the previously passive learning process.

Ireland stands at a crossroads in the education world. Population trends will see some alleviation of education pressures on the exchequer in the coming decade; the heavy Church influence will considerably lessen, almost to disappearance, as religious personnel leave the classrooms; the commitment in the Maastricht Treaty of 1991 to 'the development of quality education' should have a salutary influence on the hitherto rather inward-looking Irish system, the growing power and influence of parents as contributors to policy should balance the power of the teacher unions, and the shift of emphasis by the Church to working for social justice should help to push governments towards giving more money for the educationally disadvantaged. The educational achievements of the country have been considerable despite severe economic constraints; if those financial pressures ease, the future should be very bright.

Two events will shape the education policy of Ireland in the coming years: a government Green Paper, *Education for a Changing World*, was issued in June 1992, and a new government took office in January 1993.

The Green Paper had a long gestation and, owing to political changes at the top, it came through the hands of three Fianna Fáil ministers. Its purpose was to set the basis for a nationwide debate and lay the groundwork for a White Paper to be followed by the country's first Education Bill to underpin the entire organization of the system. The minister* introduced it thus: 'At key times there is a need to take a fundamental look at the education system, and redirect it to reflect new needs as they emerge. Such a moment is now.'[20] It was a substantial document. Containing no great revolution in thinking, nor presaging really major changes in direction, it nevertheless approached several topical issues: it touched on the need for more community control of education (alarming the Churches), the possible separation of religion from other subjects at primary level (exciting further clerical concern) and suggested much

---

*Séamus Brennan (b. 1948), appointed Minister for Education in February 1992, having previously held the Ministry for Tourism and Transport since July 1989.

greater equity in access to education. Where it touched some nerves was in a constant repetition of the need for more technology and enterprise in the education system. Among the chorus of critics were Garret FitzGerald ('do the authors of the paper see the student of the future as an embryonic "economic man" rather than an actively participating member of society in the twenty-first century?')[21] and Michael D. Higgins of the Labour Party who condemned 'this new version of education that denied creativity'.[22] Since the much-praised Culliton report on industry of January 1992 had emphasized the need for technology and enterprise to be made central to the education system, and the sponsoring minister was a well-known supporter of industry, it was hardly surprising that this element should have appeared in the Green Paper. It was depressing, however, that the arts and culture were not mentioned, and strange that they were not seen as promoting that creative thinking which is surely the basis of entrepreneurship. However, while the debate on the Green Paper was just getting into its stride, and the education world was flexing its muscles for controversy and confrontation, a general election befell the country in November.

Before the new coalition between the Labour and Fianna Fáil parties took office on 12 January 1993, the two parties had hammered out a programme for government after the results came in at the end of November. It was published early in the new year of 1993. Heavy emphasis on the word 'democratic' bore the stamp of Labour's input to the section on education, as well as 'openness'; these are usually considered Labour's code-words for lessening Church control of the system. Culture was back, but there was no mention of entrepreneurs; political and social awareness would form part of the curriculum, with particular attention paid to sex equity ... and despite their earlier condemnation of the Green Paper in the heat of an election campaign, Labour agreed that there would be an 'open and democratic' debate on it, followed by a White Paper and legislation. Improvements in pupil–teacher ratios and agreement on help to the disadvantaged at every level of education were themes running through the document. Third-level students and their parents were encouraged by an undertaking that new European Structural Funds would be used to widen access to universities and colleges.

Any education system, by its very nature, is slow to change

direction. Changes take considerable time to work their way through government and parliament, to gain agreement and cooperation from powerful interest groups, before they finally impinge on the child or young person in the classroom. The debate and promises of early 1993 in Ireland were not expected therefore to cause great waves or upheavals in the short term: but they certainly had potential for considerable transformation of a system badly in need of change.

NOTES

1. D. E. Mulcahy and Denis O'Sullivan (eds.), *Irish Educational Policy, Process and Substance,* Institute of Public Administration, 1989.
2. Preface by Patrick Lynch in S. Ó Buachalla, *Education Policy in Twentieth Century Ireland,* Wolfhound Press, 1988.
3. ibid.
4. R. Breen, D. Hannon, D. Rottman, and C. Whelan, *Understanding Contemporary Ireland*, Gill & Macmillan, 1991.
5. *Education at a Glance*, Paris, Organization for Economic Cooperation and Development, 1992.
6. *Irish Times*, 23 November 1991.
7. ibid.
8. Figures from Department of Education, 1992.
9. David Alvey, *Irish Education: The Case for Secular Reform*, Church and State Books, 1991.
10. *Irish Times*, 17 January 1990.
11. 'Second International Assessment of Educational Progress (IAEP)', *Irish Independent*, 14 February 1992; *Independent* (UK), 14 March 1992.
12. *Irish Times*, 5 April 1992.
13. John Horgan, *Irish Times*, 3 July 1992.
14. Department of Education statistics 1992.
15. *Irish Independent*, 25 July 1992.
16. *Irish Times*, 30 January 1992.
17. Eileen Kane, 'Who Doesn't Go to College?' Paper presented to a study day of the Higher Education Authority, Athlone, Ireland, 8 June 1989.
18. In conversation with the author, 8 March 1992.
19. *Irish Times*, 24 August 1991.

20. *Education for a Changing World* (Green Paper), Department of Education, June 1992.
21. Article in *Decision Maker* magazine, September 1992.
22. Lecture for RTE Radio's *The Open Mind*, November 1992.

CHAPTER 18

Women and Life in Ireland

The Irish Constitution is officially issued in a small volume, *Bunreacht na hÉireann* (Constitution of Ireland), in which the fifty Articles governing the country's life are to be found. Consulting the index for what it says about women, this is the entry:

WOMEN: See FAMILY, SEX.

In 1943, six years after the Constitution was passed by Dáil Éireann, its architect, Éamon de Valera, explained his vision of Ireland in a famous St Patrick's Day broadcast to the Irish people, which has become part of the consciousness of everyone in Ireland: its most-often-quoted paragraph is:

That Ireland which we dreamed of would be the home of a people who valued material wealth only as a basis of right living, of a people who were satisfied with frugal comfort and devoted their leisure to the things of the spirit; a land whose countryside would be bright with cosy homesteads, whose fields and villages would be joyous with sounds of industry, the romping of sturdy children, the contests of athletic youths, the laughter of happy maidens; whose firesides would be the forums of the wisdom of serene old age.[1]

It was an idyllic vision, which perhaps has never been true, of Ireland or anywhere else. Irish women, happy maidens or not, rarely enjoyed idyllic times in their newly independent State after 1922. After a brief and sparkling public participation in the exciting revolutionary period 1916–22, Irishwomen – like many of their sisters in other post-revolutionary societies – retreated into a private, secondary, limited role, which was underpinned by Church and State for several decades. A modern historian, who is also a nun and a feminist, describes what happened after 1922: 'Around Irishwomen, as in a cage, were set the structures of family life, and women were assigned a home-based, full-time role as housewives, whose talents and energies were devoted to looking after husband

and children.'² When the Constitution that remains in place today came to be written in 1936–7, it naturally contained the attitudes towards women which were the norm for the times, although, as we see later, it has been employed by Irishwomen in modern times in legal strategies to get some rights which were hardly foreseen by its authors.

A Dáil motion of 1925 prohibited divorce; a law of 1927 virtually excluded women from jury service; censorship of films and books (by all-male censors) stifled any expressions of sexual freedom ('advocating the unnatural prevention of conception' was one of the grounds for banning books); in 1935 the sale, advertising or importation of contraceptives was outlawed; and the fears of sexual licence by both Church and State were exemplified by a 1927 bishops' pastoral condemning modern dancing and immodest fashions in female dress as twin evils, while district justices were given powers to restrict and regulate local dances. A ban on recruitment of married women to the public service was put in place under the Civil Service Regulation Act of 1925, and the few women who were employed were paid less than both married and single men. It goes without saying that there was no question of abortion in Ireland; so far was it from anyone's thoughts, that it was never even considered necessary to include a prohibition in the Constitution after 1921. There was simply no discussion of the subject.

By 1937 it was no wonder that a few brave female souls were very concerned about what Mr de Valera might do in his new Constitution, now that he was firmly in political control of the country. But the Taoiseach refused to meet the Joint Committee of Women's Societies, and went on planning his *magnum opus* with the advice of a prominent Catholic cleric, later to become Catholic Archbishop of Dublin, Dr John Charles McQuaid. No woman took part in the deliberations during the writing of the Constitution, and no meaningful contribution was made by the three Fianna Fáil women in the Dáil (who became known as the 'Silent Sisters') when it came to the debate. When he belatedly met the women's group, a sample of the general attitude towards women appeared in the major Sunday newspaper of the day: 'Many men (including, it is whispered, the President) think that a woman cuts a more fitting and more useful figure when darning the rents in her husband's socks by the fireside than she could hope to cut in a Parliamentary assembly.'[3]

There is an article of the Constitution which more than any other attracted the anger and disquiet of the few women activists of the day. It is Article 41: 'In particular, the State recognizes that by her life within the home, woman gives to the State a support without which the common good cannot be achieved' and 'The State shall, therefore, endeavour to ensure that mothers shall not be obliged by economic necessity to engage in labour to the neglect of their duties in the home.'* This was, and is, considered paternalistic, patronizing, and limiting. Moreover, Irishwomen have noted that no attention was paid for nearly forty years to giving women in the home legal or financial support, which would at least show some sincerity on the part of the State. It is interesting that no constitutional case has been taken on behalf of women trying to establish exactly how far that Article obliges the State to go. As we shall see later, women were to discover in 1992 that the Article was not useful in any way to help them in or outside the home.

There are, however, no less than six Articles in the Constitution which could be read, if interpreted in a certain way, as giving women real equality. They deal with citizenship, voting, equality before the law, personal rights of the individual, including property rights, protection of marriage, and the right to an adequate means of livelihood. Indeed, as Dr Yvonne Scannell, barrister and legal academic, says: 'One might be forgiven for concluding that women in Ireland enjoy an enviable position in comparison with their sisters in other jurisdictions which do not have written constitutions.'[4] But written constitutions are exactly that: pieces of paper. The citizen depends on two things happening in order to translate possibility into reality: first that the Articles in the Constitution are tested in order to vindicate rights, and second that the interpretations themselves are favourable. Until relatively recently, neither event happened in Ireland. When it did start to happen for women in the late 1960s and 1970s, a young female barrister-cum-Senator, Mary Robinson, played a leading role in the legal processes.

Article 40.1 of the Constitution reads: 'All citizens, as human persons, shall be held equal before the law. This shall not be held

---

* Section 2, subsections 1 and 2.

to mean that the State shall not in its enactments have due regard
to differences of capacity, physical and moral, and of social function.' This Article could have been used by the constitutional courts
to ensure full equality, and to outlaw any kind of sex discrimination,
but it was not. For the most part, Irish judges of the constitutional
courts (entirely male until the late 1980s) have confined themselves
to narrow interpretations of particular articles to deal with specific
cases. For example, in a case called *Murtagh Properties* v. *Cleary*
(1972), Mr Justice Kenny, while allowing that women had a right
to an adequate means of livelihood under Article 45, was careful to
limit that right by opining that differences in salary on the ground
of sex would not be unconstitutional. Dr Scannell: 'Thus the door
was virtually closed on possibilities of achieving equal pay for
equal work by constitutional means.'[5]

For almost thirty years after the Constitution was adopted, the
position of women in Irish society hardly changed at all. The litany
of deprivation is long and almost incredible today. Laws based on
the premise that women's rights were inferior to those of men
stayed on the statute books. Women were kept in the home by
various means, including the outlawing of contraception. There
was no legal aid for women in crisis marriages. No financial help
was given to single mothers, deserted wives, or prisoners' wives –
even when they were fulfilling their 'duties in the home'. It was
virtually impossible for the battered wife to get her husband out of
the home, while if she fled, her husband had a right to damages
from anyone who enticed her away, harboured her, or committed
adultery with her (she was considered his property).* Women with
real crisis pregnancies died, suffered mental and physical ill-health,
were ostracized from society, or resorted to the dangerous and
criminal activity of backstreet abortions, until the knowledge spread
that abortion had become both safe and legal 'across the water' in
England. The traffic of furtive and secret journeys started, growing
every year.

Until 1965 a wife could be disinherited totally by her husband.
Women were not entitled to unemployment assistance. The social-
welfare system treated women only as dependants of males, even

---

*Even in early 1993, a woman cannot get a barring order against a violent
common-law husband: she must be married to him.

giving children's allowances to the father and not the mother. It was hardly surprising that the women who made it into national politics were only a handful in number, and almost entirely well-connected widows or relatives of deceased well-known male politicians, and that women were almost totally absent from positions of power or status in either the professions or the trade unions. Such women's groups as there were concentrated on women's roles as consumers or farm spouses, with only a slow awakening by very few to the many wrongs affecting every aspect of women's lives. Trade unions did little to work against the kind of conditions that male workers would have found intolerable.

Most Irishwomen accepted the situation passively, naturally influenced by the powerful messages coming from the Irish Catholic church, in their schools and Sunday Masses. The ideal was Mary, the pure, silent mother of Jesus. Girls in middle-class convent schools were taught that the highest role for women to aspire to was the religious life; the second was matrimony and the bearing of children; and the third (very inferior) was the single state in the world of work.

Sexual taboos lurked around every corner in these very enclosed schools, naturally leading to high sexual tensions. Edna O'Brien, a convent-school product from the west of Ireland, who shocked her native country with her celebrated frank accounts of sexual adventures of young girls in Ireland in the 1950s and 1960s, describes her own reactions as a young girl in a convent school; one evening, just after reading about the iniquities of gymnastics, sun-bathing, and paintings of the nude:

I read it despite myself, then continued up to bed with legs sealed, hands clenched, armpits so close that not even a little flea could crawl in there. The same routine – shoes off outside the dormitory door, strategic undressing under the shelter of one's dressing-gown, and under the same awning washing in a basin of cold water, getting into one's nightgown, and uttering further night prayers.[6]

If careers were considered at all (to fill in the years before marriage) the teaching, secretarial and nursing professions led the field: to this day, Irish nurses are sought after across the world for their high standards and caring natures. For poor women, domestic service or labour in bad conditions for low wages were the only options.

Three things changed Irish women's lives as the 1970s dawned: first, the gradual appreciation of legal means as a way to wrest basic rights from a passive, if not hostile, legislature. 'People began to seek redress in the courts for grievances that the Oireachtas had chosen to ignore.'[7] Second, the birth of the modern Irishwomen's movement as part of the worldwide awakening of women. And third, like the knight on a white charger, the European Economic Community stepped in and forced Irish employers and trade unions to begin treating women workers as equals. There was resistance by Church and/or State to some or all of these developments, but by then a lively and increasingly skilful and demanding women's movement was in no mood to take 'no' for an answer.

A watershed in the unstoppable progress of women out of the darkness of the middle decades of this century was the report of the Commission on the Status of Women in December 1972. This commission was established by a Fianna Fáil Taoiseach in 1970, as a result of determined lobbying by the hitherto relatively mild women's movement – by 1970 iron had entered their souls. Its chairperson was the only woman at the top level of the civil service, Dr Thekla Beere.* Now, at last, the facts of discrimination were laid bare for all to see: forty-nine recommendations formed the nucleus around which women lobbied politicians. The degree of interest in women's progress when it came to political power-games was, however, made clear when a new Taoiseach, Liam Cosgrave of Fine Gael, appointed only men to the Senate in April 1973, in a breathtakingly direct rejection of the whole thrust of the commission's report, and a harbinger of the struggle ahead.

In some ways, though, the government did set about implementing reforms, although it was shocked by the Equal Pay directive of 1975 from Brussels and tried to block it. Progress was made in some parts of family law, and in giving some support to single

---

*Thekla Beere (1902–91) was a rare phenomenon in the Ireland of her day. A member of the Church of Ireland, she was a brilliant scholar at home and abroad, being an early woman graduate of the Trinity College, Dublin, political science and law school, and continuing at Berkeley and Harvard – all achieved through scholarships as she had little money. She entered the civil service and eventually became Secretary of the Department of Transport and Power. She never married (she would have had to leave if she had), and was never paid equally with her male colleagues, and was the first, and by 1992, still the only woman ever to achieve that rank.

parents. Street demonstrations became a feature of women's new assertiveness, and a celebrated landmark incident epitomized the anger of women: on 22 May 1971, forty-seven Dublin feminists – members of Irish Women's Liberation – took a train to Belfast, purchased contraceptives, and flaunted them in the face of embarrassed Gardaí on their return to Dublin. General disapproval was expressed, from men and women, but this went side by side with widespread, silent, shocked glee. It was nine more years before contraception became legal, and then only for married couples. But Irish newspapers caught the changing mood, and in women's pages which featured as much consciousness-raising feminist material as recipes and home-making, women journalists helped to hurry change along. In that same spring of 1971, Senator Mary Robinson introduced her first private members' bill on contraception in Seanad Éireann, which was soundly defeated.

Women ran into blank walls of government indifference when it came to most areas requiring State expenditure, such as equalizing social-welfare entitlements or abolishing taxation inequities, and the forces of conservatism resisted strongly any attempts to introduce contraception, maternity leave, or the provision of crèches. In the early 1970s, when a Minister for Finance introduced the first system of financial support for unmarried mothers and their babies, it was whispered about as 'the whore's budget'.

In the face of women's growing demands in the sexual liberation area, in 1981 anti-abortion groups persuaded politicians (at a time of fierce political activity and competition) to insert an anti-abortion clause in the Constitution. Garret FitzGerald, too late, tried to undo the finality of the constitutional amendment by wording it so that the issue would be left in the hands of the legislature. He failed in this, and after a divisive and bitter public campaign, Fianna Fáil succeeded in having their wording placed in their founder's Constitution, as Article 40.3.3: 'The State acknowledges the right to life of the unborn, and with due regard to the equal right to life of the mother, guarantees in its laws to respect, and as far as is practicable, by its laws to defend and vindicate that right.' This Eighth Amendment was passed on 7 September 1983, by 841,233 votes to 416,136: a percentage poll of only 53.7 per cent. In view of the huge campaign by the Church in favour of the amendment, the low poll and relatively high number of 'no' votes was significant. However, the country had (it thought) reaffirmed the illegality of abortion within Ireland, but Irishwomen continued to take the boat and aeroplane to England, in even greater numbers. English agencies continually confirm that up to 4,000 Irishwomen a year were having abortions in England, and this did not take into account those women who gave addresses of relatives living in England.

It needed Europe to bring the Irish government into line on women at work – on equal pay, equal opportunities, and maternity leave. And, right up to the debate on the Maastricht Treaty on European Union, women in Ireland appreciate how much Europe has done for them. In October 1992, a further maternity directive was signed in Luxembourg, confirming leave and maternity benefits for working women; Ireland, however, shares with Britain and Luxembourg the distinction of having the poorest conditions in terms of leave and compensation for pregnant and child-bearing working women.

More than twenty years of a combination of legal actions, unremitting political pressure by the women's movement, and European directives have changed women's position in Ireland immensely. Gone are the legal discriminations against married women workers, gone is the fear of being thrown out of house and home at a male whim, gone are the grossly insensitive laws on rape* which frightened and humiliated women in courtrooms all over again. Irishwomen in the early 1990s have increasing access to contraception;† they can get protection against violent husbands speedily; they have rights to equal pay and equal opportunity at work (although the theory is superior to the reality, as we shall see) and they have statutory maternity leave courtesy of the EC – though not accompanied by any attempt at the provision of child care for ordinary working women (in 1992, the whole civil service had one crèche for its workers). One of the most significant

*The author introduced the first legislation on rape in Ireland, by a private member's bill in the Senate in 1978. It was defeated by the government but led to further legislation by government within a short time.

†In October 1992, the US Population Crisis Centre in Washington published a report ranking Ireland lowest among the world's developed countries in access to contraception. Ireland's score (40 points out of a possible 100) reflected the lack of abortion: abortion has never been considered in Ireland as having anything to do with contraception.

changes in those decades was the fall in family size. Between 1960 and 1990, the average completed family size fell from about five to little more than two; it marked the fastest recorded rate of decline in average family size in western Europe or North America in this period. When the pill and the contraceptive finally came to Ireland, they fell on fertile ground, so to speak. Ireland, having been slow to begin the process of catching up with what had happened a genera-tion earlier in other industrialized countries, crowded a lot of change into a short time. The network of laws against women, their inability to control their fertility, and legal obstacles to their participation in the full life of the country have undergone dramatic and far-reaching change.

Agencies, supported to some extent by the State, work full-time for the improvement of women's position. The Employment Equal-ity Agency (EEA)* was set up in 1977 under the European-inspired Employment Equality Act; its function is to monitor the workings of the Act and to promote continually the implementation of full equality at work, with some legal enforcement rights in both employment practices and advertisements. But things are slow to change: and the EEA complains that the legislation needs to be strengthened and widened in order to make real progress in a situation where Irishwomen in 1992 still earned less than 70 per cent of male earnings, fifteen years after the Act. Governments continually promise new and more comprehensive legislation. The EEA's grant from government in 1992 was IR£404,000. There is increasing pressure to widen the scope of the agency, and to broaden its terms of reference to a full-scale Equality Commission.

The Council for the Status of Women (CSW)† grew out of the

* The chief executive of the agency until 1992, who was also its first chairperson from 1977 to 1987, was Sylvia Meehan (b. 1929). A former second-level school vice-principal, she was one of the most indefatigable and effective agitators for women's rights during the 1970s and 1980s. She was the first female Gold Medallist in the Literary and Historical (debating) Society of UCD. In 1993, the former chief executive of the non-governmental agency, the Council for the Status of Women, Carmel Foley, succeeded Ms Meehan.

† Its chairwoman during the important years 1988–92 was Frances FitzGerald (b. 1950), a former social worker whose combined skills of communication and expertise in many areas made her a household name. She was elected to Dáil Éireann in November 1992 for Fine Gael. Her successor was Anne Taylor from Clonmel, Co. Tipperary (b. 1948), the former vice-chair.

original ad-hoc committee of women's organizations of the late 1960s which had lobbied for the setting up of the first Commission on the Status of Women. When that commission reported in December 1972, the women came together again to form a permanent representative body of women's organizations. Its history has been chequered (largely because of the awkward logistics of its unwieldy size and initially tortuous procedures), but by the 1990s it had established itself as an effective national pressure group. In 1992, despite the difficulties of getting consensus from its eighty-two different member organizations, the council gained strength and much improved credibility for its leaders' articulate and insistent criticism of government and law during and after the crisis of the X case concerning the fourteen-year-old suicidal alleged rape victim who wanted to travel to England for an abortion. It was assiduously courted by government during the referendum campaign on the Maastricht Treaty later in 1992, and reluctantly advised Irishwomen to vote 'yes', having got some promises from government about forthcoming clarifications on the abortion issue. In 1991 and 1992, its grant from government was IR£114,000.

Another officially organized women's body is a parliamentary committee, made up of Dáil Deputies as well as Senators: the Joint Oireachtas Committee on Women's Rights.* It holds public hearings, taking evidence from witnesses, carries out research and issues reports. Unfortunately, like most of the Irish parliamentary committees, its work is hampered both by the many other concerns of its members, imposed by the Irish electoral system, and its lack of power to summon ministers of the government, or to insist on its reports being debated. A former senior civil servant and lecturer in Irish public administration says: 'Owing to the priority given by TDs to constituency work . . . little importance is attached to service on committees . . . neither House has organized a procedure to discuss committee reports . . .'[8] Staff shortages and low budgets

---

*From 1987 to 1992, its chairperson was Monica Barnes TD (b. 1936). An effective and highly committed spokesperson on women's rights in Ireland and internationally, Ms Barnes was appointed to the front bench of her party (Fine Gael) rather belatedly in 1991, despite nine years of very-high-profile activity. Her appointment, by the socially conservative John Bruton, was seen as helping his own credibility with the liberal wing of the party. In the 1992 general election, Ms Barnes lost her Dáil seat in Dún Laoghaire, Co. Dublin. In 1993, Teresa Ahearn TD (b. 1951) became chairwoman.

do not help either. There is no doubt, none the less, that it is better to have such a committee than not to have one, since the media take an interest in their work, and the standing of parliamentarians of both sexes on the committee adds a little weight to women's concerns.

What should have been the most significant factor in improving the position of women in Ireland – a junior ministry for women's affairs, under the Taoiseach's aegis* – suffered a set-back in credibility in 1992. A man, Tom Kitt TD,† was appointed to the job. This factor in itself could have been positive rather than negative, since the man in question was a young, likeable, energetic, recognizably liberal politician. The problem was that he was simultaneously appointed to two other jobs: that of junior Minister for European Affairs, and also of Arts and Culture. Never had these three jobs been combined, and each one of them covered a large area which needed full-time attention. People interested in each of these areas felt that their own was automatically downgraded by being given a third of a junior minister's time. To add insult to injury, it became known that a senior woman politician, the former Fianna Fáil Cabinet Minister for Education and then Health, who was being demoted by the new Taoiseach in February 1992, had refused the job. She had then been given the portfolio for Trade and Marketing, while women's affairs, in a last-minute change, were lumped in with Minister Kitt's other two areas. So the new minister began his term of office with a considerable credibility problem. However, in the Dáil on 11 March 1992, just a month after his appointment, he pointed out that he had been given three extra staff on the women's

---

* The first such ministry was created in 1982, and filled by a strong feminist with impeccable credentials, Nuala Fennell TD, until 1987. But, because of paucity of funding and staffing, as well as unclear terms of reference and powers, her four years of office were often publicly criticized, not least by women journalists. However, the new consciousness of women's issues, and the prestige brought to them by having a junior minister in the Taoiseach's office, undoubtedly improved understanding of the issues right across the public service.

† Tom Kitt TD (b. 1952). First elected to the Dáil in 1987, one of two brothers from Galway to be elected to the Dáil, both sons of a former TD and junior minister. His liberal credentials include membership of Amnesty International, CND, and West European Parliamentarians for Action against Apartheid. Tom Kitt represents one of the most liberal constituencies in the country, the affluent suburbs of Dublin South. In 1992, he was re-elected to the Dáil and became Minister for State for European Affairs and Overseas Development.

affairs side of his portfolio, and indicated that he would place a particular emphasis on the following issues: 'More positive action for women in employment, a greater recognition of the dual responsibilities of parents in the home: and for practical support for women wishing to return to the labour force by such means as the progressive provision of training and child care.'⁹ In that speech, he also attacked in very strong language the practice of exclusion of women from sport and social clubs, without however specifying any action to be taken. He promised legislation on giving women equal rights to ownership of the family home, and the Minister for Labour promised legislation to update and widen the Equal Pay laws. But Irishwomen are uncomfortably aware that when it comes to taking a tough stance on achieving equal rights, Irish governments are reluctant. Dr Damien Hannan, one of the country's best-known social researchers, put it thus: 'Equality of opportunity, despite being a goal of State policy, has never been actively pursued by the State.'¹⁰

Nearly a quarter of a century since Irishwomen experienced their own first real revolutionary stirrings, Ireland has many thousands of confident, well-educated, achieving women across a wide range of the life of the country. They crowd into higher education, outnumbering male students in areas like medicine, challenging them in law, only being outnumbered heavily in engineering and higher computer technology. From airline pilots to bus conductors and postwomen, there is hardly an area untouched. Women artists exhibit in large numbers across Ireland, dominating new sculpture forms everywhere they go. Women writers and poets flourish in a new free Ireland side by side with Irish men. In theatre, in singing and music, both Irish traditional, rock and classical, women develop and use their gifts at home and abroad. As traditional farming suffers a massive change, women on farms take a prominent role in agri-tourism and new farming activities. Women are admitted, if not quite welcomed, into the police and the Army. On television particularly, the change has been remarkable: women presenters, current affairs reporters, and political correspondents fill positions which were unthinkable twenty-five years ago, although no woman holds any of the top management positions in the national broadcasting station or major newspapers. The clearing away of so much legislative dead wood which was choking the capacity of women to reach their potential has helped to transform their participation in most areas of public life. The election of Ireland's first woman President in 1990 by the popular vote of all the people seemed to put a seal on the new Ireland; her background of liberalism and unashamed feminism seemed further proof of what fundamental changes in thinking had occurred. There are still only four women among the 1,000 senior managers in Ireland's top 500 companies and forty-nine financial institutions, but more and more women creep up the corporate ladders at lower level.

And so the debate has moved on to the next phase. From the many faceted struggle to convince Irish males in power that basic, outdated laws had to be changed, the focus for Irish women has shifted in the early 1990s to insisting on positive steps to undo the damage to women from all those years of grave hindrance, and to make it possible for both women and men to fulfil their family and career aspirations. For, as the new young Irishwoman emerges from school and college, she finds a country full of challenges and opportunity which for the most part she can face on equal terms with her brother; but one huge area remains which will destroy that equality a few years later, and that is her biology. Sex and family, those areas which summed women up in the index to the Irish Constitution, are still convulsing the Irish body politic, and still explain why Irishwomen are found in the home as opposed to the workplace more than most of their European sisters.

In 1991, 168,000 married women in Ireland were at work, compared with 473,000 who described themselves in the census as 'on home duties'.*

As has already been mentioned, there is virtually no public provision of crèche facilities in Ireland, and very little provision by the private sector. The report of the first Commission on the Status of Women in 1972 called for the development of community-based child-care facilities. The Irish Congress of Trade Unions pointed out in 1992 that despite numerous reports and working parties on child care, Ireland still does not have it: 'If government is serious about providing women with choice and equal opportunities in the labour market, then it must provide child-care facilities.'[11] Irish-

---

* Central Statistics Office figures.

women do not relish the thought of having to wait for a strengthened European Community to deal with this outstanding gap, and saw the rise in power of the Labour Party in 1993 as a good omen for progress.

Women crowd into low-paid jobs, and jobs where part-time hours will make it possible for them to work, and then they drop out after children are born in areas where jobs with part-time hours are not available. More than three-quarters of part-time workers are women. They are therefore clustered in low-paid jobs with little security. In September 1991, women earned 68 per cent of male rates.

This central fact governing the economic and public life of women is mirrored in almost every area: women, since working and raising a family are so difficult, opt out of the struggle. This factor, added to the historical barring of married women across the public service, means that women cannot contribute their talent to the economic life of the country. There are none at the top of the civil service, while 66 per cent of the lowest grade are women. Five per cent of the Irish police are women (526 out of 10,500) and fewer than 200 women are found out of some 13,000 personnel in the Defence Forces. There are no women at or near the top of either service. Up to February 1992, nearly 2,000 men had been appointed to State boards and commissions, while 315 women had been so honoured: 16 per cent. In local-government management across the country, there are two women out of 106 senior managers, and these two are at the lower end of management. The figures repeat themselves in every area: and most seriously in areas where real power, therefore real potential for change, resides.

Twelve women held Dáil seats, out of 166 members, after the 1989 election. This was two fewer than in the previous election, 1987. The first time the number of women achieved double figures was in 1981, after the first decade of the modern women's movement. In that short-lived government, there was one woman in Cabinet;*

* Máire Geoghegan-Quinn, Minister for Tourism, Transport and Communications (see pages 129, 228 and 439n). No Irishwoman held a Cabinet post between the time of Countess Markievicz, redoubtable revolutionary and first Minister for Labour in the early 1920s, and Ms Geoghegan-Quinn, who held the Ministry for the Gaeltacht (Irish-speaking areas) for eighteen months from late 1979 to June 1981.

and two at junior ministerial level. In Seanad Éireann, six women sat with their fifty-four male colleagues.

More progress was made in the November 1992 election. Twenty women achieved election to the Dáil, causing a wave of euphoria which was tempered somewhat by the realization that they still amount to only 12 per cent. The Senate elections in early 1993 saw one more woman joining fifty-three men. Interestingly, one of the women elected from the Trinity College panel was a tireless spokesperson for the pro-choice cause, Dr Mary Henry.

There is one female High Court judge, and since December 1992, Ireland's first female Supreme Court judge.*

A week before the presidential election in November 1990, when Mary Robinson, the feminist and first woman candidate for the presidency, was looking like a winner, the government appointed a second Commission on the Status of Women, asking it to

make recommendations on the means, administrative and legislative, by which women will be able to participate on equal terms and conditions with men in economic, social, political and cultural life, to pay particular attention to the needs of women working in the home, and to consider positive action strategies for the achievement of an equal opportunity society.

The independent commission was chaired by one of the two women High Court judges, Ms Mella Carroll,† highly respected for her proven competence and no-nonsense approach to her work, and had a big majority of women members, which included the chairwoman and chief executive of the Council for the Status of Women as well as the chairwoman of the Employment Equality Agency.

A month later, on 5 December 1991, the Supreme Court found that Irishwomen who had worked at home all their lives to rear their family could not be automatically granted any beneficial right to ownership of that home, under Article 41 of the Constitution –

---

*Susan Gageby Denham (b. 1945). Educated at Alexandra College, Trinity College, Dublin, and Columbia University, New York. Called to the Bar in 1971, and to the Inner Bar in 1987. A greatly respected judge of the High Court for a short period before her elevation to the Supreme Court, she is considered both compassionate and liberal on social issues.

†Mella Carroll (b. 1934). Educated at the Sacred Heart Convent in Leeson Street, Dublin, University College, Dublin, and the King's Inns. Appointed a High Court judge in 1980.

that Article which asserts that women's life within the home is essential to the common good. Nor did the Constitution's guarantee that women could not be 'forced by economic necessity to work outside the home' give the courts any right to interpret that as having anything to do with the ownership of the home. Irishwomen – the majority of whom stay at home – were thus sharply reminded that if they had gone against 'the preferred constitutional activity'* of staying at home, and had worked to contribute towards paying for their house, they would be legally much better off. In the uproar which followed, government promised 'immediate legislation' to put this right. By late 1992, no legislation giving automatic ownership of the family home had appeared, and rumours of constitutional difficulties were rife.

Divorce remains prohibited in Ireland, despite the evidence of breakdown of Irish marriages, and the increasing payment of support to deserted wives (nearly 20,000 in 1992). A White Paper on marriage breakdown which had been promised since early 1991 made its appearance in September 1992. There was an air of *déjà vu* about it, since a Dáil/Senate committee had sat for two years from 1983 to 1985 and produced a major document on marriage breakdown; and in 1989, the Judicial Separation and Family Law Act had covered this area exhaustively in its long passage through the legislature.† The sensitivities within Fianna Fáil on this issue are well known; in 1986, a previous government under Garret FitzGerald had put a bill before the people in a referendum to remove the constitutional ban on divorce. Through a combination of conservative organizations running a skilful campaign with the open assistance of the Catholic Church and the politically astute though hardly principled 'neutral' stance of Fianna Fáil, the referendum was defeated by a decisive majority. The parties proposing the referendum had approached it in some disarray and with a lack of efficiency, leaving sufficient doubt about the economic position of dependent spouses after a divorce to allow the Opposition to instil real fears in Irishwomen; this, allied to the rural suspicion about the fate of family farms, was enough to produce a

---

* Remark of Chief Justice Thomas Finlay.[12]
† One of the very few bills to originate from a private member, Alan Shatter of Fine Gael, a lawyer specializing in family law.

'no' vote. It is generally believed in Ireland that if all the political parties were united in proposing to delete the divorce ban, they would succeed quite easily. The White Paper of September 1992 announced that 'the Government proposes to proceed with a divorce referendum after a full debate on the complex issues involved'. This was met with disappointment at the vagueness of the undertaking, since a full debate could take years. The Fine Gael party accused the government of 'kicking to touch' on the issue: 'there are tens of thousands of people locked into the legal "twilight zone" of a broken marriage. Sadly for them, this White Paper offers little hope.'[13]

In December 1991 there had been another indication of women's status: one of Ireland's biggest, most respected and expensive sports and social clubs held a special meeting to consider whether to drop its outright ban on membership by women.* Those in favour were defeated, and the rule was reaffirmed. Several judges, senior barristers from whom future judges will come, and many male leaders of public bodies, professional organizations, and private companies remain members of this and other clubs, mostly 'dining' clubs, and a great many golf clubs, which refuse membership to women. There is slow but perceptible progress among some of the oldest dining clubs in Dublin: in 1993, the Stephen's Green Club and the University and Kildare Street Club abolished the ban on women, though the old golf clubs remain locked in prejudice. Women have asked for real action to be taken on this issue, the most effective step being the refusal of renewal of club licences for sales of alcohol. It is seen by women as a symbol, an important matter of principle – and also, as a measure of the sincerity of the male legislators. Male politicians have verbally condemned such clubs: in his first address to the Dáil after his appointment as Minister for Women's Affairs, Tom Kitt used strong language about these clubs: 'I unreservedly condemn . . . odious practice . . . offensive exclusion . . . no longer tenable . . . an affront not just to women . . .'[14] – but gave no indication whatsoever if or how he intended to use any legislative means to deal with them. (In 1991, the government decided that no such clubs would be eligible for any State grants: but since most would not have been seeking them anyway, it was

* Fitzwilliam Lawn Tennis Club.

not a profoundly significant gesture.) And on 4 February 1993, the Fitzwilliam club once again voted for the continued exclusion of women; this time the ballot was a secret one, and the number voting against women was much greater.

There is a large section of women in Ireland who lead a very different life from that of their urban sisters: the 41 per cent of women who live in rural Ireland (rural as defined by the Central Statistics Office as areas outside clusters of 1,500 or more inhabitants). These half million or so women, many of them connected in some way with farming, face special difficulties: isolated as they are, they cannot avail themselves of many of the services – like family planning, women's support groups – which have become part of the life of urban women. Figures from the agricultural advisory and training authority Teagasc show that, in 1991, only 17 per cent of participants on their short courses were women. A survey in 1990,* commissioned by the Irish Farmers' Association and the *Irish Farmers' Journal*, showed that 62 per cent of women did manual farm work and that Irish farm women worked thirty-eight hours per week. Eighty-five per cent would expect to have a say in major policy decisions. Despite all this work and responsibility, the Gasson survey found that there was a lack of recognition of farm women's work, and that this was creating a 'crisis of identity' for them. They are, officially and legally, invisible. Their work on the farm is ignored in official statistics; in this difficult area of women's work at home, which in the farming world crosses over into work on the farm, the wife, farming or not, has few rights in the property and income. Neither has Ireland made much progress by European standards on the question of social security for farm women, or on maternity leave, for example: the existing relief services depend on having money to afford them. The powerful and vocal farming organizations, which have some family-oriented committees within them, nevertheless present an almost totally male face to the world, and are ruled by male farmers, despite the crucial interest of women in farming developments in the 1990s.

A bright light in the lives of rural women in Ireland has been the Irish Countrywomen's Association, the largest women's organization in the country, with a membership of more than 25,000.

---

* Survey carried out by Dr Ruth Gasson of London University.[15]

Founded in 1910,* as the women's side of the cooperative movement, it was first known as the 'United Irishwomen' and its aims
were to 'improve life in rural Ireland through educating women in
a variety of crafts, skills, etc.'.[16] Its units are called guilds, of which
there are more than 1,000 around Ireland. In 1992, its statement of
aims has changed: 'To bring women together in fellowship and
through cooperative effort to develop and improve the standard of
rural and urban life in Ireland having due regard for our Irish
culture and to encourage the use of the Irish language.'[17] The ICA's
beneficial contribution to women's lives in Ireland is immeasurable,
and through their residential college – An Grianán – in Co. Louth,
they provide a vast range of courses at low prices for women from
all over Ireland. They have gradually been developing their
interpretation of their role in society, and by 1992 were firmly
placed at the centre of the modern Irish women's movement.
Today, assertiveness courses are promoted as well as art and craft,
and the ICA uses the strength of its large membership to get
involved in social and economic issues. A measure of how things
are changing in Ireland was the survey taken by the ICA of their
members in the middle of the abortion debate in Ireland in late
1992. Seventy-five per cent felt that abortion should be available
where a woman's life was in danger, and 63.5 per cent said that it
should be available following rape or sexual abuse[18] – such opinions
would have been unthinkable even ten years ago. The ICA has in
the past been criticized for its conservatism by activists in the
feminist movement, and has been considered something of a sleeping
giant. Its presidents, elected for a three-year term of office, have
usually been strong but careful women in their public pronouncements.

A feature of the new kind of life led by women in rural Ireland
has been the recent growth of small women's groups involved in
both personal development and community activities, groups which
were constantly praised by President Mary Robinson when she

* The founder was a man, Sir Horace Plunkett, 1854–1932, who was the practical
visionary and founder of Ireland's first agricultural cooperative movement and
was both an Irish member of the Westminster parliament and a member of the
Irish Free State's first Senate. He said in 1910: 'We men can see to the better
farming and better business, but only you women can see to the better living.' Sir
Horace left Ireland in 1923 after his house was burned down by Irish 'patriots'.

toured the country: a survey in the west of Ireland in 1991 discovered over forty such groups with an average of twenty members.[19]

On 12 February 1992, something happened which was to engulf the country, and more particularly women, in yet another marathon debate on abortion. A young girl of fourteen years of age was forbidden by the High Court to leave Ireland for an abortion.

Women found that their right to travel was suddenly taken away; more precisely, of course, it had effectively been taken away in 1983. National uproar followed the High Court's action; the Supreme Court reversed the High Court decision quickly, but on grounds which made it clear that the right to travel for an abortion only applied where there was substantial and grave risk to the life of the mother, as there apparently was in the case of the unfortunate young girl, Ms X. They based their judgement, of course, on the Eighth Amendment to the Constitution. The first thoughts of Irish women turned, as has happened so often, to Europe, to an appeal to European courts – only to find that the government had inserted a protocol into the Maastricht Treaty making it impossible for European courts to deal with the application 'in Ireland' of the Eighth Amendment. And this same government was inviting the Irish people to vote in a referendum in June in favour of Maastricht, protocol and all. Coming as it did on top of other court judgements which had already banned the giving of advice or information on abortion availability, the X case ensured that the women's movement took a high-profile role in the Maastricht referendum debate.

The anti-abortion groups, which included women and men, were alarmed by the Supreme Court judgement for other reasons. They were dismayed by the judgement because it allowed abortions in the case of grave risk to the mother's life, specifically where suicide was threatened: this was not what they had intended in 1983. Once again, Ireland was plunged into an abortion debate around the Maastricht Treaty, and only after all the political parties together publicly undertook to rectify the travel and information questions in the autumn of 1992, and to deal either legislatively and/or by referendum with the main issue of abortion, did the Council for the Status of Women agree to urge women to vote 'yes'. The Maastricht Treaty was subsequently approved by a conclusive majority. As for what came to be called 'the substantive issue' – abortion itself – the government set up a Cabinet subcommittee to deal with the Supreme Court interpretation of Article 40.3.3. With considerable foreboding, bearing in mind the convulsions of 1983 – described as 'the second partitioning of Ireland'* – the country temporarily relaxed for the summer of 1992.

The foreboding was justified. On 7 October, the government circulated its proposed wording for the constitutional amendment which would deal with the question of abortion, as well as the right to travel and to have information. They were the Twelfth, Thirteenth and Fourteenth Amendments to the Constitution (the subsection 3 referred to is the Eighth Amendment):

Travel: Subsection 3 of this section shall not limit freedom to travel between this State and another State.
Information: Subsection 3 of this section shall not limit freedom to obtain or make available, in the State, subject to such conditions as may be laid down by law, information relating to services lawfully available in another State.
Abortion: It shall be unlawful to terminate the life of an unborn unless such termination is necessary to save the life as distinct from the health of the mother where there is an illness or disorder of the mother giving rise to a real and substantive risk to her life not being a risk of self-destruction.

Consternation ensued. The arguments quickly centred around the exclusion of the health of the mother and, to a lesser extent, the exclusion of a suicide threat as grounds for abortion. Public opinion was divided also on the question of whether the abortion issue should be dealt with by referendum at all. Women's leaders used words like insult, anger, outrage, offensive. And Irish people were reminded of the central hypocrisy of, on the one hand, a constitutional amendment to give women the right to know about abortion and to travel abroad for it, and on the other to forbid physically or mentally ill women from having one at home. The anti-abortion groups apparently saw no contradiction in this, but they opposed the wording on abortion on the grounds that it would allow abortion in certain circumstances. The government's defence

*This is the title of a book on the 1983 Amendment by Tom Hesketh, who wrote it initially in the form of a doctoral thesis for his studies at Queen's University, Belfast.[20]

was that the wording reflected the wishes of the people, who did not want to change what had always been medical practice in Ireland. The Dáil debate opened on 20 October, the Opposition condemning the wording on abortion as 'grossly offensive', 'brutal, divisive and ultimately counter-productive', 'profoundly misogynistic and immoral'.[21] On 28 October, one of the most influential Fine Gael women,* not known as a feminist, declared in the Senate: 'As a woman I feel abused by the Minister's treatment of me and other women by the inclusion of the words in relation to the health of the mother.'[22] The Council for the Status of Women came out strongly against the abortion wording in November, describing the proposed amendment as 'insulting to the integrity of women as individuals and mothers'.[23] They urged a 'yes' vote on the travel and information issues, describing these as human-rights matters which should never have been in doubt in the first place.

The bills allowing for the referendums were passed through both Houses of the Oireachtas, but since a general election was unexpectedly called in early November, it was decided to hold the abortion polls and the general election on the same day, 25 November. In the heat of the general-election campaign, the public debate on abortion was muted, and did not become enmeshed with the campaign, which was conducted on mainly economic issues. The results were:

Subject	Turn-out (%)	Yes (%)	No (%)
Travel	68·2	62·3	37·7
Information	68·1	60·0	40·0
Abortion	68·2	34·6	65·4

The reaction to this result was general satisfaction, except of course on the part of the proposers. Both anti-abortion and pro-choice groups were pleased. The question of abortion remains to be dealt with by legislation, as it seems most unlikely that any government

---

*Avril Doyle TD (b. 1949 in Dublin but represents Wexford in the Dáil). From a prominent political family (Belton), Ms Doyle, who holds a science degree from University College, Dublin, has been Mayor of Wexford and junior minister (Office of Public Works in Finance). Lost her Dáil seat in 1989, served in the Senate, and regained her seat in 1992. An all-rounder in politics, she is considered leadership material for her party, Fine Gael.

will try to find yet another form of words to encapsulate the complexities of the issue in the Irish Constitution. The legal situation on abortion as 1993 opened was governed by the Supreme Court decision of February 1992, allowing abortion in certain cases where a grave risk to the life of the mother exists. Since, however, no legislation has been enacted to define these circumstances, the area was unclear. In the meantime, the traffic to Britain continues.

The general election in November 1992 saw twenty women elected to the Dáil, giving Ireland with 12 per cent its highest female representation ever. Among them was Frances FitzGerald, who had led the mainstream women's movement since 1989. Women were dismayed, however, at two political full stops: the decision by a former junior Minister for Women's Affairs* to withdraw from politics just before the election; and the defeat in her Dún Laoghaire constituency of the chairperson of the Oireachtas Committee on Women's Rights.†

The government which was formed in January 1993 contained two women at senior level, in the Ministries of Justice and Education‡ respectively, and three at junior ministerial level. This was also the highest number of women at senior political level ever seen in Ireland, and broke the barrier of having only one woman in the Cabinet. All of the women could fairly be described as modern and liberal in their outlook, with both an understanding of and interest in women's issues. It also featured a new full-Cabinet Ministry for Equality, combining responsibility for the disabled, the travellers, and other disadvantaged groups with the whole women's field, under a male minister. §

*Nuala Fennell TD (b. 1935). She was a founder and leader of the modern women's movement, particularly active in the fields of battered wives and family law, author of two books on family law. Junior Minister for Women's Affairs and Justice, 1982–7. First elected to the Dáil in 1981.

†Monica Barnes.

‡ Justice: Máire Geoghegan-Quinn TD. Education: Niamh Bhreathnach. The Minister for Justice (b. 1950) was first elected to the Dáil for her native Galway in 1975. She has held several ministerial positions, and was the first woman to hold a full Cabinet post in modern Ireland. The Minister for Education (b. 1945) was first elected to the Dáil in 1992, was chairperson of the Labour Party, was their spokesperson on women's affairs, and has a background in remedial teaching.

§Mervyn Taylor TD (b. 1931). One of three Jewish Dáil Deputies, and a consistent liberal on social issues, he is an experienced lawyer. Preceded Niamh Bhreathnach as chairperson of the Labour Party, and served in local government since

For the first time in its history, Fine Gael, the main Opposition party, appointed a woman, Nora Owen,* as deputy leader, while the Progressive Democrats appointed Mary Harney† as their deputy leader. The Democratic Left, the smallest party in Opposition, finally acquired its first woman Dáil member.

The new Fianna Fáil/Labour coalition produced a set of undertakings to women in their *Programme for a Partnership Government* that included (among many other things) a commitment to an Equal Status bill as well as the following:

- New comprehensive family-law reform, including a divorce referendum by 1994;
- Major expansion of child-care facilities, including better maternity leave and provisions for paternity leave;
- Affirmative action on State boards to achieve a minimum of 40 per cent participation within four years;
- A 'sex-proofing' policy for all legislation;
- State funding of a women's officer in all political parties.

On the delicate issue of abortion, the programme promised: 'Legislation to regulate the position, recognizing the sensitivity of the issue throughout the community.'

The year 1993 opened with a new outlook for women in Ireland. They were given another, more fundamental blueprint for action early in the year with the publication of a massive document from the Second Commission on the Status of Women, a report with twelve dense chapters. The simple statement of the commission's objective in the report − 'to develop choice and opportunity for women and men and to bring about a fairer gender balance in public life' − did not by any means convey the depth and strength of the document, which was remarkable in its comprehensiveness. Every subject discussed in the foregoing chapters of this book, and many more, is fully addressed in the commission's report, with concise and uncompromising recommendations both to government and to wider society, backed up with careful research. Issues

---

1974. First elected to the Dáil in 1981, having been front-bench spokesperson on Justice and Finance, and chief whip for his party.

* See page 178n.

† See Chapter 21, 'Ireland's Environment'.

concerning disadvantaged women, whether they are low-paid, travellers, disabled or handicapped, or prostitutes are covered; lesbian women are considered; health issues, political issues, education, women in the business world. There is no doubt that Irishwomen were well served by the group working on the report. And since the new government had committed itself to 'act swiftly on the Report of the Second Commission on the Status of Women'[24] there was a new feeling of optimism in the air.

After an important twenty years for Irish women, the report came at a time when a new government was just being moulded into shape. Frances FitzGerald, one of the report's main instigators, who now sat in Dáil Eireann preparing for some years in Opposition, looked forward 'to monitoring the integration of the report into government policy'.[25] Despite the threatening economic clouds surrounding the new government, there was enough in the report which did not require expenditure to enable big changes to be made, and made quickly. With a newly motivated women's movement, women's groups active right across the country and at every social level, and a group of strong women in Dáil and government, change seemed both inevitable and unstoppable.

One result of the new assertiveness and public roles of Irish women is the highlighting of crimes against women, so long hidden. This extends also into areas such as sexual harassment in the workplace. Responding to a survey carried out by the Dublin Rape Crisis Centre in 1993, 210 respondents from a range of Irish companies revealed a 40 per cent incidence rate of sexual harassment at work, that 50 per cent had no policy to deal with the issue, and that 55 per cent had no plans to deal with it. It was significant that the new Minister for Equality attended the presentation of the survey results; it was not long ago that organizations like the Rape Crisis Centre were marginalized and almost ignored by officialdom. The minister, as well as promising legislative action to complement existing Labour court policy, praised the work of the centre. The centre's main work is to give crisis help as well as counselling to victims of rape and sexual abuse. The need for its work is constantly brought home to the Irish people, who face revelations which shock the country. In 1993, accounts of the sixteen-year ordeal of a Kilkenny woman were almost unbearable. Abused, continually beaten, and raped by her father in a Co. Kilkenny town, she bore a child by him in her twenties. He was sentenced to seven years in prison, a sentence considered extraordinarily lenient by public opinion. Such was the public outrage at the whole story, that an inquiry was set up under the direction of a barrister and former Senator, Catherine McGuinness, to try to find out how this child, girl and woman could have been abandoned to her fate for so long. The results of the inquiry showed a desperate need for updating, improving, and strengthening the legal and social provisions for child care: in response, the minister promised to spend IR£35 million over the coming three years on the full implementation of a Child Care Act which had not been implemented since its enactment some years previously, because of lack of money.

By mid-1993, a series of political initiatives and attitudinal changes were marking a major transition to a new way of thinking in Ireland. The Joint Oireachtas Committee on Women's Rights set about working for a crèche inside Leinster House, which a new woman Deputy had condemned as 'anti-woman and anti-family'.[26] The Minister for Justice, Máire Geoghegan-Quinn, showed herself to be in touch with modern thinking on feminism. She told a conference of Fianna Fáil women in May 1993 that there was 'frank prejudice' against women in politics:

If you haven't met my friend, Frank Prejudice, he's the fellow who rang the Late Late Show the night the new women deputies were on it, and asked who was minding their children while they were on television ... he's the guy who has the word 'strident' bopping around on his tongue, ready to apply to any woman who talks with decisiveness or with strength.[27]

This minister went on in 1993 to repeal the Act which criminalized homosexual acts between adults over the age of seventeen, and made clients and pimps liable for prosecution in the prostitution area. The Minister for Labour Affairs, Mary O'Rourke, described as 'a childish charade' the universal use of 'he' and 'him' in official language, particularly in legislation. Her Labour Party colleague, the Minister for Equality and Law Reform, published legislation providing for joint ownership of the family home and recognizing the work of women inside the home: this was part of the legislative prelude to a divorce referendum promised for 1994. The Minister for Health had already passed legislation providing almost unrestricted access to condoms as part of the fight against AIDS, and a woman – psychologist Maureen Gaffney – was appointed to the Chair of the National Economic and Social Forum, which for the first time involved women as 'social partners' in a major advisory body to government. Nineteen ninety-three was a year when so many steps forward were being taken that it looked as if Irishwomen might at last be on the way towards a real partnership in their country.

NOTES

1. *Irish Press*, 18 March 1943.
2. Dr Margaret McCurtain, in Eiléan Ní Chuilleanáin (ed.), *Irish Women: Image and Achievement*, Arlen House, 1985.
3. *Sunday Independent*, 7 February 1937.
4. Eiléan Ní Chuilleanáin (ed.), *Irish Women: Image and Achievement*, Arlen House, 1985.
5. ibid.
6. Edna O'Brien, *Mother Ireland*, Penguin.
7. Brian Farrell (ed.), *De Valera's Constitution and Ours*, RTE/Gill & Macmillan, 1988.
8. Seán Dooney and John O'Toole, *Irish Government Today*, Gill & Macmillan, 1992.
9. *Dáil Report*, 11 March 1992.
10. D. Hannon, *Understanding Contemporary Ireland*, Gill & Macmillan, 1990.
11. *'Programme for Progress': An Evaluation*, ICTU, 1992.
12. Reported in the *Irish Times*, 6 December 1991.
13. Fine Gael press release, 29 September 1992.
14. *Dáil Report*, 11 March 1992.
15. Ruth Gasson, 'Farm wives, their contribution to the farm business', *Journal of Agricultural Economics*, vol. 43, no. 1, 1992, pp. 74–87.
16. Irish Countrywomen's Association, *There is a Lot More to the ICA Than Meets the Eye* (leaflet).
17. ibid.
18. *Irish Times*, 21 November 1992.
19. V. McEllin, *Networking Women's Groups in the West of Ireland*, Headford, 1991.
20. T. Hesketh, *The Second Partitioning of Ireland*, Brandsma Books, 1990.

21. Alan Shatter, Fine Gael; Dick Spring, Labour; and Proinnsias de Rossa, Democratic Left, respectively: *Dáil Report*, 20 October 1992.
22. *Dáil Report*, 28 October 1992.
23. *Irish Times*, 11 November 1992.
24. *Programme for a Partnership Government, 1993–97*.
25. In conversation with the author.
26. Liz McManus TD, speaking to the Joint Committee on 26 May 1993.
27. *Irish Times*, 10 May 1993.

CHAPTER 19

Sport

Irish people love the theatre: and since sport is the great unrehearsed drama, it is not surprising that they take part in it, or flock to it at every opportunity. And since the island is so small, there is nothing they like to see more than an Irish person doing well abroad. International triumphs in recent years have brought huge numbers on to the streets to welcome the heroes home: when the Irish soccer team returned in 1990 from the World Cup tournament in Italy, having reached the quarter-finals, nearly 700,000 people turned out on the route from the airport to the centre of the city of Dublin. A few years earlier, the streets were packed for Barry McGuigan, who won the world featherweight boxing title; in 1987 when Stephen Roche won the Tour de France on his bicycle, the city came to a standstill.* And in August 1992, when an Irish Army corporal called Michael Carruth came home from Barcelona with a gold medal for boxing, accompanied by his silver-medal-winning team-mate from Northern Ireland, Wayne McCullough, the welcome and the street parties were huge and good-humoured. (Irish people in the Republic were puzzled by the low-key welcome for McCullough when he left Dublin and arrived in his native Northern Ireland among his Protestant community.) The only other such manifestations in recent history were seen for Pope John Paul II when he came to Ireland in 1979, and for John F. Kennedy, illustrious descendant of Irish emigrants, in 1963.

Add to that natural delight and innate sense of drama a young population, a relatively gentle climate, rolling green fields and wide open expanses of land, exposure to multi-channel international television, and strong national sporting traditions and you have a country

---

* The Taoiseach of the day, Mr Charles Haughey, who was nothing if not a flamboyant character, was at the finishing line in Paris to embrace the conquering hero, occasioning some acerbic comment from sports people at home. Undaunted, he triumphantly joined the Irish team in a lap of honour in Rome after the quarter-final game in the World Cup in 1990.

where sport really matters. Ireland being Ireland, there is an element of the old national struggle and division mixed in with several of the major sporting groups, and – as in other countries – success in sport does no harm at all to business, professional, or political prospects for young men. And as in other countries, perhaps more so, women's place in sport is very much at the fringes, though improving.

This avidity for all things sporting has not translated itself into financial support from government, which until 1992 managed to escape without really major provision being made. Ireland enjoys very few first-class sports facilities either in schools or nationally. It was the Olympic Gold Medal win at Barcelona which sparked off a confrontation between the Irish Olympic Council and the government: and brought some interesting facts to public knowledge. The first concerned the Irish National Lottery, established in 1987, which was conceived with the stated purpose of mainly funding sport, arts and culture. Despite the runaway success of the lottery, with a turnover heading towards IR£300 million in 1993, only 8 per cent of its grants have gone to sport. Governments (and large numbers of the population to judge by opinion polls) have felt that the millions generated by the lottery were more badly needed in areas like health care than in large-scale funding of sport. They are also aware that the major sports in Ireland – Gaelic football, Rugby Union, soccer, and everything connected with the horse – are not poverty-stricken. Neither do all sports lobby together for funding, something which the President of the Olympic Council of Ireland* feels has damaged the minor sports. His argument is that Irish sportsmen and women are the last true amateurs of Europe, that the country has a blameless reputation for high standards (no Irish athlete has ever failed a drug test), that young Irish people can do wonderful things if they get the training, but that lack of resources is rapidly getting the country the status of a Third World area in the international world of sport. After considerable media attention

---

*Pat Hickey (b. 1945). A Dublin man, running his own financial services and auctioneering business, he was elected President of the Olympic Council in 1988. Outspoken and dedicated to his voluntary work with the council, he strongly criticized the government's funding approach in 1992, causing the Fianna Fáil Minister for Finance to be given a very hostile reception and shouted down by the crowd at Dublin airport when the gold and silver Olympic medallists returned from Barcelona. This was despite his own personal friendship with, and political support of, the minister.

to this funding question, it seems likely that the Olympic Games in Atlanta will see a better trained and financed Irish team competing than ever before. In the government programme for the newly elected administration, published in January 1993, a specific undertaking is given to 'provide aid for a Programme to assist participants in international competition, including training for the 1996 Olympics'. No specific figure is mentioned, but the sum of about IR£750,000 a year for this purpose was rumoured to be available.

Hickey himself hopes for a figure of about IR£500,000 a year for general distribution to the twenty-three Olympic sports bodies, with a special fund not exceeding IR£1 million for the specific preparation of selected athletes for training.[1] The Olympic Council intend to support some very promising men and women over four years so that they can concentrate on the full-time aim of medal-winning in Atlanta.

Ireland sent fifty competitors to Barcelona in August 1992. This was thirty less than to Seoul in 1988. Two came back with medals, both in boxing. Since Ireland first started competing in the Games in the 1920s, thirteen medals have been won: four gold, three silver, six bronze. Seven of those have been for boxing. The last time a gold in a track event came to Ireland was in 1956, won by Ronnie Delaney for the 1,500 metres in Melbourne, Australia. It is not surprising that Irish athletes are finding it difficult to get medals at all; facilities are minimal, and there is no Olympic-size pool for swimmers and no national indoor sports complex.

Gaelic football and hurling, Association football (soccer), Rugby football and the various sporting events equestrian are the dominant activities engaging Ireland's sporting community. Athletics and cycling are creeping up in popularity, and golf is widely established and spreading rapidly as a major leisure activity. Boxing leapt to the forefront with the sport's first gold medal win.

The relative strength of each of the three ball games organizations in Ireland is:

Organization	Number of clubs	Number of players
Gaelic Athletic Association	2,000	306,000
Rugby Union	214	55,000
FAI (Soccer)	3,190	124,615

THE GAELIC ATHLETIC ASSOCIATION

The most powerful and wealthy sports body in the country is also the one in which a strong sense of nationalism is still the driving force. The Gaelic Athletic Association (the GAA, or Cumann Lúthchleas Gael, in Irish) was founded in 1884. It was part of the resurgence of nationalism in the late nineteenth century. The literary renaissance, spearheaded by the poet and playwright W. B. Yeats, and the Irish cultural and language movement led by Douglas Hyde,* signalled a revival of Irish cultural identity. The visionary Michael Cusack, an Irish-speaking teacher from Co. Clare, disliked intensely what he saw as the political trends in Irish sport, dominated as they were by the Protestant University (Trinity College, Dublin), the mostly Protestant and Anglo-Irish moneyed and upper classes, and the 'anglicized form of athletics spreading throughout the country, through the medium of the cricket clubs'.[2]

Three elements came together to worry Cusack: traditional Irish sports were suffering and some had almost died; sabbatarianism – the Irish Protestant tradition of no sporting or social activity on Sundays (which was the only day of leisure for the Catholic working class); plus the narrow definition of amateurism, which was actually described as 'Gentleman Amateur' and specifically excluded 'mechanics, artisans, or labourers'.[3] Together they combined to keep poor Catholics excluded from the sporting life of their own country.

Cusack launched the GAA in Thurles, Co. Tipperary, on 1 November 1884. At three o'clock on that Saturday afternoon, in Miss Hayes's Commercial Hotel, he opened the meeting in the billiard room. 'The proceedings were brief, Cusack alone being long-winded.'[4] The body had seized on an idea whose time had come: the revival of the ancient Irish sports of hurling and Gaelic football, handball and throwing, as part of the new resurgence of Irishness. 'The Association swept the country like a prairie fire,'[5] and, 'In rural Ireland the founding of the GAA caused something of a social revolution.'[6] The heady mixture of religion, the social class division, sport and nationalism all combined to catch the

*Douglas Hyde was subsequently first President of Ireland, and served from 1938 to 1945.

imagination of Irishmen across the country, North and South. Over the years, hurling and Gaelic football emerged as the central focus of the association's activities, with a lesser emphasis on handball, almost none on throwing, and with the development of the women's game of camogie, which like hurling is played with a curved stick. Hurling is an exciting, fast and dangerous game, with teams of fifteen clashing their whirling sticks in competition for the leather ball; Gaelic football is a fast-moving game too, in which handling and bouncing the ball while running towards the opponent's goal are a central feature.

One of the first things done by the GAA was to enact 'the Ban'. 'After 17th March 1885, any athlete competing at meetings held under other laws than those of the GAA shall be ineligible for competing at any meeting held under the GAA.' This remained in force until 1971, when public opinion outside and fresher, less paranoid minds inside the GAA forced the membership to repeal it. There are still echoes of that ban in the games today: the GAA will not allow its main sports field and headquarters, Croke Park,* to be used for any other games.

A famous letter from Archbishop Croke, a founding patron of the association, to mark the foundation of the GAA captures the tenor of the times:

If we continue travelling for the next score years in the same direction that we have been going in for some time past, condemning the sports that were practised by our forefathers, effacing our national features as though we were ashamed of them, and putting on, with England's stuffs and broadcloths, her masher habits and such other effeminate follies as she may recommend, we had better at once, and publicly, abjure our nationality, clap hands for joy at the sight of the Union Jack, and place England's 'bloody red' exultantly above the green.[7]

Today another ban remains: Rule 20 of the GAA states: 'Members of the British Armed forces and police shall not be eligible for membership of the Association.' Peter Quinn, a successful business-

* Croke Park takes its name from Archbishop Croke (1824–1902), Archbishop of Cashel, Co. Tipperary, in the 1880s, who lived in Thurles and was the leading nationalist member of the Catholic hierarchy. He strongly supported the GAA from its inception.

man from Northern Ireland who became President of the GAA in April 1991, explains why that ban remains: 'There are two things: one is the continuing occupation of the Crossmaglen grounds* and the general harassment of the association's members. The other is that the RUC† are not acceptable to a large proportion of the population of the Six Counties.'‡ This sort of statement fuels the anger of those who believe that the GAA is too identified with republicanism. It also partly explains the sinister rumblings from the other side of the political divide in Northern Ireland: a statement from the Ulster Freedom Fighters (the UFF, a paramilitary Unionist group) on 8 October 1991 announced that the UFF regarded members of the GAA as 'legitimate targets'[8] and accused the association of financing the IRA as well as of sectarianism. Peter Quinn, taking that kind of threat seriously, and in an attempt to calm relations in Northern Ireland, arranged a meeting with Northern Ireland loyalists in February 1992. He explained on RTE Radio on 25 February that this meeting was part of a series. By the end of 1992, the death toll in Northern Ireland had reached nearly 100 for one year, and for the first time, more murders were committed by the Protestant paramilitaries than by the IRA, including members and supporters of the GAA.

Frequent controversies flare up among sports writers who heavily criticize the GAA for various manifestations of its 'closed shop' policies: in December 1991, the central committee of the GAA stepped in at a late stage of the planning of a unique and original 'double-header' event in Dublin's RDS grounds: two GAA teams were to be followed by two soccer teams in a kind of festival of football, on the same football pitch. In what became a public-relations disaster, rules about sharing the financial proceeds were somewhat feebly invoked to prevent the matches taking place. Almost every sports writer deplored the GAA's action, while editorial writers weighed in with condemnations. The President of Ireland, Mary Robinson, chose the occasion of the GAA All-Stars

* A GAA sports field in South Armagh, border territory – and a stronghold of republicanism in Northern Ireland – used as a base by the British Army.
† The Royal Ulster Constabulary, Northern Ireland's police force.
‡ The term 'Six Counties' is often used to refer to Northern Ireland; its use is generally confined to more nationalist speakers: the political entity of Northern Ireland is composed of the six north-eastern counties of the island of Ireland.

Awards to remark in her own gentle – but pointed – way that the GAA should have confidence in its own strength and place within Irish society, and use that confidence to open itself to the rest of the world. 'The GAA is better equipped than most to embrace openly and positively new ideas and cultures.'[9]

'Nothing foreign can ever compare with Croke Park on a summer Sunday, a glorious reality that the fanatics might care to reflect on'[10] – Éamonn Dunphy, a colourful character and sports writer, was trying to explain the GAA's internal contradictions to a French colleague. He went on: 'You cannot understand how a [sporting] feud dating back to the nineteenth century can still endure, to cast a shadow that will stretch to the year 2010.'

The young players of the future were historically formed in the mostly rural primary and second-level schools of the Christian Brothers, as well as the Vocational schools, and now are coming from Vocational and newly founded Community and Comprehensive schools, encouraged by an active programme of initiatives from the GAA itself. For many years, the GAA failed to notice the serious effects on their future prospects of two modern Irish social phenomena: the steep decline since the 1960s of the number of religious in the schools, with the accompanying massive fall in the number of young men entering the teaching profession. Danny Lynch, the Kerry-born public-relations officer of the GAA, is pleased to note that such insouciance has now disappeared.

Despite all controversies, the association remains powerfully at the centre of Irish sporting and social life, with prosperous clubs all over the country, and huge crowds turning out for its national and provincial matches. It is a massive and beneficial part of community life in Ireland, and plays an important part in fostering the sense of Irish identity. Lynch reckons that about 700 of the 2,000 clubs are of a high standard with full facilities like first-class changing rooms, gymnasia, social functions, bars, and meeting-rooms. The All-Ireland finals both in hurling and football are great national carnivals held in Croke Park in Dublin, with crowds of 60,000 attending and television coverage to many parts of the world where the Irish diaspora has spread. In 1992, the finals were seen on thirteen television stations in the USA, in several European countries, in Australia, parts of Africa, and widely in Britain.

Tickets are precious, while Presidents and Taoisigh and almost the full Cabinet attend. County games and provincial finals attract intense interest too. The association's director and staff have understood and acted upon modern trends of communications, recruiting, sponsorship, and attractive conditions for players, who themselves are aware of their financial value to the association. Elaborate sunshine holidays for players and spouses are the kind of 'perk' which this multi-million-pound sporting body must provide for players who have become popular icons.

Because the GAA is so important in local towns and counties all over the country, and is almost completely voluntary in its administrative structures, it is not surprising to find that GAA players and supporters find their way in large numbers into politics. About one-third of those elected to the Dáil in each election in recent years are or were actively involved in their sport. One of Ireland's best-loved Taoisigh and leaders of Fianna Fáil, Jack Lynch,* won six All-Ireland medals for his native Cork in the 1940s (five for hurling and one for football). It would be generally agreed that he owed his initial entry into public life to his prowess on the playing pitches of the GAA. In the twenty-sixth Dáil, dissolved in 1992, the Tánaiste (deputy prime minister) John Wilson was the holder of two All-Ireland medals for his native Cavan, and Fine Gael's Dáil Deputy Jimmy Deenihan from Kerry shares that honour.

In the 1990s, plans were advancing for a huge development of Croke Park which will make it into the Irish equivalent of Paris's Parc des Princes. Estimated to cost over IR£100 million, the association would like financial assistance from the State, but only if it comes 'with no strings attached', that is, no requirement to share the facilities with other sports. Full planning permission for the plan was finally obtained in March 1993. The GAA points out that Ireland is unique in the world in that its indigenous sports predominate over all the 'international' games. Hurling in particular is a source of great national pride and protectiveness to the GAA; Danny Lynch explains that 'hurling is

---

* He first became Taoiseach in November 1966, in office until March 1973; then again served, from July 1977 to December 1979, when he resigned (to be succeeded by C. J. Haughey).

considered by many GAA people to be as precious as the [Irish] language, the Ardagh Chalice,* the heirlooms in the National Museum . . .'

The organization of the association ensures its continuing strength. It is organized along parish lines, proceeding up to county standard, interprovincial, and all-Ireland. The clubs, based on village or parish, compete for county titles, and their management elects a county board, through which are selected the all-important individuals to represent the county in further competitions. The supreme governing body of the GAA is the Central Council, a fifty-strong body which meets about five times a year. Thus, each level appeals to the fierce partisan loyalty of village, town and county, with the All-Ireland finals in September causing an outbreak of feeling behind the competing counties which has to be seen to be believed. The scenes of joy which greet the winning team as they progress royally to their own county town have remained unchanged for nearly a century.

In the 1990s, there are more GAA clubs outside Ireland than there are in the western province of Connaught. More than 200 overseas clubs manned by emigrants and their descendants in Britain, Canada, the USA and Australia are a sign of the economic situation at home, but have had a happy by-product in that fixtures abroad are a welcome 'perk' for winning county teams in this amateur sport. Irish visits are welcomed overseas as an additional fillip to the games outside Ireland. In Australia, a form of semi-professional football with its origins in Gaelic football is played according to 'Australian Rules' – and a regular international series takes place with Irish teams travelling 'down under' and vice versa, playing under compromise rules. The majority of the overseas clubs are in Britain.

Despite the introduction of modern management techniques and the ready adaptation to sponsorship and cooperation with the mass media, the GAA today retains and reaffirms its strong nationalistic tradition, as exemplified in the introduction to the 1991 *Official Guide*. It is an interesting mixture of strangely old-fashioned

---

*The Ardagh Chalice, made of silver with inlaid panels of gold and studs of amber and glass of different colours, dates from the eighth century and is one of the treasures of Ireland in the National Museum, Kildare Street, Dublin.

rhetoric and nationalistic hyperbole, and is worth quoting as the official position of the GAA:

The primary purpose of the GAA is the organization of native pastimes and the promotion of athletic fitness as a means to create a disciplined, self-reliant, national-minded manhood ... Since she has no control over all the national territory Ireland's claim to nationhood is impaired ... it would be still more impaired if she were to forsake her own games and customs in favour of the games and customs of another nation.

Rules are indeed still strictly observed and enforced, including one forbidding players from drinking in public during the times when they are in training. The GAA is therefore more than just a sporting organization, and while the games attract great numbers and strong loyalties, there is a niggling worry about the incursion of other sports, in particular the appearance of real soccer fever following Ireland's creditable World Cup performance in Italy in 1990. However, one of the country's most devoted sportsmen,* and most prominent sports broadcasters, points out that while soccer was engaging the attention of the country more and more after 1990, the numbers attending big GAA matches continued to rise. And in April 1993, in another sign of the changing times in Ireland, a popular fifty-seven-year-old Wicklow Protestant, Jack Boothman, was elected to take over the presidency of the GAA in 1994.

RUGBY FOOTBALL

With a mere 214 clubs (including schools) and 55,000 players, the Irish rugby fraternity hardly competes with the GAA. It holds, however, a position of interest and influence out of proportion to its following because of the social position of those who play it: in Ireland, rugby has been played in middle- and upper-middle-class schools, with a consequent concentration of moneyed, professional and managerial members. It benefits greatly too from its inter-national character: the annual 'Triple Crown' tournament among the countries of the British Isles, and the international championship which includes France, are hugely enjoyed by the whole country.

* Jimmy Magee of RTE.

And if Ireland can perform well in the new World Cup rugby series, joy will know no bounds.

The game came to Ireland from across the Irish Sea in 1874. Like the GAA, its membership comes from all thirty-two counties on the island, with the crucial difference that there is an almost 100 per cent Protestant membership north of the Border, and a high proportion of Protestant members in the Republic – though they still amount to a small minority overall. There is a suggestion that Catholic schools in the North of Ireland are disticly hostile to the idea of the students playing rugby. A feature of international rugby matches, which take place in Lansdowne Road stadium in Dublin, is the massive influx of Northern Ireland visitors from both communities there. It is one of the few occasions when such friendly mingling happens on the island. They all happily cheer for an all-Ireland team drawn from North and South, wearing the green Irish jersey.

When in 1971 the GAA abolished the ban forbidding players to switch between their games and 'foreign' games, they hoped that one of the effects would be the embracing by many more boys' schools of the two main GAA games. That was not to happen. The GAA's official historian noted in 1980: 'No boys' school has so far displaced rugby from the dominant and usually exclusive place it occupies in many of them, a matter that is as much a reflection on the parents who patronize such schools as on those who run them.'[11] So, schools like Blackrock College, Castleknock College, and St Mary's College held on to their rugby and ran their competitions. Their reasons are rooted in history, including a distaste by many of the middle-class professionals, particularly in Dublin, for what they saw as an excessive nationalism, as well as a class difference: the Jesuits, the Holy Ghost fathers, the Cistercians were educating the sons of professionals for the future and wanted them to be part of the ruling establishment. That establishment, formerly heavily dominated by the Anglo-Irish tradition in sport as well as business and the professions, played rugby in its schools. The Irish educators followed the English 'public'-school system in playing rugby, because, according to the IRFU's Technical Director, George Spotswood, 'they perceived those schools to be their nearest counterparts'.[12]

Rugby football is now firmly in place as a popular sport of the middle classes and retains a devoted following across the country. As with all stereotypes, there are exceptions: the game in Munster, Ireland's southernmost province, does not follow that class-based pattern. Similarly to the game in Wales, it transcends the social barriers. In 1992, Garryowen Club in Limerick, with a much more eclectic social mix in its membership (over one hundred years in existence), won the All-Ireland League, and in the following year another Limerick club, Young Munster, snatched the League from the Dublin club, St Mary's. In 1992, the province of Munster defeated Australia, a feat which the national team had failed, once more, to perform. On the other hand, Wanderers, Dublin's oldest rugby club, has been described more than once as the club of the Church and the Army: the wags added '. . . unfortunately the wrong Church and the wrong Army'.

The nurseries for rugby are, therefore, the boarding and day schools around Ireland run by religious orders like the Jesuits, the Carmelites, the De La Salle Order, the Holy Ghost Fathers, the Vincentians, as well as the Protestant schools both in the south and in Northern Ireland. Outstanding among these schools for the single-minded adherence to rugby is Blackrock College in south Dublin, which dominated the Schools' Cup tournament in the Leinster province for many years and still is a powerful force.

The main focus of the year is the international tournament between the 'Home Countries' (England, Ireland, Scotland and Wales) and which includes France. The mythical trophy for the team which defeats all the other Home Countries is called the Triple Crown; the team which can defeat France as well wins the championship. The Irish Rugby Football Union has no problems in sharing its ground, and rents it to the Football Association for big soccer games, thereby increasing its revenue. Provincial and interprovincial tournaments, and in recent years an all-Ireland league competition, as well as fiercely contested and highly prized Schools' Cups make up the rugby calendar.

'You'll know him by the sheepskin coat, the tweed cap, the slightly florid face, and the jaunty spring in his step. The high point in his year is reached on international day at Lansdowne Road.'[13] 'The Rugger supporter is wealthier and enjoys the finer things in life . . . cigars and Chablis soothe the pain of defeat.'[14] The perception of the rugby community as solidly middle-class, conservative in their views, very fond of social drinking, and operators of an 'old boys' business network is still fairly general.

The IRFU's president, Dr Tony Browne, admits that there is a 'grain of truth' in allegations of an old boys' rugby network in business.[15] That must be an inevitable result of the public exposure to the wealthier and more influential sector of Irish life, particularly when playing for the national side; it cannot do a young stockbroker any harm at all to be described as 'a cool clean sporting hero . . . intelligent, easygoing, charming and talented'.[16] The best-known businessman graduate of Irish rugby is A. J. F. (Tony) O'Reilly, chairman and chief executive of Heinz who as a schoolboy and later, playing for Ireland, became a household word. Ciarán FitzGerald, who played for, captained, and trained the Irish rugby team in the 1980s and 1990s, left the Army for the business world and says: 'Rugby may have helped to open doors for me, but that's all; if the rugby player has a business advantage it may be because of the attributes the player has developed through rugby such as self-discipline, organization and ability to handle pressure.'[17]

Like many another sport, the rugby clubs are increasingly aware of the erosion of the purely amateur status of the game. This led to a controversial decision by the IRFU in February 1992 to introduce new and stringent regulations about overseas players joining Irish clubs, in an apparent reaction to the danger of 'overseas mercenaries demanding fat salaries and perks'.[18] It followed a growing debate about how far the governing bodies of the sport can go to 'compensate' players who have to travel and lose time at their employment in the interests of the game; it has become accepted now that players should certainly not be at any financial loss for the game's sake. That debate is ongoing, and however much the traditionalists may regret it, newer voices recognize that the Irish rugby establishment is going to have to face up to and compete with the near-professionalism of the other countries playing this so-called amateur game.

A hopeful development in club rugby in Ireland has been the establishment of an All-Ireland League. This means that the top nine or ten clubs will have series of highly competitive matches against their peers, and will attract good players to their ranks, lifting – it is hoped – the standard of the game at top level, and filtering right down to the schools.

In 1992, Ireland's national rugby team had an abysmal run of defeats on the international scene, leading to considerable speculation about the governing body's organization and abilities, and to the resignation of the team coach. The most humiliating defeat was against France in March: Ireland was crushed by 44 points to 12. 'France', said the *Irish Times* rugby correspondent, 'broke nearly every International Championship record in the book, and the Irish performance broke our hearts.'[19] It was the lowest point in a low year, when Ireland came out bottom of the major international tournaments. Rugby's health, unlike that of the GAA, depends on good performance on the international front. National pride was deeply offended: 'My God, it infuriates me that we have become the butt of sniggers from commentators on the other side of the water,'[20] said Willie John McBride, one of the legendary Northern Irish rugby players of the past, reminding his readers that 'there are some guys in the current Irish team who have never known what it is to be successful at international level'.[21] At the end of the season, some pride was restored by a fine performance against New Zealand; a defeat at their hands in May by 24 points to 21 was considered almost a victory. A former Ireland coach, who had led the country to great victories in the 1980s, attacked the ruling body, the Irish Rugby Football Union; he pronounced that the IRFU's structures were stultified, key positions were held for too long, there was no accountability, self-perpetuation in power was the obsession, and 'mediocrity reaches its all-pervading hand into our club, interprovincial, and international teams'.[22] And the opening joust of the 1993 international season was not encouraging: a defeat by Scotland 15–3 in Edinburgh raised some more questions about the management of the game. However, the great unrehearsed drama was seen to full advantage when the Irish team, having started on the road back to favour by beating Wales in early March, trounced a much-favoured English team amid scenes of almost incredible jubilation in Dublin on 20 March 1993.

ASSOCIATION FOOTBALL

Another imported game, but one which has been growing fast in recent years all over Ireland, is that game controlled by the Football Association of Ireland, which to distinguish it from rugby football and Gaelic football I refer to as soccer. The first game of soccer in Ireland took place in Belfast in 1878, between the Scottish clubs Queen's Park and Caledonian. 'We scarcely think the natives will take kindly to the innovation,' said the *Irish Sportsman* of 26 October 1878.[23] The paper went on to describe the Scottish visitors 'butting at the ball like a pack of goats'.

Soccer is one of the many sports in Ireland which is not played on an all-Ireland basis, a split occurring in 1921 after the political division of Ireland. The FAI (Football Association of Ireland) controls the game in the Republic, with its 124,000 players spread among more than 3,000 clubs: 46 per cent of the activity takes place in the eastern, more urbanized province, Leinster, and only 6 per cent in the west, Connaught. It is a sport traditionally associated with the urban working class.

Until 1966, and the phenomenon of the televised World Cup finals from London which were seen in Irish homes (Ireland's television station had been established only five years before), soccer was not the widespread activity it is today. The impetus given by the televising of the FAI cup final in Ireland in 1967, and the growing involvement of the emigrant Irish population in Britain in the game, combined to stimulate the promotion of more clubs and more players. British talent scouts came to see young Irish players, who had graduated from kicking a ball in the street and frequently found themselves eventually playing for English club sides for big money: soccer at senior level is a professional game. That ready interchange between Britain and Ireland still applies.

Old-established Irish clubs such as Shamrock Rovers, Bohemians, Waterford, and Cork Celtic were joined by Athlone Town and Finn Harps and then Derry City, which took colourful supporters around the country and greatly stimulated the rising popularity of the game. On the international front, very little success was achieved until the early 1970s, when John Giles was appointed player-manager. Gradually, the Irish sides began to assert themselves, helped by the growing willingness of players in England with Irish roots to join Ireland's team. The FAI became more and more professional, appointing national coaches and press officers, seeking considerable sponsorship and bringing the game new popularity.

A watershed event occurred in 1986, with the appointment of the former English international player Jack Charlton as Ireland's manager. On the run-in to the European Championships in Germany in 1988, Ireland went twelve games in a row without defeat. The steady build-up of the standard of play resulted in the historic breakthrough of 15 November 1989, when the Republic of Ireland beat Malta 2–0 to qualify for the World Cup finals for the first time.

The big breakthrough for soccer in Ireland was the success of the Irish team in reaching the final round of the World Cup in Italy. During June 1990, an extraordinary outpouring of national senti-ment and pride was witnessed all over the country, especially in Dublin. Ireland's team reached the quarter-final of the competition, having drawn with England and Holland, and beating Romania, only to succumb to the Italians. Apart from the many thousands who went to Italy for the events, the country came to a standstill for every match, while pubs and clubs filled up with cheering supporters and giant TV screens. Men, women and children who had never been at a soccer match in their lives – including fervent GAA and rugby supporters – talked of nothing else. Street carnivals erupted spontaneously as supporters streamed out of their homes and their pubs after each match. Allied to the sudden national euphoria about the Irish team's performance was a pride in the decorous standard of behaviour of the Irish fans in Italy, in a sport which has seen the worst kinds of ugly scenes in Europe in recent years. When the team came to Ireland after the competition, with their manager, more than half a million people stood in the streets and mobbed their buses. Charlton achieved the status of sanctity in Irish eyes. 'St Jack' was considered to be an honorary Irishman.

None of the winning Irish side were living in Ireland; all of them played for British teams, although each of them had strong Irish roots: they included unlikely names like Cascarino, Aldridge, and a dusky Paul McGrath. Their absence from Ireland is a measure not only of the history of emigration from Ireland to Britain, but also of the greater financial rewards for players in bigger countries, and the superior facilities for training.

That 1990 fillip has given a new impetus to the FAI, who are busily establishing school and junior clubs as fast as they can. Not too much controversy surrounds the sport; the conflict between the 'ordinary punter' and the corporate sponsor for tickets to big games surfaces from time to time, 'touts charge exorbitant prices for tickets, and match them up with caviar, smoked salmon and bubbly'[24] for business customers: this and variations of it annoy the supporters of all the big sports.

Critics, particularly sports writer Éamonn Dunphy who played soccer for Ireland himself, consider that the style of football set by Jack Charlton is dull and uninspired, leading to too many drawn games full of dour defence play; Dunphy was extremely unpopular during the 1990 World Cup series for criticizing Charlton, and was physically threatened at Dublin airport in one of the few untoward incidents of the time.

Glossy magazines, wealthy sponsors, new management style, international television coverage, ambitious youngsters, superstar status, huge earning power – all these ingredients add up to a sport which is poised to become Ireland's premier game in terms of numbers and money. 'People are playing soccer at every level in every town; even a small town like Kanturk in Cork has two soccer teams, one rugby team and one GAA team: formerly it was a GAA stronghold,' said Dave Guiney, veteran sports writer and chronicler of Irish sporting history. It is a challenge of which the GAA are acutely aware. And as the 1994 World Cup drew near, and Ireland's team made a triumphal progress through the preliminary rounds, it looked as if soccer fever was going to be around for some time.

THE HORSE

'Ireland is simply the best place in the world to breed horses'[25] – Irish people accept this statement as given truth, with the island's limestone soil and abundance of grass: and the most recent demonstration of it is the influx of multimillionaire Arabs breeding their horses in the country.

Horses, their breeding, show-jumping, selling and racing, and their partnership in the hunt have played for centuries an important role in the life of both the ordinary and the wealthy people. From the small farmer keeping a mare or two, and enjoying the involvement in local horse shows and racing activity, to the breeding empires of Ireland's magnificent large stud farms, it is a sport, a business, and an enjoyable part of being Irish.

All over the country, in sometimes breathtakingly beautiful settings, horses race each other and people wager money on the results. Twenty-seven race courses are scattered around the country, from the beach-racing at Laytown, Co. Meath, to the fashionable venue of the Irish racing classics, the Curragh of Kildare. Racing dominates the scene, with a major industry built around the sport. Breeders, trainers, bookmakers and jockeys have their own hierarchies, fortunes are won and lost. Over a million people go to race meetings every year, from big national events to small country 'point-to-point' meetings, numbering 269 in all venues. The major racing events are the Christmas meets at Leopardstown, in south Co. Dublin, the Punchestown (Co. Kildare) festival in March, the Irish Grand National at Fairyhouse (west Co. Dublin) also in the spring, and the Irish Derby (sponsored by Budweiser) in June. In July, Galway hosts a racing festival as colourful as it is thronged, while Listowel in Co. Kerry has its own huge following. As in most areas of discretionary spending and international business, the key racing statistics for Ireland at the end of 1991 showed a decline: total betting down by 15 per cent to IR£103·6 million; sponsorship down by 11·8 per cent to IR£3·3 million; attendances down by 3·3 per cent to 1·02 million.

The Irish-bred horse is a desirable commodity internationally, and brings in about IR£65 million annually in export sales, although international competition gets more severe all the time, and the recession of the early 1990s has caused considerable disquiet in the industry. Two big sales outlets, Goff's at Kill, Co. Kildare, and Tattersalls (Ireland) at Fairyhouse not far away, dominate the scene. Only one old traditional horse fair survives, at Ballinasloe in Co. Galway, with all the traditional tricks of the trade and local colour of a long history.

The whole industry employs about 12,000 people, with 348 registered trainers and a staggering 7,000 breeders.[26]

The rich flatlands of Kildare and Meath abound in stud farms and training establishments, although Ireland's most famous contemporary breeder and trainer, Vincent O'Brien,* runs the beautiful Coolmore in Co. Tipperary, from where some of this century's most celebrated horses came. Lord Killanin,† whose many sporting interests include horse-racing, declares his love for the sport because he considers it essentially classless. Not all prominent people in the industry are happy at the way the business is run, considering it inefficient and detached from the real world, nor would they agree with Lord Killanin on the question of class: 'Racing in Ireland is governed by the Turf Club and the Irish National Hunt Committee: a club where pedigree counts for more than performance, where no politician is welcome, where 14 per cent of its members are ex one army or the other, where 15 per cent have a relation to keep things cosy, and where only 2 per cent are female' – the words of Jim Bolger, a former accountant who is one of the country's most brilliant and successful contemporary horse trainers and considered to be on his way to take on the mantle of the greats of the past.[27]

Show-jumping and eventing (dressage, cross-country, and endurance) are part of the equine scene in Ireland; the showpiece of jumping is the Dublin Horse Show in the first week of August every year, with Noel Duggan's Millstreet in Co. Cork coming second, with a post-Dublin show in August, and now a new indoor jumping event later in the autumn. The Dublin Horse Show features the Aga Khan Cup, the stylish centre-piece attended by the President of Ireland and the entire diplomatic corps, with rounds of embassy cocktail parties and balls to complete the fun.

The bray of hounds and the sound of horns are the symbols of the hunt, the old and classic fox-chase across country in smart hunting-pink jackets and jodhpurs, with Masters (even if they're women) leading the way. Ireland abounds with old and classic hunts, and even if the hunt is not among the smartest or most renowned, it is an important feature of Irish country life – the Galway Blazers, the Scarteen Hunt (Limerick), the Ward Union, each has its Master and its long history. More and more tourists join the hunt on a pricey package – another side to the horse

---

* Vincent O'Brien (b. 1917, Churchtown, Co. Cork).
† Rt Hon. Sir Michael Morris, Bt, third Baron Killanin, President of the International Olympic Council 1972–80.

business. Traditional farmers are turning more and more to the horse as a source of tourist income, with Euro-grants persuading them out of beef and dairy farming. Polo, from its original base in Phoenix Park, Dublin city's beautiful open green space, is beginning to expand (though its horses are mostly Argentine-bred). Riding-clubs with trekking offers are mushrooming everywhere, as Bord Fáilte capitalizes on one of Ireland's very special attributes.

It would take much more than one chapter of this book fully to describe the complex interaction of Irish life and Irish horses. An illustration of this interaction is the emotion with which Irish people speak of some of the great horses which have emerged, of none more so than of the steeplechaser Arkle, bred by a Dublin family in 1957. Owned by Anne, Duchess of Westminster, and trained at home by Tom Dreaper, this 'wonder horse' crowned an extraordinary succession of unbroken wins at all the big races in the British Isles with a hat-trick of wins in the Gold Cup at Cheltenham in England, from 1964 to 1966. The death of his jockey at Cheltenham, Pat Taaffe, in 1992 reminded the country of that illustrious partnership. Taaffe, in the tradition of great Irish jockeys, once said of Arkle: 'He was like a human being; he knew exactly what was required of him and did it. He loved the crowds and he was a grand quiet horse at home.'[28] Arkle's skeleton is lovingly preserved at the National Stud of Ireland in Kildare. Wherever horse-lovers gather in the world, they will recognize the great names of twentieth-century horses that came out of Ireland: Dawn Run, Shergar, Red Rum, Nijinsky, L'Escargot, Dundrum, Boomerang . . . The roll-call is very long.

GOING TO THE DOGS: GREYHOUND-RACING

'If horse-racing is the sport of kings, greyhound-racing is the sport of their van drivers,' said an (understandably anonymous) sports writer to the author in summing up the section of Irish society which has traditionally followed the dogs. Greyhound-racing is an old-established sport in Ireland: the first meeting on the island took place in Belfast in April 1927, followed by the first meeting in the South in May of that year. The sport evolved out of the rural pursuit of farmers training their dogs using hares; it is the survival of that original sport of live-hare coursing, and the alleged widespread cruelty to hares which results, that causes controversy today.

Eighteen licensed greyhound tracks are dotted around the country, eight of them owned by the national semi-State body Bord na gCon* (Irish Greyhound Board). Figures are slow to emerge from the board, but the 1991 results show a decrease in certain key areas compared with the previous year, and part of a continual pattern. (The board pointed out in its preliminary report for 1991 that greyhound tracks in the USA and Britain had experienced much greater decline in turnover and attendances.) On-course betting with bookmakers and the tote amounted to IR£33·82 million, a decrease of nearly IR£2 million on the previous year. Attendances at the 1,896 meetings was 704,000, down by 2·89 per cent. On the other hand, prize money was at an all-time high of IR£2 million in 1991, as was sponsorship at IR£584,533. Strenuous efforts are being made to inject new life into the sport, not least because of the valuable export market in greyhounds, particularly to Britain. Bord na gCon operates a sales advisory service for worldwide prospective purchasers of Irish greyhounds. In 1991, the total number of dogs exported was 10,034, with an estimated value of IR£25 million. Therefore the breeding activity is all-important, and new courses are under way to widen and improve the expertise in that area. The main track in the country, Dublin's Shelbourne Park, is being upgraded and made comfortable and welcoming to a gentler, less hardy kind of person, including women.

In 1993, twenty years' campaigning against live-hare coursing by greyhounds found an expression in Dáil Éireann: a private member's bill was brought in by a Dublin Deputy, Tony Gregory, which sought to ban it. It is an issue which rouses fierce passions, as coursing clubs around the country reject accusations of cruelty, and ugly scenes in rural Ireland result from protests. The debate about Gregory's bill was intense, particularly inside the parties, as rural and urban Deputies lined up against each other. The government promised legislation to muzzle the dogs, and to introduce mandatory veterinary inspection of hares. The Irish Coursing Club insisted that part of the reason for Ireland's healthy exports of greyhounds

---

*Bord na gCon, established in 1958, with headquarters in Limerick. Government allocation to the board in 1992 was IR£4 million.

was that they were well trained in the coursing fields, unlike those in other countries. The battle promised to be a long one.

GOLF

The climate and the scenery of Ireland combine to produce some of the most beautiful golf-courses in Europe: 148,000 golfers, men and women, are on the Golfing Union's list of registered players.[29] Of course, only a handful of these are women members, since the anti-woman bias of Irish golf goes very deep. Women instead may be associate members – and the dispute goes on. (See Chapter 18.) Two hundred and seventy-one golf courses, with more being added each year, of which nearly all are private clubs, add up to a considerable investment. Mostly a middle-class sport – though that is changing as public courses begin to emerge – membership fees in the private clubs range from IR£2,000 down to IR£700, with waiting lists at most of the well-established clubs. The burgeoning of golfing tourism, as well as the grants from Europe for agri-tourism for farmers (up to IR£50,000 for conversion of farmland to golf course), have led to an explosion of fine new courses in recent years. The most spectacular of these are millionaires' Michael Smurfit and Tim Mahony's investments in golf/country clubs around two great Irish houses, Straffan, Co. Kildare, and Mount Juliet, Co. Kilkenny.

BOXING

'Whether boxing people like it or not, it is a working man's sport,'[30] said a former Irish Olympic boxer, Mick Dowling, now a respected Irish coach, in the aftermath of Ireland's two Olympic medals in 1992. The Drimnagh Boxing Club, from which the Republic's gold-medal winner graduated, epitomizes the real heart of Irish amateur boxing. In 1992, reporters descended to examine this Olympic nursery, to find a cold hall, poorly equipped and badly in need of repair, in the centre of a modest working-class Dublin district. The shower area was extremely shabby, and one of the changing-rooms couldn't be used. A new roof was added in 1992. It cost £35,000. The State came up with £5,000 and the rest was raised by collecting money from the local area.

There are about 320 amateur boxing clubs in Ireland. The Irish Amateur Boxing Association has members in the North and South of the country: Dublin has about fifty clubs, Belfast forty. There are about 6,000 people boxing on the island, mostly youngsters who do not go on to senior level. 'They find out about girls and discos and that's that,'[31] said the vice-president of the Irish Amateur Boxing Association, Brendan O'Conaire. Many of those working in the field of boxing seem to consider their role as partly that of social worker, and point out that many of their young members could well be young offenders were it not for the activity and fulfilment given by their boxing involvement. For despite the presence of boxing clubs in the universities, the Gardaí, and the Army, the sport is firmly rooted in the urban working class, which is the victim of so much of Ireland's chronic unemployment problem.

Professional boxing is almost non-existent in the Republic of Ireland, and stars of the calibre of Barry McGuigan were trained and developed by the Northern Ireland professional bodies and managers.

Athletics and cycling grow every day because of international attention from television, and because of some great Irish role models for youngsters, though the facilities in Ireland can't compare with other more developed and bigger economies in Europe. Many Irish athletes must go abroad for training, as Ronnie Delaney, the gold medallist in 1956, did; the athletic scholarship to US colleges has been a considerable boon to Irish talent. Two of the Atlanta Olympic hopefuls in running, Sonia O'Sullivan and Catherina McKiernan, have benefited from athletic scholarships to US universities. Up to now, Olympic medals have been won in sailing, hammer-throwing, boxing, marathon running, and the 1,500 metres.

It has taken time for this developing society in Ireland to recognize the need for a long-term policy for sport, but the time might have arrived. One of the offshoots of the Olympic success was the establishment by Dublin's Lord Mayor in 1992 of a Sports Council, whose task was to set about planning to attract major international sporting events to the capital. Its president was Tony O'Reilly, and the council had a range of business people, sports stars, and sports managers. The 1993 statement of a new government at the beginning of the year was positive and encouraging. It asserted that sports policy 'will be integral to the government's education and health policies,'[32] and undertook to increase funding not only for future Olympic efforts, but for sports facilities across the country, including a 50-metre swimming-pool, and the building of an indoor national sports stadium; both of these will benefit from joint-venture arrangements with the private sector. Given the economic conditions of early 1993, with Ireland's already jobless economy being battered by a currency crisis, the sports world could only wait and hope that the promises would not fade away.

NOTES

1. In conversation with the author, January 1993.
2. Trevor West, *The Bold Collegians – The Development of Sport in Trinity College, Dublin*, Lilliput Press.
3. *Lawrence's Handbook of Cricket in Ireland 1867–88*, quoted by Trevor West, op. cit.
4. Marcus de Búrca, *The GAA*, Gaelic Athletic Association, 1980.
5. ibid.
6. ibid.
7. Gaelic Athletic Association, *Official Guide. 1988*. Published by the GAA.
8. *Irish Times*, 9 October 1991.
9. Presidential address to GAA All-Stars awards dinner, 21 December 1991.
10. Éamonn Dunphy, *Sunday Independent*, 16 February 1992.
11. De Búrca, op. cit.
12. *Irish Times*, 19 October 1991.
13. Liam Collins, *Sunday Independent*, 16 February 1992.
14. Paul Kimmage, *Sunday Tribune*, 2 February 1992.
15. *Irish Times*, 19 October 1991.
16. Description of Brendan Mullin, a graduate of Trinity College and Oxford University, who played for Ireland more than forty times (article in *Dublin Tribune*, February 1991). He works as a stockbroker with the Dublin firm J. & E. Davy.
17. *Sunday Business Post*, 27 January 1991.
18. *Irish Press*, 12 February 1992.

19. *Irish Times*, 23 March 1992.
20. ibid.
21. ibid.
22. Mick Doyle, *Sunday Independent*, 19 April 1992.
23. Quoted by Trevor West, *The Bold Collegians*, op. cit.
24. Seán Kilfeather, *Irish Times*, 16 March 1991.
25. Grania Willis, *The World of the Irish Horse*, Weidenfeld & Nicolson, 1992.
26. The Racing Board, press release, 14 January 1992.
27. *Irish Times*, 19 November 1990.
28. *Irish Times*, 8 July 1992.
29. *Sunday Business Post*, 1 March 1992.
30. *Irish Times*, 8 August 1992.
31. *Sunday Tribune*, 9 August 1992.
32. *Fianna Fáil and Labour Programme for a Partnership Government, 1993–97.*

CHAPTER 20

Irish Identity Expressed:
Irish Culture by the 1990s

> Freud said that the Irish are the only race that can't be psycho-
> analysed; they're too ready to invent dreams, or to contrive lies more
> interesting than the truth.

Writer Anthony Burgess, with claims to Irishness himself, ascribed that *obiter dictum* to Freud, in reviewing a book – yet another – about James Joyce.[1] Joyce, the colossus of letters straddling the international consciousness of Irish culture, is at once an illustration of and a glorious escaper from the darkness surrounding Irish cultural life in the first decades of Irish political independence.* Joyce fled in order to be free of what he saw as Ireland's suffocating closed-mindedness. Other writers stayed, and suffered through nearly five decades of attempted thought-control, carried out by a government and people who took that long to develop confidence that they could be both civilized and creative.

In the Ireland of the last decade of this century, there is abundant evidence that those days are part of history: Irish traditional art and culture live contentedly with their international counterparts in all areas, old and new, both taking from them and enriching them with a new exuberance in self-expression which the country has never seen before. Naturally, debate and controversy are part of this new Ireland of the arts, as well as the occasional and inevitable artistic disaster; but the country which Joyce left is unrecognizable today in its freedom and artistic ebullience.

From street-theatre extravaganzas in the west of Ireland to the

---

* James Augustine Aloysius Joyce (1882–1941); born in Dublin, educated by Jesuits and at University College, Dublin (the 'Catholic' University), left Ireland with Nora Barnacle from Galway in 1904 to live in Trieste; his masterpieces include *Dubliners*, *A Portrait of the Artist as a Young Man* (pioneering the modern 'stream of consciousness' movement), *Ulysses* (the extraordinary wanderings through Dublin city), and the massive saga *Finnegans Wake*, which challenges scholars to this day.

eloquence of women poets writing of private agonies, from the international brotherhood of Dublin rock musicians U2, to the startling artistic achievements of the Wexford Opera Festival – there is rarely any lacuna in the year-round access to high-quality work of every description. Traditional musicians form a lively backdrop to eloquent literary talk in halls and pubs in a plethora of summer schools, and new realism about poverty and deprivation and the burning question of Northern Ireland makes the Irish confront their society in a succession of high-quality films, books and plays. In the small island community which Ireland is, this means that few people are left untouched by some example of Irish excellence in the arts. Two big problems exist in tandem with the emergence of this new Irish appetite for expression of its own identity: the pressure of Anglo-American media in all their manifestations; and the gradual, and seemingly inexorable, weakening of the Irish language.

The cultural community in Ireland has flourished and developed in recent years, despite the absence of any coherent national government-driven policy. Confusion about what exactly culture is, plus administrative apathy, led to a proliferation of cultural and heritage institutions and responsibilities divided among several different government departments; and since government departments rarely communicate with each other, and jealously guard their own small empires, fragmentation and sometimes conflict becomes endemic. All this was thrown into sharp focus when a new government in January 1993 appointed the first Cabinet-level Minister for the Arts, combined it with the Ministry for the Gaeltacht, and started to draw into it the different strands from different departments – like the National Concert Hall, the National Museum, the National Heritage Council, and the heritage section of the Office of Public Works. Resistance from other departments and tension between ministers was a feature of this process. It represented, however, a new and different approach to the whole field of culture and creativity as a central and important facet of Irish life, worthy of the full attention of government, which it had never had before.

It would perhaps be better to draw a veil over the early cultural experiences of twentieth-century independent Ireland, except that they reveal the indomitable nature of the human search for freedom of expression in all its forms, and the parallel truth that it is almost impossible to destroy the creative soul of a people. Ireland had had, of course, a great deal to contend with over previous centuries, as it struggled to survive its long domination – political, economic, and cultural – by Britain. In the latter part of that struggle, the doctrine of the industrial revolution had come to overshadow everything – that doctrine of the supremacy of economics and finances over everything else, the assumption that governments' sole purpose was to ensure such supremacy, deplored by economist John Maynard Keynes as 'the most dreadful heresy, perhaps, which has ever gained the ear of a civilized people'.[2] Ireland suffered from that theory, not least in the forces which it applied to weakening, and nearly extinguishing, the Irish language and many ancient Irish traditions along with it. The continuing battle for the rescue and resuscitation of the language is illustrative of so much in the nature of Irish politics and priorities that it is described in a separate section at the end of this chapter.

THE EARLY DAYS: FROM 1922

The Irish literary revival which took place in the first years of the twentieth century, involving the revered names of W. B. Yeats, John Millington Synge, and Lady Gregory, and the foundation of the Abbey Theatre, was followed by a sort of cultural sterility which set in with independence.

As the Irish members of parliament approach Leinster House, the seat of the Dáil and Senate, they pass between the National Library of Ireland and the National Museum in order to get to their own front door. This led to an old joke that therefore Dáil Deputies entering parliament turned their back on art, literature and cultural heritage. The cynicism about politicians in that story still flourishes today, as the war of words about State support for the arts continues as merrily as in most western democracies. In an extra-ordinarily ironic turn of events, a book on the history of the State involvement in the arts in Ireland which was published in 1990 became itself the centre of a hot debate on censorship, with many accusations about intimidation and deliberate shredding of the book.*

---

* Dr Brian Kennedy's *'Dreams and Responsibilities': The State and the Arts in Independent Ireland*, 1990, commissioned and published by the Arts Council. The

There was once a 'Ministry for Fine Arts' in Ireland, which lasted all of nineteen weeks, and was quietly abolished at the signing of the treaty with Britain in 1921: abolished so quietly that no one told the only civil service staffer until he enquired one day, to find that his office had been merged with the Department of Education. There was, however, a continuing almost lone voice putting forward ideas and schemes about State support of the arts during those early decades of independence, when politicians of all sides were not at all inclined to think about that side of life as they worked to establish the new State. He was a lawyer and art expert, Thomas Bodkin,* who later became widely known for his efforts in arranging to have Ireland and Britain share a bequest of outstanding paintings which had been uncertainly bequeathed by Sir Hugh Lane. The historian of the Irish State and the arts, Dr Brian Kennedy, has no doubt about Bodkin's singularity: 'It is an understatement to say that Bodkin was ahead of his time . . . he was offering advanced arts policy proposals to politicians who had neither the resources nor the inclination to implement them.'

Amid a climate of censorship and penury, there was, however, a major arts initiative with the decision to give a State subsidy to the Abbey Theatre, the first such subsidy in the western world. In the budget of 1925, a grant of £800 was made. There was a stipulation that a Catholic should be added to the Board of Directors, which was duly done, to the surprise of the chosen man,† who gave this opinion of his appointment: 'I possessed no obvious qualifications beyond being a Catholic, which was apparently considered desirable . . . I knew nothing about the theatre and received no director's fees.'[3]

---

argument in late 1991 concerned the shredding by the Arts Council director of 200 remaining copies of the book, on the grounds that there was no room in storage for them (he already had 300). The then Taoiseach, Charles Haughey, denied all knowledge of the shredding and expressed his 'distress' at hearing about it, in the Dáil on 17 December 1991.

*Thomas Bodkin (1887–1961), Secretary to the Commission on Charitable Donations and Bequests; Director of the National Gallery of Ireland, and Professor of Fine Arts at the Barber Institute, Birmingham.

†George O'Brien, who became Professor of National Economics and later, of Political Economy, at University College, Dublin.

Interestingly, no government introduced a law censoring theatrical productions; perhaps there was no need, given the violently hostile public reaction to Seán O'Casey's *The Plough and the Stars* in 1926, when poet, Senator, and playwright W. B. Yeats fiercely denounced the Abbey audience from the stage, accusing them of 'disgracing themselves'. Despite the prevailing climate, the theatrical revival continued, and the Gate Theatre was established, bringing international drama and more adventurous production style to Dublin – in the words of Mícheál Mac Liammóir of the Gate, setting 'a faintly fluttering heart a-beat once more in Ireland's body'. That heart was taking a severe battering in the area of films and literature, with censorship laws in 1923 and 1929 gradually grinding down the will and interest of the artists concerned, many of whom were totally alienated and left the country in disgust. Condemnation from writers at home and abroad was expressed in pungent terms, often bitter and dismissive. George Bernard Shaw, an early exile, conveys the general dismay:

In the nineteenth century, all the world was concerned about Ireland. In the twentieth, nobody outside Ireland cares two-pence what happens to her ... if, having broken England's grip of her, she slops back into the Atlantic as a little grass patch in which a few million moral cowards are not allowed to call their souls their own by a handful of morbid Catholics, mad with heresyphobia, unnaturally combining with a handful of Calvinists mad with sexphobia, then the world will let 'these Irish' go their own way into insignificance without the smallest concern.[4]

Despite references to 'perpetual adolescence', 'obscurantism settling on the country like a fog' and other despairing condemnation, the censorship continued. Side by side with this, there was an uncertain and faltering development of the visual arts, of the museums and the National Library, all the while without a definite national policy for the arts; this placed Ireland firmly in line with most small western democracies.

When Eamon de Valera came to power in the 1930s, to remain the dominant figure in Irish politics for the next thirty years, things were not to get much better. According to a writer, broadcaster, and later senior arts administrator of the time, Mervyn Wall, the new Taoiseach 'hadn't the slightest understanding of, or interest in, the arts ... he couldn't see any reason for playing the works of foreign composers in Ireland as we already had our own beautiful Irish music . . .'[5] In his fifties, de Valera said he had never been in the Abbey Theatre, Ireland's national theatre; in that, he was not different from the first leader of the country, William Cosgrave, who had made the same admission in 1924. One of the underlying elements in the disdain of Fianna Fáil and a great many of its followers for anything concerning 'the fine arts' was the almost unspoken feeling that the places where such things had always been found were the 'big houses' – the homes of the landed gentry, not perceived as part of native Irish tradition. Orchestras, concerts, operas, dances, works of art were all part of English domination, nothing to do with 'Irish Ireland'. In his zeal to encourage cultural endeavour only if it coincided with his own vision of an Ireland which he wanted to re-establish, de Valera and his followers were introverted; for many, this equated with philistinism. It was, given the history, an understandable if not agreeable attitude. It persisted for a very long time.

The attitude of officialdom, in particular the all-powerful Department of Finance, was hardly encouraging. In the course of a government debate about the possible funding of a concert hall in 1937, the department delivered itself of the opinion that the arrival of the 'musical talking film' and 'the wireless set and gramophone' had ensured that 'the necessity for public concerts had become smaller and would continue to decline', and asked: 'Is it any part of the State's duty to resuscitate a Victorian form of educational recreation?'[6]

A change of government saw a slight change of heart: in 1951, the Arts bill establishing the Arts Council was passed by the Dáil, having been steered through parliament by one of the short-lived non-Fianna Fáil governments. In the bill, the definition of areas where the council would have responsibility was outlined: 'painting, sculpture, architecture, music, the drama, literature, design in industry and the fine arts, and applied arts generally'. A month after its passing, the inter-party government fell, and so the indefatigable Thomas Bodkin was not made first Secretary of the Arts Council: he was close to John A. Costello, the previous Taoiseach, and in Irish politics, that kind of association disqualifies. The 1950s was a decade of poverty, emigration, and stagnation in Ireland, not a propitious time for the new council. Having been established, however, the Arts Council gradually, if tortuously slowly over two decades, built up its influence and funding, with both the State and the council taking some small steps towards placing the arts – and associated design – slightly more centrally in Irish life.

Milestones of cultural development were the founding of Ardmore Film Studios in 1958 and the associated Irish Film Finance Corporation (alas, both were to fail); and the Kilkenny Design Workshops, which used the expertise of Scandinavian designers to improve standards. The new Abbey Theatre was built, replacing the original, which had been destroyed by a fire, and included a small experimental Peacock Theatre; a fine new extension to the National Gallery was built and an innovative director, James White, appointed. The government gave IR£300,000 towards the construction of the new Cork Opera House. Despite committees and discussions and documents, however, no national concert hall was built in those years; it took until 1974 before a government announced that the great hall of the former University College, Dublin building near the centre of the city would be adapted to fill this need. In the event, it was very successfully done by the Office of Public Works.

The coming of a native Irish television station in 1961 was the major cultural development of those decades – bringing television with its potential and dangers for the indigenous culture of any small country. The Arts Council opposed the establishment of the station, arguing that the IR£1·5 million given for initial capital investment would have been better spent on direct subvention of the arts. Television hastened the social and cultural changes already understood as inevitable by many. It 'took viewers on voyages of discovery of Irish society'[7] and was a contributory factor to the changing of the censorship law; in 1967, a new Act limited the censorship of books to twelve years (renewable). Another contributory factor was the Church sacking of a teacher, John McGahern, from his post following the banning of his second book, despite its acknowledgement as a work of art by, among others, the Arts Council.* This caused considerable uproar and embarrassment.

---

*In 1990, John McGahern's novel *Amongst Women* (Faber) was short-listed for the Booker Prize and won the Irish Guinness Peat Aviation IR£50,000 prize.

The last book by an Irish writer to be banned was Lee Dunne's *The Cabfather* – it was released from the censor in 1988. Cinema censorship had been liberalized in 1964.

The arrival of a new major figure on the Irish political scene in the late 1960s ushered in a fresh approach and a period of dynamic growth in consciousness of, and accompanying patronage of, the arts in general. Charles Haughey* became Minister for Finance in 1967, and increased the Arts Council budget to IR£60,000 from IR£40,000. His long career at the centre of Irish politics was never free from controversy, including his desire to be known as a patron of the arts. 'He cornered the market politically in that area,' said a senior arts administrator not altogether admiringly. His principal monument in the cultural life of Ireland is his radical tax measure of 1969: it freed creative writers, sculptors, composers and painters (but not performing artists) living and working in Ireland from income-tax obligations. This had a psychological as well as a practical result for Irish artists; after the long period of stagnation, suspicion, and neglect, the creative community felt it had come in from the cold, and was accepted fully into Irish life.

With new galleries, newly invigorated art colleges, and new support for the Gate Theatre, the country had at last begun to shake off its dull acceptance of cultural mediocrity. Not that there was a coherent State policy for the arts, or any equivalent to the kind of economic planning which had so assisted Ireland's emergence from a long economic decline; but at least there was a senior and powerful politician who seemed genuinely interested in the area. In 1973, with a new Fine Gael/Labour government, the impetus continued: the Arts Council was radically restructured, enlarged, given more powers, placed under the Taoiseach's department, and became accountable to the public. Among those speaking in the Senate debate on the new council was Mary Robinson, already making her mark in national politics; she wanted the council's scope broadened to include film. In view of the many major mistakes made later by governments in handling the Irish film industry, her remarks were prescient.

---

*Extensively covered in many chapters of this book, including those dealing with government, political parties, national economics and finances, and Northern Ireland.

The government grant to the council was increased in 1975 to IR£200,000; in 1972/3 it had been IR£85,000. A dramatic new feature of the new council was its openness to the press, as well as its composition: its seventeen members included professional artists and writers, and a Northern Ireland nominee, and among them were three women. And it set about, quickly, establishing its priorities, which included a demand to government that the Arts Council should be just that; in other words, while it welcomed government and ministerial interest and support of its work, it insisted on being consulted fully when any major cultural decision was being made. That area continues to be a source of controversy into the 1990s, as politicians from time to time want personal credit for grand gestures – notwithstanding the fact, so often totally forgotten by both public and politicians, that the money comes from the taxpayer, not the personal munificence of the minister temporarily in place. Allied to that has been the tendency for governments to decide unilaterally on the funding of some cultural initiative, without going through the Arts Council, which tries to follow an overall policy.

In 1975 a 'talented iconoclast',* Colm Ó Briain,† took over as director of the Arts Council, and proceeded to administer a vigorous stirring to the cultural life of the country, in particular the State-supported end of it. A restless and energetic personality, with a gift for communication, Ó Briain challenged all the assumptions and invited the innovative wherever he went: moreover, he was a committed socialist, and later went on to become, for a while, the general secretary of the Irish Labour Party. He led the Arts Council into a period of achievement and growing independence of government, in terms of policy and public statements. In 1975, too, the Arts Council was greatly strengthened when the Abbey Theatre, the Gate Theatre, the Irish Theatre Company, the Irish Ballet Company and the Dublin Theatre Festival were all removed from the aegis of the Department of Finance and put under its wing,

---

* According to Dr Brian Kennedy.

†Colm Ó Briain (b. 1943). A Jesuit education and legal training in University College, Dublin, and the King's Inns (Bar training) were the unlikely stamping-grounds of this creative television, theatre, and film director, arts administrator, and political activist. In January 1993 he was appointed special adviser to the Minister for Arts, Culture and the Gaeltacht.

increasing its power and financial clout (to nearly IR£1 million in 1976). In July 1975 the Irish President (then Cearbhall Ó Dálaigh, himself a most cultured man) opened a large extension to the Chester Beatty Library, built by public funds: this is a world-famous collection of priceless oriental treasures donated to Ireland. And local authorities around the country began to flex their muscles and spend some money on the arts, in accordance with the 1973 legislation.

A landmark in the development of the arts was the Richards report of 1976, a critique and blueprint for Irish arts policy. Following the report, the Arts Council began a programme of support for individual creative artists of all disciplines, and – most important – embarked on a strong regionally directed programme of activities. Tours began all over Ireland of the Dublin-based music and theatre groups, festivals of all kinds sprang up, as well as theatres and arts centres. In response to the clear signals emanating from the Arts Council, and as if waking from a long sleep, an astonishing mushrooming of artistic activity of every kind broke out all over Ireland. It led, naturally, to ever-increasing demands for funding, and to public demands by the Arts Council to government. Contact with the Arts Councils of Great Britain and Northern Ireland emphasized for Irish administrators how relatively niggardly their own support was in comparison with that for their peers outside the country.

A new Arts Council was appointed in 1978, under a Fianna Fáil government: Ó Briain continued to criticize and demand more and more funding, which was given relatively generously, but not often generously acknowledged. The Department of Education came in for heavy criticism, after the Arts Council commissioned a report, *The Place of the Arts in Irish Education*, by Ciarán Benson.* There were responses from the State to this constant prodding, in particular the appointment of arts officers to some vocational education bodies around the country, and the support of youth-theatre touring companies.

Charles Haughey finally became Taoiseach in December 1979. One of the most imaginative measures to support the arts happened before long: the setting up of Aosdána† – a group of creative

* Ciarán Benson was named as chairperson of the Arts Council in August 1993.
† In ancient Ireland, the *aos dána* were men of art whose skill gave them a status

artists, to a maximum of 150, who would be supported by a small income from the State, enough to allow them to avoid having to do other work to survive. The scheme was launched in March 1981, and the first eighty-nine members were named the following December. It was described by the English critic Bernard Levin in *The Times* of 18 March 1981 as 'the nicest bandwagon you ever saw'.

The 1980s saw a further expansion of the Arts Council's activities in every direction, accompanied by continual unease and controversy between council and government about funding and who exactly was in charge of national arts policy. A National Heritage Council was established in the Department of the Taoiseach, the National Concert Hall was given a direct grant and a board appointed by the Taoiseach, and Fine Gael appointed a junior Minister for the Arts in late 1982. These developments were looked on with suspicion by the council, since they might involve a bypassing of the council in designing and developing arts policy. However, the existence of the junior ministry in the Taoiseach's department was soon seen as a plus.

Major funding difficulties emerged in 1982 for the council as its grant was not increased in line with inflation, so that difficult decisions had to be made about cutting back in certain areas. Political fury ensued, as some of the decisions were interpreted as simply tools of pressure for more funds. Charles Haughey, who returned briefly as Taoiseach from February to November 1982, was not a man who liked to be defied. It was believed that he asked the council chairman to get rid of Colm Ó Briain.* This was firmly refused.

The first Minister for the Arts (this time at junior ministerial level) since the nineteen-week tenure of Count Plunkett in the pre-treaty days took office in December 1982. And in 1983, Colm Ó Briain decided to leave the council, after eight productive and controversial years, and a new Arts Council took office in January

---

beyond that due to them at birth. In 1991, controversy broke out about whose idea it was to set up Aosdána, Mr Haughey's or Colm Ó Briain and the Arts Council's. The truth seems to be a mixture of the two: it was an idea whose time had come.

*This was recounted to the Arts Council's historian, Dr Brian Kennedy, by James White, the chairman, on 23 February 1988. See notes to Chapter 9 of *Dreams and Responsibilities* by Brian P. Kennedy (Arts Council, 1990).

1984. From then on, it was a constant battle for funds, as the government of Garret FitzGerald tried to control public spending, including spending on the arts. The hapless minister, Ted Nealon, found himself constantly in the wars with the council, despite arranging for some new tax benefits for corporate sponsorship of the arts and finding IR£900,000 of unused funds lying dormant in the courts for capital funding. Theatre and other live performances were exempted from value-added tax in 1984, European Music Year was assisted, and new social-employment schemes allowed arts organizations to employ staff. A public row erupted in 1985 when the government instructed the Arts Council to replace the proposed cover of its annual report (a collage of press cuttings about underfunding of the arts) with an innocuous artistic design. Despite all these vicissitudes, the Arts Council continued with its work of chivvying government departments, in particular the hard-pressed Department of Education, which was already embroiled in bitter dispute with teachers because of lack of money. The regional policy was considerably strengthened by the new director, Adrian Munnelly,* who expanded in a quieter but workmanlike manner the initiatives put in place by Ó Briain, and took a strong personal interest in the education area.

Two hopeful signs now emerged: first, the government set about preparing a White Paper on cultural policy – the first time this had ever been done; and second, a National Lottery was established, which would assist the funding of arts and culture. After the White Paper appeared in January 1987, entitled *Access and Opportunity*, endorsing the Arts Council's policies and positions, the government changed. But the council had already submitted a historic five-year plan for the development of cultural policy and funding. The new Taoiseach – Charles Haughey again – got into public controversy with the outgoing council, who saw what they considered to be an 'Arts Council Mark 2' as lottery moneys were distributed to arts projects by the Department of the Taoiseach without reference to the Arts Council. However, in the dying days of 1988, as he prepared

---

* Adrian Munnelly (b. 1947). From Mayo, he was educated at University College, Galway, and became a teacher in Monaghan and Mayo, then education officer in Castlebar, and held the same post at the Arts Council before being appointed director in 1983.

to appoint his own Arts Council, the Taoiseach seemed to relent, and affirmed: 'It would be my intention from now on to allocate all moneys for the arts to the Arts Council ... we should establish a good Arts Council and entrust to them the task of holding the balance and deciding the priorities.'[8] Apart from the implied criticism of that adjective 'good', the Arts Council were well pleased to have elicited that affirmation of their role.

By 1992, funding of the Arts Council had reached a little over IR£10 million (see table). As a result of the acceptance of the Arts Council's five-year development plan, and more funds available because of the National Lottery, the allocation to the council jumped by 40 per cent between 1989 and 1991. There was negligible increase in 1992 over the previous year, leading to gloomy forecasts for hundreds of groups hoping for increased funding. The council compares financial support of the arts per capita in 1991 as between Ireland and Britain: Wales, IR£4·31; Scotland, IR£4·23; Northern Ireland, IR£4·00; Ireland, IR£2·85.

The Arts Council appointed in 1989 for a period to 1993 was generally regarded as a good one. An important part of any modern Irish Arts Council's make-up should be the ability to communicate effectively with the seat of power; and this council had that skill. It should also encompass a wide range of artistic disciplines, while understanding finance and planning. A council with a combination of vision and business, along with a wise overview, was the achievement of Charles Haughey who appointed that council three years before his own departure from politics. Chaired by Colm Ó hEocha, talented president of University College, Galway, and a much respected, low-profile administrator and scholar, it included the business manager of U2 and general show-business entrepreneur, Paul McGuinness. Ireland's best-known theatre managing director, Michael Colgan of the Gate Theatre, and philosopher/writer Richard Kearney were both relatively young luminaries of Irish artistic debate. An Irish-language scholar, an art-gallery owner, and a television presenter and former Irish harpist and singer made up the three women on the council: Máire de Paor, Bríd Dukes, and Kathleen Watkins, respectively. Poetry, prose, music, opera, the Irish language, and architecture were all among other areas covered in the membership. They have generally been judged a success in their practical and personally generous approach to their work. In

The Arts Council: 1992 Budget (IR£)			
Income		**Expenditure**	
Grant-in-aid	4,968,000	Literature	655,000
National lottery	4,988,000	Visual arts	1,121,000
Sundry income	130,000	Film	415,000
Total	10,086,000	Drama	3,395,000
		Dance	195,000
		Traditional music	245,000
		Opera	567,000
		Music	528,000
		Arts centres	666,000
		Education	230,000
		Community arts, festivals, etc.	305,000
		Regions	285,000
		Capital	735,000
		Sundry	94,000
			9,436,000
		Administration	700,000
		Capital account	10,000
		Total	10,146,000

Source: The Arts Council, 12 October 1992.

December 1992, the Taoiseach Albert Reynolds announced a further IR£1 million in the 1993 allocation to the Arts Council, bringing the total to IR£11 million.

Ireland certainly experienced a time-lag in coming to an understanding of the importance of the arts as the means of self-expression of a people and therefore essential to the national morale. But the Arts Council's director believes the councils through the years have 'created a climate in which the arts are an accepted part of life, working with communities across the country ... twenty years ago, the arts were never on the local agenda'.⁹ Among the most striking features of recent years has been the arrival of so many new painters and sculptors working in every part of the country, with about equal representation of women and men. High-quality festivals of whatever discipline always feature exhibitions of painting and sculpture as a *sine qua non*. Open-air street-theatre spectaculars, created and constructed to a high artistic standard by local artists, are another feature of the Irish summer, despite the uncertain climate. The explosive cultural fabric of Ireland's rock music scene – Dublin has been called the city of 1,000 rock bands, but it is not confined to Dublin – is apparently unstoppable. Traditional music has been revived in its many forms, and enthrals tourists as much as Irish people, who are themselves amazed at its richness. The suspicion and lack of confidence in coming to terms with the history of Ireland as exemplified in, for example, Dublin's Georgian architecture, has almost evaporated. The destruction of beautiful old houses, or simple village architecture, is now seen as mistaken and sad. The insularity of the country has passed, replaced by the confidence of an outward-looking young generation of artists and writers who take what they treasure about Ireland's past and combine it with their own internationally informed integrity.

One of the happiest fusions between Ireland's cultural past and present has been seen in the revival of traditional Irish music, singing and dancing. Central to this revival was an organization begun in 1951 called Comhaltas Ceoltóirí Éireann (Irish musicians' association), which started life when a group of Irish pipers held the first national Fleá Cheoil (music festival) in Mullingar in 1951 in central Ireland. Primarily an occasion for competitions in various instrumental skills, the Fleánna attracted Irish music lovers from the whole country, and then from further afield. Irish exiles came home, saw what was happening and took the good news back to their adopted countries. Comhaltas Ceoltóirí started classes and got the traditional fiddlers, flute-players, pipers, and a range of other musicians to pass on their skills in a huge teaching programme. Television and radio added impetus to the spreading enthusiasm, and new kinds of arrangements and styles saw the birth of groups like the internationally popular Chieftains, Clannad, the Bothy

Band – and today's Planxty, and Stockton's Wing ... A great international ballad boom in the 1960s found a ready market in the pubs of Ireland, fostering simultaneously a new interest in the old ('sean-nós') traditional unaccompanied songs. Today, new stars travel the world with adaptations of Irish and foreign traditional music. And in Ireland, traditional music and its variations are found in hundreds of pubs across the country, to be heard in its purest and most traditional form in Counties Clare, Galway and Sligo. It is in the playing and enjoyment of this kind of music that the visitor to Ireland comes to understand the place of the public-house – the pub – as a cultural reality in Irish life.

There are geographical gaps in this spreading of cultural activity, and one of them is in the centre of the island, where the midlands have yet to develop their response to the new feeling of exploration of the arts, although some stirrings are visible. The education system has yet to show itself capable of providing enough music in schools, so private music schools have sprung up everywhere, to the detriment of poorer children; likewise there is little in the way of theatre or drama studies in schools, surprising in a country which excels in theatre and which in 1991 and 1992 provided London and Broadway with its most successful serious drama. It is a measure of parents' motivation that young Irish musicians clamour for auditions at two thriving national youth orchestras which perform Mahler with total aplomb, and a touring Opera Theatre Company featuring young Irish voices in everything from Handel to Britten to contemporary specially written opera.

Sometimes, mistakes are made even in the most distinguished company. In 1991, the Field Day artistic group, founded by playwright Brian Friel, with its headquarters in Northern Ireland, published a magnificent three-volume anthology of 1,500 years of Irish writing in all its forms. It was, and is, an astonishing achievement: a review in the *Independent on Sunday* described it thus:

Leafing through these three huge volumes is like sitting in the pit of a theatre, looking up at a stage on which, in the crowded chorus, stellar figures mix with those of lesser fame and also with gifted strangers whose names the general reader does not know. Swift, Berkeley, Sheridan,

Goldsmith, Burke, Wilde, Shaw, Yeats, Joyce, and Beckett are all here speaking in their own voices . . .[10]

The mistake was not only in the much-criticized nationalistic emphasis of the anthology, which after all reflected the background of the principal editor, Professor Séamus Deane of University College, Dublin, a Derry man born and bred. It was in the almost complete omission of the work of women poets and writers, and of modern feminist writings. It was as if the all-male editorial board had simply forgotten their existence – an existence which has been one of the most notable features of Ireland's modern cultural revival. One of Ireland's foremost women poets, Eavan Boland, said of the anthology's failure to venture into this new area:

. . . not only has it not taken the chance, it has performed a series of exclusions which are more directly challenging and more deliberately silencing of women writers, poets, scholars, in this country than any I can remember . . . in an anthology which is eloquently concerned with the anti-colonial, this furtherance of colonialism is inconsistent.[11]

Because of the general condemnation from women, and many men, a fourth volume is in preparation entirely devoted to the work of Irishwomen. It came as a shock that this could have happened in the field where women have been considered stronger than any other in conservative Ireland.

In April 1993, the directors of Field Day announced that they were taking a six-month 'sabbatical' – and so there came a temporary hiatus in the work of one of Ireland's most significant cultural innovations. It had produced some major work by playwright Brian Friel (*Translations* was an outstanding success), as well as its major literary work. A former director, hearing the news of the withdrawal, described its place in contemporary Ireland thus: 'Field Day stands for more than any single person. It stands for a movement in Irish writing informed by the Northern situation, and more than that, it stands for committed writing and theatre.'[12]

Despite that controversy, Irish writing is enjoying a renaissance. Irish book publishing, with total sales of IR£27.7 million reported in September 1992, has expanded by 40 per cent over six years. While not approaching the world leader – Germany – in expenditure per head on books (IR£57), Ireland is respectably placed with

IR£23 per head, and 41 per cent of all books bought in Ireland are Irish-published. Most best-selling contemporary Irish writers are published abroad and sell, of course, throughout the world. Poets, novelists and playwrights like William Trevor, Eavan Boland, Séamus Heaney, Josephine Hart, Derek Mahon, Paul Durcan, Nuala Ní Dhomhnaill, Jennifer Johnston, Dermot Bolger, and Roddy Doyle have followed the generations before, and with dramatists like Brian Friel (*Dancing at Lughnasa*), Tom Murphy (*The Gigli Concert*) and John B. Keane (*The Field*), present faces of Ireland and aspects of humanity which enthral the world as much as their own Ireland. Six Booker Prize nominations over four years, and a raft of theatre awards across the world, testify to the strength of Ireland's verbalizing. Poets have gained a new place in the country. Perhaps it is fanciful to equate 'the rise of the poet with the demise of the priest', as philosopher Richard Kearney remarked in 1991,[13] but it was not so long ago that 'poets were, in the public imagination, people you found in a dark corner in McDaid's* quoting an elegant line or two when not prevented by paranoia or excessive drink'.[14] Today in Ireland, the Séamus Heaneys and Eavan Bolands are household names and highly respected and read.

Among politicians, there is still a serious lack of interest in the arts. Only a small handful are ever seen on the cultural circuit, or heard speaking on the subject in public.† In appointing his government in February 1992, Albert Reynolds showed a strange confusion about the arts; his junior Minister for the Arts was also put in charge of women's affairs and European affairs. The arts world felt that it would perhaps have been better to let the office drop than give it a corner of a junior minister's mind. Mr Reynolds himself came to office with no reputation for interest in the arts, unlike his controversial predecessor. Mr Haughey had – disparagingly – made reference to Mr Reynolds's 'country and western' image during the final political battle between the two men.

However, all that was to change in January 1993, when the

---

* A Dublin literary pub, frequented by, among others, the late Patrick Kavanagh.
† In 1982, the author was one of a group attempting to start an ad-hoc parliamentary Committee on Arts, Culture and Broadcasting. The short-lived Dáil was dissolved, the author joined the Cabinet, and the committee foundered. One of the more supportive members of that group was Michael D. Higgins, who became minister in the area just over ten years later.

politician in Dáil Éireann most identified with the arts was given a full Cabinet post of Minister for Arts, Culture and the Gaeltacht, with special responsibility for broadcasting. It was a rare moment in Irish politics, and a powerful symbol of the transformation of Irish political and social thinking. Michael D. Higgins,* a published poet and radical, long considered to be on the left of the Labour Party and former scourge of his party leader, was universally welcomed by the whole arts and culture community. Perhaps it was the unguarded remark of the leader of the small Progressive Democrats in the heat of the election that he could not imagine Michael D. Higgins in Cabinet ('Sure the man would go mad!')[15] which prompted his leader to take the plunge. Whatever it was, praise was showered on the party and its new minister. His impeccable record of passionate support of the arts and the language was recalled in all the media, and in his native Galway, fast becoming a centre of excellence in many facets of art and culture, the rejoicing was unrestrained. In wishing him well, many commentators and friends worried about the kind of demands he was about to undergo: 'A man who read the collected works of Thomas Mann while sitting through boring Senate debates on land drainage may find it hard to cope with the pressures of ministerial office.'[16] The country hoped that the minister's new office would not involve this idealist in too much pragmatism.

Minister Higgins (popularly referred to as 'Michael D.') had the backing of promises in the new government's *Programme for a Partnership Government*. In a two-page section on the arts, heritage and the film industry, a wide-ranging overhaul of provision for the arts all around the country was envisaged, along with an undertaking to use some of the massive new funding coming to Ireland from Europe under the Maastricht Treaty. Missing from the programme was any commitment to the provision of galleries, theatres and other performing places, museums, and film centres around the

---

*Michael D. Higgins (b. 1941 in Co. Clare), educated in Clare, University College, Galway, Indiana University, and Manchester University, and lecturer in sociology in UCG. A radical and outspoken commentator on human rights in Ireland and abroad, he was first elected to Dáil Éireann in 1981, having been a Senator. He was chairman of the Labour Party from 1978 to 1987. A volume of his poems, *The Season of Fire*, with drawings by Mick Mulcahy, was published (by Brandon Books) in 1993.

country, one of the more obvious deficiencies in all areas apart from two of the larger centres of population. A severe critic of the programme, Bruce Arnold,* wrote: 'There is a long-neglected programme waiting to be fulfilled: creating on a regional basis with proper funding, at least some of the facilities available in the capital city, and in a few other places around the country – notably Cork and Limerick.'[17] As if on cue, the Arts Council published a major proposal† for a capital programme for the provision of appropriate arts buildings and facilities in all parts of the country, by securing IR£35 million in structural funds from Europe. Since IR£8 billion was the magic figure which Ireland expected from Europe in the post-Maastricht push towards unity, it did not seem unreasonable. The council produced some interesting employment figures to support their case: the number of painters/sculptors, for example, was 2,300 in 1990, a 158 per cent increase since 1971. The number of actors/entertainers/musicians had increased by 75 per cent (to 2,600). Authors and journalists numbered 3,900 in 1990, an increase of 147 per cent since 1971. It pointed out that these increases took place at a time when other employment in Ireland was stagnant.‡

Signs of storms ahead immediately appeared: the new minister said that the Arts Council proposal would have to be discussed with his department, while the Arts Council's Literature and Community Arts Officer said: 'The independent Arts Council would be delighted to answer questions ... the Arts Council's independence has long been part of the fabric of national life and I hope we will continue in that spirit.'[18] This was a symptom of the difficulties for the new minister and the cultural institutions in putting in place mechanisms for the implementation of government policy from a minister who would certainly not be content to let the Arts Council or anyone else decide on national cultural and artistic aims and objectives.

---

*Bruce Arnold (b. 1936), English-born, educated at Trinity College, Dublin, has lived in Ireland since the 1950s. Political commentator, novelist, author and filmmaker on Irish artists. Was victorious in a legal case against the Irish government for damages because his telephone was tapped by the government of Charles Haughey in 1981 and 1982. Literary editor of the *Irish Independent* 1987 to date.

† *Capital Programme for the Arts, 1994–97*, Arts Council, January 1993.

‡ The council based their figures on a FÁS/ESRI survey of trends in the occupational patterns of employment in Ireland 1971–90, by T. Corcoran *et al.*, July 1992.

One of the new minister's early and popular steps was to announce the government's decision to reactivate the Irish Film Board. This board had been 'put on ice' by Charles Haughey in 1987, in the first flush of Fianna Fáil's financial rectitude. Because of the continued international success of Irish film writers, directors, and actors, the absence of an active government-funded film board to provide state encouragement and some seed funding was by 1993 a source of continual embarrassment. As films like *The Commitments*, *My Left Foot* and *The Crying Game* achieved praise and honours right up to Oscar-winning level, the new minister chose his moment well; the day after Irish writer and director Neil Jordan won an Oscar for his screenplay for *The Crying Game*, having been nominated under six headings, the Film Board announcement was made. Its first chairperson was Lelia Doolan from Galway, a well-known activist in the film movement, former television and film producer and former Artistic Director of the Abbey Theatre. Other members included Neil Jordan. The minister announced that the board's headquarters would be in his native Galway.

Out of troubled history, modern conflict, and Celtic emotion has come the cultural Ireland of the 1990s. Freud's 'Irish dreams and interesting lies' have come into their own, fighting for their place through seventy years of development. The State's policy has been carried out in the past mainly by abdicating responsibility for policy to successive Arts Councils, and not designing a coherent broad central strategy in partnership with those councils. In 1993, with a new Cabinet seat for Ireland's first full Minister for the Arts, Culture and the Gaeltacht, a new phase seemed poised to begin.

THE IRISH LANGUAGE: A FIGHT FOR SURVIVAL

One of the most encouraging signs of life for the Irish language in the 1990s was the public commitment of the President, Mary Robinson, to relearn the language herself. The gesture was all the more striking, coming from someone who had never had any public connection with the language, except the minimal educational achievements on her way to becoming a barrister. By July 1992, after a year and a half in office, it was clear that she had made considerable progress: as she addressed the Houses of the Oireachtas, her insertion of some paragraphs, spoken in the language, showed an ease and fluency which had not been evident on the day of her inauguration in December 1990. She preceded those remarks in Irish by expressing hope that the language could receive the same dedication that people were showing towards protection of the environment:

Now we need to persuade our young Irish people that a language also is a part of our environment, is a living thing, subject to stresses and neglect, likely to be mourned if it becomes extinct, and entitled, I believe, to the same excited sense of care and protection.

Irish is one of the Celtic branch of the Indo-European language family. It has a close relationship with Gaelic: at some time in the sixth or seventh century, Gaelic was brought to Scotland by the Irish.

But the language fared badly in the nineteenth century, to the extent that the formal education system – such as it was – ignored its very existence. Irish had been spoken by the vast majority of the people in previous centuries. Requests to the English government of Ireland for proper educational provision for those areas of the country where Irish was still the only language of the people were also ignored. The British aim was to make English the language of everyday use, as well as the language of the schools: this was all a part of the 'stratified, hierarchical system of the cultures'[19] which had grown up in the old United Kingdom of Britain and Ireland over many decades and previous generations. The ancient Gaelic world and its institutions were not modified and integrated into the British system, and so they gradually weakened and faded: 'They were simply condemned to inferiority and left to rot away into a cultural desert.'[20] A social and cultural élite centred around power: the English-language culture of the top echelons filtered down and influenced all the institutions, schools, the newspapers, trade and business.

Change was slow to arrive, but it did come along with the ideology of nationalism, spreading throughout Europe from the late eighteenth century onwards, which had its effects in Ireland too.

One of the results was the gradual awakening of a new interest in the old traditional Gaelic ways, and in particular, the language. By the 1890s, the clearest expression of this interest was the Gaelic League, founded in 1893 by Douglas Hyde, a fervent believer in the need to restore 'Irish Ireland' who later became the first President of Ireland.* Like many visionaries before and after him, Hyde indulged in some romantic flights of fancy, as he extolled the utopia that would follow the 'de-anglicization' of the country. There was then, and still is in modern Ireland, an ambivalence about the imitating of English culture and institutions; it is constantly done, but it annoys and irritates the Irish even as they do it.

Hyde, who was a Protestant, saw the language as a unifying rather than a divisive force. In choosing the restoration of the language as the central plank of nationalism, he thought that the dangerous area of religion could thereby be neutralized as a threat to Irishmen coming together: 'It was possible to choose one's language in a way in which it was not possible to choose one's religion.'[21] Despite the kind of hindsight we might bring to bear on the subject today, when religion, language, and nationalism have been embroiled together and used as weapons in Northern Ireland, Hyde's first ideas were certainly admirable as an expression of national identity.

The Gaelic League had many successes in the period before the foundation of the new Irish State; in particular, many schools were persuaded to introduce Irish as an extra subject, and by 1915, more than 3,000 teachers were qualified to teach the language. When the first native government of the country took office, the language was placed firmly at the centre of education policy, where it remained for six decades. And that was where many mistakes were made. Education was given the task of restoring the language, but education failed without the kind of cross-societal support which was so badly needed and never given.

Today, as the language struggles to survive, the question arises: would it have surged back to general use and central importance if Ireland had not achieved its political independence before the work of restoration had really begun? Catalans in north-eastern Spain employ their language as an emphatic mark of their separate identity within Spain – but the Irish had achieved political independence as a largely English-speaking nation, and therefore a central motivation for asserting cultural separateness was removed in 1922. Added to that factor was the emergence in the early 1900s of some of the greatest Irish writers in English that Ireland ever produced; this cruel coincidence led some prominent nationalists to deny the

* See Chapter 1, 'The Presidency'.

true Irishness of any writing in the English language, leading to lasting tensions and divisions that did the Irish-language revival no good either.

In the first Dáil, in 1919, before formal independence was achieved, the then president of the Gaelic League was appointed Minister for Irish,* and after independence, Minister for Education: therefore, the policy of the Gaelic League became the policy of the government. It was an early Minister for Finance, Ernest Blythe, who tried to widen the application of State policy for the restoration of the language: 'His vision encompassed a much wider penetration by the language in the administrative machinery of the state, in commerce, vocational training, publishing, the legal system, and the creative arts, especially the theatre.'[22] Acceptance of these efforts was by no means universal in Ireland, since English was so entrenched; it was always a losing battle.

When de Valera came to power in 1932, there was a continuation of the widespread efforts to encourage the restoration of the language – indeed, that last ambition was, and remains, one of the essential 'core values' of the Fianna Fáil Party; the other was the 'reunification' of Ireland. (The party has still survived, though weakened, as the biggest in the State, despite the failure to achieve either aim.) There was little difference between the attitude of the two main political parties towards the Irish language in the early decades of the new State, though things changed somewhat in more recent years. But at that time, the differences were more in the way things were done. Fianna Fáil brooked no criticism or examination of how effective the policies were: 'Fianna Fáil were unswerving in their attachment to the original orthodoxy and were adamant in refusing an independent commission of enquiry.'[23] Those in charge of national policy neither carefully examined nor measured the results of their energy and financial commitment as the years went by; more successful methods might have been adopted, if it had been acknowledged that the ones already tried were not working.

By 1932, three-quarters of all serving national teachers were qualified in Irish, and Irish was taught in all except a handful of national schools. There was an accompanying set of draconian rules such as Irish-only in the infant classes of all schools, and the

* Seán Ó Ceallaigh.

rating of teachers on their ability in Irish. But there was continuing concern that the population in general showed no sign of replacing English with Irish as their everyday language. Worse, the heavy Irish emphasis in the schools of the country was not helping general attitudes: by the 1940s 'Irish had become fatally associated with the purgatorial fires of the classroom, the terrors of the irregular verb, and the distortions of ingrown virginity'.[24]

The long-serving Fianna Fáil Minister for Education, Tomás Ó Deirg, in 1943 refused an enquiry despite his own admission that the out-of-school environment was rendering the education policy almost useless: but in 1948, when a new non-Fianna Fáil government was elected, some easing of the policy was initiated, and this trend continued even under Fianna Fáil governments, more by stealth than formal announcement.

The *Irish Times* editorialized in the mid-1950s that the language was of interest only to 'elder statesmen, rabid doctrinaires, and the entrenched obscurantists of the Department of Education'.[25] This seriously overstated the case: but the signs were rampant that compulsion (Irish was necessary to obtain a school leaving certificate, enter the civil service, or go to most universities) and poor teaching methods between them were engendering considerable hostility at worst, and apathy at best, among most of the population.

Until the late 1960s, second-level education was not free, therefore the teaching of advanced Irish up to the age of seventeen or eighteen was confined largely to some sections of the middle classes, in schools run by religious orders. This led to a middle-class domination, which persists today, of Irish-language organizations in whatever sphere. It also explains why there have historically been strained relations between the ordinary country people of the Gaeltacht areas and those middle-class zealous revivalists of the Irish-language organizations.

Fine Gael made an issue of liberalizing the laws on Irish, and in 1973–4 the requirement of a pass in Irish to obtain either of the two school certificates – Intermediate and Leaving – was abolished, along with the Irish requirement for most public-sector appointments. This was a tacit acceptance of what was becoming very clear, that 'compulsion had failed to convert the vast majority to any practical desire to speak the Irish they were taught at school'.[26]

The National University of Ireland, with its constituent colleges (University Colleges, Dublin, Cork and Galway, as well as St Patrick's College, Maynooth, between them providing the majority of university education), retained the Irish requirement for entry, and continue to do so. This is the last bulwark in education for preservation of the language, since the Department of Education no longer requires Irish as a prerequisite to gaining a certificate. There are, sadly, classrooms full of youngsters across the country who are required by department rules to study Irish as a classroom subject, but who, unless they are really ambitious for a place in the national university system, are bored and unmotivated. This is difficult for both youngsters and teachers, and has led to new campaigns by parents for the further abolition of remaining compulsion. Even the granting of bonus marks – up to 10 per cent – for students who answer their school leaving examinations in Irish has failed to counteract this trend. In the late 1980s, an organization called the Association for Choice in Irish mounted a campaign, echoing a campaign called the Language Freedom Movement of the 1960s: the latter caused very high passions and resulted in what are politely called 'unruly scenes' even involving members of the clergy, including a future Cardinal, Tomás Ó Fiaich.

In his study of the situation of the Irish language published in 1990, Reg Hindley of the University of Bradford is clear-eyed about the prospects of revival of bilingualism: his thesis is that Irish is dying as a living, everyday language of the people, and will only survive as a respected repository of culture like Latin. To back up this thesis, Hindley analyses and rejects the accuracy of census returns over the years, which have shown up to 30 per cent of Irish people claiming to speak Irish and English.* He quotes Bord na Gaeilge's† study showing that only 4 per cent of the population were daily users of Irish in 1983, of whom 35,000, or a quarter,

* The numbers claiming to speak Irish rose from 27·2 per cent in 1961 to 31·1 per cent in 1986 (the latest figures available). These figures bear no relationship, however, to the numbers actually using Irish as their principal language: Bord na Gaeilge's figures put that at around 4–5 per cent.

† Bord na Gaeilge, established by statute in 1978 to 'extend the use of Irish, particularly its use as a living language and a general means of communication among the people', employs twenty-three people and in 1992 was granted IR£1·5 million for its work by the State.

were in the Gaeltacht, those small areas mostly in the west of the country, where Irish is still easily spoken and which receive economic assistance to keep it that way. The reason why Irish people fill in their census form claiming to 'speak Irish and English' is that, since all of them learned Irish at school, they feel that they have it inside them somewhere, only waiting to spring back into life. Linguists know better, alas. Surveys consistently show a general concern and goodwill for the survival of the language; this, however, does not extend to agreeing actually to do something themselves about it, but rather it is to expect someone else – like the government – to do it. John Bruton, the Leader of the Opposition, remarked with some asperity: 'It is this Irish unwillingness to cast aside symbols, while ignoring them in practice, that has given us an aspirational constitution and an impractical language policy.'[27]

Attitudes towards the Irish language and other forms of traditional Irish culture differ within Irish society; as Ireland becomes more urbanized, and its business community more internationalized as well as more powerful, interest in, knowledge of, or even benevolent regard for what one might call the symbols of ethnicity have faltered. As late as the 1960s, access to powerful positions in the public service involved strong adherence to the 'politically correct' view of the language as well as its constant use. That has all changed.

Another damaging blow to the language has been the insidious impression which has arisen among many Irish people since the start of the modern phase of the Northern Ireland conflict in the early 1970s that rabid nationalism, and its extreme manifestation, violent republicanism, are somehow connected with the language-revival movement. Irish people do not identify with militant republicanism, and some leaders of public opinion endorse that view and take it further: 'Horrified by the violence of events in Northern Ireland, they have turned to the condemnation of nationalism per se.'[28] In Northern Ireland itself, the language is certainly politicized. In 1991, at a ceremony to mark the granting of IR£750,000 by the British government to a new Irish-language group, the Ultach Trust, a British junior minister for community relations deplored this reality. The language 'has been torn out of the cultural context and has become a political weapon'.[29] A year earlier, another language organization in Northern Ireland, Glór na nGael, had its grant of £90,000 withdrawn by the British government, on the grounds that it was 'improving the standing and furthering the aims of paramilitary groups'.[30] That kind of incident is quietly observed in the Republic, no doubt confirming the anti-language prejudices which many hold.

A further blow to the work of revival of the Irish language was an exhortation in 1992 by the government-appointed chairman of the State's official Irish-language agency, Bord na Gaeilge, to voters in West Belfast to support Sinn Féin President Gerry Adams in the imminent British general election. Proinnsias Mac Aonghusa,* writing in Irish in *Anois*, an Irish-language Sunday newspaper, on 5 April 1992 asked the people to vote for Adams, despite the candidature of a respected constitutional Nationalist, Dr Joe Hendron. A considerable furore followed, north and south, with general condemnation. Historian and Cork senator, John A. Murphy, summed it up: 'In short, Proinnsias Mac Aonghusa's article was a bad day's work for Ireland, a betrayal of the language cause, and of numerous language-linked cultural groups.'[31] There were many calls for his removal by the government, or his resignation; neither happened. A month later, Mac Aonghusa was re-elected unopposed to his presidency of Conradh na Gaeilge, and declared (speaking in Irish) in the context of the approaching Maastricht Treaty referendum on closer European union, 'The mind of the slave, of the hireling, and the vagabond is still fairly dominant in Ireland ... according to the false leaders, the Gaelic tradition is worth little, and it does not matter if Irish people or foreigners are running the State.'[32] Most Irish-language organizations were quick to dissociate themselves emphatically from Mac Aonghusa's support of Sinn Féin. It was generally felt that the stereotypes of the Irish speaker who had a certain political outlook were no longer relevant, and that Irish belonged to all the people of Ireland. Mac Aonghusa's

---

*Proinnsias Mac Aonghusa (b. 1933 in Ros Muc, Co. Galway). Journalist and broadcaster; member of the Arts Council, President of Conradh na Gaeilge (a voluntary and rather fiery Irish-language organization) and former activist with the Labour Party. In the 1970s and 1980s, however, he was identified with Charles Haughey, leader of Fianna Fáil and three times Taoiseach. He is married to a Northern Ireland Protestant, Catherine McGuinness, who is well known both as a liberal in her Church, a former Trinity College senator, feminist, and holder of many important State offices on commissions and committees.

comments had resurrected attitudes which people had imagined dead.

The Irish language today is weakening. Despite pockets of enthusiasm, such as the establishment of all-Irish infant and primary schools, as well as some secondary schools, the general trends continue downward. Educationists and language enthusiasts alike are concerned too that, as the language is gradually becoming less important in the schools, there is a cultural vacuum left behind. Suggestions that the study of Irish in the schools should be part of a new course embracing other traditional aspects of Irish culture have been made from time to time but never acted upon.

What is to be done? Among the gloom, there is however the optimism engendered by the growth in appreciation of traditional culture and music, and the ancient arts and archaeology of the country. Young people flock to summer colleges where Irish language and culture are the core activities, combined with well-organized and lively summer activities. It no longer seems that the language can be repossessed as the normal spoken word by most of the people, but there is still a reluctance to accept that fact. That reluctance is presumably what prevents governments from designing new stratagems. The Irish language is now seen as just one component, albeit an essential one, of the cultural factors which form Irish identity. Politicians rarely bother to use the language, except those to whom it comes readily. In certain ministries, like education, it is considered necessary to include at least a few words (*cúpla focal*) in most public speeches.

Europe's interest in helping 'lesser-used' languages through its coordinating bureau* and financial assistance is a hopeful sign. One of the early steps in a new process will be to find the political and social courage to face the realities, instead of perpetuating myths such as the proclamation – uniquely in Europe – of a language that is little used in daily life as the first official language. The first big hurdle is to engage the attention of all those who are so newly interested in the ethnic and the traditional side of the modern world, and to convince them that a wealth of experience and pride waits for them in their ancestors' language. A noted English-language scholar, broadcaster, feminist and liberal described her

---

* The EC Bureau for Lesser-used Languages is located in Dublin.

own desire to know the Irish language, while castigating herself for her apathy, that universal obstacle: 'I know that there is a feast there, but I won't give up the time to learn the language so as to sit at the table.'[33]

In the government's plan of action published in January 1993, a commitment was given to establishing a long-promised Irish-language television station, to be located in the Connemara Gaeltacht, broadcasting for a couple of hours a day. With a new Minister for the Gaeltacht, whose constituency embraced Connemara, it looked indeed as if this promise would be fulfilled. The minister lost no time in acting. He got money from the fund which had built up in RTE since the advertising 'cap', announced the imminent establishment of an Irish-language television service, and in early May 1993 introduced an eighteen-member Foundation Committee to bring recommendations to him by the end of August. That committee was headed by Gearóid Ó Tuathaigh, vice-president of University College, Galway.

The rest of the Irish-language section in the Joint Programme for Government bore a depressing resemblance to the formulas and aspirations of the past which have failed to revive or renew the language. The feast, for the moment, will remain uneaten, unless the combination of Arts, Culture and the Gaeltacht under a new and committed minister might develop new thinking on this old problem. The minister and government were publicly reminded of grim realities by an eminent scholar and supporter of the language, Sean Ó Tuama, in April 1993: 'The first thing that has to be faced up to by leaders of opinion and in particular by leaders of Irish revival organizations is that the Gaeltacht is slowly but surely dying away ... only about 4 per cent of the whole population of Ireland seem to use Irish (mostly in their homes) on any sort of continuing daily basis.'[34] Professor Ó Tuama was comforted by the network of all-Irish schools, and by the increasing use of Irish phrases in various areas. But he pointed out that there was no sign of a bilingual speech-community emerging in any urban location. Therein lies the challenge, and the opportunity, for this ancient language.

NOTES

1. *Observer*, 2 August 1992.
2. John Maynard Keynes, 'Art and the State', *The Listener*, 26 August 1936, pp. 371–4.
3. James Meenan, *George O'Brien, A Biographical Memoir*, Gill & Macmillan, 1980.
4. Julia Carlson (ed.), *Banned in Ireland. Censorship and the Irish Writer*, Routledge, 1990.
5. *The Journal of Irish Literature*, vol. 11, nos. 1 & 2, January–May 1982 (quoted in Brian Kennedy's *'Dreams and Responsibilities'*).
6. Memorandum submitted by Department of Finance to Department of the President, 21 May 1937 (quoted in Brian Kennedy's *'Dreams and Responsibilities'*).
7. J. J. Lee, *Ireland 1912–1985, Politics and Society*, Cambridge University Press, 1989.
8. *Dáil Report*, 29 November 1988.
9. In conversation with the author, 10 August 1992.
10. Brian Moore, *Independent on Sunday*, 1 December 1991.
11. In a speech at the International Association for the Study of Anglo-Irish Literature, in Trinity College, reported in the *Irish Times*, 15 July 1992.
12. Playwright Tom Kilroy in the *Irish Times*, 4 April 1993.
13. *Sunday Independent*, 14 July 1991.
14. ibid.
15. *Irish Independent*, 16 January 1992.
16. *Sunday Business Post*, 17 January 1993.
17. *Irish Independent*, 8 January 1993.
18. *Irish Times*, 27 January 1993.
19. *Why Irish? Irish Identity and the Irish Language*, Bord na Gaeilge, 1989.
20. ibid.
21. ibid.
22. Séamus Ó Buachalla, *Education Policy in 20th Century Ireland*, Wolfhound Press, 1988.
23. ibid.
24. Declan Kiberd, 'Writers in quarantine: the case for Irish studies', *The Crane-bag Book of Irish Studies*.
25. ibid.

26. Reg Hindley, *The Death of the Irish Language*, Routledge, 1990.

27. *Irish Independent*, 11 August 1990.

28. *Why Irish?*, op. cit.

29. *Irish Times*, 4 April 1991.

30. ibid.

31. *Sunday Independent*, 12 April 1992.

32. *Irish Times*, 11 May 1992 (their translation).

33. Nuala Ó Faoláin, *Irish Times*, 11 February 1991.

34. *Irish Times*, Supplement on the Irish language, 13 April 1993.

CHAPTER 21

Ireland's Environment

There are many areas where Ireland's position as a small underdeveloped English-speaking island on the western edge of the European continent has its disadvantages, not least being unemployment and emigration, plus the threat to its culture and ancient language from both the United States and Britain. Environmentally, however, the island is blessed with mostly still unspoiled countryside, open spaces, clean water and pure air. And Ireland has benefited immensely from the international movement to protect the environment, which has come in time to allow her to avoid the worst excesses of her European neighbours as she seeks to industrialize in order to create employment.

In April 1992, a ninety-four-page bill was passed by both Houses of the Oireachtas after a year of parliamentary discussion, and nearly three years of unprecedented consultation between the sponsoring minister and scores of groups and individuals. The Environmental Protection Agency Bill 1990, signed by the President on 23 April 1992, was master-minded by Mary Harney TD,* who was appointed Minister for State at the Department of the Environment,† in charge of a new office of Environmental Protection in July 1989. It was a serendipitous appointment – public interest and concern on

---

* Mary Harney (b. 1953). From a conventional Catholic background in Dublin, though Galway-born, she attended Trinity College, where she was first woman auditor of the Historical Society. In 1977 she became the youngest-ever Senator, appointed by Taoiseach Jack Lynch. First elected to the Dáil in 1981 for Fianna Fáil, she was a joint leader of the breakaway Progressive Democrats in 1985. In 1992, her party left the coalition government with Fianna Fáil, precipitating a general election. She was returned to the Dáil, and became deputy leader of her party.

† The Department of the Environment is responsible for a wide range of services provided mainly through the local government system, and is responsible for the local-government system itself, as well as for water and sanitary services, housing, building, etc. Included in its remit is the roads system, which many people feel should be with the Department of Transport. The minister since February 1992 is Michael Smith (b. 1940), from Tipperary, formerly a farmer.

environmental issues had reached fever pitch, leading to the election of local politicians and one national politician belonging to the Green Party (of which more later). The woman who took office in July 1989 had already shown her mettle and ability in her political career, and her party had made the establishment of strong measures on the environment one of their central platform points. The minister proceeded to act with determination on several fronts, the first being the politically difficult problem of smog in the city of Dublin. Because of the troubled birth of the coalition government in which she served, as well as the continual tension between her party and the Fianna Fáil majority party in government, the junior minister's job was complicated by poor relations with her senior minister at the department, Pádraig Flynn.* It was part of the general political gossip of those years – 1989 to late 1991 – that hostilities and jealousy inside the department would break out regularly. It was also believed that because of this extra challenge, the junior minister was even more active and determined to achieve her aims.

Air quality in Dublin in 1989 was not good. Industrial, but mostly domestic pollution was causing several crises every year; the citizens of Dublin learned to dread the still cold days of winter, when a cloud of immobile choking fumes settled over the city, issuing from the domestic fires burning everything, but mostly dirty coal. Minister Harney set about legislating and regulating, and stepped courageously over and through the political minefields of interest groups to arrive at a situation today where Dublin's air quality has greatly improved, mainly owing to a ban on smoky fuel. Dublin's air pollution now rarely exceeds the limits set by the European Community law – European regulations and directives which have played a major part in ensuring Irish legislation for protection of the environment.

*Pádraig Flynn (b. 1939, in Mayo). A former national schoolteacher and publican, he is known for his conservatism on social issues, and his devotion to the Fianna Fáil Party. First elected to the Dáil in 1977, he was a close ally of Charles Haughey until late 1991, when it became clear that the Fianna Fáil edifice would crumble if Haughey remained in power. Switching allegiance to Albert Reynolds, he lost his ministerial post until Reynolds took office and appointed him to the Justice portfolio in February 1992 (to the dismay of those who sought liberal social reforms). In December 1992, he was appointed Ireland's Commissioner in Europe, obtaining the portfolio of Social Affairs.

When the bill to establish Ireland's new environmental watchdog was passing through the Dáil and Senate, the minister repeatedly made the point that Ireland has the cleanest environment in the EC. This is true – but neither she nor anyone else involved in the field of environmental investigation and protection were under any illusion about the causes, and not foolish enough to claim credit. Since the country has such a sparse population, with lower population density (50 persons per square kilometre compared with an EC average of 142)* and less urbanization than almost any western country, abundant water exchange, benevolent climatic conditions and prevailing winds, and a minimal industrial base, Ireland escaped the depredations which so devastated other countries whose late nineteenth- and accelerated twentieth-century industrial and population growth brought environmental chaos in their wake. Today, less than 1 per cent of Irish water is seriously polluted, while there is virtually no air pollution, since smoke pollution has been controlled. In 1991, the European Commission noted, in its examination of the state of bathing water across the community, that 'the results . . . again confirm the excellent quality of bathing water in Ireland'.[1] Compared with many other countries, Ireland has no serious problems in respect either of the qualitative or quantitative aspects of the water cycle. The visitor to Ireland will find large amounts of clean air, rolling and empty mountains and hills, green grass, sparkling water and uncrowded towns and villages.

The wish to preserve this happy state of affairs is strong, but the political determination to take suitable action is not always obvious: for example, environmentalists deplore the failure of politicians to grasp the nettle of incinerating or providing other disposal facilities for toxic waste, while politicians protest that they cannot deal with what they describe as the national paranoia on the subject, with ferocious local resistance to any suggestion of disposal facilities in any part of the country.

The Environmental Protection Agency (EPA), the centre of so much discussion and in which so many hopes reside, came about mainly because of the uncertainty and blockages surrounding applications by industry for planning permissions and licences. This manifested itself particularly in a lack of expertise among most

* Environmental Research Unit, Dublin, December 1991.

local authorities, who found themselves ill-equipped for dealing with complex issues; in her 1992 book on environmental law in Ireland, Dr Yvonne Scannell* describes in circumspect language 'the consequent diminution in public confidence in their abilities to monitor and enforce environmental legislation'.[2] Bitter local and sometimes national opposition to some types of proposed new industry was increased by alarming legal actions, such as that taken in the 1980s by a farming family from Tipperary against the multinational chemical company Merck, Sharpe & Dohme; the family alleged illness in humans and both illness and deformity in animals from poisonous emissions from the company's plant since the 1970s. In the event, after years of legal battles, the family won, the judges of the Supreme Court giving their verdict on the 'balance of probability'. (A sign of the improved times in the 1990s: Merck, Sharpe & Dohme won a prestigious environmental award in 1992.) A particularly crass example of early mistakes is the siting of the ICI fertilizer factory in the beautiful Vale of Avoca in south Co. Wicklow, about one and a half hours from Dublin. Built in the 1950s as Nitrigín Éireann Teo (NET) to manufacture fertilizers for Irish farmers, this large factory is ugly and was obviously unsuitable for this otherwise beautiful rural area. It is a vivid reminder of how lucky Ireland was that very few such industries were established at a time when very few people in high places knew or cared about the environment.

A second reason for the establishment of the EPA was the lack of any unified mechanism for dealing with the necessary multiple authorizations for projects that range from air and water schemes to roads and buildings; the system is tortuous and an obstacle course for any developers. It was hardly a welcoming atmosphere for a country desperately needing foreign industrial investment to help allay the growing unemployment crisis.

A major source of concern to planners and environmentalists alike in Ireland over the years has been the virtually untrammelled

---

*Dr Yvonne Scannell (b. 1948). Senior Lecturer in Environmental Law, Trinity College; Consultant in Environment Law to Arthur Cox & Co. (law firm), Dublin; author of three books on her subject; also a feminist activist in the 1970s and 1980s. Recognized as one of the foremost influences on the development of environmental law in Ireland, and generally regarded as an important advisory resource for Minister Harney from 1989 to 1992.

power of local authorities to carry out projects without any need to seek planning permission, and without controls or monitoring of the environmental results of their decisions. Given the historic lack of development and reform of local government in Ireland, and the consequent haphazard quality of personnel and decisions (see Chapter 5), some disastrous planning decisions have been made. The consequences can been seen in Dublin city and elsewhere: the denuding of city centres of all habitation, the construction of concrete jungles outside the city, the erection of unsuitable and unsightly office blocks; in the country, the spread of ribbon-development housing into areas of high scenic amenity, the spoiling of traditional Irish villages. Something needed to be done.

Unfortunately, Minister Harney did not win that battle entirely when she was piloting her EPA bill through Cabinet; however, the agency has certain powers of consultation, advice, and monitoring over local authorities which are an improvement on the previous situation. It is not impossible for the agency to be given further powers at a later stage.

In general, the need for clear national standards for environmental protection, and the enforcement of these standards in an even-handed and consistent manner, were becoming critical in the new Ireland, facing every kind of challenge to its relatively protected situation. Not least of the imperatives was that of tourism, for if Ireland can keep that quality of cleanliness and purity, as well as natural beauty, which forms an important part of its image abroad, then tourism, vital to economic survival, will thrive.

The EPA was therefore given a range of powers and competences which, if the properly qualified personnel were put in place, could transform and mightily strengthen Irish environmental policy. The properly qualified personnel, as always, constitute a problem. The salary for the chief executive, the director, was set at IR£55,000, plus car; and correspondingly less for the other four directors, all of whom will be full-time. This, of course, is well below the salary at top management level of big companies in the private sector. The location of the agency headquarters, in a Victorian Gothic castle outside the town of Wexford, two hours from the capital city, is considered another drawback. Johnstown Castle is set in lovely surroundings, and has been the home of high-level agricultural research for several decades. It may in theory be an ideal setting for the EPA: in practice, the area is off the beaten track and – much to local annoyance – has no university or third-level facility. However, the autumn 1992 advertisements in Ireland and abroad for the director's post apparently attracted huge interest from applicants of high calibre, numbering 700 from home and abroad. By the end of 1992, despite the interruption of a general election in late November and a change of minister, interviews had been completed; after the new government took office in January, an announcement was expected daily.

When a new agency or board is being established, the degree of independence from the State can be gauged by the method of appointment of the key personnel. The EPA's key people are appointed by government after interview with and nomination by a panel of six: two senior civil servants, the head of a statutory environmental body, the head of the Industrial Development Authority, the general secretary of the Irish Congress of Trade Unions, and the chief executive of the major women's organization in the country, the Council for the Status of Women.

Integrated systems of licensing and control for a very wide range of developments form a crucial part of its brief; advice, support and supervisory functions for all public and private bodies concerned with the environment; coordination of monitoring, and regular reports on the state of the environment; research; supervision of water, sewage and landfill; local-authority activities; participation in environmental-impact assessment procedures . . . If the agency is equipped with the personnel and finance to do all it is empowered to do, Ireland will have an exceptionally strong and efficient environmental protection regime, certainly as far as industrial development is concerned. The agency is designed to be, in the words of the minister, 'tough, independent and fair . . . strong medicine for our environment'.[3] After the dust of electioneering and government formation had settled, the appointment of the top team for the EPA was announced. Its director-general is Liam McCumiskey, with a background of senior positions in the public service, in environmental research and protection: before taking up his new post, he had headed a team setting up environmental monitoring in Bulgaria. He had previously held the directorship of the Environmental Research Unit, which was set up in 1988 to provide the Department of the Environment with research and support services for major infrastructural development. The four directors,* two men and two women, come from the civil service, local government, and the wider public service, all with extensive experience in various environmental fields. Some disappointment was expressed that all of the top officials in the new agency were from the Irish public service; a wider range of experience and attitude had been expected. It was hoped in environmental circles that the agency would get the good start it needed, despite the fact that it was the pet project of a previous administration whose parting with Fianna Fáil was less than harmonious. Irish governments have never been noted for enthusiastic carrying through of the schemes and projects of preceding administrations.

There are, of course, many threats to the Irish environment; one which causes environmentalists in Ireland to furrow their brows is that of farming pollution. Ironically, the very European Community which has done so much to help Ireland, and which has often been the major influence in environmental protection, has also been an agency for damage. Farmers have been encouraged since the early 1970s through the Common Agricultural Policy to fertilize their land and intensify their farming. From being a country of mostly small farmers using old-fashioned non-polluting methods, Ireland saw more and more chemicals and different methodology becoming the norm. From being a benign influence, farming became a menace: fertilizers, silage, pig-breeding, intensive cattle production – all threatening, and sometimes almost destroying, the pure water quality of some lakes and rivers. During the 1980s, the most notorious case of water pollution was a beautiful lake in Co. Cavan; strong fishermen and women wept over the dense green thicket of algae which choked the fertile fishing waters of Loch Sheelin. However, the EC has stepped in with a major IR£200 million anti-pollution grant programme for farmers. Environmentalists worry that these grants are taken up by large farmers who can meet the balancing finance required, leaving medium and small farms unaided. The Department of Agriculture so far has been unable or unwilling to work out a way of making it possible to give grants to poorer farmers.

*Declan Burns, Anne Butler, Iain McClean, and Marie Sherwood.

Fish-kills are the most dramatic sign of farming pollution: a sign of the improvement taking place is that in 1991, 22 of a total of 59 fish-kills were from farmer pollution, compared with 90 of a total of 122 kills in 1987. By the end of 1991, almost 25,000 applicants had been approved for grants under the EC Control of Farmyard Pollution Scheme. A second area of concern is a great mystery: the denuding of the rivers and lakes of the Galway/Mayo area of the feisty sea-trout, beloved by those addicted to fishing. Strong suspicion abounds, but no concrete proof exists, that the proliferation of commercial salmon farms in those waters has caused a huge increase in sea lice which has killed off the trout. The controversy rages.

Britain, 'the old enemy', is the source of one of Ireland's greatest environmental concerns. Across the Irish Sea lies the British nuclear installation of Sellafield (formerly called Windscale). Attitudes towards it range from implacable opposition to its existence to careful statements expressing worry about possible radioactive contamination of Irish fish. The chairperson of the Radiological Protection Institute of Ireland (RPII), while expressing a general wariness about any radioactive emissions into any part of the Irish Sea, said on radio shortly after her appointment that 'no significant health hazard' existed for Irish consumers, and that 'the level of radioactivity in the Irish Sea had decreased quite significantly from the early 1980s'.[4] A recent decision by the British to permit the construction of a IR£1·85 billion thermal-oxide reprocessing plant (THORP) at Sellafield, otherwise known as Sellafield II, was greeted with some complacency. The RPII issued a statement in June 1992, announcing its conclusion that when THORP is in full operation, 'the total radiation dose which will be received by the most exposed member of the Irish public due to all routine discharges from Sellafield will still amount to no more than a fraction of 1 per cent of that received by a person in Ireland from all natural and artificial sources of radioactivity'. Some environmental pressure groups consider that the RPII, and its predecessor the Nuclear Energy Board, were far too relaxed about Sellafield, and point to accidents at the plant, and unexplained incidents of cancer and leukaemia in Britain and Ireland, as causes for concern. In October 1992, a massive civil action was launched against British Nuclear Fuels Ltd by two British claimants,* alleging that men working at the nuclear plant in Cumbria had fathered children who subsequently developed various forms of cancer because of damaged sperm. They were picked out as test cases by solicitors acting for more than forty other families with health-related claims.

Other activists, while accepting the judgement of the RPII on these water-radiation issues, are more worried about the possibility of air contamination in Ireland from ageing 'clapped out' British nuclear plants generally. The debate, the monitoring, and the arguments go on. The British have, of course, no intention of conducting their nuclear-energy policy according to the wishes of their nuclear-free neighbouring island. Dramatic dashes across the sea to Sellafield by the Irish rock group U2 and Greenpeace have highlighted the situation, and keep the pot boiling.

Environmental awareness in Ireland has come about from various sources. The global concern of international groups like Greenpeace and Earthwatch, the international disasters like Bhopal and Chernobyl, the waxing and waning of the various 'green' political movements, have all had an impact on the Irish consciousness, in a country so open to international media. Young teachers in schools across the country have incorporated this awareness into their teaching, with encouraging results. (Although many environmentalists note ruefully that this consciousness does not seem to extend to an understanding of the need to curb litter; Ireland, alas, is one of the least litter-conscious nations in Europe.)

One of the few individuals, as opposed to institutions, who have strongly influenced Irish thinking and policy formation on the environment is the forceful and expert journalist Frank McDonald of the *Irish Times*.† McDonald is admired by environmentalists, feared by developers (including public bodies like local authorities and the apparently autonomous Office of Public Works), and

---

*Mrs Elizabeth Reay, claiming damages for the death at ten months from leukaemia of her daughter Dorothy, in 1962; and Ms Vivien Hope (twenty-seven), left infertile and partially disabled after treatment for non-Hodgkin's lymphoma. Both Mrs Reay's husband and Ms Hope's father had worked at Sellafield.

†Frank McDonald (b. 1950 in Dublin). Student activist and magazine editor while at University College, Dublin, he started his journalistic career with the *Irish Press*, joining the *Irish Times* in 1979. Became Environment Correspondent in 1986. Recipient of many awards, he has also written *The Destruction of Dublin* (Gill & Macmillan, 1985) and *Saving the City* (Tomar, 1989).

respected by politicians. His dedication to environmental matters is described by his admirers as 'more like a vocation than a job'. If any politician thought that the establishment of the Environmental Protection Agency, or any of the other initiatives taken in recent years, would diminish McDonald's vigilance and critical stance, a broadside in September 1992 gave warning of things to come; in a survey of widespread golf-course developments and 'bungalow blitz' in recent years, he thundered: 'Ultimately, our national heritage – in all its aspects – is threatened by the short-termism which seems to infect the core of the Irish psyche ... it has become another vehicle for exploitation.'[5]

McDonald is particularly concerned about the Dublin city situation. In 1985 he published his anger in a massive indictment of speculators, civil servants, planners and architects – a book called *The Destruction of Dublin*. This, and growing public concern in the 1980s, motivated recent actions taken by the State and local authorities to halt damage and destruction to the built environment in a once gracious Georgian city. But nothing has yet been done to curb the huge traffic growth and expansion in the number of car-parking spaces in the city which has caused traffic congestion equal to the worst in Europe. Dublin, with only half the number of cars per thousand of population as the city of Munich, provides three times the number of car-parking spaces: 40,000 compared with 13,000. Every morning, over 150,000 people progress into the city. In 1967, 54 per cent of these journeys were made by public transport. By 1989 this had decreased to 34 per cent.[6] By late 1992, no decisions had been taken to provide new and efficient public transport. Dublin is a city which has not been well managed by its guardians. Europe may yet come to Ireland's rescue once again: the National Development Plan which is to go to Brussels in order to draw down the IR£8 billion promised at the 1992 Edinburgh European Summit will, it is expected, contain proposals for considerably improved public transport into the city of Dublin, including a new light rail system. And during the general-election campaign, the outgoing government announced the scrapping of a proposed controversial, long-debated massive Dublin road system called the Eastern Bypass.

While there has been considerable progress, much remains to be done. Urban renewal has recently been given a high priority on the

political agenda, with a junior minister* attached to the Department
of the Environment with responsibility for Housing and Urban
Renewal. The area in the centre of the old city called Temple Bar,
beside the River Liffey, was designated for revitalization and
renewal, with generous tax concessions for business and residential
development in its old buildings, and is rapidly becoming transformed into a lively and attractive area. Shops, restaurants, art
galleries and residential units proliferate to take advantage of the
tax reductions; life returns to the city centre. Pedestrianization of
shopping streets and the refurbishment of fine old buildings testify
to a recent awareness of the need to preserve Dublin's unique
character.

In towns and cities and rural areas across the country, EC
money and improved awareness of heritage have combined to
refurbish and revitalize city centres on a growing scale, while some
county managers and authorities have led the way for others in
both restoring and beautifying the natural and built environment.
Environmentalists single out local authorities in Galway, Kilkenny,
Co. Cork, Co. Louth, Co. Wexford, and Kildare as particularly
energetic and effective in their environment-friendly initiatives.

One of the landmarks in the development of Ireland's awareness
of its built environment was known as the Wood Quay controversy
in the late 1970s. The Dublin Corporation had embarked on the
building of massive new office blocks to house its workers who
were scattered all over the city. The problem was that the site
uncovered Ireland's most important Viking remains, the old walls,
houses and streets of Viking Dublin, under the street known as
Wood Quay. The huge buildings also threatened to dwarf and
diminish the fine old Christ Church Cathedral. More than twenty
thousand people marched in many protests in the city, while a
group of twenty prominent Dublin citizens, including the Lord
Mayor, marched in to the building site one evening and took
possession of it:† a sort of siege ensued, becoming a national *cause*

*Emmet Stagg TD (b. 1944). Representing Kildare, Stagg as a Dáil Deputy was
best known for his trenchant views and position on the left of the Labour Party.
He was one of the potential critics brought into government by the Labour leader
in January 1993, and is respected as an able politician.
†The author, an independent University Senator at the time, was one of this
group of people drawn from all walks of life from politics and the arts to the

célèbre over many weeks. The project was fought brick by brick through the courts, and eventually extra time was gained for thorough excavation, but the main battle was lost. Among the leaders of the battle of Wood Quay were an Augustinian friar and a fiery young barrister/Senator, Mary Robinson, who in 1990 became President of Ireland.

The first, IR£20 million phase of the Wood Quay civic-office buildings was completed in the late 1980s, and the buildings are variously known in Dublin as 'the bunkers', 'the filing cabinets', and 'the guns of Navarone'. In late 1992, the plan to finish the scheme was put out to competition among a group of prominent architectural firms; the architect of the original scheme, a well-known and controversial designer Sam Stephenson, was excluded. He contended that public hostility to his buildings stemmed from the fact that the scheme was never completed, and that the finished civic centre would be 'a major statement of this century, intended to be as powerful on the riverside as London's County Hall is'.[7] He did not win his argument, and the city fathers decided to proceed with a different plan which meant that there would be no more bunkers.

Other controversies over Dublin's architectural and archaeological heritage surfaced over the years as Irish citizens became ever more watchful about their capital city. They had realized that a careful eye had to be kept on proposed new developments.

Not many Irish politicians are either expert or particularly interested in environmental matters, to judge by the debates in the Dáil and Senate on these issues. One of the exceptions, and she is working in Brussels and Strasbourg rather than Ireland, is an MEP for the Dublin area, Mary Banotti.* Apart from Minister Harney, Banotti's was the political name consistently mentioned to the author by environmentalists. She takes an interest in, and often an unpopular stance on, environmental issues all over the country. She supported environmentalists in their battles against the plans of the Office of Public Works to place interpretative centres in certain areas of great scenic beauty. When the EC Commission agreed to

---

Church, who with some apprehension trespassed on to the site and settled down in tents for the night; the author shared a tent with the Irish writer Mary Lavin.

* See Chapter 9, 'Ireland and Europe'.

fund such a centre in the remote and unique Burren in Co. Clare, despite passionate opposition from Banotti and many others, she said the impact of the news was 'like a death in the family'.*⁸ The issue did not become a deathbed one, however: in a historic decision on 12 February 1993, the High Court found that the Office of Public Works did not have the authority to build thousands of its projects across the country without planning permission. The very special limestone area of the Burren, at a place called Mullaghmore, seemed to be reprieved. But emergency legislation was rushed through the Oireachtas because a veritable vacuum, affecting thousands of projects and many jobs, existed after the court decision. And, amid political embarrassment and confusion, work stopped at the disputed building site at Mullaghmore, while two government departments, headed by ministers from the two different coalition partners,† wrangled about demarcation and waited for Supreme Court decisions. Were Mullaghmore and all the other beauty spots targeted for interpretative centres under the control of the Minister for Culture or the OPW's boss, the Minister for Finance? Truly, it was an outstanding Irish example of political and planning failure, and more particularly, a spectacular omission by both the Fianna Fáil and Labour parties from the decisions made before going into government together.

A former leader of the Opposition, Alan Dukes of the Fine Gael party, Environment spokesperson of his party in October 1992, showed interest and considerable expertise during the Dáil debates on the Environmental Protection Agency, as did the Democratic Left's Éamonn Gilmore. Senators like Brendan Ryan, a chemical expert from Cork, David Norris of Trinity College, Avril Doyle of

*During 1991 and 1992 the question of 'interpretative centres' for the public, located in areas of great beauty and interest, became another national controversy. Funded largely by the EC, the argument centred around whether the centres should be located right in the middle of the area in question, or in a nearby town, which would minimize the car and bus presence on narrow country roads. The Office of Public Works, located under the aegis of the Department of Finance, was empowered until 1993 to make these decisions with or without planning permission. Ireland has imported environmental champions too: David Bellamy, world-famous environmentalist, declared that the Burren would become 'the Torremolinos of Ireland' if the interpretative centre went ahead.⁹ Bellamy has taken a particular interest in preservation of the unique Irish boglands.

†Minister for Finance, Bertie Ahern, represented by his junior minister; Minister for Arts, Culture, and the Gaeltacht, Michael D. Higgins.

Fine Gael (a former junior minister herself) were impressive too. A champion of the environment over the years has been Senator Carmencita Hederman (see Chapter 5, 'Local Government') and, for many years Dublin Dáil Deputy for the Labour Party, ex-architect Ruairí Quinn.* When the new government came into office in January 1993, environmentalists had hoped that Quinn would take the job of Environment Minister, for which he was particularly suited. This was not to be.

Until very recently, however, environmental concerns were not at the centre of Irish political debate. This is an interesting reflection, because it is a 'cause' which delivered a new entrant to the Dáil in 1989, in the shape of Ireland's first Green Party member. With just 8.8 per cent of the first-preference vote in the Dublin South constituency, Roger Garland† was elected on the eighth count to one of the five seats, to the surprise of not only his opponents, but his own party as well. The proportional-representation system showed in this instance that it can represent to a highly sophisticated degree the margins of preferences of the voters (see Chapter 3 for explanation of the system). In fact, a Green Party colleague in a neighbouring constituency‡ was considered to have a better chance of election, achieved 10.12 per cent of the vote, but was defeated by a clever 'vote-managing' operation by Fine Gael. During his time in Dáil Éireann, until he was defeated in November 1992, Roger Garland did not maximize his party's potential impact in the Dáil, perhaps from lack of previous political experience. In the 1991 local elections, the Green Party achieved significant successes in the Dublin area, getting ten councillors into power (including the election of a candidate who was out of the country for most of the campaign, and did not canvass – this astonished and annoyed

---

*Ruairí Quinn (b. 1946). First elected to the Dáil for Dublin South-East in 1977, Ruairí Quinn held two ministries between 1983 and 1987: first Labour, then Public Service. An architect by profession, Quinn became deputy leader of the Labour Party in 1989, and was one of the architects of the Fianna Fáil/Labour coalition in 1993. A popular, able and cultured man; Minister for Employment and Enterprise from 1993.

†Roger Garland (b. 1933). Formerly a finance director in the private sector, and Green Party activist since 1982.

‡Dublin South-East, where former Taoiseach Garret FitzGerald took a risk in urging people to vote for his party colleague Joe Doyle in order to spread the vote and see two Fine Gael people elected.

hard-working local politicians). Because of the strong environmental measures and high profile of the junior environment minister between 1989 and 1992, the Green Party's potential may have diminished somewhat. The young vote, however, sees the 'Greens' as having a role in the great global issues which concern them, as opposed to the local Irish issues: this factor, untapped by mainstream Irish politicians on the whole, may garner more votes for the Greens than generally imagined. In the general election of 1992, Garland was replaced by Trevor Sargent of the Green Party from the Dublin North constituency.

A major indicator of changing thinking on the environment, and a force for bringing about that change, is the Environmental Institute at University College, Dublin. Directing that institute since 1981 and simultaneously holding the Heritage Trust Chair of Environmental Studies is a man of quiet dedication and indefatigable energy, Frank Convery.* The chair he holds, and the institute he directs are unique in Ireland, but their influence is spreading into other academic areas and into every area of Irish life where there can be said to be an environmental dimension. Frank Convery's university, but not the wider community interested in the environment, breathed a sigh of relief when he was not made head of the new EPA, a post for which he had been short-listed.

In central Dublin, a public office with a high-street shop frontage called ENFO has been established by the Department of the Environment as a permanent resource, information and exhibition centre for the general public on the environment. In 1992, the minister related with satisfaction that more than one thousand people a week called at the office, with a continual discernible increase, and that there were about 350 postal and telephone enquiries each week.[10]

The pioneering voluntary organization which carried a torch for the Irish environment, when that was a lonely and isolated activity, is called An Taisce, the National Trust for Ireland. Founded in

---

*Francis Convery MAgrSc, MS, PhD (b. 1944). Educated Dublin (Agricultural Science) and New York, taught at Duke University, North Carolina; he is a visiting World Bank professor. Early specialism was forestry. Author of several environmental works, organizer of huge imaginative 'environmental shows'. The Irish Who's Who describes him thus: 'A superb communicator, a clear thinker with a passionate commitment to the environment.'

1948, An Taisce is now a body with statutory functions under the planning Acts. It is less centrally important in the 1990s because its concerns have at last become the concerns of government and many other agencies. It claims 7,000 members and thirty-one local associations: a criticism has been made that its branches are independent fiefdoms, operating locally and thereby weakening the impact of the national body. Incidents are recounted in which developers, impatient with the objections of the local An Taisce branch to their planning applications, arranged for a flood of new members to join the branch and reverse the objections. Despite such problems, the new breed of Irish environmentalists are, however, loud in their praise of An Taisce and the work it did, and does, with very limited resources on a totally voluntary basis. Through the years, many distinguished people have held office in An Taisce and have contributed significantly to the protection of the Irish heritage in all its forms.

Ireland is lucky; the modern international concern and expertise on the global environment, and the accompanying increase in awareness of each country's responsibilities in that respect, have come at a period when there is still time and opportunity to preserve the high degree of environmental advantage which the country enjoys. An informed and interested public forces political action, which has – after many years of apathy – been relatively energetic. European pressures and assistance keep the momentum going, while agencies both public and private are growing in number and confidence. Weaknesses in laws and structures which allowed destruction in the past, in particular of the built environment, are gradually being addressed. The balance between the need for new industry and the protection of the environment is being addressed by initiatives like the Environmental Protection Agency. Ireland's good and comprehensive legislation on wildlife, through the 1976 Wildlife Act, is under review in the early 1990s; the Act will be strengthened and adapted to ensure it can remain effective in its intentions, and will comply fully with EC developments in the area.

In January 1990, the government produced a ten-year environmental action programme with considerable fanfare and far-reaching statements of intent. In it were plans involving the spending of IR£1 billion over ten years. It came just in time for the Irish presidency of the European Community, which began that month; the Taoiseach had announced some time previously, taking the environment community in Ireland somewhat by surprise, that Ireland's would be a 'green' presidency. It was felt that the Taoiseach had, literally and metaphorically, 'sniffed the wind' of public and European concern, and simultaneously had realized that his coalition junior minister, Ms Harney, was riding a wave of public approbation for her work. Fianna Fáil shares with most political parties a desire not to be outshone on any major issue. The beneficiary of political competition was, happily, the Irish environment.

And in May 1992, Ireland presented a comprehensive and well-designed report on environment and development to the United Nations Conference at Rio de Janeiro.[11] Its optimistic and upbeat statement of the state of affairs and future plans for Ireland's environment was not perhaps as realistic as many activists in the field would have liked. Nevertheless, the broad statement of the current Irish state of understanding, hope and intentions about air, water and land and all the ways of dealing with possible threats to them would not have been possible ten years ago and represents a great leap forward for Ireland and its people.

A new government with a major Labour component took office in January 1993, appointing a new Minister for Environmental Protection to replace the highly regarded Mary Harney. John Browne,* in whose Wexford constituency the new Environmental Protection Agency will be based, is an unknown quantity as far as the environment is concerned. He has, however, the backing of the government's *Programme for a Partnership Government*, which promises action on waste management (recycling, no mention of toxic waste), extension of Dublin smog regulations to other areas, 'investigation of the possibilities of using Community and International Law to hasten the winding down and closure of Sellafield and particularly the new reprocessing facility . . .', and a range of other undertakings. The Programme makes clear the government's

---

* John Browne (b. 1948). Fianna Fáil. He was first elected to the Dáil in November 1982, and served for one year as a junior Minister for Agriculture (with special responsibility for Food), February 1992 to January 1993. His former occupation was as a salesman. He is remembered for asking, during the presidential election campaign, if Mary Robinson would open an abortion referral clinic in the Áras if elected.

commitment to the Environmental Protection Agency – too often in times past, the proposals of previous governments have been quietly shelved by new administrations. The Programme also makes a welcome statement on the importance of the energy area in protection of the environment. In general, it was the most comprehensive statement and set of promises on the environment ever made in a programme of its kind. It remained to be seen whether the new government would have the same energy as the junior partner in the last one when it came to implementing the programme: if not, there may well be a resurgence of the Greens in Irish politics. By mid-1993, it seemed that the environment issue had, so to speak, gone off the boil. The new agency was waiting to move into its headquarters, and nothing had been heard from it. The former Minister for the Protection of the Environment was now involved in a range of other issues in Opposition, and the new one was quiet.

But in the early 1990s, a great deal had been achieved for protection of the environment, and the potential was there for much more: in this field, as in so many others, Ireland stands at a point of transition where she has choices and opportunities, as well as positive and negative examples from outside her shores. In a country with such a young, lively, and educated population, with such strong convictions about so many things, the prospects for progress seemed excellent.

NOTES

1. *Quality of Bathing Water, 1991*, Commission of the European Communities, 1992.
2. Yvonne Scannell, *Environmental Law in Ireland*.
3. In conversation with the author, 14 October 1992.
4. Dr Mary Upton, interviewed by Pat Kenny, RTE Radio 1, on 14 October 1992.
5. *Irish Times*, 24 September 1992.
6. These figures from a paper entitled *Transport in Dublin: Facing Reality*, supplied by the Department of the Environment, October 1992.
7. *Sunday Times*, 18 October 1992.

8. *Irish Times*, 8 October 1992.
9. *Irish Independent*, 19 March 1992.
10. In conversation with the author, 13 October 1992.
11. Ireland, *National Report to the United Nations Conference on Environment and Development*, Department of the Environment, June 1992.

INDEX

censorship, 383, 418, 474, 476–7; of Sinn Féin, 346–9
Central Applications Office, 411–12
Central Bank, 246, 257, 260f, 272; forecast, 1993, 263–4
Central Criminal Court, 114
Central Statistics Office, 252, 434
Centre Party, 164
Century Radio, 334, 351
charity, 300
Charlton, Jack, 460f
Chernobyl disaster, 510
Chester Beatty Library, 479
Chief Justice, 121
child abuse, 441–2
child care, 423f, 429–30, 441–2
Child Care Act, 442
Childers, Erskine, 10n
Childers, Erskine Jnr, 10f; memorial to, 207–8
Christ Church Cathedral, 380, 512
Christian Brothers, 406, 451
Christian Democrats, 229
Chubb, Professor Basil, 68, 345
Church of Ireland, 203, 205, 377, 379–80
Churchill, Sir Winston, 220
Circuit Court, 114; judges' salaries, 121
Cistercian Order, 455
City and County Amendment Act 1955, 102
city management system, 96, 98–9, 101; 'Section 4', 102–4
Civic Guards, 132
civil service, 81–93; analysis of, 87–9; attempts at reform, 84–6; conflict with ministers, 93; decentralization, 106; head-hunting from, 86–7; influence of, 81–2; pay scales, 92–3; political impartiality of, 86; promotion, 85–6; qualifications in, 87; recruitment of, 83–4; reform movement, 88–9; Secretaries, 89–91
Civil Service Commission, 81, 98
Civil Service Regulation Act 1925, 418
civil war, 26, 81, 156, 163, 165–6, 189n
Clare, Anthony, 395
Clare, County, 308, 310
Clare Champion, 343
Classic Hits 98FM, 336
clientelism, 57, 60–61; clinics, 105
Clifford, Dr Dermot, Archbishop of Cashel and Emly, 377
Clinton, President, 23
Clonliffe Seminary, 374
club membership, 112n
Coillte, 290, 311
Colgan, Michael, 483
Collins, Gerry, 206
Collins, Michael, 149, 162, 178n
Combat Poverty Agency, 300
COMETT programme, 225
Comhaltas Ceoltóirí Éireann, 484

Commitments, The, 274, 490
Common Agricultural Policy (CAP), 226, 307–8, 312, 365, 508
Commonwealth, 25
Communications, Department of, 334–5
Communications Workers' Union (CWU), 370
Communist Party, Soviet, 173, 332, 334
Community Alert Schemes, 137
Community Schools, 404, 451
Competition Authority, 125n
Comprehensive Schools, 451
Confederation of Irish Industry (CII), 258, 361–2
Conference of Major Religious Superiors (CMRS), 374, 389, 392
Congo, The, 143
Connaught Tribune, 343
Connell, Dr Desmond, Archbishop of Dublin, 377, 390
Connolly, James, 170, 194
Conradh na Gaeilge, 497
conscription, 221
Conservative Party, 200
Considine, Tom, 260–61
Consilio, Sister, 389
constituencies: demands of PR system, 44–5; importance of ministers, 45–6; selection conventions, 61–2; TDs' activities in, 31, 32–3, 66–7
Constituency Commission, 56
Constitution of Ireland, 1922, 163–4
Constitution of Ireland, 1937, 74, 122, 157–8; adopted, 25–6; amendment on Seanad representation, 77; Articles 2 and 3, 21, 158, 191–3, 194, 202; Catholic Church influence, 373, 382–3, 397; courts system, 110–11; Dáil and Senate in, 54–5; Eighth Amendment (abortion), 110–11, 216–17, 423–4, 436–9; FitzGerald crusade, 36; position of women in, 417–20, 429, 431–2; presidency in, 12–13, 17, 54–5; referendums, 13, 55, 374n, 395, 432–3; Supreme Court interpretations, 12, 55, 110, 431–2, 439
Construction Industry Federation (CIF), 362
contraception, 112f, 395, 418; condoms, 442–3; Cosgrave votes against bill, 167; legalized, 424–5; O'Malley splits from FF, 174–5; Robinson bill, 423
Convery, Professor Frank, 107, 516
Cooley, Dr Mike, 321
Cooney, Patrick, 33n
Cooper, Charles, 270, 280
Corish, Brendan, 171
Cork, 298, 489
Cork, County, 45–6, 512
Cork Examiner, 339
Cork Opera House, 476
Cosgrave, Liam, 36f, 166–7, 422
Cosgrave, Liam Jnr, 166n

ENFO, 516

Enniskillen, Co. Fermanagh, Remembrance Day bomb, 77n, 187f

Enterprise and Employment, Department of, 282–3

entrepreneurs, Irish, 318; as role models, 322–4; success stories, 324–30

environment, 502–19; future plans, 517–19; nuclear threat, 509–10; urban renewal, 511–12

Environment, Department of the, 98, 104, 296–7, 502, 507–8, 512; ENFO, 516

Environmental Institute, UCD, 516

Environmental Protection, Department of, 518

Environmental Protection Agency Act 1990, 502–4, 506, 514–15

Environmental Protection Agency (EPA), 176, 502–8, 511, 517, 518–19; structure and functions, 507–8

Environmental Research Unit, 507–8

Eogan, George, 77n

Equal Opportunities Policy, 87

equal pay, 362, 420, 422, 428

Equality and Law Reform, Department of, 50, 439, 441f

Erasmus programme, 225

Esso Petroleum, 329

European Bureau for Lesser-used Languages, 498

European Commission, 146, 504, 513–14 Commissioners, 13, 223–8, 503n

European Community (EC), 22, 150, 166, 213–38, 243, 269, 303, 430; and abortion question, 119; assessment of membership, 47, 214–16, 235–8; committee on EC legislation, 232–3; effect on agriculture, 306–8; encouragement of forestry, 311; and the environment, 503–4, 508–9; equal-pay directive, 362, 422; Irish in Brussels, 223–8; Irish presidency of, 233–5, 517–18; labour legislation, 363; money for interpretative centres, 288; poverty programme, 300; subventions from, 213–14, 237–8, 253, 264; and women's rights, 422, 424; see also currency crisis

European Court of Human Rights, 123

European Democratic Alliance, 229

European Environmental Bureau, 230

European Law, Centre for, 232n

European Monetary System, 213

European Music Year, 481

European Parliament, 79, 201n, 225, 236–7; elections, 228–9, 230; Irish members of, 228–31

European People's Party, 229

European Social Fund, 272, 410

European Structural Funds, 286, 414

extradition, 193

Fair Trades Commission, 125, 127

family home, right of spouse to, 113, 431–2

family law, 68, 431–2

family-planning legislation, 30

Fanning, Ronan, 15, 206

farmers, 363–5; influence of, 257–8

Farmyard Pollution Scheme, 509

Farrell, Brian, 30

FAS, 272n, 405

Faul, Fr Denis, 203

Federated Union of Employers (FUE), 361–2, 365

Federated Workers' Union of Ireland (FWUI), 366

Fennell, Nuala, 427n, 439

Fennelly, Niall, 124n

Fianna Fáil, 9, 26, 29n, 64, 67, 103, 153, 154–62, 163, 167, 170, 179, 205, 305, 351, 508; 1990 presidential campaign, 15–18; abortion amendment, 423–4; Ard-Fheis, 180; Arms Trial, 14, 35, 93, 166, 174; and the arts, 475, 490; broadcasting policy, 332, 334–5, 336; and business controversies, 295f; and Catholic Church, 382; civil-war origins, 172; coalition with Labour, 28, 30, 36–7, 48–53, 228, 261–2; coalition with PDs, 18, 37, 41, 181, 253; and Constitution, 418–19; and divorce, 432; EC Presidency, 234; economic policy, 242–5, 249, 256, 263, 269, 360n; and education, 413–14; election, 1992, 181–4; and the environment, 503, 514; in European Parliament, 229; and Fine Gael, 165–6, 169; and Irish language, 493–4; and Irish Press, 342–3; judicial appointments, 115, 118; liberal wing, 129; local elections, 1991, 106f; and neutrality, 220; and New Right, 371; and Northern Ireland, 192–3, 210; PD origins in, 174–5; political advisers, 46–7; and PR, 57; presidents, 11–12; Reynolds takes over, 37–9; in the 1990s, 177f; special advisers, 82–3; and sport, 446n, 452; working-class vote, 171; see also Programme for a Partnership Government

Field, The, 304, 487

Field Day, 485–6

film industry, 337, 476f, 490

Finance, Department of, 85, 97, 237, 264, 296, 361, 405–6, 514; and the arts, 475, 478; decision-makers, 258–61; officials head-hunted, 86–7; Secretary, 90, 92, 257

Finance, Minister for, 27, 39, 42–3; at Cabinet meetings, 30

Financial Times, 261

Fine Arts, Ministry for, 473

Fine Gael, 10, 14, 24, 36, 64, 68, 153f, 160, 162–70, 171, 177, 179, 227, 340, 422; 1992 election, 50–51, 181–4; 1990 presidential campaign, 16; and agriculture, 364; Anglo-

Justice, Department of: first woman minister, 129; and Garda Síochána, 133f, 136n, 138–40; lack of research, 141
Juvenile Liaison Scheme, 137

K

Kane, Dr Eileen, 411
Kavanagh, Patrick, 298, 303, 487n
Keane, John B., 304, 487
Kearney, Richard, 483, 487
Kelly, John, 220–21
Kennedy, Dr Brian, 472f, 478n, 480n
Kennedy, Geraldine, 24n
Kennedy, John F., 445
Kennedy, Sr Stanislaus, 389
Keogh, Professor Dermot, 233
Kerry Cooperative, 312n
Kerryman, 343
Keynes, John Maynard, 472
Kildare, 512
Kildare, County, 462–3
Kilkenny, 512; abuse case, 441–2
Kilkenny Design Workshops, 476
Killanin, Lord, 463
Kitt, Tom, 427, 433

L

Labour, Department of, 361, 368, 430n
Labour Court, 358–9, 441
Labour Party, 9, 14, 64, 68, 119, 122, 153f, 170–72, 177, 193, 250, 497n; 1992 election, 181–4; 1990 presidential campaign, 15; and the arts, 477, 488; broadcasting policy, 332, 336; business and financial support, 295; coalition with Fianna Fáil, 28, 30, 35f, 37, 48–53, 228, 261–2; coalition with Fine Gael, 166–7f, 171–2; and Dáil reform, 71; and Democratic Left, 174; economic policy, 246–8, 263; and education, 414; and the environment, 514; in European Parliament, 229; family appointments, 31, 52; local elections, 1991, 107; and neutrality, 221; and Northern Ireland, 159n, 194; and position of women, 430; and PR, 57; and privatization, 293, 367; in the 1990s, 178–9; special advisers, 31, 45, 46–7, 83, 257; and trade unions, 170, 172; *see also Programme for a Partnership Government*
Labour Relations Commission, 358, 368
Land Commission, 304–5
Landy, Vincent, 124n
Lane, Dr Dermot, 386–7, 388f
Lane, Sir Hugh, 473
Language Freedom Movement, 495
Laois, County, 311–12
Larkin, James, 170
Late, Late Show, The 16, 138, 199, 349f, 442
Lavin, Mary, 513n
Law Reform Commission, 117, 119, 120, 127–8

Law Society, 116, 125, 127
Lawson, Nigel, 328
Leaving Certificate, 405, 494; points race, 411–13
Lebanon, 146
Lee, Professor Joseph, 19, 164, 274–5, 320; on civil service, 83–4
Legal Aid Board, 124
legal profession, 110–30; accessibility of justice, 123–5; criticisms of, 128–30; judiciary, 114–16; payment of judiciary, 121; solicitors and barristers, 116–17, 125–30
Leinster House, 28, 31–3, 54, 442, 472; library, 66n
Leitrim, County, 311
Lemass, Seán, 35f, 37, 84n, 158–9, 160n, 220, 269; on Catholic Church, 381–2; economic expansion, 242–3; on RTE, 345–6
Lenihan, Brian, 13, 47, 138; Minister for Defence, 150–51; presidential campaign, 1990, 9–10, 15–18
Levin, Bernard, 480
Lillis, Michael, 87n, 209
Limerick, 298, 489
Limerick University, 409–10
literary revival, 472–4
'Live Aid', 300
Live Register, 271–2
Liveline, 352
living standards, 299
Lloyd George, David, 25, 189n
Local Appointments Commission, 98–9
local government, 95–108; centralized finance, 97–8; costs of, 99–100; elections, 106–8; and the environment, 505–6, 510; and national politics, 104–5; planning abuses, 102–4; powerlessness of, 96–8, 101–2; recommendations for reform, 98, 107–8; structures of, 96–101; *See also* councillors
Local Government and Public Services Union (LGPSU), 366
Local Government Bill 1991, 102, 105
Loch Sheelin, Co. Cavan, 508
Lomé convention, 234
Louth, County, 512
Lynch, Danny, 451, 452–3
Lynch, Jack, 35, 37, 45, 159–60, 174n, 175n, 234, 245, 452; economic policy, 244–5
Lyons, Patrick, 125n

M

Maastricht Treaty, 55n, 161, 213–14, 233, 289, 307, 395, 488, 497; and abortion question, 39, 110–11, 119–20, 176, 216–19, 426, 436–9; convergence criteria, 236; ministerial broadcast, 338n; and neutrality, 220–22; referendum on, 222–3
Mac Aonghusa, Proinnsias, 497–8

McBride, Willie John, 458
McCarthy, Justice Niall, 35, 111, 118
McCartney, Robert, 205
McClean, Iain, 508
McCreevy, Charles, 43–4, 52
McCullough, Wayne, 445
McCumiskey, Liam, 507–8
McCurtain, Dr Margaret, 389
McDonald, Frank, 510–11
McDowell, Major Tom, 340
McGahern, John, 383, 476
McGilligan, Patrick, 164
McGonagle, Stephen, 77n
McGovern, Jimmy, 139n
Mac Gréil survey, 387
McGuigan, Barry, 445, 467
McGuinness, Catherine, 442, 497n
McGuinness, Martin, 347–8
McGuinness, Paul, 483
McKenna, General Dan, 145
McKiernan, Catherina, 467
McLaughlin, Commissioner Patrick, 139n
Mac Liammóir, Mícheál, 474
McManus, Liz, 444n
McQuaid, Dr John Charles, Archbishop of
   Dublin, 382, 397, 418
Macra na Feirme, 363, 365
MacSharry, Ray, 224, 225–6, 227–8, 249, 253,
   309, 329n
Magee, Jimmy, 454
Mahon, Derek, 487
Mahony, Tim, 466
Major, John, 199f, 206
Mallon, Séamus, 195, 202
Mansergh, Dr Martin, 46
Mara, P. J., 46
Margetson, Ernest, 124
Marine, Department of the, 152
Markievicz, Countess, 430n
Martin, Michael, 78
Masterson, Dr Patrick, 409
Mater Dei Institute of Education, 388
maternity leave, 423f, 434
Mates, Michael, 199
Maud Committee, 97
Mawhinney, Brian, 191n
Maxwell, Greg, 366n
Maxwell, Robert, 341
Mayhew, Sir Patrick, 194, 199, 202
Mayo, County, 308
Meath, County, 462–3
media, 331–55; advertising battles, 331–2,
   336–7, 343–5; beginnings of broadcasting,
   337–8; independent radio, 336, 345; national
   share, 333; newspaper readership, 353–5;
   newspapers, 336–7, 339–43; pirate radio,
   331–2, 334; political control of, 345–9; Sinn
   Féin ban, 346–9; television, see Radio Telefís
   Éireann (RTE)

Meehan, Sylvia, 425n
Mellor, David, 339
Merchant Banking, 135n
Merck, Sharpe & Dohme, 505
Mercy Order, 408n
Methodist Church, 203, 205, 377
Mills, Michael, 130
Millstreet, Co. Cork, 463
Ministers: Cabinet meetings, 28–30; and civil
   service, 33, 82–3, 93; pressures on, 30, 31–3,
   44–5; role of, 44; salaries and pensions, 47–
   8; special advisers for, 31, 82–3, 257; state
   cars, 45–6; women as, 430–31, 439–40
Ministers of State, 28
Mirror Group, 341
miscarriages of justice, 129
Mitchell, Dr Thomas, 408, 411
Mitchell, Gay, 22
Mitchell, Jim, 98
Molloy, Bobby, 41n
Monaghan, County, 298
Morgan, Professor David Gwynn, 123
Moriarty, Paddy, 277
Mount Juliet, Co. Kilkenny, 466
Mulcahy, General Richard, 165, 398
Mulcahy, Mick, 488n
Mullaghmore, Co. Clare, 514
Mullin, Brendan, 468n
Mulvey, Kieran, 358
Munnelly, Adrian, 481
Munster Express, 343
Murphy, Annie, 351–2
Murphy, Christina, 412
Murphy, John A., 222, 497
Murphy, Tom, 487
Murphy, William Martin, 340
Murray, Frank, 89–90
Murtagh Properties v. *Cleary*, 420
music, 484f
Muslims, 379
My Left Foot, 490

N
Nally, Dermot, 89
Nangle, Garda Tom, 139n
National Adult Literacy Agency, 401
National Army Spouses Association, 147
National City Brokers (NCB), 297
National College of Art and Design, 319
National Concert Hall, 471, 476, 480
National Council for Curriculum and
   Assessment, 402n
National Development Plan 1993–9, 264, 511
National Economic and Social Council
   (NESC), 270–71, 361
National Economic and Social Forum, 443
National Gallery, 476
National Heritage Council, 471, 480
National Labour Party, 170